Le Cordon Bleu

COMPLETE

Cooking Techniques

Le Cordon Bleu

Complete

Cooking Techniques

Jeni Wright & Eric Treuille

TED SMART

A CASSELL BOOK

First published in the United Kingdom by Cassell plc.,
Wellington House, 125 Strand, London WC2R 0BB

First published 1996

This edition produced for The Book People Ltd.,
Guardian House, Borough Road, Godalming,
Surrey GU7 2AE

Created and Produced by
CARROLL & BROWN LIMITED
5 Lonsdale Road
London NW6 6RA

Publishing Director Denis Kennedy
Art Director Chrissie Lloyd

Project Editor Laura Price
Editor Jo-Anne Cox

Designers Vicki James,
Adelle Morris, Karen Sawyer

Production Manager Wendy Rogers
Assistant Kate Disney

Production Consultant Lorraine Baird

Photographer David Murray

British Library Catalogue-in-Publication Data
A catalogue record for this book is available from the
British Library

ISBN 1-85613-351-6

Reproduced by Colourscan, Singapore
Printed and bound in Italy by Graphicom

Introduction

For over a century, Le Cordon Bleu has been at the heart of French gastronomy: explorer of new trends, yet ambassador for the traditional disciplines of classical French cuisine and pâtisserie. Today with schools on all continents it teaches the widest range of students the skills necessary to recreate dishes of all kinds.

WITH MORE THAN one hundred years' worth of culinary expertise behind it, *Le Cordon Bleu Complete Cooking Techniques* is the repository of more skills and know-how than many people could learn in a life-time. Created by master chefs, but with the home cook in mind, the book is a unique and indispensable reference work that is destined to become one of the world's great culinary classics. In its clear, close-up, colour photographs, readers will be able to see how to select the best ingredients, how to prepare them most effectively, how to cook them successfully in a multitude of ways and, finally, how to present them at the table with mouth-watering finesse.

EVERYTHING YOU WANTED TO KNOW ABOUT INGREDIENTS ... The variety of ingredients that can be found on sale today can be as bewildering as it is exciting yet, as every great chef knows, careful selection of the raw ingredients is the first step towards a successful dish.

In *Le Cordon Bleu Complete Cooking Techniques*, readers can see what characterizes the freshest foodstuffs, how to look beyond the ordinary, and how to choose from among the many culinary products now available with confidence and pleasure. Here, too, they will be able to familiarize themselves with the many new and unusual vegetables, fruits and flavourings that are appearing so regularly on supermarket shelves. Much of this information is essential to the enjoyment of preparing and eating dishes from the various ethnic cuisines so popular today.

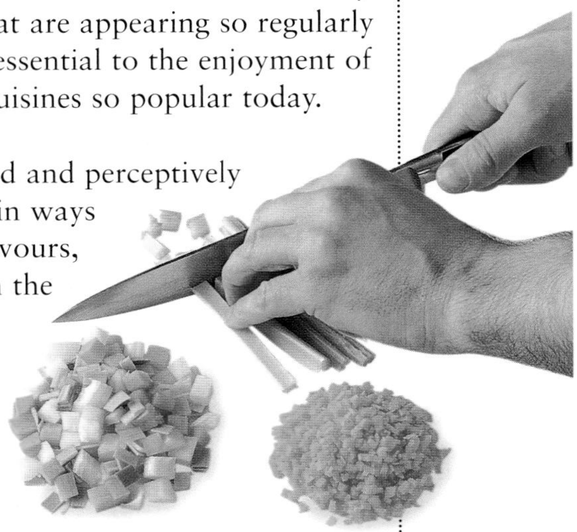

PREPARING THE FOUNDATIONS ... Even the most splendid and perceptively chosen ingredients need to be prepared to be cooked in ways that at once preserve their nutrients, enhance their flavours, and show them off at their best – techniques in which the chefs at Le Cordon Bleu excel.

Throughout the fifteen chapters, and in hundreds of individual steps, the skills that will enable cooks to ready an enormous range of ingredients for cooking are shown in specially taken photographs.

Here readers will discover how to best store and clean shellfish of every description; scale, trim and fillet fish; bone and truss poultry; and create doughs of many kinds, including yeast breads and pasta. Meat preparations of all sorts are detailed, while step-by-step directions will help you to master the skills needed to chop, shred and slice vegetables; peel, stone and skin fruit; melt and temper chocolate; beat cream; concoct soups and sauces and incorporate batters – to highlight just a few.

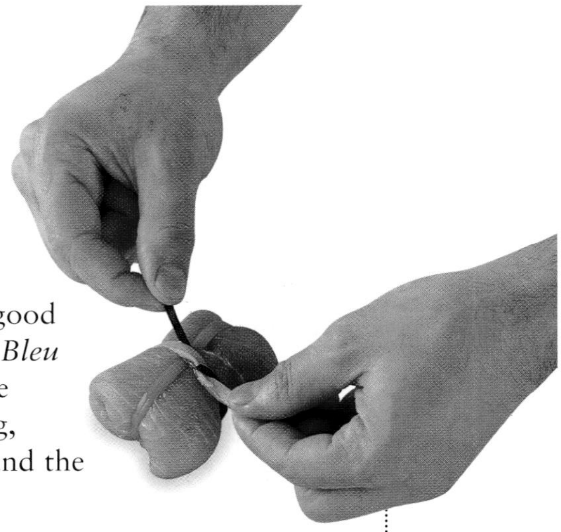

OUT OF THE FRYING PAN ... Once correctly prepared, ingredients offer themselves to be cooked in myriad ways and served up with stunning results.

For everything that needs doing there are, of course, good methods, and better methods! Throughout *Le Cordon Bleu Complete Cooking Techniques* readers will discover the correct ways of roasting, braising, pan-frying, poaching, steaming, stir-frying, baking, grilling and barbecuing, and the best ones to choose for each foodstuff.

A WORLD OF FLAVOURS ... Take a culinary tour with *Le Cordon Bleu Complete Cooking Techniques* and discover how sushi, saté, Chinese dumplings, tempura, Oriental duck and dashi are made. Learn to assemble a croquembouche, poach a ballotine, fry fish Cajun-style, steam tamales and simmer a tagine. Unveil the mystery of icing éclairs, curling chocolate, creating decorations, swirling coulis and piping sorbet – *Le Cordon Bleu Complete Cooking Techniques* shows them all.

RECIPES, EQUIPMENT AND MUCH, MUCH MORE ... While designed to help readers achieve success with any recipe – no matter what the source – *Le Cordon Bleu Complete Cooking Techniques* also contains more than 200 classic and contemporary recipes. Master chefs from the schools have contributed their favourite recipes, from well-known cookery staples such as French onion soup, Coq au vin, Braised lamb and Austrian cheesecake to crowd pleasing standouts such as Sichuan fish, Snail-stuffed ravioli, Stuffed quail, and Gâteau des Deux Pierre, with exciting garnishing ideas for each main chapter.

Nor is this all. Dotted throughout are informative charts with details on portion control, cooking times, equivalencies and substitutions and a detailed glossary, covering the well-known and the more arcane cookery terms, rounds off the book. The batterie de cuisine listing selects everything necessary for the well-equipped kitchen, though specialist tools are showcased throughout. Herbs, spices and flavourings – both Eastern and Western are set out along the way, and sprinkled among the pages are tricks of the trade, details of the types and variety of foods available and fascinating historical information on dishes and ingredients.

THE NEW KITCHEN BIBLE ... For all these reasons and more, this is the book that all keen cooks will want in their kitchens. Whether readers are just beginning their culinary adventures or perfecting pre-existing skills, *Le Cordon Bleu Complete Cooking Techniques* will empower them to create the dishes of their dreams as well as everyday fare. Fashions change and chef-inspired, ingredient-led or occasion-oriented cookbooks may wax and wane, but *Le Cordon Bleu Complete Cooking Techniques* will never go out of style. The clear, concise text, plethora of pictures and visual excitement of the material, will both instruct and inspire all who read it.

LE CORDON BLEU IN HISTORY ... In the sixteenth century, King Henry III of France created *L'ordre du Saint-Esprit* (the Order of the Holy Spirit) whose members became almost as renowned for their sumptuous banquets and feasts as for the broad blue ribbons they wore. Ever since, the name Cordon Bleu (Blue Ribbon) has been synonymous with culinary excellence.

Over 300 years later, the launch of culinary magazine *La Cuisinière Cordon Bleu* in 1895 by Marthe Distel heralded the start of the Paris Academy, with the first demonstration of cooking held the following year. This past century, Le Cordon Bleu has perfected a complete regime of culinary training, as more than thirty full time master chefs pass on their standards of excellence and culinary brilliance.

LE CORDON BLEU TODAY ... Incorporating influences from all over the world, with schools in London, Paris, Tokyo, Sydney and North America, Le Cordon Bleu is at the cutting edge of culinary art. The unique step-by-step teaching method of its master chefs, valued by students the world over, has been captured in *Le Cordon Bleu Complete Cooking Techniques*.

THE MANTLE OF EXCELLENCE ... *Le Cordon Bleu Complete Cooking Techniques* was made possible through the invaluable advice and expertise of Le Cordon Bleu chefs, all enthusiastically supported by their president, André Cointreau. Jeni Wright and Chef Eric Treuillé, both of whom worked previously with Le Cordon Bleu on the *Le Cordon Bleu Classic French Cookbook* ably describe and demonstrate the techniques. Carroll & Brown Limited developed the original concept and their impressive organisation provided invaluable help with the creative work in terms of design, editorial and photography. Le Cordon Bleu is very proud to have collaborated with Amy Carroll and Denise Brown who are among the top cookbook producers in the world.

HOW TO USE THIS BOOK

Le Cordon Bleu Complete Cooking Techniques opens the doors of Le Cordon Bleu to the home cook.

Its extremely accessible format leads you through 15 chapters, each focusing on a different food or food category – from Stocks and Soups to Cakes and Biscuits.

Each begins with essential information about choosing the best ingredients; the following pages demonstrate favoured preparation methods and cooking techniques. These pages are bursting with information boxes on everything from equipment to serving ideas and many chapters have a special section on finishing touches, with a step-by-step guide to the more elaborate finishes.

In each chapter you will also find a Chef's Special – every one a signature dish of Le Cordon Bleu's master chefs. These demonstrate what the home cook can achieve in terms of a stunning presentation.

The book opens with a batterie de cuisine – listing all the essential equipment a cook will need, while the final chapter delves into the mysteries of flavours, herbs and spices from the East and the West, finishing with a series of quick-reference equivalency charts, a glossary of cooking terms, and a comprehensive index.

Reader, enquire within... and, whatever your cookery question, it will be answered.

Contents

Introduction 5

Batterie de Cuisine 10

Stocks & Soups 15

Eggs, Cheese & Cream 29

Fish & Shellfish 47

Poultry & Game 87

Meat 117

Vegetables & Salads 157

Pulses, Grains & Nuts 193

•

Pasta 205

•

Sauces & Dressings 221

•

Bread & Yeast Cookery 231

•

Fruits 247

•

Desserts 271

•

Pastry 293

•

Cakes & Biscuits 307

•

General Information 327

Glossary 336

Index 340

Recipe Index 351

Acknowledgements 352

Batterie de Cuisine

Along with the best ingredients, the right tools for preparing and cooking foods are essential for successful results. Although some cooks are able to make do with a few, multi-purpose utensils, specialist equipment can make many techniques easier to master, and may be required for an authentic presentation of ethnic dishes.

Measuring Equipment

The first necessity for culinary success is to ensure that the right amounts of ingredients are used. Dry foodstuffs must be levelled off – unless heaped teaspoons or tablespoons are called for – and liquids should be viewed from eye level to ensure they reach the required depth. Spoons and measures are generally sold in both metric and imperial sizes.

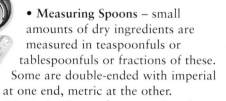

• **Measuring Spoons** – small amounts of dry ingredients are measured in teaspoonfuls or tablespoonfuls or fractions of these. Some are double-ended with imperial at one end, metric at the other.
• **Measuring Jugs** – for measuring the volume of ingredients, especially liquids. The best jugs have metric and imperial markings, plus American cups (see below).
• **Scales** – essential when recipes call for ingredients by weight. There are many varieties, from balance scales to digital display types. The best provide both metric and imperial weights.
• **American Measuring Cups** – the volume of both dry and liquid ingredients can be measured in cups and fractions – ¼, ⅓ and ½ – of a cup. Usually sold in nesting sets.

General

This catch-all category takes account of the basic utensils required for preparing and handling both raw and cooked ingredients. Among their many uses are lifting, draining, shaping, stoning, grating and mashing.

• **Timers** – ranging from simple sand-in-glass vial devices to battery-operated bell ringers, these help keep track of important preparation and cooking stages.
• **Thermometers** – there are three different types: deep-fat, meat and sugar. They are essential to ensure that the safe and desired internal temperatures of meat and poultry are achieved and that fat and sugar reach their required temperatures.
• **Kitchen Scissors** – choose sturdy all-purpose scissors with a comfortable grip. They should be made of stainless steel for easy cleaning. Poultry shears (see page 93) are designed to cut poultry bones easily.
• **Vegetable Peelers** – several varieties are available: those with swivel blades are especially good; some have a bean slicer in the handle and a pointed tip for coring.
• **Cutting Boards** – use either wood or polypropylene; these do not blunt sharp knives. Keep different boards for different purposes, those for raw meats and strong-smelling items, such as garlic, should be kept separate from general purpose boards. Clean boards thoroughly after use.
• **Tongs** – a "V"-shaped piece of stainless steel that comes together when squeezed. Used for picking up and transferring delicate foods.
• **Ladles** – come with various capacity bowls attached to a long handle. Used for serving liquids, some ladles have a lip on one side to make pouring more accurate.
• **Slotted Spoons** – wide flat spoons with holes pierced through the surface and with slightly pointed tips. Used for lifting and draining foods out of hot liquid or oil; also for skimming.
• **Stoner or Pitter** – use to remove cherry and olive stones. Made of stainless steel or aluminium, it consists of two arms hinged together in the centre. One has a holder for the fruit, the other a prong that pushes out the stone.
• **Canelle Knife** – has a short rounded stainless steel head with a small "V"-shaped blade running horizontally across it. Use to peel fine strips of zest from citrus fruits or vegetables, such as cucumber. When sliced, the fruit or vegetable has an attractive ridged edge.
• **Zester** – the stainless steel rectangular head has five holes along the top edge, designed to remove fine shavings of citrus zest, leaving behind the bitter white pith.
• **Graters** – the most common type is a hollow box with various cutting perforations on each side. Rotary graters with different blades are also available, and specialist single-sided graters for citrus zest and Parmesan cheese. For nutmeg, there is a concave version with a compartment for the whole spice.
• **Mouli-légumes** – a stainless steel or plastic hopper that clamps over a bowl and is used for puréeing soft fruits and vegetables. It comes with a selection of fine and coarse discs, one of which is placed in the hopper. A crank is used to turn the chosen disc and push the food through the Mouli into the bowl below.

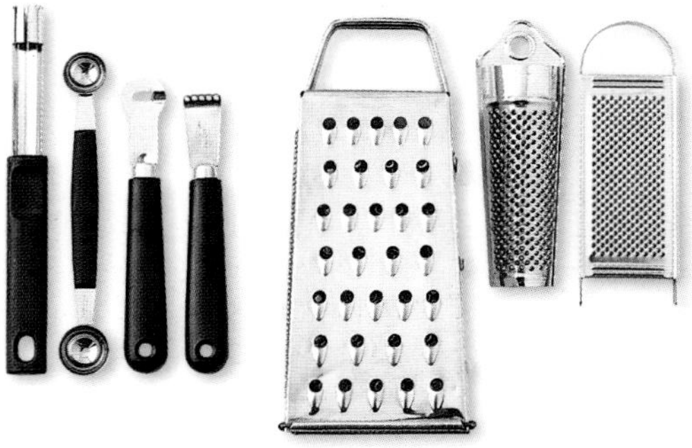

• **Skimming Spoon** – large flat round head with a series of very fine holes or mesh in the centre. Used for removing scum and fat from the surface of hot liquids, such as stock.
• **Fish Slice** – a large square or rectangular blade that will slide easily under delicate flat foods, such as fish fillets. It has holes to let fat or liquid drain through and is available in metal or plastic; it can have a non–stick coating.
• **Palette Knife** – available in various sizes. The blade is thin, flat and flexible with a rounded end. Use for turning and transferring flat items such as fish fillets or biscuits and for spreading decorative icings.
• **Angled Spatula** – sometimes called a cookie spatula, the long flexible rectangular blade is angled to help lift food from edged pans and dishes.
• **Bulb Baster** – A giant syringe-like object, used to suck up fat from meat juices and gravy.
• **Tweezers** – Small pincers, usually about 8 cm long, useful for removing fish bones and placing delicate garnishes and decorations in position.
• **Scrubbing Brush** – rectangular brush with hard bristles. Designed for scrubbing seafood shells and vegetables.
• **Wooden Cocktail Sticks** – about 10 cm long, for holding small pieces of food and for securing cut openings.
• **Apple Corer** – a cylindrical blade that fits neatly around the core of an apple, on the end of a shaft long enough to go through the fruit and remove the core in one piece.
• **Melon Baller** – two bowl-shaped blades, one slightly larger than the other, fixed either side of a central handle. Make the balls by rotating the blade.
• **Ice-cream Scoop** – comprised of a hollow handle through which body heat is conducted and a large bowl-shaped scoop at one end, usually made of stainless steel or aluminium. The conducted body heat warms the bowl and makes scooping and releasing the ice cream easier Trigger scoops are also available – the ice cream is released from the scoop by activating a lever which pushes it cleanly out.

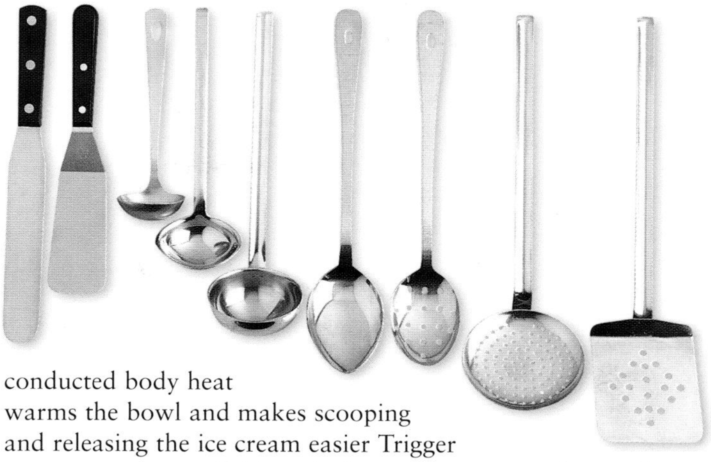

• **Lemon Squeezers** – most popular type is made of glass or plastic and has a ridged, pointed cone in the centre for squeezing the juice from halved citrus fruit. The wooden variety, called a reamer, has a similar-shaped cone attached to a handle; the juice is extracted by holding the cut fruit over a bowl and inserting the squeezer.
• **Potato Masher** – a perforated disc attached to two prongs which are shaped and connected to a handle. Used to pulp down cooked potato and other root vegetables, such as carrots and parsnips.
• **Potato Ricer** – two hinged arms, one has a basket with a fine mesh base that holds the food, the other has a flat disc that pushes the food through the holes. Produces very finely mashed, almost puréed results.
• **Cake Slice** – a flat triangular metal blade, shaped to a rounded point to fit easily under a wedge of cake or pie.

Knives

Vital for a large number of tasks, the accomplished cook should have on hand a range of both general-purpose and task-specific knives. These should be kept sharp, and stored in wooden blocks to prevent dulling.

• **Cleaver (Western)** – the weight of the large flat rectangular blade is heavy enough for cutting through bone and meat joints.
• **Chef's Knife** – also known as a cook's knife, this has a long triangular-shaped blade ranging in length from 15–30 cm. The slightly curved edge enables you to rock the knife for easy chopping.
• **Filleting Knife** – has a long flexible blade about 20 cm in length. Ideal for raw fish, fruits and vegetables.
• **Boning Knife** – has a long rigid blade (9–15 cm) curved to a fine sharp tip to make boning meat and poultry easier.
• **Serrated Knife** – a small 13-cm long knife cuts cleanly through fruits and vegetables. A larger knife is good for slicing bread and cakes neatly and evenly.

• **Small Paring Knife** – shaped like a chef's knife but with a blade only 6–9 cm long, this is one of the most useful knives. Because of its size, it has excellent control for cutting fruits, vegetables, meat and cheese, etc.
• **Mezzaluna** – Italian for "half moon", a curved steel chopping blade (also called a crescent cutter) with a vertical wooden handle at each end. Used with a rocking motion.
• **Carving Knife and Fork** – a knife with a long narrow blade is suitable for slicing hot cooked meats; a fluted one with a rounded tip is for slicing cold meats. A carving fork has two long prongs to secure meat during carving. It should have a good grip and may be fitted with a guard to protect your hand.
• **Knife Sharpener** – a long rod of coarse-textured steel. To sharpen, run the edge of the knife blade along the steel at an angle of approximately 45°.

STOVETOP

For top-of-the stove use, cookware should have long, fireproof handles, be of sufficient weight to rest securely on a burner but not be too heavy to lift, and should distribute heat evenly.

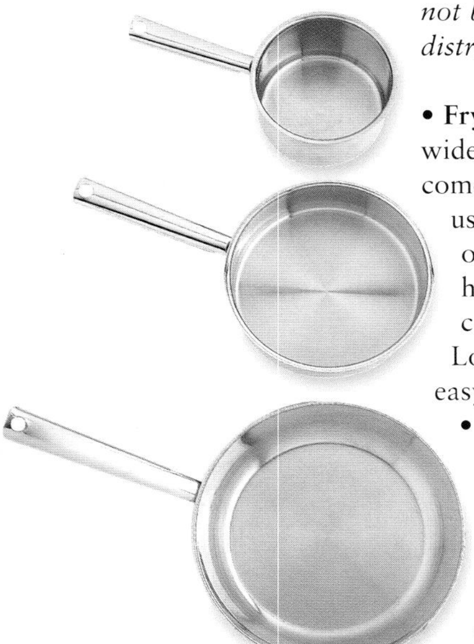

- **Frying Pans and Skillets** – these wide, shallow, flat-bottomed pans come in a variety of sizes. Generally used for cooking thin, flat pieces of food quickly in fat, so pans of heavy gauge, good heat-conducting metals are best. Long, straight handles make them easy to manoeuvre.
- **Non-stick Frying Pans and Skillets** – special coatings line these pans, precluding the use of fats. Special care must be taken to prevent the lining from becoming scratched.
- **Saucepans** – the workhorses of the kitchen, these are found in many different sizes and shapes. Some are short and squat, others tall and deep. Generally differentiated by capacity – either litres or pints or both – they are normally sold complete with lids. Heavy-gauge stainless steel pans are good conductors of heat.

- **Double Boiler** – a two-saucepan set with a large bottom pan and a thin small pan that fits inside or on top. Use as a *bain marie* for cooking delicate foods over boiling water to buffer direct heat.
- **Stockpot** – also useful for cooking pasta, this should be taller than it is wide and of a large capacity.
- **Steamer** – a perforated container that fits into a saucepan and permits vegetables to be cooked without them touching the water. Special stacking steamer pans are also available.
- **Griddle** – A heavy (usually cast iron), flat cooking utensil, sometimes with non-stick coating, with excellent heat-transferring abilities. Use to cook drop scones and pancakes. Ridged cast-iron types are good for cooking fish, meat and vegetables to give a "chargrilled" effect.
- **Crepe Pan** – traditionally made of cast iron, this shallow-sided, pan is ideal for producing perfect crêpes. It should be "proved" or seasoned before use and wiped clean rather than washed.

ASIAN EQUIPMENT

Designed for preparing food for traditional fast cooking over a high heat, these tools are usually sold alongside specialist ingredients in Asian shops.

- **Chinese Cleaver** – has a large flat blade with short wooden handle. Suitable for all sorts of chopping and slicing, it is an excellent all-in-one knife. The wide blade makes a useful scoop.
- **Chopsticks** – use long wooden ones for handling and arranging delicate food and for stirring; use the shorter more elegant variety (avoid slippery finishes) for eating.
- **Wok and Shovel** – a bowl-shaped iron pan that comes with one handle (best for stir-frying) or two handles (for greater stability when deep-frying, braising or steaming). For family use, a 35-cm wok is ideal; some have domed lids, which are useful for steaming and braising. The metal shovel or wok spatula, has a long handle with a flat head. It is curved along the outer edge to fit neatly into the shape of the wok and has a lip around the back to catch the food as it is turned about during stir-frying.
- **Bamboo Mat** – made of flexible woven bamboo, place inside cooking pots or woks to prevent meat from sticking to the base during long, slow cooking, or use to roll sushi. Wash after use and dry thoroughly before storing.
- **Wooden Saté Skewers** – come in a variety of lengths, the long ones are mainly used for skewering meat and vegetables ready for grilling or barbecuing. Soak in water for 30 minutes before using to prevent the wood from charring.
- **Japanese Omelette Pan** – a square-shaped shallow pan made of cast iron or aluminium with a sturdy wooden handle. The pan is used to make thin symmetrical omelettes. To clean, wipe with oil then a damp cloth.
- **Large Oriental Straining Spoon** – has a long bamboo handle with a flat wire head, used for lifting and straining food from hot oil or liquid.
- **Bamboo Steamer** – consists of three parts: two round 5 cm-deep baskets with lattice bases which allow the steam to circulate, and a woven lid. Ideal for steaming a selection of foods in a wok or over a large pan of water. Different ingredients can be cooked in layers at the same time.
- **Small Thin Rolling Pin** – usually about 60 cm long, and can be even in width or tapered at the ends. Ideal for rolling out very thin pieces of pastry or bread dough. Wipe with a damp cloth after use – do not soak or the wood may crack or warp.

• **Omelette Pan** – Heavier and larger than a crêpe pan, this special frying pan should have a thick base to distribute heat evenly, and curved, gently sloping sides that permit the cooked omelette to easily slide out onto the serving plate. An angled handle makes manoeuvring easier. Omelette pans should be seasoned before use and wiped rather than washed.
• **Fish Kettle** – a long narrow pan, as deep as it is wide, this contains a perforated rack on which to lift the fish in and out of its poaching liquid.
• **Deep Fryer** – a heavy, lidded saucepan and wire basket set, the latter's handle should enable it to be lowered into fat and supported for draining.
• **Pressure Cooker** – deep, heavy, lidded saucepan incorporating pressure gauge and safety valve, this uses internal steam to cook food in about half the normal time.

OVENWARE

Baking dishes, pans and pots made to withstand high temperatures or to conduct heat are available to suit specific tasks. Many are sufficiently decorative to be used at the table.

• **Casseroles** – cast iron, earthenware and china are popular materials for deep, lidded, single or double-handled cooking pots. Some are flameproof – for use on top of the stove as well.
• **Terrines** – generally of earthenware, usually oval and lidded with air vents in the top, these straight-sided containers are designed for cooking minced and chopped meat mixtures.

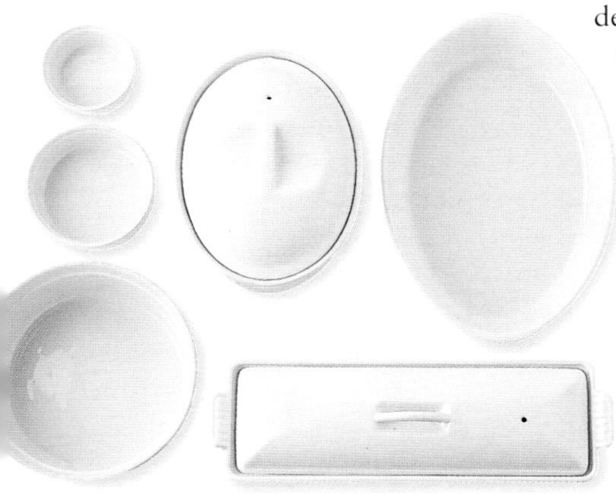

• **Soufflé Dishes** – straight-sided, round dishes of glass, porcelain or stoneware, these are traditionally fluted. An unglazed underside allows heat to penetrate quickly.
• **Ramekins** – individual-sized soufflé dishes that are also useful for baking custards and cold or hot puddings.
• **Gratin Dishes** – wide and shallow with straight or sloping sides and handles. Usually flameproof so they can be used under the grill and in the oven to produce dishes with crusty tops.
• **Roasting Tins** – rectangular or oval, flat-based metal tins with straight or slightly sloping sides, used for cooking meat and baked dishes. Deep tins usually have integral racks.
• **Racks** – primarily used to allow fat and juices to run free from roasting poultry and meat into the tin below, these footed grills can be cradle-shaped or rectangular.
• **Metal Skewers** – long and thin with a sharp pointed end to cut through chunks of meat and vegetables; for making kebabs, piercing baking potatoes and testing for doneness.

BAKEWARE

The home baker requires a wide variety of specialist items to turn out perfect breads, pies, tarts, cakes and biscuits.

• **Cake Tins** – metal, square, round or rectangular tins for making single and multi-layered cakes, which can be deep or shallow. Decorative shapes are also sold. Some tins have loose bases, which enable the cake to be removed easily.
• **Ring Mould** – when baking heavy batters, the central hole ensures that heat reaches the centre of the cake. With light and airy mixtures, the ring supports the cake on rising.
• **Springform Cake Tin** – has removable base and a spring-clipped side that make extraction easier.
• **Swiss Roll Tin** – shallow, rectangular metal tin designed specifically for cooking sheet of whisked sponge.
• **Baking Sheets** – thin, metal, rectangular sheets, sometimes with lipped edges. Good-quality heavy sheets are essential for even conduction of heat and to prevent buckling.
• **Loaf Tins** – plain, rectangular tins with deep sides for baking breads and pâtés. Long, narrow baguette tins for French bread are usually made of tinned or blued steel.
• **Pie Tins** – shallow, slope-sided round tins may be made of glass or metal, or porcelain for serving at the table.
• **Flan Tins** – round and shallow, often fluted with removable bases. Can be made of tinned steel, black steel or ceramic; used for tarts, flans and quiches.
• **Flan Rings** – plain or scalloped metal hoops used with a baking sheet for tarts, flans and quiches; can also be used for layering cakes.
• **Baking Beans** – ceramic or metal beans help to weight down pastry in its tin when baking blind without a filling.
• **Tartlet Tins** – small, decoratively shaped metal tins often with fluted sides are ideal for petits fours and small pastries. Eclairs, madeleines, cup cakes, muffins and other small buns can be baked in tins that contain multiple moulds.
• **Cake Racks** – round or rectangular, these footed open metal grids enable air to circulate beneath food during cooling.
• **Decorative Moulds** – can be used for making breads, steamed or baked puddings, jellies, mousses, ice creams and bombes etc.
• **Biscuit and Pastry Cutters** – sold individually or in sets, these thin, metal straight-sided cutters come in geometric and naturalistic shapes and in varying sizes.
• **Pastry Wheel** – wooden-handled cutter with fluted wheel, used to trim edges of pies decoratively.

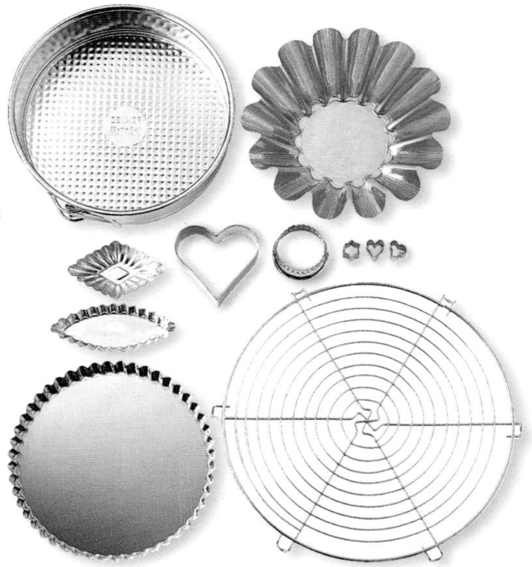

Sieves, Strainers and Sifters

Designed to separate parts of, drain water from or incorporate air into ingredients, there are a number of essential tools.

• **Sieves** – metal, plastic or wooden frames with different-sized mesh. Conical ones, called *chinois*, are ideal for straining liquid ingredients into jugs and jars; bowl and drum sieves fit over bowls and are best for dry ingredients.

• **Colander** – perforated basin for draining water from cooked vegetables and pasta or washing fruits and vegetables. Comes in various sizes, with either single or double handles.
• **Dredgers** – ideal for incorporating air into flour or sprinkling sugar in decorative patterns, these can be simple shakers with wide openings or mesh-bottomed cups with integral triggers.
• **Salad Shaker** – plain wire basket or plastic spinner that removes excess water from salad leaves without bruising.
• **Egg Separator** – a round spoon with holes or slots. Allows the egg white to drain through while trapping the yolk.

Machines

Though every task in the kitchen can be accomplished by hand, electric tools can help save time and labour.

• **Food Processor** – multi-purpose machine, ideal for chopping, mincing, and puréeing a wide variety of ingredients. Most are sold with slicing and shredding discs and blades for making and kneading dough.
• **Mixer** – hand-held and table models exist for mixing doughs and batters, whipping cream, whisking egg whites and creaming cake mixtures. Heavy-duty tabletop versions have a variety of attachments.
• **Blender** – ideal for making purées, pâtés and dips, soups, sauces and drinks. Also useful for chopping dry ingredients.
• **Ice-Cream Maker** – small model churns the mixture in the freezer; large free-standing model, called a sorbetière, which produces a smooth professional result, has an integral stirring and cooling mechanism.
• **Grinder** – small-scale machine useful for grinding coffee beans, nuts and spices.
• **Deep-fat Fryer** – free-standing electric models with in-built fryer baskets are the safest. They have their own thermostats to regulate temperature of oil.

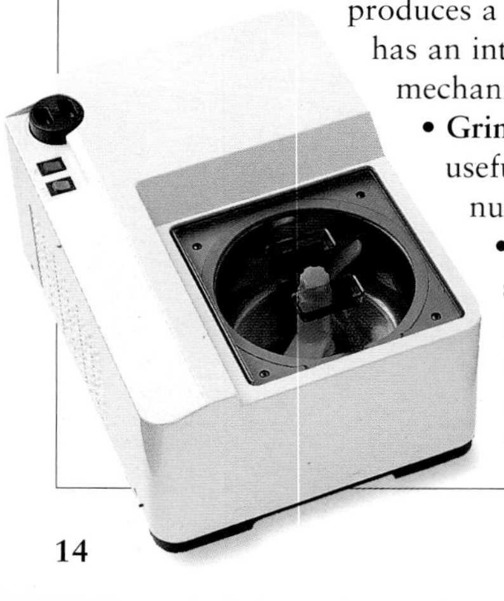

Mixing, Rolling and Decorating

Preparing foods – whether by stirring, beating or shaping – and decorating the finished item require a number of different, but important tools.

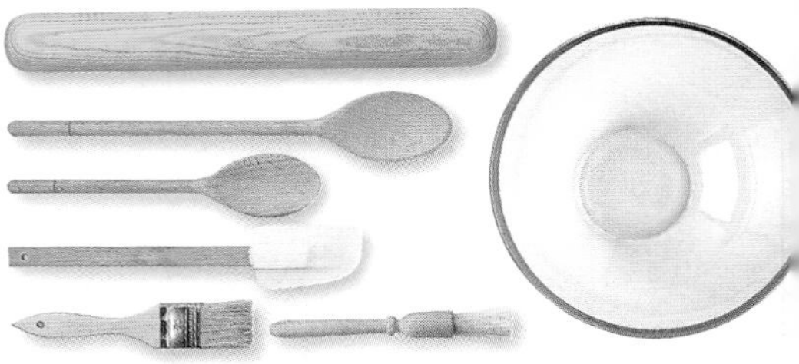

• **Mixing Bowls** – come in a large number of sizes. Stainless steel bowls are durable and good conductors of heat and cold; glass and ceramic bowls are sufficiently heavy to sit firmly on a counter while ingredients are beaten.
• **Wooden Spoons** – ideal for stirring, mixing, beating, and creaming, they are strong and inflexible and poor conductors of heat. Wood absorbs flavours, so always wash, dry and air spoons thoroughly after use.
• **Rubber Spatula** – useful for folding in whisked egg whites, as well as removing all traces of batter from mixing bowls, this flexible scraper is essential for non-stick pans.
• **Pastry Brushes** – for applying glazes to many different foods before or after baking, they may be round or flat and contain hog's head or plastic bristles.
• **Pestle and Mortar** – the mortar is a small bowl usually made of stone or marble, that has a rough inner surface. The pestle has a round unglazed end shaped to fit the contours of the bowl. Use for grinding spices and seeds and making pesto.
• **Rolling Pin** – plain, smooth, heavy hardwood roller may be handleless or have integral handles. Some rolling pin handles are fixed to a central rod in the roller.
• **Pasta Machine** – purpose made for both rolling and cutting out pasta, it is sold with a variety of cutters to make ribbons and noodles of varying widths.
• **Whisks** – hand-held balloon ones with wire loops and coiled metal handles are preferred by chefs for light and airy whisked egg whites, to blend sauces and to create lump-free batters. They are sold in various sizes to suit different tasks.

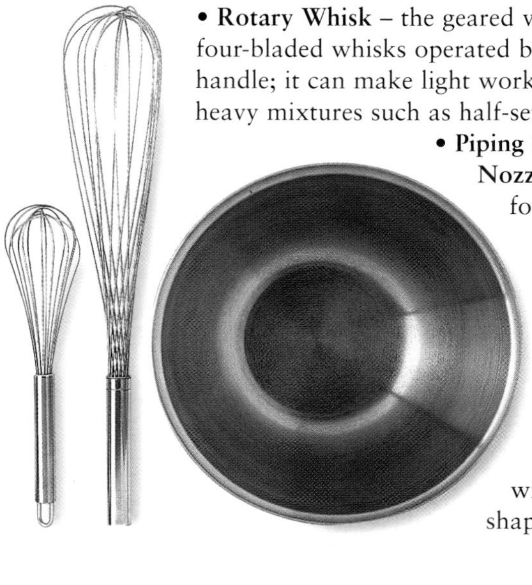

• **Rotary Whisk** – the geared version has two four-bladed whisks operated by a small handle; it can make light work of beating heavy mixtures such as half-set ice cream.
• **Piping Bags and Nozzles** – essential for creating piped decorations, differently sized bags accommodate small metal or plastic nozzles (also called tubes) with variously shaped openings.

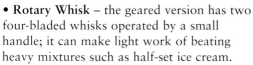

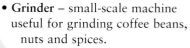

Stocks & Soups

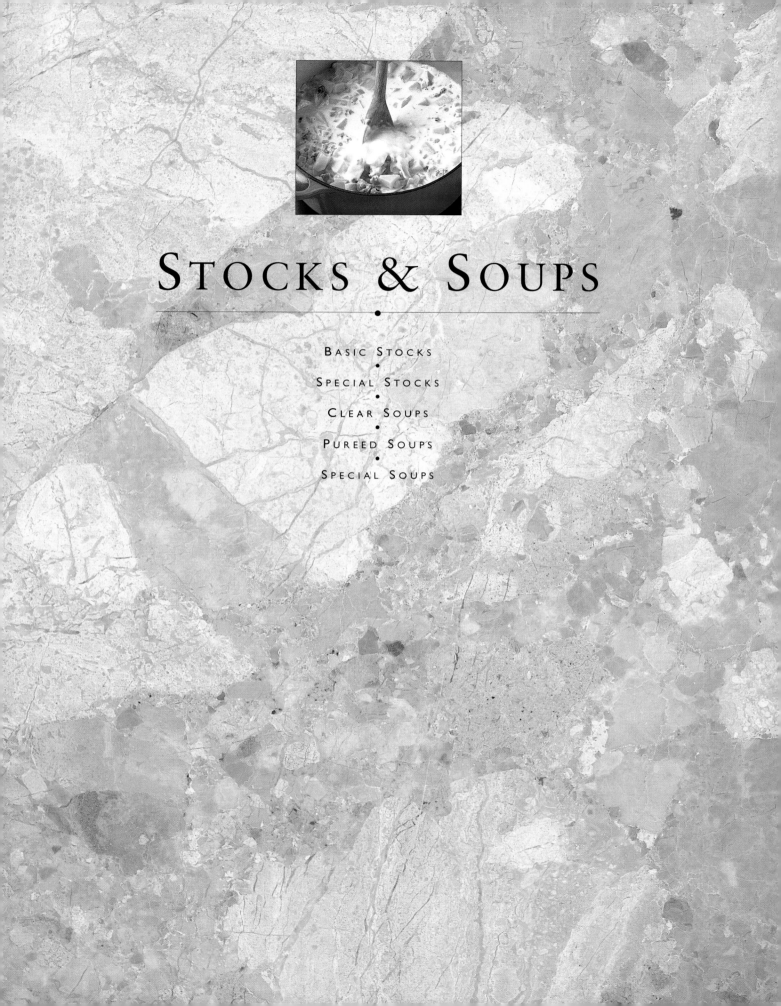

Basic Stocks
•
Special Stocks
•
Clear Soups
•
Pureed Soups
•
Special Soups

BASIC STOCKS

Stock, the strained liquid that results from cooking poultry, meat or fish with vegetables and seasonings in water, forms the basis of many soups, sauces and stews. Homemade stocks produce a finer, more aromatic and less salty flavour than shop-bought cubes, granules and canned broths. They also freeze well, so you can always have them to hand.

CHICKEN STOCK

About 750 g chicken bones and carcass
About 150 g mixed onion, celery and carrot, roughly chopped
1 clove
1 bouquet garni
2 garlic cloves, chopped (optional)
6 peppercorns
1.5 litres water

Blanch the bones and carcass, drain and rinse. Place in a pan with the remaining ingredients and bring to the boil. Simmer for 2–3 hours, skimming often. Strain the stock and let cool, then refrigerate for up to 3 days. Makes about 1.5 litres.

CHICKEN STOCK

Pale and golden in colour, this classic can be made from raw chicken bones and carcass or the bones and scraps of a cooked chicken. Blanching the bones first is a chef's technique to remove excess fat; an alternative method is also given.

1 Add bones to vegetables in pan, cover with water and bring to the boil. During simmering, skim often.

2 Ladle into a fine sieve set over a bowl. Press the solids with the ladle to extract all of the liquid.

REMOVING FAT
Refrigerate stock overnight, then lift off any surface fat with a slotted spoon.

BROWN STOCK

1.5 kg beef or veal bones
1 onion, unpeeled and quartered
2 carrots, 1 leek and 1 celery stick, chopped
3 litres water
2 tbsp tomato purée
1 bouquet garni
6 peppercorns

Roast meat bones at 230°C for 40 minutes, adding vegetables halfway. Deglaze with a little water. Transfer to a pan, add remaining ingredients and simmer for 3–4 hours, skimming often. Strain and let cool. Refrigerate up to 3 days. Makes about 3 litres.

BROWN STOCK

This meaty stock, which can be made with beef or veal bones, has a good, strong colour and flavour because the bones are roasted first. Roasting caramelizes the outside of the bones and so adds colour to the stock; it also renders the excess fat. For a white stock, omit roasting.

1 Add vegetables to bones halfway through roasting time and stir to mix.

2 Skim stock as often as possible during simmering, to remove fat and scum.

3 Ladle into a fine sieve set over a bowl. Press the solids with the ladle to extract all of the liquid.

Fish Stock

For a delicate flavour, use the bones and trimmings of white fish such as sole, turbot, plaice or haddock, or pale pink fish such as the salmon shown here. Do not use strong-flavoured oily fish such as mackerel. Simmer fish stock for 20 minutes only; longer cooking will make the stock bitter.

1 Cut the bones and fish trimmings into pieces using a chef's knife. Remove the eyes and gills. *Dégorge* the bones and trimmings by soaking them in cold salted water for about 10 minutes (this removes any blood and "muddy" taste). Drain the bones and trimmings and place in a pan.

2 Cut the vegetables into even pieces and place in the pan with the remaining ingredients.

3 During simmering, skim off the scum as it rises to the surface of the liquid, using a large slotted spoon.

4 Ladle into a fine sieve set over a bowl. Press the solids with the ladle to extract all of the liquid.

Making Stock Cubes

You can prepare stock in large quantities and freeze it for later use (it will keep in the freezer for up to 6 months). After cooling the stock and removing any solidified fat, boil it until reduced and concentrated, then let cool and follow the technique shown here. Frozen cubes can be dropped straight into a soup or stew as it simmers.

1 Pour cold concentrated stock into ice-cube trays, then open-freeze for about 4 hours until solid.

2 Once the cubes are completely frozen they are ready for use or storing. Remove them from the tray and place them in a plastic freezer bag. Seal the bag and return the cubes to the freezer until ready to use.

FISH STOCK

2 kg fish bone and trimmings, chopped and dégorged
1 onion, 1 carrot and 1 celery stick
250 ml dry white wine (optional)
12 peppercorns
2 bay leaves
Juice of ½ lemon
2.5 litres water

Put the ingredients in a pan and bring to the boil. Simmer for 20 minutes, skimming often. Strain the stock and let cool, then refrigerate up to 3 days. Makes about 3 litres.

TRICK OF THE TRADE

Quick Skimming

Professional chefs use this method to remove traces of fat from hot strained stock. It is quicker than leaving the stock to chill before removing solidified fat (see opposite page).

While the stock is still hot, pass a double thickness of paper towels through it; the paper will quickly absorb any fat.

SPECIAL STOCKS

Different ingredients and techniques give these stocks unique textures and flavours, completing the culinary repertoire of stocks that are most frequently used. For basic stocks, see pages 16–17.

VEGETABLE STOCK

Light and mild, this stock can be used as a vegetarian substitute for chicken or meat stock (see page 16). Use about 450 g mixed vegetables, such as the carrots, onions, leek and celery shown here, a bouquet garni and 2 litres water to make about 1.5 litres stock. After cooling, refrigerate up to 3 days, or freeze up to 1 month.

1 Put chopped vegetables, bouquet garni and water in a pan. Bring to the boil and simmer for up to 1 hour.

2 Ladle into a fine sieve held over a bowl. Press the solids with the ladle to extract all of the liquid.

SEAWEED STOCK

Called dashi *in Japanese, this clear seaweed stock has a delicate fishy flavour. It is very quick and easy to prepare, and will keep refrigerated up to 3 days.* Kombu *(dried seaweed) and* bonito *(dried fish) flakes are generally available from large supermarkets and Japanese stores. For the recipe, see box, left.*

1 Add *kombu* seaweed to *bonito* flakes in pan of water and bring to the boil.

2 Slowly strain the liquid through a muslin-lined sieve set over a bowl.

DASHI

1 litre water
25 g bonito flakes
25 g kombu seaweed

Pour the water into a pan and add the *bonito* flakes and *kombu* seaweed. Bring the water to the boil, then remove the pan from the heat and let the *bonito* flakes settle. Slowly strain the liquid through a muslin-lined sieve into a clean pan and simmer for 10 minutes. To concentrate the flavour, return the *bonito* flakes and *kombu* seaweed to the stock and repeat as above. Makes about 1 litre.

GAME STOCK

The carcasses of mature game birds make flavourful stock, especially if they are browned in butter first. To make about 2 litres stock, use 1 kg chopped carcasses, about 450 g chopped vegetables, such as onions, carrots and celery, and 2 litres water.

1 Brown carcass pieces in butter to heighten the colour and flavour of stock.

2 Add vegetables and water and bring to the boil. Simmer for 1–2 hours, skimming frequently. Strain, then cool and refrigerate for up to 3 days.

CONSOMME

A clear stock-based soup, consommé is prepared from chicken, beef or veal stock (see page 16), which is clarified by the addition of egg whites and vegetables. The vegetables also enhance flavour and colour.

MAKING CONSOMME

This easy method of clarifying stock uses a mixture of egg whites, a mirepoix *of vegetables (see page 166) and an acid in the form of lemon juice. Chicken consommé is made here, but the same technique applies to making beef or veal consommé.*

1 Whisk 3–4 egg whites with a fork until frothy. Add 2 tbsp lemon juice and about 350 g *mirepoix*.

2 Add the egg mixture to 2 litres warm stock; bring to the boil. Whisk until a crust forms, 4–6 minutes.

3 Make a hole in the crust for the liquid to simmer through. Simmer gently for about 1 hour – do not stir.

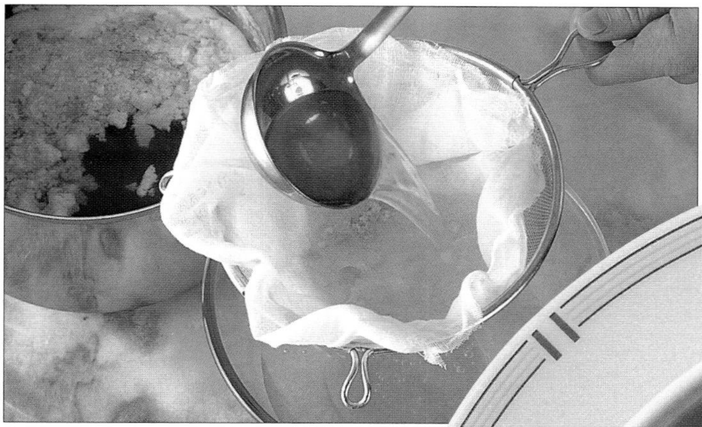

4 Line a sieve with damp muslin and hold it over a large bowl. Break the crust and ladle the consommé through the muslin. Reheat in a clean pan and garnish just before serving with a black truffle *julienne* and leaves of fresh chervil, as shown here. Or sprinkle with a vegetable *brunoise* (see page 166), the traditional garnish.

MAKING ASPIC

Add gelatine to consommé to make aspic that is firm enough to cut decoratively into shapes as a garnish. Liquid aspic is often used to set savoury moulds, mousses and terrines, and for glazing fish, meat and poultry (see page 225).

Soak gelatine leaves for 2–3 minutes in a little of the measured amount of cold consommé (allow 7 g gelatine for every 500 ml liquid). Warm the remaining consommé, then add the gelatine and its soaking liquid. Stir over a gentle heat until the gelatine has melted. Test by chilling 1 tbsp on a saucer.

CLEAR SOUPS

These are based on a stock or broth combined with other ingredients. They can be light and delicate – finely sliced vegetables, seafood or shredded meats in a flavoursome liquid such as *dashi* – or more substantial – like Scotch broth and minestrone, in which hearty ingredients have been simmered for a long time. The quality of these soups depends on using a good homemade stock (see pages 16–17).

VARIATIONS

Clear soups are enlivened by the addition of tasty ingredients. Here are some suggestions:

- A *julienne* of mixed vegetables.
- Thinly sliced mushrooms.
- Chopped spring onions.
- Chopped or shredded cooked chicken.
- Small cooked prawns or sliced scallops.
- Croûtons.
- Shavings of Parmesan or Gruyère.
- Grated citrus zest.

SIMPLE ADDITIONS TO STOCK

By adding just a few ingredients to homemade stock you can have a delicious soup in minutes. Some additions give extra taste, while starchy items like pasta, rice or dumplings give body to the soup. For other ideas, see box, left. Here two quick-and-easy Italian soups are illustrated, both using 1 litre chicken or fish stock. Both will be sufficient for four first-course servings.

PASTA IN BRODO
Bring stock to the boil, then reduce to a simmer. Add 225 g uncooked tortellini; cook for about 7 minutes.

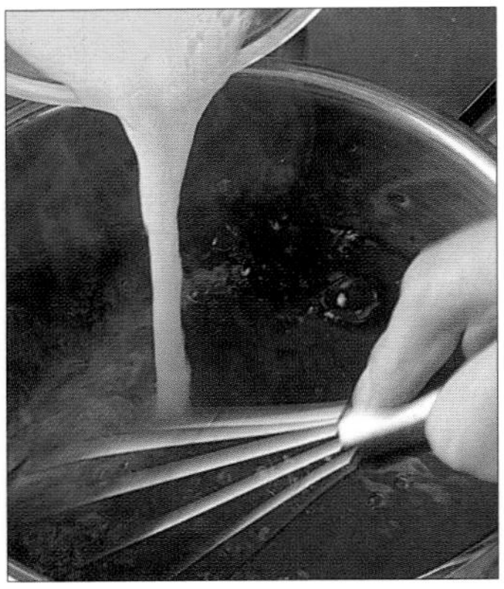

STRACCIATELLA
Beat 2 eggs and whisk into simmering stock. Remove from the heat so that the hot stock cooks the eggs.

FRENCH ONION SOUP

450 g onions, thinly sliced
75 g butter
1.5 litres brown stock (see page 16), made with beef bones
200 ml dry white wine
1 bouquet garni
Salt and freshly ground pepper

Sweat the onions in the butter in a heavy-based pan for about 20 minutes or until tender and caramelized. Add the stock, wine, bouquet garni and salt and pepper to taste and bring to the boil, stirring. Lower the heat, cover and simmer for 30 minutes. Remove the bouquet garni and check seasoning. Serves 4–6.

MAKING A FRENCH ONION SOUP

This classic broth-based soup is made by first cooking the onions in butter, then simmering them slowly in beef stock. The essential technique is to caramelize the onions in the first stage. This ensures that the finished soup is deep brown in colour and rich in flavour.

1 Sweat the onions over a moderate heat stirring frequently until caramelized, about 20 minutes.

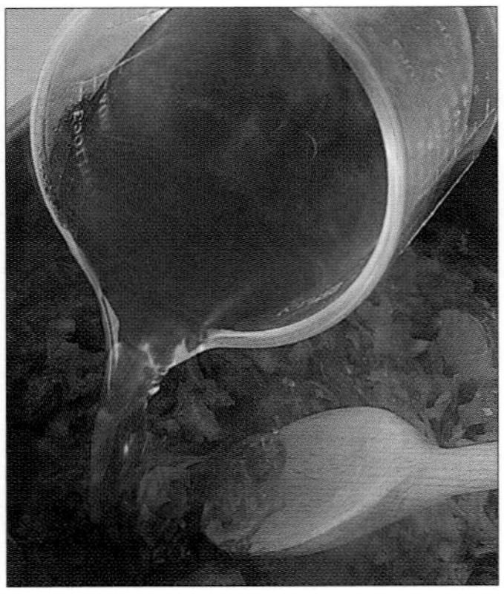

2 Add the stock and wine when the onions are a rich brown. Bring the liquid to the boil, stirring.

3 For a gratin topping, ladle the soup into heatproof bowls and sprinkle with grated Gruyère (see page 44).

Making a Chinese-style Soup

This type of soup can be made in moments by adding Oriental ingredients and flavourings to simmering fish or chicken stock. Here sliced fresh shiitake mushrooms, dried oyster mushrooms that have been reconstituted and shredded, and strips of chicken breast are used as the main ingredients; for flavourings and other ideas, see box, right.

1 Add oyster mushrooms to shiitake mushrooms in simmering stock in wok. Cook for 1 minute.

2 Add strips of chicken breast and simmer, stirring frequently, for 3–5 minutes or until opaque.

3 Pour a beaten egg into soup off the heat and stir with chopsticks so the egg forms long threads.

A Taste of the East

The following ingredients will give an instant Chinese flavour to clear stock. You can add just one or two, or several:

- Light or dark soy sauce.
- Rice wine or dry sherry.
- Peeled and thinly sliced or shredded fresh root ginger.
- Cubes of tofu (bean curd).
- Cellophane noodles.
- Canned sliced bamboo shoots or water chestnuts.
- Shredded Chinese cabbage or *pak choi*.
- Bean sprouts.
- Dried prawns.
- Fresh coriander leaves.
- Sliced spring onions.
- Sesame oil.

Japanese Soups

Dashi *(see page 18) is the classic Japanese stock, used as a base for many Japanese soups. Each soup takes its character from the individual ingredients that are added to the stock. These can be a few delicately prepared items, such as those shown here, or a more substantial mixture of noodles, vegetables, meat and seafood.*

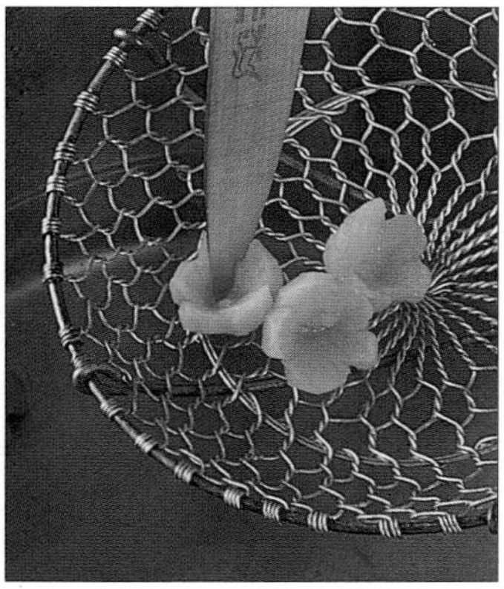

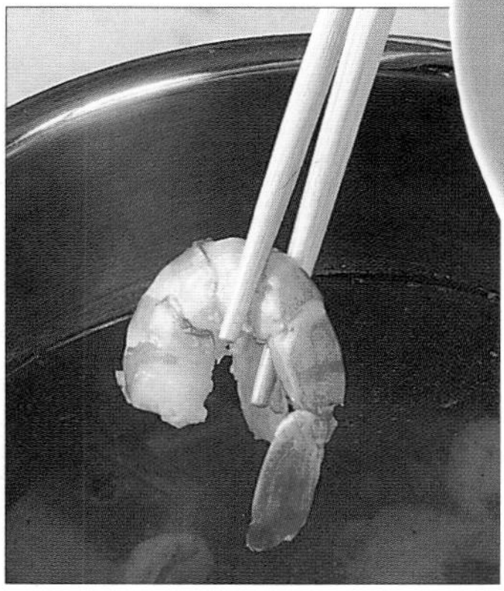

Carrot-flower soup
Make honeysuckle blossoms from 2 medium carrots (see page 104). Bring 1 litre *dashi* to the boil, then lower the heat to a simmer. Add the carrots and simmer for 2 minutes. Ladle into warmed bowls and garnish with bean sprouts and coriander leaves.

Prawn soup
Peel and devein 150 g cooked prawns, leaving the tail shells intact. Bring 1 litre *dashi* to the boil, then lower the heat to a simmer. Add the prawns and heat through for about 2 minutes. Serve in warmed bowls, with coriander leaves.

Creole Bouillabaisse

Here the classic Provençal seafood stew is given a West Indian flavour by the addition of hot chilli, peppers and rum. Use a mixture of fish, such as monkfish, cod, haddock, sea bass, bonito and John Dory – the best and most fresh you can buy.

SERVES 6

2.5–3 kg mixed fish (gutted and cleaned weight, including bone)

12 fresh oysters in shell

100 ml olive oil

1 onion, finely chopped

1 celery stick, finely chopped

1 red pepper, deseeded and diced

1/2 green pepper, deseeded and diced

2–3 garlic cloves, finely chopped

1/4–1/2 tsp dried chilli flakes

Pinch of saffron strands

2 tbsp chopped fresh parsley

1 1/2 tsp fresh thyme leaves

1 bay leaf

500 g ripe tomatoes, skinned, deseeded and chopped

1 litre fish stock

Salt and freshly ground pepper

500 g raw king or tiger prawns in shell, peeled and deveined

1–2 tbsp dark rum

TO SERVE

Chopped fresh thyme

Rouille (see box)

Croûtes (see page 246)

Remove any scales from the fish and, if necessary, remove the heads and tails. Whether you fillet the fish or leave it on the bone, cut them into large, uniform pieces. The bones will add flavour to the stew. Open the oysters carefully, and reserve both the oysters and the liquor from their shells.

Heat the oil in a large flameproof casserole and add the onion, celery, peppers, garlic and the chilli flakes. Crumble the saffron strands between your fingers and add to the vegetables. Cook gently for about 5 minutes, stirring occasionally, until all of the vegetables are softened and lightly browned.

Add the herbs, tomatoes, fish stock and seasonings, stir to mix, and bring to the boil. Lower the heat and simmer for about 30 minutes, stirring from time to time.

Bring the liquid back to the boil, then add the pieces of firm-fleshed fish, putting rich, oily fish in first and white fish on top. Boil rapidly for about 8 minutes, stirring gently once or twice. Add pieces of soft-fleshed fish and continue cooking for 6 minutes, adding the prawns after 2 minutes and the oysters and their liquor for the last minute or two. Remove the casserole from the heat and discard the bay leaf. Stir in the dark rum to taste, and taste and adjust the seasonings.

Serve the bouillabaisse hot, sprinkled with chopped fresh thyme, in a warmed large soup tureen. Hand the rouille separately. This can be added to the soup to taste or spread on to croûtes.

Making Rouille

Rouille is a thick sauce from Provence in the south of France. It is a fiery mayonnaise-like sauce, so named because of its colour: rouille *means rust.*

Put 1 roasted red pepper, deseeded, in a food processor with flesh of 1 baked potato, 1 tbsp tomato purée, 1 egg yolk, 1 garlic clove and 1/4 tsp each salt and cayenne.

Work the ingredients in the machine to a purée, then add 125 ml extra-virgin olive oil while the machine is running and work until smooth and thick. Taste for seasoning.

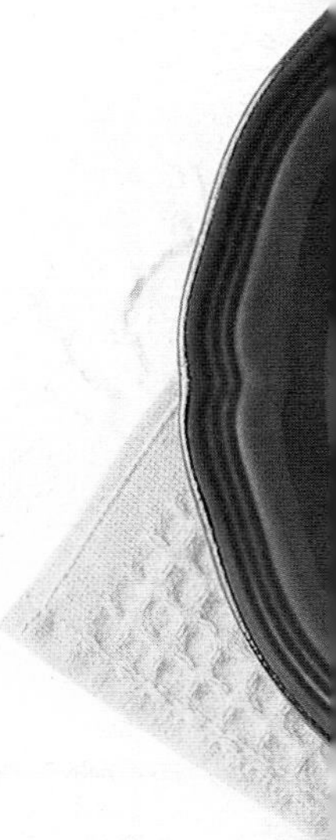

Pureed Soups

Puréeing ingredients that have been cooked in stock, water or milk and then enriching the purée with cream or eggs or both is a simple method of making soup. It can be applied to almost any combination of ingredients, even fruit, and is a useful way of using up leftover vegetables.

FRUIT SOUPS

The puréeing method is ideal for fruit soups. Replace the stock with wine or fruit juices. Pair complementary fruits enhanced with fresh herbs or spices to make refreshing summer soups to serve chilled. Try the following:

- Sour cherry and nectarine.
- Raspberry, strawberry, cinnamon and nectarine.
- Strawberry and rhubarb.
- Melon, mango and basil.
- Apple, pear and cinnamon.
- White peach, apricot and cardamom.
- Papaya, peach and mint.

Making Pureed Vegetable Soups

These are made with one vegetable, such as the carrots here, or with several. Leeks or onions are usually added for flavour. The technique is to cook the vegetables until very soft for easy puréeing. For enriching after puréeing, see opposite page.

1 Sweat diced vegetables in butter over a moderate heat, stirring frequently, for 3–4 minutes until they soften.

2 Add stock or water to cover, and seasonings to taste. Simmer until very soft, about 20 minutes.

3 Purée in a blender, then reheat in a clean pan. Check both the seasonings and the consistency.

Alternative Methods of Pureeing

Vegetable mixtures can be puréed in a number of ways depending on the ingredients they contain. Stringy vegetables, such as green beans and celery, and those with coarse skins like peppers and broad beans, need to be blended and sieved after cooking but before adding stock.

Food processor
Can be used as an alternative to a blender, but softened vegetables must be puréed without liquid in order to prevent splashing.

Hand blender
For blending small amounts of soup quickly. For hot soups, blend in the pan; for cold soups, decant into a large bowl.

Food mill
Good for coarse-textured vegetables because the fibres are left behind in the mill. Drain vegetables from cooking liquid before milling.

Fine sieve
Essential for vegetables with skins such as the roasted yellow peppers shown here. Rub flesh through sieve, then discard skins from sieve.

Making a Pureed Fish Soup

There are many types of puréed fish soup, the most famous of which is the classic French soupe de poissons *from Marseille, made with a variety of Mediterranean fish. Another French classic is the* bisque, *a velvety smooth purée of shellfish, traditionally lobster. The techniques for making these soups are similar; here a puréed crab soup is shown.*

1 Soften chopped carrot, onion, potato and celery in butter in a heavy-based pan. Add about 12 small crabs and stir over a moderate heat until deep brown.

2 Flambé a few spoonfuls of brandy and pour over the crab, then sprinkle in 2 tbsp plain flour and stir for 1–2 minutes until the flour has mixed completely with the liquid.

3 Add 2 litres fish stock, 150 ml dry white wine, 2 tbsp tomato purée, 1 bouquet garni and seasonings to taste. Cover and simmer for 45 minutes.

4 Discard the bouquet garni and work the mixture in a food processor.

5 Transfer the mixture to a very fine sieve (a conical one is best) and press through with ladle. Reheat and enrich with cream (see box, above right).

ENRICHING SOUPS

The taste and texture of puréed soups can be enriched by the addition of creams and yogurt. Stir them in at the last minute to prevent curdling.

CREAM: Use double cream or other dairy products such as crème fraîche and sour cream. Their high-fat content keeps them stable when heated (as opposed to lower fat products, which tend to curdle). They add both richness and an attractive gloss. They can also be used to decorate soups (see page 27).

YOGURT: Because it has a more fragile composition than cream, yogurt and low-fat dairy products such as fromage frais should never be allowed to boil or they may curdle.

EGG YOLK LIAISON: This mixture of egg yolks and double cream must be tempered with a little hot soup before it is stirred into the soup – this prevents the yolks from scrambling. Use 2 egg yolks and 1 tbsp double cream to enrich 1 litre soup.

Finishing Touches

Add colourful visual appeal to soups just before serving with a stylish garnish – even the most simple topping helps transform a plain soup into a special dish. Use tweezers or a small spoon to position small and delicate pieces of ingredients with precision.

KEEP IT SIMPLE

Your choice of garnish for a soup does not have to duplicate an ingredient in the soup, but it should complement all the flavours, and often the simplest of ingredients is the best. This is why many chefs favour using fresh herbs.

Clear and cream soups are most suitable for the more elaborate garnishes, while chunky soups are better finished with simple touches, such as finely chopped herbs or freshly grated cheese. Here are some more ideas for simple garnishes:

- A single sprig of herbs.
- A *chiffonade* of spinach or sorrel.
- Fennel fronds.
- Small celery leaves.
- Heart-shaped croûtons dipped in finely chopped fresh parsley.
- A light sprinkling of ground spices tapped off the end of a pastry brush.
- Coarsely crushed peppercorns or coriander seeds.
- Lightly toasted sesame or pumpkin seeds.
- Finely grated hard cheese, such as Parmesean or pecorino.
- Blanched, julienned strips of citrus zest.
- Grated citrus zest.
- Flaked white crab meat.
- A single prawn in the shell.
- A few peeled cooked prawns.
- Petals from an edible flower, such as pansy, rose or violet, strewn over a chilled fruit soup.

Ring of herbs
Arrange fresh herbs, such as these tiny dill and sage leaves, decoratively in the centre or around edge of soup.

Tomato and herbs
Accent a pale chilled soup with a *concassée* of tomatoes (see page 178) arranged with delicate herb leaves.

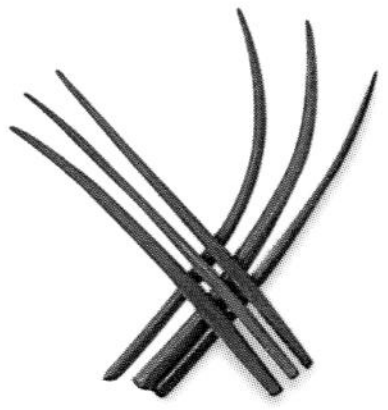

Classic chives
Chives are a classic garnish. Arrange them criss-cross fashion, as here, or finely snip over surface of soup.

Toasted nuts
Add extra texture and colour to cream soups with lightly toasted golden almonds (see page 203) or other nuts.

Olive petals
Cut stoned black olives into slivers. Arrange as a flower with a small parsley sprig in the centre.

Decorative julienne
Echo vegetable flavours in a soup with delicate sticks (see page 166), such as these cut from celeriac and carrot.

Ribbon curls
Use a vegetable peeler to pare thin ribbons (see page 167) from long vegetables, such as carrots and courgettes.

Vegetable melange
Liven up the looks of clear and pale soups with finely diced carrot, courgette and celeriac.

Cheese and caviar
For a luxurious presentation, shape full-fat soft cheese into quenelles and arrange with caviar or lumpfish roe.

Pepper pieces
Use tiny aspic cutters to make unusual shapes from different coloured peppers. Blanch the pieces before using.

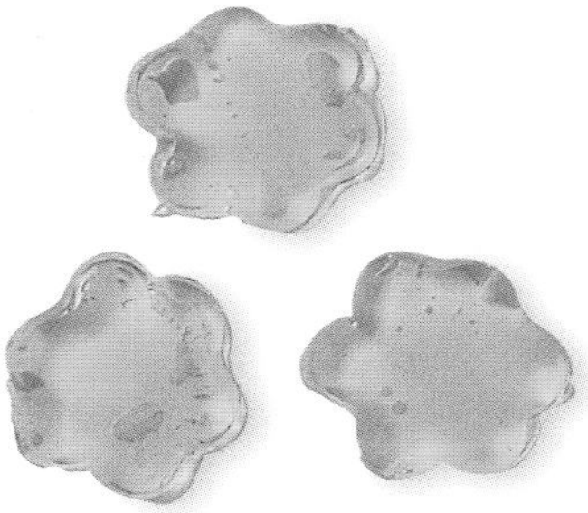

Aspic accents
Float tiny aspic shapes on top of chilled consommé. Cut the shapes from a layer of aspic chilled in a tin.

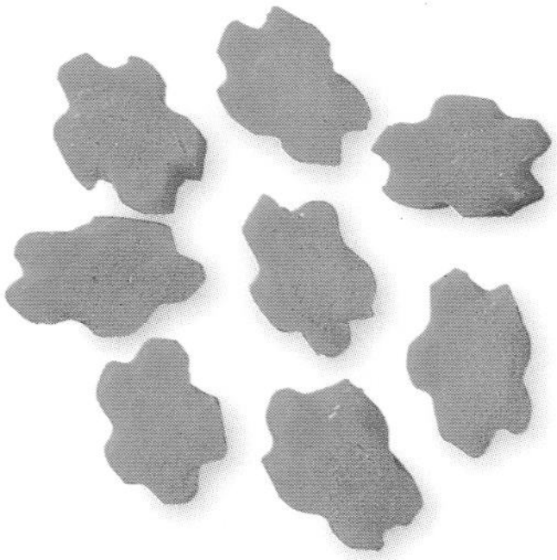

Carrot flowers
Use a canelle knife to cut long grooves in a carrot, then slice crosswise. Float in clear broths.

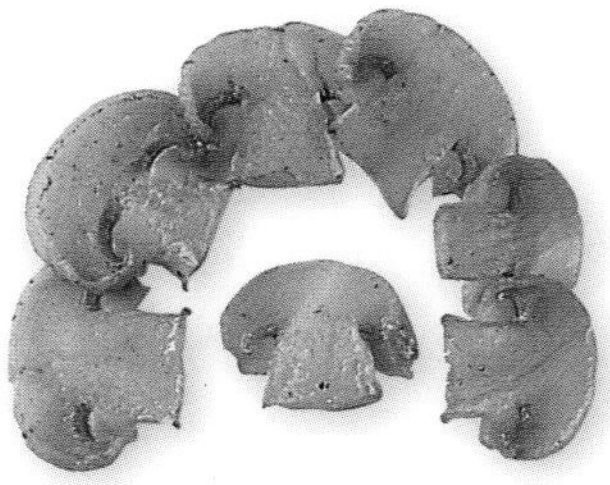

Mini mushrooms
Garnish mushroom-flavoured soups with thin mushroom slices that have been lightly sautéed in butter or olive oil.

Crispy croutons
Sprinkle hot soups with deep-fried or toasted croûtons for a traditional garnish that adds texture.

Decorating with Cream

For a dramatic presentation of a brightly coloured cream soup, spoon or swirl cream in the centre, or use it to make these pretty patterns. The key to success is to make sure the consistency of the cream is similar to that of the soup – in most cases, the cream should be lightly whipped first. Make the pattern just before serving.

Catherine wheel
Stir a little pesto into lightly whipped cream. Place 1 tbsp in the centre of each serving. Draw the tip of a knife away from the centre to make a swirl.

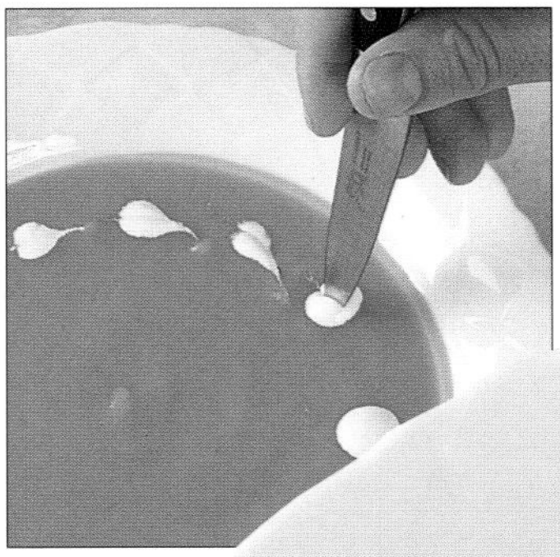

Romantic rim
Drip cream on to the soup in a circle. Draw the tip of a knife through each drop to form connecting hearts.

Special Soups

Some soups have such unique cooking methods and diverse ingredients that they create a category all of their own. Gumbo is one such example. Spicy and aromatic, this New Orleans speciality has a thick consistency and sultry flavour. Clam chowder is another regional American soup made thick and chunky with diced potato and onion.

Making Gumbo

There are two essential techniques for making a good, full-flavoured gumbo. The first is to cook the roux for at least 15 minutes to give the finished soup a nut-brown colour and rich depth of flavour. The second is to thicken it to the right consistency with filé powder, a special seasoning made from ground dried sassafras leaves.

1 Stir the roux constantly over a low heat for at least 15 minutes until rich brown. Watch the roux carefully, or it may burn.

2 Add the okra towards the end of cooking so they retain their shape and firm texture; if cooked too long, they will become slimy.

3 Add just enough filé powder to thicken the gumbo slightly. It must be added off the heat or it will become stringy.

Making a Chowder

Two of the world's most famous chowders are from Manhattan and New England. Both have a base of diced potatoes and onion, but Manhattan chowder is fresh and piquant with tomatoes and herbs, while New England chowder is pale and rich with milk and cream. Clams are the classic addition to both chowders.

Manhattan
Sweat diced potatoes and onions in butter until softened. Add stock, chopped tomatoes, thyme and salt and pepper to taste and simmer for 20 minutes. Add canned clams and their juice and heat through.

New England
Sweat diced potatoes and onions in butter until softened. Add milk and salt and pepper to taste and simmer for 20 minutes. Add canned clams and their juice, heat through, then enrich with double cream.

CREOLE GUMBO

2 tbsp vegetable oil
25 g butter
25 g plain flour
1.2 litres chicken stock
1 large onion, chopped
1 celery stick, chopped
400-g can chopped tomatoes
1/4 tsp dried thyme
1/4 tsp cayenne pepper
400 g okra, cut into 2-cm pieces
Salt and freshly ground pepper
1-2 tbsp filé powder

Heat the oil and butter in a heavy-based pan. Stir in the flour and cook over a low heat for 15 minutes, stirring constantly, until nut-brown. Add the stock and bring to the boil. Add the onion, celery, tomatoes with their juice, thyme and cayenne pepper. Cover and simmer for 20 minutes, stirring occasionally. Add the okra and seasonings to taste and cook for 10 minutes or until the okra are just tender. Off the heat, add the filé powder and check the seasoning. Serves 4.

WHAT'S IN A NAME?

The name chowder comes from the French *chaudière*, a cauldron used by fishermen to make stews with their catch. At one time chowders were always made with seafood, but now meat and vegetables are also used.

Eggs, Cheese & Creams

Choosing & Using Eggs

Cooking Eggs

Omelettes

Batters

Choosing Cheese

Fresh Cheese

Using Cheese

Creams

Choosing & Using Eggs

Eggs are one of our most valued and useful ingredients in the kitchen – many recipes simply wouldn't be possible without their aerating, thickening and emulsifying capabilities.

FREE-RANGE

Around 85% of eggs in the UK are produced using the "laying cage system" or battery method. For eggs to be called free-range, the birds must have access to runs and a variety of vegetation, such as grass and corn. Although they have more freedom, these hens are more affected by weather conditions and predators and, as a result, they are a little more expensive.

SHELL COLOURS

The colour of an egg shell is determined by the breed of hen and its diet. The colour can range from speckled (quail's egg) to blue (duck's egg). Hen's eggs, either white or brown, are most commonly used – they taste the same, the difference in colour having no effect on flavour.

Clockwise, from bottom left: duck egg (off-white); duck egg (blue); hen's egg (white); pullet's egg (small brown); hen's egg (brown); quail's egg (small and speckled).

How to Test for Freshness

First check the "best before" date (see Safety First box, opposite page). If there is no date, test the freshness by immersing the egg in water as shown here. As the egg gets older it loses water through the shell, making the air pocket larger – so the older the egg the lighter it will be.

A fresh egg is heavy due to its high water content. It will settle horizontally on the bottom of the glass.

With a less fresh egg the air pockets will expand and make the egg float vertically, tip down, in the water.

An old, stale egg contains too much air and will float to the surface of the water. Do not use the egg.

Separating Yolk from White

It is easiest to separate eggs when they are cold – the yolk is firm, and there is less chance that it will run into the white. Whites will not whisk properly if there is any yolk in them.

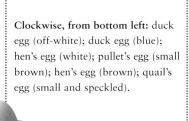

Hand method
Crack egg into a bowl, then lift it up and cup it in your hand to let all the white drip through your fingers.

Shell method
Crack egg shell in half. Pass the yolk backwards and forwards between the halves until the white is in the bowl.

Safety First

- Use eggs within the "best before" date. Check for the Lion Mark which ensures hygienic production standards greater than those required by UK or EC law.
- Salmonella bacteria can enter eggs through cracks in the shell, so only buy eggs with clean, undamaged shells.
- Wash your hands before and after handling egg shells.
- The elderly, people who are suffering an illness, pregnant women, babies and children are vulnerable to the risk of salmonella. All should avoid eating raw eggs and foods containing them.
- It is important to cook all egg dishes thoroughly – heat destroys salmonella.

TRICK OF THE TRADE

Blending Albumen Strands

Egg yolk is anchored in the white by thick albumen strands. The strands should be sieved or blended into the whites so that they help to stabilize the foam.

Sieving
Work the egg white through a fine sieve held over a bowl with a spoon to break up the albumen strands.

Blending
Put the egg whites in a bowl and use chopsticks or a fork to lift the whites and break up the albumen strands.

Whisking Egg Whites

To achieve greater volume and stability before whisking egg whites, let them stand at room temperature for about 1 hour in a covered bowl. Whether whisking by hand or machine, make sure all utensils are free of grease and that the bowl is deep enough to hold the volume of whisked whites.

By Hand

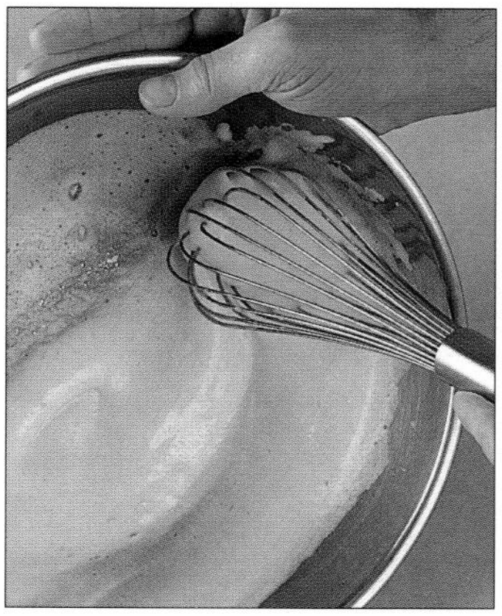

Put whites in a stainless steel or glass bowl. Whisk them from the bottom of the bowl upwards in a circular motion. For greatest volume, use a large balloon whisk.

By Machine

With the whisk attachment of a tabletop electric mixer, start whisking slowly, to break up the whites, then increase the speed as they thicken. A little salt relaxes the albumen and makes whisking easier.

Making Egg Wash

A mixture of egg yolk and water is brushed over bread or pastry before baking to give a rich, golden colour and a glossy glaze.

Mix 1 egg yolk with 1 tbsp water and a pinch of salt. Whisk with a fork until combined. Brush the egg wash over bread or pastry with a pastry brush just before baking.

Storing Eggs

- Refrigerate eggs as soon as possible after buying them.
- Store eggs in their carton, away from strong-smelling foods.
- Store eggs pointed-end down to keep the yolks centred.
- Separated whites and yolks or shelled whole eggs should be refrigerated in airtight containers. Whites will keep for 1 week, yolks and whole eggs up to 2 days.
- Use food containing raw eggs within 2 days.
- Hard-boiled eggs in their shells will keep for up to 1 week.

Nutritional Value of Eggs

Eggs are a valuable source of protein (one large egg contains 12–15% of the recommended daily allowance for an adult), supplying all essential amino acids needed by the body.

They also contain the minerals iron, iodine and calcium and vitamins A, B, D, E and K. Indeed, vitamin C is the only vitamin that is not present in an egg.

Eggs are also low in calories, supplying about 75 calories each. In the past, a limit on the number of eggs consumed per person per week was advised because of the cholesterol content, but more recent research shows that the dietary intake of saturated fat is the main cause of increased blood cholesterol levels. So, despite the fact that an egg contains 213 mg of cholesterol, all of which is within the yolk, the level of saturated fat is very low.

Although egg intake is restricted in some special diets, the current UK dietary guideline for egg consumption for an adult is 2–3 eggs per week.

COOKING EGGS

The art of cooking a perfect egg is simple – once you know how. The techniques shown here may seem very basic, but they are an essential part of every good cook's repertoire.

BOILING

Some cooks put eggs in cold water to start, others in hot. The hot-water method shown here is best for accurate timing. Always use fresh eggs at room temperature – the shells of eggs taken straight from the refrigerator are more likely to crack.

1 Put the eggs in a pan of gently bubbling water and add a pinch of salt. Start timing from the moment the water returns to the boil.

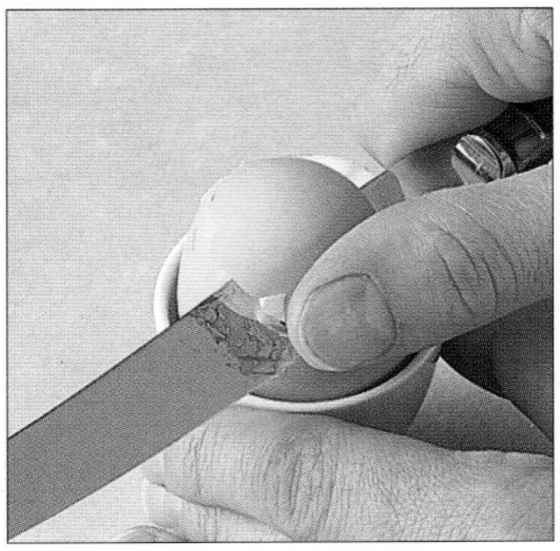

2 For soft-boiled eggs, simmer gently for 3–4 minutes. Remove with a slotted spoon and cut off the tops with a knife.

3 Remove the top part of the shell and any small pieces that have fallen into the egg. The white should be just set, the yolk runny.

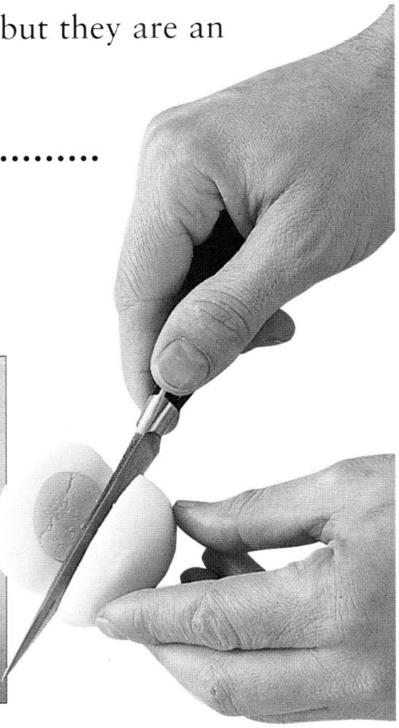

HARD-BOILED
Simmer for 6–10 minutes. Plunge immediately into cold water, to prevent greying around the yolk, then peel.

TRICK OF THE TRADE

CAVIAR EGGS
For an elegant breakfast or brunch, serve soft-boiled eggs Russian-style.

Soft-boil the eggs and cut off the tops following the directions above, then spoon in a little caviar, or red lumpfish roe as shown here.

POACHING

Very fresh eggs and a wide, shallow pan are essential for successful poaching. For accurate timing, cook no more than four eggs at a time.

Add 1 tbsp wine vinegar and a tarragon sprig to boiling water. Do not add salt. Turn off the heat, crack in the eggs and cover. Let stand until the whites are opaque, 3 minutes.

BAKING

It's tricky to get the whites set and the yolks runny at the same time when baking eggs. Here are two methods, the classic French oeufs en cocotte *and the more unusual Mexican* huevos rancheros. *Stand the dishes on paper towels when baking in a* bain marie, *to prevent overcooking and cracking the china.*

OEUFS EN COCOTTE
Put eggs in buttered ramekins and add 2 tbsp cream and seasonings to each one. Cover and bake in a *bain marie* at 180°C for 6–8 minutes.

HUEVOS RANCHEROS
Put cooked sliced peppers and onions in individual gratin dishes. Top each with an egg. Cover and bake at 180°C for 8–12 minutes. Top with *salsa*.

Scrambling

The secret of making perfect, creamy-textured scrambled eggs is to cook them over a low heat and patiently stir them all the time. Never attempt to rush scrambled eggs or they will be stiff and rubbery. For two servings, allow 4 eggs, 2 tbsp cream or milk and seasonings to taste.

1 Put the eggs in a jug with the cream or milk and salt and pepper to taste. Whisk with a fork for 1 minute. The seasoning prevents streaking.

2 Heat enough butter to coat the bottom of a frying pan. When the butter is foaming, pour in the egg mixture.

3 Stir constantly with a wooden spoon over a low heat for 5–8 minutes, then stir for 1–2 minutes off the heat. Serve immediately.

Additions to Scrambled Eggs

Many ingredients can be whisked into eggs before they are scrambled or while cooking to add texture and flavour.

- In the Basque dish *pipérade*, onions, peppers and mushrooms are fried, then the eggs are stirred in. Alternatives include chopped ham or pesto.
- One famous dish, Hangtown Fry, originated during the 1849 gold rush in California. It combines deep-fried breaded oysters with scrambled eggs.
- The Chinese make a dish called "red, green and yellow" – cubes of tomato and cucumber mixed with scrambled eggs.

Shallow-Frying

For most people, the perfect fried egg has a runny yolk and a set white. There are two ways of achieving this – by keeping the egg yolk "sunny-side up" during frying and basting it with hot fat, or by turning it "over easy" halfway through. This second method is less popular because the yolk can easily be broken during turning, and it loses its bright yellow colour.

Sunny-side up
Heat a shallow layer of oil or butter in a frying pan until hot but not smoking. Add the eggs and fry over a moderate heat, basting constantly with the hot fat, for 3–4 minutes. Baste the white only to keep the yolk runny, or the white and the yolk, as you like.

Neatly-shaped eggs
Coat the bottom of a frying pan with oil, then place a metal pastry cutter (stainless steel is preferable) in the pan and heat until hot. Slide the egg into the cutter and fry as for sunny-side up eggs (see left). Remove cutter carefully before removing the egg.

Deep-Frying

This French technique is often used for eggs that are to be served on croûtes. Olive oil gives a delicious flavour, but other oils can be used. Butter is not suitable – it will burn.

Heat about 2 cm oil in a deep frying pan until it is very hot but not smoking. Add 1 egg, spoon the hot oil over it and fold the white over the yolk to enclose it. Cook for 1 minute. Remove the egg with a slotted spoon and drain on paper towels. Repeat with more eggs.

Deep-Fried Eggs Escoffier Style

4 tomatoes, halved
Salt and freshly ground pepper
4 tbsp fresh white breadcrumbs
1 tbsp chopped fresh parsley
1 shallot, finely chopped
4 eggs

Place tomatoes, cut-side up, in a baking dish and season well. Mix together the breadcrumbs, parsley and shallot and spoon over the tomatoes. Bake at 180°C for 10 minutes. Deep-fry the eggs (see left) and serve on warmed plates the tomato halves alongside. Serves 4.

Omelettes

In classic French cuisine, an omelette is a folded, fluffy creation, simply made by whisking eggs and cooking them quickly in a traditional pan. In other parts of the world, however, an omelette is quite a different thing.

Flavourings for Omelettes

Add flavourings to the egg mixture before cooking or spoon fillings into the centre of the omelette and fold over to enclose. The following combinations are delicious.

- Grated cheese and finely diced tomatoes.
- Snipped bacon sautéed in walnut oil until crisp with fresh spinach leaves.
- Sliced or diced peppers and shallots sautéed in butter with sliced mushrooms.
- Smoked salmon shavings and a little fresh dill.
- Chunks of cooked sausage and caramelized onion slices.
- Strips of smoked ham and blanched asparagus tips.

Making a Folded Omelette

This is the classic French omelette which is traditionally cooked in a well-seasoned cast-iron pan, although here a non-stick frying pan serves the same purpose. For best results, allow 15 g butter and 3 eggs per omelette in a 20-cm pan.

1 Immediately before cooking, lightly beat the eggs and seasonings with a fork. Do not overbeat the mixture or the finished omelette will be stiff.

2 Heat the butter over a high heat until foaming. Pour in the eggs. Mix with a fork for even distribution.

3 Cook quickly, drawing in the edges with a fork to allow the uncooked egg to run underneath.

4 Tilt the pan and fold the omelette over towards one side of the pan, pushing it with the fork to help it roll.

Making a Japanese Omelette

Japanese omelettes offer a symmetrical shape and light texture. They are traditionally made in a 20-cm square pan, and they are rolled as they are fried. If you do not have a pan of this shape, use a round pan and trim the sides of the omelette once cooked. Allow 1 egg and 2 tbsp water for each omelette; the addition of water thins the batter to create light texture. Serve cut into slices or shreds (see opposite page).

1 Brush the pan with a little oil and heat. Pour in half the egg mixture. Tilt the pan to make an even layer. As surface bubbles appear, loosen the edges with a palette knife.

2 Roll omelette towards you with chopsticks. Cook until set, about 1 minute. Make another omelette with remaining mixture.

Making Omelette Shreds

In Asian cooking, shreds made from very thin omelettes are used as toppings and garnishes. For a dish to serve four, use 1 egg beaten with a pinch of salt. Cook the omelette in a wok.

1 Heat 1 tbsp oil. Swirl in egg. Cook over moderate heat for 1–2 minutes.

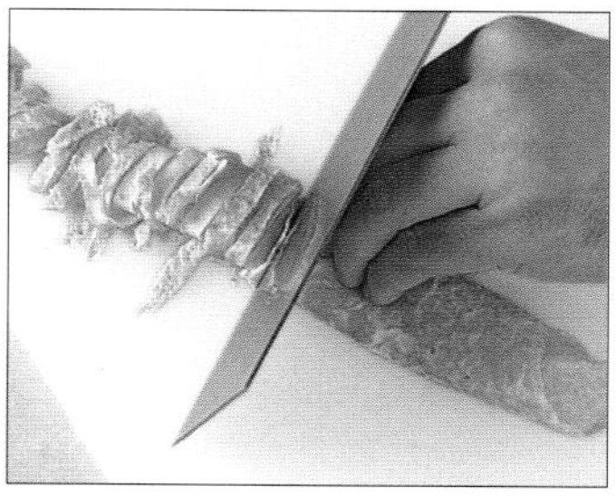

2 Slide the omelette out of the wok, roll up and let cool. Shred crosswise.

Making a Souffle Omelette

This type of omelette is made by separating eggs, beating the whites until stiff, then folding them into the yolks. As its name suggests, the finished omelette is therefore lighter and fluffier than a conventional omelette. In classic French cuisine, soufflé omelettes are often sweet, and the yolks are beaten to the ribbon stage with sugar before the whites are folded in.

Whisk 3 egg whites until stiff. Fold into 3 seasoned and whisked yolks. Cook as for a folded omelette (see opposite page), without mixing with a fork in step 2.

Making an Eggah

A traditional Persian dish, an eggah *is a kind of thick, firm omelette baked in the oven and served sliced or cut into wedges, hot or cold.* Eggahs *can be made plain, with a touch of spice, but adding other ingredients is more traditional. Chopped spinach is used here, but fresh herbs, onion, garlic, peppers or other vegetables may be used.*

1 Mix 6 beaten eggs with chosen flavourings. Pour into an oiled baking dish.

2 Bake at 170°C until firm, 15–20 minutes. Cut into wedges to serve.

SPANISH TORTILLAS

This omelette is similar to an Italian *frittata*, except for the cooking technique and some of the flavourings used. Onions and potatoes are fried in a generous amount of olive oil, then beaten eggs are added. Unlike *frittata*, which is finished by browning under the grill, a *tortilla* is always flipped over in the pan to brown and set both sides.

Making a Frittata

A thick, flat Italian omelette, a frittata *is partially cooked on top of the stove in a heavy-based pan, then grilled until brown and set. For a 30-cm* frittata, *use 1–2 tbsp olive oil, 7–10 eggs and flavourings of your choice. The chopped peppers illustrated here are traditional, so too are asparagus, globe artichokes, sliced green beans, mixed chopped herbs, grated Parmesan, tomatoes, chopped onions and garlic.*

Whisk eggs with flavourings and pour into hot olive oil. Cook for 15 minutes over a low heat, then brown under the grill for 1–2 minutes.

Cheese Soufflés

These light-as-air cheese puffs are rightly called soufflés, despite their unconventional sabayon-type base. They are served floating on a rich cheese cream, called a fondue *after the French word for melt.*

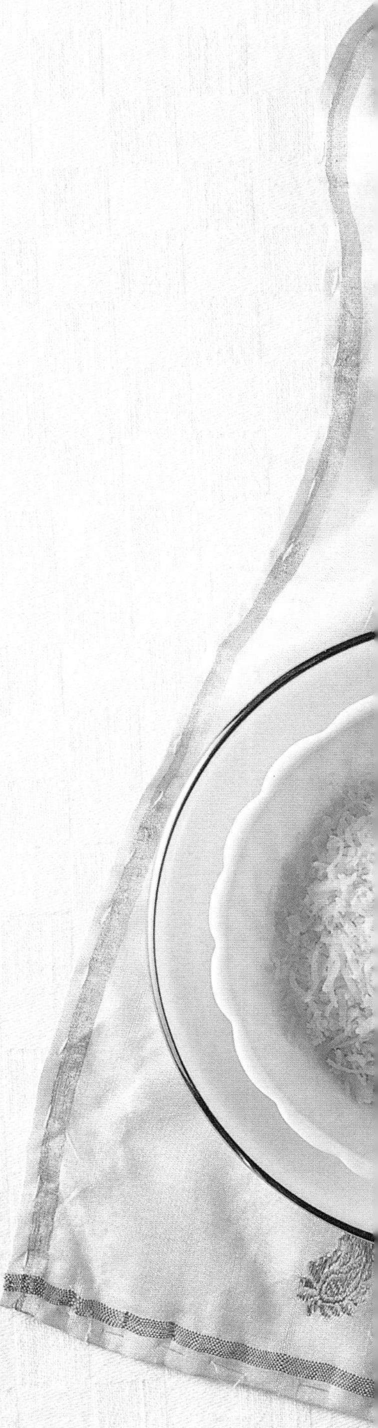

SERVES 4

4 eggs, separated

100 ml dry white wine

Salt and freshly ground pepper

100 g Parmesan cheese, freshly grated

FOR THE FONDUE

200 ml double cream

100 g Gruyère or other easy-melting cheese, grated

TO SERVE

Snipped chives

Freshly grated Parmesan cheese

Put the egg yolks and wine in a large heatproof bowl set over a pan of gently simmering water (bain marie) and whisk them together until they reach the ribbon stage. Remove the bowl from the bain marie and whisk until the mixture is cool.

In another bowl, whisk the egg whites until stiff. Fold the whites gently but thoroughly into the egg yolk mixture and add salt and pepper to taste.

Bring the cream to the boil in a pan and stir in the Gruyère until melted and smooth. Pour into four shallow ovenproof dishes.

Using two spoons, shape the egg mixture into quenelles (see page 76) and float on the fondue. Sprinkle each quenelle with one-quarter of the grated Parmesan. Bake at 180°C for 10 minutes or until the soufflés are puffed up and golden brown. Serve at once, sprinkled with snipped chives, with grated Parmesan cheese handed separately.

ALTERNATIVE FLAVOURINGS

- Replace the Gruyère with blue cheese.
- Add a little rouille (see page 22) to the fondue.
- Add freshly chopped herbs to the fondue.

Making a Soufflé

Soufflés have a light, fluffy texture due to the incorporation of air. Here, a standard whisk is used over a bain marie; for even greater volume, use a large balloon whisk or a hand-held electric mixer. The bowl for the egg whites must be spotlessly clean or they will not whisk.

Whisk the egg yolks with the wine until the mixture is pale and thick enough to leave a ribbon trail when lifted.

Whisk the egg whites at a steady pace to a white foam that will hold a stiff peak.

Fold together using a scooping and cutting action to ensure you lose as little of the whisked-in air as possible.

BATTERS

Many cooks lack confidence when it comes to making crêpes, pancakes and Yorkshire puddings, and yet there is no mystique about them. Follow the techniques shown here for smooth batters and successful results every time.

MAKING CREPES

French chefs use a special well-seasoned pan (see box, left) to make wafer-thin crêpes, but you can use a non-stick frying pan. Don't worry if the first few crêpes tear or stick. There are many elements to get right: the temperature of the pan, the temperature and amount of butter, and the consistency and amount of batter.

1 Put a knob of butter in the pan and heat over a moderate heat until foaming. Pour off the excess melted butter into a bowl, then pour in a small ladleful of batter, starting in the centre of the pan.

2 Tilt the pan to swirl the batter over the base and reach the edges, adding more batter if necessary.

3 Cook for about 1 minute until golden underneath and bubbles appear. Loosen and turn with a palette knife.

4 Cook the second side for 30 seconds–1 minute, then turn the crêpe out, first side facing down.

CIGARETTES

PANNEQUETS

FANS

CREPE BATTER

125 g plain flour
½ tsp salt
2 eggs, beaten
300 ml milk or milk and water

Sift the flour and salt into a bowl, make a well in the centre and add the eggs. Gradually beat in the flour from the sides and slowly pour in the liquid to make a smooth batter. Sieve if necessary (see opposite page). Cover and let rest for 30 minutes or overnight. Beat thoroughly before using. Makes about 12 crêpes.

CREPE AND BLINI PANS

Crêpe and blini pans are made of cast iron, which conducts heat well and cooks food evenly. The only difference is the size – crêpe pans are usually 22 cm in diameter, blini pans 12 cm. Once the pan is "proved" or seasoned, it is practically non-stick. To prove, heat the pan and rub with salt. Wipe clean and repeat with oil. Do not wash the pan after use, just wipe it clean.

Making Yorkshire Puddings

For well-risen, crisp and light puddings, use very hot fat, otherwise the puddings will not rise.

Put about 1/2 tsp white vegetable fat or oil in each cup of a Yorkshire pudding tin and heat at 220°C until very hot, almost smoking. Pour in the batter and bake for 20–25 minutes.

Making Griddle Pancakes

Traditional American pancakes are about 10 cm in diameter. Also popular are the fun-sized "silver dollars" shown here, so-called because of their shape. Like Scotch pancakes, they are about 5 cm in diameter. Make them on a griddle, or in a heavy-based frying pan. Test the temperature of the pan by sprinkling over a little water; it should sizzle and evaporate. Grease lightly before spooning on the batter.

1 Make the batter (see box right). Place tablespoons of batter on the hot griddle, spacing them well apart.

2 Cook until the edges are brown and the tops bubbling. Turn with a palette knife; cook until golden.

TRICK OF THE TRADE

Making a Smooth Batter

If making batter by hand, blend the flour and eggs with a balloon whisk for best results, and add the liquid gradually. If lumps occur, pour the batter through a sieve. For a foolproof method, work all the ingredients together in an electric blender there should be no need to sieve.

After making batter by hand, pass it through a fine-meshed sieve to ensure smoothness.

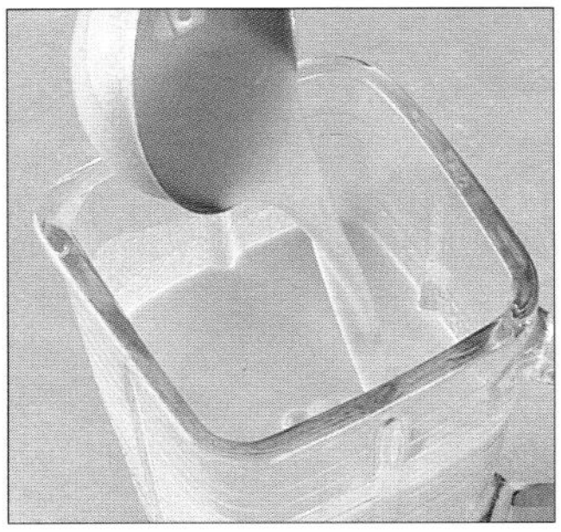

For an ultra-smooth batter, work the ingredients in an electric blender for 1 minute until smooth.

VARIATIONS ON A THEME

You can make different batters by adapting the basic crêpe batter recipe (see box, opposite page). It is important that any batter you make is left to rest for at least 30 minutes before cooking, to allow time for the starch grains to absorb the liquid.

Yorkshire pudding batter
Substitute strong plain flour for the plain flour in the original recipe – the extra gluten creates a more elastic batter, giving a better and more stable rise. Use a mixture of equal parts milk and water rather than all milk. The addition of the water will help to lighten the batter.

Griddle pancake batter
A thick batter is used for griddle pancakes because they need to hold their own shape as they cook unsupported on the griddle. Use 225 g plain flour (almost double the amount given in the crêpe batter recipe) to each 300 ml liquid and add 1–2 tbsp melted butter and 1–2 tsp baking powder. The butter will enrich the batter; the baking powder will aerate it.

SHAPES FOR CREPES

For rolled or folded crêpes as shown on the opposite page, spread filling in centre, then proceed as follows:

- For cigarettes, fold in two opposite sides, then roll up from one of the other sides.
- For pannequets, fold in two opposite sides, then fold in the other sides and turn over.
- For fans, fold in half, then fold in half again.

Choosing Cheese

It pays to use a reliable supplier; a shop that has a wide stock and a fast turnover is more likely to sell cheese of the required degree of ripeness. The vast differences in taste and texture discernible in individual cheeses are a result of the type of milk used, the manufacturing process and the length of ageing. As a general rule, the longer a cheese has been aged, the stronger the flavour, the drier the texture and the longer it will keep.

Soft cheese rind should be evenly coloured and slightly moist with a "bloomy" look.

Hard cheese rind should not be not too dry or cracked, nor look moist or "sweaty". When matured in cheesecloth, it should cling to the paste

Hard cheese should have a clean, firm or crumbly texture with no discoloration

Soft Cheeses

Containing a high percentage of fat and moisture, these have been briefly ripened, have a creamy texture and are easy to spread. When fully ripe, some soft cheeses, such as Brie and Camembert, ooze gently. These have a characteristic "bloomy" rind, while others, such as Pont l'Evêque and Livarot have a "washed" rind and sharper, richer taste. Soft cheeses should be springy to the touch, and smell nutty, sweet and aromatic. Avoid any with a chalky white centre or a strong smell of ammonia. **Semi-hard cheeses** such as Reblochon and Port Salut are matured longer and because they contain less moisture, are slightly firmer, and hold their shape when cut.

Hard Cheeses

Often high in fat, though low in moisture, these long matured cheeses have flavours ranging from mild to sharp and textures from "flexible" to crumbly. Some cheeses in this category such as Emmenthal, have characteristic holes, caused by the gas-producing bacteria introduced within the ripening cheese. **Hard-grating cheeses** such as Italian Parmesan and Pecorino, are the driest of the hard cheeses. Aged until they have a dry, granular texture, they will keep for months in the refrigerator if wrapped tightly. Taste the cheese before buying if you can and reject any that taste over-salty or bitter. The rind should be hard and yellow and the paste yellowish white.

Fresh Cheeses

These are unripened, rindless cheeses which range in consistency from the creamy and smooth – fromage frais, cream cheese and mascarpone to thicker curd mixtures – ricotta, pot cheese and cottage cheese. The fat content varies, with many low-fat, skimmed-milk versions available. It is very important to use fresh cheese within the "use-by" date on the packaging.

Blue Cheeses

These have had a bacteria culture introduced which creates their characteristic blue-green veining. Immature blue cheeses have little veining near the rind. Look for a firm, crusty rind with no signs of discoloration underneath. Blue cheeses may smell strong but should not smell of ammonia. Sample before purchase if possible, and avoid cheeses that taste over-salty or chalky.

HARD BLUE CHEESE should have even veining throughout and a creamy-yellow paste
FRESH CHEESE should be moist and white, with no sign of mould
SOME SOFT CHEESE has a "washed" orange rind. This should be evenly coloured with no visible cracks.
GOAT'S CHEESE RIND varies with age. The more mature cheese has surface mould

Goat and Sheep Cheeses

Curds made from goat's milk are lightly packed into small moulds to produce cheese in a variety of shapes and sizes.They can be sold at any stage of the maturing process, the age determining the character of the cheese. Initially soft and mild, they mature to become firm with a tangy, strong flavour.

Buy goat's cheese from a shop with a rapid turnover to ensure freshness. When fresh, goat's cheeses should be moist with a slightly sharp, but not sour, flavour.

Of a medium fat content most ewe's milk cheeses are milder in taste than those of cow's milk. Famous exceptions include Roquefort, pecorino and ewe's milk feta.

TESTING A SOFT CHEESE FOR RIPENESS

When a soft cheese develops its characteristic texture, flavour and aroma it is deemed ripe. Eat soft cheeses at their peak, because they deteriorate very quickly, especially after cutting.

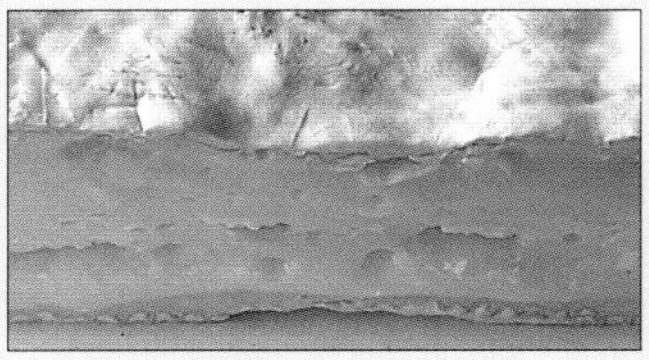

A Brie that is just ripe should feel spongy in the centre and be creamy throughout.

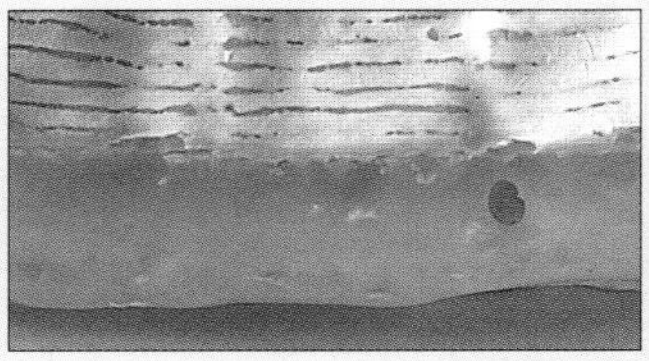

Over-ripe Brie has thin, patchy rind, a bitter flavour, smells of ammonia and "oozes" excessively.

Fresh Cheese

Characterized by a mild, clean, taste and soft texture, fresh cheese is simple to make. Here the technique of making a fresh cheese is demonstrated, plus ways to enhance fresh cheeses with coatings, marinades and flavourings.

Fresh Cheeses

The following varieties offer varying degrees of texture and richness. Most fresh cheeses are soft enough to eat with a spoon, however some are dried and as moisture evaporates, they thicken. Fat content varies, as they can be made from whole or skimmed milk, or even cream.

- Fresh chèvre cheese is made from 100 per cent goat's milk.
- Cottage cheese is made from whole or skimmed milk curds.
- Mascarpone is a high-fat, soft Italian cream cheese with a rich, smooth texture.
- Ricotta is an Italian unripened whey cheese with a mild, almost bland flavour.
- Fromage frais is a soft, slightly acidic curd cheese often enriched with cream.

Coatings for Fresh Cheese

When fresh cheese is 2-3 days old it is usually firm enough to form into loose rounds. Coating the rounds with herbs, spices or nuts will add interest to the mild flavour of the cheese. The following coatings are suitable.

- Cracked mixed peppercorns.
- Paprika or cayenne pepper.
- Toasted sesame seeds.
- Snipped chives.
- Lightly crushed dried chillies.
- Coarsely chopped walnuts or hazelnuts.

Making Fresh Cheese

Pasteurized milk is warmed to a temperature of 27°C, then buttermilk is added to provide the bacteria necessary for curds to form. Once the whey is drained off, use the cheese within a day; if salt is added, it will keep in the refrigerator for 2–3 days.

1 Combine 250 ml each buttermilk and warm milk; let stand at room temperature for 24 hours until curd forms.

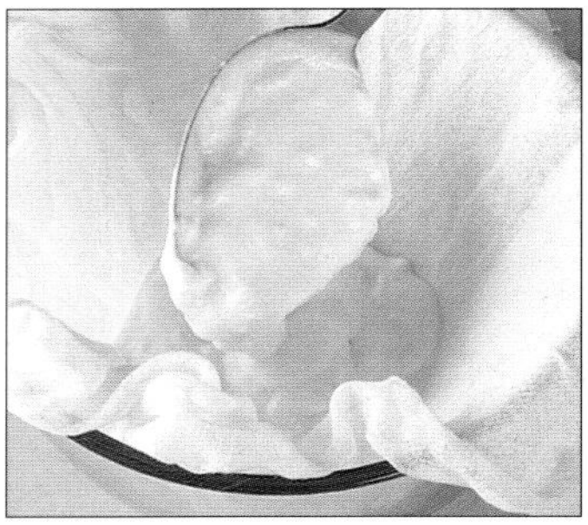

2 Line a bowl with a double thickness of sterilized muslin. Carefully spoon in the curd and cover.

3 After about 5 hours, gather up the muslin and tie with string. Squeeze the whey out firmly with your hands, then hang above the bowl to drain.

4 Let drain for 1–4 hours until firm. Cut the string, turn the cheese on to a plate and peel off the muslin.

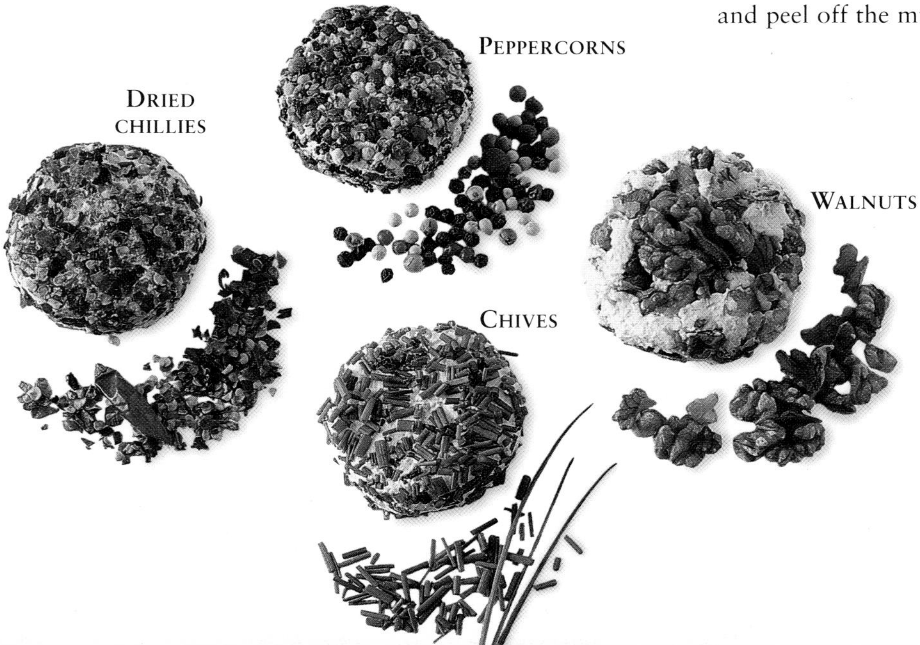

Flavouring Fresh Cheeses

Firm fresh cheeses gain flavour from a marinade (see box, right). They can be marinated for just a few hours, or refrigerated in sterilized Kilner jars for 2–3 weeks. Small round goat's cheeses (crottins de Chavignol) *are used here; cubes of Greek feta cheese are also suitable.*

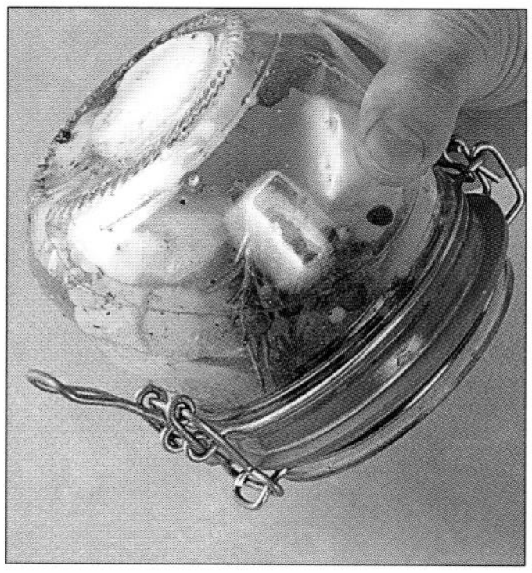

1 Place discs of cheese in a sterilized Kilner jar. Add flavourings of your choice (see box, right).

2 Pour olive oil over the cheeses until they are completely covered. Seal the jar tightly.

3 Store in the refrigerator for up to 2–3 weeks, turning the jar occasionally to redistribute the flavourings.

Marinades for Fresh Cheeses

Fruity extra-virgin olive oil makes the best base for a marinade; it also acts as a preservative. Add one or more of the following:

- Fresh herb sprigs, especially rosemary, thyme, oregano or marjoram.
- Whole peppercorns.
- Dried chillies or halved fresh chillies.
- Bay leaves.
- Fennel seeds.
- Pared lemon or lime zest.
- Whole cinnamon sticks.
- Bruised garlic cloves.
- Sun-dried tomatoes.

Piping Fresh Cheese

Fresh cheeses are extremely versatile because they are soft enough to be piped. Here homemade fresh cheese (see opposite page) is mixed with herbs and piped into an array of vegetables – hollowed-out cherry tomato halves, blanched and scooped-out patty pan squash, blanched and opened-out mangetouts.

1 Mix cheese with chopped fresh herbs and seasonings to taste until evenly blended.

2 Put cheese in a piping bag fitted with a star tube and pipe into prepared vegetables.

Flavourings for Fresh Cheese

When flavouring cheese, you can choose contrasting tastes and textures. Try the following:

- Chopped toasted pine nuts and chopped basil.
- Finely chopped spring onions and fresh root ginger.
- Chopped fresh coriander and Thai curry paste.
- Ready-made tapenade and chopped fresh parsley.

USING CHEESE

Cooking with cheese requires care. Consistency, fat content and flavour all influence how it will behave in a recipe. Here are hints for picking the right variety – and method – for what you are making.

ROTARY GRATER

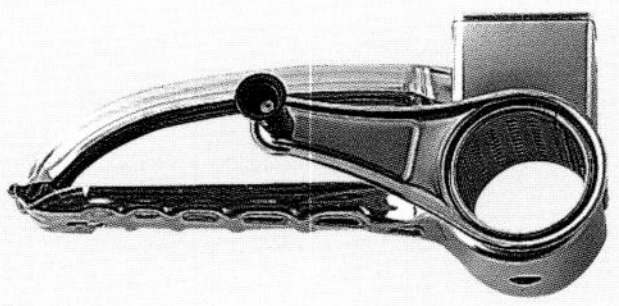

Equipped with a selection of drums, this time-saving tool (also called a Mouli grater) grates hard cheese easily into shreds of various sizes.

GOOD MELTING CHEESES

Several cheeses are prized for their ability to achieve a specific consistency when heated. Soft cheeses such as mozzarella, for instance, melt easily when simply sliced. A hard cheese like Gruyère is best grated.

- Mozzarella is the traditional topping for pizza. It melts evenly to produce gooey "strings" of cheese.
- Fontina is a well-tempered, nutty-flavoured cheese that withstands high temperatures. It can even be coated in breadcrumbs and deep-fried.
- Gruyère, France's favourite cheese for gratins, is best grated for even melting. Use well-aged Gruyère for fondue.
- Goat's cheese holds its shape well when warm, and colours to an appetizing golden brown. It is good on croûtes.
- Cheddar melts and browns well. It is excellent for grilling.

GRATING

Different graters can be used according to the type of cheese you are grating and the size of shreds required. Use cheese straight from the refrigerator for best results.

FINE SHREDS
A rotary grater (see box, left) makes light work of fine grating. Simply put the cheese in the hopper and turn the handle.

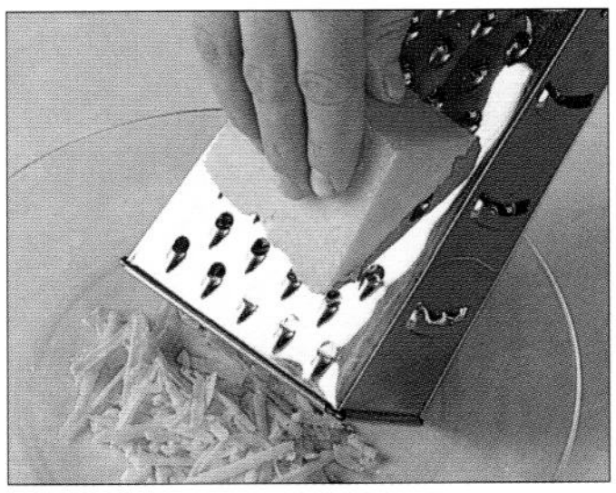

COARSE SHREDS
An upright grater creates thick shreds that hold up in a salad, or melt evenly.

PARMESAN
Use a special small Parmesan grater to grate this very hard cheese into tiny shreds.

MAKING A GRATIN TOPPING

Dishes that are to be finished by browning under the grill or in the oven are often topped with grated cheese. The cheese melts quickly (see box, left) and forms a crisp, golden crust, making a delicious gratin topping.

Grated Gruyère is sprinkled on French onion soup (see page 20) and put under a hot grill 2 minutes before serving.

MELTING

Always melt grated cheese slowly over a low heat in a heavy-based pan. This will help prevent the melted cheese becoming stringy or grainy, or separating the oil. Not all cheeses melt well: each has a different fat and moisture level, which react differently to heat. For recommended melting cheeses, see box, left.

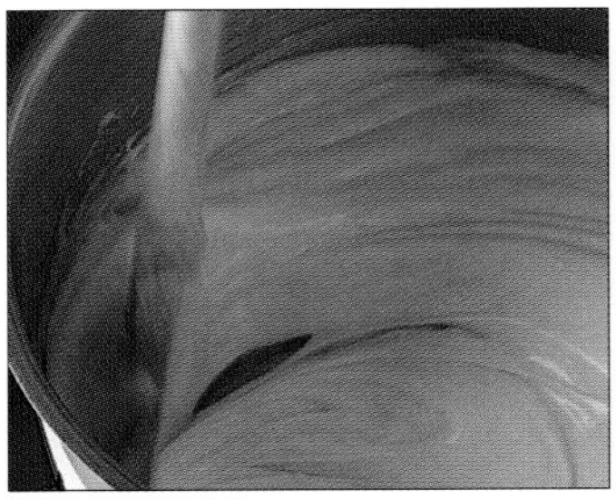

CORRECT
Cheese that is melted gently over a low heat is smooth and glossy.

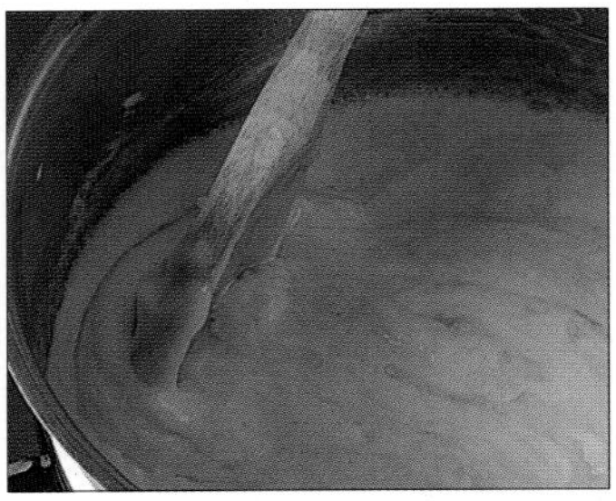

INCORRECT
Cheese that is melted too quickly over a high heat will separate into oily lumps.

MAKING SWISS CHEESE FONDUE

The word fondue *is French for melted, in this case for cheese melted in alcohol. Success depends on using a heavy-based pan and keeping the heat beneath it constantly low – the same technique that is essential for melting any cheese (see opposite page). Warm the wine before adding the cheese and stir until melted. Adding a little cornflour will help to stabilize the mixture.*

1 To help prevent mixture sticking to the pan, stir constantly with a wooden spoon over a low heat.

2 Use long-handled forks for dipping bread into the fondue. Turn forks after dipping to stop fondue drips.

CHEESE FONDUE

1 tbsp cornflour
450 ml dry white wine
1 garlic clove, halved
250 g Emmental cheese, grated
250 g Gruyère cheese, grated
250 g Comté cheese, grated
Pinch of grated nutmeg
Salt and freshly ground pepper

Blend the cornflour with 2 tbsp of the wine. Rub the inside of a fondue dish with the cut side of the garlic and pour in the remaining wine. Bring to the boil, then lower the heat. Gradually add the cheeses, stirring constantly to ensure they have melted after each addition. Add the cornflour mixture and stir until thick and creamy. Stir in the nutmeg and seasonings to taste. Serves 6–8.

GRILLING

Grilled cheese on toast is a time-honoured favourite. Here it's given a modern twist by using slices of fresh goat's cheese cut from a log and basted with a spicy dressing of olive oil and peppercorns. If you like, you can use marinated cheese (see page 43), Italian mozzarella or Greek halloumi, varying the dressing by adding chopped herbs or ground spices to taste.

1 Put cheese on rack in grill pan. Brush with olive oil dressing. Grill 3 cm away from heat for 1–2 minutes.

2 Put the cheese on warm croûtes (see page 246) and serve on a bed of salad leaves, with more dressing.

DEEP-FRYING

This technique is perfect for individual portions of Camembert. The wedges are coated in beaten egg and breadcrumbs that become crisp during frying and protect the cheese from melting and oozing out into the oil. Use cheese that is ripe but firm, and chill it before frying so that it will retain its shape on the outside yet be perfectly runny in the middle.

1 Dip Camembert wedges in beaten egg, then in dried breadcrumbs. Chill for 1 hour in the refrigerator.

2 Deep-fry at 190°C for 2–3 minutes until crisp and golden. Drain on paper towels.

CREAMS

Milk products, such as cream, yogurt, buttermilk, crème fraîche, clotted cream and soured cream, have a myriad of uses in sweet and savoury dishes. Though commercially available, the latter three are easily made at home.

BUTTERMILK AND YOGURT

- Buttermilk is a non-fat or low-fat milk to which bacteria is added to thicken it and give it tartness. It features in American soda breads, biscuits and pancakes.
- Yogurt is a fermented low-fat milk product, with a slightly sour taste. Greek yogurt often has a higher fat content, and is creamier. Plain yogurt can be substituted for sour cream.

CREAMS

The fat content of cream denotes its stability when heated and its whipping quality. The higher the fat content the more stable it is.

- Double cream is favoured in cooking because, with 48% fat, it can boil without curdling.
- Whipping cream has just enough fat, 35–39%, for heating and whipping. Make your own with a 2:1 ratio double cream to single cream.
- Single cream contains about 24% fat and is mainly used as a pouring cream; it can be used to add body and a creamy texture to liquids as long as it is not boiled.
- Sour cream has a spooning consistency. Although it can be stirred into warm sauces to enrich them, it has a fat content of about 21%, so it is not stable at high heat.

CREME FRAICHE

This partially soured, tangy cream has the added bonus of not separating during cooking. It is made by mixing buttermilk, sour cream or yogurt with double cream, heating it, then letting it stand. Stir, cover and refrigerate crème fraîche after it has thickened. Use it as the French do – as a flavouring for soups, sauces and savoury dishes. It is also delicious with fruits and sweet dishes.

1 Mix 500 ml buttermilk and 250 ml double cream. Put bowl over a pan of hot water and heat to 30°C.

2 Pour warm mixture into a glass bowl; partially cover. Let stand at room temperature for 6–8 hours.

CLOTTED CREAM

A renowned West Country speciality, this deep-yellow thick cream is made by gently heating the cream to scald it and make a crust. It will keep for up to 5 days in the refrigerator.

1 Pour 600 ml double cream into a heavy-based pan. Heat gently until cream thickens, 25–30 minutes.

2 Chill the cream until it has set and a crust has formed on the surface.

3 Remove the crust of clotted cream with a large metal spoon. Reserve the cream and discard the liquid left underneath.

MAKING SOUR CREAM

This technique for making sour cream, a favourite with Mexican and Eastern European food, can also be applied to milk for making Devonshire scones.

Stir 1 tbsp fresh lemon juice into 250 ml double cream in a glass bowl. Let the mixture stand at room temperature for 10–30 minutes or until it has thickened. Cover the bowl and refrigerate until ready to use.

Fish & Shellfish

Choosing Fresh Seafood

Using Fish & Shellfish

Preparing Whole Round Fish

Preparing Whole Flat Fish

Fish Steak & Fillet Preparations

Smoked & Salted Fish

Poaching

Steaming

Grilling

Baking

Frying

Fish Mixtures

Lobster

Crab & Prawns

Mussels

Oysters & Clams

Scallops & Whelks

Squid

Choosing Fresh Seafood

Seafood falls into four categories: seawater, freshwater, preserved fish (smoked, salted and dried) and shellfish. All but preserved fish should be eaten as fresh as possible. It is only really possible to judge the freshness of a whole fish; fillets, steaks and pieces are more difficult to assess. Freshwater fish should smell fresh and clean, while marine fish should smell of the sea.

EYES should be full, moist, bright and bulging. Avoid fish with dull, dry, shrivelled or sunken eyes
GILLS should be clean, red and bright, with no signs of greying or traces of slime
BODY should be firm, smooth and quite stiff, not limp, floppy or lumpy

Buying Fillets and Steaks

It is better to buy fillets or steaks that are cut from the whole fish while you wait, rather than pre-cut, or to buy the fish and cut or fillet it yourself (see pages 55 and 57). Very large fish, such as monkfish, shark, tuna and large cod, are almost always sold ready prepared. When judging the freshness of fillets and steaks, the smell and texture of the fish can be used as a guide. The fish should smell fresh (smelling of the sea in marine fish) and look moist, firm and springy, not dry.

Handling Seafood

Fish and shellfish deteriorate much more quickly than meat, so they must be cooked on the day of purchase or as soon as possible afterwards.

Oily fish such as mackerel, herring and salmon, spoil more quickly than white fish because their natural oils turn rancid. If seafood has to be stored overnight, wrap it in damp cloths and keep it in the coldest part of the refrigerator. Whole fish will keep longer if gutted first.

BUYING SHELLFISH

LOBSTERS AND CRABS If you are buying live, choose an active specimen that feels heavy for its size. If buying cooked, check that the shell is undamaged and the claws intact. The smell should be fresh and not strong.

MUSSELS, CLAMS AND COCKLES Avoid those that are excessively covered in mud or barnacles, or that appear to be cracked or damaged. Discard any that remain open when tapped.

SCALLOPS These are most often sold opened, cleaned and trimmed rather than in their closed shells. Check that they smell sweet; if so, they are fresh. The flesh of fresh scallops is slightly grey and translucent, not perfectly white.

OYSTERS The shells must be undamaged and tightly closed. When tapped they should sound solid. Traditionally, they were picked when there was an "r" in the month to avoid infection during warm weather. They are now generally sold all year round because of modern techniques of oyster farming and improved methods of transport.

PRAWNS These are sold in several ways: cooked in or out of their shells, or raw in their shells. Cooked prawns should be bright pink and firm, not watery. Raw prawns should also be firm, with shiny grey shells. Avoid any prawns with black spots – a sure sign of ageing.

SKIN should be shiny and damp to the touch, not dry or dull. Any natural markings and colouring should be undimmed. For example, red mullet and snapper should be a bright pinky red; trout, herring and mackerel should be irridescent; salmon a shimmering silver; and parrot fish a brilliant blue

UNUSUAL FISH

There are many exotic fish on sale at large supermarkets and city fishmongers, many of them beautifully marked with spectacular, irridescent colours.

- Emperor Fish, also called *capitaine rouge*, *capitaine blanc* and *lascar*, has a strong flavour and is quite bony. Bake whole.
- Gurnard is tasty and firm fleshed, good in fish stews and soups.
- Sea Bream has sweet, firm flesh and is inexpensive. Gilt-head bream – *daurade* in French – is especially good. Bake whole with or without stuffing.
- Shark steaks are meaty and firm with very little bone. Good for chargrilling and in stews.
- Tilapia has firm white flesh and good flavour. It can be steamed, baked, grilled or barbecued, whole or in fillets.

Using Fish & Shellfish

Fish and shellfish are delicate foods to cook – they have fragile flesh that requires careful handling. Choose the freshest you can, and make sure they are thoroughly cleaned before use. Cook fish just long enough to set the protein and turn the flesh opaque; if overcooked, fish will become tough and dry. When substituting one fish for another, make sure it is of a similar structure, texture and flavour.

Round Fish

This variable family runs the gamut in size and shape. Their flesh is typically firm and "meaty" tasting, meaning they pair well with other assertive ingredients.

Fish	Cooking Methods
Bass/ Mullet	Poach, steam, bake, barbecue
Bream	Bake, braise
Catfish	Stew, braise, grill
Cod/Haddock	Pan-fry, deep-fry, grill, poach, bake
Dogfish	Bake, stew, grill
Eel	Bake, stew, grill
Hake	Bake wrapped, steam, pan-fry
Mackerel	Pan-fry, grill, barbecue
Monkfish	Pan-fry, bake, grill, barbecue
Salmon/Trout	Pan-fry, poach, steam, bake, grill, barbecue
Sardines	Grill, barbecue, pan-fry, bake
Snapper/Mahi Mahi/ Orange Rough	Poach, pan-fry, grill, barbecue, bake
Swordfish/Tuna/ Shark	Grill, barbecue, pan-fry, bake, stew, braise

Flat Fish

To showcase the subtle flavour of these fine-textured varieties, choose for preference a swift cooking process that uses as few other ingredients as possible. Braising works particularly well because this moist-heat method tends to concentrate the natural, and often very delicate, flavour of the fish.

Fish	Cooking Methods
Brill	Bake wrapped and unwrapped, steam, poach, grill, pan-fry
Grouper	Bake wrapped and unwrapped, steam, poach, grill, pan-fry
Halibut	Poach, pan-fry, braise
John Dory	Poach, grill, pan-fry
Plaice	Pan-fry, deep-fry, poach, steam, grill, bake
Ray/Skate	Pan-fry, bake
Sole	Grill, pan-fry, deep-fry, steam, bake
Turbot	Bake wrapped and unwrapped, steam, poach, grill, pan-fry

SHELLFISH

Some molluscs require special attention. A live shellfish yields the best flavour, so store mussels or clams in salted water (4 tbsp salt to 1 litre water) not fresh water, which will kill them. Bearding mussels more than a few hours before cooking can spoil them.

SHELLFISH	WHAT TO LOOK FOR	COOKING METHODS
CLAMS/COCKLES	*Shells should be tightly closed, not chipped or broken* *Shucked clams should be plump and smell fresh throughout*	Steam – in shell Grill, bake – half shell Stew, pan-fry – shucked
CRAB	*Active and heavy* *Shell undamaged and claws intact*	Boil, steam
LOBSTER	*Heavy for size* *Tail curled under* *Claws intact and undamaged*	Boil, steam – in shell Grill – split
MUSSELS	*Shells tightly shut and undamaged* *Not light and loose when shaken*	Boil, steam – in shell Grill, bake – half shell Pan-fry, stew – shucked
OYSTERS	*Shells tightly closed and undamaged* *Shucked oysters should be plump and uniform in size with clear liquid*	Serve raw Bake, grill – half shell Pan-fry, stew – shucked
PRAWNS	*Firm meat that feels full in the shell* *Moist appearance and fresh smell* *Avoid any that smell of chlorine or have black spots on the shell*	Pan-fry, deep-fry, stir-fry, grill, barbecue, bake, poach, steam
SCALLOPS	*Free of liquid with a sweet fresh odour whether on half shell or shucked* *Check the body section is plump and creamy white* *Coral pink and moist* *Avoid any with a sulphurous smell*	Bake, grill – half shell Poach, pan-fry – shucked
SQUID/ OCTOPUS	*Clear eyes, fresh smell* *White moist flesh*	Deep-fry, pan-fry, poach, bake, stew
WHELKS/ WINKLES	*Should smell sweet* *Move into shell when prodded* *Lid should be moist and firmly in place*	Boil – in shell Stew – shelled

FISH ON THE MENU

From coast to coast, great cooks pair their region's catch with local ingredients and cooking techniques to create internationally appealing dishes.

FRANCE – *Bouillabaisse* (a lusty fish stew of Mediterranean fish and shellfish with saffron and fennel) originated in Marseille.
GREECE – *Kalamari* (squid deep-fried in a light batter and served with lemon wedges and chilled retsina) is a favourite midday snack on the Aegean.
ITALY – *Spaghetti alle vongole* (with clam sauce) is a staple in trattorias throughout Italy.
MEXICO – *Ceviche* (raw fish "cooked" not by heat, but by the acidity of lime juice) is refreshing with a tart tang.
SPAIN – *Paella* (shellfish and squid with saffron rice, tomatoes and garlic) is a favourite festive dish.
UNITED STATES – *New England Clam Chowder* (a soup made with potatoes, clams and cream) dates back to the early 1700s. *Manhattan Clam Chowder* (a spicy tomato- and clam-based soup) came to fame later, in the 1930s.

Preparing Whole Round Fish

Round fish are so named for their body shape – a round belly as opposed to a flat one, with an eye on either side of the head. Popular varieties include trout and salmon. Round fish yield two fillets, one from each side of the backbone. Though most often gutted before being sold, round fish can be cleaned at home if you like. Once gutted, round fish can be boned and stuffed or filleted.

TRICK OF THE TRADE

Slippery Fish

Many fish are slippery and tricky to handle – a natural condition, not a sign of poor quality. Rinsing the fish in hot water or a vinegar and water solution, prior to scaling, will help reduce slipperiness.

Fill a container large enough to hold the fish with a solution of 1 tbsp vinegar to every litre of water. Submerge the fish and rub its sides with your fingers. Drain and pat dry with paper towels.

VANDYKING

An English technique of preparing a fish to be served whole, is to cut its tail into a "V". This is known as vandyking in honour of the painter's V-shaped beard.

Sir Anthony Van Dyck (1599-1641)

Trimming and Scaling

Most fish, such as the salmon pictured here, have scales that need to be removed before cooking. Removing scales is a simple but messy task, so work as near to the sink as possible. Trimming any fins beforehand will make scaling more straightforward and, because some fins are spiny, will be gentler on your hands and make the fish easier to handle. Trim the fins with a pair of kitchen scissors but use a large chef's knife to remove the scales. Fish scalers are also available from specialist kitchen shops.

1 Cut off the three fins that run along the stomach of the fish from the head to the tail – the pectoral, ventral and anal fins – with kitchen scissors.

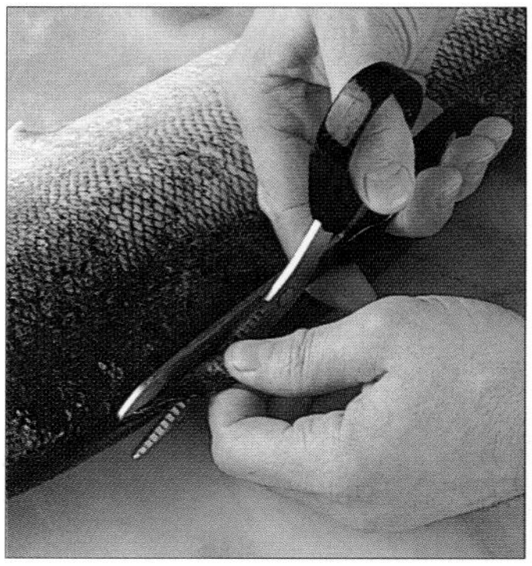

2 Turn the fish over and cut off the dorsal fins that run along the back of the fish with the kitchen scissors. It is important to cut off the fins as they harbour bacteria.

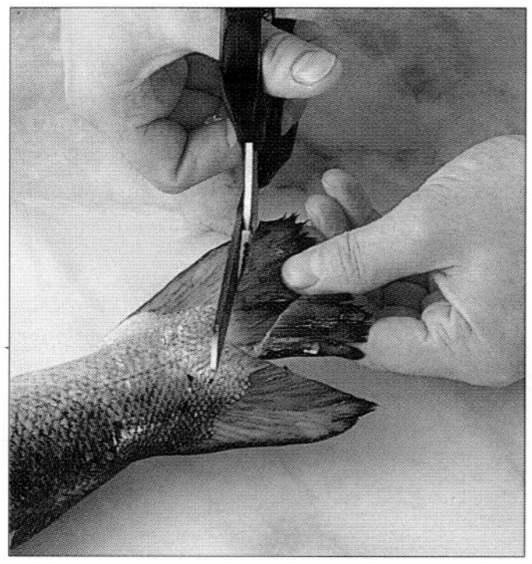

3 For fish that are to be served whole, you can make the tail look more attractive by cutting it into a neat "V" shape (see box, left) with kitchen scissors.

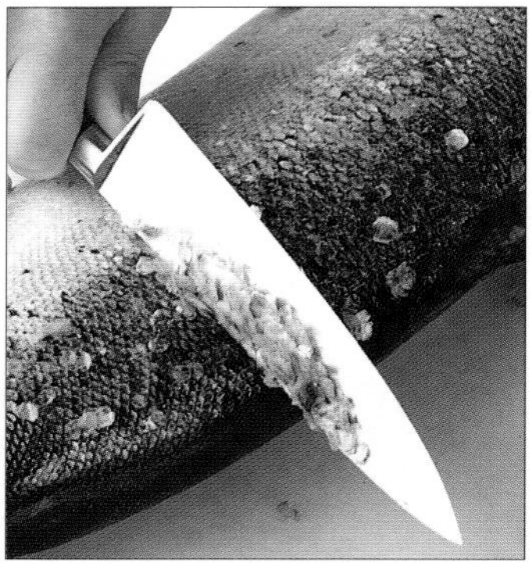

4 Hold the tail of the fish firmly. Scrape the scales off the fish with the back of a large chef's knife, working from the tail to the head. Rinse the fish thoroughly.

Gutting Through the Gills

Round fish that are to be served with their heads on should have their internal organs (innards) removed through their gills. This method retains their shape, ensuring a neat presentation. The fish can then be stuffed or left unstuffed. If the latter, bone the fish along its backbone (see page 55).

1 Locate and lift up the gill flap behind the head of the fish and cut out the gills with kitchen scissors. Discard the gills.

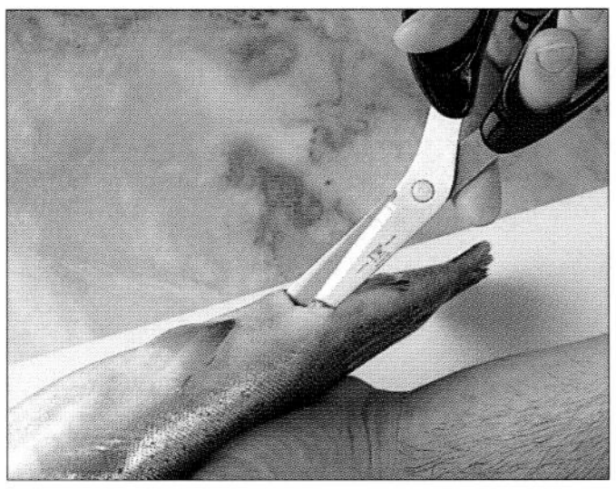

2 Hold the fish belly up. Make a small cut at the bottom of the stomach and insert the points of the scissors or your fingers through it. Cut through the innards to loosen them from the fish.

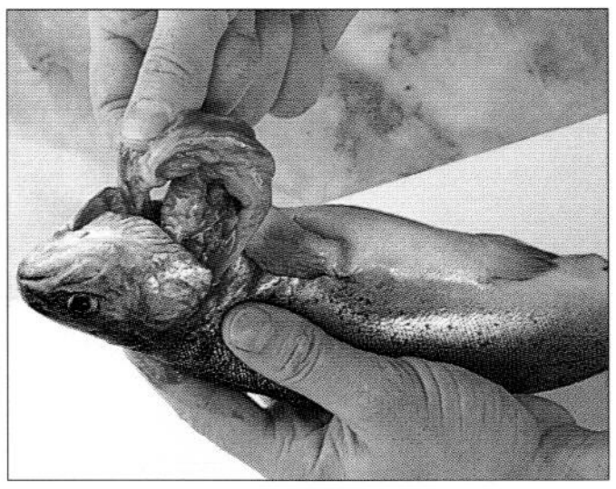

3 Insert your fingers inside the gill opening. Grasp hold of the innards and pull them out. Check the hole cut at the bottom of the stomach, making sure no organs remain. Discard the innards.

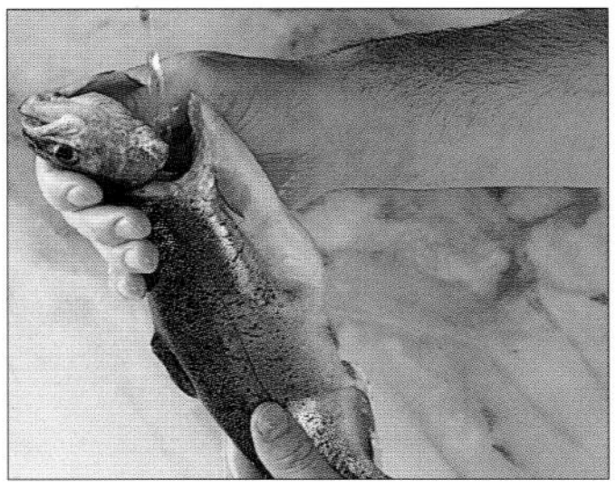

4 Hold the fish under cold running water and let the water run through the inside of the fish from the gill opening to the tail. Rinse until the water runs clear. Pat dry with paper towels.

Scoring

Today's chefs dress up plain grilled, barbecued or steamed fish by making cuts in the flesh and inserting sprigs of herbs. Slices of garlic can also be inserted or, for an Asian dish, lemon grass, spring onions and fresh root ginger can be used. The flavours of the herbs penetrate the fish flesh during cooking.

Make 2–3 slashes in one side of the fish, cutting through to the bones. Turn the fish over and repeat on the other side. Tuck the seasonings into the slashes. The fish is now ready for cooking.

Gutting Through the Stomach

The easiest and most common way to remove the innards from a fish is through its stomach. Use this method for fish that are to be served whole, stuffed or unstuffed, and where a pristine shape is not required, particularly if the fish is to be boned before or after cooking.

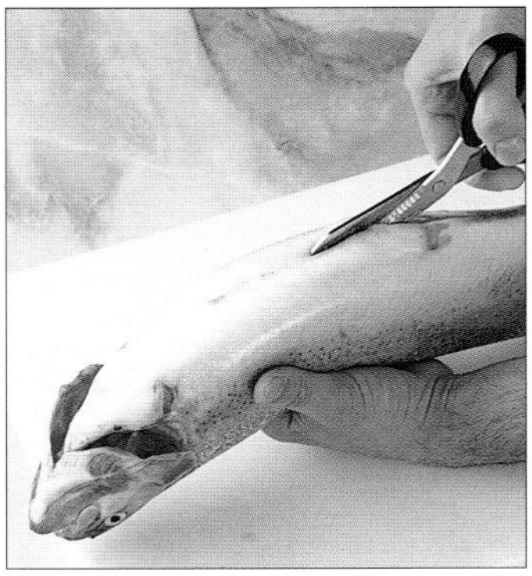

1 Cut out the gills behind the head and discard. Make a small cut at the bottom of the stomach, then cut along the underside, stopping just below the gills.

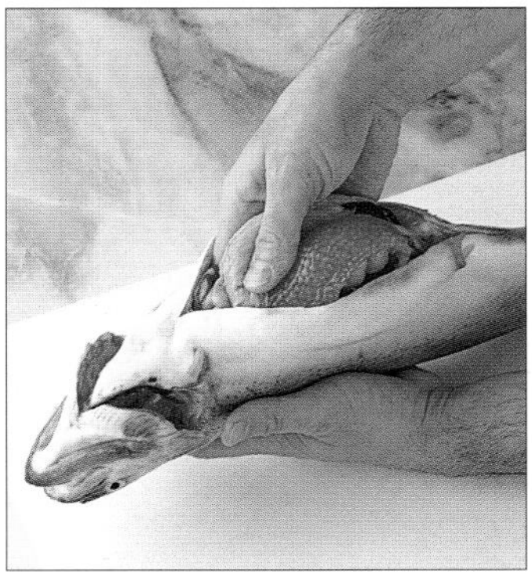

2 With your hand, grasp hold of the innards and pull them out. Discard the innards; they are not suitable for the stockpot.

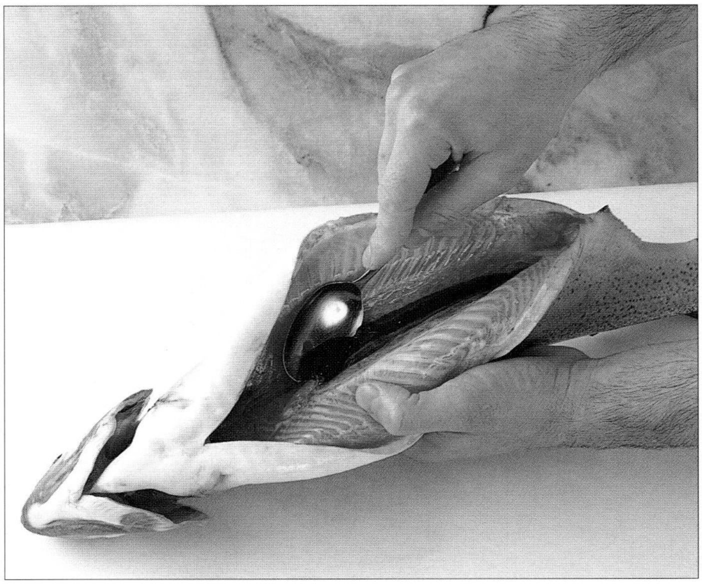

3 Run along each side of the backbone with a tablespoon. This removes any blood vessels which detract from the fish's appearance and can make it taste bitter when cooked. Rinse the fish under cold running water, then pat dry with paper towels. The fish is now ready for cooking.

Boning Small Round Fish

Small, oily fish, such as the sardine shown here, have such soft bones that they can be boned with your fingers rather than a knife.

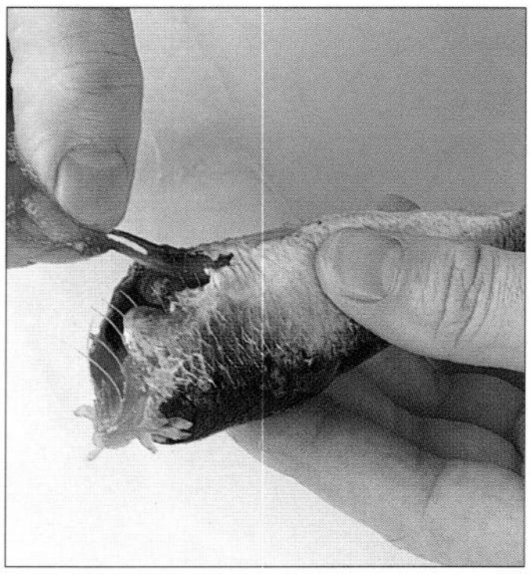

1 With your fingertips, break off the head of the fish behind the gills. Discard the head and gills. Insert your forefinger into the head end of the fish and run it down the belly so that it slits open. Working from head to tail, pull out the innards and discard them.

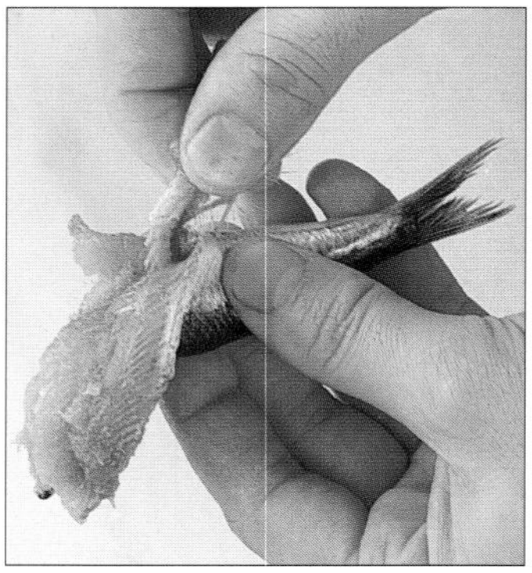

2 Open the fish out and, working from head to tail again, pull out the backbone. Release the backbone at the tail end by snapping it off with your fingers. Rinse the fish thoroughly and pat dry with paper towels. The fish is now ready for cooking.

Boning Through the Stomach

Once the innards have been removed through the opening in the stomach of the fish (see page 53), you should also remove the backbone through the stomach. Gutting and boning a fish through its stomach, as with the salmon shown here, creates a natural cavity for stuffings.

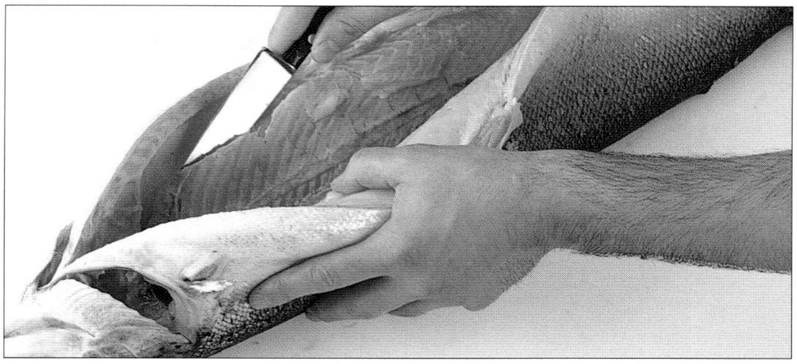

1 Hold the fish on its back and use a filleting knife to cut upwards between the rib bones and the flesh on one side of the backbone so that the rib bones are loosened.

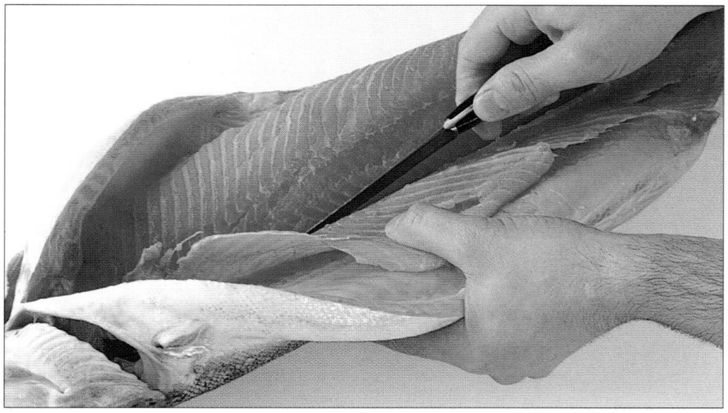

2 Slide the blade of the knife down the rib bones close to the backbone so that all the ribs on this side are detached from the flesh. Repeat from step 1 to free the ribs from the other side of the flesh.

3 Cut the backbone from the fish with a pair of kitchen scissors, and discard along with the ribs.

4 Remove the fine pin bones from both sides of the fish's spine with a pair of tweezers. Run your fingers from the head to the tail, again on both sides, feeling for pin bones you may have overlooked. Wipe the fish dry with paper towels. The fish is now ready for cooking.

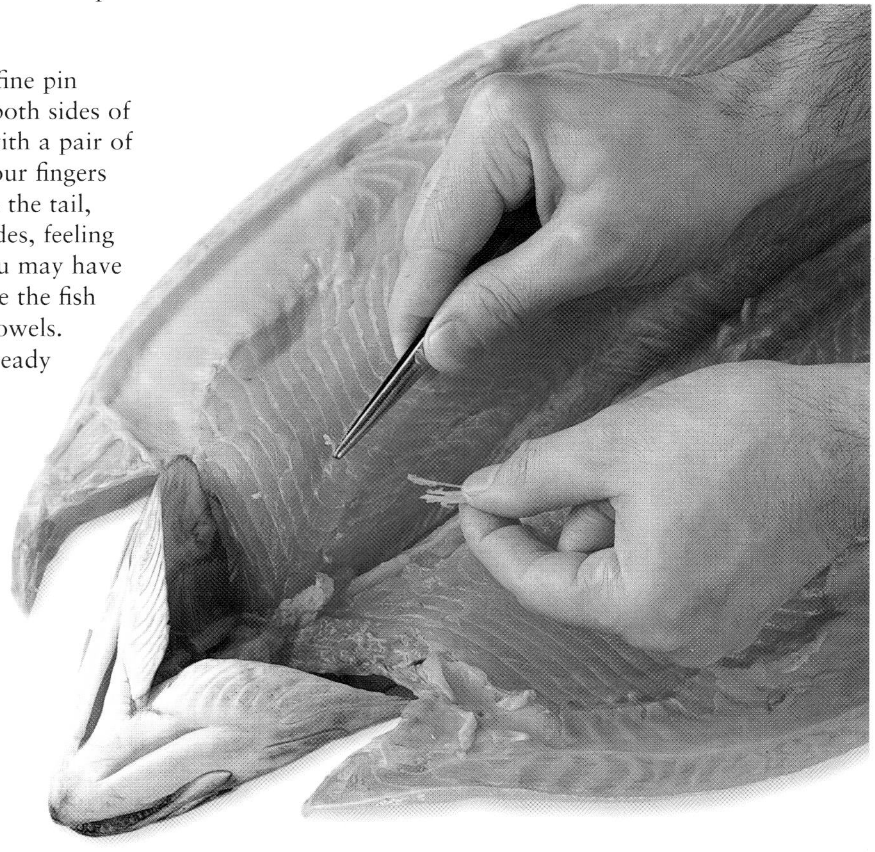

Boning Along the Backbone

To preserve the shape of a whole round fish, leaving the stomach cavity intact for stuffing, bone it along the back. The fish, such as the trout shown here, should be gutted through the gills.

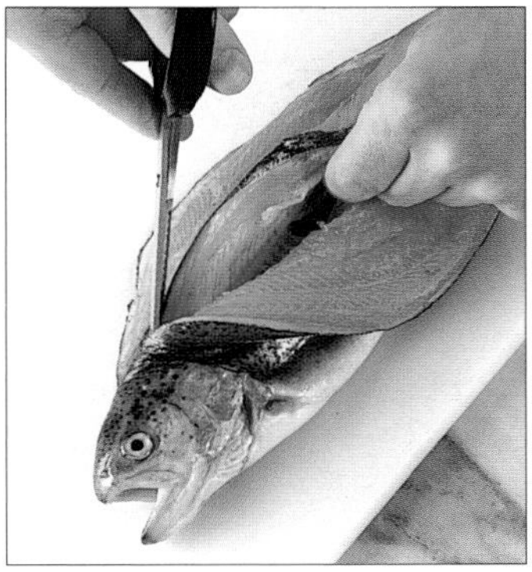

1 Working from the tail to the head, cut along each side of the backbone with a pair of kitchen scissors.

2 Carefully detach the backbone at both the head and tail ends of the fish, using a chef's knife. Lift out the backbone and discard. Wipe the fish thoroughly dry with paper towels. The fish is now ready for cooking.

Filleting Round Fish

Once a fish has been scaled, trimmed and gutted through the stomach (see page 53), it can be filleted or cut into large boneless slices. Two fillets – one from each side – can be cut from round fish, such as the salmon shown here. Use a sharp, flexible filleting knife and work carefully to leave as little flesh on the bones as possible. Check the fillets for pin bones (see page 54).

1 Make a cut around the back of the head then, working from head to tail, using the rib bones as a guide, cut along one side of the backbone. Holding the knife flat use long, even strokes to cut the flesh away. Run the knife over the rib bones, holding the free flesh with the other hand.

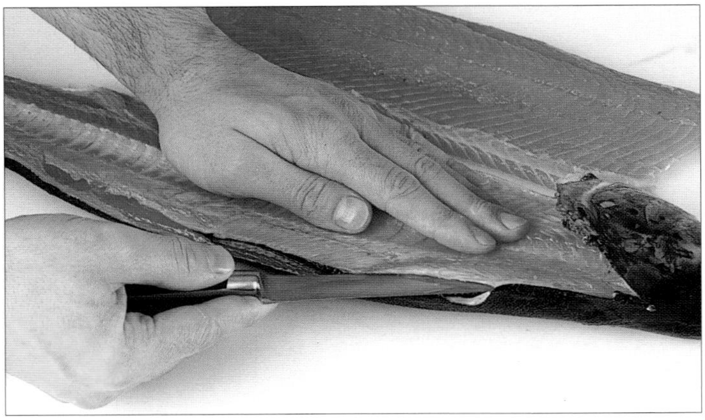

2 Turn the fish over and repeat step 1 to remove the remaining fillet. The head and carcass will be left. Use the bones along with the head, but not the gills, to make fish stock (see page 17), if you like. The fillets may be skinned as for flat fish (see page 57) before cooking, depending on what the finished dish calls for.

Boning Monkfish

If you buy monkfish on the bone you will need to know how to remove the bone if a recipe calls for fillets.

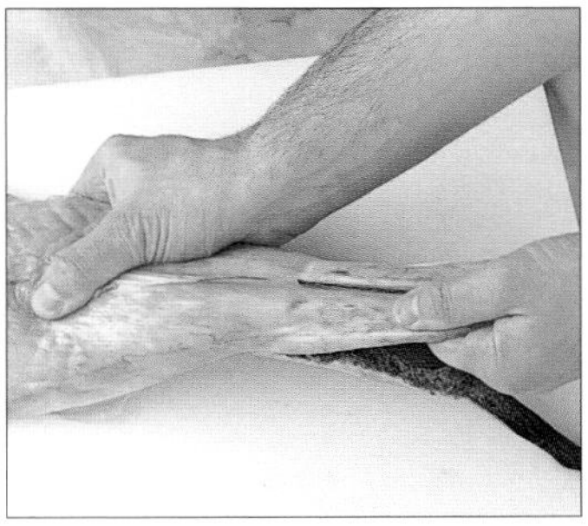

1 Lay the monkfish down, grasp hold of the skin and pull it back towards the tail of the fish.

2 Cut along both sides of the backbone with a chef's knife, separating the flesh of the fish into two fillets. The backbone can then be used to make fish stock (see page 17).

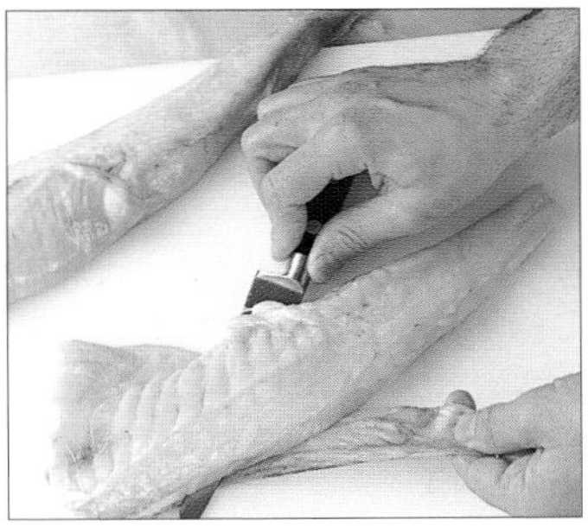

3 Carefully remove the dark membrane from the underside of each fillet. Wipe the fillets thoroughly with paper towels. They are now ready for cooking.

Preparing Whole Flat Fish

Flat fish are so named because they are flat-shaped. Popular varieties include plaice, sole, turbot and brill. Flat fish swim on their sides and have both eyes on their top side, or back, which is dark for camouflage. The underneath of flat fish is white. In order to preserve their shape, flat fish are always gutted, from behind the head and gills. Because gutting is done at sea, they are invariably sold ready-gutted.

Scaling

You will need to remove the scales from the skin of the fish if you are planning to serve the fish whole or if you have bought a fish that is not already scaled by the fishmonger.

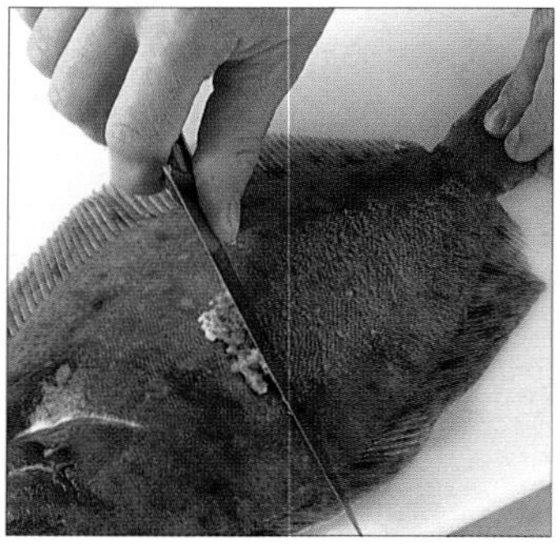

This is a messy job, best done near the sink. Lay the fish dark-side up and hold the tail firmly. Working from tail to head with the back of a chef's knife, scrape the scales off the fish. Hold the fish by the tail under the cold tap and rinse it thoroughly, washing away the scales by rubbing the skin vigorously with your hands.

Skinning

If you are serving a flat fish whole, only the dark skin needs to be removed – the white skin is left on to help hold the fish together during cooking. If you plan to serve the fish as fillets, you can remove both dark and white skins while the fish is whole, as with this Dover sole, or you can skin individual fillets.

1 Working on the dark side first, scrape the skin away from the tail with a knife to loosen it from the flesh.

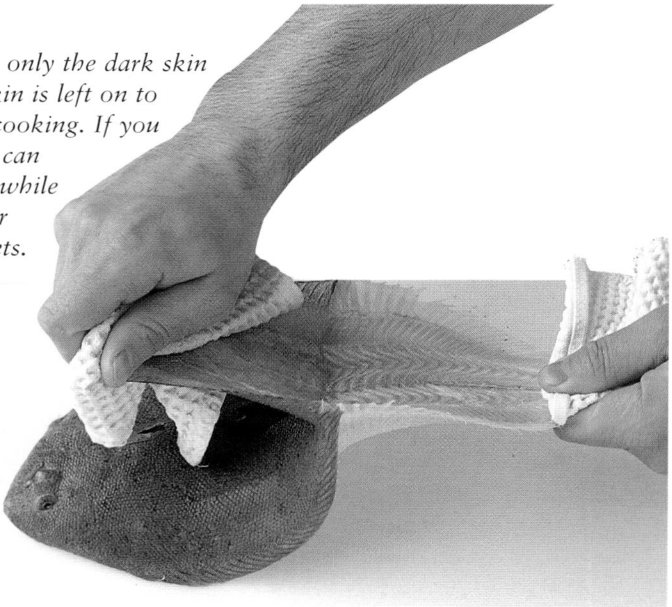

2 Grasp the skin and tail using a tea towel to prevent your hands from slipping. Pull the skin away from the tail and over the head, detaching it completely from the fish.

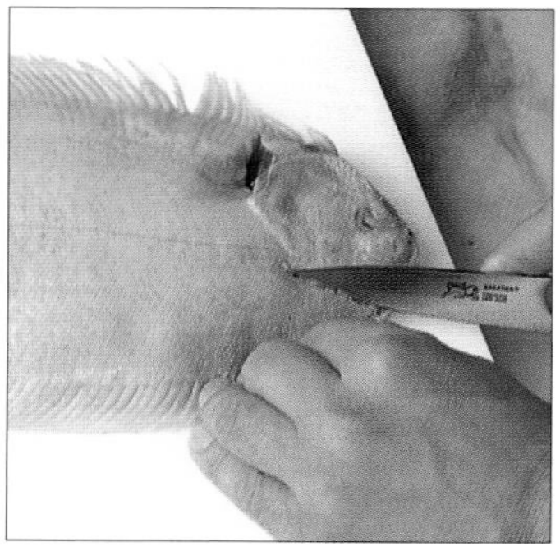

3 Turn the fish white-side up. Cut around the head of the fish to loosen the skin.

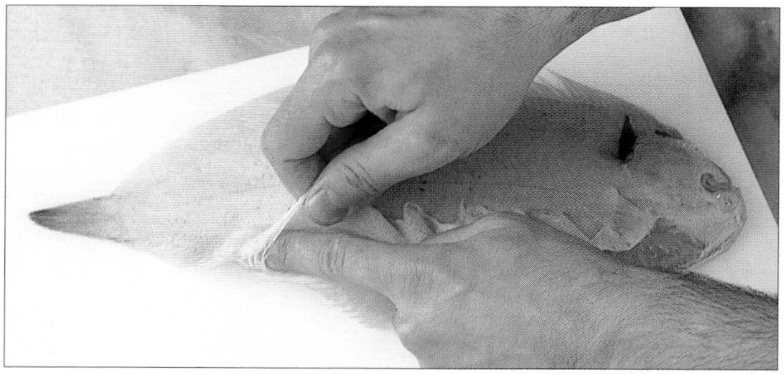

4 Working from head to tail on both sides, use your fingers to loosen the skin and pull it back from around the edge of the fish. Once the skin is well loosened, grasp it at the tail end and pull it away from the flesh, detaching it completely.

FILLETING

Depending on its size, a flat fish yields two or four fillets. Whether you are going to skin the fillets or not, you should always trim and scale the fish before filleting. Here a large brill is separated into four fillets.

1 Lay the fish dark-side up on a cutting board. Cut around the outside of the fish with a filleting knife where the flesh meets the fins, carefully tracing the shape of the fillets.

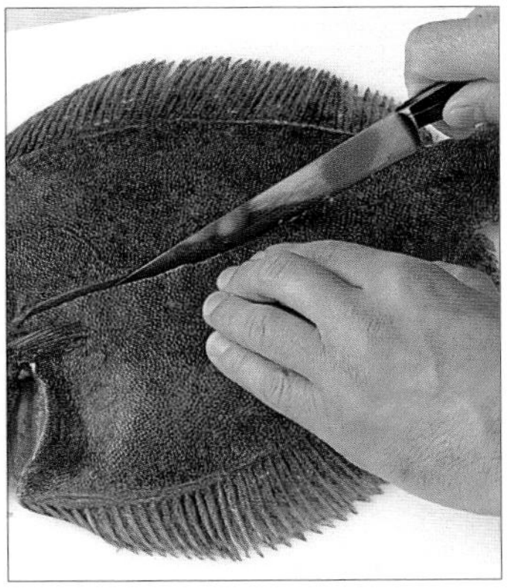

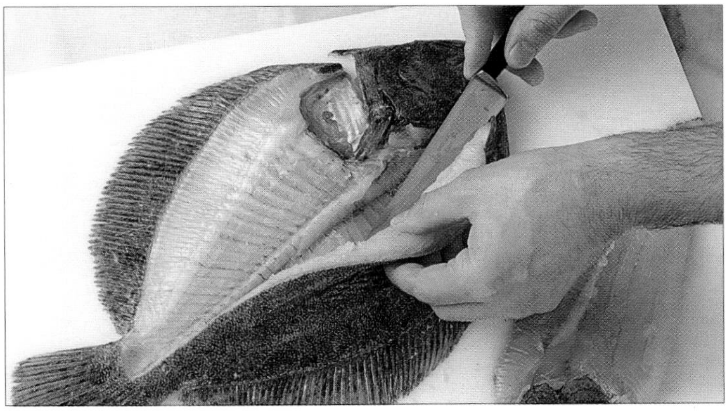

2 Cut down the centre of the fish from head to tail with a sharp knife, cutting right down to the bone.

3 Working from the centre of the fish to the edge, cut away one fillet with long, broad strokes of the knife. Take care to leave as little flesh still on the bones as possible. Turn the fish around and remove the second fillet in the same way.

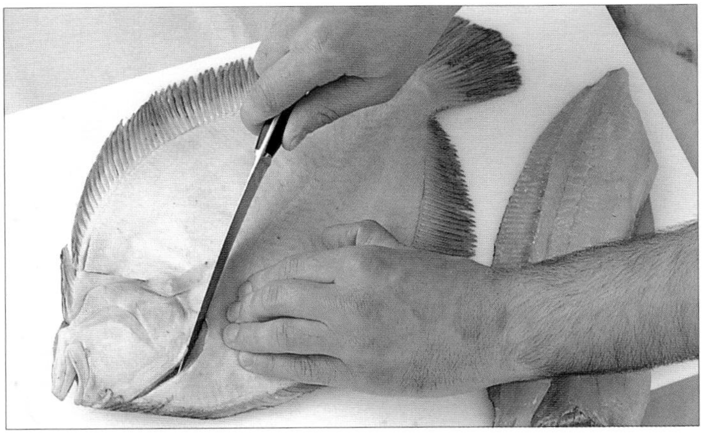

4 Turn the fish over. Make a cut around the back of the head and around the outside edge of the flesh. Cut down to the bone along the centre of the fish, working from head to tail. Follow step 3 to remove the two remaining fillets.

Fillet from one half of a Dover sole

Fillets cut lengthwise in half for paupiettes

SKINNING A FISH FILLET

Even when bought packaged from the supermarket, fish fillets most often come with their skins on – which helps them to maintain their shape. The technique of skinning a fish fillet is important; if the skin and the flesh are not separated properly, the flesh may come away with the skin or be ragged and torn.

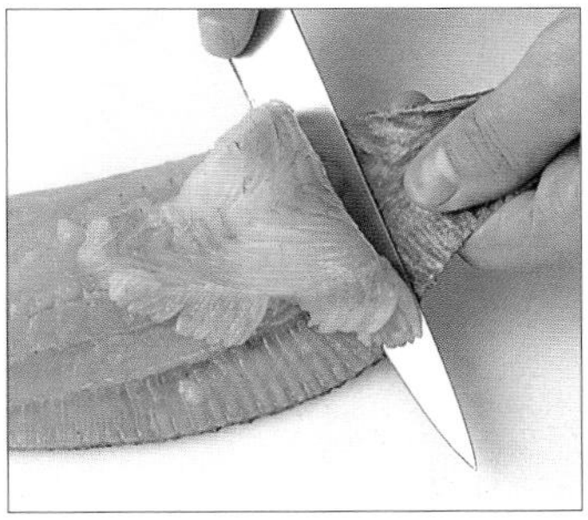

Lay the fillet skin-side down and make a cut across the flesh at the tail end. Dip your fingertips in salt to help you get a good grip, grasp the tail end and insert the knife in the cut. Working away from you and using a sawing action, hold the knife at a shallow angle. Move the knife between the flesh and skin until you reach the other end of the fillet.

Sichuan Fish

A Chinese classic, your choice of a whole, firm-fleshed fish such as red snapper, sea bass or grey mullet, is deep-fried in a wok, then braised in an aromatic sauce flavoured with garlic, ginger and chilli.

SERVES 4

1 whole fish, weighing about 1 kg

Salt

500 ml groundnut oil

1 tsp cornflour

2–4 garlic cloves, shredded

2.5 cm piece of fresh root ginger, peeled and cut into very fine shreds

2 tbsp Shaoxing rice wine or dry sherry

1–3 tbsp chilli bean sauce

2 tbsp light soy sauce

150 ml fish stock or water

2 spring onions, cut into very fine shreds

2 fresh red chillies, deseeded and cut into julienne

1 tsp caster sugar

1 tsp Oriental sesame oil

Fresh coriander sprigs, to garnish

Prepare the fish and remove any scales if necessary. Score both sides of the fish with three diagonal cuts, spacing them evenly along its length. Sprinkle the fish with salt on both sides.

Heat a wok over a high heat until it is hot, then slowly pour in the oil down the side. When the oil is very hot, carefully add the fish and deep-fry, turning once until golden brown on both sides, about 4 minutes.

Carefully remove the fish with two fish slices and allow to drain on paper towels. Pour off the hot oil, leaving about 1 tbsp.

Mix the cornflour to a paste with 2 tsp water; set aside. Add the garlic and ginger to the hot wok and stir-fry briefly, then add the rice wine, chilli bean sauce and soy sauce and stir to mix. Pour in the stock and add the cornflour paste. Bring to the boil, stirring. Reduce the heat, slide the fish back into the wok and braise gently for about 5 minutes.

Remove the fish. Stir the spring onions, chillies, sugar and sesame oil into the sauce and simmer until reduced. Return the fish to the wok, spoon over the sauce and garnish with fresh coriander.

CHILLI BEAN SAUCE

Commercial chilli bean sauces range from mild to very hot, so add the amount you favour according to the brand used and your taste. You can make your own sauce by mixing dried red chillies, ground in a food processor or pestle and mortar, and yellow bean sauce. A ratio of one part ground chillies to two parts bean sauce will produce a moderately hot result.

Deep-frying and Braising

Because of its gently sloping sides, a wok is an excellent vessel for deep-frying a whole fish in hot oil, and then braising it in a sauce. For safety's sake, use a two-handled wok – it will be more stable than the type with one handle.

Heat the oil in the wok until it is just smoking (about 190°C). Slide in the fish and deep-fry until golden brown on both sides, turning it over with two fish slices.

Braise the fish in the sauce, basting it constantly, until it is cooked through. If the fish is very thick, turn it over with two fish slices halfway through cooking.

FISH STEAK & FILLET PREPARATIONS

Steaks and fillets can be cut from both round and flat fish. The French distinguish between *darnes*, steaks cut from round fish, and *tronçons*, steaks cut from large flat fish. Fish steaks are cut thicker and are quite robust; fish fillets are thinner than steaks and therefore more fragile.

CUTTING ESCALOPES

Large round fish fillets, such as the salmon illustrated here, can be cut into thin slices or escalopes for use in a variety of preparations. Escalopes can be cut from a fillet with or without its skin and should be about 1 cm thick. Often, they are then pounded between sheets of baking parchment to flatten them, making them even thinner. Check for pin bones and remove any you find before you start (see page 54).

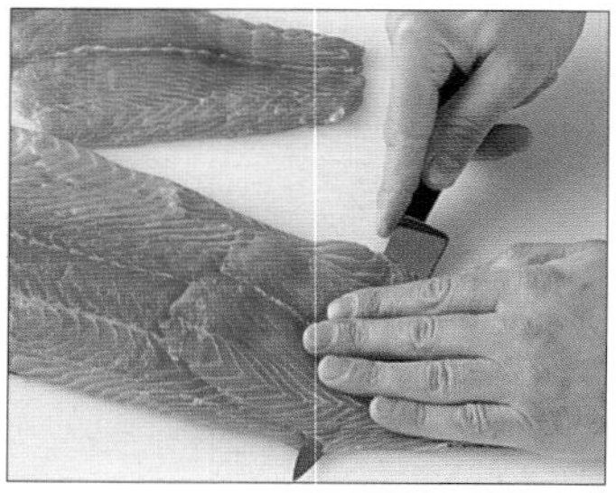

Starting near the tail end of the fillet and working your way towards the head, with a sharp, thin-bladed knife, cut evenly sized pieces. Keep the knife almost flat against the fillet as you cut, and always face the tail.

CUTTING STEAKS

Steaks cut from a round fish are made by cutting across one that has been scaled, trimmed and gutted. Use a chef's knife or cleaver. Steaks are usually cut 2.5 cm thick and can be pan-fried, grilled, roasted or poached. Sea bass is shown here.

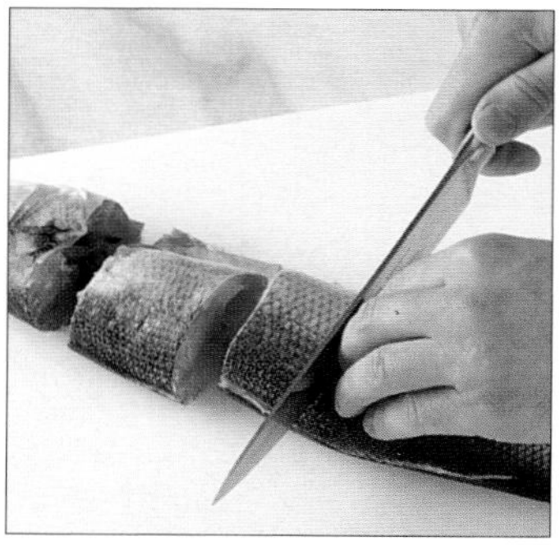

1 Make evenly spaced marks along the side of the fish. Cut down forcefully through the flesh and backbone at each mark with the knife.

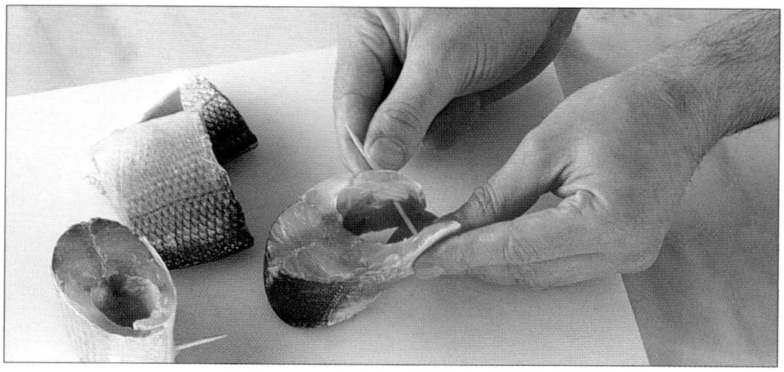

2 Fold the ends of each steak in towards the centre; secure the ends with a wooden cocktail stick to keep the ends from curling during cooking. The steaks are now ready to cook and they can be served with or without the backbone.

MAKING PACKAGES

Thin pieces of fillet called escalopes (see left) can be wrapped around a filling to make a savoury package. Fish packages are fragile and are best poached or carefully pan-fried. Salmon is illustrated here.

1 Put the escalope between two sheets of baking parchment. Pound with a cleaver's flat edge until flat.

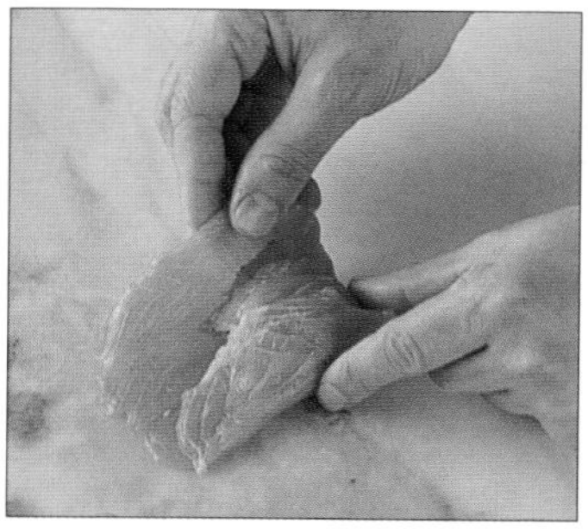

2 Wrap the escalope around your chosen filling, making as neat and square a package as possible.

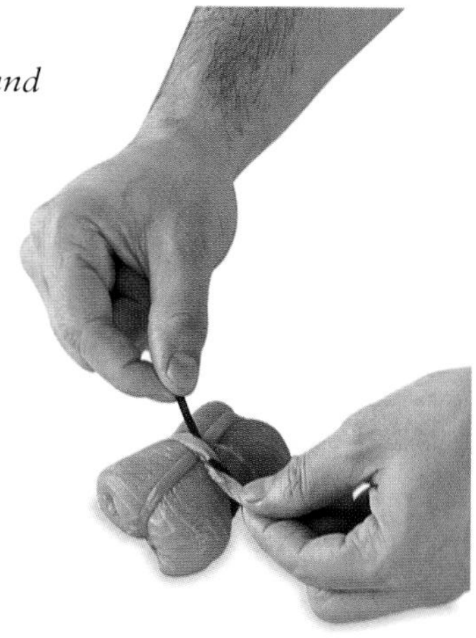

3 Turn the package over seam-side down, and secure it by tying a strip of spring onion around it.

Making Pillows

A pillow is a piece of fillet in which a pocket is cut to contain a stuffing. Any thick, firm fish, like the salmon shown here, can be used. Cut fillets into 7.5 x 4 cm pieces to accommodate the stuffing. Because they are fragile, pillows are best poached.

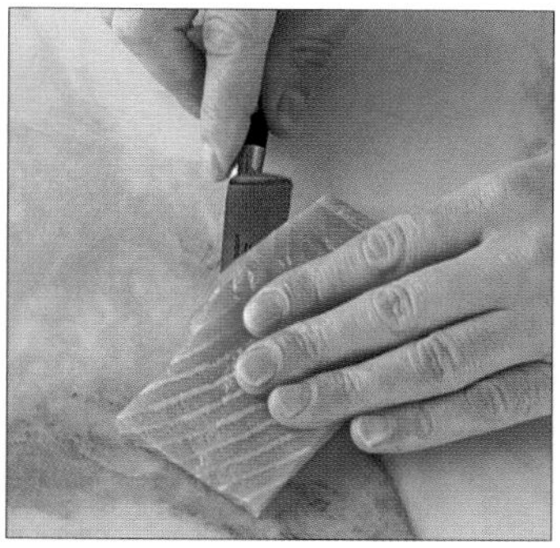

1 Starting and ending 1 cm in from each side, cut a pocket in the front of the fillet (do not cut through the back, top or bottom).

2 Hold the pocket open with one hand and spoon the stuffing into the pocket. Do not overfill or the stuffing may burst out during cooking.

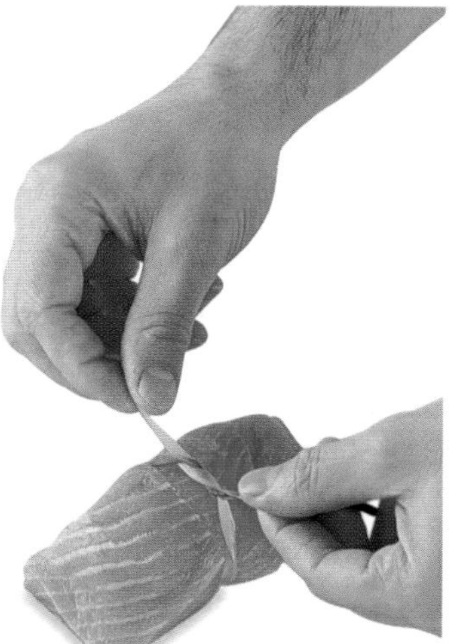

3 Secure the opening by tying a strip of spring onion around it. The pillow is now ready for cooking.

Making Fish Plaits

A variety of round and flat fish fillets with contrasting flesh and thin colourful skins, such as the mackerel, snapper and sole shown here, can be used to good effect in this easy but impressive presentation. To preserve the delicate texture of the fillets, steaming is the best cooking method.

1 Cut each fillet into strips about 20 x 2 cm. Lay three strips, one from each fillet, skin-side up on the cutting board. The strips should be close together.

2 Interweave the strips, keeping the plait as even as possible. Plait the strips loosely because they shrink a little when cooked.

3 Steam the plaits (see page 70) over simmering *court bouillon* (see page 66) or fish stock (see page 17).

Making Paupiettes

For this technique, skinless fish fillets are halved lengthwise and rolled. They are stuffed before cooking, either by spooning the stuffing on one end of the fish and then rolling it up, or by spooning in the stuffing when the fish rolls are upright. Any flat fish fillet can be used, but the sole shown here, is a classic. Paupiettes are best poached, steamed or baked.

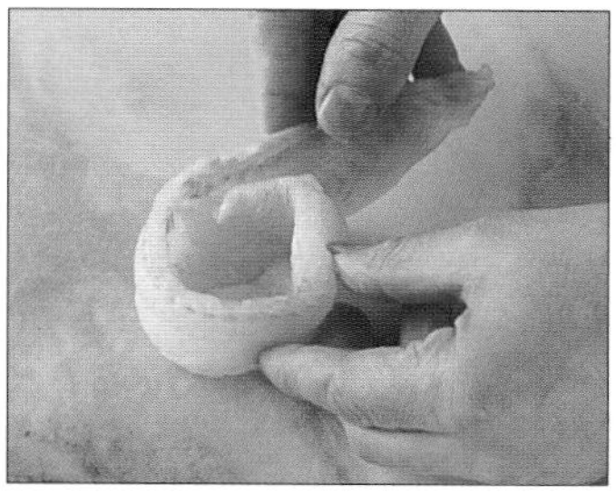

Coil the fillet, skinned-side in, into a turban – the tail end on the outside. To hold the coil, stand them close together during cooking or secure them with wooden cocktail sticks.

Fillings for Fish Packages, Pillows and Paupiettes

Vegetables, fish mousse, soft cheese and herbs are all appropriate. Try one of these:

- A fine julienne (see page 166) of blanched carrots and leeks tossed in vinaigrette.
- Soft cheese and chopped fresh herbs such as parsley or dill.
- A brunoise (see page 166) of mango, cucumber and fresh root ginger with baby prawns.
- Mushroom duxelles (see page 170).
- A light, creamy risotto with a hint of lemon.

SMOKED & SALTED FISH

Preserving fish by smoking and salting is traditional. The extra flavour this preparation adds ranges from the subtle to the strong, but preserved fish usually has to be treated further before it is ready to eat.

TARAMASALATA

4 thick slices of white bread, crusts removed
6 tbsp milk
100 g prepared smoked cod's roe (see right)
2 garlic cloves, chopped
100 ml olive oil
100 ml vegetable oil
About 75 ml lemon juice
2 tbsp hot water
Freshly ground pepper

Tear the bread into a bowl and add the milk. Mix well with your hands, then squeeze the bread and discard the milk. Put the bread in a food processor and blend with the smoked cod's roe, garlic, olive oil, groundnut oil and 75 ml lemon juice. Add the water, then taste and add pepper, and more lemon juice if you like. Blend again until mixed.

Turn out the mixture into a bowl, cover and let chill in the refrigerator for at least 4 hours, preferably overnight. Serves 4–6.

PREPARING SMOKED ROE

The roe, or eggs, of the female salmon, trout or cod (as shown here) is often sold salted and smoked. Once soaked, it can be eaten raw, thinly sliced and sprinkled with lemon juice and ground pepper. It can also be used in creamy dips such as Greek taramasalata *(see box, left).*

Cut the smoked cod's roe into pieces, place in a bowl and pour over enough boiling water to cover. Soak for 1–2 minutes, then drain thoroughly. Peel away the skin with your fingers and discard. The flesh is now ready to use.

DESALTING ANCHOVIES

Anchovies are sold in cans or jars, salted and packed in oil. The best of the preserved anchovies are the fillets that come from the Mediterranean, available here in continental delicatessens. They are bottled in olive oil and are not too salty. Canned anchovies contain more salt and will therefore need to be desalted. This technique will make them slightly softer in texture and milder in flavour.

1 Turn the anchovies into a sieve set over a bowl and let the oil drain through. Discard the oil. Turn the anchovies into the bowl.

2 Pour in enough cold milk to cover the anchovies and let soak for 20 minutes. Drain off the milk, rinse the anchovies under cold running water and pat dry.

PREPARING SALT COD

Salt cod is very popular in Portugal, where it is called bacalhau, *and in Spain, where it is known as* bacalao. *The whole gutted fish or fillets are soaked in brine or layered with dry salt, then dried. It is available from ethnic shops and delicatessens. Before cooking it must be soaked to reconstitute it and remove the excess salt.*

Cut the fish into pieces, place in a bowl and cover with cold water. Let soak for at least 2 days for heavily salted fish, changing the water 5–6 times. After soaking, drain the fish, then place in a pan of cold water and bring to just below boiling point. Simmer for 20 minutes or until tender. Flake into meaty chunks, discarding all skin and bones.

TRICK OF THE TRADE

Using Sliced Smoked Salmon

Line ramekins with salmon, fill with *taramasalata* (see opposite page) and turn out.

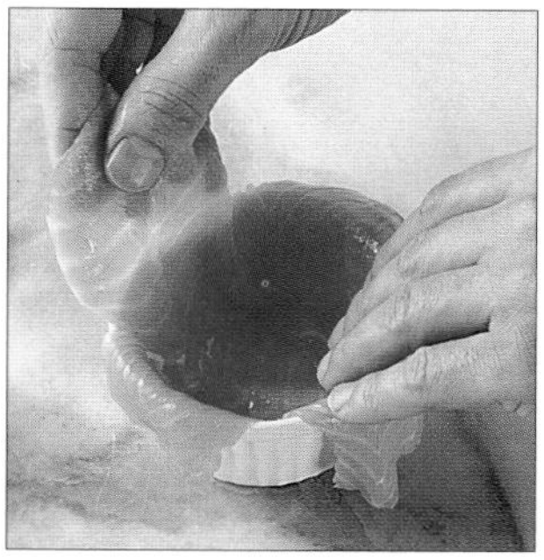

Slicing Smoked Salmon

For a large party it is more economical to buy a whole side of salmon and slice it yourself than to buy it ready sliced. A smoked salmon knife (see box, right) makes light work of this technique, although any long, thin flexible knife can be used.

Trim and discard the dark fatty edges and remove any pin bones (see page 54). Holding the knife as parallel to the fish as possible and starting at the tail end, cut wafer thin slices with a gentle sawing action. Work along the fish towards the head end, cutting slices in "V" shapes so the dark fatty flesh in the centre is not included. For easy serving, interleave the slices with non-stick paper.

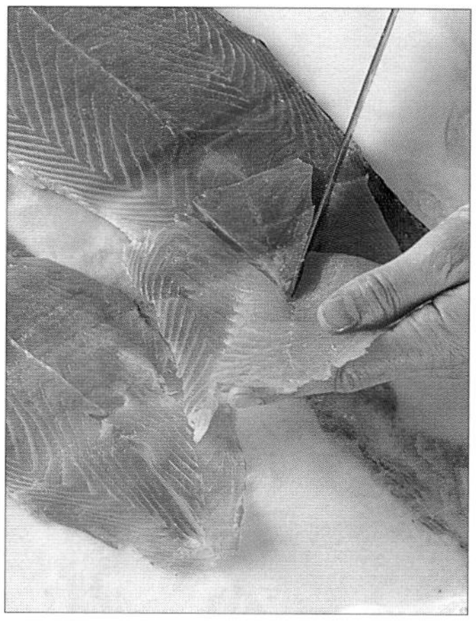

Smoked Salmon Knife

To slice smoked salmon very thinly you can buy a special smoked salmon slicer. This is a knife with a long, narrow, flexible blade. The cutting edge is straight but the blade can be smooth or fluted and is usually rounded at the tip. Its smoothness and flexibility enables it to slice through the soft salmon flesh without tearing it. The knife can also be used to slice *gravadlax* very thinly on the diagonal (see below).

Making Gravadlax

In Sweden, they have perfected the art of salting fish to produce the famous gravadlax. *Use unskinned salmon fillets; once cured, store wrapped in the refrigerator for up to 2 days.*

1 Lay two 900 g salmon fillets skin-side down in a shallow glass dish. Combine 75 g sea salt, 125 g sugar and 2 tsp crushed white peppercorns and sprinkle over the fish. Sprinkle 1 large bunch of coarsely chopped dill evenly over the salt mixture.

2 Lay the uncoated fillet, skin-side up over the other. Place foil-covered cardboard over the fillets and weight it down. Refrigerate for 3 days, turning every 12 hours until the seasonings have penetrated the flesh.

3 To serve, separate the two fillets and cut each one crosswise on the diagonal into thin slices. Fan the slices out on individual plates and serve with lemon and dill, and a mustard and dill sauce.

Sushi & Sashimi

These well-known Japanese dishes are much enjoyed in the West. Sushi is based on vinegared rice rolled in seaweed, with strips of raw fish or a vegetable such as cucumber or avocado hidden in the centre. Sashimi is simply very fresh raw fish, served with a horseradish paste called wasabi. *Both are exquisitely presented, and are eaten with chopsticks.*

Sushi Rolls

MAKES 32 SLICES

1 piece of very fresh tuna fillet, about 200 g, skinned

4 sheets of nori *seaweed, each measuring 20 x 18 cm*

Rice vinegar

600 g vinegared rice *(see page 197)*

Wasabi *(see box, right)*

TO SERVE

Pickled ginger roses *(see page 69)*
Cucumber crowns *(see page 139)*
Japanese soy sauce

Cut the tuna crosswise into strips, each 1 cm wide.

If the nori is not labelled "*yakinori*" – pre-toasted – hold each sheet with tongs and wave one side over a gas flame for a few seconds until crisp (see page 329).

Place a rolling mat flat on the work surface and put a sheet of nori on top, close to one of the short edges of the mat. Dip your fingers in water mixed with a dash of rice vinegar, and spread a layer of vinegared rice over the nori. Make a line of wasabi paste in the centre of the rice and cover with tuna.

Roll the nori around the rice with the mat. Press the mat around the roll to keep the shape tight. Run a wet fingertip along the exposed edge of the nori to seal it. Using a moistened chef's knife, cut the roll across into eight pieces. Repeat four times.

Arrange the sushi rolls, cut side-up, on a platter. Serve with ginger roses, cucumber crowns and soy sauce.

Sashimi

SERVES 4

1 piece of very fresh red mullet fillet, about 200 g, scaled but not skinned

1 piece of very fresh salmon fillet, about 400 g, skinned

About 300 g very fresh mackerel fillet, unskinned, with membrane removed

TO SERVE

Cucumber crowns
Wasabi *(see box, right)*
Japanese soy sauce

Before cutting the fish, check that all bones, especially fine pin bones, have been removed. The fish will be much easier to cut thinly if it is very well chilled.

Cut the piece of red mullet fillet into very thin slices against the grain.

Cut the mackerel fillets lengthwise in half. Holding the halves together, skin-side up, cut the fish across into thin slices, the same thickness as the red mullet and salmon.

Arrange the mullet, salmon and mackerel slices on plates, keeping them separate. Serve with cucumber crowns, wasabi and soy sauce.

WASABI

Known as Japanese horseradish because of its hot, pungent flavour, wasabi comes from the root of an Oriental plant. It is used freshly grated in Japan, but in the West it is normally sold as a paste, ready prepared in tubes. Look for it in large supermarkets.

Making Sushi Rolls

Individual sushi rolls are cut from one long roll to reveal the filling hidden in the centre. For shaping the long roll you need to use a mat. Special bamboo rolling mats can be found in Oriental shops, or you can use an undyed, flexible straw place mat.

Lay tuna over the line of wasabi paste to cover it completely. You may need more than one strip of tuna.

Lift up the short end of the mat nearest to you and roll the nori around the rice, rolling it away from you.

Cut the long sushi roll across into four equal lengths, then cut each length in half to make eight pieces.

POACHING

Fish is often cooked in liquid kept just below boiling point because this gentle method of cooking helps preserve the delicate nature of the flesh. Large whole fish are traditionally poached in a *court bouillon.*

COURT BOUILLON

2.5 litres water
700 ml dry white wine
250 ml white wine vinegar
2 carrots, chopped
2 onions, chopped
1 large bouquet garni
1½ tsp rock or sea salt
2 tsp black peppercorns

Combine all ingredients, except vinegar, in a large pan. Bring to the boil, then simmer, uncovered, for 15–20 minutes, adding the vinegar for the last 5 minutes. Cool before use. Store in the refrigerator for up to 5 days. Makes about 3 litres.

POACHING IN A KETTLE

Whole fish with the head on, or off such as the salmon used here, must be trimmed, scaled and gutted before cooking. Stovetop poaching affords you most control. A fish kettle is made for this task – the entire fish fits comfortably on a rack in the cooking vessel, with enough room for the poaching liquid to cover it.

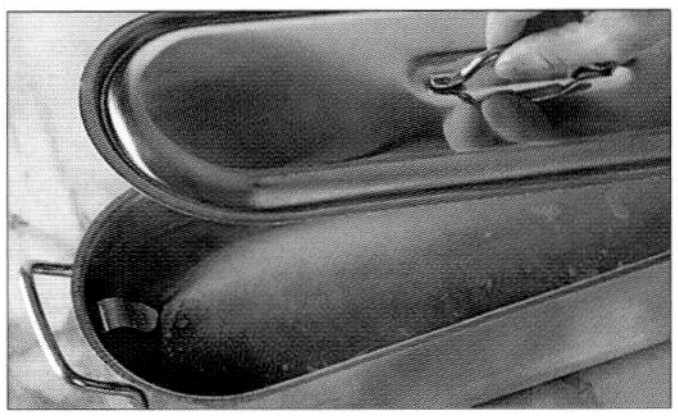

1 Measure the thickest part of the fish. Put the fish on the rack and lower into the kettle. Cover the fish with cold *court bouillon*. Check seasoning. Bring to the boil.

2 Reduce to a simmer. Poach the fish for 10 minutes for each 2.5 cm width. Cool the fish in the kettle to retain moisture. Remove and turn out on to baking parchment (see page 67).

MICROWAVE TIMES

Delicate fish flesh requires quick cooking. The speed of the microwave ensures that the flesh remains moist and cooks evenly. The cooking times shown below are for 600–700 watt ovens set to 100% power.

- STEAKS
  2–3 mins per 250 g
- FILLETS
  45 secs–1 min per 175 g
- PACKAGES AND PAUPIETTES
  1½–2 mins each
  with precooked filling
- WHOLE FLAT FISH
  1½–2 mins per 250 g
- WHOLE ROUND FISH
  2½–3 mins per 250 g unstuffed

POACHING WITHOUT A KETTLE

Fish kettles are convenient for cooking a large whole fish, such as a salmon or sea bass, but if you don't want to go to the expense of buying a piece of equipment that may be used only rarely, you can improvize with everyday equipment.

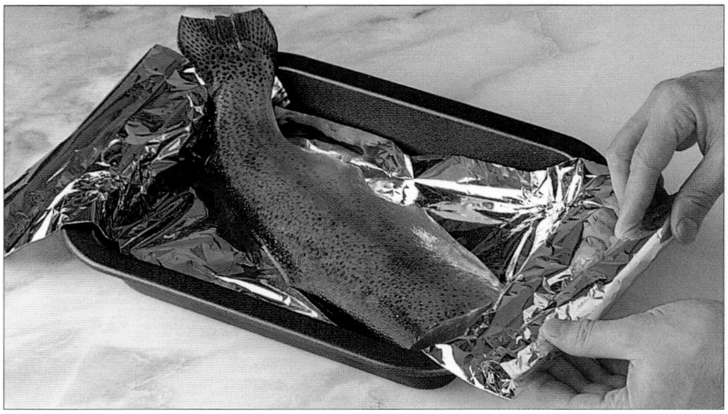

Cut and fold a double or triple thickness of foil slightly larger than the fish. Lay the fish on one of its sides on the foil and place in a large roasting tin. Pour cold *court bouillon* (see box, above left) over the fish to just cover it, then cover the pan with foil and cook and cool as in the fish kettle (see above). Lift out the fish with the aid of the foil. The fish can now be prepared for serving (see page 67).

SHALLOW POACHING

This technique suits steaks, fillets, and small whole fish that are scaled and gutted.

Lower the fish into a pan of simmering *court bouillon.* Bring back to a simmer and cover. Poach, allowing 5–10 minutes for fillets and 10–15 minutes for steaks, until opaque throughout.

Poaching Smoked Fish

Smoked fish, such as haddock and cod, is usually poached in seasoned milk rather than court bouillon *or water. Milk helps rid the fish of excess salt and mellows its smoky flavour.*

1 Pour milk or an equal mixture of milk and water into a pan and add 1–2 bay leaves and a few peppercorns. Add the smoked fish, bring to a simmer over a moderate heat, then remove from the heat and cover tightly. Let stand for 10 minutes. Remove the fish and discard milk and flavourings.

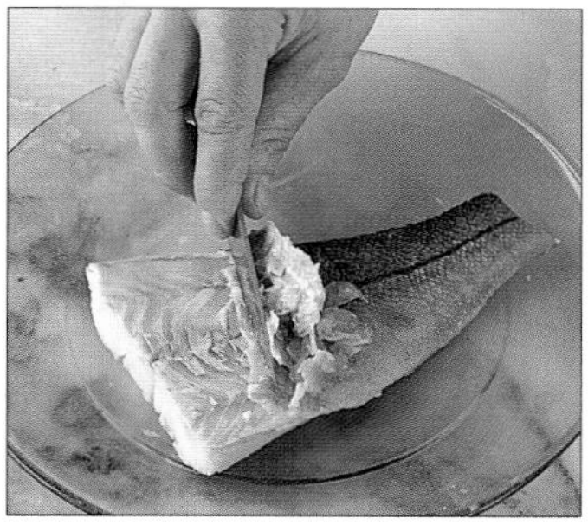

2 Scrape away the skin and any dark flesh with a paring knife. Turn the fish over and remove any bones with tweezers.

USING POACHED SMOKED FISH

Even a small amount of smoked fish will add a unique flavour to many dishes. After poaching flake the flesh and use it as follows:

- Mix with curried rice and chopped hard-boiled eggs to make a kedgeree.
- Use to flavour a hot soufflé.
- Toss with salad leaves and serve with horseradish cream.

Preparing a Whole Poached Fish for Serving

For easy serving and eating, remove the skin and bones of a whole poached fish, such as the salmon shown here. If you follow the method below, the fish can still be presented whole so it will look attractive, an important consideration if you are serving the fish as a table centrepiece. The fish can be served hot or cold.

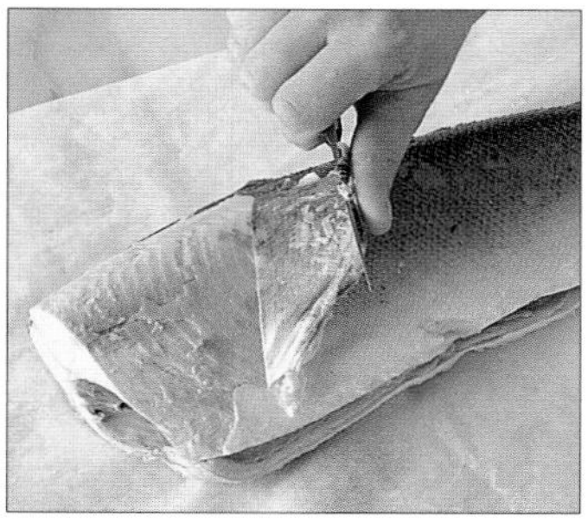

1 After poaching (see page 66) turn the fish on to baking parchment. Cut along the backbone. Working from head to tail, peel away skin.

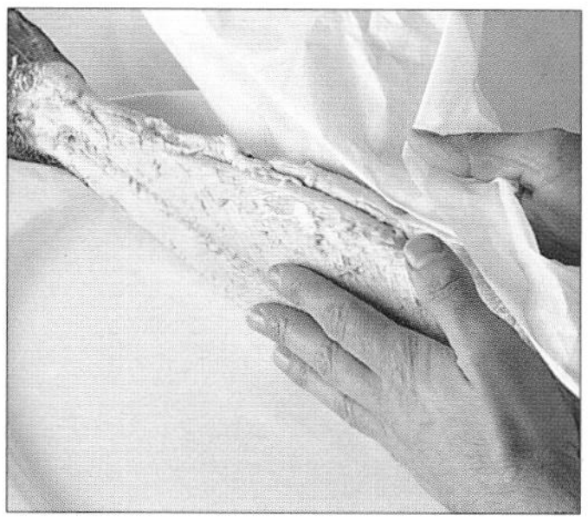

2 Scrape away any dark flesh with a chef's knife. Roll the fish from the paper on to a serving plate.

3 Repeating steps 1 and 2, peel away the skin and scrape the dark flesh from the reverse side. Carefully split the top fillet of the fish using a chef's knife, then lay the pieces to either side.

4 Lift out the backbone, bringing the rib bones out with it, if necessary, cutting it from the tail end of the fish with kitchen scissors.

5 Put both of the top fillets back in place. The fish is now ready to coat with a sauce or garnish (see pages 68-69).

Finishing Touches

Lemon slices and fresh parsley are classic garnishes for fish dishes and the latter is useful to hide an open eye. Other fruit, vegetable and herb decorations, however, will add interest and colour to the presentation. Rose petal scales secured in aspic (see opposite page) are the most fanciful.

Zesty knots
Use a canelle knife to cut 4-cm strips of lime, lemon or orange zest. Blanch (see page 336), then dry and knot.

Caper flowers
With your fingertips, gently pull back some of the outer layers of drained capers to make petals.

Anchovy loops
Drain canned anchovy fillets and pat dry, then cut into strips. Wrap anchovy strips around capers.

Kumquat cups
Make small angled cuts all round a kumquat's middle, then pull apart. Top with mayonnaise and fresh dill.

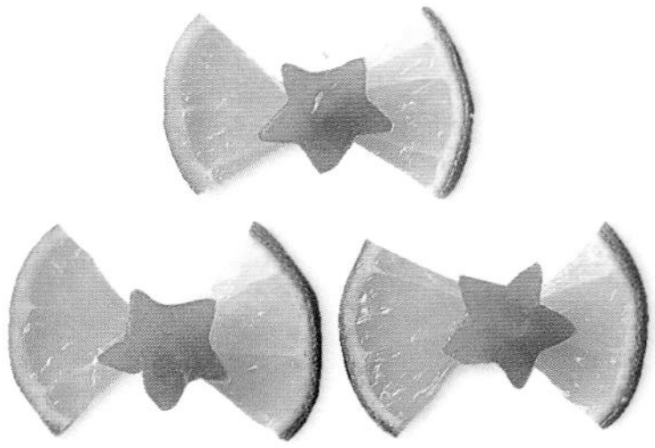

Lime butterflies
Cut lime slices into quarters, then join 2 points to make a bow. Top with a star cut from a blanched red pepper strip.

Pastry fleurons
Cut shapes from rolled-out puff pastry. Brush with an egg-yolk glaze; bake at 190°C until golden, 5–7 minutes.

Lemon special
Cut top and bottom off lemon. Cut strips of zest, leaving them attached at top. Weave strips as shown.

Citrus curls
Cut a 15-cm strip of orange peel with a canelle knife. Curl around a skewer until the peel holds the shape.

Winged lemon
Canelle a lemon. Cut around 180° leaving one end attached; rotate lemon and repeat. Fold one cut point over another.

Presenting a Whole Fish

Small fish are normally served whole, skin and bones in place, larger fish are more often skinned and filleted, then reformed and presented whole. This is usually the case with poached salmon (see page 67), which is classically garnished with overlapping cucumber "scales". For a colourful and summery presentation, use fresh rose petals instead of cucumber (see opposite page), dipping their tips in aspic or mayonnaise so they will adhere to the fish. Courgette scales are another option.

Keep It Simple

- Serve lemon wedges for squeezing fresh juice over fish. For formal occasions, wrap the wedges in muslin so the seeds do not scatter on the fish.
- Use dainty bunches or sprigs of fresh herbs, such as those on the opposite page. Chervil, chives, lemon balm and watercress are other options.
- Add finely chopped herbs or watercress to mayonnaise (see page 228) and serve with poached fish, especially salmon.
- Serve hot fish topped with pats of chilled maître d'hôtel (parsley and lemon) butter. Anchovy and citrus butters are also good with fish.

Asian decorations

Chinese and Japanese steamed whole fish and stir-fried dishes benefit from traditional decorations made from ingredients sold in Asian food stores and large supermarkets. Buy sliced, not shredded pickled ginger.

Deep-fried ginger
Blanch julienned peeled fresh root ginger; pat dry. Deep-fry in 180°C oil for 10 seconds, then drain.

Mooli julienne
Cut a peeled mooli crosswise into thin slices, then into julienne strips. Keep crisp in iced water, then pat dry.

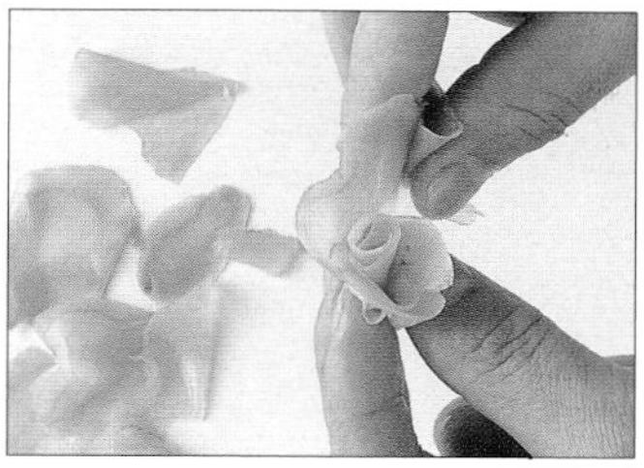

Pickled ginger rose
Roll up one slice to form the centre, then wrap 3 more overlapping slices around the first to form "petals".

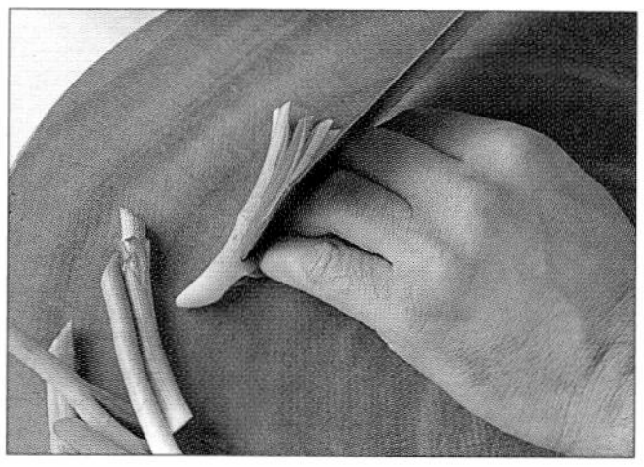

Spring onion tassel
Slice the green end of a spring onion lengthwise, leaving one end uncut. Chill in water for 2–3 hours until curled.

Deep-fried herbs
Deep-fry leafy herbs, such as purple basil and flat-leaf parsley, in 180°C oil for 10 seconds. Drain well.

Cucumber twirls
Rib a cucumber with a canelle knife (see page 179) and cut into wafer-thin slices. Slit each slice and twist.

Herb bouquet
Fan out sprigs of fresh parsley, dill or thyme next to freshly cooked fish. Tarragon is also suitable.

Lemon zest rose
Use a very sharp knife to pare a long strip of zest in a spiral, giving it a "frilly" edge. Roll up to make a rose blossom.

Courgette scales
Blanch a courgette, cut into slices, then quarters. Lay quarters over fish so they overlap like scales.

STEAMING

The vapour produced by a simmering liquid cooks fish by steaming. This method is ideal for delicate fish, such as sole and plaice, and shellfish. Water can be used, but a vegetable or herb broth adds flavour.

FLAVOURING THE FISH

Steamed fish can be bland so give flavour to it by adding vegetables, herbs and spices, and other seasonings to the liquid in the wok or steamer, or by sprinkling them over the fish itself.

- Chop a mixture of herbs and vegetables – onions, carrots, celery, fennel, parsley stalks or coriander leaves – and add to the steaming liquid.
- Place the fish on the steaming rack on a thick bed of fresh fennel fronds and fresh sprigs of thyme or dill.
- Cover the fish with chopped spring onions, slivers of fresh root ginger or garlic and slices of lemon and a sprinkling of fennel seeds.
- Marinate the fish before steaming. Olive oil, lemon juice, white wine and soy sauce are are all good with fish.

STEAMING TIMES

Fish is cooked when opaque throughout and the flakes separate easily with a fork. If overcooked, the fish will be dry and fall apart.

- FILLETS
  3–4 mins
- PLAITS
  8–10 mins
- WHOLE FISH
  6–8 mins (up to 350 g)
  12–15 mins (up to 900 g)

CONVENTIONAL METHOD

Metal steamers contain perforated baskets that sit above the simmering liquid at the bottom. Steam filters through the perforations and cooks the fish. Here, plaits of mackerel, snapper and sole (see page 61) are steamed over a simmering court bouillon.

1 Add *court bouillon* to cover the bottom of the steamer and bring to a simmer. Arrange the fish in a single layer in the basket. Place the basket over the simmering liquid. Cover and steam (see chart, below left).

2 The fish is ready when it is opaque. Test it with a fork: the flesh should feel moist and tender.

BAMBOO STEAMER METHOD

A woven basket can be placed in a wok over simmering broth. The aromatic steam helps flavour the fish, while herbs, spices and other seasonings can be added to the fish itself. Steaming preserves the attractive colour of fish, such as the red snapper shown here.

1 Half fill a wok with water and bring to a simmer. Add chopped vegetables (see box, above left).

2 Score the fish and insert flavourings of your choice (see page 53) so the flavours enter the flesh. Lay the fish flat in the basket and sprinkle over more flavourings. Place the basket in the wok.

3 Place the lid on the basket to intensify the flavour imparted by the vegetables and other additions. Steam according to the times given in the chart, left. Serve with the steamed vegetables and seasonings.

GRILLING

The high heat of the grill and barbecue cooks fish quickly which is by far the best way. Fatty fish such as sardines and mackerel are ideal, their natural oils help keep the flesh moist during cooking.

GRILLING SMALL WHOLE FISH

Skin and bones keep fish moist so it is best to grill fish whole. Trim, scale and gut the fish (see pages 52–53) before cooking and score (see page 53) if you like. For additional flavour, marinate in olive oil, crushed garlic and chopped parsley as shown here with the sardines.

1 Remove the fish from the marinade and place on an oiled grill rack. Grill under a high heat for 2 minutes.

2 Turn the fish over and brush with the marinade, or with olive oil if a marinade was not used. Grill for another 2 minutes, or until the skin is crisp and golden.

BARBECUING WHOLE FISH

The heat of the barbecue sears the fish keeping the flesh moist and flavourful. Trout is shown here but other suitable fish include mackerel, shark, tuna and bass. For even cooking, score the fish (see page 53), and for ease of handling, use a fish rack (see box, above right).

Place the fish in an oiled rack, with sprigs of fresh herbs or vine leaves if you like, and close the rack tightly. Place the rack on the grid of a hot barbecue. Cook the fish for about 3 minutes on each side, basting frequently with olive oil or marinade. Check for doneness: the skin should be crisp and golden and the flesh fork-tender.

FISH RACKS

Whether barbecuing whole fish, fillets or steaks, a special hinged fish rack can make the job more manageable. Brush the fish rack with olive oil to prevent the fish from sticking to it.

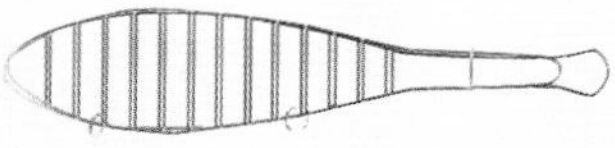

FISH-SHAPED RACK

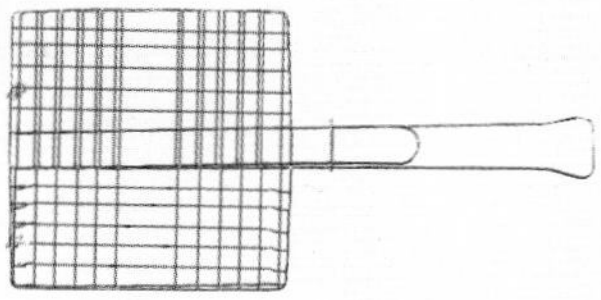

SQUARE RACK

SALSA FOR FISH

Contrast a cooked fish straight from the barbecue with a chilled spicy salsa.

A traditional accompaniment in Mexican cooking, *salsa* combines pungent garlic, onion and chillies with the sharp tang of lime. Served chilled *salsa* brings out the subtle flavours of hot fish.

BAKING

This is an excellent method for cooking large and medium-sized whole fish and for thick steaks and fillets. Fish can be baked without a covering, or wrapped in parcels of foil, paper or leaves or, for a whole fish, baked with a salt crust. For a more substantial dish, fish can be stuffed before baking; this will also give the fish more flavour.

FLAVOURINGS FOR OPEN BAKING

The simplest flavouring is fresh herbs pushed into the stomach cavity. Some alternatives are:

- Asian flavourings such as fresh ginger and lemon grass.
- Fresh breadcrumbs with herbs, spices or chopped nuts bound with egg.
- Prawns with garlic or parsley.

OPEN BAKING

Medium-sized whole fish such as red snapper are ideal for cooking this way.

Place a single layer of fish in a greased roasting tin. Sprinkle over flavourings (see box, left) and just cover with liquid. Bake, uncovered, at 180°C for 30 minutes or until the flesh is opaque and the skin crisp. If you like, strain the pan juices and serve with the fish.

STUFFING AND BAKING IN FOIL

A foil wrapping allows fish to cook in its own juices, keeping it deliciously moist. The fish can be wrapped unstuffed or, depending on the boning method can be stuffed through the stomach or back. Stuffed fish take a little longer to cook.

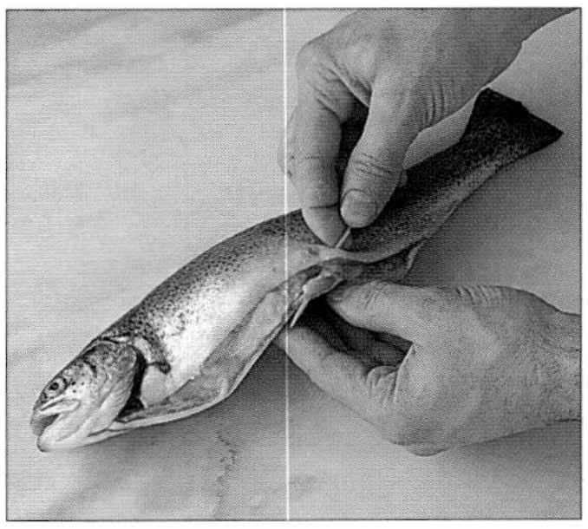

1 Spoon your chosen stuffing into the stomach cavity of the fish. Secure the stomach opening with 1–2 wooden cocktail sticks.

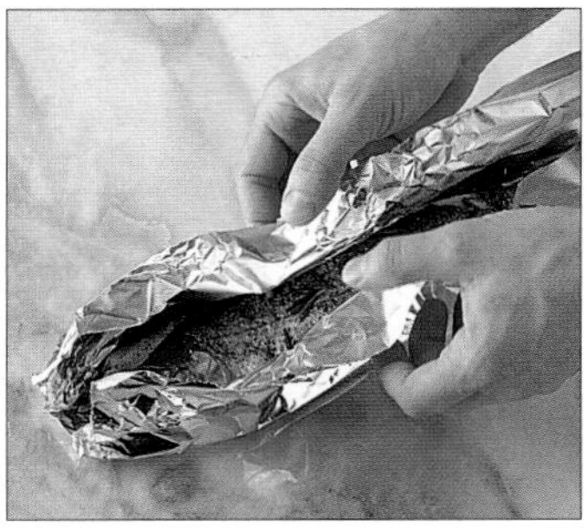

2 Wrap fish individually in oiled or buttered foil. Seal the foil tightly to prevent juices escaping during cooking.

3 Bake in a roasting tin at 180°C, 25 minutes for a small fish, 35–40 minutes for a large fish. Open the foil wrapping at the table.

STUFFING THROUGH THE BACK BEFORE BAKING

Though the back cavity is smaller than the stomach, stuffing the back enables the fish to maintain a good shape. For the technique of boning a whole fish through the back, see page 55.

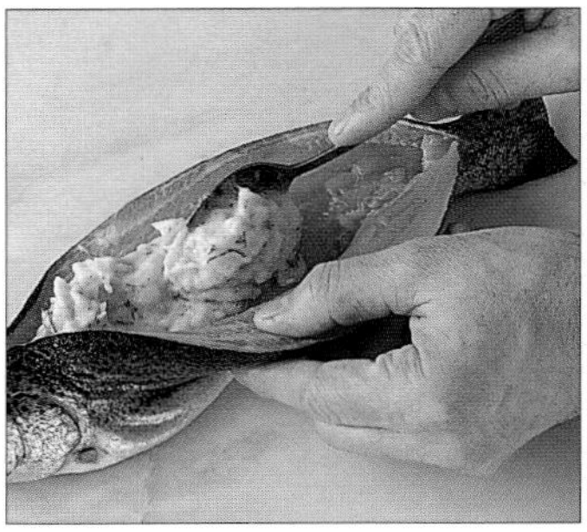

Spoon the stuffing into the cavity in the back of the fish. Wrap and bake as for the fish shown left.

Baking en Papillote

The term en papillote *is French for "in a paper bag". This technique protects the fish (brill is shown here) and helps keep it moist. The topping of herbs, vegetables and white wine adds flavour during cooking. For maximum effect, open the parcels at the table.*

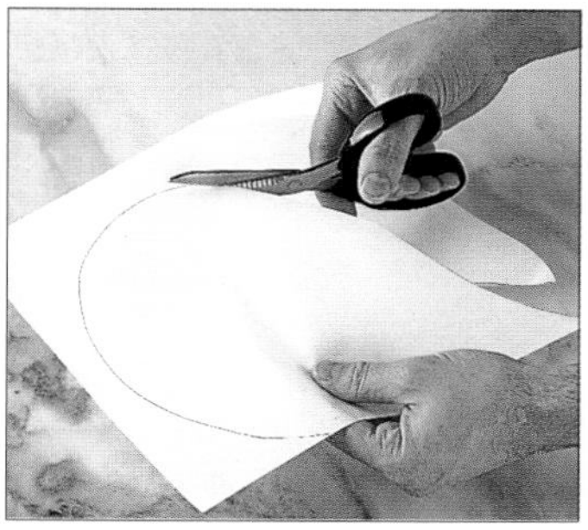

1 Cut a heart shape, 5 cm larger than the fish, out of baking parchment, greaseproof paper or foil, and oil it.

2 Put the fish on one half with 4 sprigs of coriander, 2 carrots, julienned (see page 166) and 4 tbsp white wine.

3 Fold over the other half of the paper and twist to seal the edges. Place on a baking sheet and bake at 180°C for 15–20 minutes, until puffed.

Baking in Leaves

Vine and banana leaves keep fish moist during cooking and they also flavour the fish.

Set the fish in the centre of a leaf. Roll and wrap the leaf around the fish. Tie in place with a blanched strip of leek if necessary.

Baking in a Salt Crust

Fish baked in this way will have a crispy skin and moist flesh – without being over salty. The salt crust will help the fish to retain moisture and add flavour. Before cooking, trim, scale and gut, then wipe the fish dry with paper towels.

1 Spread a 5 cm layer of sea salt evenly over the bottom of a heavy-based casserole dish. Lay the fish on top of the salt and cover with another salt layer (1.3 kg salt will cover 900 g fish as shown here).

2 Sprinkle the salt with water. Bake the fish at 220°C for about 30 minutes.

3 Chip through the top layer of salt with a small hammer. Remove the fish, keeping it in one piece. Brush away the excess salt and serve immediately.

Trick of the Trade

Plaited Monkfish

Plait rindless streaky bacon rashers around a monkfish fillet, tucking in a few thyme leaves as you go. Bake at 180°C for 20 minutes. During baking the bacon imparts flavour to the fish and forms a crunchy coating; the fat seeps into the fish to moisten it.

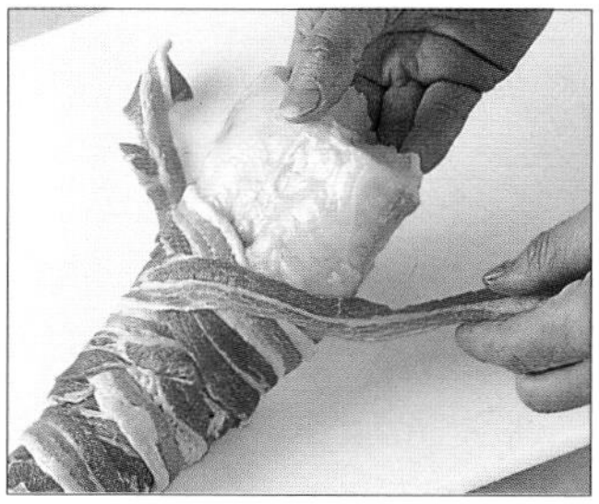

FRYING

Choose pieces of fish of equal thickness to ensure even cooking. The temperature of the fat, whether oil or butter, is vital – too low and the coating will be soggy and fall apart, too high and it will cook too quickly.

COATINGS FOR FISH

A light coating protects delicate fish fillets and helps keep them moist during frying.

- Make a dry blend of Cajun herbs and spices – paprika, onion and garlic powder, dried thyme and oregano, white, black and cayenne pepper and salt.
- Mix fragrant herbs and spices such as chopped fresh dill, crushed fennel seeds and coarsely ground pepper.
- Mix snipped chives and a little grated lemon zest into fine breadcrumbs or flour.

SHALLOW PAN-FRYING

Use equal parts butter and vegetable oil for successful pan-frying. Season and coat the fish first (see box, left) and ensure the butter is foaming before adding fish.

1 Place the fish, skin-side down, in foaming butter and oil. Fry for 5 minutes then turn the fish over.

2 Fry the fillets for another 3–5 minutes, until golden brown. Insert a fork into the thickest part of the flesh – it should feel firm and be opaque throughout.

NUT-BROWN BUTTER

Called beurre noisette *in French, this is the classic butter for frying white fish, especially skate wings. Remove the dark skin and coat with seasoned flour.*

Heat 4 tbsp butter in a frying pan until it turns a light nutty brown. Add the skate wings and fry for 8–10 minutes, turning once.

CAJUN-STYLE

Fish fried Cajun-style, from New Orleans and the states around the Gulf of Mexico, has a dark, peppery-hot crust. This comes from the special coating that is generously rubbed over it before cooking (see box, above left).

Place coated fish fillets (red snapper is shown here) in hot fat. Fry until the coating is charred, about 6 minutes, turning once.

COATING WITH A HERB CRUST

This technique creates an attractive crust, which adds contrast in flavour and texture to the moist fish. Use firm textured fillets such as salmon, cod or monkfish. A non-stick pan reduces the oil required, allowing the crust to "toast".

1 Spread a mixture of fragrant herbs and spices (see box, above left) over a plate. Press skinned fish fillets, skinned-side down, into the mixture to ensure an even coating.

2 Pan-fry the fillets, crust-side down, in a little hot oil for 7–10 minutes without turning. Press firmly with a metal spatula to encourage the juices to rise to the surface and the heat to penetrate upwards into the flesh.

Deep-frying Fish in Batter

Batter provides a protective coating, which keeps fish succulent and moist. A high cooking temperature (180–190°C) is necessary for the best result, and the oil should be carefully chosen, both for its ability to reach the required temperature and how it affects the flavour of the fish; vegetable oils are best. Cut the fish into even pieces or use steaks or fillets.

1 To test the temperature of the oil, drop in a cube of white bread, it should brown all over in about 30 seconds. Remove the bread and discard.

2 Lower the batter-coated fish into the hot oil. Cook large pieces of fish one at a time for 7–10 minutes to ensure even cooking.

3 When golden and crisp, lift the basket out of the fryer. Shake the basket to remove excess oil, then drain the fish on to paper towels. Season before serving.

Making Goujons

Cut strips from skinned fish fillets, working across the grain of the flesh: this helps the goujons retain their shape. The oil will rise in the pan, so fill to the recommended level – a deep pan should be filled to one-third of its capacity.

1 Cut the skinned fish fillets into 1-cm strips, working across the grain and using a chef's knife.

2 Put the strips of fish in a plastic bag containing seasoned flour. Twist the top to seal, and shake to coat evenly.

3 Heat the oil to 180–190°C. Lower the goujons into the oil using a slotted spoon or fryer basket. Deep fry for 3–4 minutes until golden. Remove and drain on paper towels.

Deep-fat Thermometer

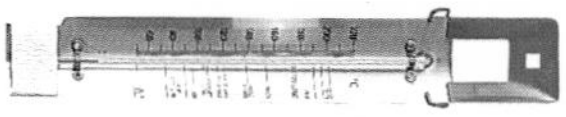

This has a hook to fix it to the side of the pan, avoiding the need to have your hands over hot oil. Position it when the oil is cool and wait until the reading is correct before immersing food.

Batters for Fish

The mixture should be smooth (see page 39) and lightly coat the fish. Change cooking oil regularly as flavourings may taint the batter.

- Add a little oil or melted butter to enrich batter.
- Use beer instead of milk for a light coating with added colour.
- Flavour flour with cayenne, chilli or curry powder.
- Use tempura batter (see page 269) to coat prawns or goujons and serve them with soy sauce.

Fish Mixtures

Many fish can be puréed or flaked and the resulting mixtures have many applications. Fish mousse can be moulded, layered or shaped into dumplings, and flaked fish can be formed into cakes. Enliven the basic fish mousse shown here with chopped herbs, ground spices or other seasonings.

FISH MOUSSE

450 g fish fillets (whiting, plaice, sole or salmon)
Salt
2 egg whites
350 ml whipping or double cream
Ground white pepper or cayenne

Trim and skin the fish fillets and remove all of the bones, checking carefully for any pin bones. Purée the flesh in a food processor with salt to taste, then add the egg whites. For a velvety texture, pass this mixture through a fine sieve into a bowl (this will also help eliminate any fine pin bones that may remain). Gradually fold in the cream over an ice bath to prevent the mixture from splitting. Season with salt and pepper. Makes about 850 g.

WHAT'S IN A NAME?

QUENELLES: The word derives from the German word for dumpling, *knödel*, but it now means any egg-shaped sweet or savoury mixture such as mousse and sorbet. Small quenelles can be used to garnish clear soups.
TIMBALES: This is the name given to small, round, deep moulds and also to any food that is shaped or baked in them, as long as it forms a single serving. The name can be applied to fish, meat or vegetable preparations.

Making a Fish Mousse

Chilling the mixture over an ice bath when adding the cream prevents the mixture from separating.

1 Chop the fish into chunks and purée evenly with the salt in a food processor fitted with the metal blade. Add the egg whites and process until evenly incorporated.

2 Work the mixture through a sieve into a bowl, then set it over a bowl of water and ice cubes. Fold in the cream with a rubber spatula.

Making Fish Timbales

One of the simplest ways to use the fish mousse above is to bake it in dariole moulds.

1 Divide the mousse between 6 chilled dariole moulds. Cover with buttered greaseproof paper. Set in a roasting tin and pour in hot water almost to the top of moulds.

2 Bake in a *bain marie* at 160° C until firm, about 25 minutes. Turn out on to individual plates.

Making Fish Quenelles

These dumplings, made from the fish mousse above, are shaped with tablespoons that have been dipped in water.

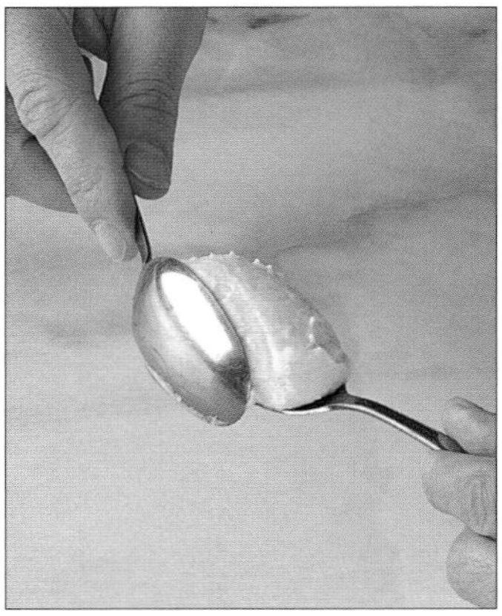

1 Take one spoonful of mousse and round each side with another spoon until smooth and egg-shaped. Repeat to make 18 quenelles.

2 Poach the quenelles until firm, 5–10 minutes. Remove with a slotted spoon, and drain on paper towels.

Making Fish Cakes

These can be made from a variety of different raw fish: white fish such as cod or hake, or oily fish such as mackerel or salmon. A mixture of fresh and smoked fish is also good, and the fish can be coarsely flaked or finely minced, whichever you prefer.

Leftover cooked fish can also be used in fish cakes, using equal quantities of fish and potatoes.

1 Flake raw fish with a fork. Mix with mashed potato and enough egg to bind, using a spatula. Add chopped parsley and seasonings and blend into the mixture.

2 Form the mixture into balls, flatten them and coat in dried breadcrumbs. Let chill for 30 minutes. Pan-fry in hot oil for 5–6 minutes on each side or until golden.

Making a Layered Fish Terrine

Here the basic fish mousse (see box, opposite page) is given an elegant treatment in a terrine with three layers. One layer uses the basic mixture, another uses the basic mixture with liquefied herbs, and spinach-wrapped prawns are sandwiched in between. If you like, add contrast by making half the mousse with salmon or trout. The terrine can be served hot or cold.

1 Line a buttered terrine mould with blanched spinach leaves, making sure that there are no gaps.

2 Roll up the prawns in blanched spinach leaves and place on top of the plain mousse in three rows.

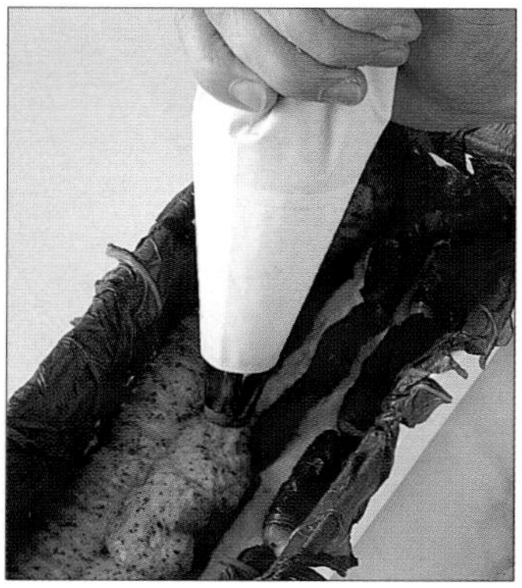

3 Cover the spinach-wrapped prawns with the fish mousse to which liquefied herbs have been added. Pipe it in even rows so that the finished texture will be smooth. Once baked, turn out and serve sliced. If serving the terrine cold, as shown here, serve slices on a saffron sauce garnished with saffron strands.

Fish Terrine

850 g fish mousse (see opposite page)
300 g cooked peeled prawns
12–15 large spinach leaves, blanched
30 g mixed chervil and dill, chopped

Liquefy the chopped chervil and dill in a food processor. Divide the mousse in half and add the liquefied herbs to one half until the mousse is a rich green colour.

Line a buttered 1.5 litre terrine with blanched spinach. Pipe a layer of the plain fish mousse in the terrine. Wrap the prawns in blanched spinach, arrange on the plain mousse and pipe a layer of the herb mousse on top. Cover with baking parchment. Bake in a *bain marie* at 150°C for about 1 hour or until a knife inserted in the centre comes out clean. Turn out and serve sliced, hot or cold.

LOBSTER

A lobster's flesh is meaty, sweet and delicate. For absolute freshness, lobsters are best bought live and prepared at home. Choose active ones that feel heavy for their size.

HUMANE KILLING

Some chefs recommend placing the live lobster in the freezer for an hour to desensitize it before killing.

Hold the lobster, back up and claws bound, firmly on a cutting board. Locate the centre of the cross-shaped mark on the back and pierce through to the board with the point of a chef's knife. This kills instantly, but there may be some twitching from the severed nerves. You can now cut the lobster as required.

WHAT'S IN A NAME?

The term *en bellevue* is used to describe cold dishes of shellfish, fish and poultry glazed in aspic jelly, giving them a smooth, attractive finish. For lobster, the meat is sliced, glazed and arranged in the shell.

It seems that the name came from the Château de Belleville, owned in the 1750s by Madame Pompadour, who stimulated the appetite of Louis XV with attractively presented dishes.

COOKING A LIVE LOBSTER

Lobsters are usually bought with rubber bands tied around the claws and the tail braced with string tied to a piece of wood.

1 Leaving the body support intact, plunge the lobster into a deep pan of boiling *court bouillon* (see page 66).

2 Bring back to the boil and cook until the shell turns red, 5 minutes per initial 450 g, plus 3 minutes for each extra 450 g. Transfer the cooked lobster with a slotted spoon to a colander. Drain and let cool.

REMOVING THE TAIL MEAT FROM ITS SHELL

Cooked lobster can be served in numerous ways. The tail meat, one of the most succulent parts, is generally removed in one piece and sliced into neat pieces known as medallions.

1 Remove body support. With the lobster belly-side up, cut through the shell along each side of the tail.

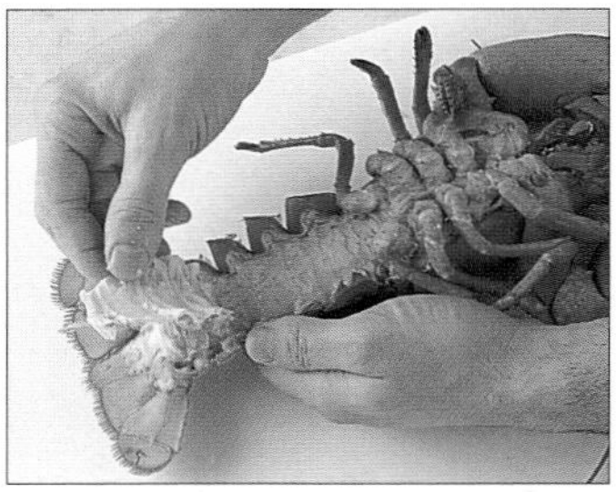

2 Pull the shell back, exposing the meat of the lobster tail.

3 Pull tail meat from shell, keeping it whole. Make a shallow cut along the inner curve. Remove dark vein.

4 Cut away the white flesh from the top of the tail meat, then cut the remaining flesh into even slices. Present them overlapping along the back of the lobster – when glazed with aspic this presentation is called *en bellevue* (see box, left).

Removing Meat from the Half-shell

The orangey-red shell of a cooked lobster makes an attractive serving "dish". The entire tail section can be detached from the head, rinsed out and used for serving. Alternatively, and especially when the lobster is intended for two, you can serve the meat on the half-shell.

1 Cook the lobster as described on the opposite page. When it is cool enough to handle comfortably, cut the string and remove the body support. Holding the lobster with its back uppermost, and cut it in half lengthwise from head to tail with a large chef's knife.

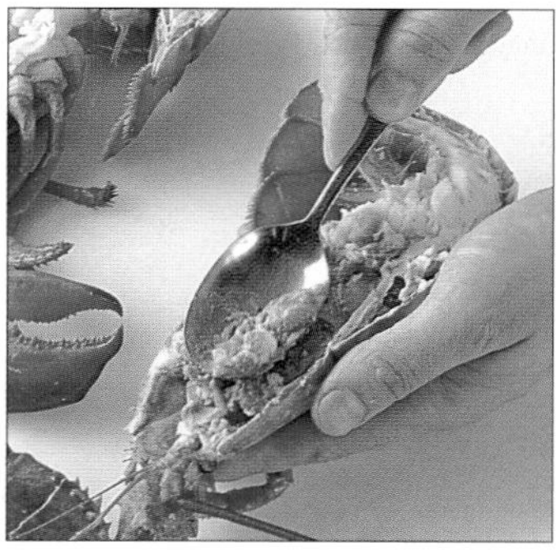

2 Spoon out the green liver, or tomalley, and reserve. Female lobsters may contain roe, or coral, which is pink when cooked and should be saved. Discard the gravel sac.

3 Gently pull the tail meat from each side of the shell. Remove and discard the intestinal vein.

4 Crack each claw just below the pincer, without damaging the meat. Remove meat from base of claw shell.

5 Pull the small pincer away from the rest of the claw, bringing with it the flat white membrane. Remove the meat from this part of the claw. Pull the meat from the large pincer shell, keeping it in one piece.

Lobster Crackers

Lobster claws are especially tough. To remove their meat, use a cracking tool or small hammer.

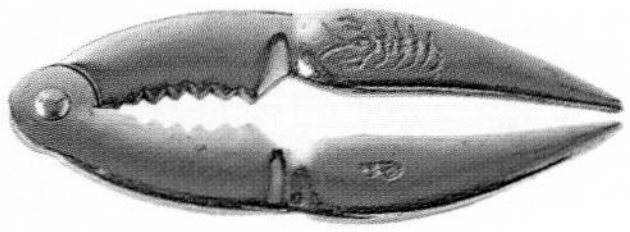

Lobster crackers are similar to the hinged type of nut crackers but are rather sturdier. The inner edges near the hinge are ridged to provide grip on the smooth shells. Some have a prong at the end to tease out the claw meat. You can also buy lobster pincers designed to crack the claws and extract the meat.

Parts of a Lobster

The lobster's shell accounts for two-thirds of its weight, but very little of the rest is inedible. Blue-black when raw, the shell turns scarlet when cooked.

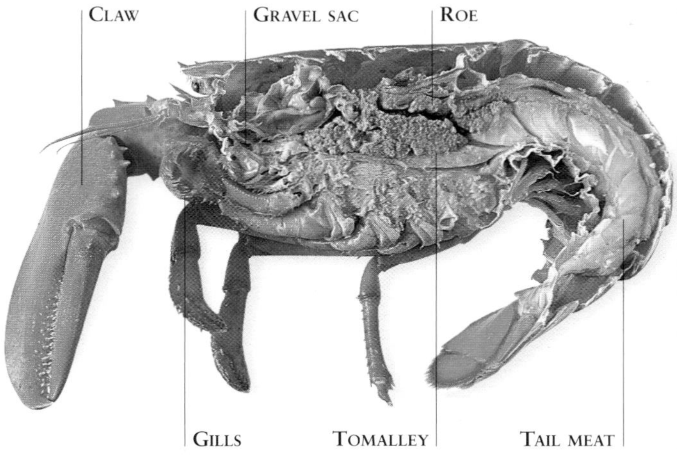

Edible parts
- The most meaty part is the lobster tail.
- The two claws are also full of delicious flesh.
- The green, creamy liver (tomalley) is a delicacy.
- In the female, the roe can be eaten. It is black when raw and scarlet when cooked.

Inedible parts
- The shell and legs.
- The bony membranes in the two claws.
- Small gravel sac (the stomach).
- The intestinal channel which runs down the back to the tail.
- The feathery gills in the body section between the lobster's head and tail.

CRAB

There are over twelve edible varieties of crab, the large-bodied species being the most common in the kitchen. You can buy crab whole, alive or cooked – live ones should be active and feel heavy for their size. Crabs are usually cooked whole and then cut up afterwards.

BOILING A CRAB

The cooking liquid can vary from water or the classic court bouillon *(see page 66) to a spicy broth (see box, left). Before you start, put the live crab in the freezer for 1 hour to desensitize it. The crab will then be easy to handle.*

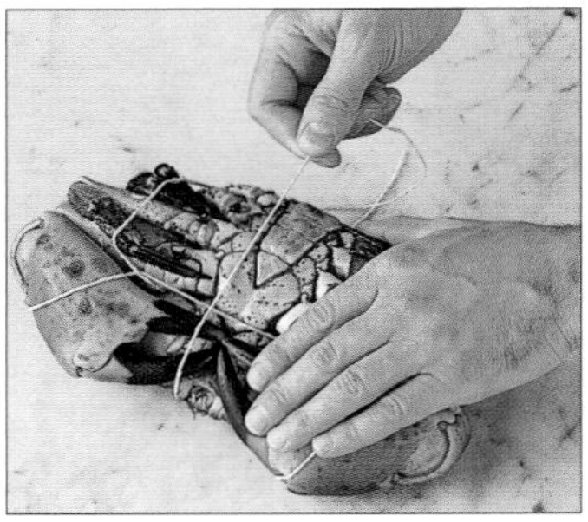

1 If not already done by the fishmonger, tie the crab with string to keep its claws still. Fill a pan with enough *court bouillon* to cover the crab. Bring to the boil.

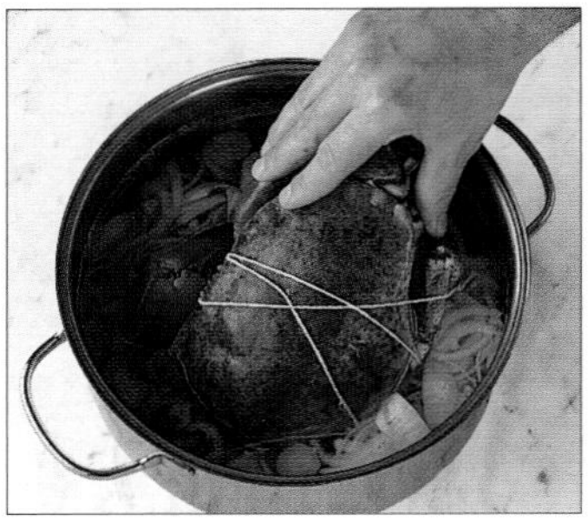

2 Add the crab and cover the pan; bring back to the boil and cook until the shell of the crab turns red, about 5 minutes per 450 g.

3 Remove the cooked crab from the pan with a slotted spoon. Transfer to a colander to drain. Let cool, then remove the cooked meat from the shell (see below).

REMOVING COOKED CRABMEAT FROM THE SHELL

Although size and shape vary from one species to another, the essential parts of the body need a similar approach. The larger the crab the easier it is to remove the meat. A variety of utensils are available to extract the meat. For the legs, snip open the shell and remove the meat with a pick. Use a spoon to scoop out the yellowish-brown meat from the shell. Opt for a skewer or larding needle to poke out the white fibres from the central body. To dress a crab, see box (left).

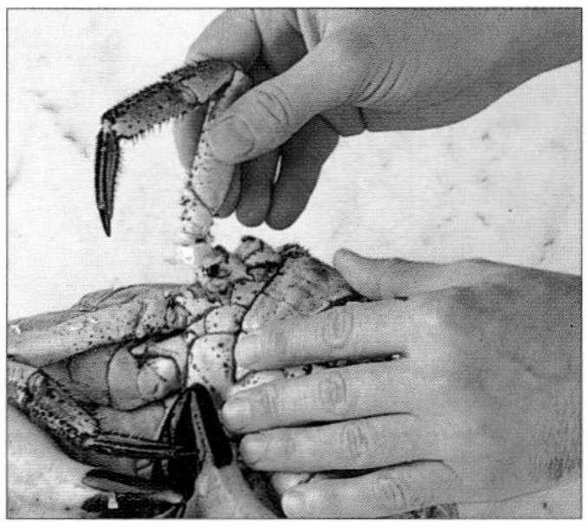

1 Hold the legs and claws close to the body and twist to remove. Discard the legs.

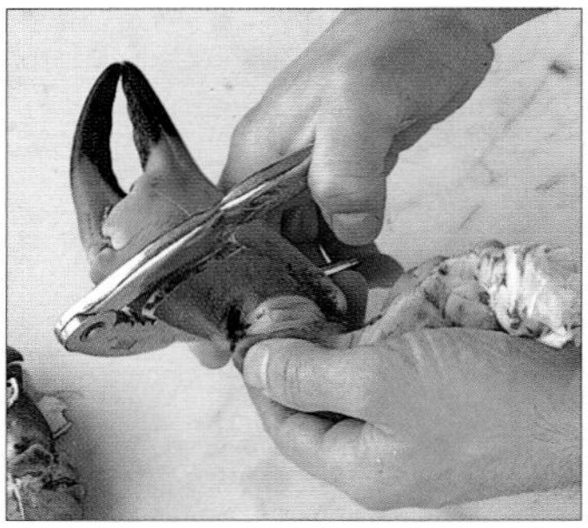

2 Crack the claws without damaging the meat inside. Remove the meat in large chunks.

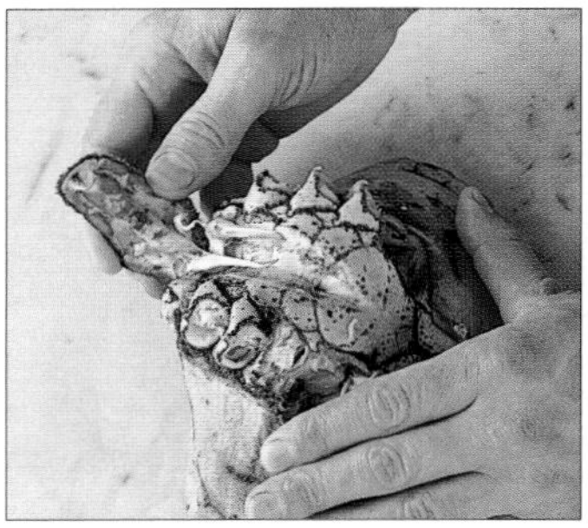

3 Remove the pointed tail or apron flap by snapping it back with your fingers.

LOUISIANA CRAB BOIL

As an alternative to a traditional *court bouillon*, consider a Louisiana crab boil, which gives the meat a peppery flavour. In this unique cooking method, crab is cooked in a fiery herb broth heady with lemon, allspice, thyme, chillies, onion, garlic and peppercorns. The recipe stems from states around the Gulf of Mexico, which are rich in Creole and Cajun tradition. Creole cooking, a sultry blend of French, Spanish and African influence, is considered to be the more refined of the two. Cajun cooking, brought by the French, is spicier than Creole.

HOW TO DRESS CRAB

This classic presentation turns the large shell into an elegant container for the crab. Remove meat, keeping pieces as large as possible. Pick over crab and remove any membrane or shell. Cut around the line rimming the edge of shell. Scrub out shell and dry. Arrange white meat in one half of shell. Mix any brown meat with a little mayonnaise and pile into the other half. Garnish with finely chopped fresh parsley, finely chopped hard-boiled egg white and sieved hard-boiled egg yolk; serve with additional mayonnaise.

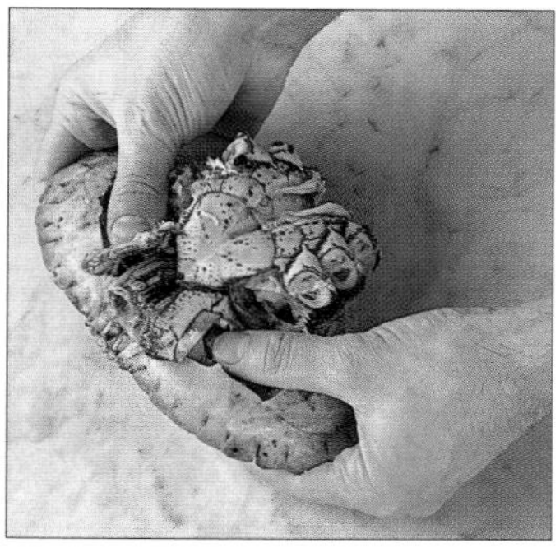

4 Break the shell by pressing down each side of the body with your thumbs. Lift out the body section. Scrape away the soft brown meat from the shell, keeping it separate from the white claw meat.

5 Discard the stomach sac and soft gills (also known as dead man's fingers) as they are inedible. If you intend to use the shell for serving, clean it thoroughly.

6 Cut the body of the crab in half lengthwise with a chef's knife. Remove the meat from the body of the crab with the handle of a small spoon or a chopstick, keeping it separate from the brown shell meat.

PRAWNS

The different varieties and sizes of prawns available are enormous, but no matter what sort you buy, the techniques for dealing with all of them are the same. Whether raw or cooked, you need to know how to shell them and how to remove the dark intestinal vein.

PREPARING PRAWNS

Most large prawns have a black intestinal vein running along their backs. This is unsightly, and its gritty texture is unpleasant to eat, so it should be removed. If you buy raw prawns, remove these veins before cooking.

1 Peel off the shell, being careful to keep the prawn intact and leave no flesh on the shell. All the shell can be removed, including the tail end, or you can leave the shell on the tail for an alternative presentation.

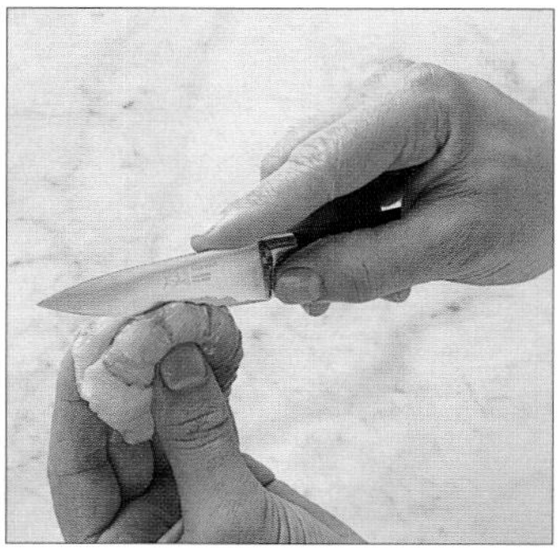

2 Make a shallow cut along the back of the prawn with a small knife, to expose the dark vein. Carefully loosen any overhanging membrane that may tether the vein to the prawn.

3 Remove the dark intestinal vein with the tip of the knife. Discard the vein. Rinse and pat dry with paper towels.

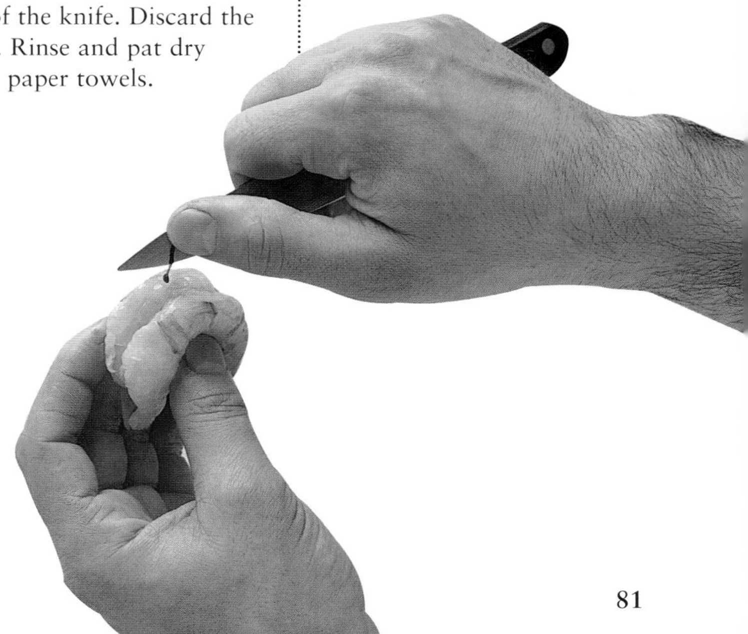

CRAYFISH

Although crayfish resemble tiny lobsters, they are in fact prepared and cooked in a similar way to prawns. The intestinal vein is best removed before cooking. Twist the centre section of the tail, then pull it away from the body – the vein will come away too.

TRICK OF THE TRADE

KEEPING PRAWNS STRAIGHT

Oriental chefs use this simple technique to prevent prawns from curling during cooking.

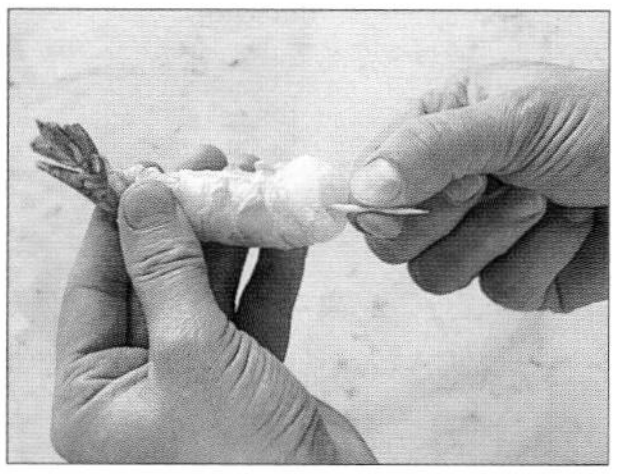

Before cooking, insert a long wooden cocktail stick through the centre of each prawn. Remove the sticks before serving.

MUSSELS

Choose undamaged, fresh-smelling mussels. Avoid those that feel heavy – they may be full of sand – or light and loose when shaken – they are probably dead. Ensure all are tightly closed; reject any that do not shut when tapped.

MOULES A LA MARINIERE

25 g butter
2 shallots, chopped
2 garlic cloves, chopped
200 ml dry white wine
1 tbsp chopped fresh parsley, plus extra for garnishing
450 g live mussels, cleaned
Salt and freshly ground pepper

Melt the butter in a large, deep pan and sauté the shallots and garlic for 5 minutes or until soft. Add the wine and parsley, bring to a simmer, then add the mussels. Cover the pan tightly and steam for 6 minutes or until the mussels open. Discard any that remain closed. Lift out the mussels, draining their liquid back into the pan. Strain the liquid to remove any sand; rinse out the pan. Return liquid to pan and boil to reduce; season. Serve with the liquid poured over and garnished with parsley. Serves 4.

CLEANING

About three-quarters of mussels on sale today are cultivated. The rest are harvested from the wild. Mussels filter seawater through their bodies to extract nutrients and may pick up any toxins in the water. Whether cultivated or wild, they must be carefully cleaned before being cooked.

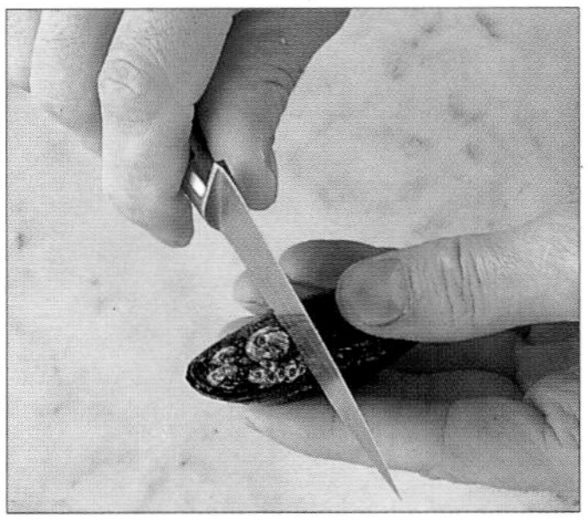

1 Scrape off any barnacles from the outsides of the shells with the back of a small knife.

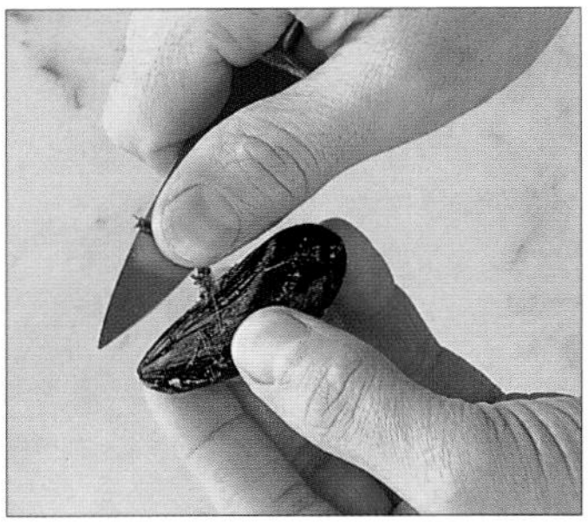

2 With your thumb against the blade, pull out and detach any hair-like "beards" from the hinges of the shells.

3 Scrub each shell briskly under cold running water with a stiff brush. This will remove any sand and thoroughly clean the mussels before cooking. Discard any mussels with cracked shells and any that do not close when tapped. Place cleaned mussels in a bowl of lightly salted cold water for about 2 hours or until ready to use.

From left to right: New Zealand green-lipped mussel; Young marine mussel; Mature marine mussel

SAFETY FIRST

- Do not collect mussels from the wild unless you are certain the water is not polluted, and never collect them in the summer.
- If possible cook mussels on the day of purchase or picking – keep them in a bowl of lightly salted cold water for 2 hours, fresh water will kill them.
- If shells are muddy, or you want to cook them the next day, soak them overnight in cold water with 1 tbsp flour and 50 g salt.
- Discard mussels that stay open when tapped or are cracked.
- Discard all mussels that do not open when cooked.

Steaming Open

To open mussels, and cook the meat at the same time, they are steamed in a small amount of liquid with flavourings such as shallots, garlic and herbs. You can use water for the liquid, but fish stock or cider will give a better flavour. Another choice is dry white wine, as in the steps here for moules à la marinière *(see recipe, opposite page). Always clean the mussels well.*

1 Clean the mussels (see opposite page), then add to the hot wine mixture.

2 Cover pan and steam the mussels for 6 minutes. Shake the pan occasionally to ensure even cooking.

3 Remove the mussels using a slotted spoon; discard any that are shut. Serve with the strained, reduced liquid.

Removing the Rubbery Ring

The rubbery ring that forms a brown edge to the mussel flesh should be removed.

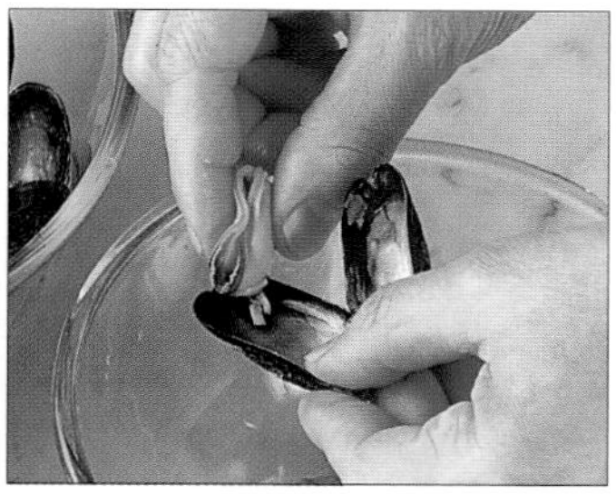

1 Clean mussels and steam them open. Remove them from the cooking liquid and then from their shells.

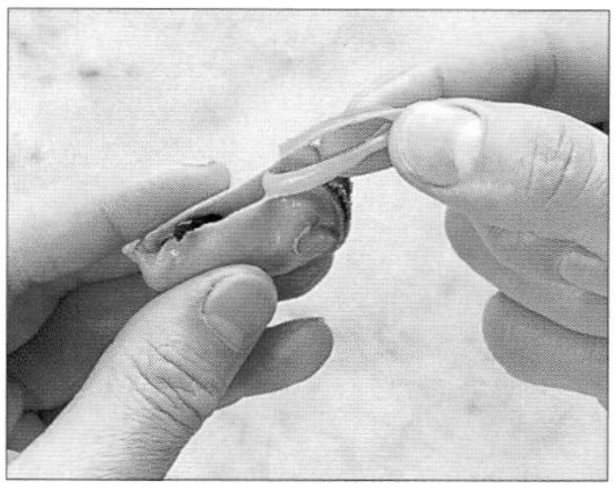

2 Carefully pull off the rubbery ring that surrounds the flesh with your fingers and discard it.

Serving on the Half-shell

Once opened, the meat of the mussels can be removed from the shells and used in recipes, or left in and served in the shells with a sauce, or topped with herb butter or breadcrumbs mixed with chopped fresh herbs. If they are large mussels, their tough, rubbery rings should be removed (see right).

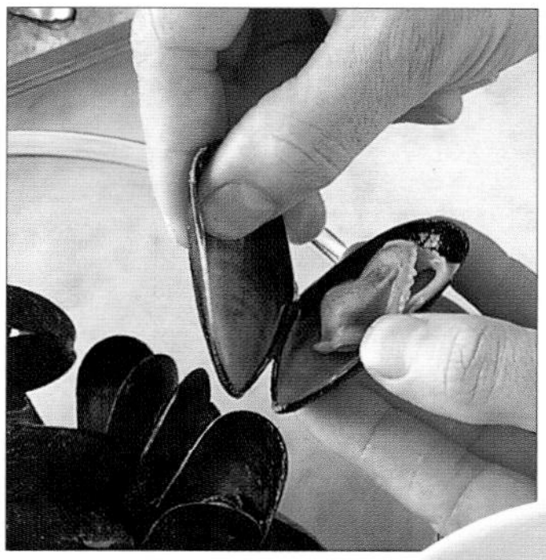

1 Clean mussels open (see opposite page) and steam them open as above, with liquid and flavourings of your choice. Remove them from the liquid and let cool, then prise them open with your fingers and discard the top shells. Loosen the mussels from the bottom shells.

2 Arrange the half shells on sea salt in a heatproof dish. Top each mussel with ½ tsp pesto (see page 330) or garlic and herb butter (see page 127), and grill for 2–3 minutes. Garnish with a *concassée* of tomatoes (see page 178) and basil leaves.

OYSTERS & CLAMS

Both oysters and clams can be eaten raw, or removed from their shells and simmered in soups and stews, baked, or deep-fried. Left on their half shells, they can be topped with a sauce or stuffing and grilled.

SHUCKER

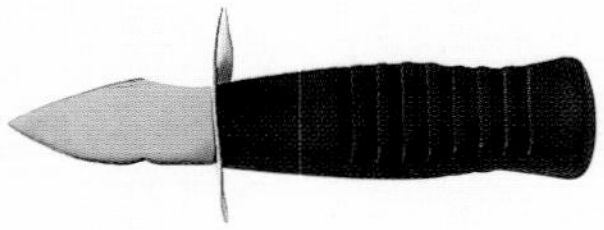

To open live oysters or other shellfish you need a short strong knife. A shucker is specially made for this task. The blade is sharply pointed, tapering on two sides. A prominent guard serves to protect your hand from the blade and the equally treacherous edges of the oyster shells.

OPENING CLAMS

There are many varieties of clam, from the small ones called vongole *in Italy, which can be steamed open like mussels (see page 83), to the larger* palourdes, *or Venus clams, and the huge hard clams or* quahogs *essential to American clambakes and chowders. Scrub all clams well before opening to remove grit and sand, and discard any open or damaged ones.*

1 Hold the clam firmly and insert the knife blade between the shells. Twist the knife to prise open the shells and sever the hinge muscle.

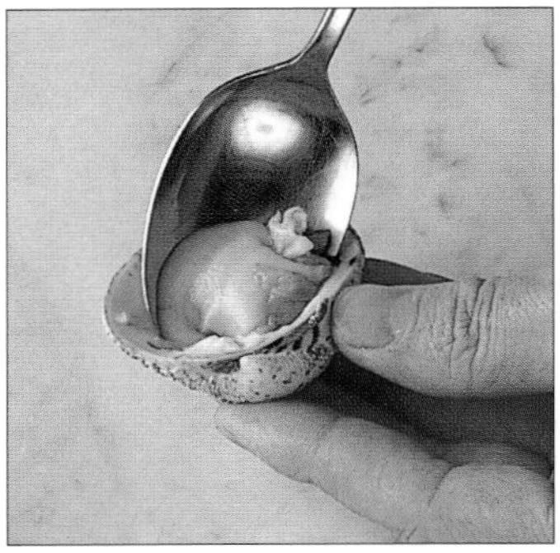

2 With a spoon, loosen the muscle in the bottom shell. If serving clams without their shells, tip both the meat and juices into a bowl.

SHUCKING OYSTERS

Oysters are usually eaten raw and should be opened (or shucked) only just before eating. Discard open or damaged ones. Scrub the shells well before opening.

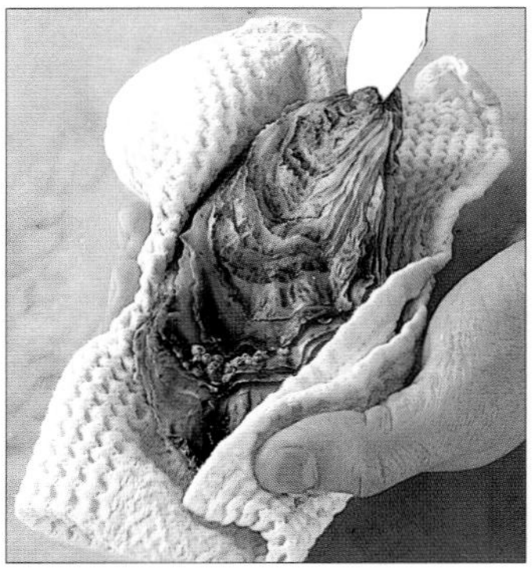

1 Using a cloth, hold the oyster, rounded-side down, in your hand. Insert the shucker just below the hinge.

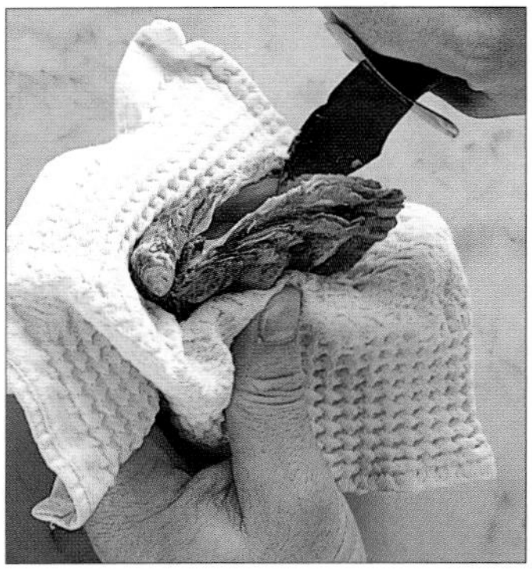

2 Work the shucker further between the two shells. Twist the shucker to separate the shells.

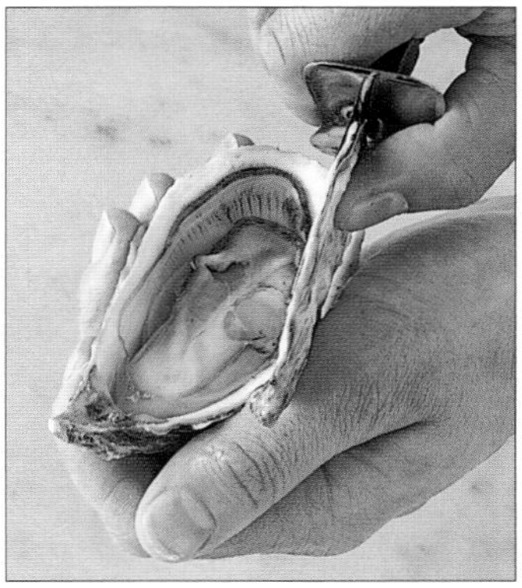

3 Carefully scrape the oyster from the top shell, cut the muscle and remove the top shell. Detach the oyster from the muscle underneath the meat on the bottom shell. Serve on the half-shell on a bed of crushed ice with lemon halves for squeezing. Garnish with blanched samphire, if you like.

Scallops & Whelks

Scallops can be bought on the shell or ready cleaned and shucked. They do not have to be live when cooked, but they should be very fresh and sweet smelling. So too should whelks, although they are not eaten raw.

Opening and Preparing Scallops

In Europe, shelled scallops are available with their orange roe (coral) intact; in the United States this is usually absent. Scallops on the shell must be opened and trimmed before cooking. To open scallops, split them with a shucker as shown here, or with a small knife.

1 Hold the scallop with its rounded side down in the palm of your hand. Insert an oyster shucker (see opposite page) between the shells close to the hinge.

2 Work the shucker further between the shells. Twist the shucker to separate the shells. Cut the scallop from the flat top shell by scraping it with the shucker.

3 Carefully detach the scallop from the muscle underneath the meat in the bottom shell with a spoon. Scoop the scallop out; set the shell aside if you are going to use it in the presentation.

4 Pull away the dark organs from the white adductor muscle and the orange coral with your fingers. Discard the dark organs; rinse scallop under cold running water.

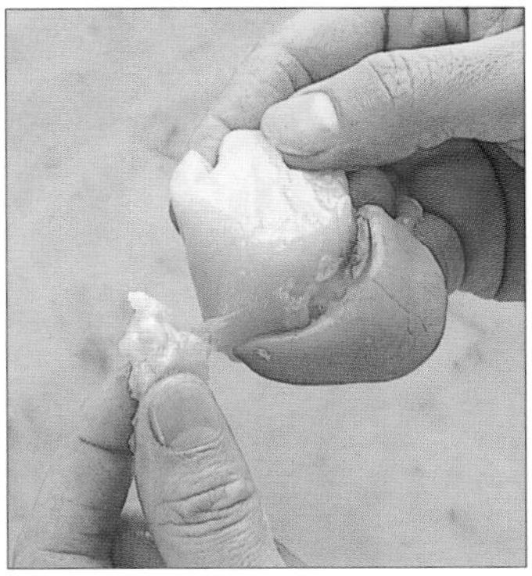

5 Pull off and discard the crescent-shaped muscle on the side of the scallop. The scallop may be cooked with or without the coral. If using the shells for serving, scrub and boil them for 5 minutes.

Pilgrim Scallops

Fan-shaped scallops are also called pilgrim scallops or *coquilles Saint-Jacques* in French. This is because the shell is the badge of the pilgrims who worship at the shrine of Saint Jacques, patron saint of Spain; the badge is always pinned to their wide-brimmed hat. Pilgrims travel through France to Santiago de Compostela in northern Spain, where legend has it that the saint is buried.

Whelks

These must be cooked in their shells because their meat is difficult to extract while they are still alive. Bring a pan of court bouillon *(see page 66) to the boil and add the whelks. Simmer until they are firm but tender.*

Lift the whelks out of the pan with a slotted spoon. Remove the whelk from the shell with a fork. Clean the whelk if there is any sign of sand.

Squid

With a sweet flavour and pleasantly firm bite, squid has long been prized in coastal cuisines. The following techniques prepare squid for numerous dishes, including pasta, stir-fries and seafood salads.

Preparing

When cleaning whole squid, you need to deal with all of its parts. The pouch, fins, tentacles and ink are all edible; the rest should be discarded. In addition to being used in soups and fish stews, the various parts of the squid can be stir-fried, deep-fried, poached, grilled and even eaten raw in Japanese sushi.

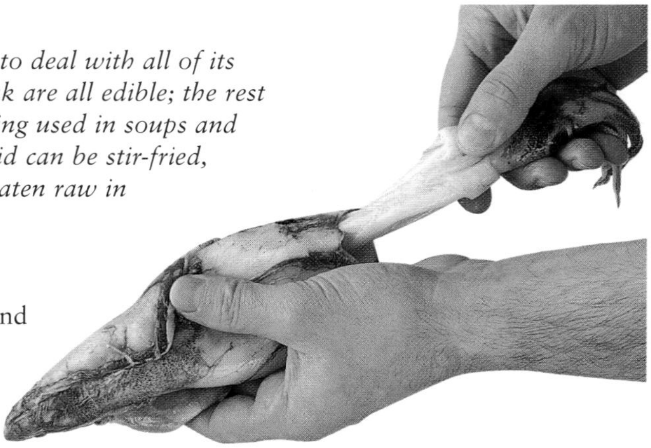

1 Hold the body firmly in one hand and pull off the head and tentacles. Drain the ink and set it aside if you are going to use it in cooking (see box, below).

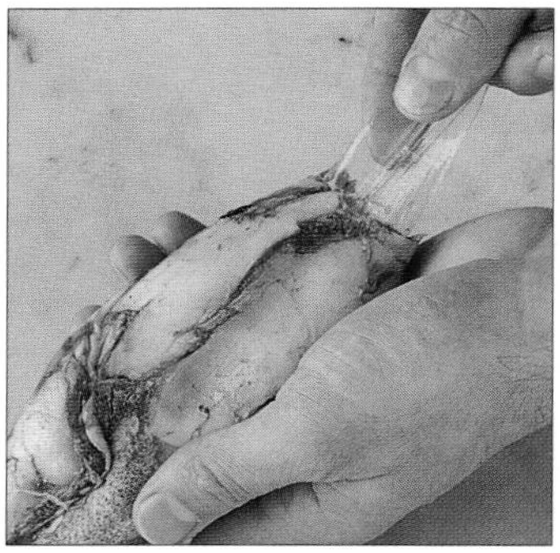

2 Pull out the "pen", which looks like a long piece of clear plastic, and discard.

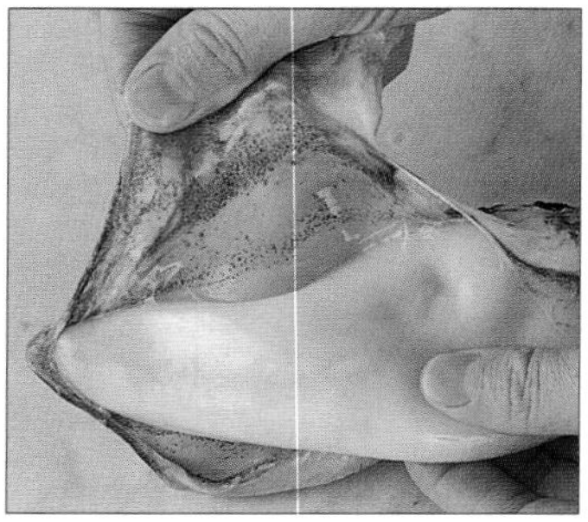

3 Peel off all of the purple skin covering the body (pouch) and the fins; discard the skin.

4 Remove the fins from the pouch with a chef's knife and reserve. Cut the tentacles from the head and reserve.

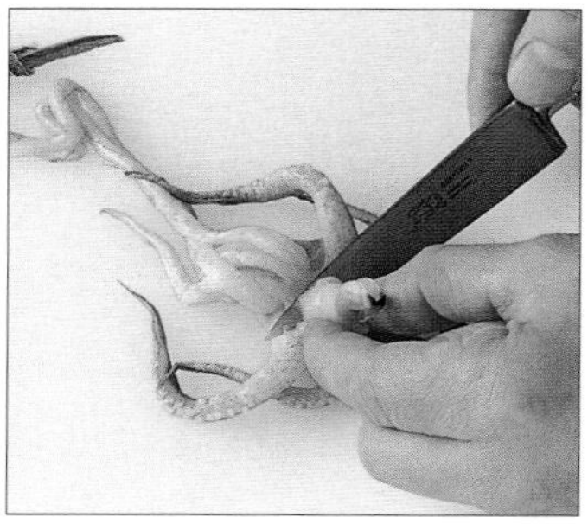

5 Squeeze the tentacles to remove the beak; cut off and discard. Cut off eyes and mouth; discard.

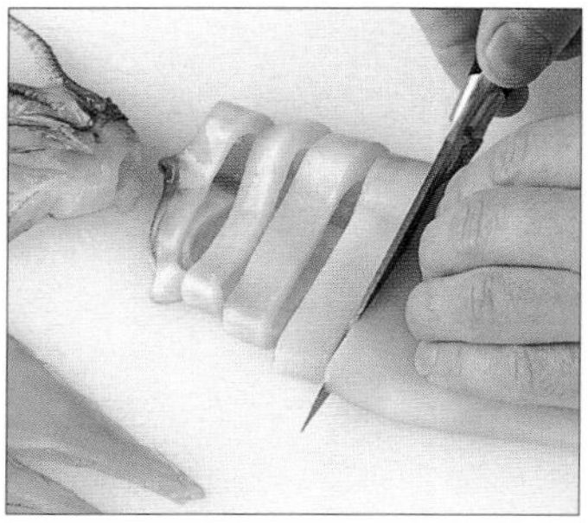

6 After cleaning, cut the pouch into rings or leave it whole for stuffing. Chop the fins and tentacles.

Squid Ink

Black ink is contained in a sac inside the squid. If the sac doesn't break during cleaning, remove it, pierce it and reserve the ink. Sacs can also be bought separately from fishmongers.

In Italy, squid ink is used to colour and flavour pasta; in Catalonia it is used with rice, especially paella. The Spanish dish *calamares en su tinta* is squid cooked in its own ink.

Stuffing

When left whole, the pouch, or body, of the squid makes a perfect natural container for stuffing. Leave a little room at the top because the stuffing swells during cooking. Use the chopped tentacles in the filling, along with other full-flavoured ingredients. A popular Spanish stuffing includes ham, onions and breadcrumbs. A Middle Eastern mixture of couscous, sausage, red pepper and mint makes a delicious alternative.

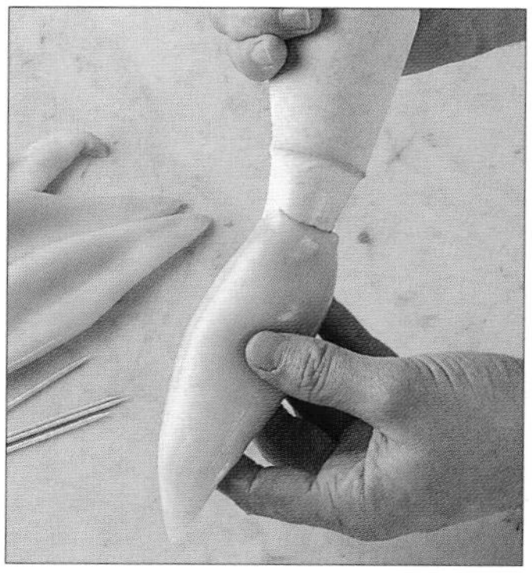

1 Hold the pouch in one hand. Pipe or spoon the stuffing into the pouch with a large tube.

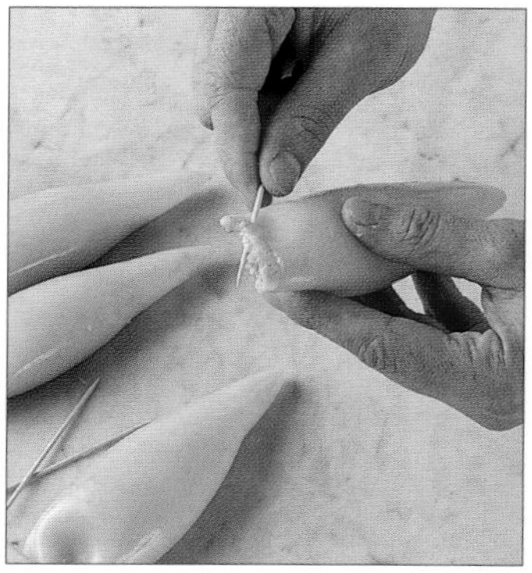

2 Secure openings with wooden cocktail sticks or sew closed with a trussing needle and string.

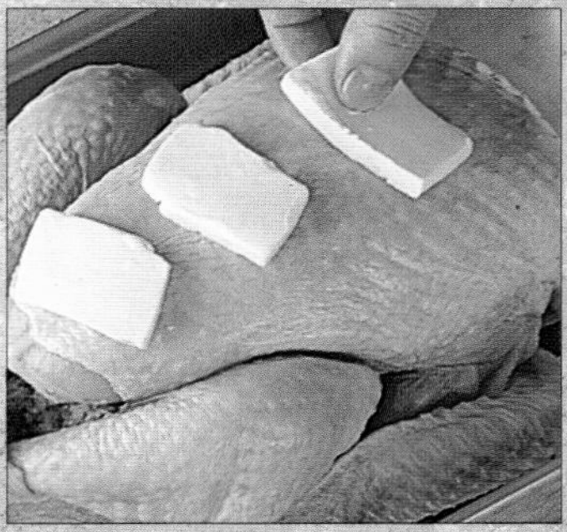

Poultry & Game

Choosing Poultry
•
Preparing Whole Birds
•
Jointing & Cutting
•
Preparing Pieces
•
Making a Ballotine
•
Roasting Birds
•
Oriental Roast Duck
•
Frying
•
Poaching
•
Grilling & Barbecuing
•
Casseroling & Pot Roasting
•
Pates & Terrines

Choosing Poultry

Whether fresh or frozen, look for well-shaped plump birds that have blemish free, light, even-coloured skin. That of fresh birds should look moist but not wet; wetness can indicate the bird has been partially frozen. Feed and breed can affect the colour of the skin and the flavour of the meat.

MAKE SURE the legs are pliable and the skin intact
SELECT BIRDS with moist, even coloured skin, there should be no signs of bruising or feathers
WHEN SELECTING younger birds gently bend the tip of the breastbone, it should be flexible
THE BODY SHOULD be compact, well rounded in shape with plump, firm breasts
THE BIRD SHOULD smell fresh, any smells from the wrapping should disappear quickly

Buying Poultry

Most supermarket birds are conventionally reared and have a consistently bland taste. Free range birds, which are more expensive, are more flavourful as a result of their varied diet and free roaming conditions. The words "free range", "traditional free range" or "free range total freedom", on labels all indicate the birds have been allowed to grow in specially designed houses, however the number of birds per square metre varies.

When choosing frozen birds make sure the wrapping is sealed and intact and that there are no ice crystals or discoloration – a sign of freezer burn on the skin. Use the chart on the opposite page to select an appropriate bird for each occasion and to check the suitable cooking methods. When considering game, domestic rabbit is generally included with wild birds.

Handling Poultry

Remove the original packaging from a fresh bird then place on a rack over a plate. Cover loosely and store in the refrigerator (1–5°C) away from cooked meats. Store any giblets separately in a covered bowl.

Always check the label on frozen birds and portions for freezer storage times. Frozen poultry must be defrosted completely before cooking. Thaw in the original packaging on a plate in the refrigerator allowing 3–5 hours per 450 g. Remove any giblets as soon as possible. Cook the bird within 12 hours of thawing and do not refreeze. Raw poultry is susceptible to bacterial growth so clean work surfaces and all preparation utensils after use.
To store cooked poultry, cool it quickly then cover and store in the refrigerator for 2–3 days.

Poultry & Game

Chicken and turkey suit everyday and special occasion meals while other birds are generally reserved specially for the latter. Select young tender birds for quick cooking such as stir-frying and grilling and older birds for slow, moist methods, like stewing, which will help to tenderize the flesh and draw flavour from the bones. Ask your butcher for help with selection advice.

Bird	What to Look For	Cooking Methods
Boiling Fowl	*Lean breast with firm breastbone* *Slightly mottled skin* *Flesh a little darker than chicken*	Braise, stew, casserole, boil, poach, steam
Chicken	*Creamy-white smooth skin, should look fresh and moist*	Roast, pot-roast, braise, casserole, steam, poach, pan-fry, deep-fry, stir-fry
Duck	*Supple, waxy looking skin* *Dry appearance* *Long body with slender breasts*	Roast (whole) Pan-fry, grill (breasts) Use fat for roasting potatoes
Goose	*Plump breast with flexible backbone* *Light coloured waxy skin* *Yellow fat in body cavity*	Roast, pot-roast Braise, stew (portions)
Grouse	*Moist fresh-looking skin* *Deep red flesh, with no "shot" damage*	Roast, pot-roast, braise, casserole, stew
Guinea Fowl	*Long lean breasts* *Golden skin and fat, dark coloured flesh*	Bard and roast, pot-roast, casserole
Partridge	*Plump, pale coloured, soft flesh* *Obvious gamey aroma*	Roast, pot-roast, braise, casserole, stew
Pheasant	*Good even shape with no "shot" damage* *Limbs intact and not broken* *Strong gamey aroma*	Bard and roast, stew, braise
Poussin	*Moist creamy-white skin* *Plump legs and lean breasts*	Roast (whole) Grill, barbecue (spatchcock)
Quail	*High proportion of meaty flesh to bone* *Good round shape, plump flesh*	Roast, pot-roast, braise, casserole, grill, barbecue (spatchcock)
Rabbit	*Even covering of flesh and rounded back* *Lean, moist, pale pink flesh* *Very little visible fat*	Pan-fry, grill, roast, braise, stew, casserole
Turkey	*Plump, well rounded breast and legs* *Moist skin with no blemishes* *Very little odour*	Roast (whole) Roast, braise, casserole (portions) Stir-fry, pan-fry (breast meat)

Chicken On the Menu

Inexpensive, easy to prepare and perfect with a vast range of seasonings and accompaniments, chicken is a popular dish practically everywhere.

China – *Bang Bang Chicken* (shredded, poached chicken served with cucumber shreds and a spicy dressing) is a favourite appetiser dish.

Eastern Europe – *Chicken Paprikash* (chicken pieces cooked in a tomato and paprika-flavoured sauce) is a Hungarian classic while *Chicken Pojarski* (deep-fried minced chicken and brioche balls in a tomato-mushroom sauce) was once a favourite of the Russian royal family.

France – *Coq au vin* is a slowly simmered chicken that gets its rich flavour from red wine, bacon and mushrooms.

Great Britain – *Hindle Wakes* (chicken with a fruit, vinegar and mustard stuffing) is a time-honoured Yorkshire classic.

India – *Tandoori Chicken* is marinated in spicy yogurt and cooked in a clay oven.

Italy – *Chicken Cacciatore* (or "hunter's style") is made with a mushroom and wine-infused tomato sauce.

United States – *Southern-fried Chicken* (chicken pieces dipped into seasoned flour and fried) is a picnic staple all over the country.

Preparing Whole Birds

All birds, both domestic – chickens, ducks and geese – and game birds such as partridges or grouse, need careful preparation, not least because keeping the bird's shape during cooking makes carving easier. Before trussing, clean away feathers and down, rinse inside and out, and dry with paper towels.

Removing the Wishbone

The wishbone is located at the neck end of the bird. It is not necessary to remove it, but if you do it will be easier to carve the breast. This is particularly important if you are dealing with a large chicken or a turkey. Use a small pointed knife.

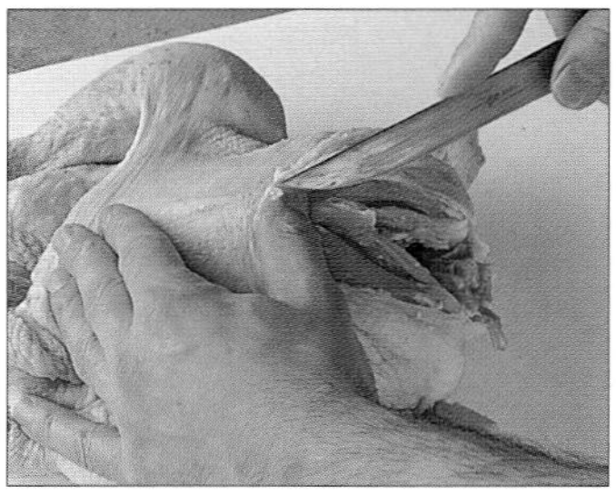

1 Pull back the skin from the neck cavity of the bird. Cut around the wishbone.

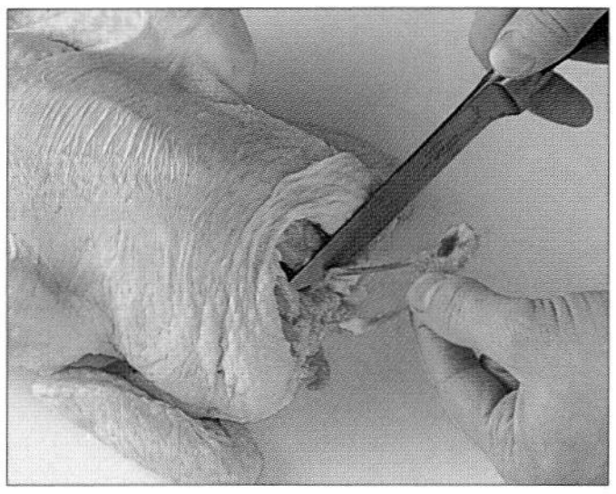

2 Scrape the meat from the wishbone, then cut away at the base.

Trussing Small Birds

Trussing gives the bird a neat shape and helps keep stuffing in place. Use a string to tie quite small birds, such as poussins, partridges, pheasants, grouse and quails, around their legs and bodies. Before you begin to tie up the birds, tuck the wing tips and the neck flap underneath.

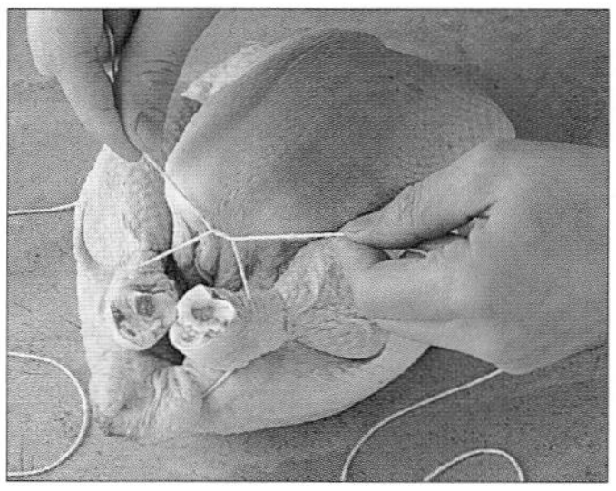

1 After seasoning, with the bird breast-side up, tie string around the legs and under the skin-flap at the tail.

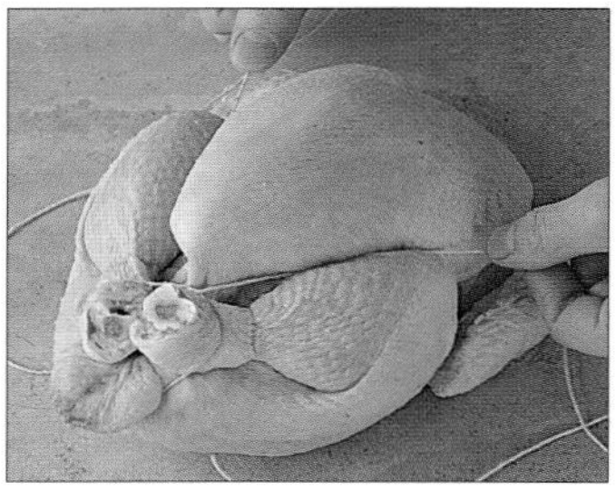

2 Bring the string towards the neck end of the bird, passing it down between the legs and body.

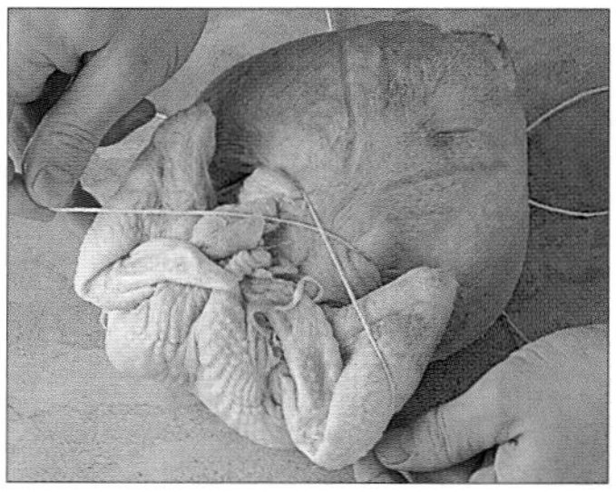

3 Turn the bird over. Cross the string over the centre of the bird. Wrap the string around the wings to keep them flat against the bird.

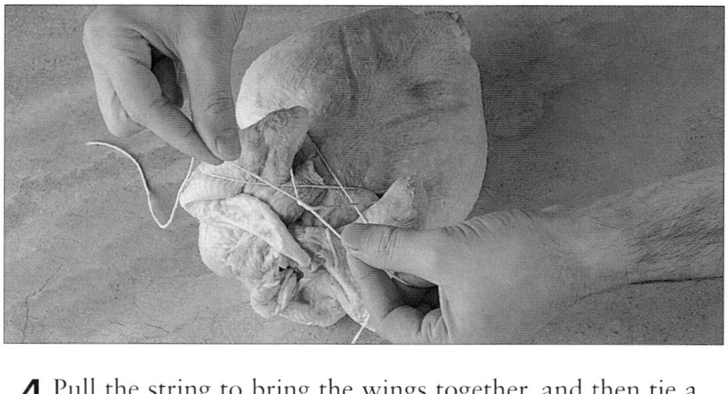

4 Pull the string to bring the wings together, and then tie a firm, double knot. The bird is now ready for cooking – roasting, pot-roasting, barbecuing or casseroling.

GIBLETS

The giblets consist of the neck, gizzard, heart and liver of the bird as well as the lungs and intestines (though the last two are generally not included in ready-prepared birds). Unless you clean the bird yourself, you will usually find the giblets packed in a plastic bag inside the body cavity. Often, however, they are absent from ready-prepared birds. Occasionally, you can buy them separately from a butcher if you wish to prepare stock.

To make stock for gravy (see page 101), trim the giblets, discarding the membrane and yellow gall bladder from the liver. Simmer them with a few tablespoonfuls of chopped onion and carrot, a bouquet garni (see page 185) and a few black peppercorns.

The livers of poultry (see page 94) and some fresh game birds are delicious in their own right, although the giblets of well-hung game birds are best discarded.

Handle and cook giblets as you would poultry. Store them separately, in a covered container away from cooked meats, in the refrigerator for 1–2 days. Always cook thoroughly before eating.

TRUSSING LARGE BIRDS

Trussing with a needle and thread is beneficial for large birds, and professional chefs always truss birds this way to ensure a neat, compact shape. Trussing helps the bird retain its natural juices, keeping the flesh moist and flavourful.

1 With the bird breast-side up, push the legs back to the centre of the breasts. Insert the needle through the joint in one of the legs, push it through the body, and out through the other leg. A 15-cm piece of string should remain where the needle first entered the bird.

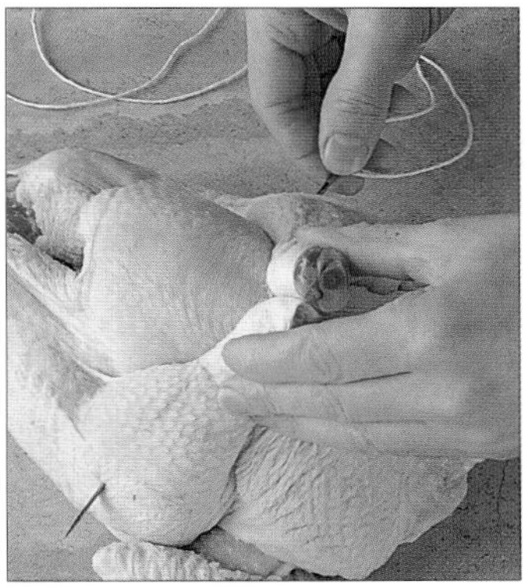

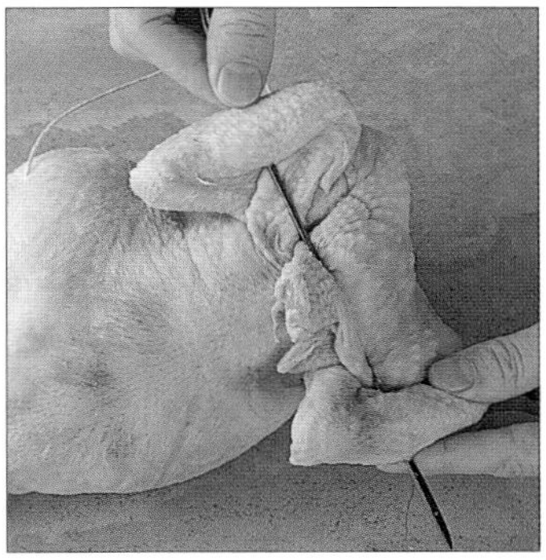

2 Tuck the wing tips under the body, and fold over the flap of skin from the neck. Thread the string through the wings and flap of skin.

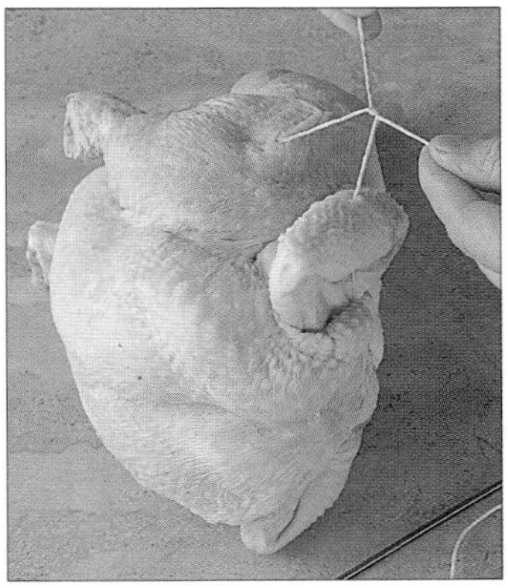

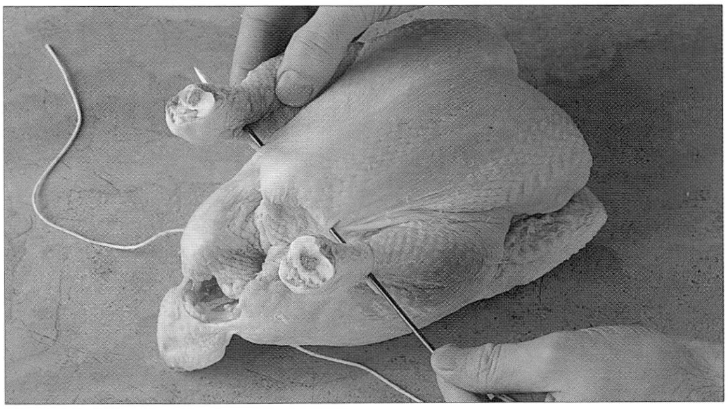

3 Make a double knot by tying the end of the string threaded through the wings with the end left at the leg. Trim both ends of the string.

4 Thread the needle under the legs through the tail end, leaving a 15-cm piece of string where the needle first entered the bird. Insert the needle through the end of one leg, push it through the breast, and out through the other leg.

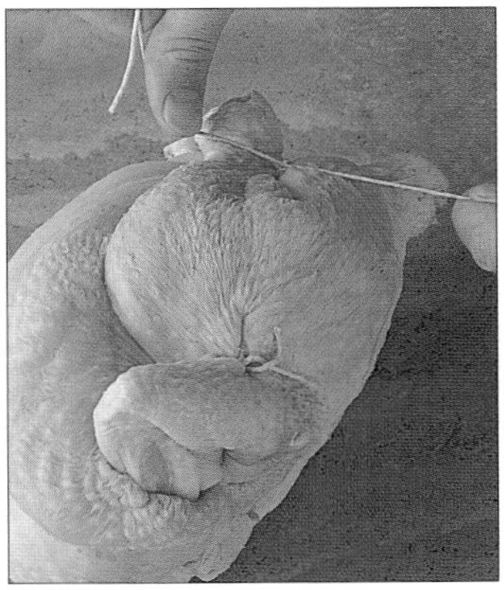

5 Make a double knot by tying the end of the string that has been threaded through the legs with the end left at the tail. Cut both ends of the string.

6 Turn the bird, breast-side up. It is now ready for cooking – roasting, pot-roasting, poaching or barbecuing (see pages 100, 110 and 113 respectively).

TRUSSING NEEDLE

To truss a large bird you need a special trussing needle. These are available in various lengths from specialist kitchenware shops. Make sure you use one which is long enough to pierce the bird fully through both legs and body. A small turkey, for example, will require a trussing needle of about 25 cm in length.

Trussing needles have very sharp points and eyes large enough to allow easy threading. The thread should be black, to show up on the cooked meat and not plastic-coated or otherwise treated.

TRICK OF THE TRADE

QUICK TRUSSING

Large birds that are to be roasted without a stuffing or barbecued can be quickly and simply secured by the insertion of two large metal skewers. One is pushed through both sections of the wing, into the neck skin and out through the other wing. The other skewer is pushed through the thighs and tail cavity. Thus secured, the bird will hold its shape and is ready for cooking.

JOINTING & CUTTING

Birds are usually left whole for roasting, pot-roasting and poaching, but for most other cooking methods they are cut up into pieces, unless they are small birds such as poussins or quail. The number of pieces depends on the size of the bird. Some small birds like pheasant, for example, may be spatchcocked or cut in half. Others are jointed into four, six or eight pieces.

SPATCHCOCKING

The derivation of this very strange-sounding culinary term is slightly obscure. An old word dating back to the 16th century, most likely of Irish origin, it is said to have come from the habit of catering for unexpected guests by speedily killing a bird and roasting it over the fire – "despatching the cock" – hence spatchcock. The word has now come to mean the cutting and removing of the backbone so that the bird can be cooked flat – and therefore more quickly.

SPATCHCOCKING A BIRD

Small birds such as the poussins used here are perfect for barbecuing or grilling. To make them the same thickness throughout so that they cook quickly and evenly, the backbone is removed, then the birds are flattened and secured with metal skewers – called en crapaudine *in French.*

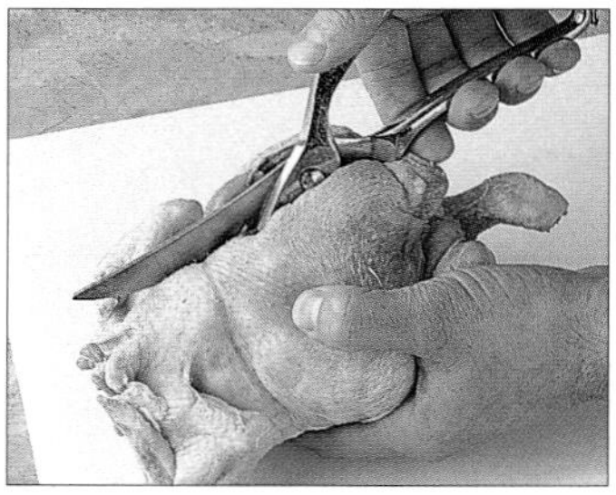

1 Tuck under the wings and remove the wishbone. Turn the bird over, cut along each side of the backbone with poultry shears and remove it.

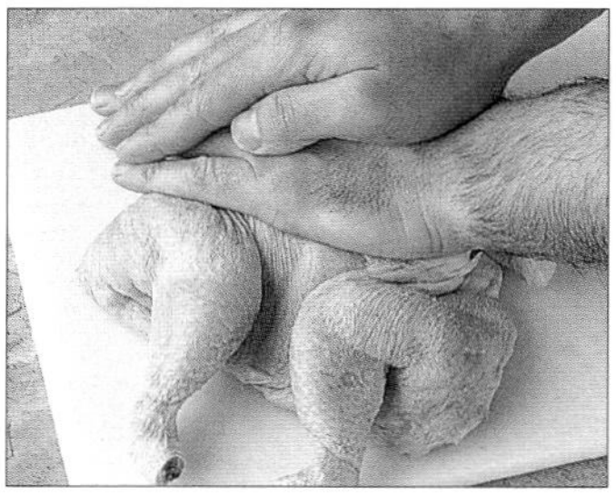

2 Push down on the bird to break the breastbone, flattening it against the cutting board.

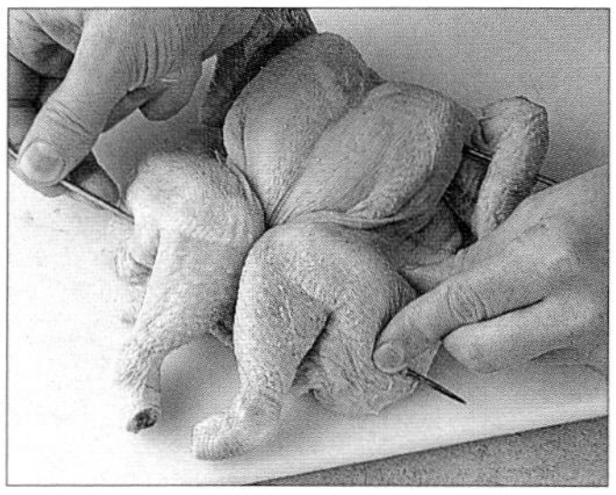

3 Keeping the bird flat, push a metal skewer through the wings and breast. Push another metal skewer through the thighs.

CUTTING A DUCK INTO FOUR PIECES

Ducks are less economical than chickens, because they have less meat in proportion to their weight, and more fat stored under the skin. They are also a different, more awkward shape for jointing, and are therefore best cut into four pieces so that each portion contains a good amount of meat to bone. The joints can be roasted or casseroled.

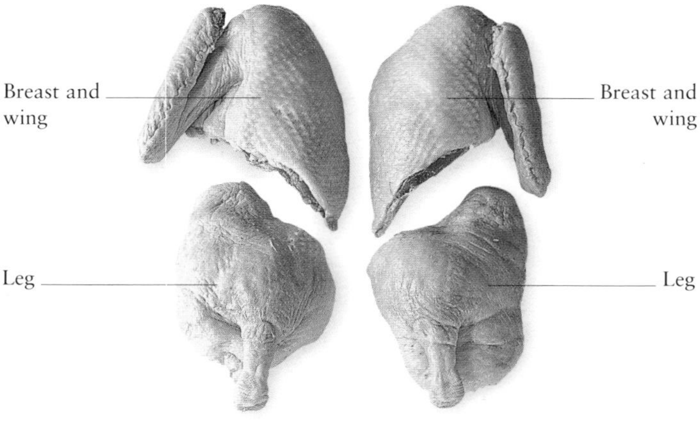

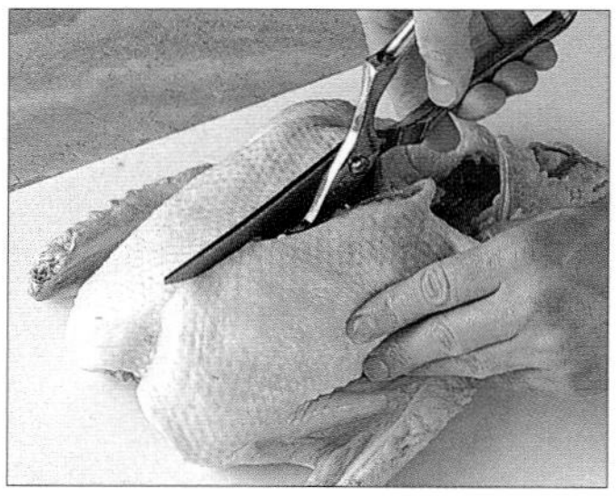

1 Trim wing tips and remove wishbone (see page 90). Cut breast in half from tail to neck, splitting the breastbone with poultry shears.

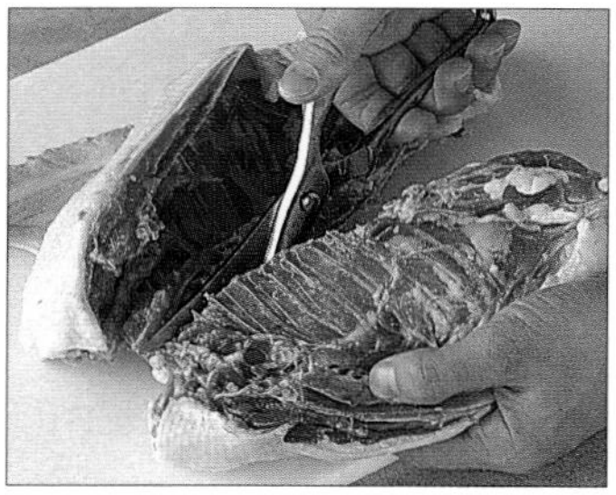

2 Separate the bird into two halves by cutting along each side of the backbone and removing it.

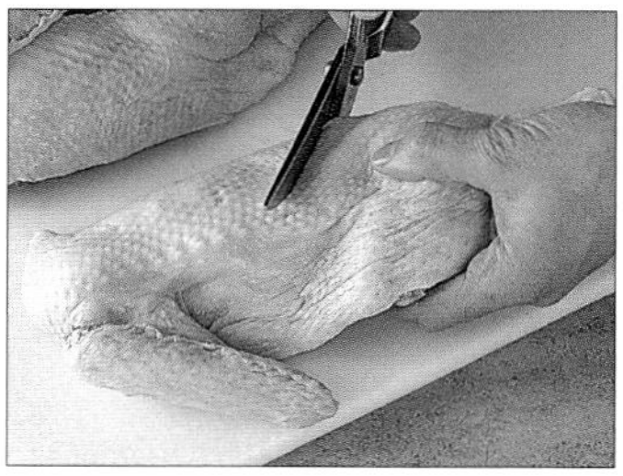

3 Cut each piece of duck diagonally in half with poultry shears. The duck is now ready for cooking.

Cutting a Bird into Eight Pieces

A medium-sized or large bird can be jointed into four, six or eight pieces. For some dishes you may wish to keep the breasts and/or the legs intact, but to ensure there is some white and dark meat for each serving, breasts are cut in half with the wings attached and the legs are split into thighs and drumsticks.

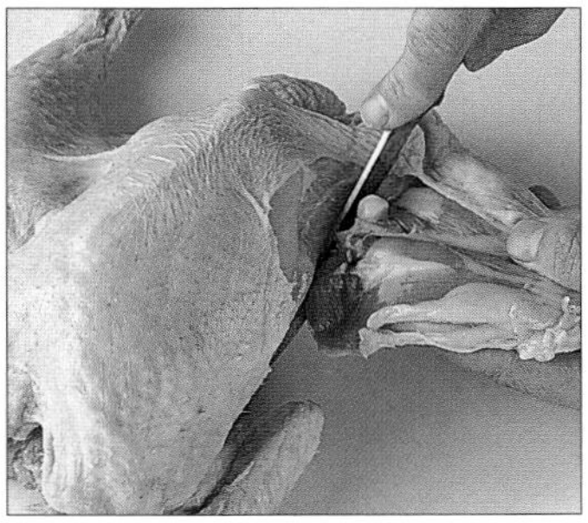

1 Place the bird breast-side up and cut one leg away from the bird. Cut through the thigh joint, to separate the leg from the body. Repeat.

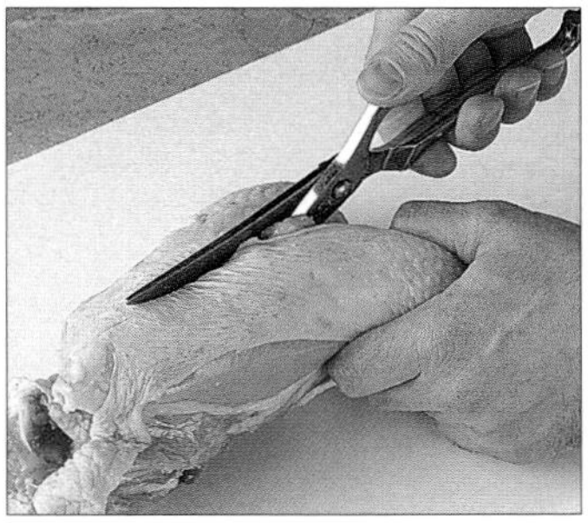

2 Holding the wing, cut the breast in half, splitting the breastbone. Turn over and cut alongside the backbone to separate the body.

3 Cut out the backbone with the poultry shears – it can be used to make stock (see page 16). Leave the wing joints attached.

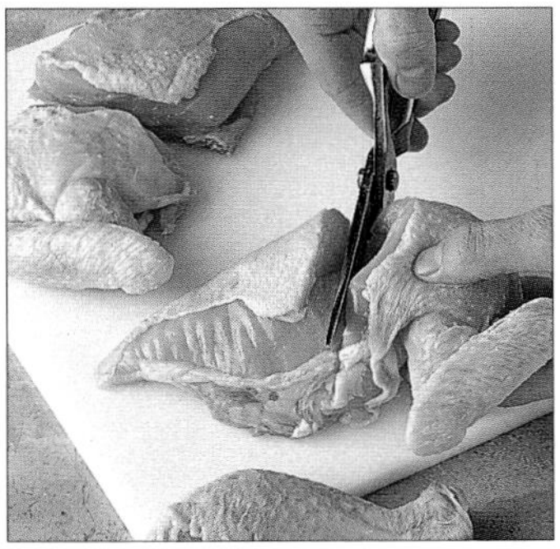

4 Cut each breast in half diagonally with the shears, so that one piece of breast has the wing attached.

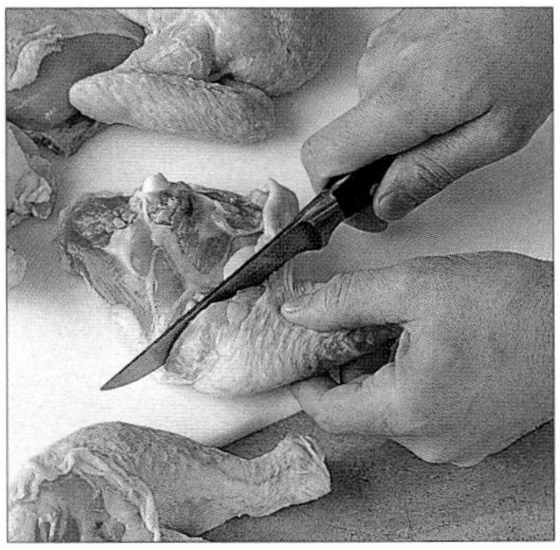

5 Cut each leg in half through the knee joint, following the line of white fat on the underside. Cut off wing tip at first joint.

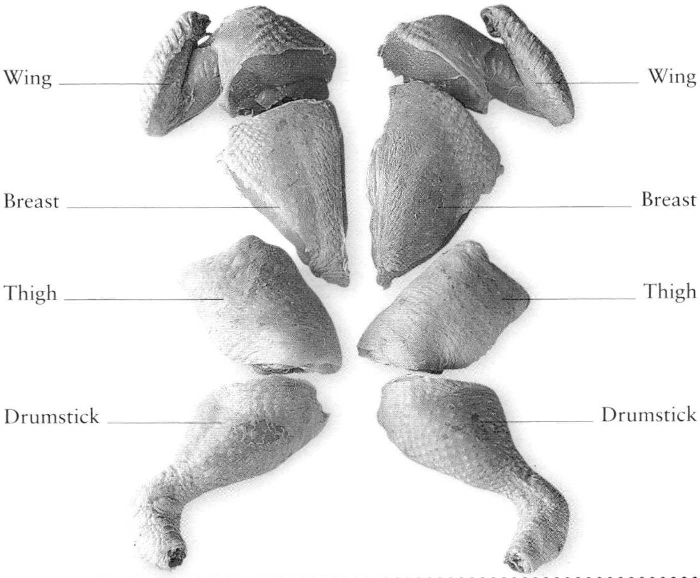

POULTRY SHEARS

Professional chefs joint poultry with a large knife, but for cutting the breastbone and backbone, you may find poultry shears easier.

Poultry shears have strong upward-curving blades, one with a straight edge and one with a serrated edge. Some have a notch in the lower blade which helps get a grip on bones. The handles are strongly sprung and are closed with a loop that holds the blades shut when not in use.

Cutting up a Rabbit

Rabbits can be roasted whole, but it is more usual to joint them for slow-cooking in casseroles and stews. It is only wild rabbit that you may need to joint, since domestic rabbit is mainly sold ready jointed. A whole rabbit, depending on size, can be jointed into six to nine pieces which will feed three to five people. Boneless rabbit meat is a good choice for pâtés and terrines (see page 116).

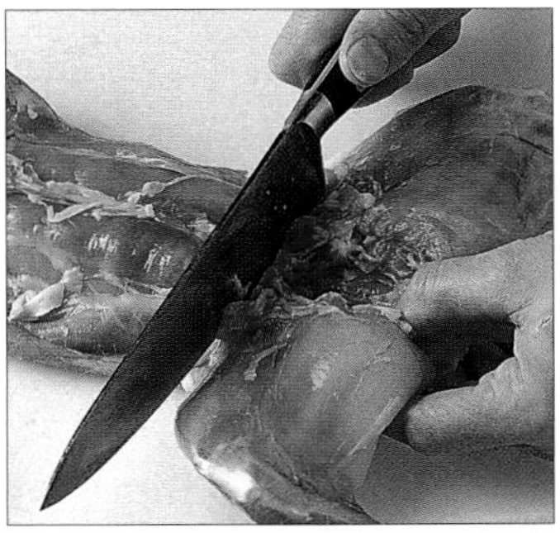

1 Cut the back legs from the carcass with a large chef's knife. Cut down the centre to separate. Cut each leg in two.

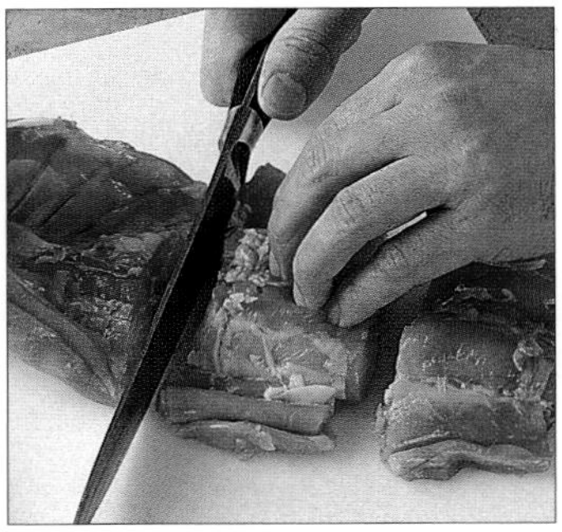

2 Cut the body crosswise into three or four pieces with the knife, making one cut below the ribcage.

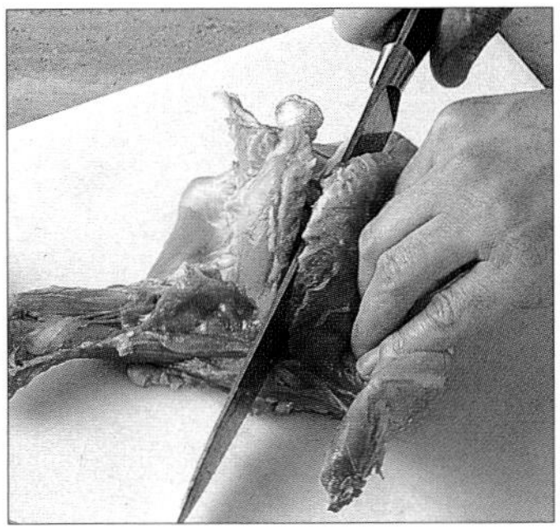

3 Cut the rib section in half through the breastbone and backbone with the knife or kitchen scissors.

Preparing Pieces

Poultry is immensely versatile: it can be cut into suprêmes and escalopes for pan-frying, chargrilling, stuffing and poaching as well as into strips for stir-frying. Thighs provide lean chunky pieces for casseroles and kebabs.

Making Supremes

These are skinless, boneless chicken breasts. Traditionally, they include the wing bones, but are often prepared without. Although available ready-prepared, preparation at home is more economical. Joint the bird (see page 93), cutting off both wings but keeping the breasts whole.

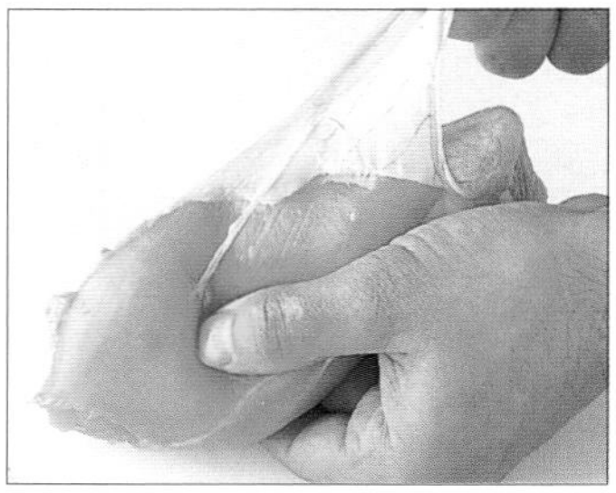

1 With your fingers, pull the skin and membrane away from the chicken breast. Discard skin and membrane.

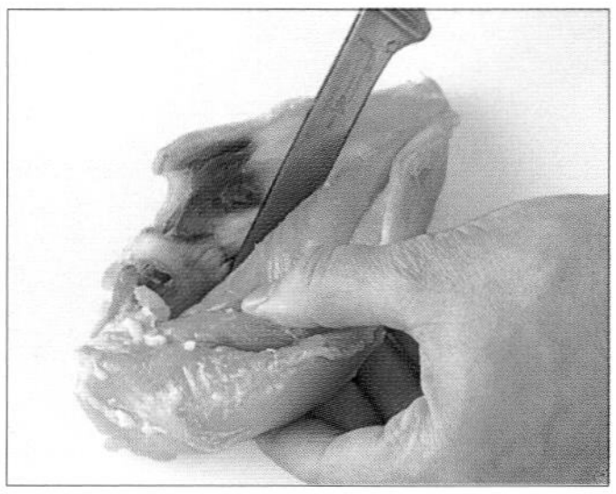

2 Turn the breast over and cut away the rib cage. Remove the tendons from the breast (see below).

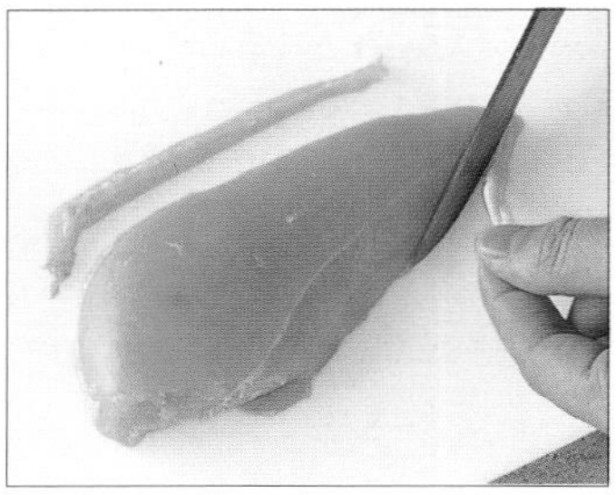

3 Turn the breast over, skinned-side up, and trim away fat and rough edges. The suprême is now ready.

Preparing Poultry & Game Livers

Poultry livers and those of some fresh game birds can be gently sautéed and served on toast or with dressed salad leaves; they are also very good in pâtés and terrines.

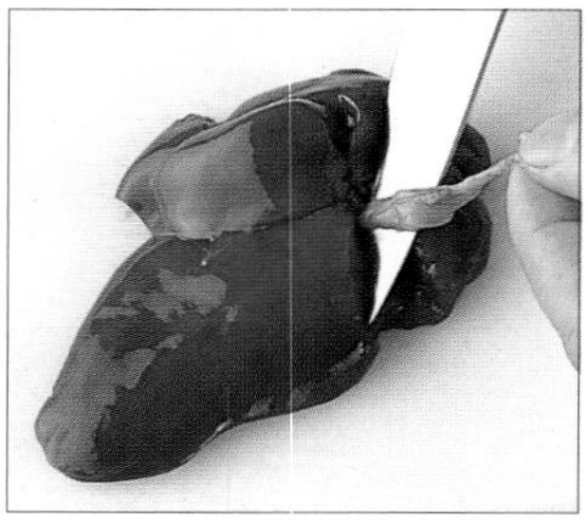

Poultry livers consist of smooth lobes surrounded by membranes and sinews. Trim the livers, removing all tubes, membrane and fine, stringy sinews that would be unpleasant in the mouth. Remove the gall bladder and cut away any dark brown or yellowish patches around it.

Removing the Tendons

There are two tendons in a chicken breast, one in the small fillet and one in the main breast. Removing them is not essential, but it does make for easier slicing and eating. In step 2, the main sinew is removed prior to slicing strips for stir-frying.

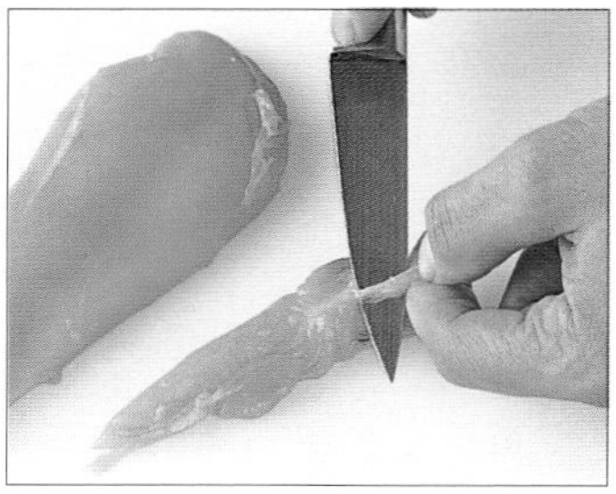

1 Pull away the small fillet. Cut out the tendon with a chef's knife.

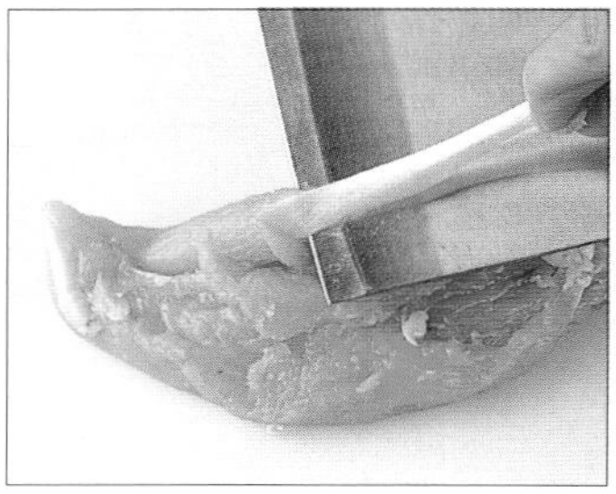

2 Cut away the tendon from the breast, using a cleaver or chef's knife.

Making Escalopes

A chicken breast provides two escalopes, a turkey breast, three or more. Escalopes can be pan-fried plain or coated (see page 108), chargrilled (see page 109), or made into pinwheels (see page 111).

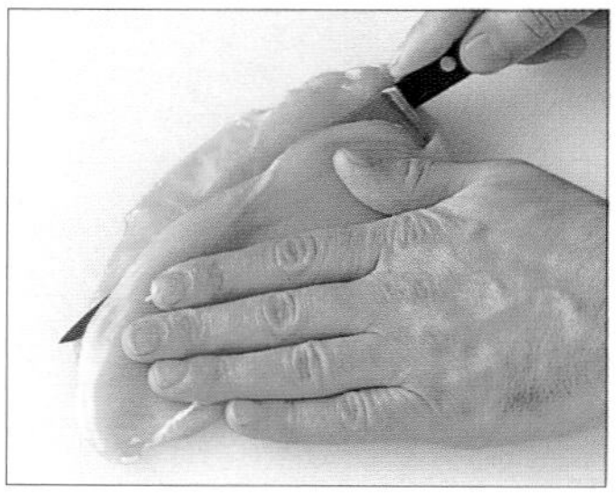

1 Remove the skin and tendons (see above). Split in half horizontally with a knife.

2 Place each piece of chicken between two sheets of baking parchment. Pound all over with a rolling pin until flattened.

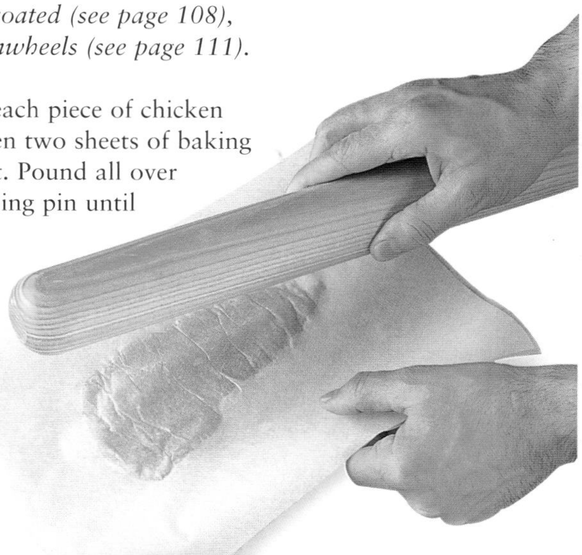

Cutting Poultry for Stir-frying

Poultry meat is ideal for stir-frying because it cooks rapidly, quickly becomes tender and marries well with the strong flavours of Asian cooking. Skinless, boneless breast of chicken, turkey and duck are most often used, and the strips marinated to heighten flavour. For the technique of stir-frying poultry, see page 109.

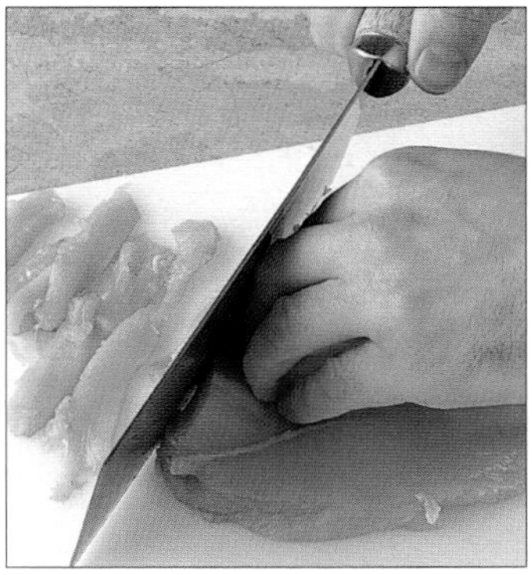

Trim the breasts of any fat and remove the tendons (see opposite page). Put the breasts between two sheets of baking parchment and pound with the flat side of a cleaver. Remove the paper and thinly slice the breasts, working diagonally across the grain of the meat (see box, right).

GOING AGAINST THE GRAIN

Meat that is cut "cross-grain" as the Chinese call it, has three advantages: a greater cut surface area is exposed to the heat making cooking very quick; long fibres are cut which makes the flesh more tender; and the strips hold their shape during cooking.

Preparing Thigh Meat for Kebabs

Thigh meat is good for kebabs as it is firmer than breast. A marinade adds flavour and moisture – soaked at least an hour before cooking, preferably overnight. Another trick is to leave the skin on for cooking, then remove it just before serving.

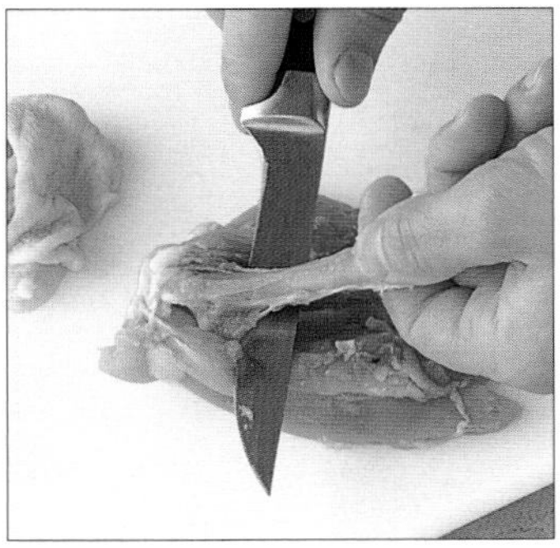

1 Remove the skin. Cut the flesh from one end of the thigh bone. Lift the bone and scrape away the flesh. Cut the bone from the meat.

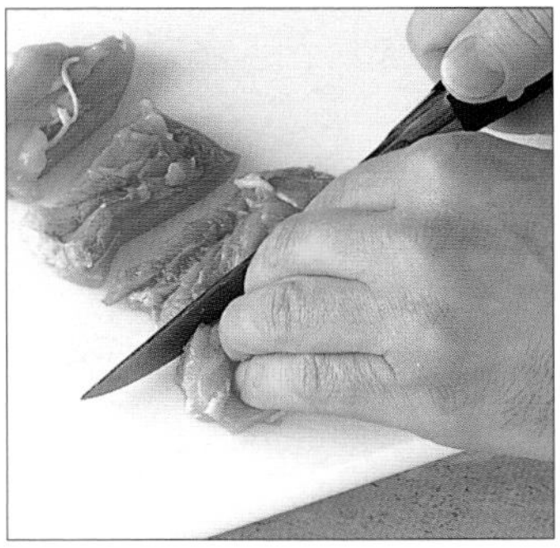

2 Cut the thigh into large pieces, across the grain of the meat. Cut away any sinew or bone that may be attached to the meat.

3 Marinate the meat if you like, then fold the pieces in half and thread on to skewers. Alternate the meat with cubed or sliced vegetables, to add colour and make the meat go further.

Preparing a Whole Breast of Duck

The breasts are the best part of the duck. They are long, thick, meaty and boneless, and can be pan-fried, roasted, grilled or chargrilled whole and carved crosswise into neat, elegant slices to serve. The french word magret *is used to describe any duck breast, although it originally only related to Barbary duck. Breasts can be cut from a whole duck (before it is jointed) using a boning knife, or can be bought ready-cut. They are not usually skinned.*

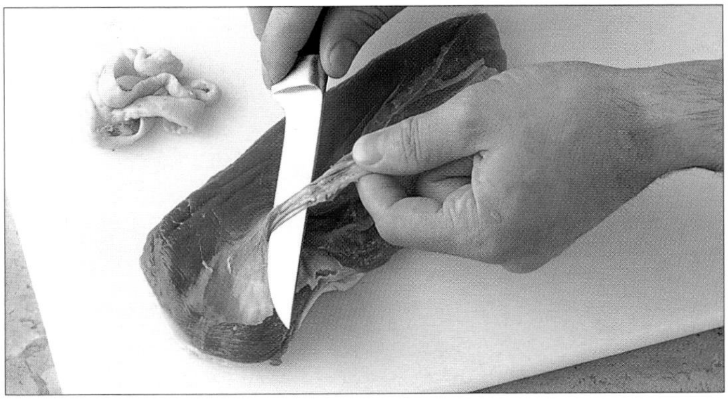

1 Trim away the rough edges of skin from the duck breast. Turn the breast on to its skin and trim away the tendon from the flesh with a boning knife.

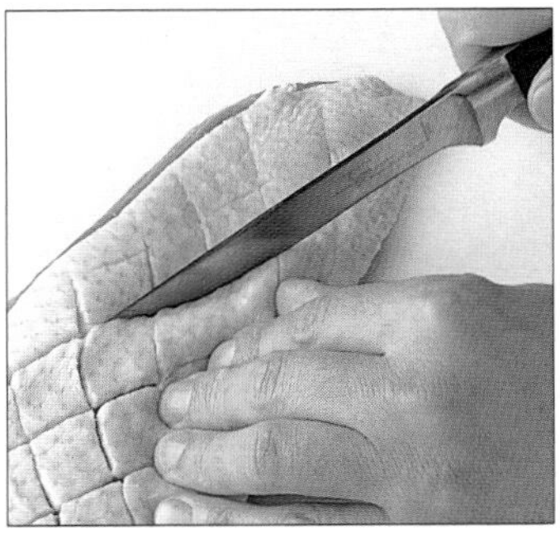

2 Score a diamond pattern in the skin. This makes it more attractive for serving, and helps release fat during cooking (see page 108).

MAKING A BALLOTINE

The word ballotine comes from the French *ballot*, meaning bundle, a neat parcel of stuffing encased in lean, boneless poultry meat. Here, a whole bird is boned and then stuffed with a forcemeat mixture. Poultry breast meat or truffles are sometimes included in stuffings for ballotines, so too are whole or chopped nuts or stoned olives.

FORCEMEAT STUFFING

350 g skinless boneless chicken breasts, cut into pieces
60 g fresh breadcrumbs
2 tbsp milk
1 tbsp butter
1 shallot, chopped
1 garlic clove, chopped
1 egg white
1 tbsp mixed fresh thyme and tarragon, chopped
Salt and freshly ground pepper

Mince the chicken in a food processor or mincer and place in a bowl. Soak the breadcrumbs in the milk until it has been absorbed, then squeeze out the excess milk and add the bread to the chicken. Melt the butter in a pan and sauté the shallot and garlic until softened, about 5 minutes. Let cool, then add to the chicken and breadcrumbs and mix well. Bind the mixture with the egg white and then add the chopped herbs and salt and pepper to taste. Makes enough stuffing for a 1.25 kg bird.

BONING THE BIRD

Ballotines are usually made with duck, turkey or, as here, chicken, but game birds such as pheasant or grouse are also suitable. You can ask your butcher to bone the bird for you, or do it yourself following the techniques shown here. Reserve the carcass for stock (see page 16). A ballotine is almost always served cold, so start making it the day before you wish to serve it to allow time for the meat to settle and cool after cooking.

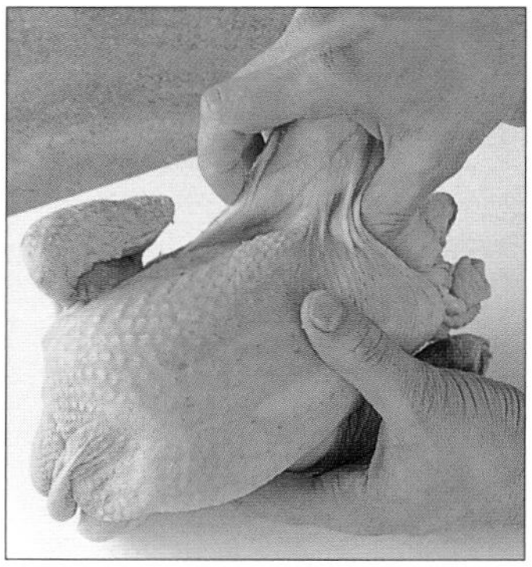

1 Dislocate each leg by breaking it at the thigh joint. Carefully remove the wishbone with a boning knife (see page 90).

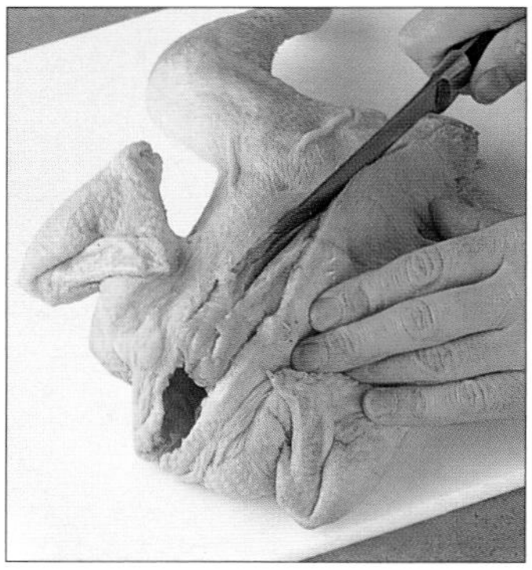

2 With the bird breast-side down on the cutting board, cut down the centre of the backbone from the neck to the tail end.

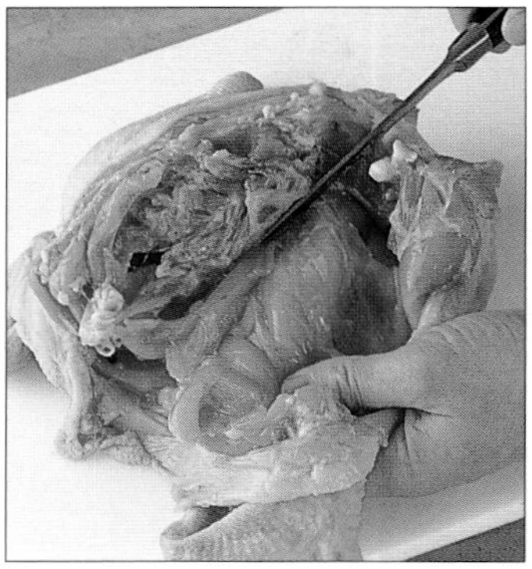

3 Working from the front of the bird to the back, carefully scrape away the flesh on one side of the backbone, cutting into the bird to expose the ribcage.

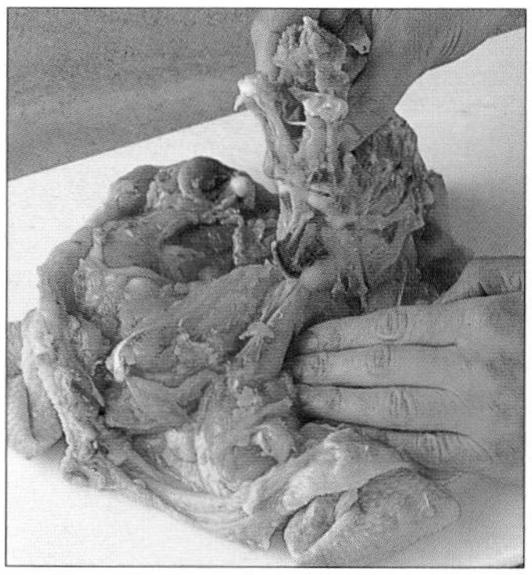

4 Repeat on the other side of the backbone, being careful not to pierce the breast skin with the knife. Pull the rib and backbone from the flesh of the bird.

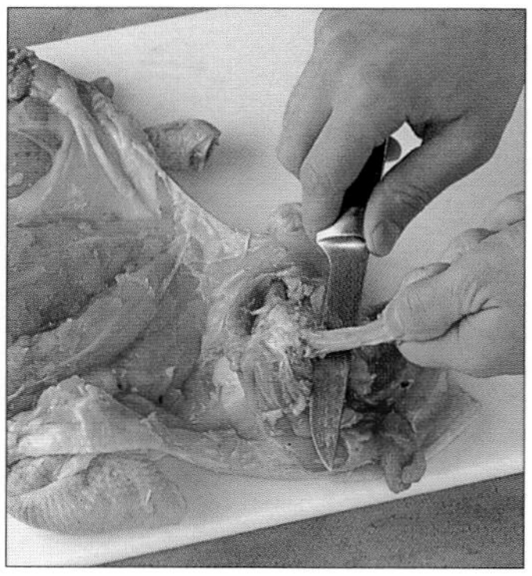

5 Scrape away the flesh from each thigh bone and cut away the bone at the joint with a knife or poultry shears. Scrape all the flesh away from the wings up to the first joint.

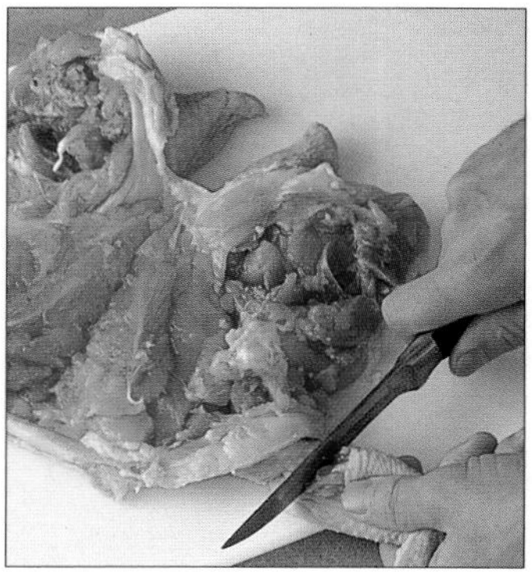

6 Remove the exposed wing bone by cutting away the rest of the wing at the joint. Cut away the tendon from each fillet and breast. The chicken is now ready for stuffing and rolling.

STUFFING AND ROLLING

After careful boning and stuffing, the bird is rolled into a neat sausage shape, wrapped in baking parchment, and foil, then tied securely with string. This holds the meat and stuffing tightly and makes a neat shape for easy slicing.

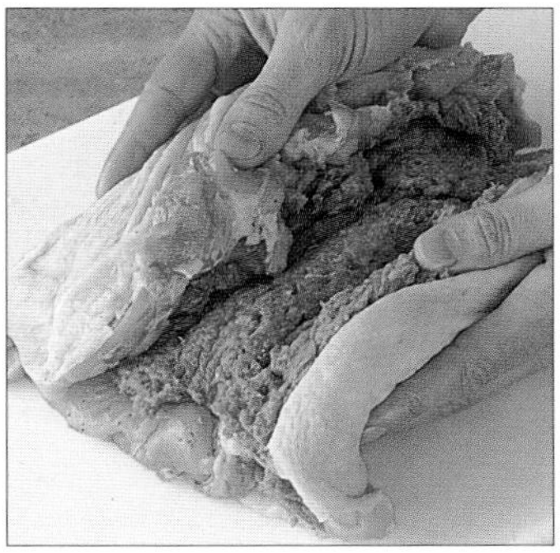

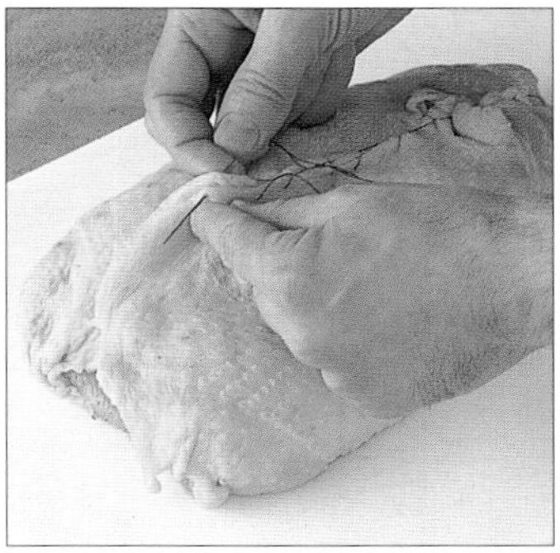

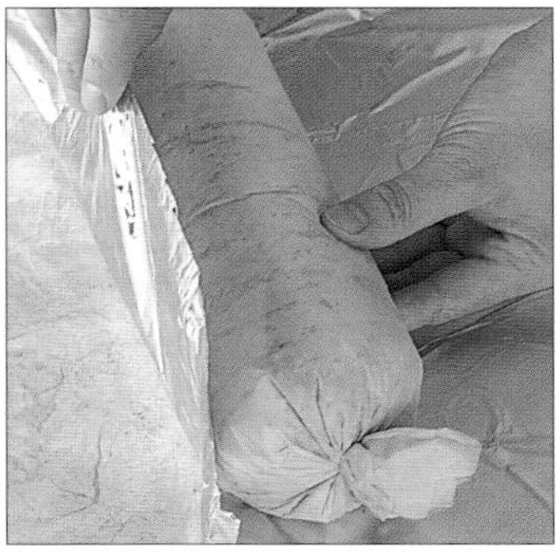

1 Season the inside of the whole boned bird with salt and pepper. Spread the stuffing (see page 96) evenly over the inside of the bird and pull up the sides of the bird to cover the stuffing.

2 Stitch the bird closed from the tail to neck end with a trussing needle (see page 91) and thread. Season the outside of the bird by rubbing the skin with salt and pepper.

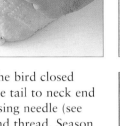

3 Dampen a large piece of baking parchment with water. Place the stuffed bird parallel to one long end of the paper, and roll the paper tightly around it, to make a cylinder. Twist the ends to seal. Place the wrapped bird on a large piece of foil and roll up in a similar way.

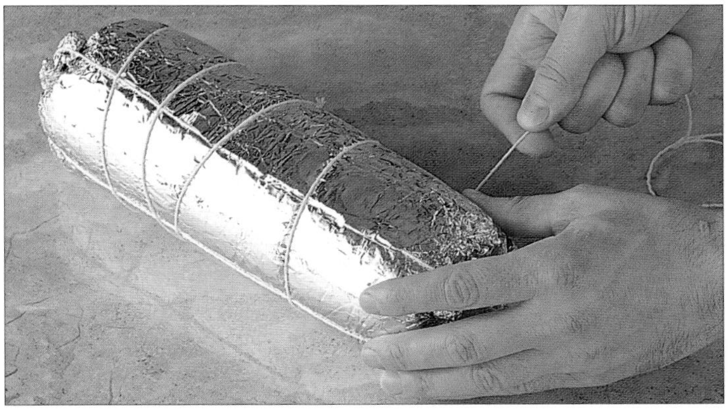

4 Cut a piece of kitchen string about 1 metre long. Wrap the string first around the length of the cylinder, then several times around its width at regular intervals, securing the ends of the string with double knots.

POACHING AND SLICING

Ballotines are usually poached very slowly in water, stock or another flavoured liquid, then left overnight and served cold. Cooling the meat in its wrapping allows it to set in the cylinder shape and as a result makes slicing easier. Ballotines can also be braised on a bed of vegetables, in which case they are rolled and tied but left unwrapped and generally served hot.

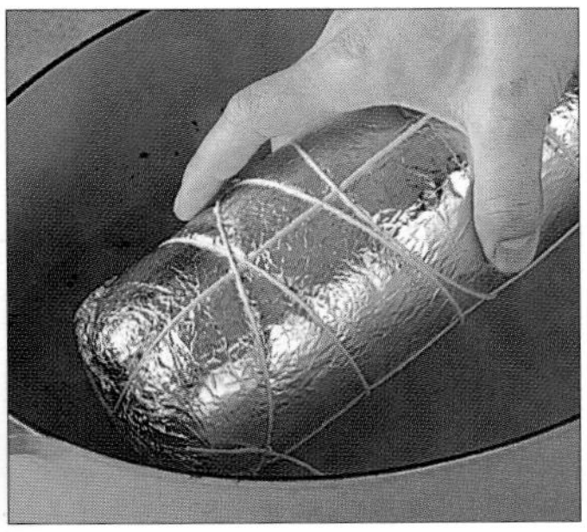

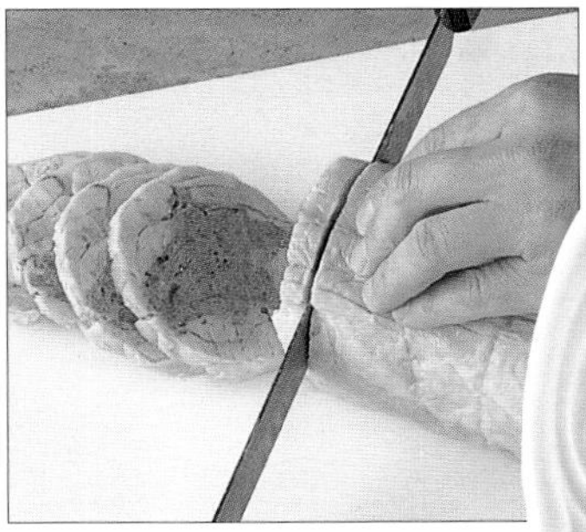

1 Weigh the ballotine and calculate the cooking time, allowing 20 minutes per 450 g. Place in a pan, cover with stock and weight it down if necessary. Bring to the boil, then lower heat and poach for the calculated time.

2 Let the ballotine cool in the liquid. Lift out of the pan, cut string and unwrap. Snip one end of the thread and pull it out. Slice the ballotine and serve cold, with a garnish of your choice (see page 115).

Cailles Rôties Farcies Madame Brassart

This wonderfully rich dish of stuffed quails is named after the founder of Le Cordon Bleu, Madame Brassart. Boned quails, filled with a mixture of wild rice, foie gras and ceps, are roasted and served with two sauces.

SERVES 4

4 quails

Goose fat or a mixture of butter and oil

Salt and freshly ground pepper

FOR THE STUFFING

90 g wild rice

300 ml chicken stock

100 g foie gras, cut into small cubes

150 g fresh ceps, cleaned and finely chopped

2 shallots, finely chopped

30 g mixed fresh herbs (parsley, chervil, basil), chopped

1–2 tbsp port or cognac

Pinch of quatre-épices or ground mixed spice

Fresh parsley and rosemary, to garnish

Bone the quails whole (see box, below). Roast the carcasses at 200°C for 10 minutes, then use the bones to flavour the port sauce (see box, right).

Make the stuffing: simmer the rice in the stock for 30–40 minutes, until tender and set aside. Season the foie gras with salt and pepper and sauté in a hot frying pan until the cubes are sealed on all sides. Add to the rice.

Heat 1 tbsp goose fat in the frying pan and sauté the ceps until wilted. Add the shallots and herbs and sauté until the shallots are soft. Reserve a few ceps for garnish; add the rest to the rice with the port and spice. Check seasoning and let cool.

Season inside the quails; fill them loosely with stuffing and truss. Heat 3 tbsp goose fat in a roasting tin, and brown the quails on all sides. Roast the quails at 200°C for 15-20 minutes, basting occasionally. Remove from the oven and arrange the birds on a platter.

Reheat the port sauce and spoon some sauce around the quails. Garnish with parsley, rosemary and the reserved ceps. Serve crème d'ail (see box, below left) and remaining sauce separately.

PORT SAUCE

200 g shallots, sliced
60 g butter
4 roasted quail carcasses
50 ml sherry vinegar
250 ml port
750 ml chicken stock
1 sprig of fresh thyme

Sweat the shallots in butter. Add the carcasses and vinegar and boil until almost evaporated. Stir in the port and reduce by half, then add the stock and thyme and simmer for 20 minutes. Strain and season to taste.

CREME D'AIL

12 garlic cloves, peeled
200 ml double cream

Blanch garlic cloves, drain and refresh. Put in a pan with cream. Cook for 10 minutes until garlic is soft. Continue cooking until reduced by half, then purée in a blender. If too thick, thin with chicken stock. Check seasoning.

Boning a Quail Whole

This clever technique removes the carcass from a tiny bird so that the bird is left whole with its skin intact. When the bird is stuffed, it therefore retains its shape. Because quails are so tiny, use a small pointed knife and your fingertips.

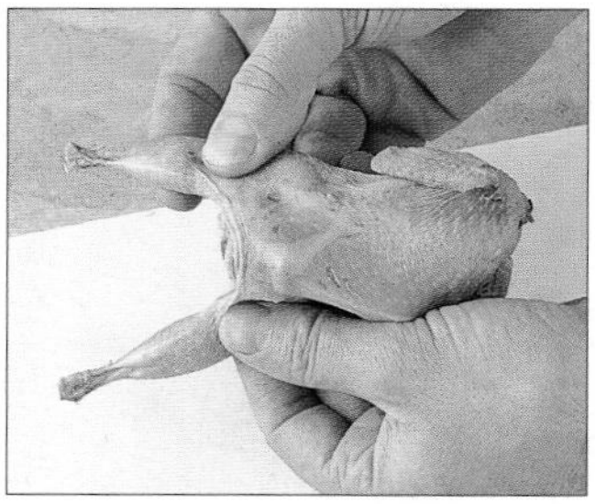

Remove the wishbone (see page 90). Loosen the leg bones from the carcass. Cut the wings from the carcass.

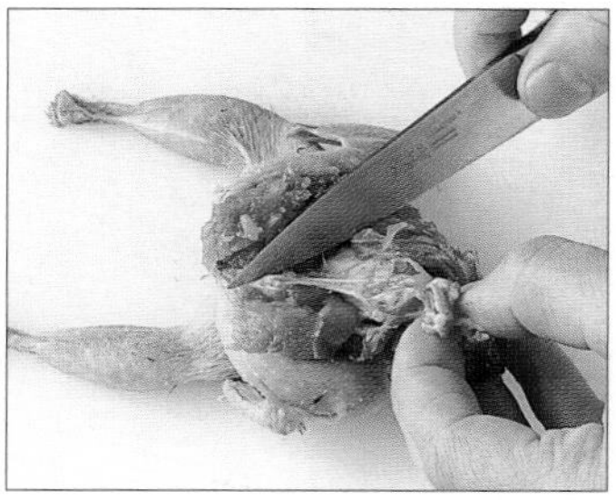

Insert a small knife between the rib cage and the flesh and scrape all around to free the flesh from the carcass.

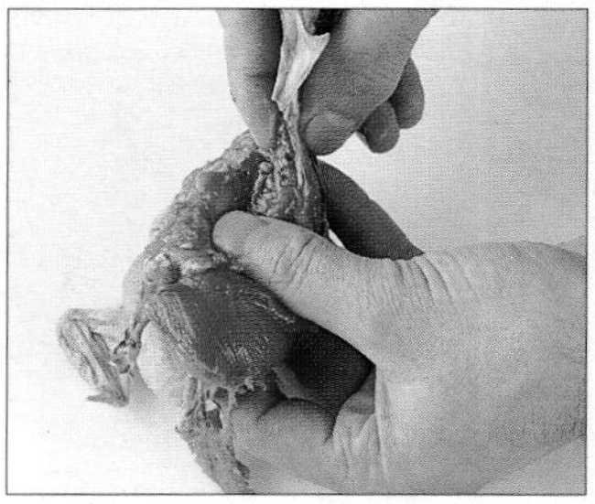

When the carcass is free, pull it out with your fingers and roast the bones for using in the port sauce.

Roasting Birds

Use a roasting tin that is only a little larger than the bird and cook on a rack or a bed of vegetables to prevent it from being fried underneath. Cover large birds halfway through cooking to prevent overbrowning.

Roasting Times

The following roasting times are approximate, so test for doneness (see page 101) to be absolutely sure the bird is properly cooked. Before cooking, weigh the bird and calculate the total cooking time.

- CAPON
  190°C for 25 mins per 450 g
- CHICKEN
  200°C for 18 mins per 450 g plus an extra 18 mins
- GUINEA FOWL
  200°C for 15 mins per 450 g plus an extra 15 mins
- POUSSIN
  200°C for 25–40 mins
- TURKEY
  180°C for 20 mins per 450 g under 4.5 kg
  16–18 mins per 450 g over 4.5 kg

Roasting a Whole Bird

*Poultry and game birds have little natural fat, so to make sure the meat stays moist during roasting place fat on the skin before placing in the oven. Butter gives a good flavour and blends with sediment in the tin to make rich-tasting juices (*jus *in French) or gravy (see opposite page).*

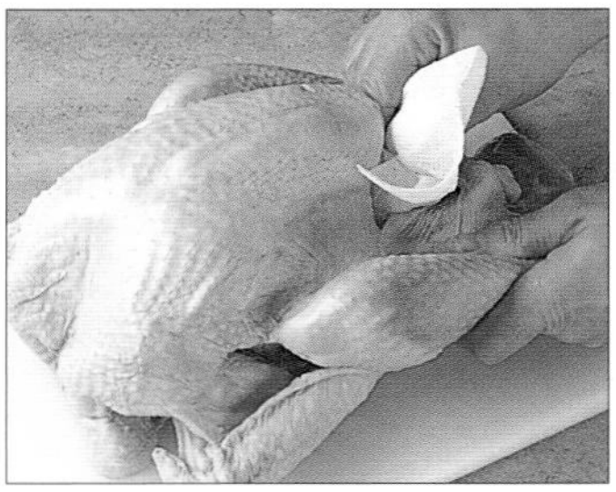

1 Wipe the bird inside and out with paper towels. Season the cavity and insert flavourings (see below, right).

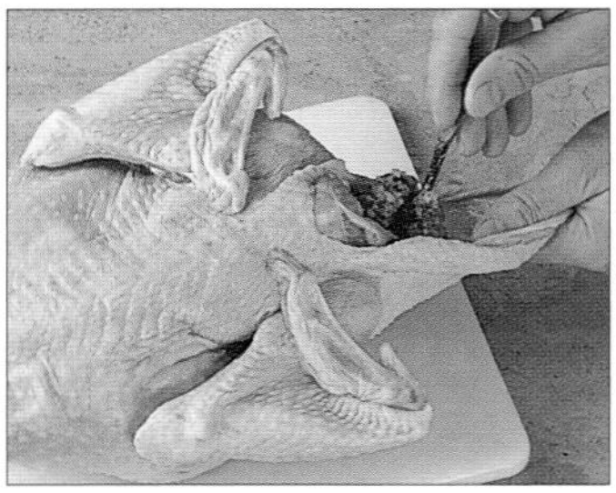

2 With the bird breast-side down, season the neck end and spoon in stuffing if you like (see below left).

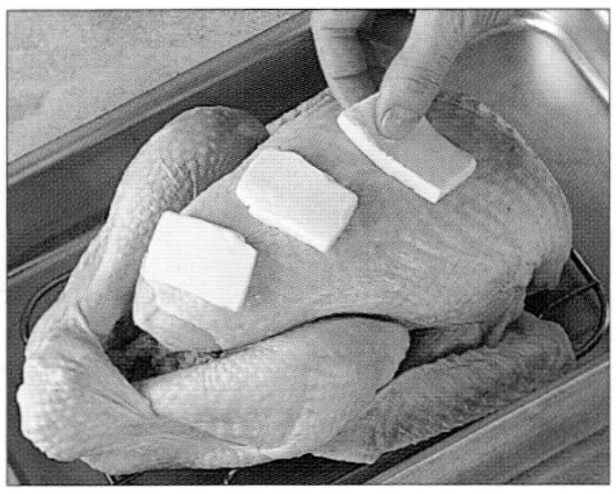

3 Tuck drumsticks under tail skin, put the bird on a rack in tin. Cover the breast generously with butter.

4 Roast the bird (see chart, left), basting frequently. Start cooking the bird on one of its sides for 15–20 minutes then turn it over and cook on the other side for the same length of time. Turn breast-side up for the remainder of the roasting time.

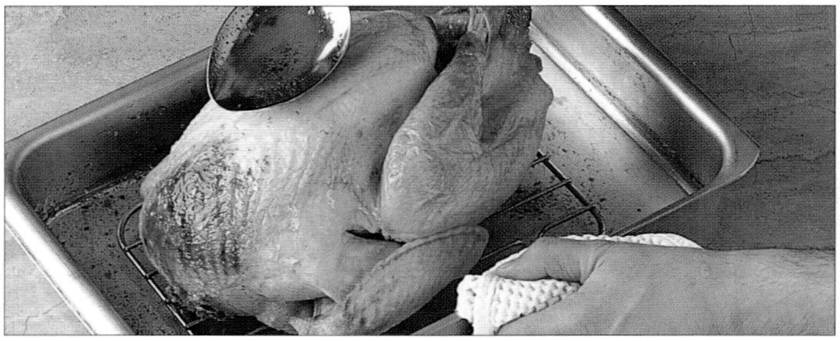

Stuffings for Poultry

Sausagemeat, breadcrumbs and cooked rice are all good stuffing bases. Add seasonings and, for different textures, nuts and dried fruit. Prepare about 225 g for a 2.25 kg bird and chill for at least 2 hours. Loosely stuff the neck end. Stuffing the body cavity can prevent heat from penetrating the centre and is not recommended for large birds. Stuff the bird shortly before you roast it, letting it come to room temperature to ensure even cooking.

For a tasty meaty stuffing, mix sausagemeat, chopped onion, nuts, parsley, raisins, apricots and breadcrumbs. Bind with egg and season.

Keeping Poultry Moist

When roasting any bird, but especially the drier kind like turkey and pheasant, it is important to keep the meat as moist as possible. Placing softened butter under the skin can help, or you can cover the bird loosely with buttered paper or foil. To brown the skin, remove the paper or foil for the last 20–30 minutes of cooking time. You can also cover the breast with streaky bacon (see page 103) or with back fat, as the French do.

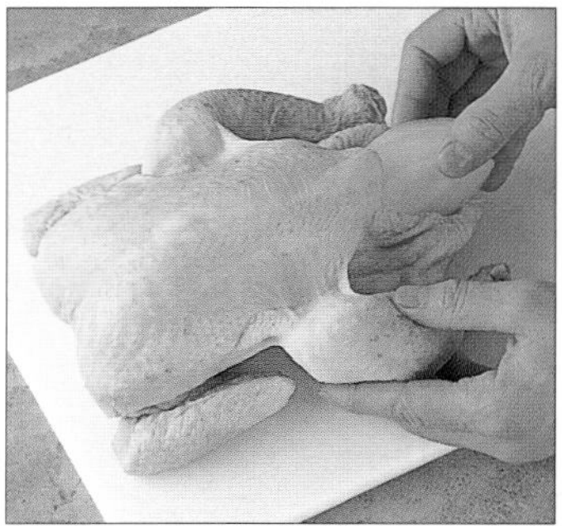

Another method to help keep a bird moist during roasting is to insert half an onion or a lemon wedge inside the cavity of the bird before roasting.

Testing for Doneness

After roasting a bird for the recommended time, always check it is properly cooked.

Hold the bird above the tin. If the juices run clear, not pink, it is fully cooked.

Cutting Up a Roasted Bird

Before cutting up small and medium-sized birds, let them rest for about 15 minutes under a loose tent of foil so the meat can relax and the juices settle. This will make carving easier. After resting, remove any trussing string and cut up the bird using a large chef's knife or carving knife. A two-pronged fork can be used to steady the bird.

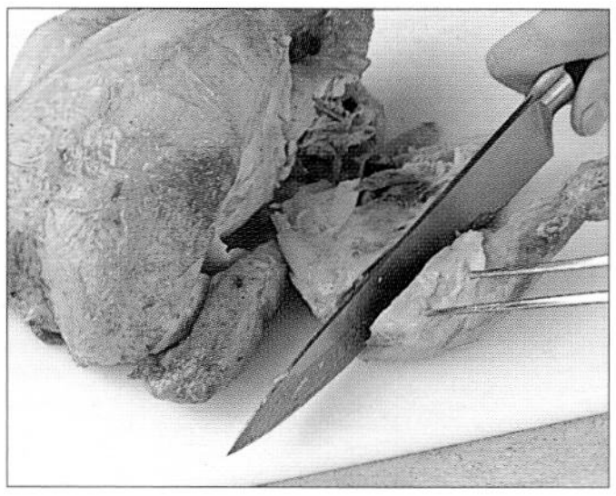

1 Place the bird breast-side up. Cut each leg from the bird and then in half to separate the drumstick and thigh, following the line of white fat on the underside.

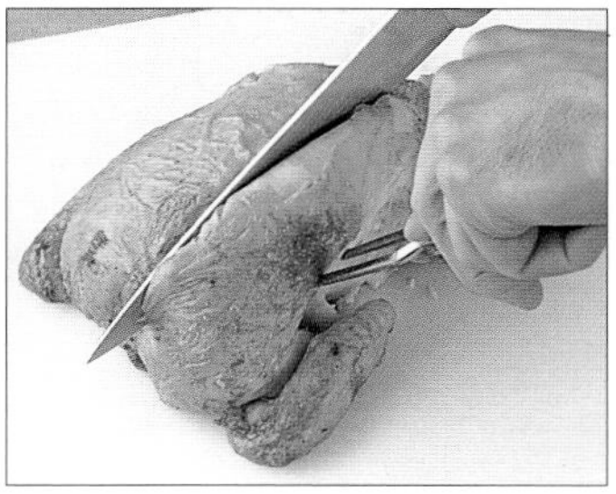

2 Hold the bird steady on the cutting board with a two-pronged fork. Carefully cut the breast in half by splitting the soft breastbone and backbone.

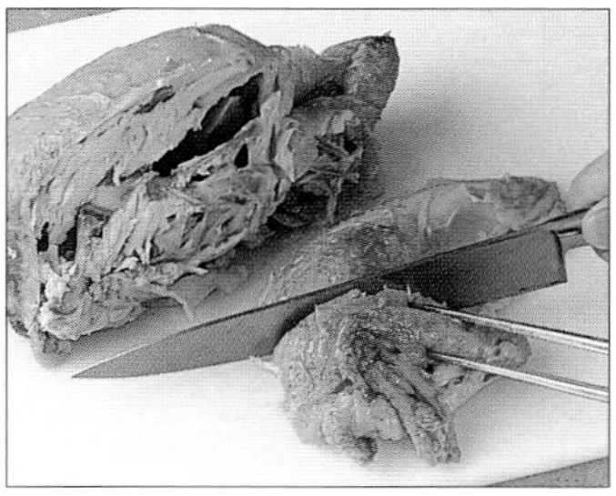

3 Cut each breast piece in half diagonally, leaving a good part of the breast meat attached to the wing. Arrange the pieces on a warmed serving platter.

Carving a Roasted Bird

Turkeys and large chickens are best served with their meat carved into neat slices. Before carving let the bird rest, as above, then snip away any trussing string and then carve. The dark meat can also be sliced from the drumstick, if you like.

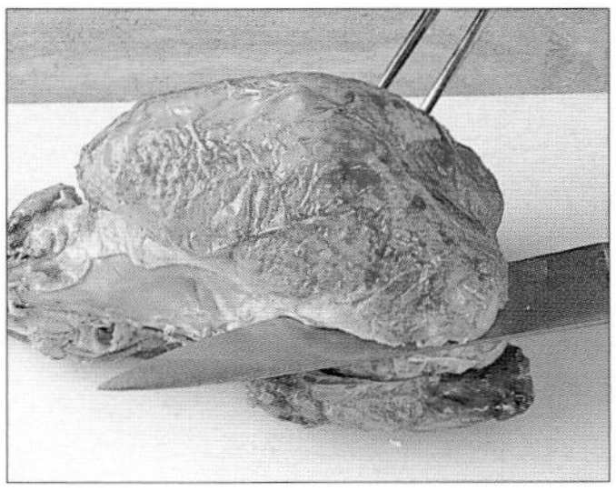

1 Remove the legs, cut them in half and transfer to a warmed platter. Hold the bird steady with a fork and make a horizontal cut into the breast above the wing, cutting all the way to the bone.

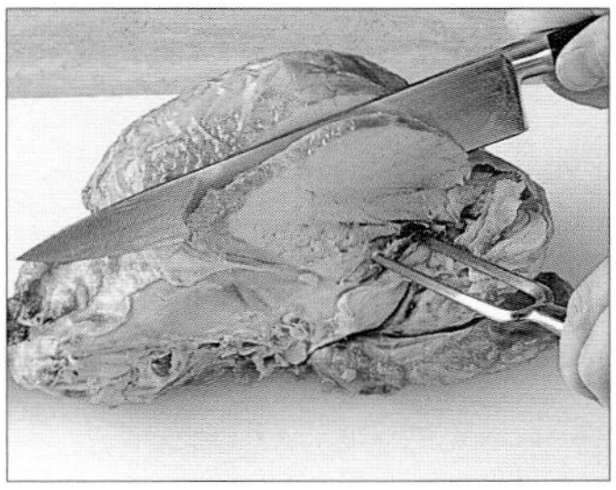

2 Carve neat, even slices from the breast, holding the knife parallel to the ribcage. Repeat on the other side.

3 Arrange the slices of white meat, overlapping, on the platter with the drumsticks and thighs.

Making Gravy

In France the juices (jus) *from the tin are served with the bird; here they are thickened to make gravy.*

Remove the bird from the tin and pour off all but about 1 tbsp fat. Put the tin over a low heat, sprinkle in 1 tbsp plain flour and stir well.

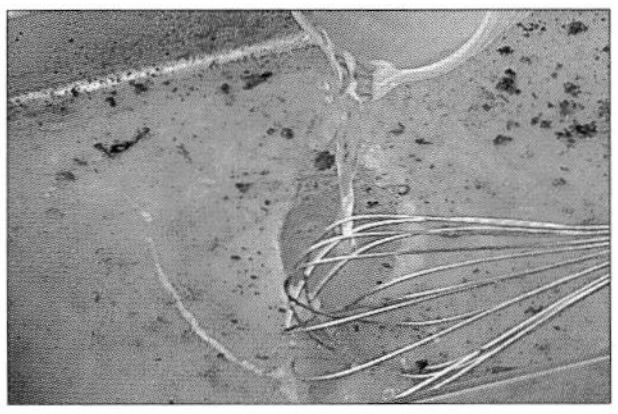

Gradually whisk in 500 ml hot stock or water. Increase the heat and bring to the boil. Simmer, whisking, for 1–2 minutes. Check seasoning. Serves 6–8.

ROASTING TIMES

- DUCK
  180°C for 30 mins per 450 g
- GOOSE
  200°C for 15 mins per 450 g plus 15 mins
- GROUSE
  200°C for 35 mins
- PARTRIDGE
  200°C for 40 mins
- PHEASANT
  230°C for 10 mins, then 200°C for 30 mins
- QUAIL
  190°C for 15–20 mins

Preparing a Fatty Bird for Roasting

When roasting a fatty bird such as a duck (shown here) or goose, remove as much fat as possible beforehand and place the bird on a rack so that it does not sit in melted fat during roasting. Cooking times are given in the chart, left.

1 With bird breast-side up, cut away excess fat from tail and tail cavity. Remove the wishbone (see page 90).

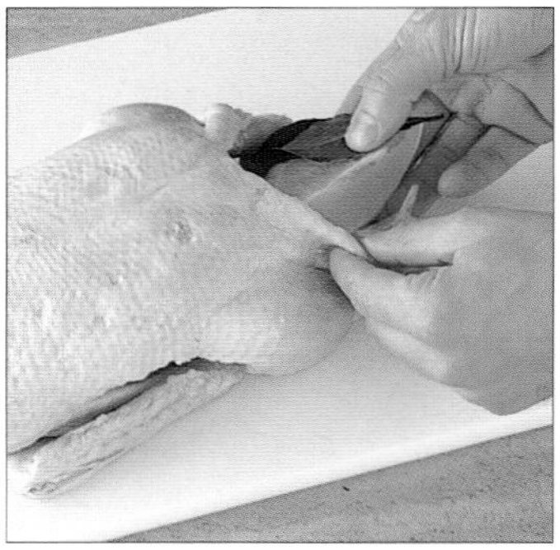

2 Season inside the tail cavity with salt and pepper, then insert 1–2 bay leaves and a wedge of orange.

3 Place the bird breast-side up on a rack in a roasting tin. Pierce the bird all over with a metal skewer.

Roasting and Carving Duck

Weight for weight, duck serves less people than chicken but, because of its rich flavour, portions can be smaller. Small roast ducks are difficult to carve; they are best cut into four pieces as for an uncooked bird (see page 92).

1 Roast the bird (see chart, above left) first on one of its sides, then on the other. Turn it breast-side up for the remainder of the time until the juices from the thickest part of a leg run clear. Let the duck rest, loosely covered with foil, for 15 minutes.

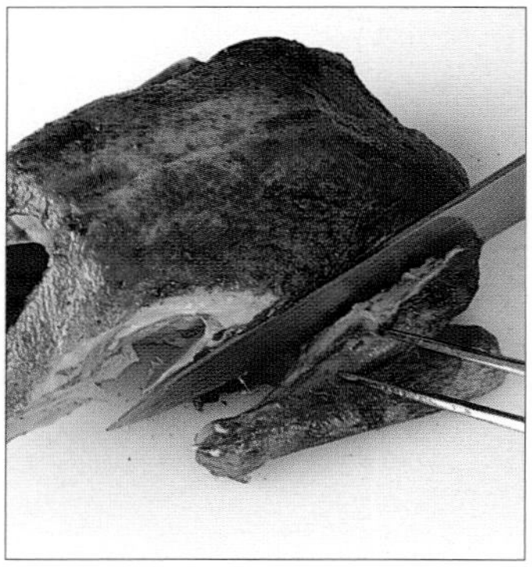

2 Place the duck breast-side up and cut the legs from the bird with a large chef's knife or carving knife. Cut down through the thigh joints, to separate the legs from the body. Cut each wing away from the body of the duck at the shoulder joint.

3 On the main body of the bird, cut away one side of the breast meat in slices, moving inwards towards the breastbone. Repeat on the other side of the breast. Arrange the sliced breast, legs and wings on a warmed serving platter.

Preparing and Roasting a Game Bird

The meat of young game birds is very lean and therefore tends to dry out easily during roasting. Barding the bird with fatty bacon helps make the flesh moist and flavoursome. A simple recipe for roast pheasant, using the techniques shown here, is given in the box, right.

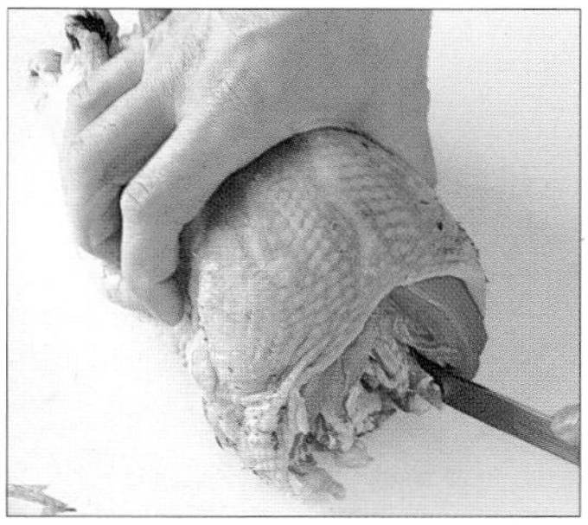

1 Remove the wishbone (see page 90) before roasting so that the breast of the bird will be easy to carve.

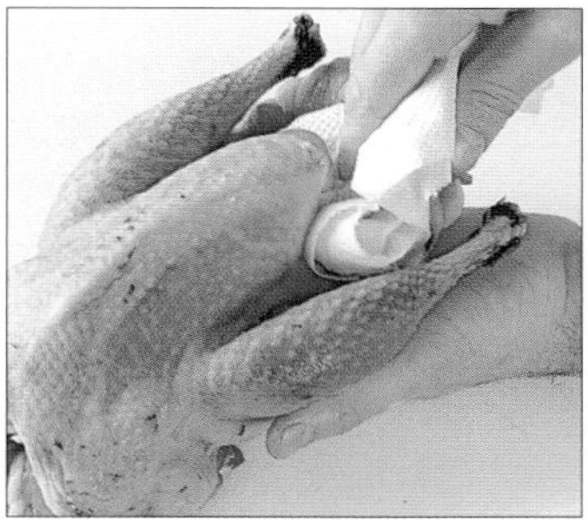

2 Trim the wings by cutting through the second joint. Rinse the cavity, then wipe dry with paper towels. Truss the bird (see page 90).

3 Season the skin if you like, then cover loosely with bacon rashers around the breast and thighs.

4 Roast the bird (see chart, opposite page) until the juices from the thickest part of a leg run clear, and the tip of a knife feels warm to the touch when withdrawn. Leave to rest, covered loosely with foil, for 10–15 minutes before carving.

Roast Pheasant with Wine Gravy

1 kg pheasant
Salt and freshly ground pepper
3–4 streaky bacon rashers
2 tsp plain flour
300 ml red wine

Prepare the pheasant for roasting (see steps 1–3, left), then place on a rack in a roasting tin. Roast at 230°C for 10 minutes, then at 200°C for 30 minutes.

Remove the bird, cover loosely with foil and let rest for 10–15 minutes. Place the tin on top of the stove. Sprinkle in the flour, stir over a low heat for 2 minutes, then gradually whisk in the wine. Increase the heat and bring to the boil, then simmer, whisking, until thickened. Check seasoning. Serve the pheasant hot, with the gravy and accompaniments (see box, below). Serves 2.

Accompaniments for Game Birds

There are many traditional accompaniments for game birds, and these are given in the box on page 104. Here are some additional ideas that can be used as well, to highlight the texture and flavour of the bird.

- Glazed carrot bâtons.
- Roast parsnips.
- Bunches of fragrant fresh herbs.
- Garlic flowers (see page 189).
- Watercress bundles.
- Braised sliced red cabbage, onion and apple with port.

Finishing Touches

Use fruit and vegetables to complement the rich flavours of poultry and game dishes, as well as adding visual appeal to the presentation. Saucy dishes, such as casseroles and stews, are best served with croûtes (see page 246), which will absorb the flavourful juices.

Classic Garnishes for Game

Wild game is available during limited seasons, making it ideal for special occasions. These are the traditional accompaniments:

Fried straw potatoes: Very thin sticks of potato, called *pommes pailles* in French (see page 169), deep-fried until crisp.
Fried breadcrumbs: An English garnish (see page 246).
Croutes: Can be fried or toasted (see page 246). For extra flavour, spread croûtes with smooth liver pâté before topping with small birds, such as woodcock or grouse
Bread sauce: An English sauce made with bread, butter, cream, onions, milk and seasonings.
Cumberland sauce: A fruity sauce made of redcurrant jelly, port, orange and lemon zest and juice, traditonally spiked with cinnamon or ginger and mustard.

Turned mushrooms
Trim stalk. Cut channels from centre of cap to edge. Use the knife tip to shape the top into a star.

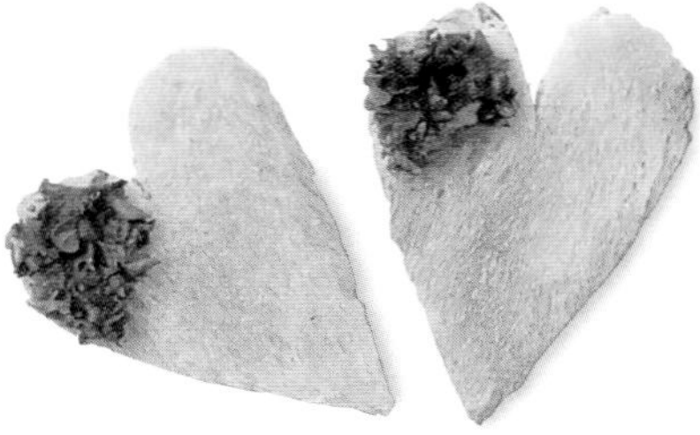

Herby hearts
Brush corners of heart-shaped croûtes (see page 246) with water and press very finely chopped parsley on to them.

Gherkin fans
Make thin lengthwise cuts in gherkins, leaving stalk ends intact. Fan out by pressing with your finger.

Pepper twists
Make two parallel cuts in a square of pepper, leaving opposite ends of the two cuts intact. Lift cut ends and twist.

Tomato roses
Cut a long and continuous strip of of tomato skin in a spiral with a sharp knife. Roll up to form a rose.

Cucumber chevrons
Quarter cucumber lengthwise; cut into chunks. Cut two V-shaped wedges in flesh, one deeper than the other; fan out.

Carrot blossoms
Cut lengthwise grooves in a carrot. Make angled cuts around end. Twist off; repeat. Fill each with a pepper dot.

Vegetable bundles
Tie steamed asparagus tips together in bundles with a long strip of blanched and refreshed leek skin.

Hot berries
Place halved strawberries and whole raspberries on a baking sheet and grill until lightly browned, 2–3 minutes.

Glazed apples
Sprinkle unpeeled yellow apple slices with caster sugar, then grill until golden and bubbling, 2–3 minutes.

CHICORY BOATS
Separate chicory into leaves and spoon a little *concassée* of tomatoes (see page 178) into the base of each leaf.

BITTER SHREDS
Use a sharp knife to cut purple chicory into fine strips. Or, as an alternative, use vibrant red radicchio.

FRIED FLOWERS
Deep-fry dry courgette flowers in 180°C oil until lightly browned, 15 seconds. Remove and drain on paper towels.

CARAMELIZED ORANGES
Briefly cook orange slices in a light caramel (see page 281) until caramelized. Remove and garnish with parsley.

NUTTY FIGS
Make fig flowers (see page 263) and fill each with half a walnut. Put under a hot grill for 2–3 minutes.

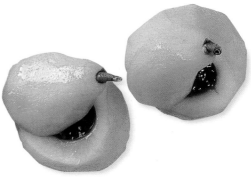

POACHED PEARS
Slice tops off poached pears at an angle. Remove core with a melon baller. Fill with redcurrant jelly. Replace tops.

CHAUDFROID DE CANARD

Prepare chaudfroid and duck slices (see page 225). Flood platter with a thin layer of chaudfroid; chill to set. Arrange orange wedges on sauce; flood and set again. Decorate the duck slices as below and arrange on the plate.

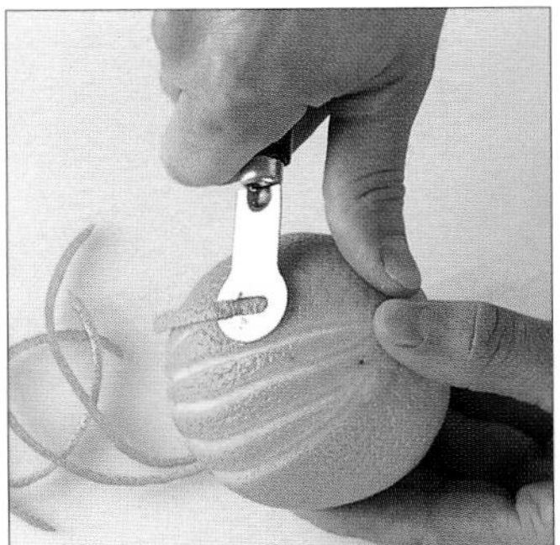

1 Cut thin strips of orange zest with a canelle knife and blanch (see page 336); refresh and dry.

2 Pipe pâté on duck. Decorate with orange zest and coat with chaudfroid.

Oriental Roast Duck

Based on Chinese tradition, a duck is often hung to dry, glazed and then roasted. Peking duck with its crispy, lacquered skin is the most famous example of this roasting method. There are various stages to the technique.

Making Chinese Seasoning Mix

An aromatic mixture of garlic, ginger, chillies and spring onions is combined with spices and herbs to impart a delicate Oriental flavour to roast duck.

Heat a wok until hot. Add 2 tsp vegetable oil and heat until hot but not smoking. Add 3 finely chopped garlic cloves, 1 tbsp crushed fresh root ginger, 2 finely chopped and seeded fresh red chillies and 2 sliced spring onions and stir-fry until fragrant and just soft, about 2 minutes. Add 2 tsp toasted and crushed Sichuan peppercorns, 2 tbsp each yellow bean sauce and soy sauce and stir-fry to mix, then remove from the heat and let cool. Stir in 2 tbsp chopped fresh coriander, just before applying to the skin of the bird to be roasted.

Preparing the Duck

Before roasting, boiling water is poured over the duck. This tightens the skin and seals the pores so that the skin will be crisp when cooked.

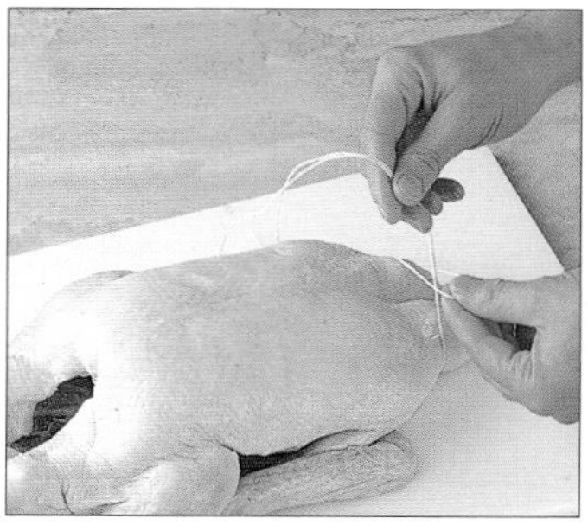

1 Trim away the excess fat from the tail end of the duck. Cut a long piece of kitchen string and tie it in a double knot around the fat at the neck end of the duck.

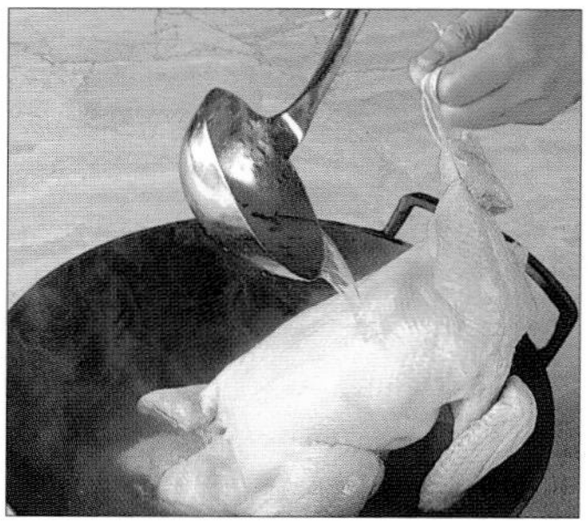

2 Bring about 2 litres water to the boil in a wok. Hold the duck in the water and ladle it over the duck until the skin becomes taut. Remove the duck and pat dry.

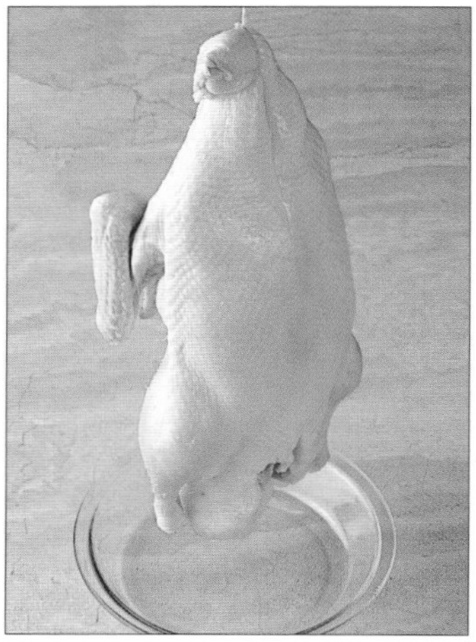

3 Hang the duck over a dish to catch the drips. Leave in a cool (10°C), airy place until the skin is dry, about 3 hours.

Roasting the Duck

Once the duck is dried, the cavity is stuffed with Chinese seasoning mix and the skin is basted with maltose mixed with water. During roasting the flesh of the bird will take on the flavour of the Chinese seasoning and the skin will become crisp and dark in colour.

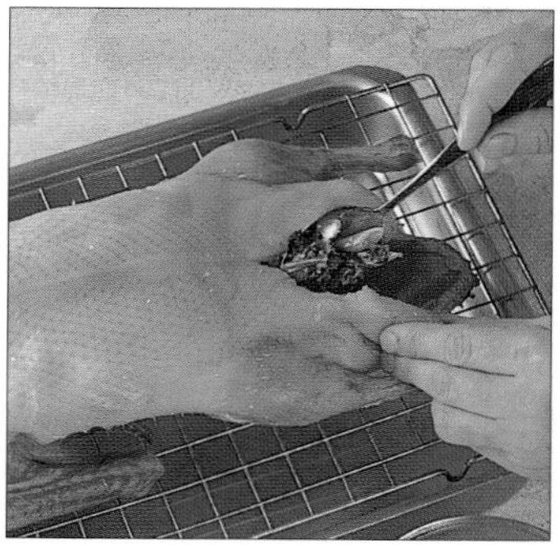

1 Soak a bamboo skewer in water for 30 minutes. Cut the string from the air-dried duck. Put the duck on a rack over a roasting tin. Spoon Chinese seasoning mix (see box, left) into the body cavity.

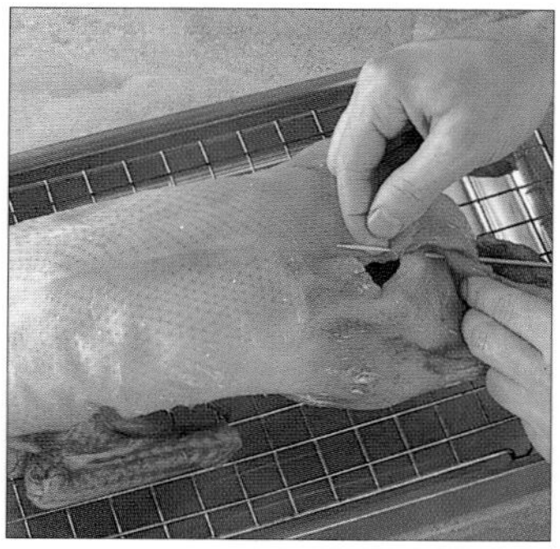

2 Thread the soaked bamboo skewer through the skin at the tail end of the duck to ensure that it remains closed while cooking. Roast the duck in a 200°C oven for 15 minutes.

3 Remove the duck from the oven and brush with maltose (see opposite page) and water. Lower the heat to 180°C and continue to roast, basting every 15 minutes, until the duck is dark brown, 1½–1¾ hours.

Carving the Duck

This is the classic Chinese method for carving roast duck. The pieces are reassembled on the serving plate in the shape of the bird. Garnish with sprigs of fresh coriander, if you like.

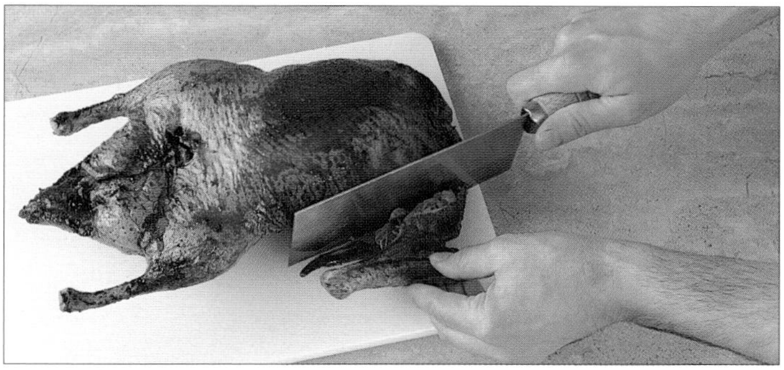

1 Let the duck rest for 15 minutes to allow the meat to retain its moisture and then place, with the breast-side up, on a cutting board. Carefully remove the bamboo skewer from the tail-flap. Cut each wing away from the body at the shoulder joint with a cleaver or large chef's knife. Cut each wing in half at the middle joint.

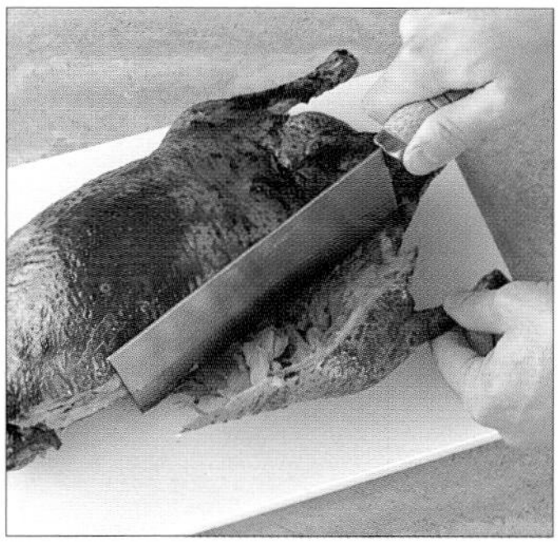

2 Remove each leg from the bird, cutting down through the thigh joint with a cleaver to separate it from the body. Cut the thigh from the drumstick at the joint between them.

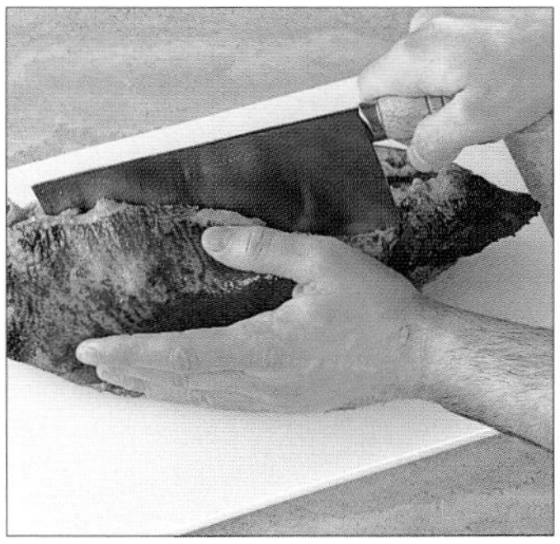

3 Turn the duck on its side and cut away the whole breast from the body, cutting through the rib bones and leaving the backbone behind. Cut the backbone and the meat still attached to it across into pieces.

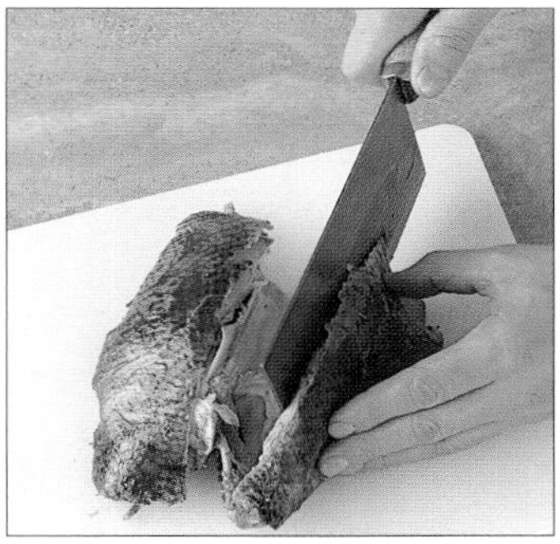

4 Cut the breast in half lengthwise, splitting the breastbone with the cleaver. The breastbone is quite soft and splits easily.

5 Cut each half-breast across into roughly equal pieces, cutting down through the breastbone.

6 Arrange the meat on a warmed platter in the shape of the duck, starting with the wings, thighs, and drumsticks. Pile the pieces of back on top, followed by the pieces of breast.

MALTOSE

This dark syrupy sugar solution is made from the fermented grains of barley, wheat or millet in a process sometimes called malting. It has been produced in China since the 2nd century BC and is commonly used in Chinese cooking for darkening the skin of roasted poultry and meat. Kept sealed, it will last indefinitely. Look for it at Oriental stores and large supermarkets.

To use it for Oriental roast duck, mix 1 tbsp maltose with 4 tbsp boiling water. If maltose is not available, you can use molasses instead.

FRYING

Pieces of poultry and game can be pan-fried, deep-fried, sautéed or stir-fried. These are all quick-cooking methods so small joints or breasts are the most suitable. The pieces can be fried plain, coated or stuffed.

PAN-FRYING A BREAST OF DUCK

Duck breasts can be "dry-fried" in their own fat and juices because they are so fatty. For successful results, trim and score the fat first (see page 95). Begin skin-side down, in a dry pan over a moderate heat, so the fat runs into the pan.

1 Season the duck breast and place skin-side down, in a frying pan. Cook for 3–5 minutes, pressing with a palette knife to extract the juices and keep the breast flat.

2 Turn the breast and cook for another 3–5 minutes (duck breast is best medium rare). Remove from the pan and let rest, covered. With the skin-side up and knife at a slant, cut thin diagonal slices.

MAKING SCHNITZELS

Escalopes cut from the breast (see page 94) can be pan-fried plain or coated with seasoned flour. Coating them in egg and breadcrumbs protects the delicate flesh. If you refrigerate them, uncovered, for one hour before pan-frying, the coating will harden to give a crisper result.

1 Season each escalope; dip in flour and beaten egg, then coat in fresh or dried breadcrumbs, pressing them firmly on to the meat.

2 Make criss-cross scores on the escalope with the back of a chef's knife. Heat enough oil and butter in a frying pan to just cover the bottom.

3 When the butter is foaming add the escalope. Cook over a moderate heat for 2–3 minutes on each side. Drain on paper towels. Serve.

STUFFING AND FRYING A CHICKEN BREAST

Boneless chicken breasts make perfect pockets for holding stuffings. Butter or soft cheese mixed with crushed garlic and/or herbs is the classic stuffing; chopped mushrooms, garlic and fresh herbs also work well, so too do chopped spinach and ricotta. Take care not to overfill the pocket or it may burst during cooking. The parcels can be fried plain or coated as for schnitzels above.

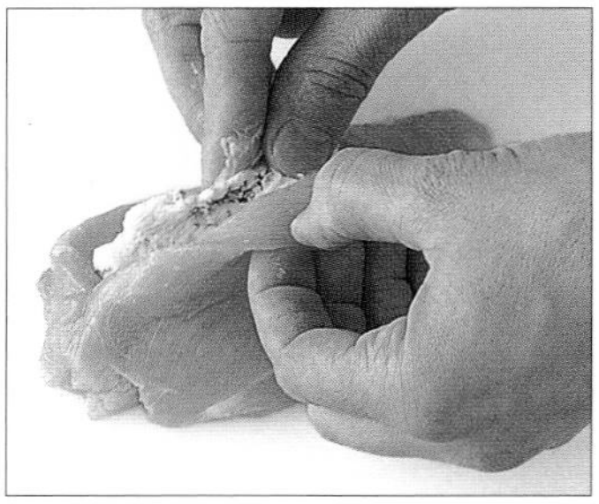

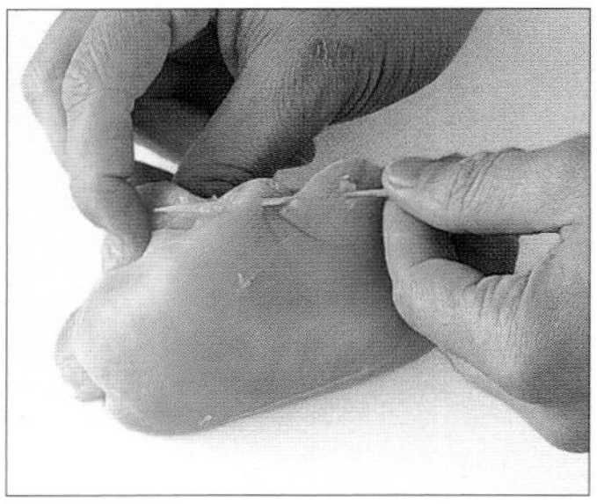

1 Cut a pocket 3–4 cm deep in the side of the breast, without puncturing the base of the pocket. Fill with stuffing.

2 Secure the opening by threading a soaked wooden cocktail stick through the cut edges of the breast.

3 Heat a little olive oil in a non-stick frying pan – just enough to cover the bottom of the pan. Add the parcels and cook, turning once, until golden on both sides, about 15 minutes. Remove the cocktail sticks before serving.

Chargrilling Escalopes

One of the simplest ways to fry escalopes is on a ridged cast-iron stovetop grill pan. The ridges on the pan give the meat a striped "chargrilled" effect, which looks most attractive and as if the meat has been barbecued. The escalopes are best simply fried in a good-quality virgin olive oil or a nut oil, or a mixture of oil and butter if you like. Deglazing the pan with balsamic vinegar adds to the flavour and is one of the simplest ways to make an instant sauce.

1 Brush a little olive oil over the pan and heat until hot but not smoking. Add the escalopes and cook over a moderate heat for 5 minutes, turning once. Add 1–2 tbsp balsamic vinegar and stir into the pan juices to make a tasty sauce.

2 Serve the escalopes on a bed of crisp rocket, as shown here, or on other leaves such as baby spinach or oak-leaf lettuce. Spoon the pan juices over the top of the escalopes and salad leaves as a dressing.

Sauteing Pieces

Sautéing is the technique of turning joints or pieces in a pan over a high heat to seal and brown the skin. Turning prevents the meat from burning on the outside before the inside is properly cooked. Use a good-quality virgin olive oil or a mixture of oil and butter. Duck can be sautéed in its own fat.

In a flameproof casserole or sauté pan, heat about 2 tbsp oil to a high heat. Add the poultry pieces and cook until they begin to brown, turning them frequently with a fork or tongs to ensure they colour evenly. Reduce the heat to moderate and cook for 25–30 minutes or until done – the juices should run clear.

Stir-frying Strips of Poultry

Cut skinless, boneless breasts of chicken, turkey or duck across the grain into strips (see page 95). Coat and stir-fry as shown here, then stir-fry vegetables, liquid and flavourings in the wok according to your chosen recipe. Finally return the strips to the wok and toss with the other ingredients.

1 Stir the poultry strips in a mixture of egg white and cornflour until evenly coated. For 250 g chicken use 1 egg white and 1 tbsp cornflour, mixed until smooth.

2 Heat a wok until hot. Add 2 tbsp vegetable oil and heat until hot but not smoking. Add the poultry. Toss over a moderate to high heat for 5 minutes, or until tender. Remove with a slotted spoon.

Poaching

A whole chicken poached in a flavoursome broth is one of the most delicate dishes. You can also poach chicken breasts or thighs, with or without stuffing. Poached chicken meat is perfect for pie fillings and sandwiches.

Poaching a Whole Bird

Gentle poaching is one of the classic ways of cooking a chicken. It leaves the meat tender and juicy, and produces a delicious broth. Trussing the chicken first (see page 90) ensures it retains its shape during cooking, while the weight of the bird determines the poaching time – allow 20 minutes per 450 g, poaching over a gentle heat on top of the stove.

1 Truss the chicken, including the neck end if you like, and place in a large pan. Pour over enough cold water to just cover the chicken. Bring the liquid slowly to the boil over a moderate heat.

2 Skim the surface with a slotted spoon. Lower the heat and add sliced carrots, onions and a bouquet garni. Poach, partially covered, for the calculated cooking time.

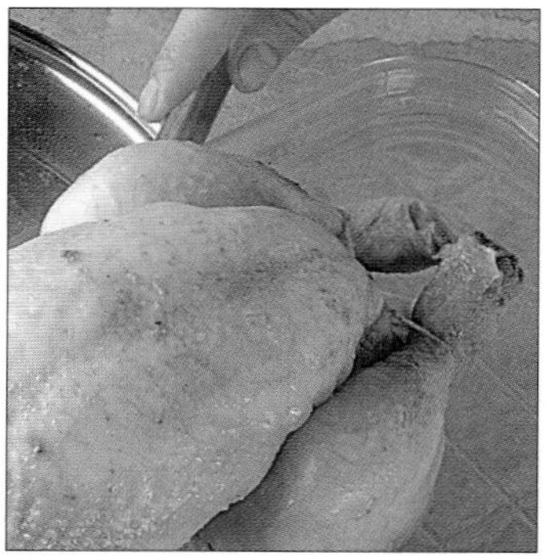

3 When the chicken is tender, remove from the poaching liquid, holding it over the pan so that as much liquid as possible drains from the bird. Remove the trussing string and cut the chicken into pieces (see page 92). Use the poaching liquid as a basic chicken stock or reduce and thicken to make a sauce.

Shredding Poached Poultry

The firm breast meat is best suited to this technique. Remove the breasts from the carcass while still warm – they will come away more easily. Begin shredding at the tip of the breast and work along to the other end, using a fine-pronged large fork.

Place the chicken breast-side up on a cutting board and pull off the skin. Remove the breasts from the carcass and shred the meat with the prongs of a fork. Remove the leg and wing meat from the carcass with your fingers; use as bite-sized pieces or shred if you like.

POULE AU POT

A whole poached chicken was the favourite dish of the French king, Henri Navarre, so much so that he wished his subjects could eat it on every Sunday of the year. *Poule au pot* is now one of the great classics of French cooking, and there are many regional variations. It may be stuffed with a mixture of breadcrumbs, sausagemeat and its own chopped liver, or with tarragon and lemon, or with truffles under the skin.

Henri Navarre (1553–1610)

SHREDDED POULTRY

Shredded poultry absorbs flavours and combines well with many flavoursome ingredients.

- Add to béchamel sauce, chill, then fill crêpes. Bake, topped with grated Parmesan.
- Mix shredded chicken or duck with sliced spring onion, grated ginger and soy sauce. Use to fill filo bundles or Chinese wontons.
- Serve shredded poultry on a bed of salad leaves, spoon over warm chilli and garlic dressing and top with croûtons.

Poaching Pinwheels

This clever technique is surprisingly simple – chicken breasts are cut open, then rolled around a filling. After cooking, the rolls are sliced crosswise to reveal pinwheel shapes. For the filling, choose colourful and juicy ingredients, such as pepper strips, spinach, herbs and soft cheese. Here the rolls are foil-wrapped and poached; they can be wrapped in bacon and roasted.

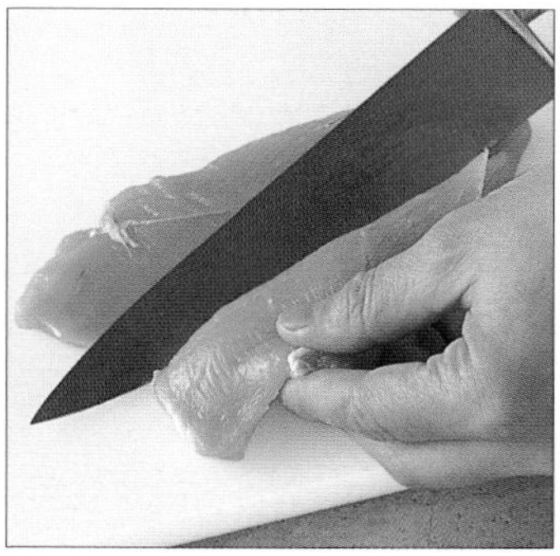

1 Cut through one long side of a skinless, boneless chicken breast, leaving it attached on the opposite side. Detach the fillet and set aside.

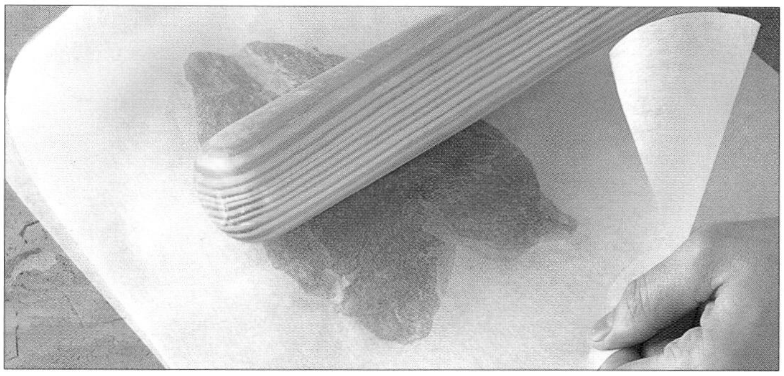

2 Open the breast out flat, cut-side up. Put it between two sheets of baking parchment and pound with a rolling pin or meat mallet to flatten and stretch it. Remove the top sheet of parchment. Spread your chosen stuffing (in this case goat's cheese and chopped spinach) evenly over the cut side.

3 Replace the fillet in the centre of the breast, parallel to the long sides. Starting from one long side, roll the meat into a cylinder.

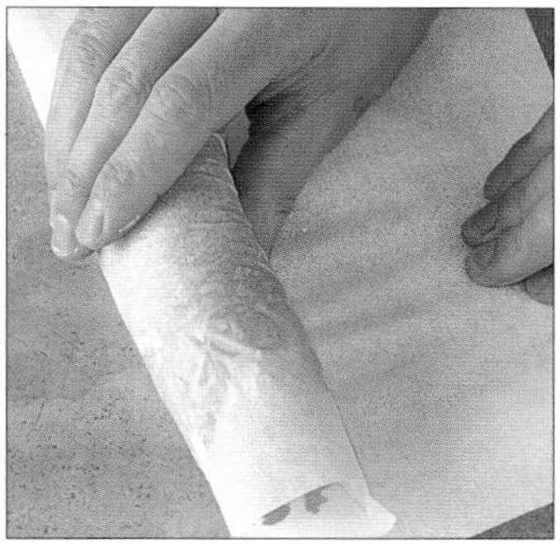

4 Roll the paper around the cylinder, pulling it tightly as you go, and twist the ends to seal. Wrap in foil and twist the ends as before.

5 Bring a pan of water to the boil and add the roll. Poach, covered, over a gentle heat for 15 minutes or until a metal skewer feels warm when withdrawn from the centre. Remove from the pan, unwrap and slice crosswise on the diagonal.

The Asian Alternative

Asian chefs often prefer to retain the succulence of chicken breasts by poaching or steaming them in wrappers that also enclose flavour-imparting ingredients, such as lemon grass stalks.

1 Cut a banana leaf into four squares, each one large enough to envelop a chicken breast. Brush each centre with a 1:1 hoisin and soy sauce mix. Place a chicken breast on each and top with lemon grass and a few slices of fresh root ginger. Spoon over more soy sauce.

2 Wrap each leaf square around the chicken breast to make a neat parcel and secure with string if necessary. Place 1–2 packages at a time in a steamer basket over simmering water and cook for 15 minutes. Serve the chicken breasts in their banana leaves to be unwrapped at the table.

GRILLING & BARBECUING

The intense dry heat of both grill and barbecue crisps poultry skin and imparts a unique flavour. Small pieces, joints or whole birds can be cooked this way. For juiciest results, leave them unskinned or marinate before cooking.

MARINADES

- For a hot and spicy flavour, mix together crushed chillies, chopped fresh rosemary and garlic, and olive oil.
- Flavour plain, yogurt with Indian curry paste and chopped fresh coriander. For a Thai alternative, use green or red curry paste with the yogurt.
- To create a Mediterranean taste, combine olive oil, crushed garlic, and chopped fresh herbs.

GRILLING DRUMSTICKS

The meat of chicken drumsticks is especially suited to the grill or barbecue because it stays moist and tender even when cooked by intense heat. Using an oily marinade prevents the drumsticks from sticking to the rack. Cook slowly until the skin is crisp and golden.

1 Brush drumsticks all over with marinade (see box, left). You can slash the skin to help the marinade penetrate the meat. Cover and refrigerate for 1 hour.

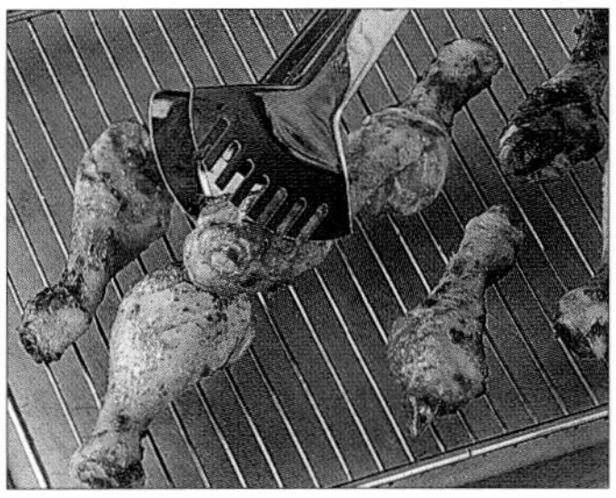

2 Put the drumsticks on the rack of the grill pan and cook under a hot grill, about 6 cm away from the heat, for 15–20 minutes. Turn and baste frequently.

CHICKEN SATE

4 skinless boneless chicken breasts
1 small onion, grated
2 garlic cloves, crushed
2 tbsp soy sauce
2 tbsp vegetable oil
2 tsp sugar
1 tbsp chopped fresh coriander
1 tsp turmeric
Peanut sauce, for serving

Slice the chicken into strips across the grain and mix with the onion, garlic, soy sauce, oil, sugar, coriander and turmeric. Cover and leave to marinate in the refrigerator overnight. Thread the strips on to soaked bamboo skewers and grill or barbecue for only 5 minutes, turning them frequently and brushing with the marinade. Serve hot, accompanied by peanut sauce. Serves 4–6.

MAKING SATE

Saté are small kebabs made with very lean chicken, meat or fish. Here they are made with succulent chicken breast meat. The secret of making good chicken saté is to wind the chicken on to the sticks and not to overcook it or it will be dry. A simple recipe for chicken saté, using the techniques shown here, is given in the box, left.

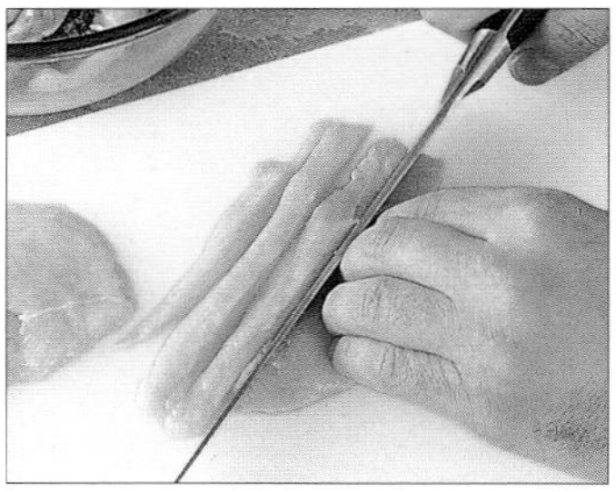

1 Remove the tendons from the chicken breasts (see page 94), then cut the flesh into thin slices, working diagonally across the grain. Marinate the strips for 1 hour, preferably overnight.

2 Soak bamboo skewers in water for 30 minutes, then drain. Thread the marinated chicken on to the skewers, winding them in a spiral pattern.

3 Cook the chicken under a very hot grill, about 6 cm away from the heat. The chicken will cook very quickly, so do not cook for longer than stated in the recipe. Turn the skewers frequently and brush with the marinade. Serve warm or at room temperature.

Barbecuing a Whole Bird

A kettle barbecue allows you to cook a bird whole. This type of barbecue has a domed lid or hood which closes over the bird, in effect roasting it but with a chargrilled flavour.

1 Season the bird and place, uncovered, on a rack in a roasting tin. Place the tin on the barbecue grid and cover with the kettle lid.

2 Barbecue the chicken until the juices run clear (see page 101), allowing $1^1/_2$–$1^3/_4$ hours for a 2 kg bird. Lift the lid of the barbecue occasionally during cooking, and baste with the juices that have collected in the tin.

BARBECUE TIPS

Outdoor cooking is quick, but requires constant attention. Prepare all your accompaniments in advance.

- Always barbecue outside – charcoal gives off carbon monoxide fumes.
- Light the barbecue at least 30 minutes before cooking and don't put food on it until the flames have died down and the coals have turned grey or are glowing embers.
- For extra flavour, strew the coals with woody herbs, such as rosemary, or fennel stems
- For safety's sake, use long tongs rather than ordinary kitchen forks to turn the food.

Grilling a Bird

Grilling or barbecuing is an ideal method for small birds such as poussins because they cook quickly and remain tender and moist. They cook faster when spatchcocked (see page 92), and have juicier flesh if marinated or their skins rubbed with olive oil and seasonings.

1 Mix together the marinade ingredients of your choice (see box, opposite page). Put the bird in a non-metallic dish and prick all over with a fork. Pour over the marinade, cover and let marinate in the refrigerator for at least 4 hours, preferably overnight.

2 Preheat the grill until very hot. Put the spatchcocked bird, skin-side up, on the rack of the grill pan and grill about 7.5 cm from the heat for 30–40 minutes, turning frequently and occasionally brushing with the marinade.

3 Remove the bird from the rack and place on a cutting board. Remove the hot skewers with the help of a fork and a tea towel. Cut the bird in half lengthwise to serve, allowing one half per person.

CASSEROLING & POT-ROASTING

These are long, slow-cooking methods that give depth of flavour and unrivalled tenderness to any type of poultry or game, both whole birds and pieces on the bone. Cooking can be on top of the stove or in the oven.

MARINATING AND CASSEROLING IN WINE

Poultry pieces are tenderized by being steeped and slowly simmered in a concentrated cooked red wine marinade. This is the technique behind the classic French coq au vin *(see box, left). For a fuller flavour, let the casserole go cold, preferably overnight. Reheat well before serving.*

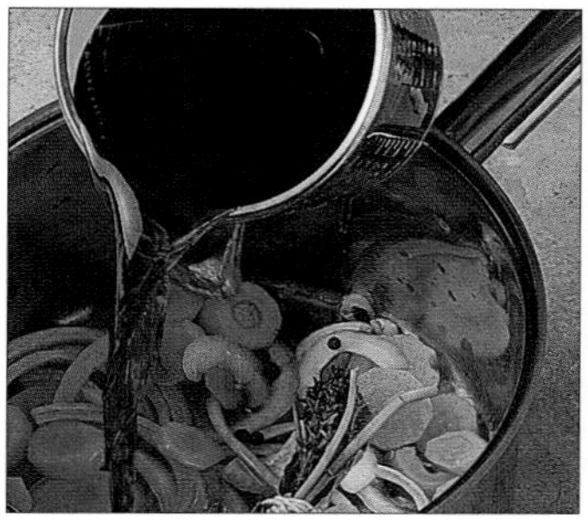

1 Cook the vegetables for the marinade in wine so that they will soften and impart flavour.

2 Let the chicken cool before adding to the marinade or the chicken will begin to cook before marinating.

3 Sprinkle oil over the surface of the marinade to help contain strong odours during marinating.

4 Make sure the chicken pieces are thoroughly dry before adding them to the hot oil otherwise they will not brown evenly.

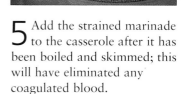

5 Add the strained marinade to the casserole after it has been boiled and skimmed; this will have eliminated any coagulated blood.

6 When the chicken is done, the sauce will be thick and rich and the chicken will feel tender when pierced with a skewer. Let stand for 10–15 minutes before serving, to allow the flavours to mellow and the fibres in the meat to settle.

COQ AU VIN

1 whole chicken, cut into 6 serving pieces (see page 93)
4 tbsp vegetable oil
1 tbsp plain flour
250 g carrots, sliced
1 onion, chopped
2 bay leaves
Salt and freshly ground pepper
175 g mushrooms, sliced

MARINADE
700 ml red wine
1 carrot, chopped
1 onion, chopped
2 garlic cloves, chopped
1 bouquet garni
4–5 juniper berries
1 tsp whole black peppercorns
200 ml red wine vinegar

Cook marinade ingredients, except vinegar, for 15 minutes. Transfer to a bowl and let cool. Stir in the vinegar; add the chicken. Sprinkle over half the oil, cover and refrigerate overnight.

Remove the chicken and strain the marinade. Heat the remaining oil in a flameproof casserole, add the chicken. Sauté until brown. In another pan, boil the marinade. Skim any blood from the surface.

Sprinkle the chicken with flour, add the remaining ingredients and stir over a moderate heat for a few minutes. Add the marinade and bring to the boil. Cook in a 180°C oven for 1 hour or until tender. Add the mushrooms for the last 15 minutes. Check seasoning. Serves 4–6

Pot-roasting Tough Game Birds

Small game birds, such as quail and grouse, can be dry and tough, so they are suited to slow, moist methods of cooking. Wrapping the birds in bacon adds flavour and protects the flesh; tying helps to keep the birds in a neat shape. Marinating before cooking (see box, right) will help moisten, flavour and tenderize the flesh.

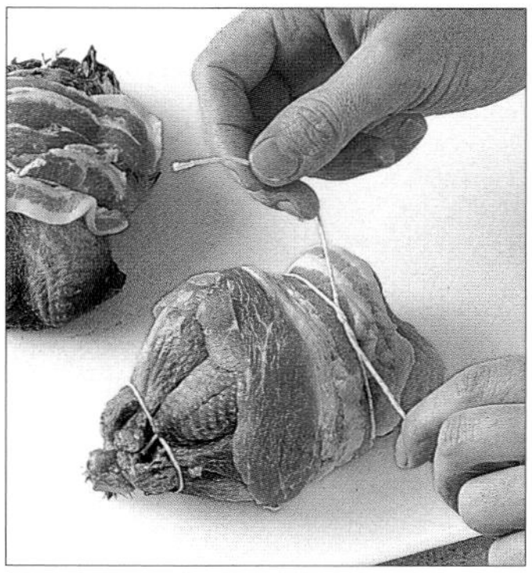

1 Tuck the neck skin and wings underneath the birds and tie the legs together with string. Season the birds, then wrap streaky bacon rashers around them and tie it in place with kitchen string.

2 Heat 2 tbsp oil in a large flameproof casserole. Brown the birds, turning them occasionally by hooking a two-pronged fork under the trussing string.

3 Add carrots and onions to the pan, with salt and pepper to taste. Sweat the vegetables for 5 minutes over a gentle heat, stirring with a wooden spoon to incorporate any sediment from the bottom of the pan.

4 Pour enough red wine to half cover the birds. Cover and simmer very gently until the birds are tender and the sauce reduced, about 30 minutes on the stovetop, or 1 hour in a 180°C oven. Check seasoning and serve.

Marinades for Tough Birds

Marinades add flavour to meat, and help to tenderize it. This is because most marinades contain an acid such as wine or fruit juice which helps break down tough fibres. Fresh pineapple juice is most effective as it contains a special enzyme that breaks down proteins and tenderizes meat.

- Fresh pineapple juice mixed with grated lemon zest.
- Lemon juice, crushed garlic and dried red pepper flakes.
- Red wine, cranberry juice and juniper berries.
- Orange juice, lime juice, cracked peppercorns, coriander seeds and chopped fresh chilli.
- White wine, cider vinegar, cumin seeds, allspice berries and cinnamon stick.
- Red wine, cinnamon stick and cracked cloves.
- Sherry vinegar, oil, thyme, sage and bay leaf.
- Red wine, rosemary and marjoram.

TERRINES & PATES

Any bone and sinew free poultry or game meat can be ground up turned into a spreadable pâté, or moulded and cooked as a terrine. Don't overcook the meat; pâtés and terrines are at their best when moist and juicy.

CHICKEN LIVER PATE

250 g chicken livers
125 g unsalted butter, softened
2 tbsp brandy
Salt and freshly ground pepper
25–50 g lukewarm liquid clarified butter (see page 227)

Toss chicken livers in about one-third of the butter until they change colour, about 5 minutes. Remove from the pan and purée in a food processor with the remaining butter and the brandy. Add seasonings to taste, Transfer the pâté to four ramekins, smooth the surface, then cover with clarified butter. Cool, then chill in the refrigerator. Serves 4.

FARCE FOR RABBIT TERRINE

1.5 kg rabbit
2 shallots, roughly chopped
2 eggs
150 ml double cream
2 tbsp shelled pistachios
1 tbsp dried cranberries
2 tbsp chopped fresh parsley
Freshly grated nutmeg
Salt and freshly ground pepper

Cut up the rabbit (see page 93), then remove the meat from the bones. Set aside the best pieces and mince the rest in a food processor with the shallots. Work in the eggs and cream, then turn the mixture into a bowl and mix in the nuts, dried cranberries, parsley and seasonings to taste.

MAKING A PAN-FRIED LIVER PATE

One of the easiest ways to make a pâté is by pan-frying livers quickly, working them to a fine or coarse purée in a food processor, then chilling until firm in the refrigerator. Chicken livers are favoured because of their mild flavour and soft texture. Take care not to overcook them or they will toughen.

COOKING THE LIVERS Keep them moving in hot butter in the centre of the pan, so they do not stick or burn, until pink-tinged.

ADDING CLARIFIED BUTTER Spoon liquid clarified butter over the pâté to keep it airtight – the mixture may discolour in contact with air.

MAKING A RABBIT TERRINE

The technique here is to contrast a creamy, smooth farce with thin slivers of tender meat to make an easy layered terrine. The addition of aspic after baking helps keep the terrine moist. It also gives the terrine a professional-looking finish.

1 Line a 1.5 litre terrine with about 15 rindless streaky bacon rashers. Make sure there are no gaps and allow the ends to overhang.

2 Put half the farce (see box, left) in the terrine, cover with pieces of rabbit in an even layer, then spoon in the remaining farce.

3 Fold over the overhanging rashers, arranging them in an attractive pattern. Cover the mould and bake in a *bain marie* at 180°C for 2 hours.

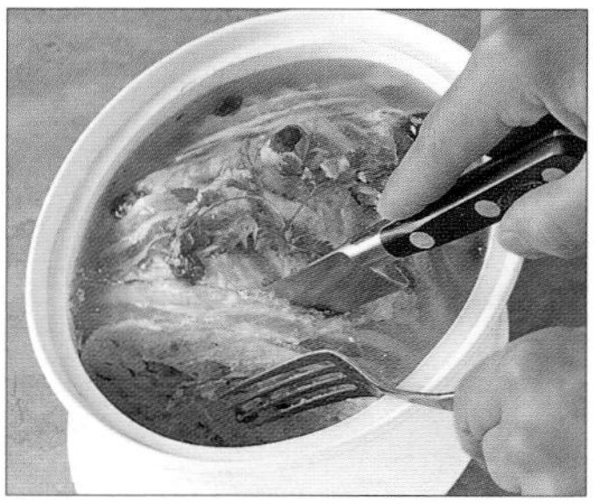

4 Slowly pour 300–350 ml liquid aspic (see page 19) over the terrine. Add it a little at a time so that it soaks in. Let cool, then refrigerate until set before slicing.

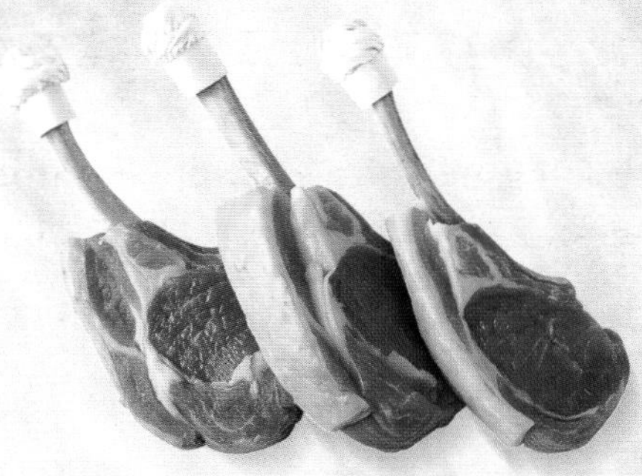

Meat

Choosing Beef & Veal
•
Preparing Beef & Veal for Cooking
•
Quick Cooking Beef & Veal
•
Slow Cooking Beef & Veal
•
Choosing Lamb
•
Preparing Lamb for Cooking
•
Roasting & Braising Lamb
•
Quick Cooking Lamb
•
Choosing Pork
•
Preparing Pork for Cooking
•
Roasting & Braising Pork
•
Quick Cooking Pork
•
Sausages, Bacon & Ham
•
Using Minced Meat
•
Offal

Choosing Beef & Veal

Buy your meat from a reliable source, a high turnover will help to indicate fresh stock. Look for good butchering techniques – joints should follow the contours of the muscle and bone, cuts should be neat and well trimmed with little sinew, and any bones should be smooth with no sign of splinters.

SMOOTH fine-grained flesh that is creamy white with a pale greyish-pink tinge is best. Any outer fat should be firm and white
AN EVEN marbling of fat in the meat is a good indication of high quality
OUTER LAYER of fat should be creamy white and smooth; yellow fat can indicate the meat is past its best except in grass-reared beef
LOOK FOR deep red, moist-looking meat with a generous marbling of fat throughout

Buying Beef and Veal

Though the age of the animal from which it came, and its breed and feed will be reflected in the meat, the best beef and veal will smell fresh and have clean-looking flesh that is not too bright in colour. Meat with a greenish-grey tinge and an "off" smell should be avoided.

Look for cuts that are uniform in thickness to aid even cooking, and that have a moist, freshly cut surface; avoid wet meat that is slimy to the touch. Always check the "use-by" dates. Leaner cuts last longer than fatty cuts because fat goes rancid before meat.

Buying the freshest and best quality meat is always worthwhile, but you must be prepared to pay a little more for organically-raised beef or that from particularly fine breeds noted for their succulent meat, such as Aberdeen Angus.

Handling Beef and Veal

Remove meat from its original wrapping as soon as possible after purchase and place on a plate or in a dish to catch any blood. Loosely cover, then store in the coldest part of the refrigerator (1–5°C) away from cooked meats.

Minced meat and small cuts of veal are best eaten on the day you buy them. Joints, chops and steaks will keep for 2–3 days and large roasts up to 5 days.

Freezing beef and veal quickly reduces the chance of damage to the texture or succulence of the meat; smaller pieces freeze more successfully than large joints. For convenience, freeze cuts tightly wrapped in individual portions; use veal within 6 months and beef within 1 year. Defrost, loosely wrapped, in the refrigerator allowing 5 hours per 450 g.

Beef & Veal Cuts

Beef cuts are the most variable of meats and offer the cook the greatest culinary scope. Milk-fed veal is very delicate in flavour and texture and should be cooked in ways that preserve these qualities such as grilling or barbecuing. Calves that are fed both milk and straw will have darker pink flesh but this does not alter the eating quality. Choose cuts suitable for the chosen cooking method – leaner cuts benefit from quick cooking, tougher joints require long, slow cooking to tenderise them.

Beef Cuts	What to Look For	Cooking Methods
Chuck or Blade	*Large lean joint, with some connective tissue Marbled with some outer fat Also sold boned or cubed*	Stew, braise
Fillet/Tenderloin	*Lean with light marbling No outer layer of fat*	Roast (whole), grill, pan-fry, barbecue (smaller cuts)
Fore/Wing/ Prime Rib	*Lean meat with obvious layers of fat and some marbling Creamy white bone Even layer of outer fat*	Roast, braise, pot-roast (boned and rolled).
Minced meat	*Pale meat indicates high fat content; darker colour means leaner mince Look for % fat declared on packet*	Use for pasta sauces, meat pies, burgers, stuffings
Sirloin	*Lean with light marbling Even outer layer of creamy, white fat*	Roast (with bone or boned)
Steak	*Lean meat with light marbling Creamy-white bone with no splinters*	Grill, pan-fry or barbecue
Topside	*Lean with little marbling Separate layer of fat tied around outside*	Braise, pot-roast, roast

Veal Cuts		
Breast	*Lean meat with light marbling Thin even outer layer of white fat*	Roast, pot-roast, braise, stew, roast, braise (boned and stuffed)
Cutlet	*Very light marbling, smooth, white bone Even outer layer of white fat*	Grill, barbecue
Knuckle	*High proportion of white bone – smooth, no splinters Pink lean flesh, some connective tissue*	Braise (osso buco), stew
Loin	*Lean meat, bones smooth and white Thin uneven outer layer of white fat*	Roast (whole), pan-fry, grill, barbecue (chops)
Pie/Stewing	*Lean with some connective tissue Usually cubed*	Stew, casserole
Shoulder	*Clear pink flesh with light marbling Visible connective tissue, white outer fat*	Roast, braise
Topside/Cushion (Escalopes)	*Very lean, pale pink No outer fat*	Lard and braise or roast (whole), grill, pan-fry, barbecue

Beef and Veal On the Menu

Generally more expensive than poultry, there are beef and veal classics that range from the rustic to the divine.

France – *Boeuf Bourguignon* (a slow-simmered beef stew flavoured with smoked bacon, red wine and mushrooms) creates a deliciously butter-soft meat in a rich sauce.
Hungary – *Goulash* (cubes of chuck steak simmered in a paprika-scented stock) is thickened with sour cream and sprinkled with additional paprika before serving.
Italy – *Osso Buco* (veal braised in a rich vegetable, tomato and wine stock) was originally created by chefs in Milan.
Japan – *Teriyaki Beef* (steak with a soy sauce, sherry and sugar marinade) is stir-fried with peppers and onions.
Mexico – *Fajitas* (steak marinated in spices and lime juice) is served in *tortillas* with avocado, sour cream and *salsa*.
United States – *Chilli con carne* (cubed chuck steak, beef stock and red kidney beans. Modern variations may include tomatoes, peppers, black beans, fresh coriander and sour cream) may have a Spanish name, but the flavours are pure Texas.

Preparing for Cooking

Beef and veal offer a wide range of cuts from lean, tender steaks that need only brief cooking, to tougher, but flavourful cuts such as shin that benefit from slow braising. Correct and careful preparation is essential.

What's in a Name?

Very lean meat requires extra fat to help keep it moist as it cooks. Use pork fat that is well chilled to make handling easier.

Larding: This technique is used for moistening lean meat flesh from the inside during cooking. As the lardons of pork fat melt they are absorbed by the flesh, making it more succulent. To add extra flavour, season the fat or marinate it for at least 1 hour before larding.

Barding: Lean meat can be wrapped in pork fat to keep it moist and help retain the shape of the meat. The barding fat will disappear during cooking; if any remains it should be discarded before serving, unless decoratively applied (see right).

Preparing Joints

Some joints, such as the rib shown here, have thick outer layers of fat which need trimming before cooking.

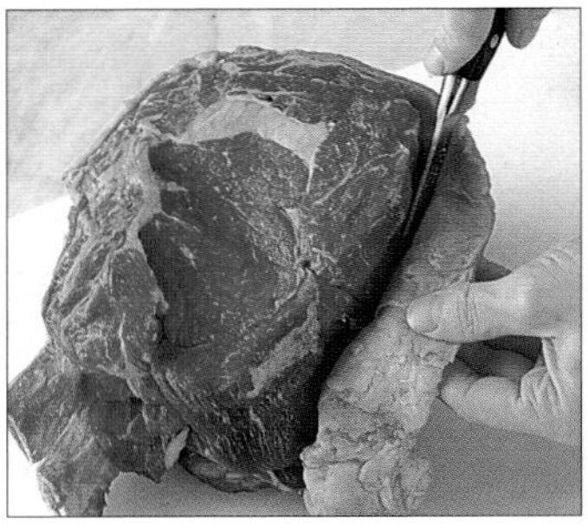

Trim the fat from the underside of the joint. Leave a thin layer on the surface to help keep the flesh moist.

Preparing Steaks

Steaks need to be trimmed and dressed before cooking. First cut away some of the excess fat, leaving an even layer sufficient to flavour the meat during cooking, then cut through the fat into the thin membrane at regular intervals. This prevents the steak from curling as it cooks. Sirloin steaks are illustrated here; rump steaks require the same technique.

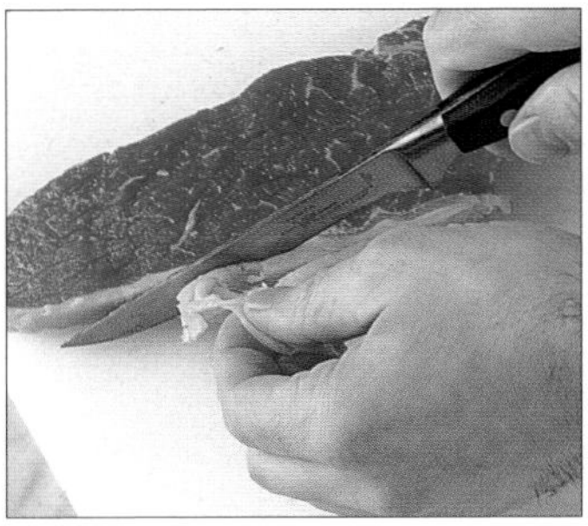

1 Trim off the outer layer of fat with a boning knife, leaving 1 cm fat next to the meat. Discard the fat.

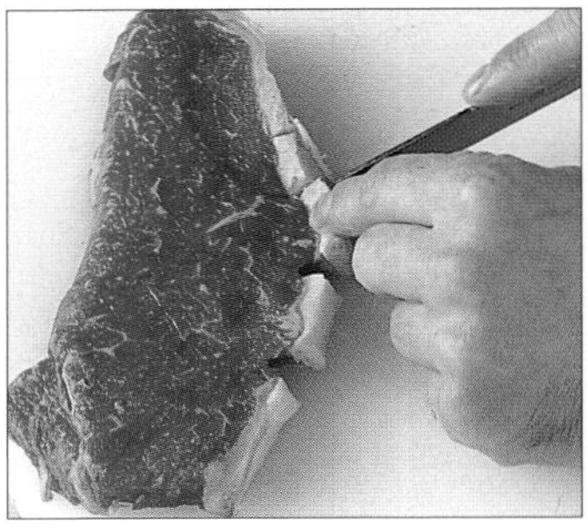

2 Cut through the fat at regular intervals with a chef's knife or snip with kitchen scissors.

Larding and Barding

Some cuts lack natural fat, and if they are to be roasted or braised it may be necessary to add fat to keep them tender and succulent. This can be done internally by larding, or externally by barding.

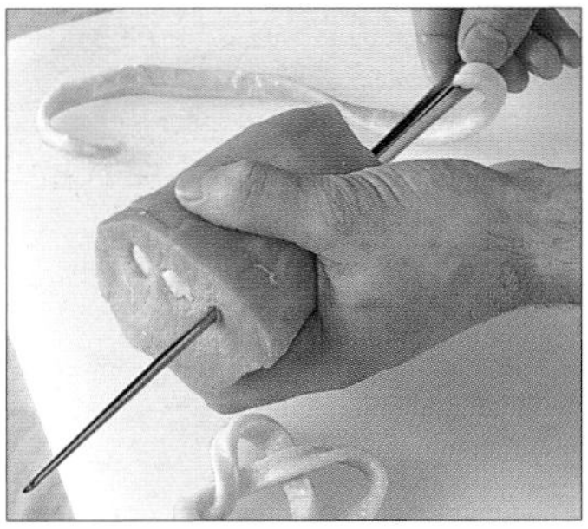

Larding
Insert a larding needle into the meat following the grain. Thread the needle with chilled pork fat, then pull through.

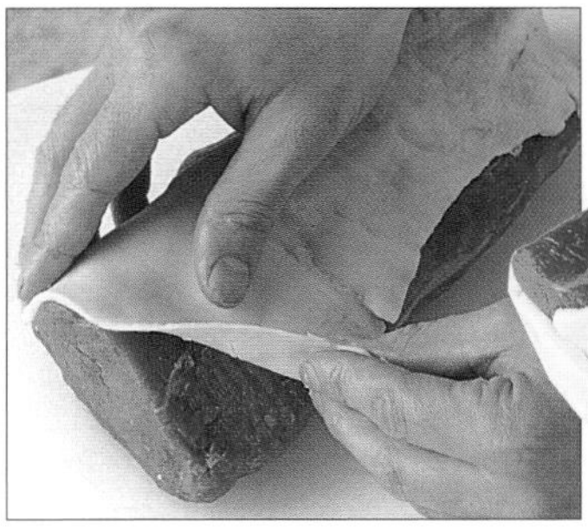

Simple barding
Wrap a thin layer of fat around the outside of the meat and tie in place with string (see opposite page).

Decorative barding
Wrap sides of meat with sheets of fat. Place a zigzag strip of fat along the top, tucking in the ends.

Boning a Breast of Veal

Joints can be cooked with the bone in or out. Boned joints cook more evenly and are much easier to carve into neat slices. After boning, the meat is ready for rolling and tying, with or without a stuffing, or for cutting into pieces.

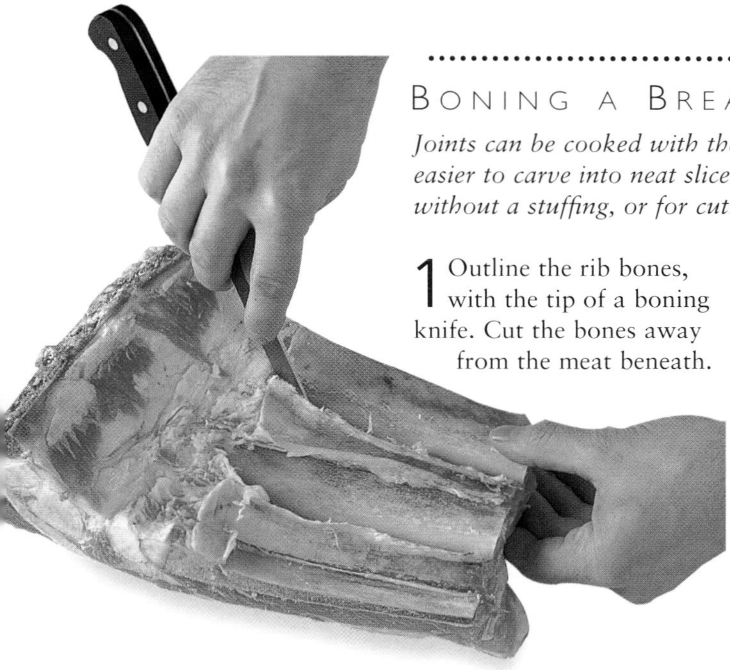

1 Outline the rib bones, with the tip of a boning knife. Cut the bones away from the meat beneath.

2 Cut through the cartilage and around the breastbone. Remove the bone.

3 Remove the rib bones. Trim the breast of any cartilage, sinew or excess fat.

Rolling, Stuffing and Tying

Boneless joints can be tied to make neat packages for roasting or braising, or to hold barding fat in place (see opposite page) or a rolled stuffed joint together. Stuffings for joints add flavour and help lubricate the meat from inside; they also help "stretch" the meat and make it go further.

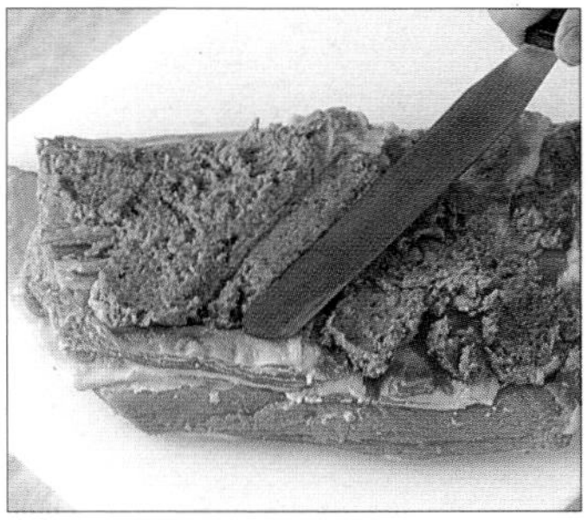

1 Place the boned breast, skin-side down, on a board. Spread the stuffing evenly over the surface.

2 Starting from the thick end, roll up the joint, smoothing it into a neat shape for tying.

3 Wrap the string twice around the length of the roll. Tie off, but do not cut.

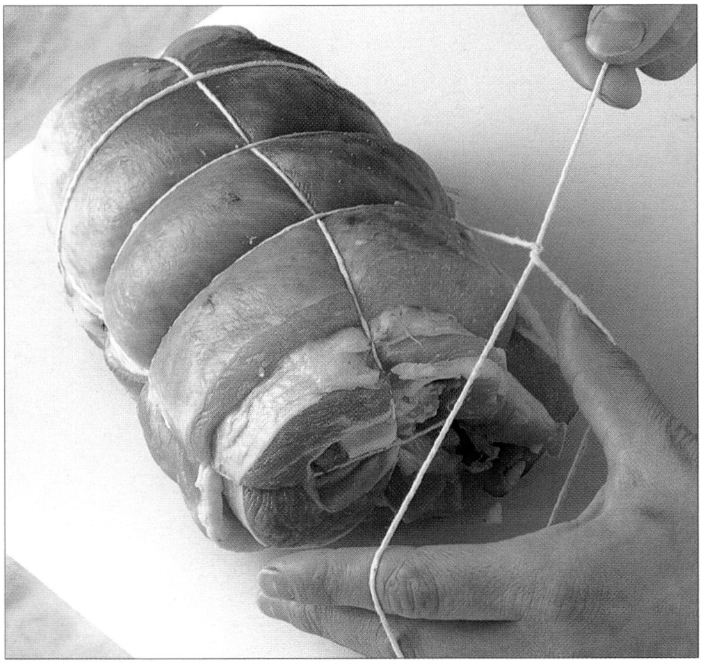

4 Wrap the string around one hand and tuck the end of the string over it to create a loop. Slip the loop on to the meat and tighten. Repeat along the roll. Knot the ends to secure.

Trick of the Trade

Simple Tying

Instead of the butcher's technique in steps 3 and 4 left, you can use a series of knots to tie a whole beef fillet into a neat shape for even cooking.

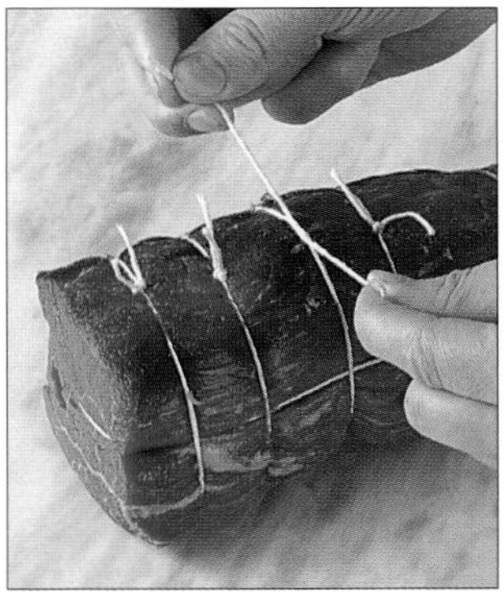

Wrap a length of kitchen string lengthwise around the fillet, tie it securely and trim the ends. Tie another piece of string around the centre of the fillet. Secure this piece with a double knot and trim the ends. Starting at one end, work towards the centre of the fillet, tying pieces of string at about 2 cm intervals knotting and trimming the ends as you go.

BEEF CARPACCIO

600 g fillet of beef in one piece
Salt and feshly ground pepper
75 ml extra virgin olive oil
Juice of 1 lemon
Shredded fresh basil
A few capers
Parmesan curls
(see box, page 236)

Trim the beef of any excess fat and membrane (see right), then wrap in foil, freeze and slice very thinly (see right).

Arrange the slices of beef on individual serving plates, slightly overlapping them so they completely cover the surface of the plates.

Just before serving, lightly season the slices with salt and pepper, drizzle with the olive oil and lemon juice and sprinkle with shredded basil, capers and Parmesan curls. Serves 4

TRICK OF THE TRADE

TENDER STEAKS

Meat that is to be cooked quickly can be tenderized by pounding, which helps break up the connective tissues. A rolling pin can be used instead of the cleaver shown here.

Place the steak on a cutting board. Pound the steak all over, using the flat side of a cleaver.

TRIMMING AND SLICING A FILLET OF BEEF

The fillet is the finest cut of beef – lean and meltingly tender. It is a classic joint for roasting, either plain or stuffed, with or without a pastry casing (see page 125). Sliced, it can produce tournedos *or fillet steaks,* châteaubriand, *very thick steak from the centre of the fillet, or strips for stir-frying.*

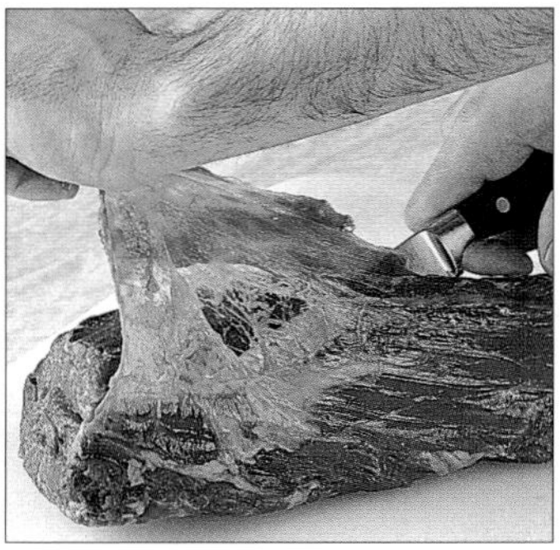

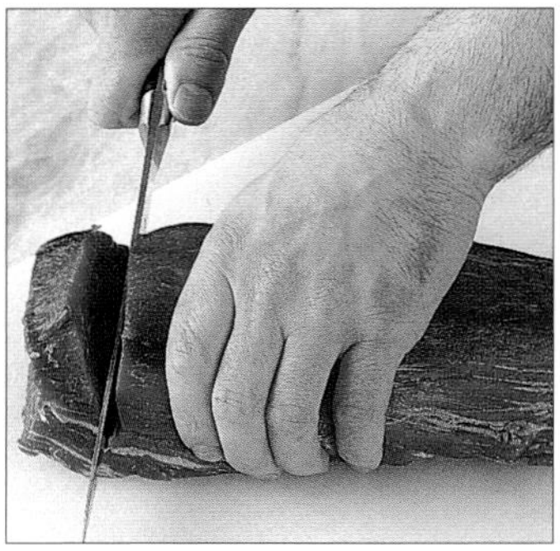

1 Remove the chain muscle from the side of the main fillet. Cut away the sinewy membrane, sliding the blade of the knife underneath and holding the membrane away with the other hand.

2 Slice the fillet crosswise into slices about 2 cm thick. Cut them thicker at the narrow end, then pound them with the flat side of a cleaver or meat mallet.

SLICING BEEF WAFER THIN

Placing meat in the freezer firms up the fibres and makes it very easy to slice. Use this technique for carpaccio *(see box, left) or stir-fries.*

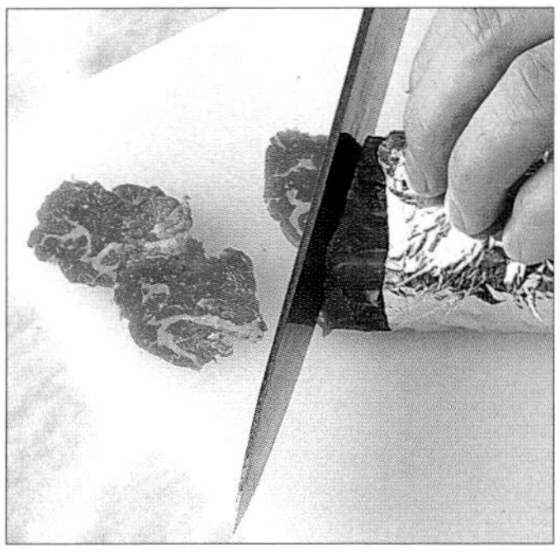

Wrap a piece of trimmed beef fillet tightly in foil and place in the freezer for 1–4 hours, depending on size. Remove from the freezer and slice very thinly using a sawing action. Allow to thaw.

CUTTING MEAT FOR STEWING

For long, slow cooking, such as stewing and braising, you can use cuts like the chuck steak shown here, skirt or shin of beef or shoulder or breast meat of veal. During the cooking process the tough muscle should soften and the gelatinous tissues break down and melt into the sauce, making it rich and velvety. For this to happen the meat must be cut into even-sized pieces, either cubes or strips, so that they cook evenly.

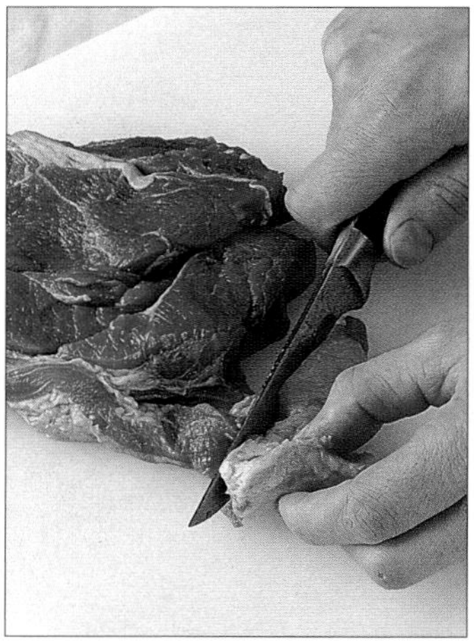

1 Trim any excess fat and sinew from around the meat using a boning knife. Discard the fat.

2 Cut the meat across the grain into 3–4 cm wide slices, using a chef's knife. Turn each slice on its side and cut in half lengthwise.

3 Cut across each slice of meat to give 3–4 cm cubes. The meat is now ready for stewing or braising.

MINCING

Although minced meat can be bought ready prepared, mincing your own means you can choose the cuts you use. Lean cuts with a little marbling are the most suitable. This simple technique can be done using a mincer or by hand, using a pair of heavy chef's knives with very sharp blades that will cut the meat cleanly. For burgers, meat can also be chopped (see page 152).

BY MACHINE

This is suitable for large amounts and for tough cuts such as neck or flank. It produces a smooth texture ideal for sausages or burgers. Cube the meat (see opposite page) and feed small amounts at a time through the machine. Process a slice of bread at the end to ensure all the meat is pushed through.

BY HAND

This is the best method for small amounts or prime cuts such as rump or fillet (it is always used for steak tartare in France). With a chef's knife in each hand, chop cubed meat using a rhythmic action.

ROLLING VEAL ESCALOPES

Escalopes are lean pieces of veal cut at an angle from the leg fillet; the large, even slices require a light pounding before being coated and pan-fried. When rolled around a filling they are called paupiettes *in French,* saltimbocca *in Italian. The same techniques can be applied to beef fillet and topside.*

1 Lightly pound the escalope on a board between two pieces of baking parchment. Remove the paper and cut the escalope crosswise in half.

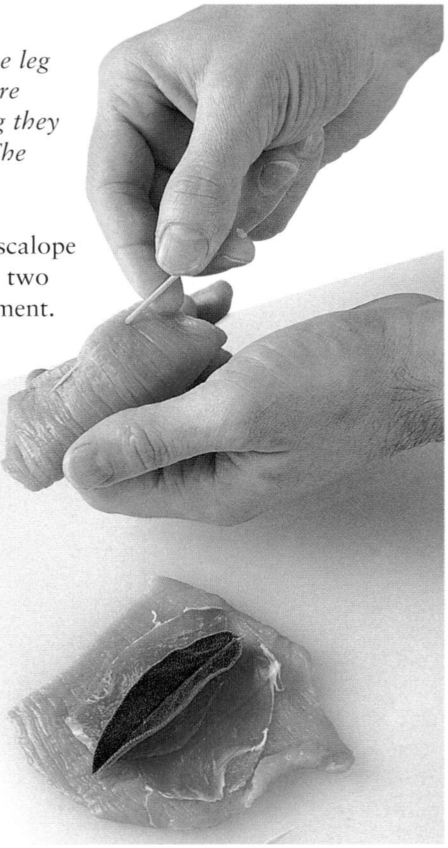

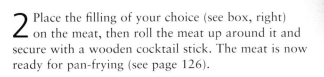

2 Place the filling of your choice (see box, right) on the meat, then roll the meat up around it and secure with a wooden cocktail stick. The meat is now ready for pan-frying (see page 126).

STUFFINGS FOR VEAL ESCALOPES

Choose stuffings that are moist and provide a contrast in flavour and texture to the meat.

- For *saltimbocca* (see page 126), roll the veal around Parma ham and fresh sage leaves.
- Spread veal with a mixture of ricotta cheese and chopped spinach moistened with a little cream, sprinkle over a few toasted pine nuts and roll up.
- Mix strips of roasted peppers with fresh breadcrumbs and shredded basil leaves.
- Combine minced veal with raisins, chopped chestnuts and chopped fresh herbs.
- Mix together equal quantities of cream cheese and crème fraîche and flavour with a few capers and grated lemon zest.

QUICK COOKING

Methods of quick cooking include roasting, for large prime cuts of meat such as rib or fillet of beef, and pan-frying or grilling for small, tender pieces such as steaks and escalopes. For roasting, bones can be left in, or they can be removed and the joint stuffed and rolled. The high heat sears the joint and produces a glossy crust, which seals in the juices.

MEAT THERMOMETER

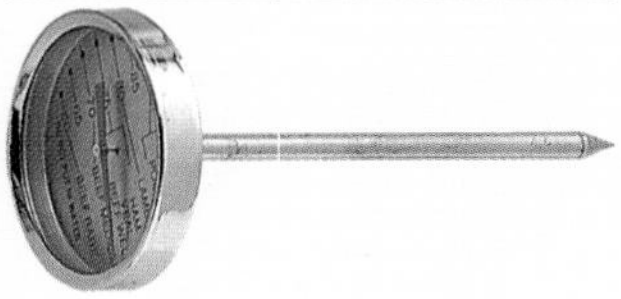

The best way to tell if a roast is done is to use a meat thermometer. After searing the meat, insert the spike of the thermometer into the thickest part of the joint. Be careful not to touch any bone as this will give you an inaccurate reading. The reading should be 60°C for rare, 70°C for medium and 75°C for well-done.

ROASTING TIMES

All timings are approximate, and are based on minutes per 450 g at 180°C.

• BEEF ON THE BONE

Rare	20 mins plus an extra 20 mins
Medium	25 mins plus an extra 25 mins
Well-done	30 mins plus an extra 30 mins

• BEEF OFF THE BONE

Rare	15 mins plus an extra 15mins
Medium	20 mins plus an extra 20 mins
Well-done	25 mins plus an extra 25 mins

• VEAL ON/OFF THE BONE

25 mins plus an extra 25 mins

ROASTING A RIB OF BEEF

Before cooking, let the joint come to room temperature for about 2 hours, then trim (see page 120). Weigh the joint, calculate the cooking time and preheat the oven (see chart, bottom left). Season the joint. Coat the bottom of the tin with oil, and heat on top of the stove until hot but not smoking. Place the joint in the tin and sear on all sides, about 5 minutes. If using a meat thermometer, insert it in the thickest part of the meat (see box, left).

1 Roast the joint in the preheated oven for the calculated cooking time, basting occasionally with a large metal spoon.

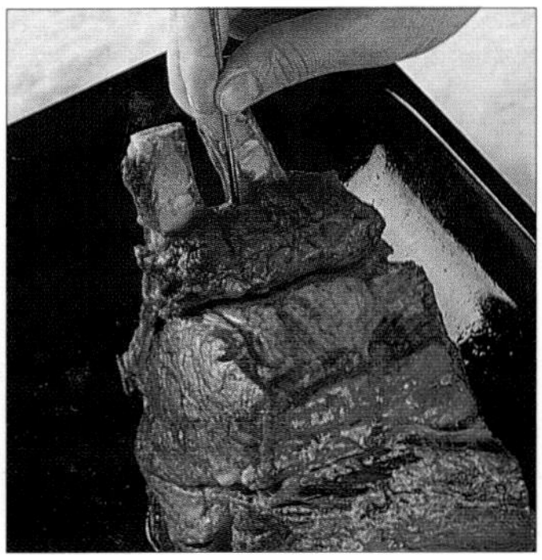

2 If no thermometer is used insert a skewer in the meat for 30 seconds. If cool when withdrawn the meat will be rare; if warm, medium.

CARVING A RIB OF BEEF

After removing the joint from the oven, cover it loosely with foil and let it rest for 10–15 minutes. This allows the juices on the surface to be reabsorbed into the flesh. When carving, use a two-pronged fork just to steady the joint; take care not to let it pierce the meat.

1 Place the rib upright on a board and steady it with a fork. Cut down along the bone between the meat and the ribs. Remove the bones.

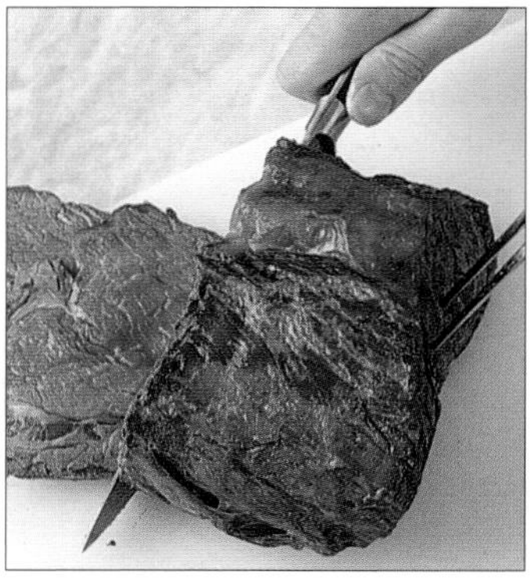

2 Turn the joint on its side. Holding the joint with the fork and without piercing the meat, carve thin, even slices across the grain.

CARVING A ROLLED JOINT

Boned and rolled joints, such as the breast of veal here, are very easy to carve. Rest the joint 10–15 minutes, then remove the string and carve.

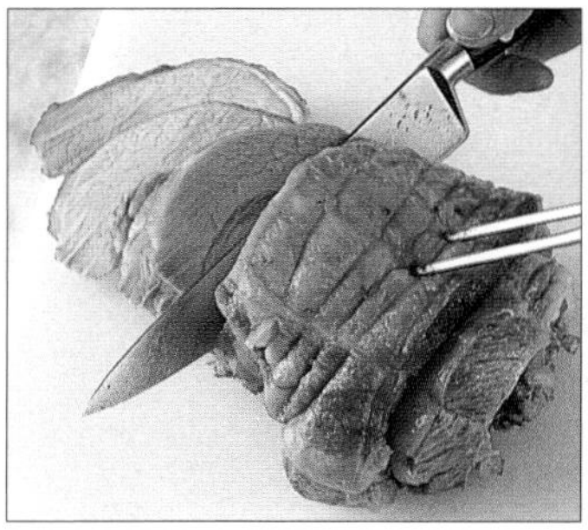

Place the joint seam-side down on a board. Holding it steady with a fork, carve the meat crosswise into slices with a sawing action.

Roasting a Whole Fillet of Beef

Sear the trimmed and tied joint in hot oil before roasting to seal and brown the outside, then insert a meat thermometer, making sure the tip of the spike is in the centre of the meat. A 1.5 kg beef fillet roasted at 220°C should take about 20 minutes for rare meat, 25–30 minutes, medium-rare.

1 Season joint, then sear in hot oil, turning with tongs. Insert thermometer and place in preheated oven.

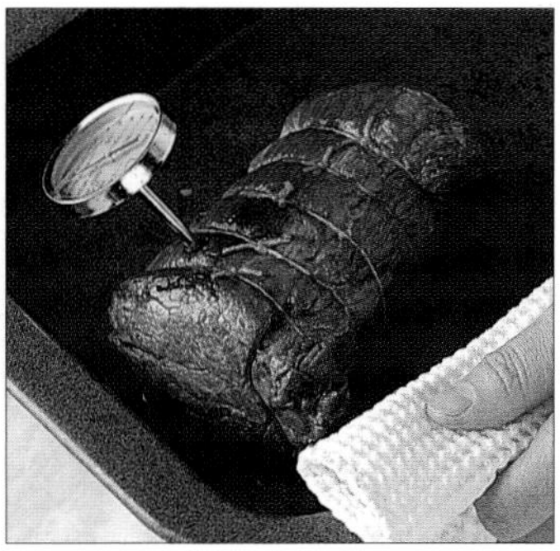

2 Baste frequently during roasting to keep meat moist. Check thermometer reading; remove from oven.

Roasting a Whole Fillet of Beef en Croute

This French technique produces rare beef in the centre and crisp pastry on the outside. The secret lies in first seasoning and searing the fillet as in step 1 above, partially roasting it at 220°C for 20 minutes until just rare, then letting it cool and encasing it in crêpes to prevent the meat juices leaking into the crust.

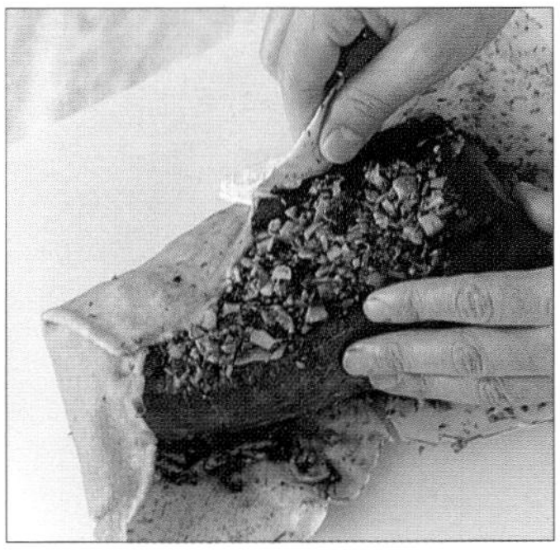

1 Press *duxelles* (see page 170) around cooled 1.5 kg beef fillet. Wrap in three 25 cm thin herb crêpes.

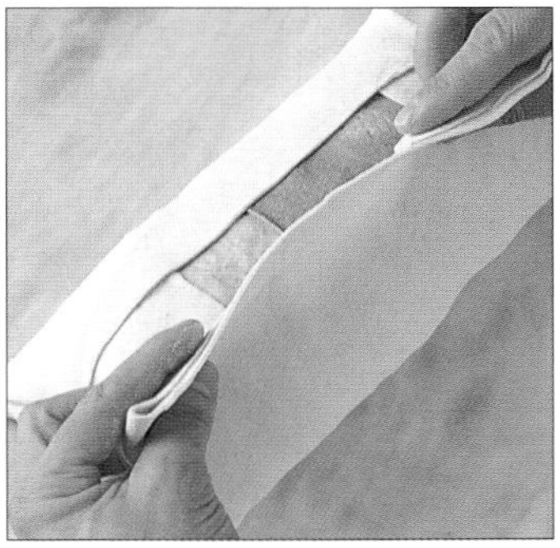

2 Roll out 700 g puff pastry to 5 mm thickness, then wrap around the fillet to enclose it completely.

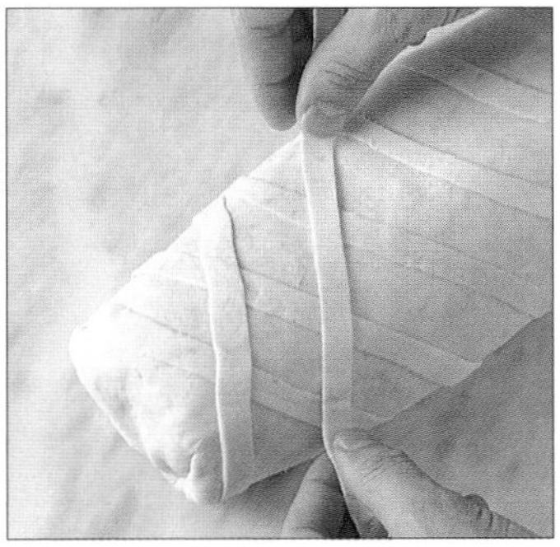

3 Place parcel seam-side down and decorate the top and sides with a lattice of pastry trimmings.

4 Place the parcel on a dampened baking sheet and brush with egg wash (see page 31). Bake at 200°C for 10 minutes, then lower the heat to 180°C and bake for another 20 minutes until golden and crisp. Let rest for 10 minutes, then cut into slices to serve.

Trick of the Trade

Stuffing a Fillet

Professional chefs often slice and stuff a whole fillet of beef before roasting. This adds flavour and helps the meat retain moisture during cooking.

Sear the fillet (see step 1, above left) and let cool. Slice thickly, almost all the way through, then spoon *duxelles* (see page 170) or the stuffing of your choice between each slice. Reform the fillet, wrap in thin herb crêpes and pastry and roast (see left).

BEEF WELLINGTON

Filet de boeuf en croûte (fillet of beef in pastry) was a French culinary classic long before Wellington's time, but in honour of the hero of the Battle of Waterloo it was renamed Beef Wellington – and the name has stuck. The dish was popular at early 19th century banquets, and was known to be a particular favourite of the Duke of Wellington. Traditionally it is made with a mushroom stuffing mixed with diced bacon and fresh chopped herbs.

Duke of Wellington (1769–1852)

SALTIMBOCCA

4 veal escalopes, halved and rolled around Parma ham and fresh sage leaves (see page 123)
1 tbsp each butter and olive oil
3 tbsp Marsala
150 ml double cream
1 tbsp chopped fresh sage
Salt and freshly ground pepper

Pan-fry the veal in the butter and oil. Remove veal; add the Marsala and mix with the pan juices. Add the cream, sage and seasonings and pour over the veal.

TRICK OF THE TRADE

COATING STEAKS

Coatings not only enhance the flavour of steaks, they also provide a protective crust which helps seal in the natural juices of the meat. Crushed black peppercorns are used for the classic steak au poivre *shown here, but you can use mixed peppercorns such as white, green and pink.*

For 4 fillet steaks, coarsely crush 2–3 tbsp peppercorns in a pestle and mortar or put them in a bowl and crush them with the end of a rolling pin. Spread them on a plate and coat both sides of each steak, pressing them firmly so they adhere to the meat.

PAN-FRYING

Pan-frying is an excellent way of cooking lean, thin slices of meat, such as the veal in the saltimbocca *shown here. The high temperature and hot fat seal the meat immediately, making sure it remains moist and succulent. Use a non-stick frying pan with a heavy base and just enough fat to prevent the meat from sticking. The delicious pan juices are combined with Marsala and cream at the end of cooking to make a rich accompanying sauce.*

1 Add the meat when the butter is foaming. Turn it quickly several times to sear it, then cook over a moderate heat for 3–4 minutes.

2 Stir the cream vigorously over a moderate heat so that it blends with the Marsala and pan juices to make a smooth sauce.

MAKING FAJITAS

In Mexican cooking, the technique of pan-frying is used for cooking beef to make fajitas, *strips of marinated steak that are served sizzling hot in warm* tortillas. *Skirt or rump steak can be used, cut into strips across the grain.*

1 Coat strips of steak in a marinade of chilli oil, lime juice and crushed black peppercorns. Cover and marinate in the refrigerator for at least 2 hours, preferably overnight.

2 Brush a stovetop grill pan with olive oil. Heat until very hot. Add the beef strips, with pepper slices if you like. Toss over a high heat.

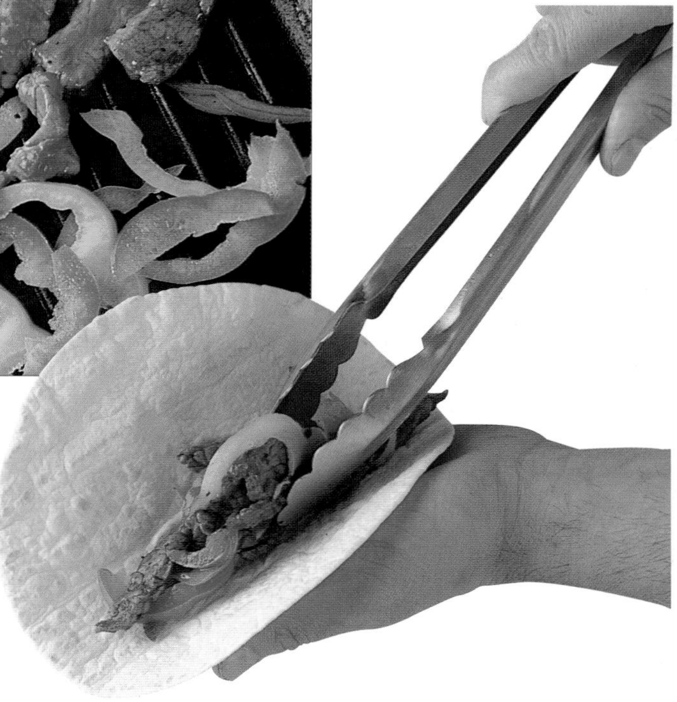

3 When the beef strips and pepper slices are tender and browned all over, remove them from the pan with tongs and serve in warm *tortillas* (see page 240).

GRILLING

Grilling is ideal for lightly marbled tender cuts that need quick cooking to keep them tender and moist. Suitable cuts include veal cutlets and chops, and beef steaks such as rump or sirloin and fillet shown here. For exact cooking times, see the box below.

1 Preheat the grill to high. Prepare the steak (see page 120), place on the grill-pan rack, and brush with olive oil, chopped garlic and ground black pepper.

2 Place the steak under the grill and sear one side. Turn the steak over, brush with more olive oil mixture and grill the second side.

CHARGRILLING FILLET STEAK
Heat a stovetop grill pan until hot but not smoking. Brush fillet steak with oil and cook according to times in box below, turning once.

GRILLING TIMES FOR STEAKS

Cooking times depend on the heat of the grill, distance from the grill and thickness of the steak. These timings are for 2.5 cm thick steaks, 5 cm from a preheated very hot grill.

VERY RARE – *BLEU*
From 1 minute on each side for fillet to 2 minutes for rump. The meat feels very soft, the interior is blueish purple.

RARE – *SAIGNANT*
From 2 minutes each side for fillet to 3 minutes for rump. The meat feels soft and spongy, the interior is still red.

MEDIUM – *A POINT*
From 3 minutes each side for fillet to 4 minutes for rump. The meat offers resistance when pressed and is pink in the centre.

WELL-DONE – *BIEN CUIT*
Sear for 3 minutes on each side and cook at a lower temperature for 6–10 minutes more, turning once. The meat is firm and brown.

BARBECUING

This technique is ideal for steaks and veal loin chops and cutlets. Prepare the barbecue following the guidelines given on page 113. For extra tenderness and flavour, and to prevent meat drying out, marinate beforehand in olive oil, herbs and seasoning of your choice.

Place the steaks on the oiled grid of the barbecue and cook according to times given for grilling (see box, left), turning once. Baste them with marinade during cooking, using a brush or a bunch of twiggy herbs such as thyme or rosemary.

FLAVOURED BUTTERS

Chilled butters are a classic topping for hot grilled meats, especially steaks.

Beat unsalted butter until soft, using a wooden spoon, then beat in flavourings of your choice, such as chopped shallots softened in red wine. Roll the butter in baking parchment, twist the ends to secure. Chill or freeze until firm, then cut into rounds. Alternatively, roll the butter between two sheets of baking parchment until 5 mm thick; leave to chill. Stamp out rounds when firm.

TRICK OF THE TRADE

CROSSHATCH STEAKS

Create an attractive design on steak as it cooks on the barbecue.

Sear the steak until the rack markings are clearly visible across the meat, then give it a quarter turn and sear again on the same side. Turn the steak over and repeat. This will create a professional "chargrilled" effect.

Slow Cooking

Tough, sinewy cuts of meat require gentle slow cooking in aromatic liquids to allow time for fibrous tissues to soften and flavours to develop. Whole joints and pieces of meat can be cooked using this technique. For maximum flavour and tenderness, cool the meat in the liquid and reheat the next day.

Pot Roasting

Less prime joints benefit from slow cooking in liquid. This tenderizes sinews and imparts a rich flavour to the meat. Suitable cuts are boned and rolled brisket, topside and silverside of beef; shoulder and silverside of veal. A 1 kg boned and rolled joint takes about 2½ hours to cook.

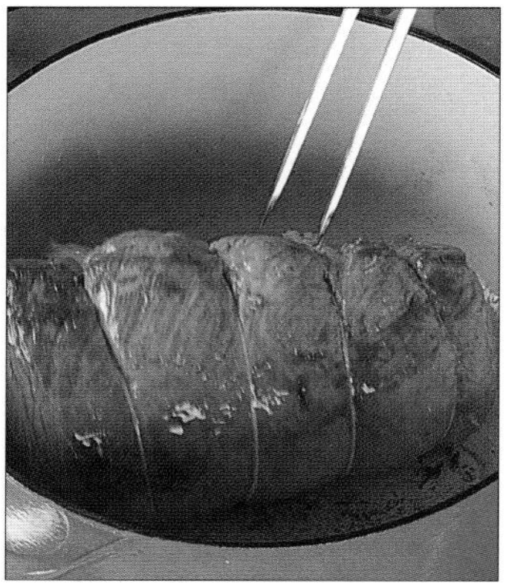

1 For a good flavour and colour at the end of cooking, first sear the joint over a high heat in a little oil, turning until evenly browned.

2 After browning, add stock or wine or a mixture of the two, chopped vegetables such as onions and leeks, plus a bouquet garni and seasonings. Simmer gently or cook at 170°C until tender. Add root vegetables about 30 minutes before the end of cooking.

Making a Stew

Stewing or casseroling is a very moist method of cooking, perfect for less prime meat such as flank, shin and chuck. For best results, trim meat of excess fat and sinew and cut into equal-sized cubes, then brown in a flameproof casserole. Add liquid just to cover and cook in the same casserole, either on top of the stove or in a 170°C oven. A stew made with 1 kg meat takes 2–2½ hours to cook.

1 If the meat has been marinated, dry thoroughly on paper towels, then brown in batches over a high heat to seal in juices and add colour to the sauce.

2 Test for doneness by inserting the point of a small knife into one of the pieces of meat. The blade should slide easily through the fibres.

Trick of the Trade

Kneaded Butter

This liaison of butter and flour, called beurre manié *in French, is often used in French recipes to thicken stews and casseroles.*

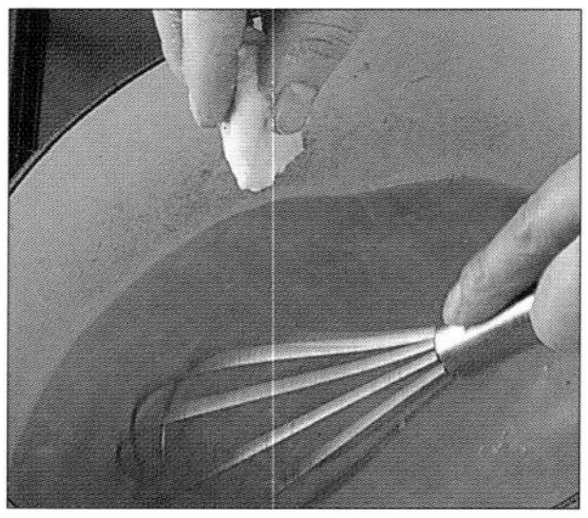

Put equal parts of unsalted butter and plain flour on a plate and cream together with a fork until a smooth paste is formed.

Put the pan of liquid to be thickened on top of the stove and add the kneaded butter in small pieces, whisking vigorously.

Bring the liquid to the boil and simmer, still whisking until thickened, adding more kneaded butter as necessary

Braising Sinewy Cuts

When choosing beef or veal for braising, select tough cuts with a good amount of bone but not too much fat, such as the shin of veal shown here. Sinew and gristle break down during cooking to enrich the sauce. Only a small amount of liquid is used, so keep the dish tightly covered. A simple recipe for osso buco, using the techniques shown here, is given in the box, right.

1 Brown the veal in hot oil. The coating of flour will form a crust around the meat and help thicken the sauce.

2 Turn the meat once or twice during braising so that it cooks evenly and takes on the flavour of the sauce.

OSSO BUCO

1 kg shin of veal, sawn into 5 cm pieces
1 tbsp plain flour
2–3 tbsp olive oil
2 carrots, diced
2 onions, chopped
125 ml dry white wine
125 ml brown stock (see page 16)
400 g can tomatoes
1 tsp dried mixed herbs
Salt and freshly ground pepper
Gremolada (see page 330)

Toss the meat in the flour. Heat the oil in a flameproof casserole and brown the meat. Remove, then add carrots and onions and sweat for 10 minutes. Return the meat to the pan and add the wine, stock, tomatoes, dried herbs and seasonings to taste. Cover and cook at 170°C for 2 hours or until tender, turning occasionally. Check the seasoning. Serve hot, sprinkled with gremolada. Serves 4.

Cooking Salt Beef

Before refrigeration, meat was preserved by drying or salting in brine flavoured with herbs, spices and sugar. Today this is not necessary, but salt beef is still popular for its unique flavour and attractive pink colour. It is available at specialist butchers and some supermarkets.

Before cooking, soak salt beef in cold water overnight to remove excess saltiness. Drain and rinse in cold water, then place in a pan with roughly chopped vegetables, such as carrots, parsnips and potatoes, and freshly ground pepper. Cover with water and bring to the boil, then cover and simmer gently for 2 hours or until tender.

Cooking in a Clay Pot

In the Middle East meat is often slow cooked in a clay pot – the steam condenses inside the tight-fitting lid of the pot, drips back into the stew and makes the meat wonderfully moist. The conical lid of the pot shown here, a Moroccan tagine, *is especially effective for this cooking method.*

1 First brown cubes of beef in hot oil in a frying pan, then place in the bottom of the pot with dried fruit such as prunes or apricots, thinly pared lemon or orange zest, hot beef stock and seasonings.

2 Cover the pot tightly with its lid, sealing it with a flour and water paste if you like. Cook in a 170°C oven for 2 hours. Serve hot, sprinkled with chopped fresh herbs.

Thai Beef

A salade tiède, *or warm salad, this stunning dish is made with lean, tender beef in a zesty Asian dressing, garnished with crisp cucumber and sweet mango, and served with rice cooked in coconut milk.*

SERVES 4

750 g piece of rump steak, cut 2.5 cm thick

Vegetable oil

10 g fresh coriander leaves

10 g fresh mint leaves

3 stalks of lemon grass, trimmed and finely chopped

FOR THE DRESSING

2 small fresh chillies, halved, deseeded and chopped

2 garlic cloves, peeled

4-cm piece of fresh root ginger, peeled and chopped

Juice of 1 lime

3 tbsp light soy sauce

2 tbsp vegetable oil

2 tsp light soft brown sugar

TO SERVE

1 fresh red chilli, halved lengthwise

1 cucumber, scored lengthwise and thinly sliced

1 large ripe but firm mango, peeled and sliced

Coconut rice (see box, below)

Heat a stovetop grill pan over moderate to high heat until very hot but not smoking.

Lightly brush the steak with oil and place on the hot pan. Grill for about 3 minutes on each side; the steak should be rare to medium-rare (it will continue to cook a little after it is removed from the heat). Move steak to a plate. Let rest while you make the dressing.

Put the dressing ingredients in a blender and blend until they are quite fine.

Chop the coriander and mint leaves, keeping a few leaves whole for garnish.

Cut the beef into thin slices. Put in a bowl, add a few spoonfuls of the dressing and toss together with the chopped herbs and lemon grass.

Pile the beef mixture on a platter, top with the pieces of chilli and arrange the cucumber and mango decoratively around the edge. Serve with the remaining dressing and the coconut rice.

COCONUT RICE

600 ml coconut milk
300 ml water
1 stalk of lemon grass, bruised
1/2 tsp salt
275 g Thai jasmine rice

Put the coconut milk and water in a pan and add the lemon grass and salt. Bring the mixture to the boil, add the rice and stir. Half cover the pan with the lid and simmer very gently for 20 minutes. Remove from the heat, cover tightly and let stand for 5 minutes. Discard the lemon grass and fluff up rice with a fork.

Cooking and Shredding Thai Beef

If the steak is pressed constantly during chargrilling this will loosen the fibres in the meat and make the meat easy to slice.

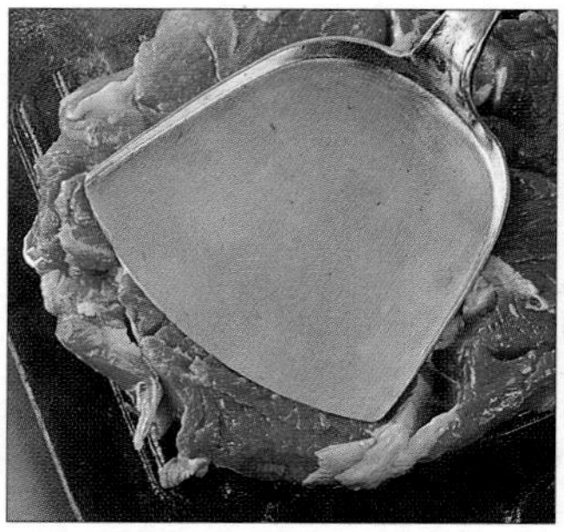

While chargrilling the steak, press it constantly with a wok scoop to keep it flat.

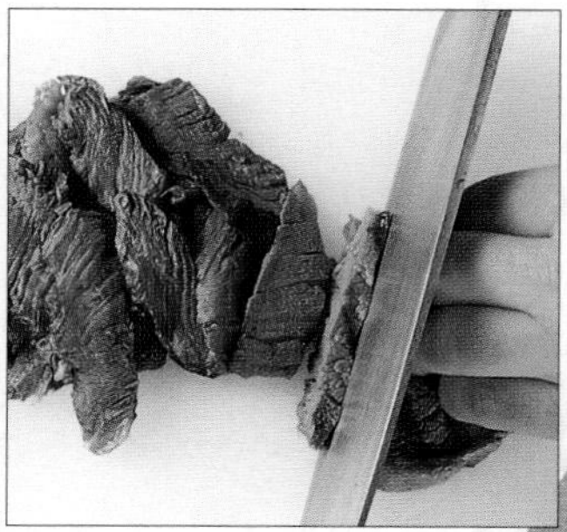

Cut the steak across the grain into slices about 1 cm thick, using a cleaver.

Choosing Lamb

Modern methods of breeding and farming have improved the taste and texture of lamb and fulfilled the demand for leaner, less fatty cuts. Meat from milk-fed baby lamb is very pale and looks similar to veal; meat from sheep less than a year old (spring lamb) has slightly darker pink flesh with a delicate flavour. Although not readily available, mutton (meat from sheep over two years old) has a stronger more gamey taste and darker coloured flesh.

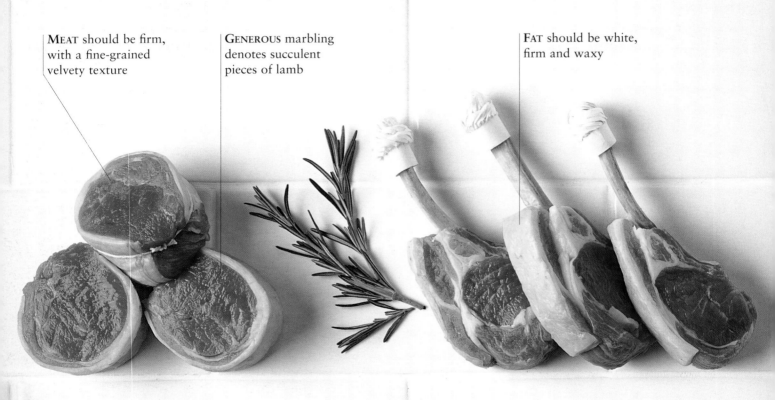

MEAT should be firm, with a fine-grained velvety texture
GENEROUS marbling denotes succulent pieces of lamb
FAT should be white, firm and waxy

Buying Lamb

Lamb freezes well with little damage to the meat so that frozen lamb is a good choice when fresh meat is unavailable.

Choose firm, pinkish meat with visible marbling, avoiding meat that appears dark, wet and mushy. As a general rule, the pinker the flesh the younger the lamb. Don't choose cuts that are surrounded by yellow fat; check for an even layer of creamy white, firm fat.

Large joints are often sold with the papery outer skin – this should feel fresh, moist and pliable, not dry or wrinkled. Also called the "fell", this skin should be removed from steaks and chops before cooking, but left on roasting joints because it helps keep the meat moist and imparts a stronger flavour.

Handling Lamb

Store lamb in its original wrapping, tightly sealed, in the coldest part of the refrigerator (1–5°C), away from cooked meats. Always check the "use-by" dates. Chops and steaks will keep 2–4 days, large joints up to 5 days. Minced lamb deteriorates quite quickly, so use within 24 hours.

Cooked lamb will keep in the refrigerator for up to 2 days. Make sure it is thoroughly cooled before putting it in the refrigerator. Store, wrapped in foil, within 2 hours of cooking.

Lamb freezes well – store tightly wrapped small cuts for 3–4 months and large cuts 6–9 months. To defrost, place the lamb on a plate to catch the drips and thaw slowly in the refrigerator allowing about 6 hours per 450 g; use within 2 days.

Lamb Cuts

Ranging from inexpensive cuts, that are best braised, stewed or casseroled to moisten and tenderize their less succulent meat, to exquisite chops, cutlets and elegant crown roasts and guards of honour for special meals, there is a cut of lamb to suit every culinary occasion. Although lamb is available year-round, new-season lamb is the sweetest and most tender. It is a traditional Easter dish in many countries where it heralds the arrival of spring.

Lamb Cuts	What to Look For	Cooking Methods
Best end of neck	*Even layer of creamy white outer fat* *Marbling throughout meat* *Bone moist with no splinters*	Roast, casserole, grill (chops and cutlets)
Breast	*Heavy marbling* *High ratio of creamy white fat to meat* *Some connective tissue*	Roast, braise
Crown roast/ Guard of honour	*Fat trimmed away from rib bones* *Bones clean but moist; "chine" bone may be sawn* *Moist lean meat*	Roast
Leg	*Fat and "fell" intact* *Cut end of bone red and moist* *Lean meat with some marbling* *Visible connective tissue*	Roast, grill, barbecue (boned)
Loin		
Chump and loin chops	*Lean meat with light marbling* *Bones red and moist – "T" bone in loin, round bone in chump* *Creamy white layer of fat around edge of chop*	Grill, barbecue, pan-fry, braise
Middle neck and scrag end	*High proportion of fat and bone meat* *Moist, lean meat with some connective tissue*	Stew, casserole, braise, grill, pan-fry ("eye"or neck fillet)
Noisettes	*Very lean moist flesh* *Thick layer of creamy white fat tied around outside*	Pan-fry, sauté, grill, barbecue
Saddle	*Pink lean meat* *Lightly marbled* *Even layer of fat (may need trimming)*	Roast
Shank	*White bone* *Creamy white fat* *Full of connective tissue*	Stew, casserole, braise
Shoulder	*Moist, pink meat with obvious marbling* *White moist bone surrounded by visible connective tissue* *Thick layer of outer fat*	Roast, braise, stew (boned and cubed)

Lamb On the Menu

Whether it's delicately perfumed with fresh herbs or boldly seasoned with exotic spices, lamb is very much an international favourite.

Greece – *Moussaka* (minced lamb layered with sliced eggplant and a cinnamon-scented bechamel sauce) is a rich and satisfying dish.

India – *Lamb curry* (cubed meat with spices such as curry, cumin and coriander) may also include vegetables, chick peas, or even nuts.

Britain – *Shepherd's Pie* (chopped lamb, with a mushroom and tomato gravy, and a mashed potato topping) is a consumate cold-weather meal.

France – *Gigot D'Agneau* (flavoured leg of lamb) is prized throughout the country. In Provence it's typically flavored with garlic, rosemary and thyme and in Burgundy, juniper. At a Parisian bistro, it may be served on a bed of creamy white beans.

Morroco – *Lamb Tagine* (cubed lamb gently simmered with onions, peppers, fennel, olives, preserved lemons, and nuts and raisins) is a richly delicious stew traditionally served with couscous.

Preparing for Cooking

The techniques shown here may require a little skill, but the results are well worth the effort taken. A boned joint is easier to carve than one with the bones left in, and a spectacular crown roast is a must for special occasions.

Boning a Shoulder

A shoulder of lamb is an awkward joint to carve; removing the blade and shoulder bones prepares the joint so that it can be rolled and tied with or without a stuffing, then roasted or braised. You will then find it easier to carve. Cut away excess fat as you bone the joint.

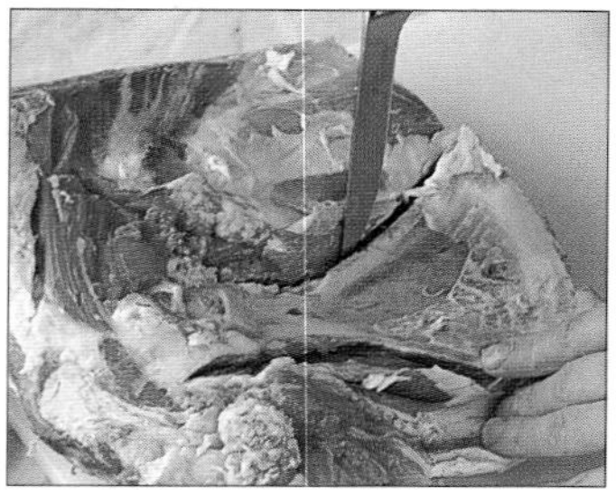

1 Cut through the meat on either side of the blade bone, using a boning knife.

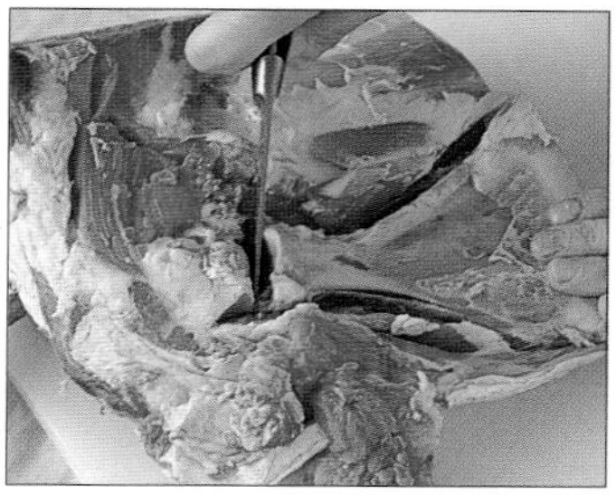

2 Cut through the ball and socket joint to separate the blade, and shoulder bones.

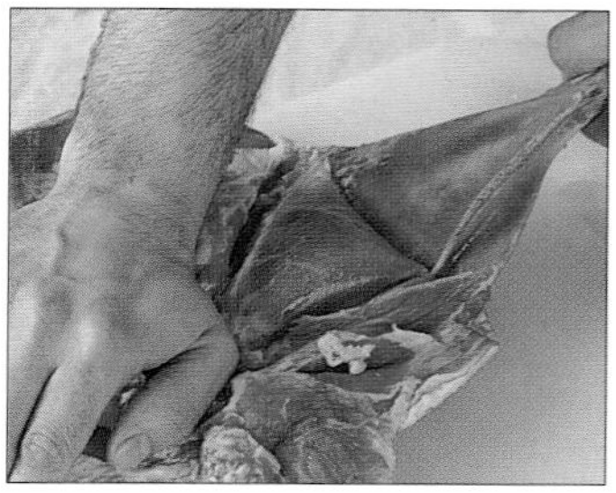

3 Holding the joint firmly, pull the bladebone sharply away from the meat.

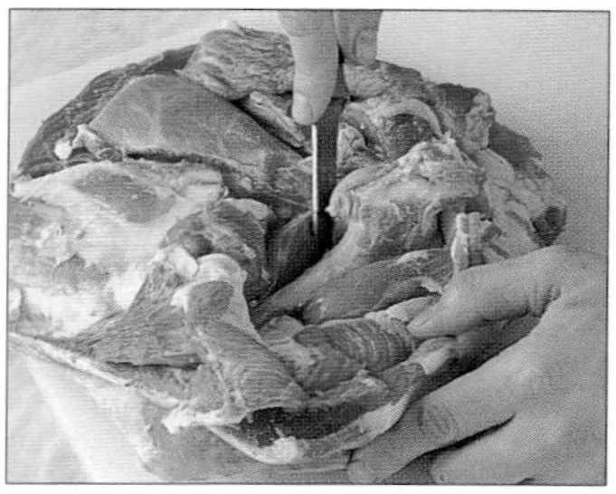

4 Scrape the meat away from the shoulder bone; when free, pull the bone out.

Tunnel Boning a Leg

This technique prepares a leg of lamb for stuffing, creating a neat pocket for the filling. It also makes carving easier. Trim off the fat from the outside of the joint and cut through the tendons at the base of the shank before you start boning.

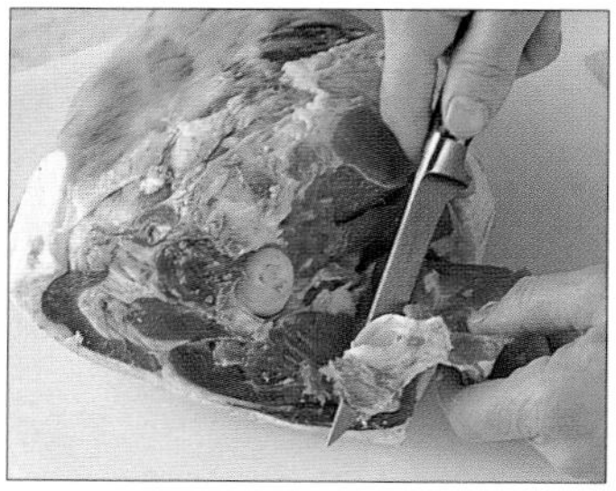

1 Cut around the pelvic bone and through the tendons. Remove the bone.

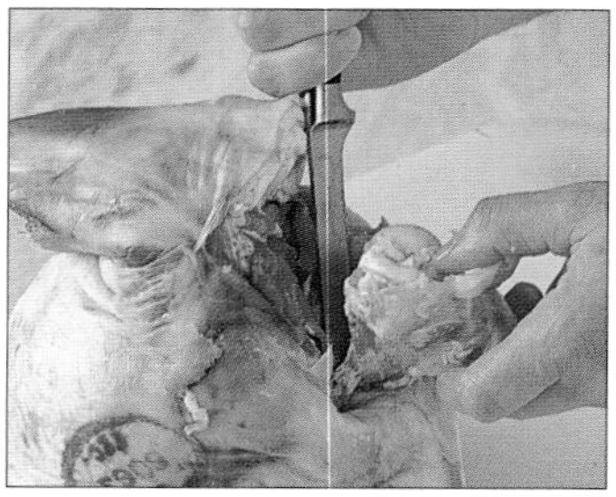

2 Scrape flesh from shank bone; cut tendons at leg joint and remove shank bone.

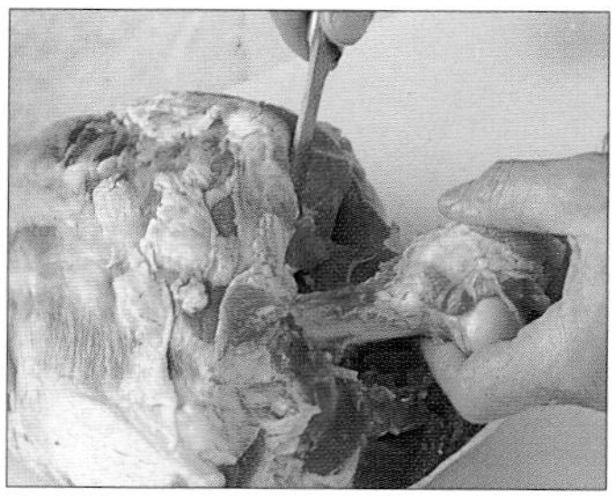

3 Cut around leg bone when exposed, twist and pull out to remove.

Butterflying a Leg

This technique prepares the joint for grilling or barbecuing. The term "butterfly" refers to the shape of the joint after it has been split and cut almost through. Before butterflying, tunnel bone the joint (see left).

1 Insert the knife into the leg bone cavity; cut to one side to split the meat open.

2 Open out the meat and make a shallow cut down the centre to keep it open.

Preparing a Rack

The best end of neck, or rack of lamb, is one side of the animal's ribcage. There are usually 6–9 cutlets in a rack, which can be roasted. Before preparing the rack, cut off the skin and all but 1.25 cm of fat.

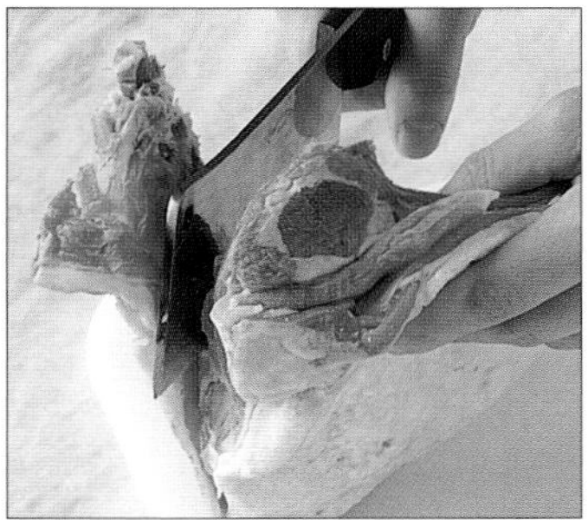

1 Place the rack of lamb on its side. Cut off the chine (back) bone.

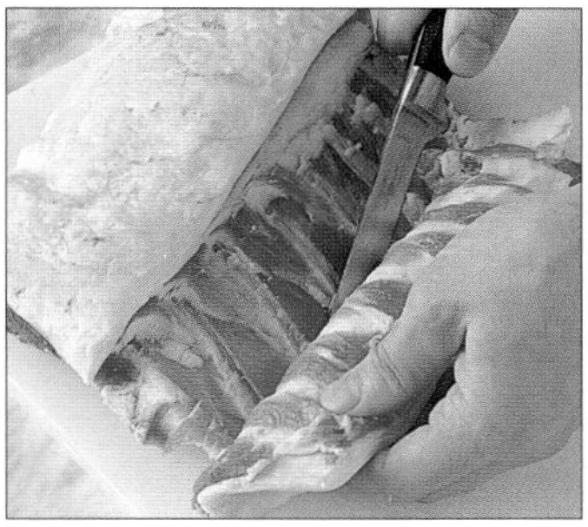

2 Cut fat from ribs 5 cm from bone ends. Turn over and score between bones.

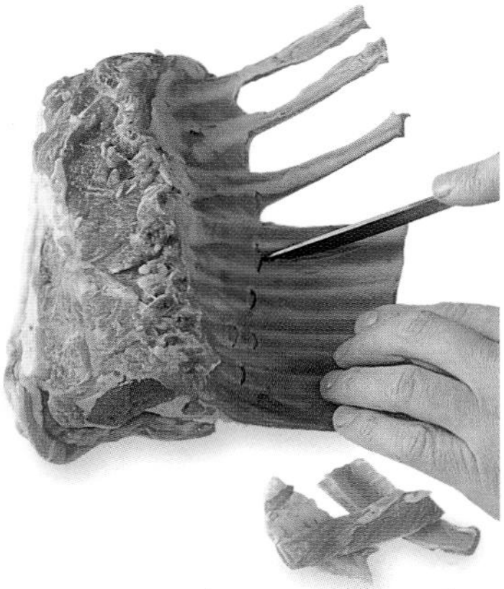

3 Cut and scrape away the meat and tissue from between the bones.

What's in a Name?

French culinary terms are often confusing, and the names given to cuts of lamb are no exception. The following list includes the most commonly used cuts.

- *Carré d'agneau* is a rack of lamb.
- *Côte d'agneau* is a chop taken from the loin or rack (best end).
- *Couronne* is a crown roast.
- *Gigot* is a leg of lamb.
- *Garde d'honneur* is a guard of honour.
- *Noisette* is a boneless cut from the saddle, tied with string.

Making a Crown Roast

This joint takes its name from the fact that when one or two racks are tied together they look like a crown. Before making the crown roast, prepare a rack following steps 1–3 above. Stuffing can be packed into the central cavity of the crown before roasting if you like, or it can be baked in a separate dish.

1 Cut the membrane between the ribs so the rack can be bent.

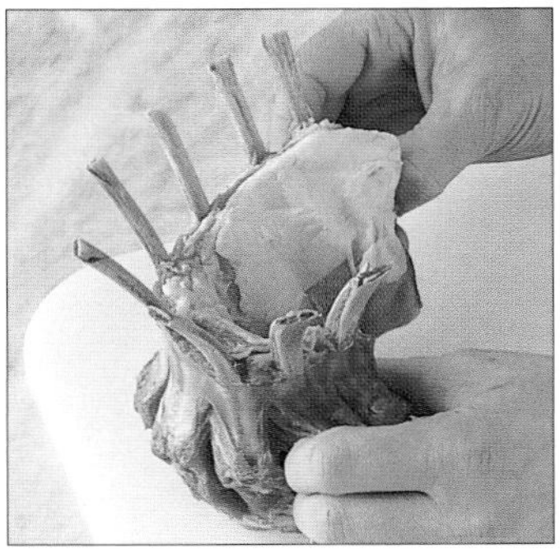

2 Stand the rack meat-side out; curve to form a crown shape.

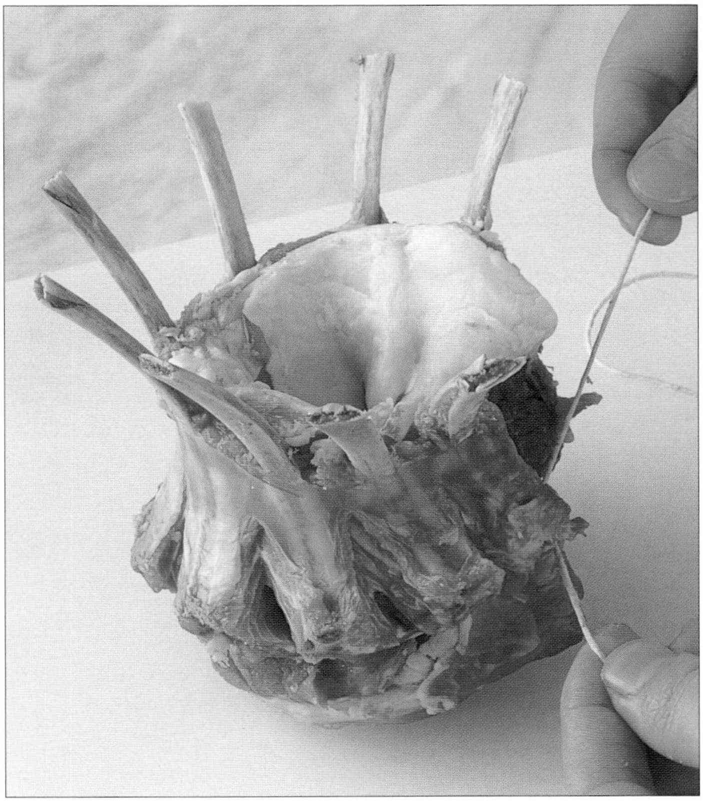

3 Bend the ribs outwards so the crown can sit upright. Tie string around the middle to hold the rack in place. Sew ends together, if you like. The joint is now ready for roasting.

Making a Guard of Honour

When the bones of two racks interlock like swords, a "guard of honour" is formed.

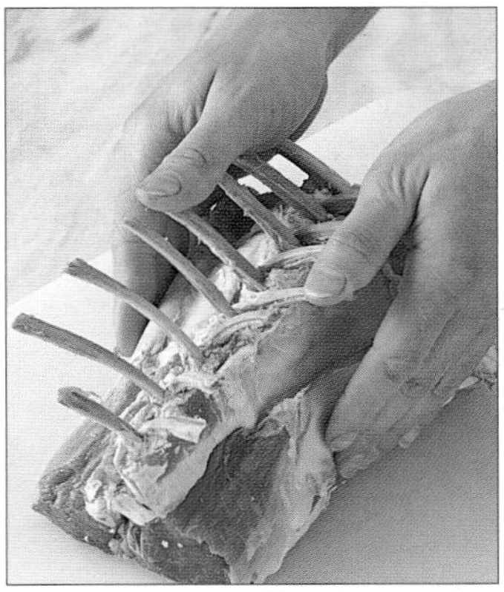

Prepare two racks as in steps 1–3 above, removing all outside fat if you like. Holding one rack in each hand with the meat and ribs facing inwards, push the racks firmly together so the bones interlock. The joint is now ready for roasting (see page 136).

Roasting & Braising

The leg, shoulder and best end of neck are ideal joints for plain roasting, while the best end of neck and shoulder are good braised with simple vegetables, but they all gain additional flavour and moisture with a stuffing or crust. These techniques are demonstrated here, together with instructions on how to carve lamb on the bone.

Stuffing and Roasting

Here a tunnel-boned leg of lamb (see page 134) is stuffed and tied, then roasted with a meat thermometer. The same roasting technique can be applied to a leg on the bone, but take care not to let the thermometer touch the bone.

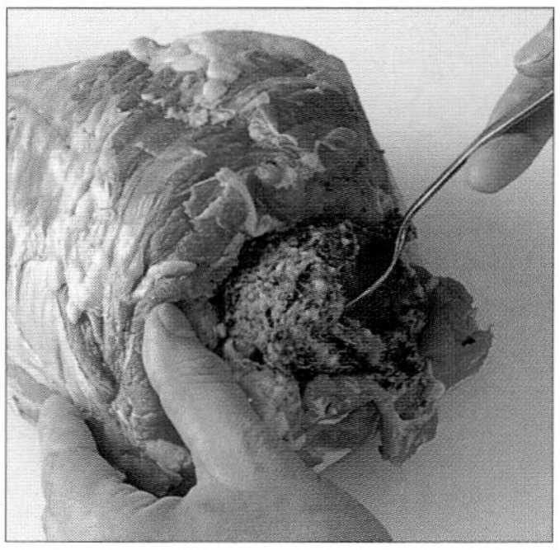

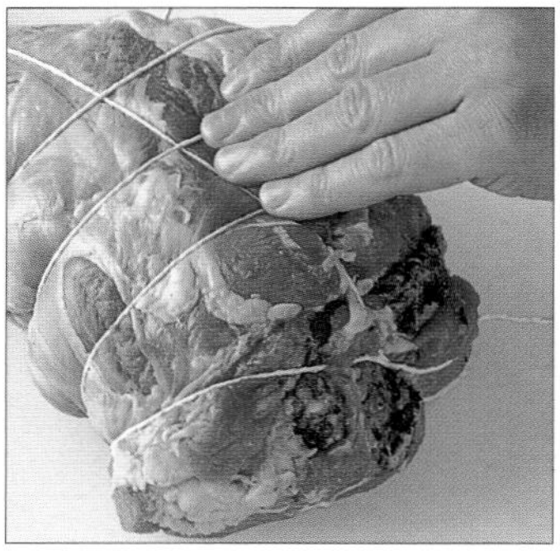

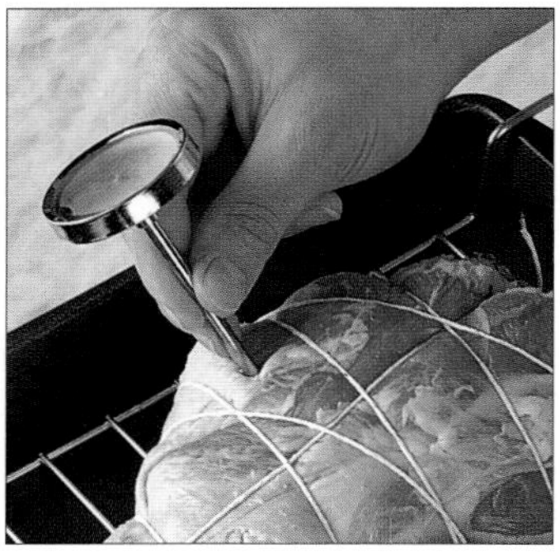

1 Spoon stuffing into the pocket left by the removal of the bone, then push it in with your fingers.

2 Tie the joint with string (see page 121) to neaten its shape. Place the joint on a rack in a roasting tin.

3 Insert the thermometer in the leg, rub the leg with olive oil and seasonings, then roast (see chart, left)

Flavouring Joints

Impart flavour – and good looks – to a seared joint of meat by spreading the outside with a paste of strong-tasting ingredients such as herbs, spices, mustard, garlic and anchovies. Or, for a homestyle presentation, stud the fat and flesh of raw meat with garlic and/or herbs.

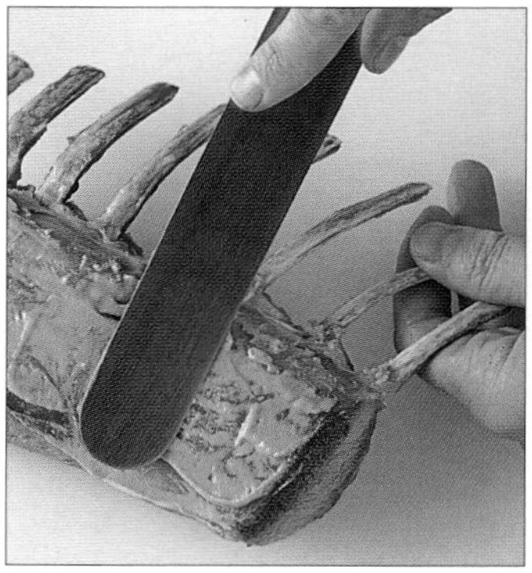

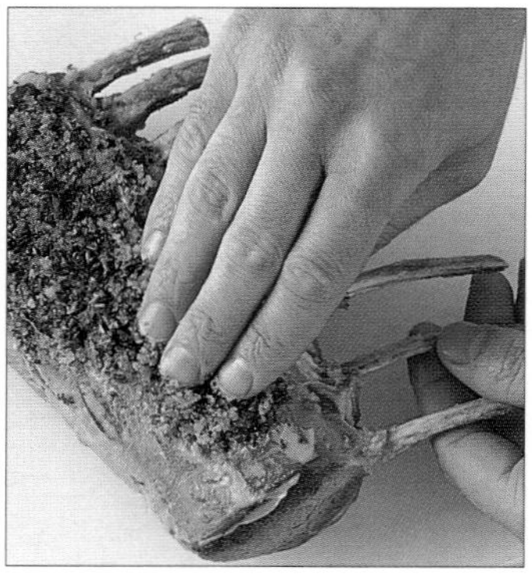

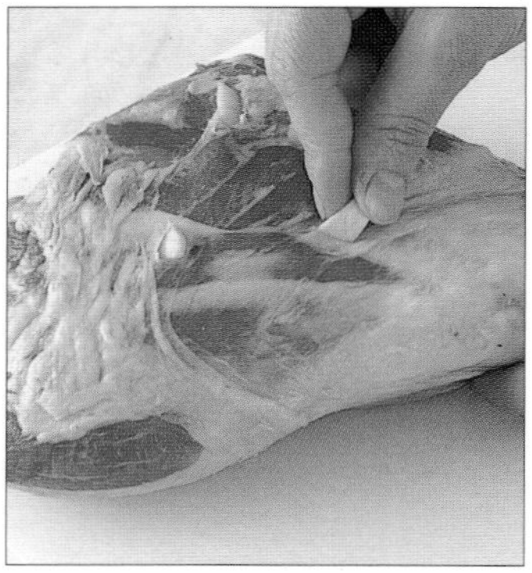

1 Sear the lamb in hot oil and leave to cool, then spread the fat side evenly with 1 tbsp Dijon or other French mustard.

2 Press a mixture of chopped fresh herbs and dried breadcrumbs into the mustard with your fingers.

Inserting garlic
Before roasting a leg or shoulder of lamb, cut deep slits in the meat and insert chunks of peeled garlic.

Roasting Times

In France, lamb is generally served rare or medium-rare. Roast at 230°C for 10 mins, then at 180°C for 18 mins per 450 g. Internal temperature should be 60°C.

- ROAST in a preheated oven at 230°C for 10 mins, reduce to 180°C and follow times below:
- MEDIUM Internal temp 70°C 25 mins per 450 g plus an extra 25 mins
- WELL-DONE Internal temp 80°C 30 mins per 450 g plus an extra 30 mins

Wrapping a Joint

In France, a boned leg of lamb is sometimes cooked in pastry to produce both a succulent joint and an attractive presentation. Brioche pastry (see page 243) is traditional, but you can use bought puff or filo pastry if you prefer. First roast the lamb, with or without stuffing, at 200°C for 40 minutes, then let the meat cool and remove the string. Wrap the pastry around the meat and place, seam-side down, on a buttered baking sheet. Brush with egg wash (see page 31) and bake for about 45 minutes until the pastry is golden. Let rest for 15 minutes before serving

Carving a Leg on the Bone

After removing the joint from the oven, lift it out of the tin and let it rest, covered loosely with foil, for 10–15 minutes. Use a fork to steady the meat, not pierce it, during carving.

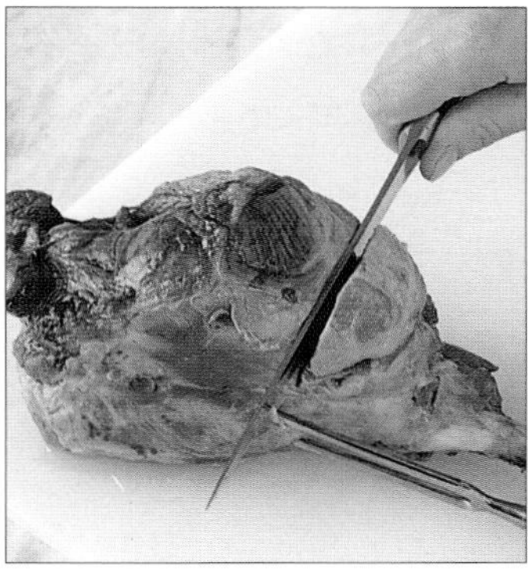

1 Insert a chef's knife into the knuckle end of the joint. Make two deep cuts, one vertical and one horizontal, to form a wedge.

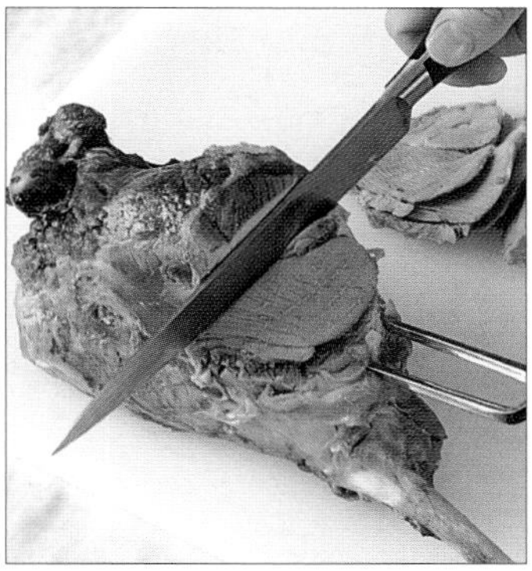

2 Carve neat slices from either side of the wedge. Turn the leg over; with the knife at a shallow angle, slice off the meat.

Carving a rack
Place the rack, ribs facing down, on a cutting board. Hold the rack steady and cut between the ribs with a chef's knife, using a sawing action.

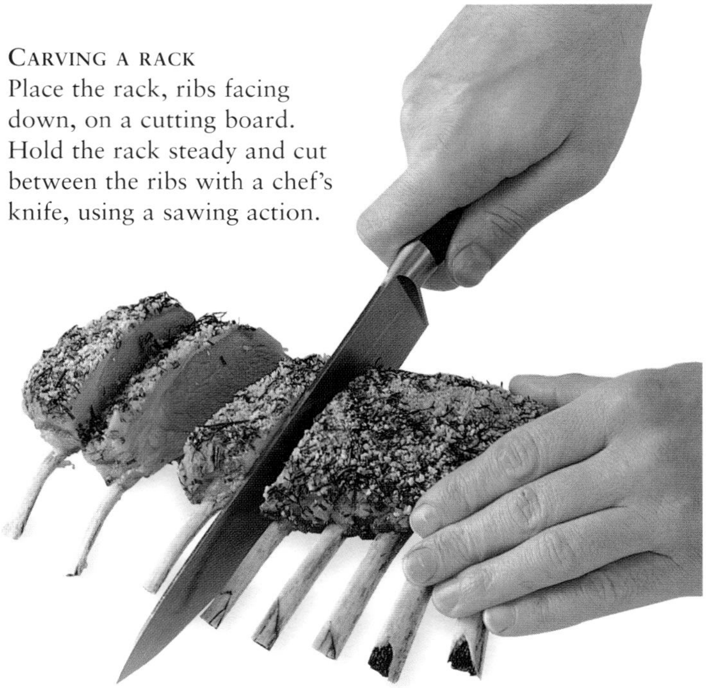

Stuffing and Braising a Shoulder of Lamb

This method produces very tender, flavoursome meat for a boned shoulder and has the added bonus of a moist stuffing that makes the meat go further. After rolling the meat around the stuffing, tie it with string according to the instructions on page 132 so that it keeps a compact shape and is easy to slice.

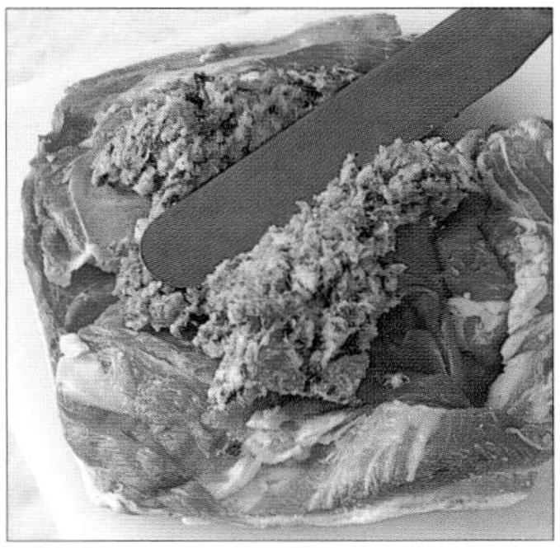

1 Open out the meat and spread the stuffing evenly, leaving the edges bare.

2 Brown the rolled joint of lamb thoroughly over a moderate to high heat before adding the onions. This helps give a good, rich colour and flavour to the finished dish.

Braised Lamb with Herb Stuffing

2 kg shoulder of lamb
4 tbsp chopped fresh herbs
2 garlic cloves, finely chopped
1 shallot, finely chopped
100 g fresh breadcrumbs
Salt and freshly ground pepper
1 egg, lightly beaten
2 tbsp olive oil
100 g baby onions, peeled
300 ml brown stock (see page 16)
3 carrots, sliced

Bone the lamb (see page 134) and finely chop the meat trimmings. Combine the chopped meat with the herbs, garlic, shallot, breadcrumbs and seasoning, then bind with the egg. Spread the mixture over the meat, roll and tie, then season and brown in hot oil in a flameproof casserole. Add the onions and stock, cover and braise at 170°C for 1½–2 hours, adding the carrots for the last 30 minutes. Check the seasoning. Serves 4–6.

Finishing Touches

Use edible decorations to enhance the presentation of whole roasted joints and individual cuts and slices of beef, veal, lamb and pork. Place the decorations around joints on a serving platter or alongside the slices of meat on individual dinner plates, not on the sauce or gravy.

DRESSING UP MEAT

When serving hot meat, make sure that any accompanying decorations that are to be eaten are also served hot. Traditional garnishes and accompaniments are given here, plus a few more unusual suggestions.

- With roast pork, serve traditional apple sauce plus apple rings fried in butter and sprigs of fresh sage.
- With roast lamb, serve mint sauce or jelly, or redcurrant jelly. Fresh mint sprigs are the traditional garnish.
- Serve roast beef with mustard or horseradish, and garnish with watercress.
- Roast veal, in classic French cuisine, is served with *jus* and garnished with parsley sprigs.
- *A la bourguignonne* is a classic French presentation for beef. Sauté quartered button mushrooms and blanched pearl onions in butter until they are tender. Spoon them around beef with a red wine sauce.
- With roast veal or grilled veal chops, serve tiny vegetable fritters or rösti (see page 190).
- With roast meat of any kind, toss turned potatoes in melted butter and very finely chopped parsley or mint.
- To tie bundles of cooked vegetables, use blanched leek or spring onion strips, chive stems, sliced bacon or strips of julienned citrus zest instead of red pepper strips (see right).

Piped potatoes
Enrich puréed potatoes with egg yolks and butter. Pipe on to baking sheet and bake at 200°C for 5 minutes.

Turned vegetables
Boil turned vegetables (see page 167), such as courgette, turnip and carrot, until tender; they can also be glazed.

Rice moulds
Pack oiled moulds with hot boiled rice mixed with finely chopped vegetables and herbs, then unmould.

Vegetable bundles
Use blanched thin red pepper strips to tie up small bunches of cooked French beans or asparagus tips.

Baby vegetables
Leave some green stalks on peeled and blanched baby vegetables, such as carrots and turnips.

Roast shallots
Toss unpeeled shallots in vegetable oil and roast at 200°C until the skins are crisp, 20 minutes.

Confit shallots
Lightly drizzle peeled shallots with goose or duck fat and cook at 120°C for 1 hour or until soft.

Crispy leeks
Deep-fry the very finely shredded green part of leeks in 180°C oil until just crisp. Drain on paper towels.

Oriental Decorations

Present stir-fries, salads and buffet dishes with these striking vegetable decorations. They can be made in advance, but keep them in iced water until required for a crisp, fresh appearance. Use a thin, sharp knife to ensure an expert finish.

Courgette fireworks
Make crosswise cuts in a thick ribbon of courgette, leaving one long edge intact. Roll up and stand, cut-edge up.

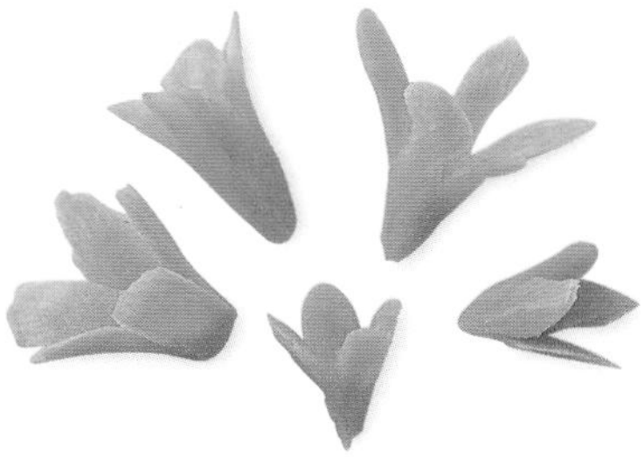

Carrot flowers
Make four angled cuts around the sharpened tip of a carrot to form petals. Twist off flower and repeat.

Cucumber crowns
Slice a 3-mm thick strip of peel. Cut strip into 4-cm wide pieces, then cut in a zigzag to form spikes.

Radish roses
Cut the tops off radishes, then cut thin criss-cross slices without cutting into the stem. Chill in iced water to open.

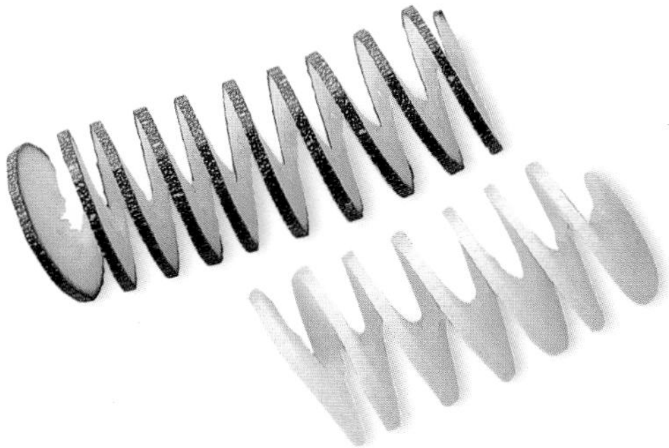

Vegetable spirals
Thread a chunk of mooli or courgette on a skewer. Cut, spiralling along the length, turning vegetable as you go.

Chilli flowers
Make 5 thin cuts from the stem of a long chilli almost to the tip. Chill in iced water until the petals open out.

Guards on Parade

Typical of traditional French style, these succulent racks of lamb are served with courgette boats, stuffed baby turnips, and cherry tomatoes stuffed with duxelles (see page 170). Keep hot with a little stock in a covered tin in the oven.

Stuffed baby turnips
Use a mellon baller to hollow out blanched baby turnips. Pipe in creamed broccoli purée.

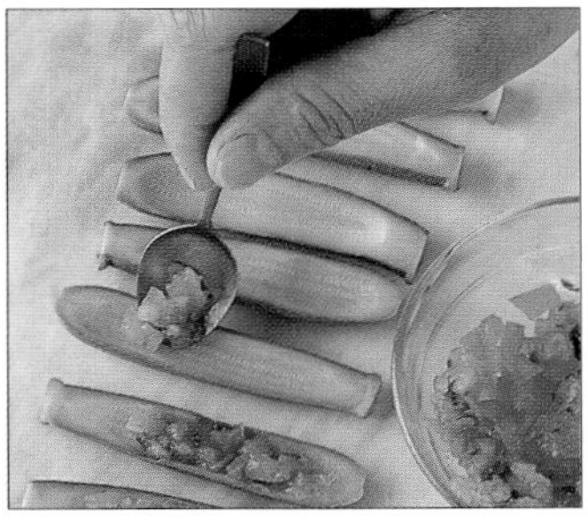

Courgette boats
Spoon a *concassée* of tomatoes (see page 178) into blanched hollowed-out baby courgette halves.

Quick Cooking

The techniques of quick cooking include grilling, frying and barbecuing, where the close contact with intense heat seals the meat and retains the juices. Lean cuts of lamb such as cutlets, chops and noisettes can be cooked this way, so too can cubes of leg, shoulder and neck fillet.

GRILLING TIMES

The cooking times given are approximate and cook the lamb to medium. Turn the meat halfway through cooking. Let the lamb rest, loosely covered, for 5–10 minutes before serving.

BUTTERFLIED	20–30 mins
CHOPS	8–10 mins
CUTLETS	6 mins
KEBABS	6–8 mins
NOISETTES	10 mins

MARINATING LAMB

Lamb can be grilled or barbecued with just a light brushing of olive oil, herbs and seasonings, but a marinade adds flavour and moistens the meat. Even one hour of marinating makes a difference, but overnight marinating is best.

- Make an acid-based marinade with oil, wine vinegar, and thyme, oregano and tarragon, plus Dijon mustard.
- Add garlic, turmeric, cumin seeds, ground cloves, cardamom and cinnamon to yogurt for an Indian taste.
- Blend yogurt with paprika and a little cayenne pepper sharpened with lime juice.

Cooking Cutlets

This simple technique from the south of France makes tender cutlets both look and taste good. Here the cutlets are cooked on the barbecue, but they can also be grilled.

1 Trim off the excess fat around the outside of the cutlets with a chef's knife.

2 Secure the loose flesh by making a slit through the fat into the flesh and inserting a rosemary sprig.

3 Place the cutlets on the oiled rack of a preheated barbecue; cook for about 3 minutes on each side.

Making Kebabs

Lamb is an excellent meat for making kebabs because it is lean and tender and cooks quickly. Leg of lamb can be used, so too can shoulder and neck fillet, both of which have a light marbling of fat that helps baste the meat during cooking.

1 Cut trimmed lamb into 3-cm cubes and mix with the marinade of your choice (see box, left).

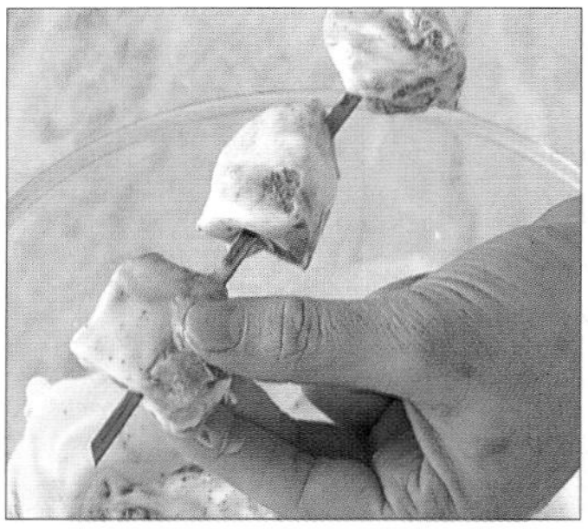

2 Thread the marinated cubes on oiled skewers, leaving space in between to ensure even cooking.

3 Place kebabs on the oiled rack of a preheated barbecue and cook, turning, for 6–8 minutes. Alternatively, cook the kebabs under a hot grill, about 5 cm away from the heat, for the same length of time as before.

Cooking a Butterflied Leg of Lamb

The beauty of this technique is that the meat can be cooked in a quarter of the time it takes to roast a whole leg of lamb. Here barbecuing is shown, but the lamb can also be grilled. For the technique of butterflying, see page 134.

1 Rub seasonings and olive oil over the lamb. Place, meat-side down, on the oiled rack of a preheated barbecue.

2 Cook for 20–30 minutes, turning once, until the outside is charred and the meat is tender when pierced.

3 Put the lamb on a board, cover loosely with foil and let rest 10 minutes. Carve crosswise into slices.

Sauteing Tender Cuts of Lamb

Use this technique for escalopes cut from a leg of lamb as shown here, or for noisettes cut from the saddle (see page 142). Both of these are very lean and tender, perfect for quick pan-frying. Escalopes take 2–3 minutes on each side, noisettes take 4–5 minutes.

1 Add lamb to foaming oil and butter and sauté for 4–6 minutes, turning once.

2 Transfer the lamb to a serving plate. Add double cream and fresh thyme to the pan juices and simmer, stirring, until reduced by one-third. Spoon over the lamb.

Pan-frying in Caul

Pig's caul (see box, page 153) is used by professional chefs for pan-frying delicate meat such as the small nuggets of lamb shown here. The caul protects the meat and melts into it during cooking, making it moist.

Wrap about 25 g caul around each nugget of lamb. Heat oil and butter in a sauté pan until the butter is foaming. Add the lamb and pan-fry for 4–5 minutes on each side. Drain well before serving.

Chargrilling

As an alternative to grilling and barbecuing, chargrilling is perfect for quick cooking small cuts. Chump chops are shown here; noisettes can also be chargrilled.

Brush a stovetop grill pan with olive oil and heat until very hot but not smoking. Add the chops and cook for 10–15 minutes until tender, turning once.

STOVETOP GRILL

This ridged cast-iron pan is good for cooking meat on top of the stove. Even at extremely high temperatures it is virtually non-stick, so needs only a very small amount of oil. The ridges on the pan produce seared markings on the meat similar to those achieved on a barbecue.

Noisettes d'agneau au thym, tian provençale

Boneless lamb noisettes, cut from the saddle, are succulent and tender. Here they are scented with thyme and served with individual gratins of courgettes, onions and tomatoes. These take their name from the French word tian, *for the earthenware dish in which they were traditionally baked.*

SERVES 4

1 saddle of lamb

50 ml olive oil

1 bunch of fresh thyme sprigs

Salt and freshly ground pepper

50 g unsalted butter

FOR THE JUS

1 tbsp olive oil

Lamb bones, chopped

150 g mirepoix *of onion, carrot and celery (see page 166)*

2 garlic cloves, crushed

1 litre veal stock

1 tbsp tomato purée

1 bouquet garni containing a lot of thyme

TO SERVE

Petits tians (see box, above right)

Fresh parsley sprigs

Bone the saddle of lamb and cut into noisettes (see box, below); reserve the bones.

Put the noisettes in a dish, pour the oil over them and add the thyme sprigs and pepper. Turn the noisettes to coat with the oil and thyme, cover and leave in a cool place to marinate overnight.

To make the jus, heat the oil in a saucepan and brown the reserved lamb bones. Add the *mirepoix* and garlic and brown with the bones, then add the stock and stir well. Add the tomato purée, mix well, and cook for 1 minute. Add the bouquet garni. Bring to the boil, skimming the surface, then lower the heat and simmer gently for 30 minutes. Strain and season.

Melt the butter in a large frying pan, then increase the heat to high. Shake excess oil from the noisettes, season to taste and add them to the pan. Pan-fry for 4 minutes, turning once, until the noisettes are richly browned on both sides but still quite pink in the centre

Arrange the noisettes on warmed plates with the petits tians. Pour jus around the noisettes and garnish with parsley sprigs.

PETITS TIANS

Sweat 300 g finely chopped onions in 50 ml olive oil. Put one-quarter in a 7.5-cm metal ring on an oiled baking sheet. Slice and blanch 200 g courgettes. Slice 150 g cherry tomatoes. Arrange a few courgette and tomato slices over the onions, alternating them in a circle; season. Remove ring and repeat to make 4 tians. Sprinkle with breadcrumbs, chopped thyme and olive oil. Bake at 180°C for 10 minutes.

Cutting Noisettes

The double loin of lamb, which is joined along the backbone of the lamb, is called the saddle. Once the saddle is boned, these two loins can be cut into 3–cm thick slices and chargrilled or fried. These slices are called noisettes *in French.*

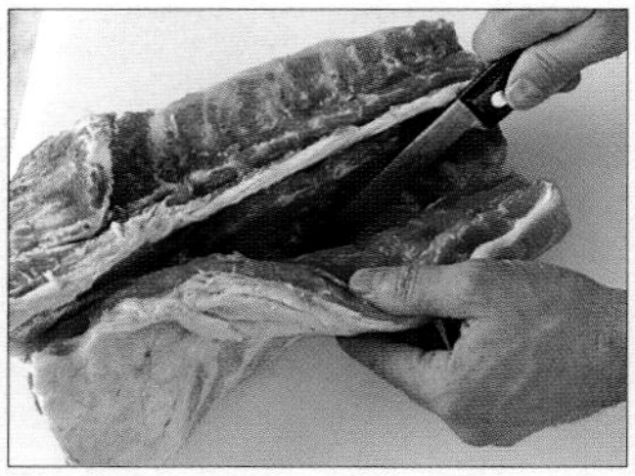

Place the saddle fat-side down, and cut off the flaps on either side of the backbone with a boning knife.

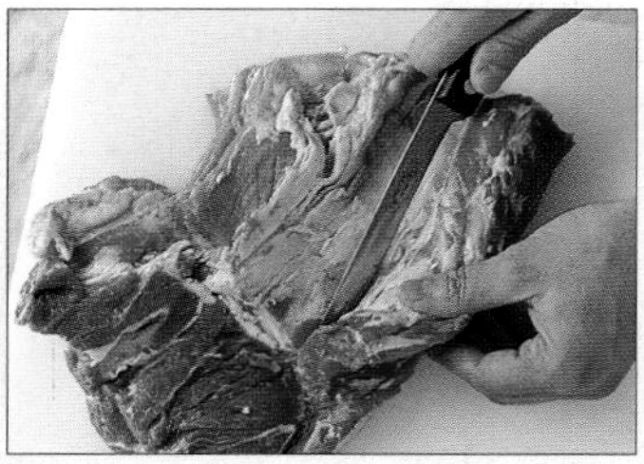

Holding the knife close to the bone, cut and scrape down both sides of the backbone to release the two slender fillets.

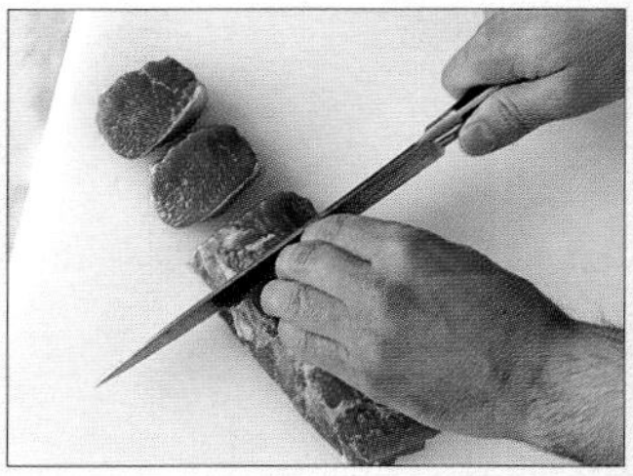

Cut each fillet crosswise into 6 even slices using a chef's knife. Flatten each slighlty using the side of the knife.

Choosing Pork

Once considered a fatty meat, pigs are now bred to produce much leaner meat. In fact, some cuts are so lean that they require basting as they roast. Pork is sold fresh as both large and small cuts and is also available cured and smoked. Different curing methods produce variously flavoured bacon and ham, which can then be smoked. Bacon that is left unsmoked is often referred to as "green".

THERE IS GENERALLY little marbling within pork meat
THE PALE PINK flesh will be darker in the leg and shoulder cuts
THE MAIN LAYER of fat encases the flesh and should be well trimmed by the butcher before purchase

Buying Pork

Larger roasts will often be sold with the papery outer skin – this should feel fresh and moist and be free of hairs and elastic. Always select pork that has smooth pink flesh that is moist but not damp or oily looking. The fat should be firm and white. Avoid cuts that have waxy, yellowing fat.

Bones may have a blue tinge and any cut ends should be red and spongy – the whiter the ends the older the animal before slaughter and as a result the meat may be less tender.

Ham is the cured hind leg of a pig, smoked or salted and smoked. Ham is sold cooked or raw. When buying raw ham such as Parma ham, choose pieces with creamy white fat and deep pink flesh. Slices should look moist and lay flat, not dry and curled at the edges.

Handling Pork

Because it can harbour a parasite that causes worms, pork must be thoroughly cooked (see page 145). Store pork in its original wrapping in the coldest part of the refrigerator (between 1–5°C), away from cooked meats. Always check the "use-by" dates. Fresh pork will keep for 2–3 days (smaller cuts do spoil more quickly), cooked pork 4–5 days and ham up to 10 days.

Bacon is often vacuum wrapped and marked with a use-by date; in general, it will keep in the refrigerator for up to 3 weeks.

Bacon and ham do not freeze well – their high salt content causes deterioration. Fresh pork, however, can be frozen, tightly wrapped, for up to 6 months, though minced pork should be used within 3 months. To defrost, place on a plate in the refrigerator; allow about 5 hours per 450 g.

Pork Cuts

All pork cuts are relatively tender but no matter the cooking method, the meat must be cooked until the juices are no longer pink and they run clear. Although today cases are rare, there is a danger of contracting trichinosis from undercooked pork. Use a meat thermometer (see page 124) when cooking roasts. The joint should register an internal temperature of 80°C on the thermometer to ensure that any bacteria in the meat is killed. Some hams produce an irridescent film on the surface which can be off-putting. This is a normal reaction between the natural fats and the curing process, which is harmless and does not affect the quality of the meat.

Pork Cuts	What to Look For	Cooking Methods
Bacon	*Clear, pink, moist meat* *An even layer of white fat*	Grill, fry
Belly	*Visible layers of fat through meat* *Meat and fat in equal proportions* *Skin intact and smooth*	Roast, pot-roast Grill, barbecue, stew (slices)
Chump chops/ Steaks	*Very light marbling* *Thin layer of creamy white fat* *White bones with red spongy centre*	Barbecue, grill, fry, roast, stew, braise
Escalope	*Deep pink flesh* *An even, smooth texture* *No outer fat or skin*	Grill, fry, barbecue
Ham	*Sweet smelling, moist, but not wet, meat*	Roast
Leg	*Lean moist meat with very little visible marbling* *Some connective tissue* *Even outer layer of fat under rind which should be hairless, elastic and scored*	Roast, pot-roast, braise
Leg/Shoulder steaks	*Some marbling visible throughout* *Dark pink, moist flesh* *No outer fat or skin*	Grill, fry, barbecue, stew, braise
Loin	*Very lean with no visible marbling* *Clean cut bone with no splinters* *Thin even outer layer of fat* *May have skin intact*	Roast, pot-roast, braise Grill, fry, barbecue, stew (chops)
Mince	*Clear pink meat with specks of fat*	Pasta sauces, stuffings, meatloaf
Shoulder (hand and spring)	*Light marbling* *Some connective tissue* *Even outer layer of white fat* *Elastic skin*	Roast, pot-roast (whole) Grill, stew (boned and cubed)
Spare ribs	*Pink moist flesh with very light marbling* *Clean cut bones with no splinters*	Grill, roast, barbecue
Tenderloin/Fillet	*Leanest cut, no visible fat* *Moist pink flesh*	Roast, grill, fry, barbecue

Pork on the Menu

From East to West, versatile pork pairs with a myriad of flavours to excite a multitude of cultural palates.

China – *Sweet and Sour Spare Ribs* (ribs marinated in a savoury soy, hoisin, sherry, ginger and garlic sauce) is a very popular, and highly exported, dish.

Cyprus – *Afelia* (pork stew marinated then cooked in red wine) gets its distinctive flavour from typical island spices such as cumin, coriander and cinnamon.

Germany – *Knackwurst* (pork sausage with cumin and garlic) is a quintessential and much loved pork snack.

Great Britain – *Roast Pork* (pork roasted and topped with crackling) is a comforting, old-fashioned favourite, usually served with sage and onion stuffing.

United States – *Boston Baked Beans* (salt pork with beans, molasses, tomato and mustard) was introduced by Puritan settlers in New England.

Preparing for Cooking

The correct preparation of pork is a very important part of a cook's repertoire, because so much of the pig is suitable for cooking and the range of pork dishes is vast. The techniques shown here include boning, stuffing and rolling a whole pork loin, cutting pockets in chops, and preparing and stuffing tenderloins.

Stuffings for a Boned Loin

- Fresh sage leaves and whole dried apricots soaked in a little white wine.
- Diced apple, onion and fresh breadcrumbs moistened with cider vinegar.
- Snipped bacon, plump raisins and cooked rice seasoned with black pepper and chopped fresh parsley.

Trick of the Trade

Tunnel Stuffing

This simple technique makes a pocket in a boned and rolled loin of pork. It saves having to untie and reroll the joint.

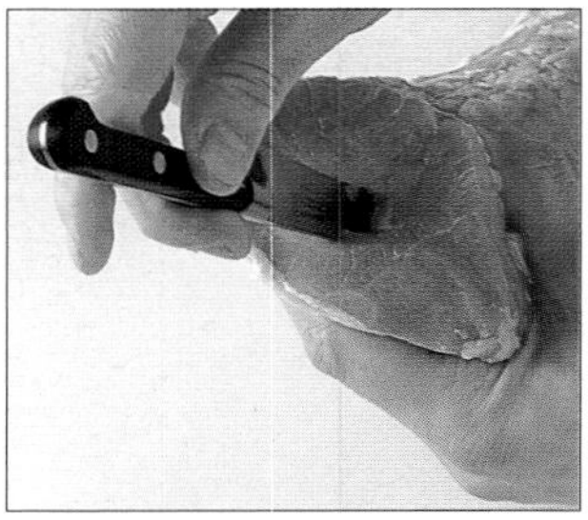

Insert the tip of a small knife into the eye of the loin and work to make a tunnel right through. Spoon stuffing into tunnel.

Boning a Loin

Although most butchers will bone a loin of pork if asked, you can easily do the job yourself with a boning knife. Remove any skin and trim the excess fat before boning, stuffing, rolling and roasting (see page 148).

1 Holding the loin, cut between the ribs; do not cut the meat deeper than the thickness of the ribs.

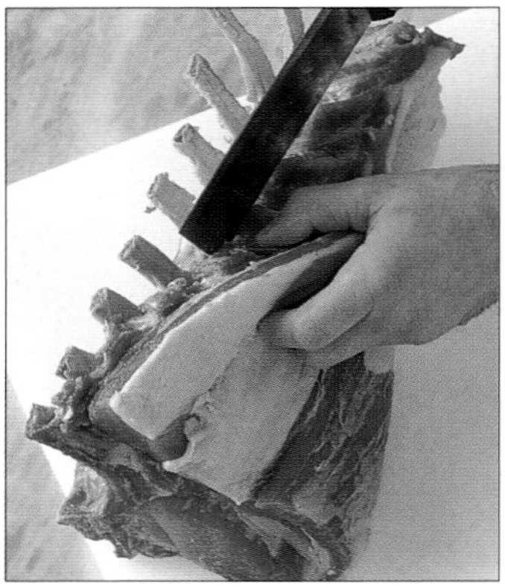

2 Cut down behind the ribs using a cleaver, cleaning as much meat off the bones as possible.

3 Work the knife around and under the chine bone, lifting it away from the meat as you cut.

4 Open the loin out flat and then cut two lengthwise slits through the meat, taking care not to cut right through. Insert stuffing (see box, above left).

5 Roll up the loin, starting at one of the long sides, and tie securely with kitchen string (see page 121). The joint is now ready for cooking.

Stuffing Pork Chops

By making a single horizontal cut in a pork chop you can create a pocket to contain a stuffing. This adds flavour and helps make the meat go further, as well as basting the meat on the inside during cooking and making it moist. The most suitable chops for this technique are those cut from the loin. They can be pan-fried or grilled, or braised in the oven (see page 149).

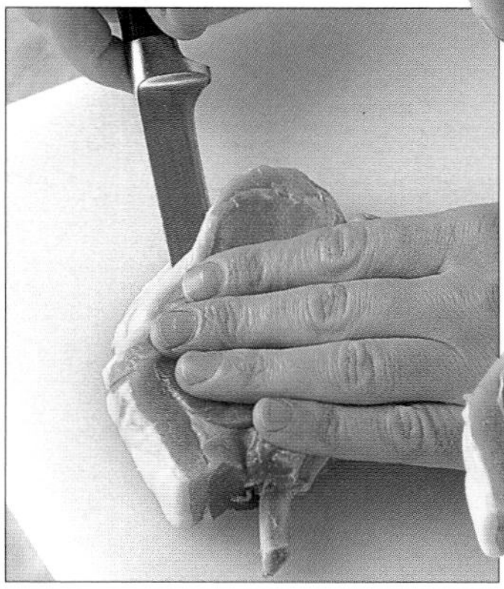

1 Insert a boning knife in the fatty side of the chop and work it horizontally to the bone to make a pocket.

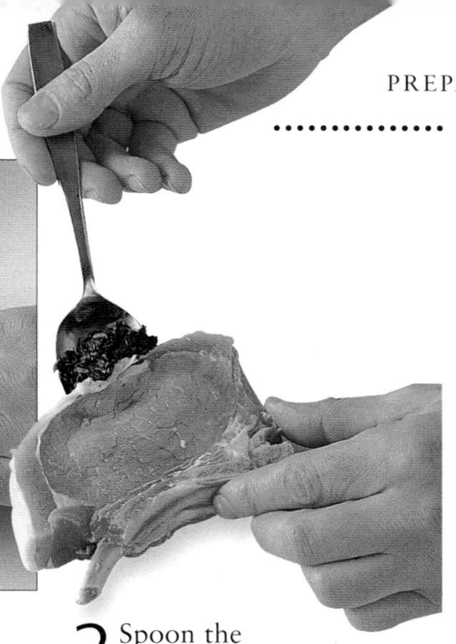

2 Spoon the stuffing (see box, right) into the pocket and press the edges firmly together.

Stuffings for Chops

- Chopped spinach seasoned with freshly grated nutmeg or tossed with chopped Parma ham.
- Shredded rocket and snipped sun-dried tomatoes.
- Roughly chopped prunes and chestnuts with finely grated orange zest.
- Spoonfuls of fruit chutney
- Chopped roasted peppers and crushed garlic.

Preparing a Tenderloin

Boneless lean tenderloin, also called pork fillet, requires very little in the way of preparation. The tendon and sinew are chewy, so they must be cut away before cooking. A whole tenderloin can be roasted or braised, with or without a stuffing (see below) or it can be cut into noisettes for grilling and pan-frying, or strips for stir-frying.

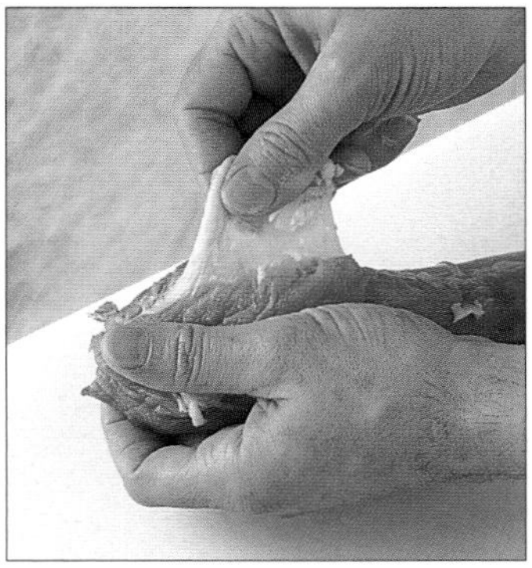

1 Carefully pull any fat and membrane away from the tenderloin. Discard the fat and membrane.

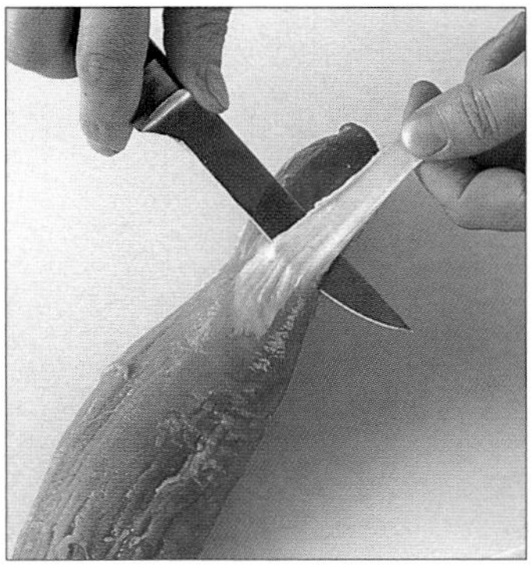

2 Cut just underneath the tendon and sinew with a boning knife, pulling it away from the flesh.

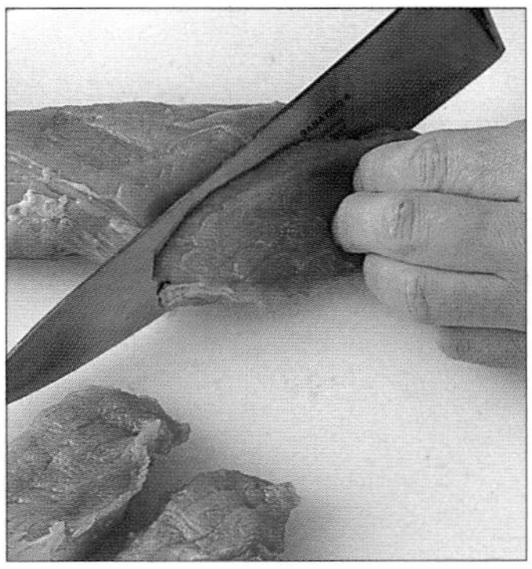

Making noisettes
Cut the tenderloin diagonally into 1–2 cm thick slices, using a chef's knife.

Stuffing Tenderloins

There are several ways in which pork tenderloins can be stuffed. The first shown here splits a whole tenderloin so that it can be opened out, flattened slightly, stuffed and reshaped; the second goes one step further and ties two split tenderloins together around a stuffing to make a larger, more substantial joint. Both can be roasted or braised as they are, or wrapped in streaky bacon before tying.

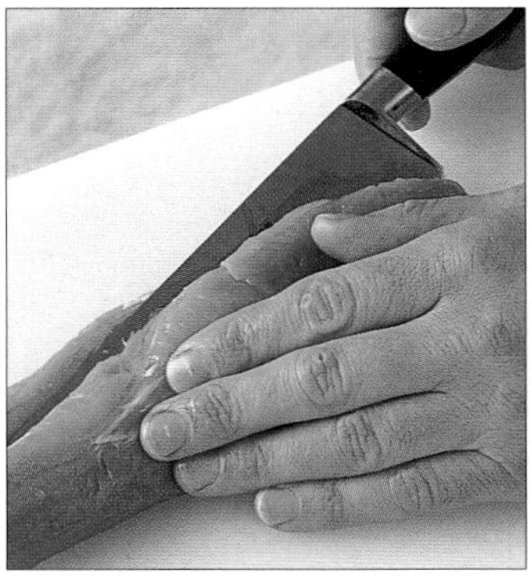

1 Cut the tenderloin lengthwise two-thirds of the way through with a chef's knife. Open out and pound gently to flatten.

2 Spread stuffing of your choice along the centre of the tenderloin and roll it up lengthwise to enclose the stuffing. Tie with kitchen string (see page 121).

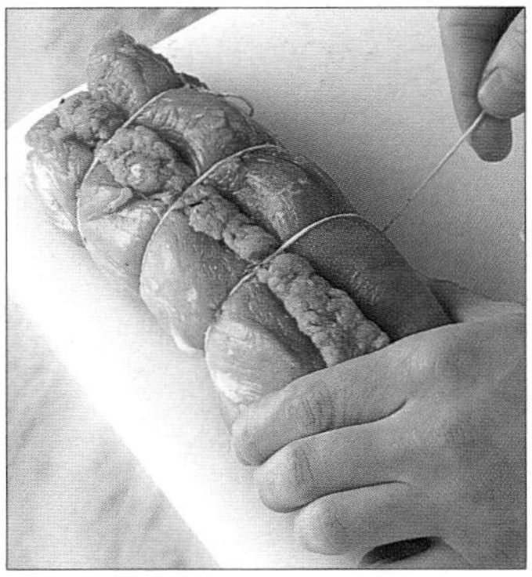

Stuffing two tenderloins
Split and flatten two tenderloins, following step 1, left. Sandwich together around a stuffing, then tie to secure.

Roasting & Braising

Using the prepared cuts of pork (see pages 146–147) for roasts and braises can yield splendid results if you follow these simple instructions and timing guidelines. Rubs, stuffings and glazes will boost the flavour of the meat.

ROASTING TIMES

Pork is usually roasted until well-done, to an internal temperature of 80°C. All times are approximate.

- ROAST at 230°C for 10 mins. Reduce to 180°C and follow times below.
- JOINTS ON THE BONE 30 mins per 450 g plus an extra 30 mins
- BONED, ROLLED JOINTS 35 mins per 450 g plus an extra 35 mins (For stuffed joints allow an extra 5–10 mins per 450 g)

CRANBERRY SAUCE

Fruits are traditionally served with pork to offset its richness. Apple sauce is the classic; this tangy cranberry sauce is more unusual.

Simmer 225 g cranberries in 300 ml water until the berries begin to burst, about 10 minutes. Remove from the heat, add 225 g sugar and 2 tbsp port and stir until the sugar dissolves. Chill and serve.

Roasting a Joint of Pork

Leg, loin and shoulder of pork are all suitable cuts for roasting, either with the bone in or boned, rolled and tied, with or without stuffing. The technique is the same, but cooking times vary (see box, left). If you like crackling, buy the joint with its skin intact, score it and pat it dry, then rub with oil and salt. Do not baste it during roasting or it will not be crisp. Make deep incisions through the skin and insert slivers of peeled garlic, if you like.

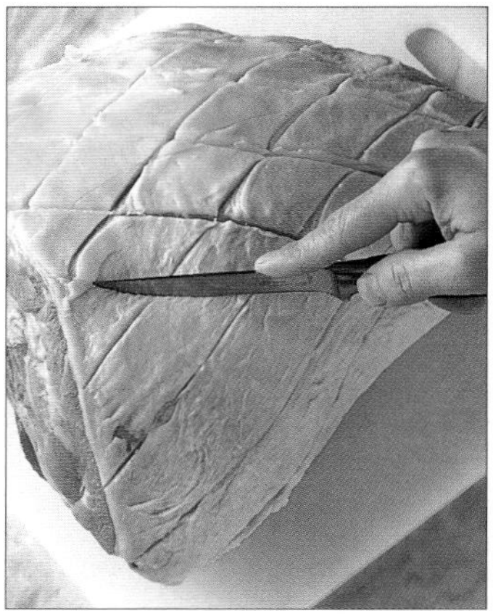

1 If the skin has been removed, as shown here on a leg of pork, score in a diamond pattern with a boning knife. Brush with a little oil and rub with salt and pepper or a dry spice mix such as cinnamon, mustard powder and brown sugar.

2 Place the joint on a rack in a roasting tin and roast until well-done (see chart, left). If there is no crackling, baste the joint with the fat from the tin every 30 minutes.

Roasting Pork Tenderloin

Tying the tenderloin around a contrasting stuffing (see page 147) makes an attractive presentation when sliced. Roast the tenderloin in a roasting tin at 220°C for 30–35 minutes, turning it halfway. For a special French touch, make a jus to accompany the meat by deglazing the cooking juices with wine or port.

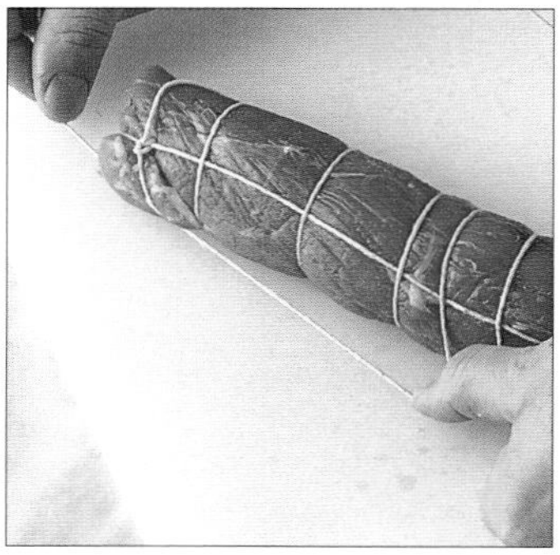

1 Tie the rolled tenderloin along its length. Brush with oil, season and roast (see left), basting with the juices.

2 Let rest, loosely covered with foil, for about 5 minutes. Remove string and slice on the diagonal.

ROASTING SPARERIBS

Don't confuse these ribs with meaty sparerib chops from the belly of the animal – these are best braised at 180°C for 45 minutes per 450 g. The ribs here are the Chinese finger-food ribs which need to be roasted so the meat is crisp enough to bite off the bones. If they are sold in a sheet, separate them with a cleaver or chef's knife.

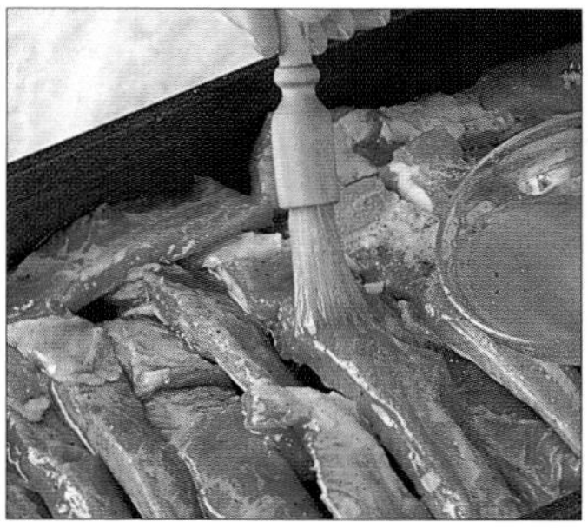

1 Put the ribs in a single layer in a roasting tin, brush with your chosen glaze (see box, right). Let marinate for at least 1 hour.

2 Roast at 220°C for 20 minutes, then reduce to 200°C and roast for 40–45 minutes. Turn often to cook evenly; remove with tongs.

GLAZES FOR RIBS

Glazes flavour the ribs and help to produce a sticky coating during roasting.

- Mix clear honey, pineapple juice, oil and a little wine vinegar. For extra bite, add a spoonful of chilli sauce.
- Mix soy sauce, oil, rice wine and five-spice powder.
- Mix grain mustard and honey and thin with a little oil.

ROASTING PORK CHOPS

The best cooking method for thick pork loin chops is roasting. The technique shown here works well with plain or pocket-stuffed chops (see page 147). The apple rings add flavour and moistness to the pork and pulp down into the juices, but they are not essential.

1 Heat a little oil in a frying pan, add the chops and sear over a moderate heat.

2 Roast in a baking dish with the pan juices at 180°C for 30–40 minutes.

PORK IN MILK

2 kg boned and rolled loin of pork
2 tbsp olive oil
1.5 litres milk
5 garlic cloves, crushed
2 tbsp fresh sage leaves
Grated zest and juice of 2 lemons
Salt and freshly ground pepper

Sear the pork in the oil in a deep casserole. Add the remaining ingredients and bring to the boil. Cover and braise at 180°C for 2–2½ hours. Serve sliced, with the sauce spooned over.

BRAISING PORK IN MILK

This unusual method of cooking pork is traditional in Italy. During long gentle cooking, the milk and the fat in the pork intermingle, making the most delicious sauce and moist succulent meat. Don't be put off by the slightly curdled appearance of the sauce – this is as it should be.

1 Sear the rolled loin in hot olive oil. Keep the heat moderate to high and turn the joint constantly to make sure the fat browns evenly on all sides. Use the fork to steady the meat, not pierce it.

2 Add the seasonings and milk, bring to the boil, cover and braise. Stir the cooking liquid and spoon it over the joint during cooking. This will amalgamate the fats and the flavours.

QUICK COOKING

The simple methods of grilling and frying lend themselves to small cuts of pork, producing tender and flavourful meat in a matter of minutes. Grilling, in a ridged pan on the stovetop or under the grill, is perfect for cooking chops or pork kebabs; stir-frying in a wok over high heat is best for cooking pork strips.

STIR-FRIED PORK

450 g pork tenderloin, cut into thin strips
1 onion, sliced
1 garlic clove, sliced
1 red chilli, finely chopped
125 ml dark soy sauce
125 ml sesame oil
1 tbsp vegetable oil
2 peppers, sliced
2 tsp cornflour

Marinate the pork, onion, garlic and chilli with the soy sauce and sesame oil for 30 minutes. Remove the pork and vegetables and stir-fry in batches in the vegetable oil. Add the peppers and stir-fry for 3–4 minutes, then blend the cornflour with the marinade, add to the wok and stir-fry until thickened. Serves 4.

CHARGRILLING PORK CHOPS

For succulent and tasty meat, chargrilling on a stovetop grill pan is one of the best ways to cook thin or medium cut pork loin chops and it's healthier than pan-frying because it uses less fat. You can use the same technique for cooking under a conventional grill. Allow 6–8 minutes on each side, 5 cm away from the heat.

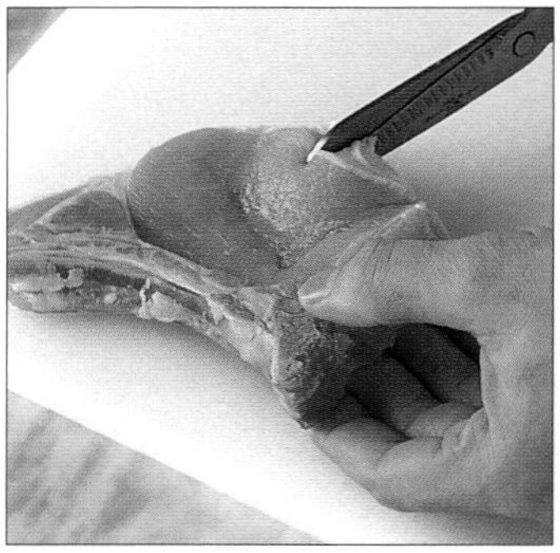

1 Snip fat and membrane at regular intervals. Brush with oil, press sage leaves into the meat and season.

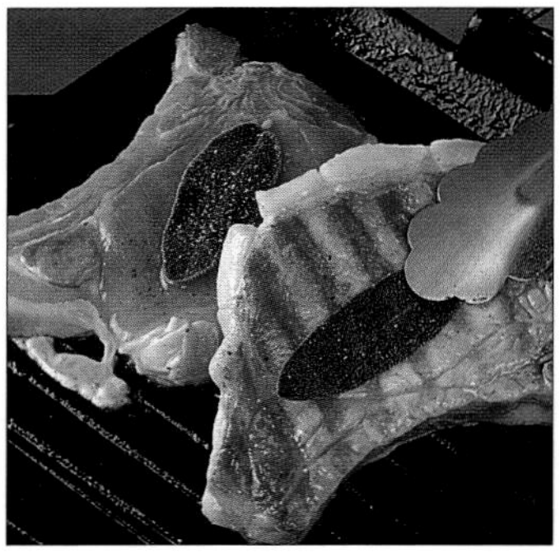

2 Heat a stovetop grill pan until hot but not smoking. Add the chops and cook for 12-16 minutes, turning once.

STIR-FRYING

Pork tenderloin, sliced on the diagonal (see page 147), can be cut into strips and stir-fried. A recipe for stir-fried pork, using the techniques shown here, is given in the box, left.

1 Before stir-frying, marinate the pork strips for at least 30 minutes at room temperature or overnight in the refrigerator. The highly flavoured ingredients of the marinade will make the meat more tasty and tender.

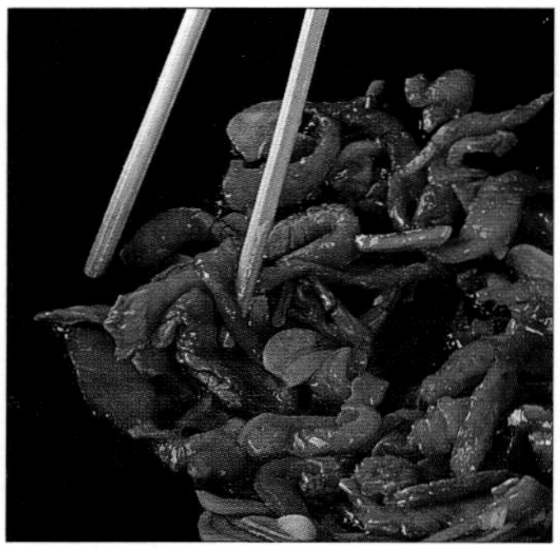

2 To stir-fry the pork, first heat a wok over a moderate heat until hot, then add the oil and heat until hot but not smoking. Add about one-third of the drained pork and toss it in the wok for 2–3 minutes, separating the strips with chopsticks. Repeat twice until all the pork is cooked, then return all the pork to the wok. If you follow these directions the meat will cook quickly and evenly and will not stick to the wok.

SAUSAGES, BACON & HAM

How ever you cook sausages or bacon, it is essential to use the correct techniques to enjoy them at their best. The preparation and presentation of a whole ham is a particularly useful technique when entertaining guests.

COOKING SAUSAGES

As sausages cook the meat expands; to ensure they do not burst, pierce the skins before cooking. Sausages have quite a high fat content, which helps keep them moist. To counteract their richness, they can be glazed with a sweet mixture such as mango chutney or honey.

PRICKING THE SKINS
To prevent sausages bursting, during cooking, prick all over with a cocktail stick or fork.

GRILLING
Most sausages take about 10 minutes to grill. Coil Cumberland sausages and secure with skewers.

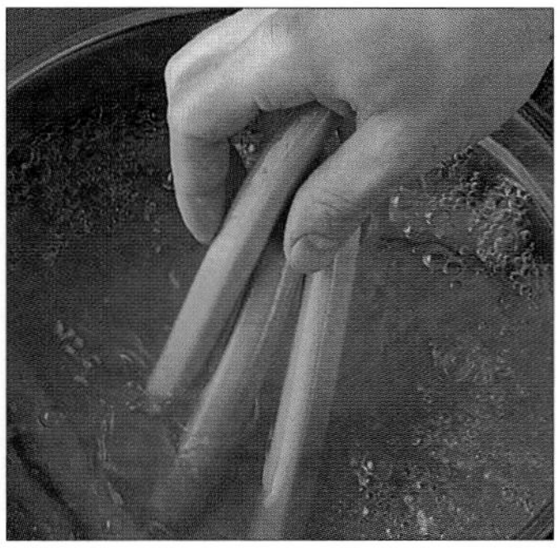

POACHING
Add sausages to boiling water, cover and simmer for 3–5 minutes; Frankfurters only need 1–2 minutes.

USING BACON IN COOKING

Rindless streaky bacon rashers are used to line terrines and loaf tins, or rolled around a filling to be served as an hors d'oeuvre. They need to be stretched before use, to prevent shrinkage during cooking. Bacon lardons *are used in French cooking as a flavouring ingredient – their strong, often salty, taste is essential in many classics such as* boeuf bourguignon *and* coq au vin.

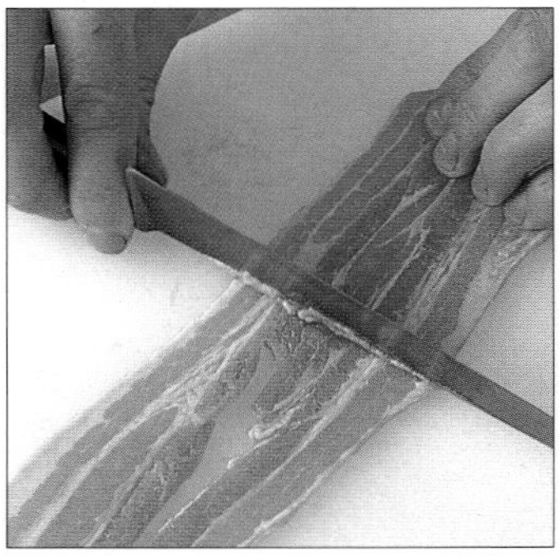

STRETCHING
Hold two rashers together and run the back of a chef's knife along their length.

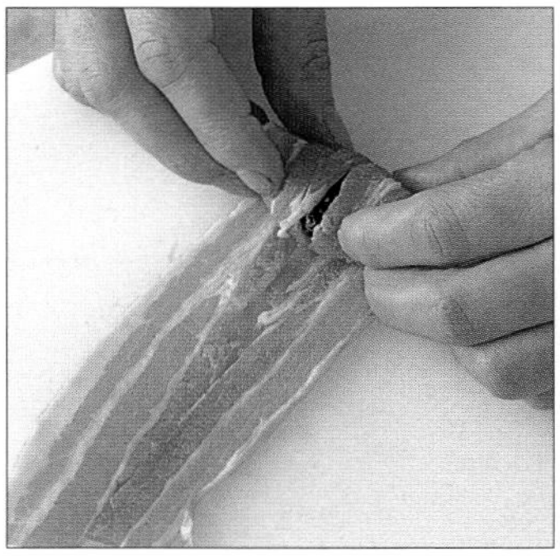

ROLLING
Roll stretched rashers around filling; secure with wooden cocktail sticks.

MAKING LARDONS
Cut thick rashers lengthwise into strips. Stack the strips and cut crosswise into dice.

TYPES OF SAUSAGES

Most sausages are made of pork, although beef, veal and lamb varieties are becoming more widely available. They can be plain or seasoned with herbs and spices.

VARIETIES FOR GRILLING:
Choose French varieties such as *andouillette* and *boudin noir* or English ones like chipolatas, Cumberland and Lincolnshire.

VARIETIES FOR POACHING:
Sausages that are most suitable for poaching are the French *andouille*, *cervelat* and *boudin blanc*, and the German *Frankfurter*, *Bockwurst* and *Knackwurst*.

TYPES OF BACON

The flavour varies according to the curing ingredients (such as sugar for a sweet cure), and the wood that is used in smoking.

- Unsmoked bacon is also referred to as "green" and has a white rind. When smoked, the rind turns brown.
- Streaky bacon is from the chest of the pig; it is a fatty bacon called *lard* in French.
- *Petit sale* and *pancetta* are similar cuts from the belly of pork. The curing process makes them quite salty, with a strong smoky flavour.

GLAZED HAM

4–5 kg gammon joint
100 g brown sugar
4 tbsp English mustard

Soak the gammon in cold water overnight. Drain, weigh it and calculate the cooking time, allowing 30 minutes per 450 g. Put in a pan of cold water, bring to the boil and simmer for half the cooking time. Drain and cool slightly, then remove the skin. Score the fat, warm the sugar and mustard and spread over the fat. Bake, covered loosely with foil, on a rack in a roasting tin at 180°C for the remaining time, removing the foil for the last 30 minutes. Serves about 12.

PREPARING AND PRESENTING A HAM

A boiled ham must have its skin removed before serving or it will be very difficult to carve, but the fat underneath the skin is unappealing. A recipe for glazed ham, using the simple technique for scoring and glazing shown here, is given in the box, left. This is essential for an attractive presentation if you are planning to serve the ham whole at the table.

1 Score the fat of the boiled ham attractively in a diamond pattern with the tip of a small knife. This will allow the glaze to penetrate and flavour the meat.

2 Warm the glaze until melted, then spread it evenly over the fat with a palette knife. Take time to work the glaze into the cuts so that it will seep into the meat and flavour it.

USING MINCED MEAT

Use lean meat with a light marbling of fat for best flavour and succulence. Minced meat is extremely versatile: it absorbs seasonings well and can be made into a variety of dishes from *moussaka* to meatballs. Try mincing your own meat (see page 123) and experiment with lamb, veal and pork.

BURGER BUDDIES

Add texture and flavour by topping or accompanying burgers with tasty extras.

- Top a cooked burger with a slice of mozzarella or crumbled blue cheese and grill to melt.
- Stir chopped roasted peppers into *salsa* – spoon on to melting cheeseburger.
- Pan-fry sliced red onions until caramelized, adding a few sliced mushrooms towards the end. Season with Worcestershire sauce and grain mustard and spoon over burgers.

MAKING BURGERS

You can make burgers with minced meat, but this food processor method makes a chunkier burger more like an American-style chopped steak. For best results, use meat such as chuck steak that has 20 per cent fat and take care not to overwork the meat or it will be rubbery.

1 Put chunks of beef in a food processor fitted with the metal blade. Pulse just until roughly ground.

2 Place the chopped meat in a bowl. Add onion, garlic and seasonings of your choice. Mix until combined.

3 Shape the mixture into even-sized balls, then flatten them until they are about 4 cm thick.

Making Different Shapes

When shaping minced meat, use your hands moistened with a little water and keep the shapes fairly loose – if you make the shapes too compact the texture of the cooked meat will be dense and rubbery.

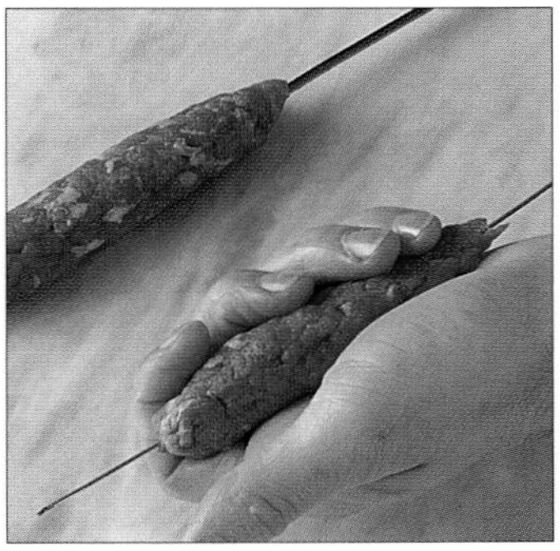

Brochettes
Take a small handful of minced meat (lamb is traditional) and shape it around metal skewers, pressing with your fingers.

Meatballs
Roll minced meat between the palms of your hands to form a ball, or roll it on a work surface if you prefer. Size can vary from 2.5–5 cm.

Making a Meatloaf

For this classic American dish, use slightly fatty minced meat from cuts such as shoulder. A combination of beef, veal and pork is best for flavour and moisture, and the addition of milk-soaked breadcrumbs is important to absorb meat juices.

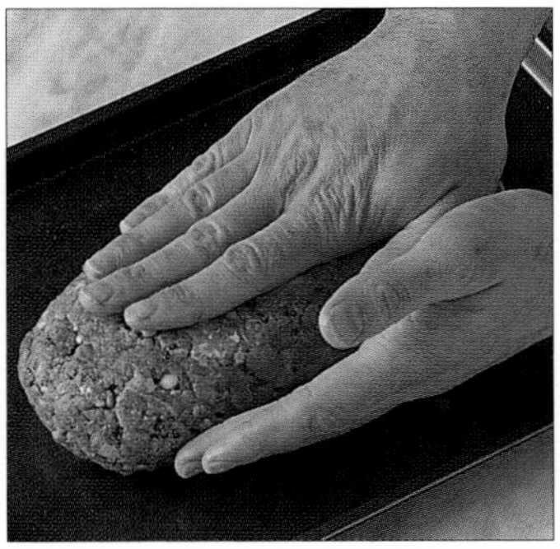

Freeform
Moisten your hands with water to prevent sticking, then form meat into a rectangular loaf shape on a lightly greased baking sheet.

Moulded
Press meat into a lightly greased loaf-shaped dish. Level the surface with a spoon, then turn it out on to a lightly greased baking sheet.

Making Crepinettes

These little French delicacies are a kind of homemade sausage – minced meat with breadcrumbs and seasonings encased in a parcel of caul (see box, right). Traditionally, pork sausagemeat is used, but you can use minced lamb, veal or poultry. Crépinettes *can be pan-fried as directed here, or grilled or oven-baked for the same length of time.*

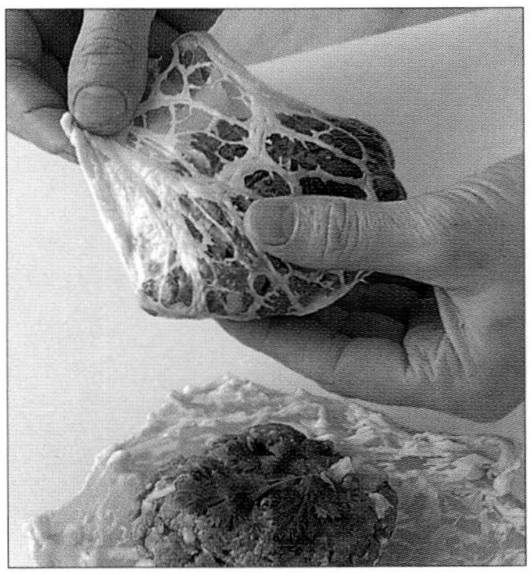

Mix minced meat with finely chopped onion, breadcrumbs and seasonings. Form into patties with your hands, then place a herb sprig on top of each (this will show through the melted caul and look attractive when serving). Wrap in squares of soaked and drained caul and pan-fry in hot oil and butter for 3–4 minutes.

CAUL

This is the thin membrane, veined with fat, that encloses an animal's stomach; pig's caul is the most readily available. Called *crépine* in French, it is used to moisten and flavour food and to hold ingredients together during cooking. Depending on thickness, caul either melts completely during cooking, or it will remain and can be discarded before serving. It can be obtained from butchers, but it may have to be specially ordered. Soak for 1–2 hours in cold water before use.

Making Steak Tartare

A dish of finely chopped raw beef topped with a raw egg yolk, steak tartare *is one of the great French classics. In France it is usually served with* cornichons *(baby gherkins), capers and Tabasco sauce, with a pot of mustard on the side. Only the freshest and finest quality fillet steak is used, chopped by hand just before serving.*

Trim fillet steak, allowing 125 g per person, of all fat, membrane and sinew, then chop the meat with two knives (see page 123). Mix with finely chopped onion and fresh flat-leaf parsley and salt and pepper. Shape into rounds, place on individual plates and hollow out the centres slightly with the back of a spoon. Slide egg yolks into the hollows. Serve immediately.

SAUSAGE CASINGS AND FILLINGS

Most butchers sell casings for sausages. Beef and pig intestines provide a natural alternative to man-made casings.

- For an Italian style, mix meat with chopped sun-dried tomatoes, garlic and basil.
- Try Indian flavourings such as curry powder, chopped fresh coriander and mango chutney to moisten and bind.
- For more traditional flavourings, try mint and onion with lamb, sage and apple with pork, and horseradish or mustard with beef.

MAKING SAUSAGES

The bonus of making your own sausages is that you know exactly what goes into them. Minced pork is the classic meat, but beef, lamb and venison are equally good. Casings can be natural or man-made, and you can vary the flavourings and seasonings to taste (see box, left).

1 Soak the casings in a large bowl of cold water for 1–2 hours. This will remove any excess salt and make the casings more pliable.

2 Fill a piping bag fitted with a large plain nozzle with sausagemeat. Hook the casing over the nozzle and squeeze in the filling.

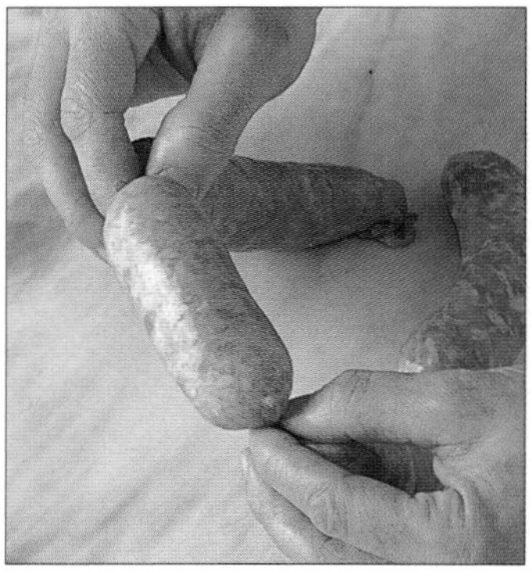

3 When the casing is full, twist sausage at intervals into links. Secure twisted ends with string. Remove string after cooking.

OFFAL

Offal are the innards and extremities of the animals we eat. Ranging from familiar liver and kidneys to more adventurous parts, all are nutritious, and with careful preparation and cooking, as delicious as any meat.

SAFETY FIRST

Offal needs careful handling, and freshness is crucial. Choose moist and shiny flesh with no dry patches; avoid offal with a greenish colour, slimy surface or strong smell. Store fresh offal in the refrigerator and use within two days. Wash all offal very thoroughly before using.

TYPES OF LIVER

- Calf's liver is very mild and tender. It is best grilled, sautéed or pan-fried.
- Lamb's liver tends to be drier and less delicate than calf's liver, but it can also be sautéed.
- Pig's liver is strong, and is good for pâtés and terrines.
- Chicken livers are mild and delicate; they are usually pan-fried and used for pâtés.

PREPARING LIVER

Chicken livers are sold whole; other livers are generally pre-sliced but can be ordered whole. When preparing a whole liver, divide the lobes and cut off any exposed ducts or connective tissue. Cut away any blood vessels, taking care not to damage the flesh. Calf's liver is being prepared here.

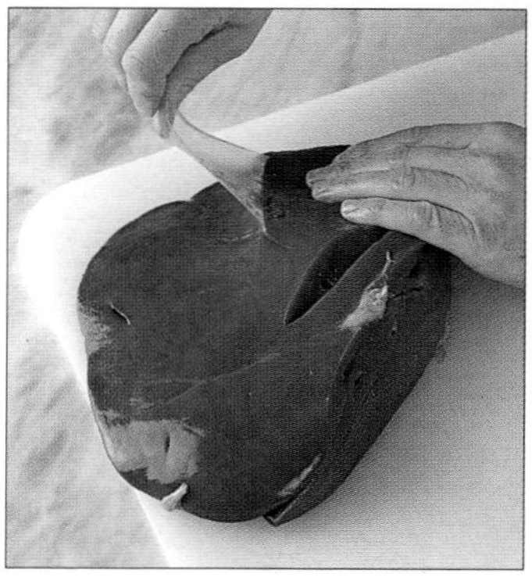

1 Peel off the opaque outer membrane with your fingers, holding the liver down to stop the flesh tearing.

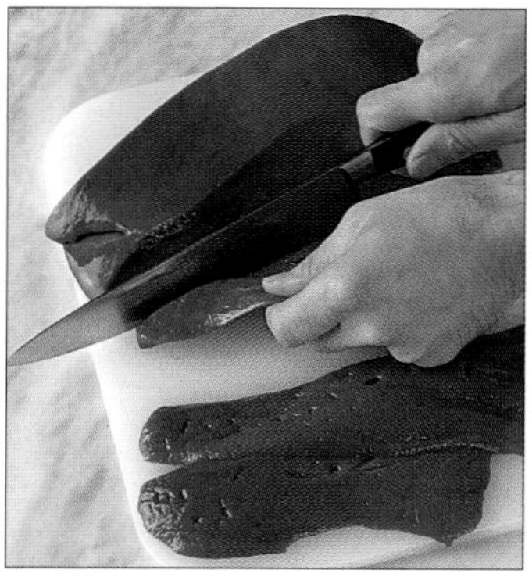

2 Cut the liver into slices about 5 mm thick with a chef's knife, and cut away any internal ducts.

TRICK OF THE TRADE

SOAKING LIVER

Pig's liver has a strong, pronounced flavour. Soak it in milk to "sweeten" it before cooking.

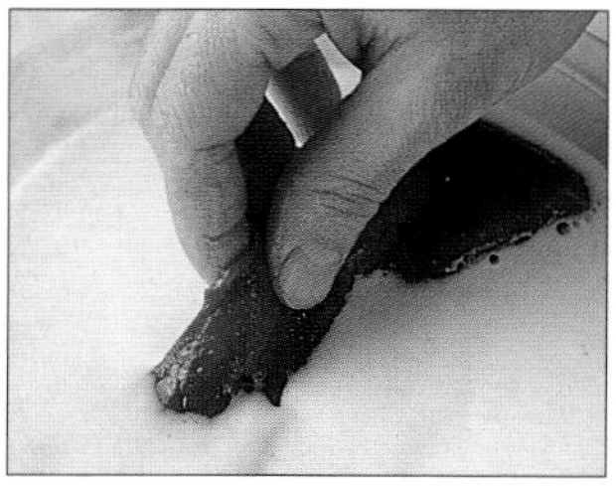

Prepare the liver (see left). Fill a bowl with enough cold milk to cover it, add the liver and turn to coat. Let soak for about 1 hour.

Preparing Kidneys

Beef, veal and pig's kidneys should be plump, firm, and encased in a shiny membrane. When buying kidneys encased in fat, it should be off-white (see box, right). Avoid kidneys with a strong odour.

1 Trim away any fat and connective tissue, then pull off the outer membrane with your fingers.

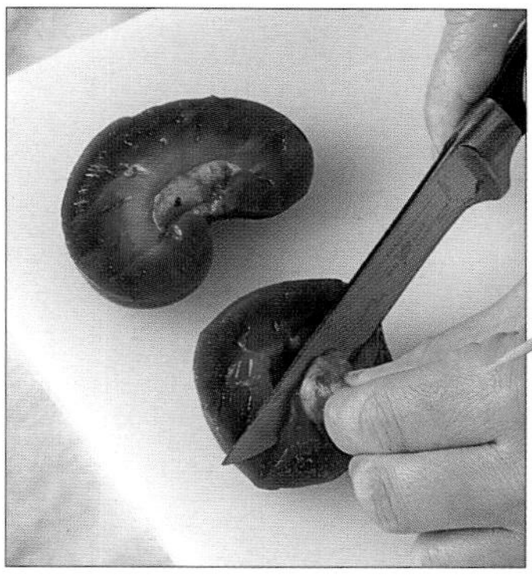

2 Cut the kidney in half lengthwise, slicing through the fatty core. Hold the core with your fingertips and cut it away with a boning knife.

3 Thread the prepared kidney halves on to a skewer to keep them flat. They are now ready for grilling or pan-frying.

Preparing Heart for Pan-frying

Heart has a firm texture and rich flavour, but it can be tough if not properly handled. To prepare heart, trim away any visible fat. After removing the tubes, cut away any sinew with kitchen scissors. Rinse the heart and pat dry with paper towels before slicing.

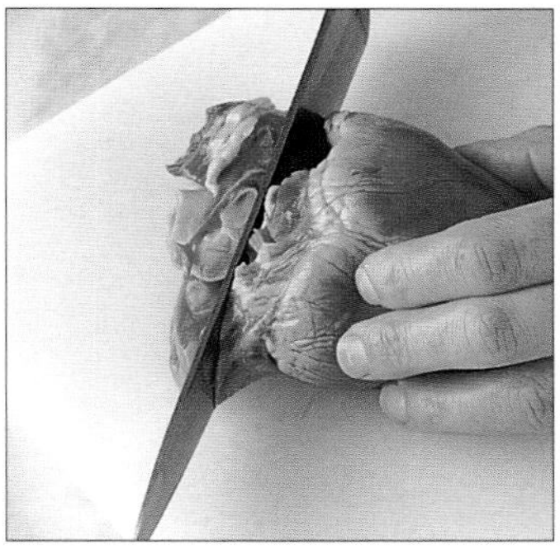

1 Cut off the tubes from the top of the heart using a chef's knife.

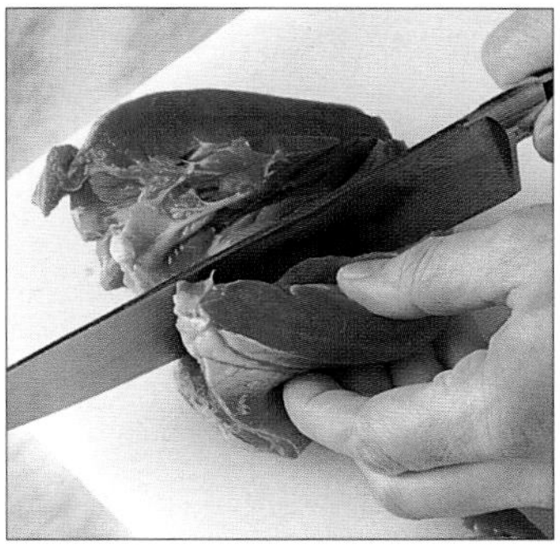

2 Cut the heart in half lengthwise and then cut it into slices or cubes.

Stuffing Heart

The natural cavity in a heart can be filled with a variety of stuffings. All hearts can be stuffed, but large beef hearts should be skewered or tied to retain their shape during cooking. Heart is lean so requires slow cooking, stewing or braising, to keep it moist. Each stuffed heart will serve 2, apart from beef heart, which serves 4.

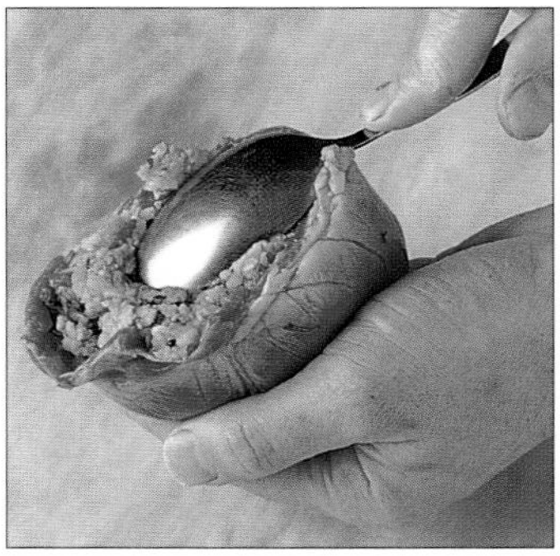

1 Follow step 1 above. Cup the heart firmly in one hand and spoon stuffing into the cavity; press down firmly.

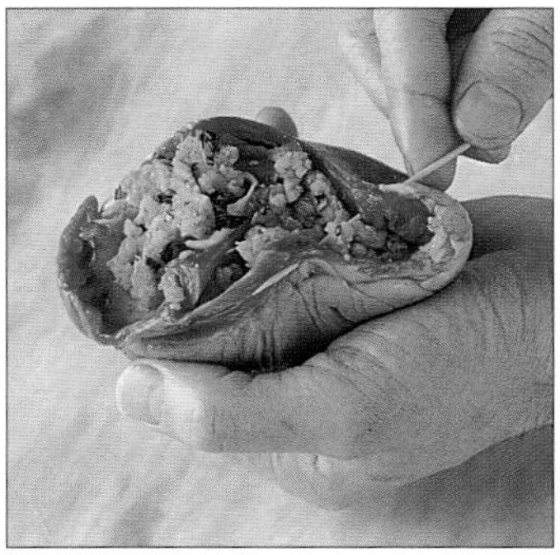

2 Thread 2–3 wooden skewers through the top edge of the heart to secure the stuffing during cooking.

Kidneys and Suet

Kidneys can be bought with or without fat (called suet). The suet should form an even layer around the flesh and be creamy white in colour. Carefully peel it away from the kidney.

Fresh suet can be bought separately and should be chilled before use. Processed suet is convenient and has less flavour.

Fresh suet is a good cooking fat, in its natural state or in rendered form – melted over low heat to remove any non-fatty particles and then chilled to separate the water and impurities.

To make a light dough for meat pies, crumble fresh suet and mix it with twice as much plain flour, then bind with milk or water.

Stuffings for Heart

Ensure stuffings are full of flavour and moist enough to withstand long cooking times. Season the heart inside and out with salt and pepper before stuffing.

- Mix together sautéed chopped mushrooms, onion and bacon seasoned with fresh herbs. Wrap the heart with bacon before securing with wooden cocktail sticks or a skewer.
- Fill with an Asian-style mixture of cooked rice, dried fruits and exotic spices.
- Combine olives, tomatoes, shredded basil leaves, a little wine with a hint of garlic.
- Soak bread in milk, then fork together with chopped onion and fresh sage for a classic combination.
- Flavour minced pork or sausagemeat with a selection of Thai seasonings – ginger, lemon grass, lime juice and chilli.

PREPARING AND COOKING TONGUE

Soak tongue in several changes of cold water for 2–3 hours – this will draw out the blood from a fresh tongue, salt from a salted tongue. Put the tongue in a large pan, cover with cold water and bring to the boil. Blanch for 10 minutes, then drain and refresh under cold running water.

Poach the tongue in water to cover with flavouring vegetables, such as a *mirepoix* of onion, carrot and celery, and a bouquet garni until tender, 2–4 hours according to the type of tongue. Let cool in the liquid until tepid, then lift out and cut away bones and gristle from the root end with a sharp knife. Slit the skin lengthwise with the knife, then strip it off with your fingers.

The tongue is now ready to slice and serve hot, or to press and served cold. Espagnole sauce (see page 225) is a classic accompaniment to hot tongue.

PREPARING AND COOKING OXTAIL

Trim away the excess outer fat from the oxtail with a paring knife. Chop off the base of the tail with a meat cleaver and discard. Chop the tail crosswise into 8-cm pieces.

To bone oxtail, slit the tail lengthwise to expose the bone and, with a sharp knife, scrape the flesh away from the bone until it is released. Discard the bone. Roll up the oxtail, starting at the wider end. Tie with string.

Pieces of bone-in or boned oxtail are good braised slowly with strong-flavoured ingredients, such as beef stock, red wine, bouquet garni and garlic. Cook for at least 2 hours.

SWEETBREADS

Sweetbreads are the thymus glands of young lambs and calves. They are highly perishable and should be soaked and cooked on the day of purchase. Once prepared as shown, they can be coated in egg and breadcrumbs and fried; in classic French cuisine, they are served with sauce poulette *(see page 223).*

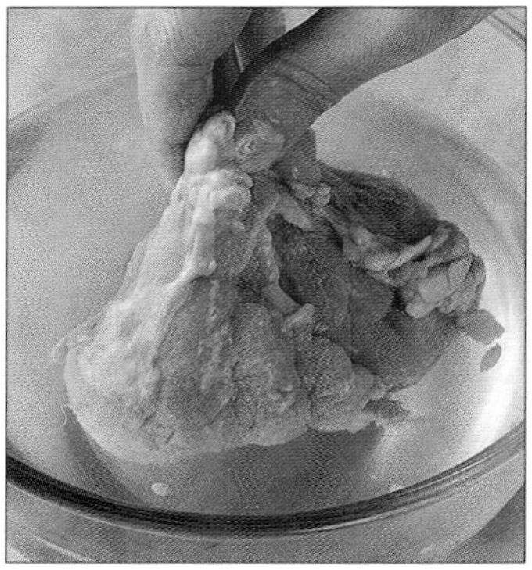

1 Soak for 2 hours in several changes of cold water. Rinse, put in a pan and cover with cold water. Bring to the boil and blanch 3 minutes.

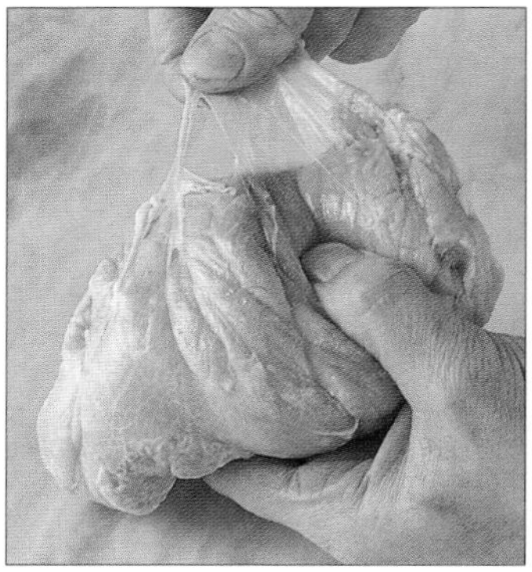

2 Drain and refresh under cold running water, then remove outer skin and any pieces of membrane.

3 Place sweetbreads between two plates, put a weight on top and chill for 2 hours until firm.

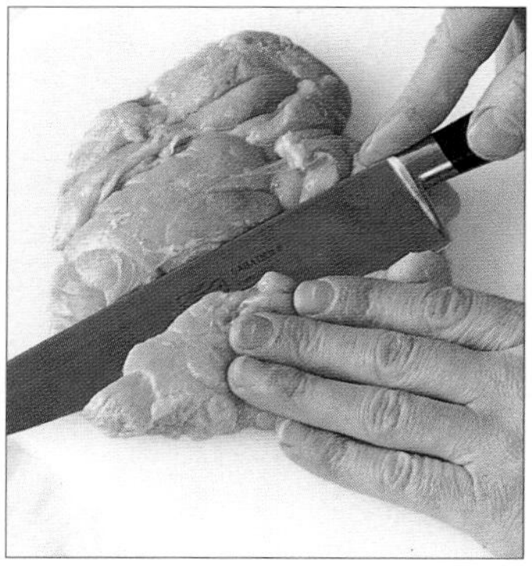

4 Slice the sweetbreads at an angle using a sharp knife. The sweetbreads are now ready for cooking.

PIG'S TROTTERS

These are usually braised, or served cold in a vinaigrette (see page 230). Before this, first scrape away the hairs between the toes, halve or bone them as shown here, then poach in stock for about 1½ hours.

HALVING
Cut lengthwise right through the middle of the trotter, between the bones.

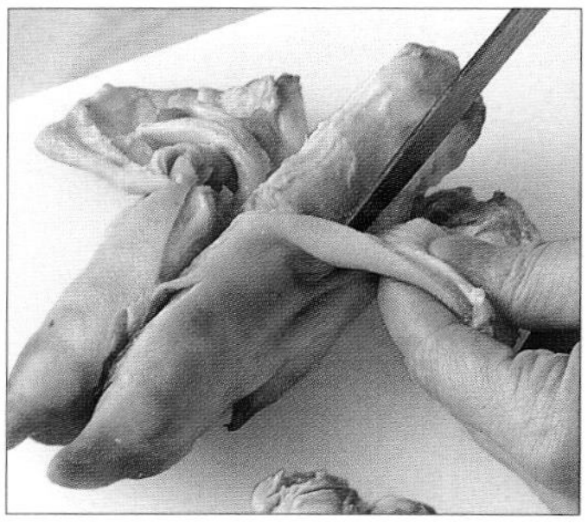

BONING
Cut through the skin of the trotter down to the bones, then lift and scrape the flesh away from the bones until it is released.

TRIPE

The muscular lining of an ox's stomach, ivory-coloured tripe is usually sold "dressed", that is cleaned, soaked and scalded, but further blanching is required before cooking to sweeten its smell. It is usually stewed, either with milk and onions, or in an Espagnole sauce (see page 225), with sliced carrots added at the end.

Rinse the whole sheet of tripe thoroughly in cold water to remove any traces of dirt. Drain in a colander, pat dry with a tea towel, then cut into strips or squares with a chef's knife. Place the tripe in a pan with a bay leaf, an onion stuck with cloves, and cold water to cover. Bring to the boil, then drain. The tripe is now ready for cooking.

Vegetables & Salads

Choosing Vegetables
•
Brassicas
•
Leafy Greens
•
Stalks & Shoots
•
Globe Artichokes
•
Roots & Tubers
•
Potatoes
•
Mushrooms
•
Pods & Sweetcorn
•
The Onion Family
•
Unusual Vegetables
•
Vegetable Fruits
•
Peppers & Chillies
•
Salad Leaves & Fresh Herbs
•
Boiling & Steaming
•
Roasting & Baking
•
Frying
•
Making Mash & Moulds

Choosing Vegetables

Choose vegetables in season when they are at their freshest and most readily available; this is when they will taste their best and be at their most nutritious. Always look for crisp, fresh looking vegetables that have brightly coloured leaves. Avoid any that have brown patches, wilted leaves, bruised or pulpy flesh.

CARROTS should have fresh looking, healthy leafy tops, not discoloured or wilting
ONIONS should have dry papery skins; red onions should have no brown discoloration
POTATOES should be firm and well shaped with no "eyes" or green patches
TOMATO SKIN should be smooth and firm with no cuts or blemishes

Roots & Tubers

Carrots, potatoes, beetroots, swedes, celeriac and radishes should have firm, heavy flesh and wrinkle-free skin. Avoid soft patches or sprouting.

Mushrooms

Choose firm, fresh looking mushrooms that have a soft "bloom" and fresh smell. The stalk end should be moist; if dry they may be slightly old.

Onions

Choose firm bulbs with even-coloured skins and no signs of sprouting. Avoid any that look damp or smell musty. Leeks and spring onions should have dark green leaves and fresh looking roots.

Vegetable Fruits

Tomatoes, aubergines, peppers and avocados should have firm, smooth, shiny skins and a deep, even colour. Avoid any that are soft, pulpy or wrinkled.

SALAD LEAVES

Choose lettuces and cresses that smell fresh and look slightly damp on the surface. Check the heart is well formed. There should be no wilting or brown patches on the leaves.

LEAFY GREENS

Choose endive, Swiss chard and spinach with crisp, fresh looking greens. Leaves should feel springy to the touch; avoid any that appear limp or wilted. There should be no sign of insect damage.

STALKS & SHOOTS

Celery, globe artichokes, fennel, asparagus and chicory should have tightly packed, firm heads with no visible brown patches on outer layers.

ASPARAGUS should have plump stalks with tight buds, even in size and colour

LEAFY GREENS should have full, well formed head, crisp leaves with fresh green tips

PEAS should not have any visible dry or brown patches

SPINACH LEAVES are best when small and moist, with fine stalks

PODS & SEEDS

Select peas and beans with bright green pods that are full and plump. Choose sweetcorn with tight green husks and plump, even, shiny kernels. The kernels should be tightly packed on the cob.

BRASSICAS

Look for cauliflower, broccoli, Brussels sprouts and cabbage with undamaged tight compact heads. Outer leaves should be fresh with no signs of wilting or yellowing. Stalks should look moist and freshly cut.

BROCCOLI of the purple "hearting" variety should have dark coloured tightly formed florets, firm stalks, no signs of yellowing

BRASSICAS

This large family of vegetables includes cabbages, cauliflower, broccoli, and Brussels sprouts, as well as Oriental greens like mustard cabbage and *pak choi.*

SETTING THE COLOUR OF RED CABBAGE

Once cut, red cabbage has a tendency to turn blue or purple. This simple technique helps it keep its red colour.

1 Pour hot red wine vinegar over shredded cabbage (about 4 tbsp is enough for ½ small head of cabbage). Mix well and let stand for 5–10 minutes, then drain off excess vinegar.

2 Serve the red cabbage raw, tossed in a vinaigrette dressing (see page 230) and sprinkled with chopped parsley, or use in cooked dishes.

CORING CABBAGE

The hard white core at the centre of all cabbage is tough and inedible and should be removed to allow easy shredding and even cooking of the cabbage leaves.

Remove any outer, damaged leaves. Cut the cabbage lengthwise into quarters with a chef's knife. Cut off the base of each quarter at an angle to remove the hard white core. The cabbage is now ready to be shredded.

SHREDDING CABBAGE

After cutting a cabbage into quarters and coring it (see above), it can be shredded for eating raw in salads and coleslaws (see below), or for stir-frying, steaming or simmering in soups such as minestrone. Cabbage can be shredded either by hand or in a food processor.

BY HAND

Lay each cabbage quarter on a cutting board. Cut across to form even strips.

BY MACHINE

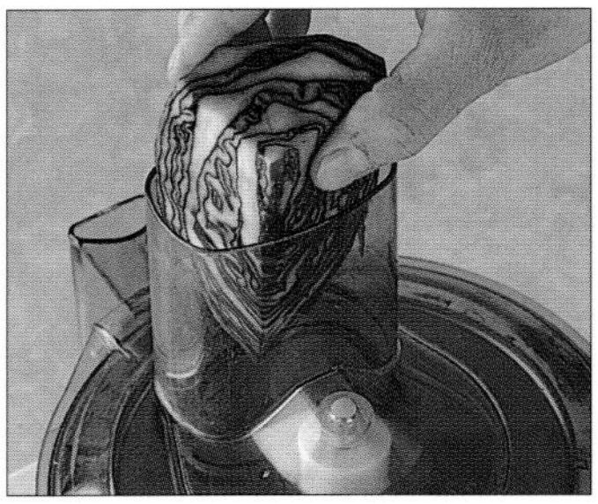

With the processor running, feed each cabbage quarter into the machine and shred.

COMBINING COLOURS

A colourful mixture of shredded red, white and green cabbage leaves looks very attractive and, with its mix of textures and flavours, makes an excellent winter salad.

Shred the cabbage either by hand or machine (see above) and place in a bowl. Toss in a vinaigrette or cooked dressing (see page 230), or in mayonnaise (see page 228).

Preparing Broccoli and Cauliflower

The delicate florets and hard stalks of broccoli and cauliflower cook at different rates so you need to separate them before cooking. Broccoli is illustrated here.

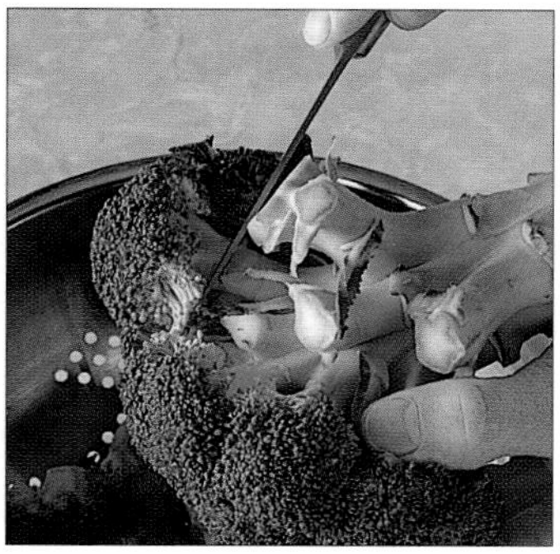

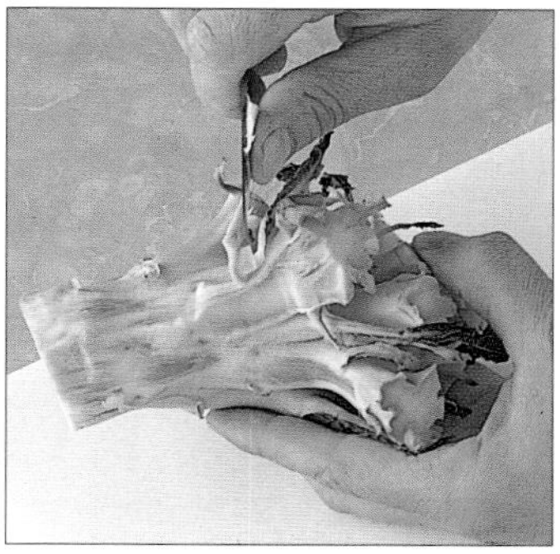

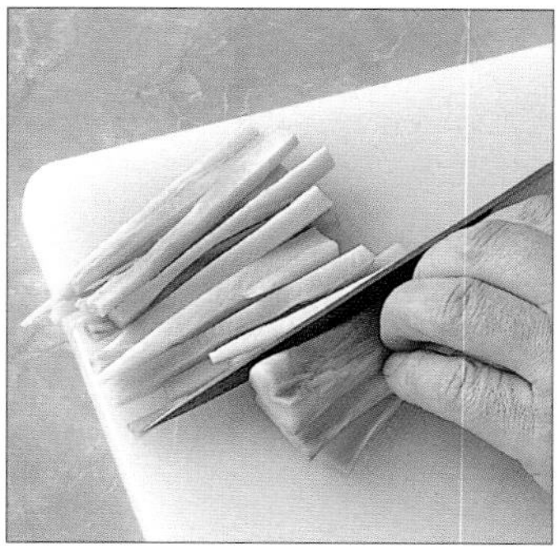

1 Holding the vegetable over a colander, cut off the florets leaving only the stalk. Divide the larger florets into smaller ones.

2 Remove the leaves from the stalk. Peel away the tough, outer layer with a vegetable peeler, then cut the stalk lengthwise in half.

3 Put the stalk cut-side down and remove the ends. Cut the stalk lengthwise into slices; cut the slices lengthwise into sticks.

SUPERSTAR VEGETABLE

Brassicas are all good sources of vitamin C and minerals, but broccoli is particularly high in many vital nutrients.

- 100 g broccoli provides over half the recommended daily intake of vitamin C.
- Broccoli is rich in carotene. High intakes may provide protection against cancer and heart disease.
- Broccoli is rich in folate (folic acid) which is needed by the body to form DNA and process proteins.
- The minerals iron, potassium and chromium are found in significant amounts in broccoli.

Preparing Brussels Sprouts

To ensure even cooking of large sprouts, a cross is cut in the base. This is not necessary for small sprouts.

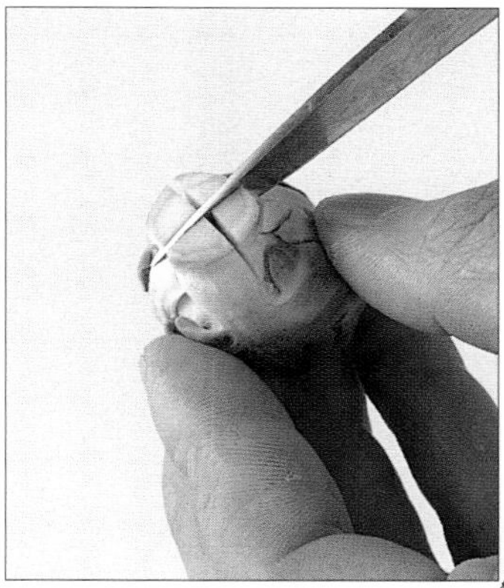

Cut a cross shape in the base of sprout with a chef's knife. Cut only a quarter of the way into the sprout, or it may fall apart during cooking. Trim the base stalks and remove any discoloured outer leaves.

TRICK OF THE TRADE

Preventing Discoloration

White vegetables, such as the cauliflower shown here, have a tendency to discolour when cut and exposed to the air. To prevent discoloration, put the prepared vegetable in a bowl, cover with cold water and add 1 tbsp lemon juice or white wine vinegar. This acidulates the water and preserves the colour of the vegetable.

From left to right: Broccoli; Brussels sprouts; Cauliflower

LEAFY GREENS

Although they are all prepared in much the same way, these greens run the gamut in flavour and texture. Young, tender varieties generally have a mild taste and can be eaten whole and raw. Large tougher-textured leaves need their stalks removed before cooking.

OTHER LEAFY GREENS

From the sweet and earthy to the sharp and peppery, greens have a wide variety of tastes. All require thorough rinsing to remove surface dirt before use.

CHINESE MUSTARD GREENS: With its strong, peppery bite, this green is best cooked; trim stalk before using.
FRENCH DANDELION: This jagged-leaved vegetable needs its tough root removed before use. Cultivated varieties have a milder taste than wild dandelions. Eat raw or cooked.
GRAPE LEAVES: These serve as a wrapper for other foods. Fresh leaves should be blanched, those sold in brine simply rinsed before use.
SORREL: Trim stalks of this tart, lemony green before eating raw or in cooked dishes.
SWISS CHARD: Separate the leaves from the white central stalks. Both leaves and stalks can be cooked.

PREPARING SPINACH

Young spinach leaves are tender so they can be eaten whole, either raw or cooked. Mature varieties have a tough stalk that needs trimming before the leaves are briefly cooked in just the water that clings to the leaves after washing. A technique that makes a stylish presentation for raw or gently sautéed spinach is the classic chiffonade *illustrated here.*

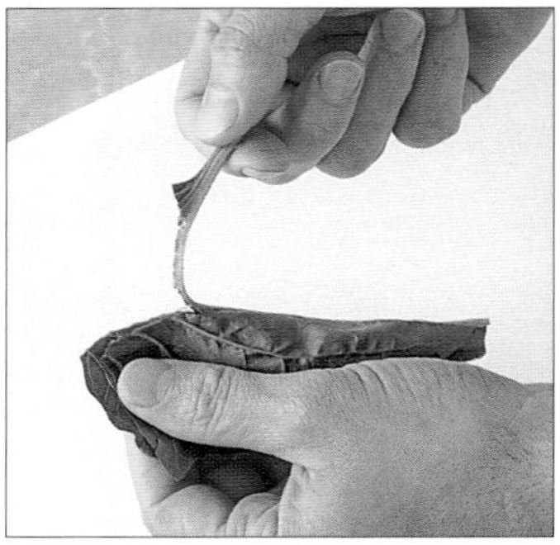

1 Fold each spinach leaf lengthwise along the central rib with the rib facing outwards. Tear the rib away from the leaf.

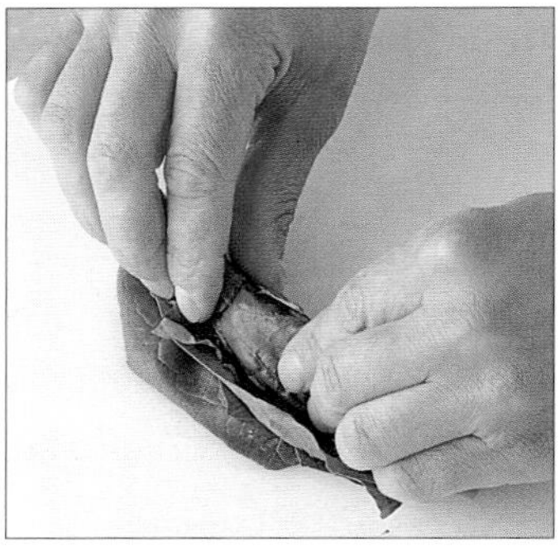

2 Stack a few leaves and roll them lengthwise into a cylindrical bundle. Hold the bundle with one hand.

3 Cut across the bundle with a chef's knife, using your knuckles as a guide, to make thin strips.

From left to right: sorrel; Chinese mustard greens; Swiss chard; French dandelion; spinach

Stalks & Shoots

These vegetables provide juicy crunch and versatility. Served raw, for instance, celery and fennel offer a sweet crispness. By contrast, when cooked, they offer invaluable depth of flavour.

Preparing Asparagus

Always choose green asparagus with even-sized, smooth spears and tips that are tightly furled. The very thin variety known as sprue, which is prized for its piquant flavour, is prepared as shown here, but it does not need peeling as in step 2. For white asparagus, see box, right.

1 Snap off the pale woody ends of the asparagus. The spears should break easily where the pale flesh begins. Rinse the spears well in plenty of cold water, gently rubbing them free of any dirt.

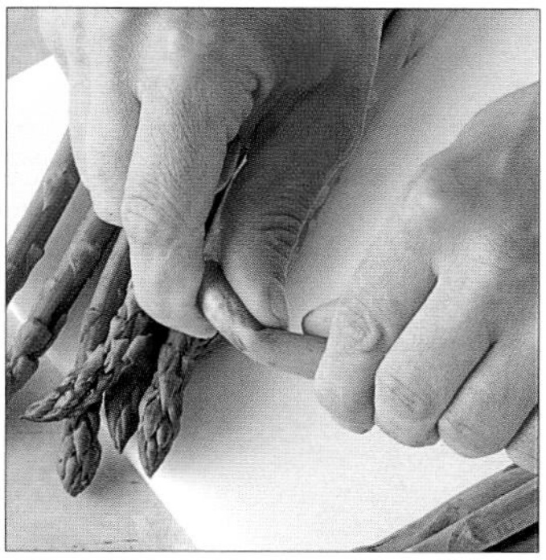

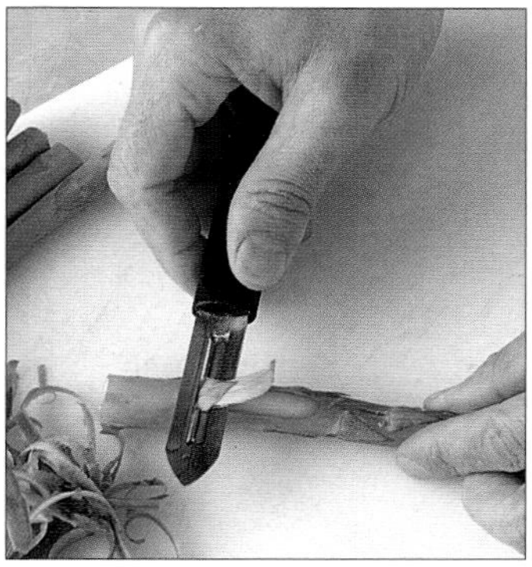

2 Carefully peel away the tough skin from the bottom half of the spears with a vegetable peeler.

3 Trim away the spiky leaves from the flower ends of the spears with the tip of a small knife.

4 Tie the spears into small bundles, making them easy to handle. To cook asparagus, see page 186.

Other Stalks and Shoots

Cardoon: A Mediterranean favourite that looks like celery but is from the same family as globe artichoke, which it resembles in flavour. Discard outer stalks, strip away leaves and peel strings from ribs. The stalks will brown in contact with air, so keep cut stalks in acidulated water to combat this. Boiling is the best cooking method.

Swiss chard: A member of the beetroot family with thick white ribs and coarse leaves. Steam the stems, whole or sliced. Leaves are cooked separately, often as a substitute for spinach.

White asparagus: A favourite Continental variety that grows underground and is fat with yellow tips. Must be peeled and cooked twice as long as green asparagus (see page 186).

Preparing Celery

Only use crisp celery that snaps easily. Flexible sticks indicate staleness. Before using raw or cooked, any tough strings must be removed from the coarse outer sticks.

Trim the top and root ends from a bunch of celery, cutting off any green leaves and reserving them for garnishing. Separate into sticks. Peel the tough strings from the sticks with a vegetable peeler.

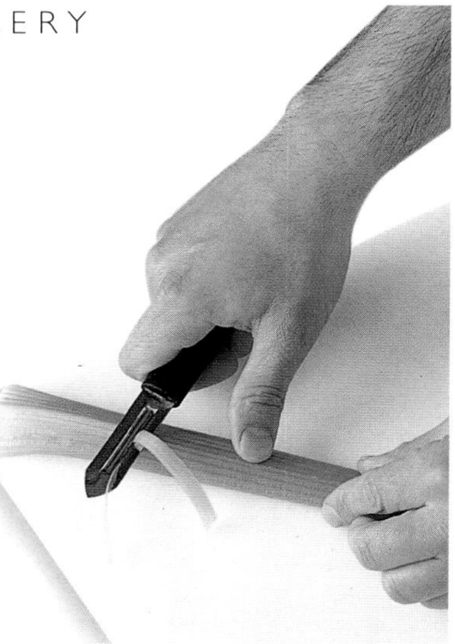

Preparing Fennel

Keep pieces of cut fennel in iced water – they brown when exposed to air. For flavour, choose mature bulbs that are well-rounded and plump.

Trim the top and root end of the fennel bulb, saving any green fronds for garnishing. Rinse the bulb. To cut into chunks, cut lengthwise in half. Cut each half into quarters. To slice, cut the bulb in half lengthwise and place cut-side down. Cut crosswise into slices.

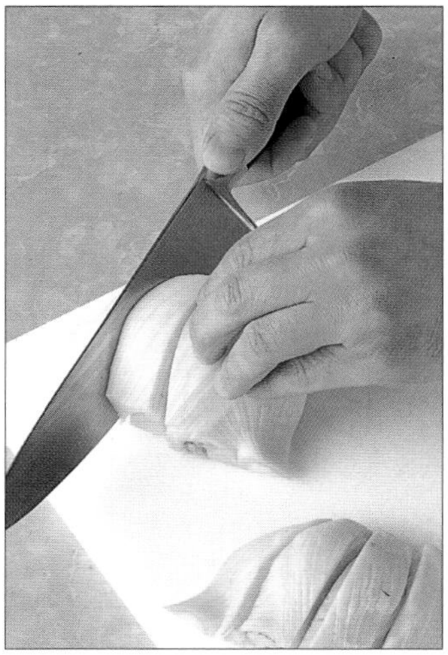

Globe Artichokes

These are members of the thistle family. What we eat are actually the flower buds, which can be put to different uses depending on the way they are prepared. You can cook the whole artichoke or just the heart.

Serving Whole Artichokes

Boiled whole artichokes are traditionally used as a receptacle for dressings, into which the outer leaves are dipped. Some dressing ideas are listed here, plus more substantial fillings.

- Vinaigrette dressing (see page 230).
- Flaked crab meat, mixed with mayonnaise and lemon juice.
- Lemon-butter sauce flavoured with finely snipped chives.
- Hollandaise sauce spiked with Dijon mustard and grated orange zest.
- *Tapenade* (olive purée) thinned with olive oil.
- *Aïoli* (see page 229).
- Pesto stirred into finely chopped tomatoes, seasoned with red wine vinegar.
- Crème fraîche or fromage frais dressing flavoured with chopped fresh dill.

Preparing and Cooking Whole Artichokes

In mature artichokes, sets of green fleshy leaves tightly enclose the tender heart and purple hairy choke. Only the base of these leaves, the heart and sometimes the stalk (see box, below) are edible. Mature artichokes are always served cooked.

1 Hold the artichoke firmly and break off the stalk at the bottom, pulling out the tough fibres that are attached to it.

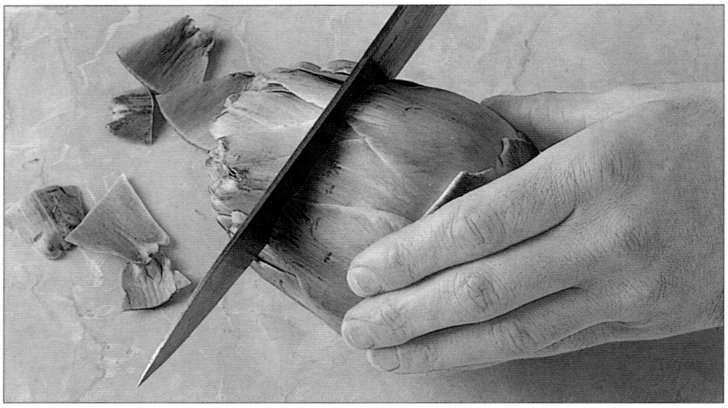

2 Cut off the top third of the artichoke and trim any tough outer leaves; discard. Place artichokes in a pan of boiling salted water with the juice of 1 lemon. Weight down with a plate and simmer for 20–35 minutes, depending on size.

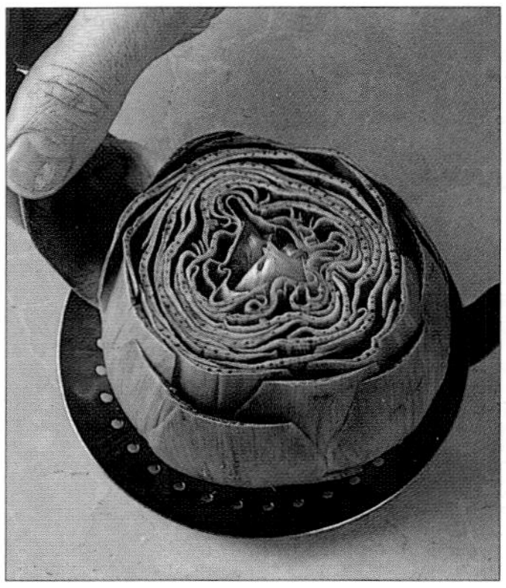

3 Test for doneness by pulling gently at one of the leaves, which should come away easily.

Trick of the Trade

Waste Not, Want Not

The stalks of very fresh, young artichokes are deliciously tender when cooked if they have been properly prepared.

For best results, simply peel off the outer fibrous layer with a small paring knife, then cut lengthwise into sticks. Cook in boiling salted water with a squeeze of lemon juice to help retain colour.

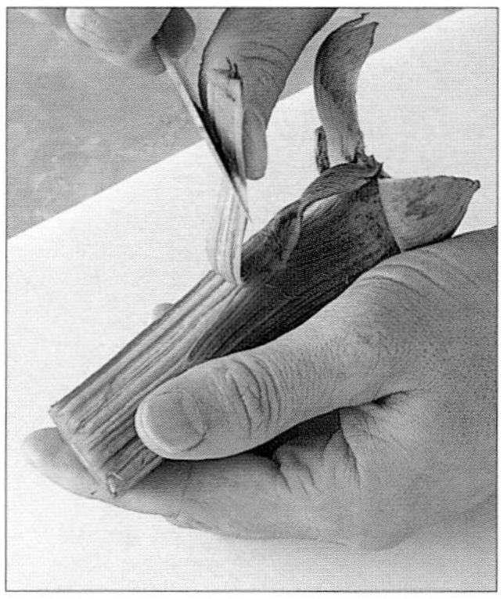

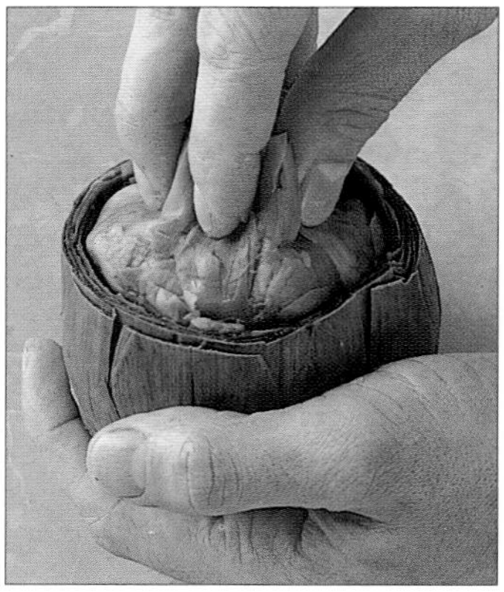

4 Pull out the central cone of leaves and reserve. Remove the hairy choke with a spoon and discard.

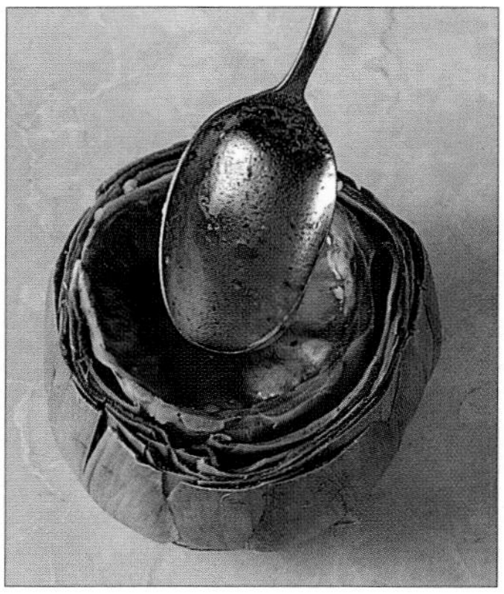

5 Put the cone back in the artichoke, upside-down. Spoon in a filling of your choice (see box, above left).

Preparing Artichoke Hearts

The heart or bottom of the artichoke is the tenderest, most delicious part, often eaten on its own without the outer leaves. In classic French cuisine, hearts are simmered in a blanc *(see page 336) to help them keep their colour, but this is not absolutely essential. After cooking, serve hearts whole with a sauce or stuffing in the centre, or slice and toss in a dressing.*

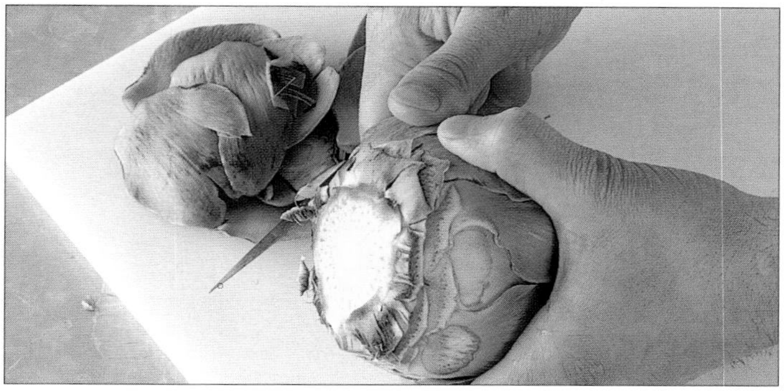

1 Carefully trim off the tough outer green leaves from the artichoke with a chef's knife. Break off the stalk with your hands, then cut the base flat.

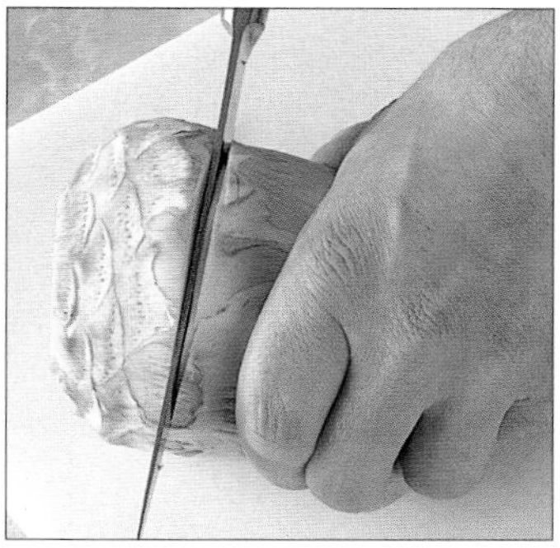

2 Hold the artichoke firmly and cut off the bottom third, taking care to include the heart; discard the top two-thirds.

3 Put the artichoke hearts in a bowl of cold water with half a lemon. This will help to prevent the artichokes from discolouring.

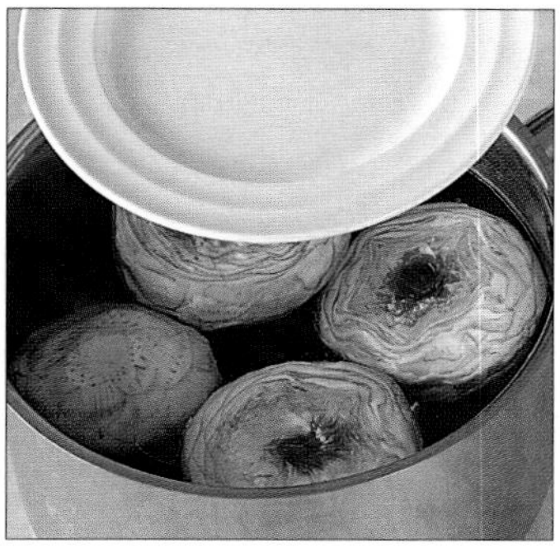

4 Place the hearts in a pan of boiling salted water, weight down with a plate and simmer for 15–20 minutes.

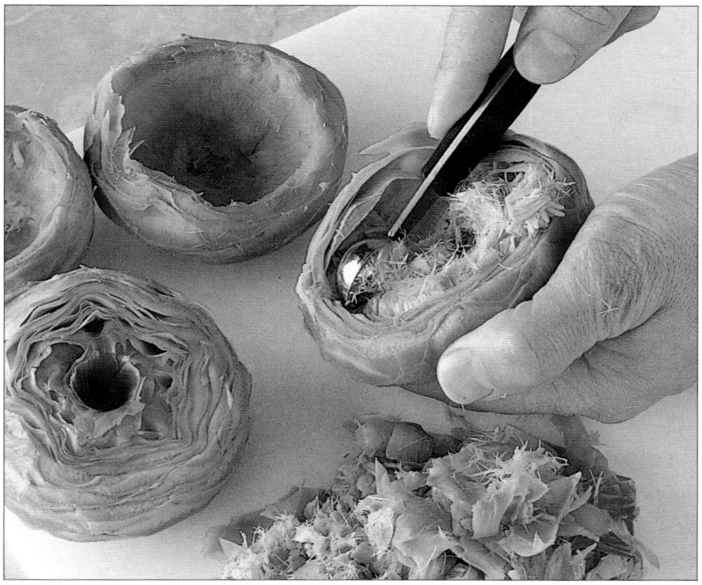

5 Test for doneness by piercing the heart with the tip of a paring knife. Drain well. When cool enough to handle, scoop out the hairy choke with a melon baller, and discard.

Baby Artichokes

Baby artichokes are a particular delicacy. They can be eaten whole including the stalk and outer leaves and even the choke, which is barely developed. Here are some serving suggestions.

- Boil them for 3–4 minutes until tender, quarter them and serve warm with a vinaigrette dressing (see page 230).
- Thinly slice them raw, then mix with olives and cherry tomatoes and dress with fruity extra-virgin olive oil and coarsely ground sea salt.
- Fry them whole in olive oil to make the Italian speciality *carciofi alla giudea*.
- Halve them and bake in a sauce made of fresh tomatoes, garlic, olive oil and basil.
- Simmer them until tender in water with olive oil, lemon juice, thyme, bay leaves and coriander seeds to make *artichauts à la grecque*. Let them cool in the liquid before draining and serving.

ROOTS & TUBERS

Beetroot, carrot, parsnip, turnip, radish and salsify all grow underground, hence their name and their hard fibrous constitution. Knobbly vegetables – celeriac, Jerusalem artichokes and kohlrabi – are included in the same category, and have similar techniques.

MAKING JULIENNE

Most root vegetables, such as the turnips illustrated here, have firm flesh suitable for cutting into long, thin sticks known as julienne. Prepared this way they need only brief cooking – boiling, steaming or sautéing – and make attractive garnishes.

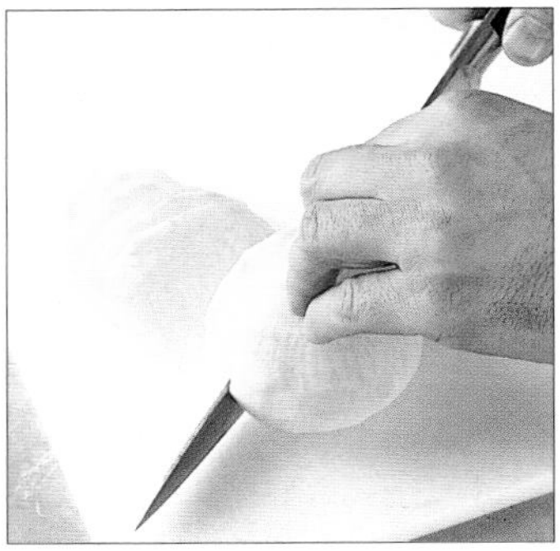

1 Peel the vegetable and cut it into thin slices with a chef's knife.

2 Stack the slices, a few at a time, and cut into thin, even-sized strips.

ROLL CUTTING

This method of cutting, favoured in Asian cooking, produces uniform pieces with maximum surface area. This is ideal for quick-cooking methods such as stir-frying and sautéing. Long roots, such as the carrot shown here, are best suited to this technique.

Peel the vegetable and top and tail. Starting at one end, cut at a 45° angle. Roll the carrot through 90° and cut at the same angle again. Repeat along the length of the carrot.

DICING

This produces even-sized cubes that cook quickly and make a neat and attractive presentation. Diced vegetables are often used as a base for soups and stews (see box, right), and are good for puréeing. Sweet potato is illustrated here.

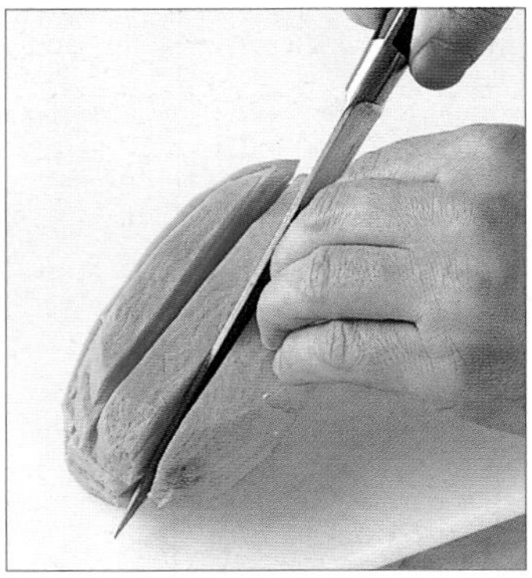

1 Peel the vegetable and cut into even slices. Stack the slices, a few at a time, and cut lengthwise to make equal-sized bâtons.

2 Cut across the bâtons to make equal-sized dice. The size of the dice may vary (see box, right).

TRICK OF THE TRADE

MAKING MIREPOIX AND BRUNOISE

These diced vegetable preparations are classics in French cooking. Mirepoix, a basic flavouring for soups and stews, takes its name from its creator, the 18th-century Duc de Lévis-Mirepoix. Brunoise is the classic consommé garnish.

Mirepoix is a roughly diced mixture of raw carrot, onion and celery. Leek is also often included.

Brunoise is very finely diced raw carrot, celery, leek or courgette. Use singly or mix together.

MAKING RIBBONS

These are thin shavings made with a vegetable peeler. The technique is perfect for long root vegetables, especially carrots, because they have a hard, fibrous texture, and also for courgettes. Use vegetable ribbons as a side dish, and in salads and stir-fries. They also make an attractive garnish.

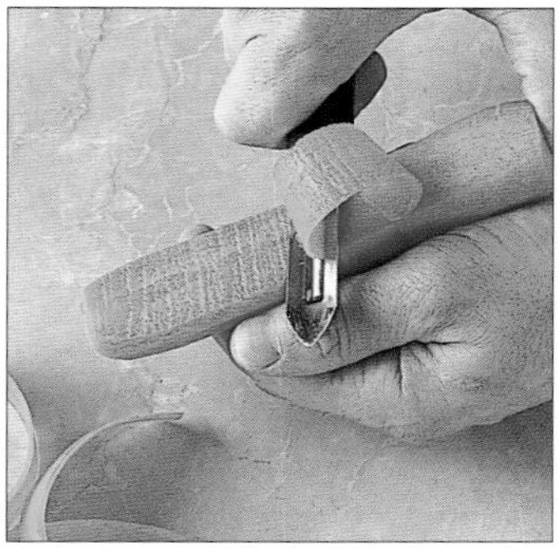

Peel the vegetable and discard the peelings. Holding the vegetable firmly in one hand, peel it all along its length with a vegetable peeler, using firm pressure. If the ribbons are not to be used immediately, keep them in iced water.

TURNING

This classic French technique "turns" vegetables into neat barrel or olive shapes, traditionally with five or seven sides, to resemble baby vegetables. Turnips and carrots are turned here; potatoes, celeriac, courgettes and cucumber can also be prepared this way.

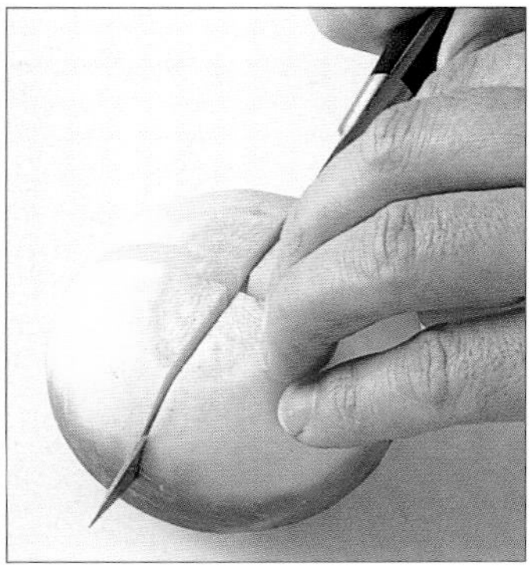

1 Cut round vegetables into quarters, tubular vegetables such as carrots into 5-cm lengths.

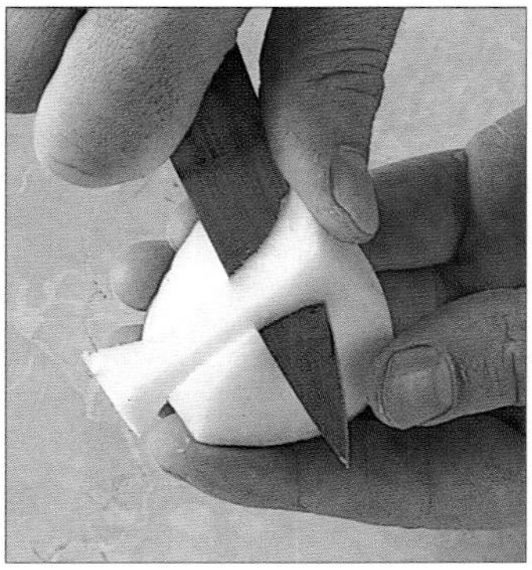

2 Carefully trim off all of the sharp edges, using a small paring knife, to form a curved shape.

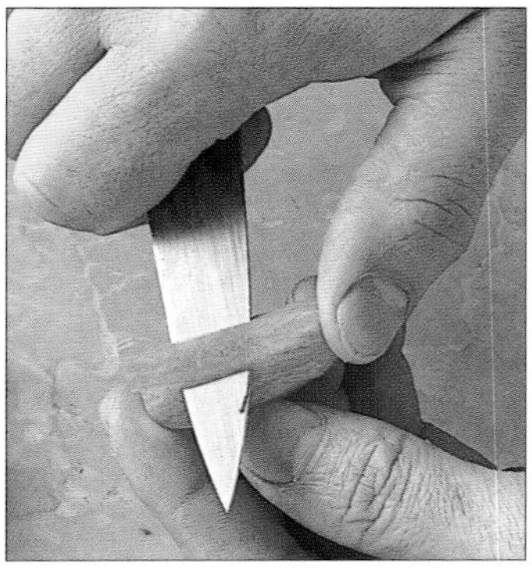

3 Pare down the vegetable from top to bottom, turning it slightly after each cut until it is barrel-shaped.

PREPARING KNOBBLY VEGETABLES

Celeriac, Jerusalem artichokes and kohlrabi are all knobbly vegetables that look difficult to deal with, but the technique of preparing them is remarkably simple. First peel off the skin with a small paring knife, then slice, chop, shred or grate the flesh, depending on future use (see box, right). Once the flesh is cut, immerse the pieces in acidulated water immediately to prevent discoloration (see box, page 161).

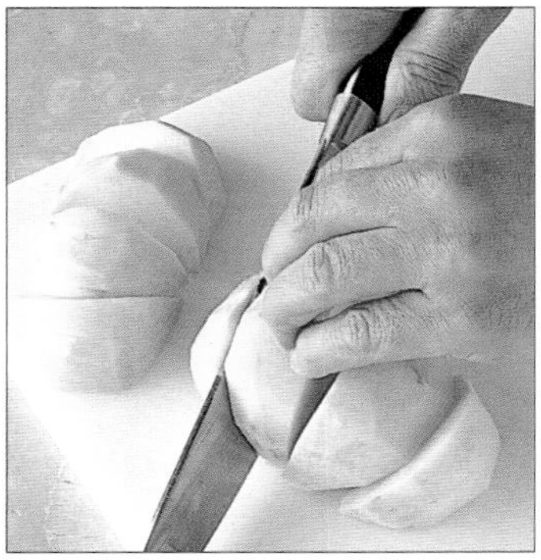

SLICING KOHLRABI
Cut the kohlrabi in half lengthwise, place each half cut-side down on a cutting board and cut into quarters.

SHREDDING CELERIAC
Set the coarse shredding blade of a mandolin (see box, above) to 5-mm thickness. Work the celeriac against the blade.

MANDOLIN

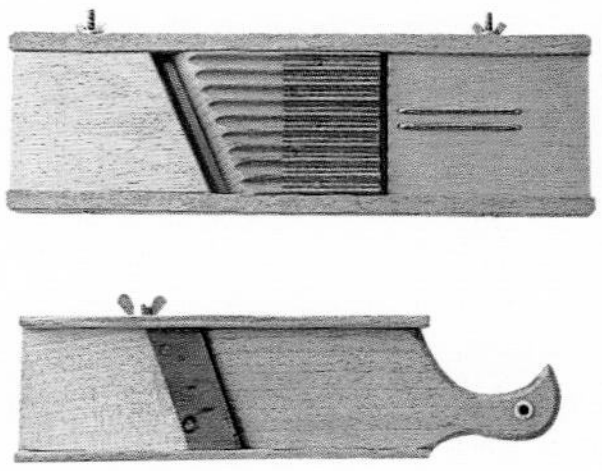

For slicing firm vegetables, such as roots and tubers, you can use a mandolin, called *mandoline* in French. The professional type is made of stainless steel (see below and page 169). It has one straight blade, coarse and fine shredding blades, and a rippled cutter for making *pommes gaufrettes* (see page 169). It also has a carriage to protect your fingers and steady the vegetable.

Simpler mandolins are made of wood with steel blades (see above). You can use the mandolin to slice very rapidly by placing the vegetable in the carriage and moving it back and forth over the blade. The thickness of the slices is adjustable.

KNOBBLY VEGETABLES

Despite their strange appearance, knobbly vegetables are as versatile as potatoes.

- Slice or chop, then boil or steam. Toss in butter or olive oil and chopped fresh herbs.
- Slice or chop, then par-boil. Roast with herbs and seasoning.
- Slice or chop, then boil and mash with butter or olive oil, crushed garlic and seasoning.
- Shred or grate raw and toss in vinaigrette or mayonnaise.

POTATOES

Although potatoes appear in many shapes and colours (see box, opposite page), they fall into two basic categories – waxy and floury. For best results it is crucial to choose the right variety. Waxy potatoes have a high moisture and low starch content, ideal for sautéing, boiling and salads. Floury varieties have more starch, hence a light, fluffy texture. They are the prized "bakers" and offer the creamiest results in purées and gratins.

EXOTIC VEGETABLE

Potatoes are commonplace vegetables today but at one time they were as exotic as yams or eddoes are now. A staple food of the Peruvian Incas, they were brought to England in the 16th century by Sir Francis Drake. Surprisingly, at first they were thought fit only for animals, and were held responsible for diseases such as leprosy.

Sir Francis Drake (1540-1596)

SCRUBBING

Potato skins are full of nutrients and flavour, so it is best not to remove them before cooking. Scrub or scrape clean rather than peel.

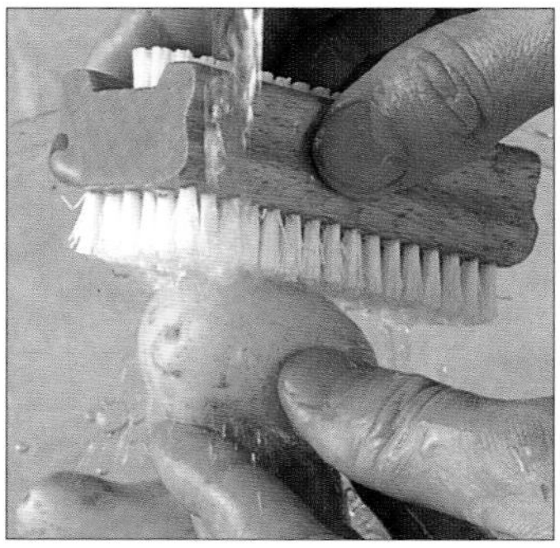

Hold the potato under cold running water and remove "eyes" with a knife tip. Scrub the skins all over with a stiff brush to remove any earth.

PREPARING FOR ROASTING

Potatoes can be roasted unpeeled or peeled. Small potatoes can be left whole, but for even and quick cooking, large potatoes are best prepared hasselback-style, or cut into smaller shapes. Pommes châteaux *are the classic French shape. For two different roasting techniques, see pages 188 and 189.*

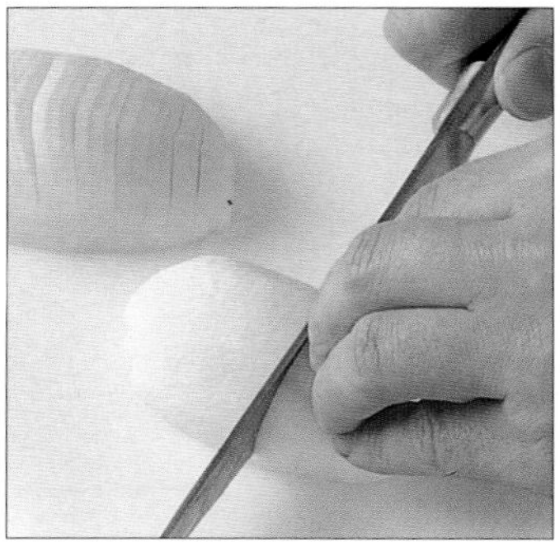

HASSELBACK
Slice off the bottom of the potato to steady it. Make thin parallel cuts from the top almost to the bottom.

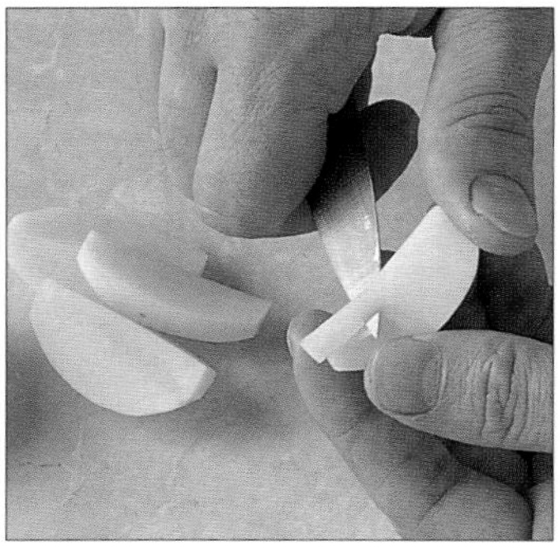

POMMES CHATEAUX
Cut potato lengthwise into quarters with a chef's knife. Shave off the flat edge of each quarter to round it.

PRICKING FOR BAKING

Large, floury potatoes are best for baking in the oven in their jackets. To prevent them bursting during cooking, the skin should be pierced by pricking it with a fork. If you like, rub with oil and salt to crisp the skin during cooking, or bake them on a bed of salt. You can also cook them on metal skewers – the heat is conducted through to the centre of the potatoes quicker this way.

Scrub potatoes (see above) and prick them all over with a fork, piercing right through to the flesh. Bake at 220°C, 1–1¼ hours.

MAKING POMMES PARISIENNES

This is the classic French way to prepare potatoes for sautéing. The name comes from the melon baller used to cut the potatoes, called cuillère parisienne *or Parisian spoon. It produces small balls that cook in butter, or a mixture of butter and oil, to an even brown colour. Large floury potatoes are best – they produce a crisper result than waxy potatoes.*

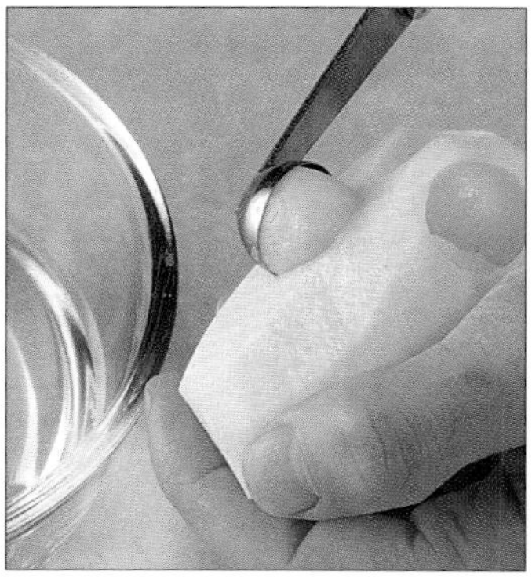

Press a melon baller into peeled potato and scoop out as many balls as possible. Drop the balls into a bowl of cold water as you work.

PREPARING POTATOES FOR DEEP-FRYING

There are many ways potatoes can be prepared for deep-frying, from ordinary chips to elaborate latticed potatoes or gaufrettes*. They are usually peeled first, and must always be uniform in size and thickness. Drop them into cold water as you cut them to prevent discoloration. This also removes some of the starch and helps to make them crisp. Drain the shapes and dry them thoroughly before immersing in hot oil –* *see page 191 for the technique of deep-frying potatoes.*

BY HAND

A sharp chef's knife can be used to cut thick sticks, such as the pommes pont neuf *shown here.* Pommes frites *and* allumettes *can also be cut by hand, but they are easier and more regular cut on a mandolin.*

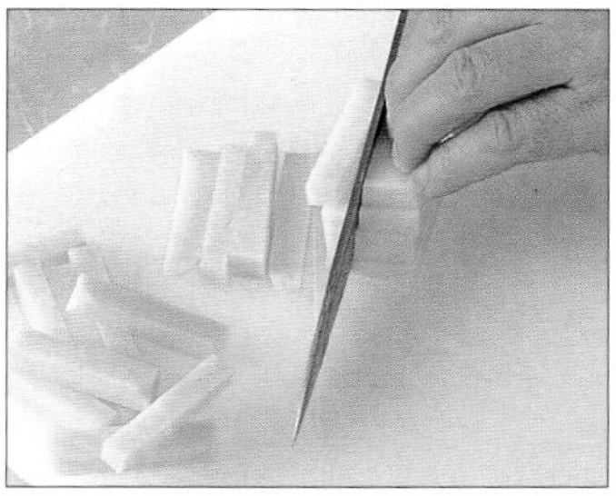

POMMES PONT NEUF
Named after the oldest bridge in Paris, these are always served stacked. Trim the ends and sides of potato to make a rectangular block, then slice 1 cm thick. Stack the slices and cut into sticks 1 cm wide.

BY MACHINE

A mandolin, with its choice of blades and cutters, is the best tool to use for these classic wafer-thin French fries. *See the box on page 167 for information on mandolins.*

POMMES ALLUMETTES
Work potato against the fine shredding blade set to 3-mm thickness. *Pommes pailles* (straw potatoes) are made in the same way, with the ramp positioned in line with the straight blade.

POMMES FRITES
Work potato against the coarse shredding blade set to 5-mm thickness.

POMMES GAUFRETTES
Work potato against the rippled cutter set to 1-mm thickness and discard the first slice. Turn the potato 90° and cut the next slice. Repeat along the potato, turning it 90° after each slice.

POMMES SOUFFLES
Slightly thicker than game chips. Work potato against the straight blade set to 3-mm thickness.

ALLUMETTES

FRITES

PONT NEUF

GAUFRETTES

SOUFFLES

OLD POTATOES

These are available from September to June. Their starch content increases with maturity.

CARA: White skins and flesh, moist texture. For boiling, baking.
DESIREE: Red skins, pale flesh. For boiling, frying, baking.
KING EDWARD: White skins with pink patches, floury texture. For mashing, frying, roasting, baking.
MARIS PIPER: White skins, cream flesh, floury texture. For boiling, frying, roasting, baking.
PENTLAND SQUIRE: White skins, cream flesh, floury texture. For mashing, roasting, baking.
ROMANO RED: Red skins, cream flesh, soft dry texture. For boiling.

NEW POTATOES

These appear from early May and are still immature. They have a sweet flavour and waxy texture.

ESTIMA: Pale yellow skins, pale creamy flesh, firm moist texture. For boiling, frying, baking.
JERSEY: Yellow skin, creamy waxy flesh. For boiling, salads.
MARIS BARD: White skins, white to cream flesh. For boiling, salads.
ROCKET: White skin, white, firm waxy flesh. For boiling, salads.
WILJA: Yellow skins, pale yellow flesh, firm dryish texture. For boiling, mashing, frying, baking.

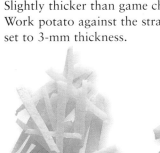

MUSHROOMS

The term "mushroom" is used loosely to mean the whole family of edible fungi. There are three broad categories: common cultivated white mushrooms, exotic cultivated ones such as shiitake and oyster mushrooms, and wild fungi such as chanterelles, ceps and truffles.

PREPARING CULTIVATED MUSHROOMS

Mushrooms can be eaten raw or cooked. Ordinary white mushrooms are grown in pasteurized compost, so need only wiping. If very dirty, rinse briefly. Do not soak them or they will become soggy. Button mushrooms can be left whole or halved, larger ones may be sliced or chopped.

1 Trim off the woody ends of the stalks with a small knife. Save the trimmings for use in stocks and soups.

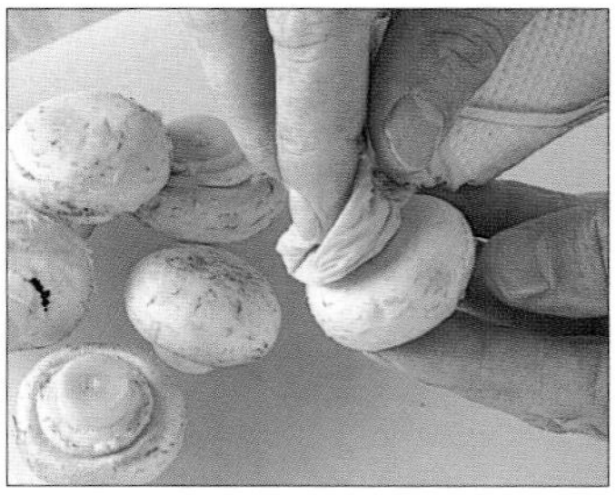

2 Wipe the mushrooms gently with damp paper towels, removing any compost still clinging to them.

SLICING
Put the mushrooms stalk-side down on a cutting board. Slice lengthwise with a chef's knife.

PREPARING WILD MUSHROOMS

Fresh wild mushrooms deteriorate quickly, so use them as soon as possible. If storing briefly, keep them in a paper bag in the refrigerator. Most wild mushrooms do not need washing or peeling, but check with your supplier.

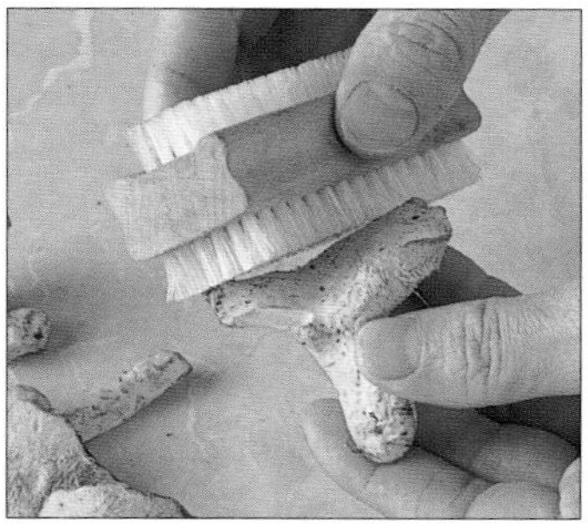

1 Gently brush off any earth that is still clinging to the mushrooms with a small brush or a clean cloth. Be careful not to damage the delicate flesh of the caps.

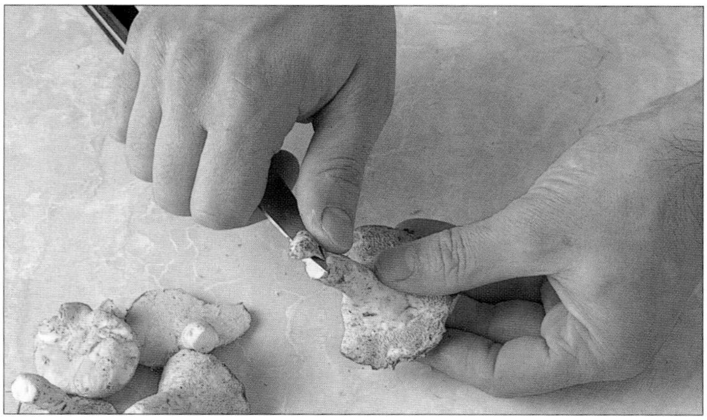

2 Trim off the woody ends of the stalks with a small knife. Leave as much of the flesh as possible. Many wild mushrooms are left whole or simply halved lengthwise, to preserve their attractive shape, but they can also be sliced in the same way as cultivated mushrooms.

DUXELLES

Duxelles is a classic French combination of finely chopped mushrooms and shallots or onions sautéed in butter until quite dry. Used as a stuffing (see Beef Wellington, page 125) or garnish, it is said to have been created by La Varenne, chef of the Marquis d'Uxelles.

TRICK OF THE TRADE

FINELY CHOPPING MUSHROOMS

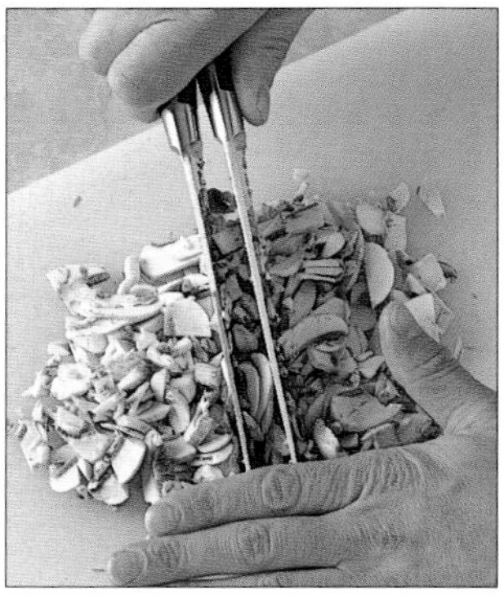

A quick method of chopping mushrooms for duxelles is to use two chef's knives held together in one hand. Secure the tips of the blades with your other hand and then chop, using a rocking motion. This limits the time the mushrooms are exposed to air and helps prevent discoloration. For a whiter duxelles, use only the mushroom caps.

Preparing Wood Ears

Also known as cloud ears, wood ears are an Asian fungus, commonly sold in dried form. Like dried mushrooms below, they must be reconstituted before use, when they swell into clusters of dark gelatinous lobes up to five times their dried size. They are used in stir-fries, soups and braised dishes.

Soak wood ears as for dried mushrooms below, then rinse thoroughly under cold running water to rid them of sand and grit lodged in the crevices. Dry thoroughly with a tea towel before use and trim off and discard the hard central stalks. Slice or chop wood ears according to individual recipe instructions.

Reconstituting Dried Mushrooms

Many different varieties of mushroom can be bought dried. These include Asian varieties such as shiitake and oyster mushrooms, and wild ones such as morels, ceps and chanterelles. Dried wild mushrooms are expensive but their flavour is highly concentrated, so even a very small quantity added to a dish will give a superb richness and depth. Add to dishes such as sauces, soups, omelettes, risottos, pasta sauces and stir-fries.

1 Put mushrooms in a bowl and cover with warm water. Leave to soak for 35–40 minutes or until they have softened.

2 Drain, then squeeze to extract the liquid. Strain the liquid and use with mushrooms.

Truffles

There are two main types – the French black truffle from Périgord and the white truffle from Piedmont, northern Italy. The black truffle is eaten raw, used in stuffings and sauces, and braised or baked in pastry. White truffles are usually eaten raw.

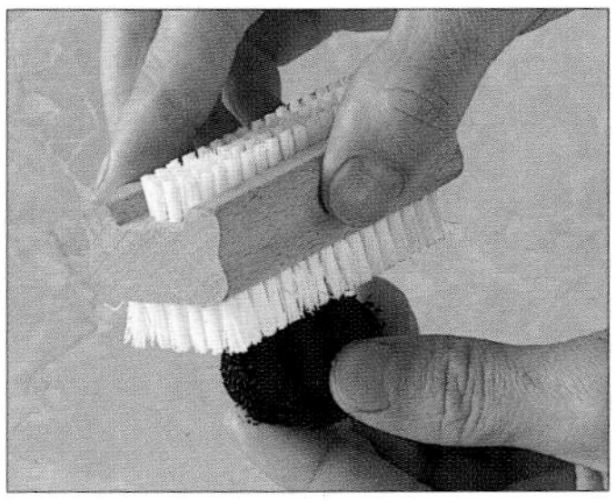

Cleaning a black truffle
Carefully scrub the truffle with a brush. If you like, peel off the knobbly skin with a vegetable peeler, finely chop the peelings and use in cooked dishes.

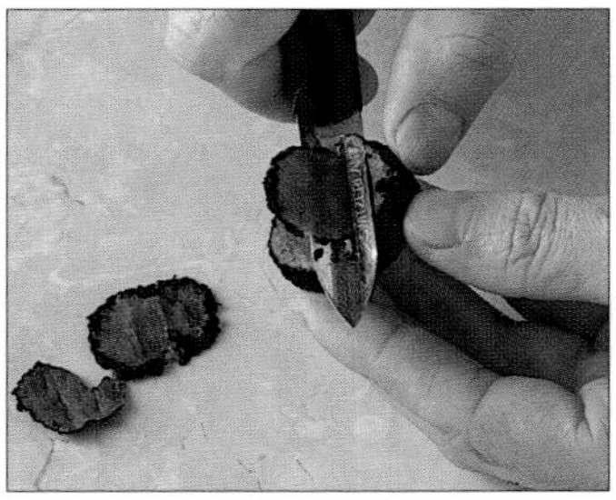

Slicing a truffle
Shave black or white truffles as thinly as possible with a vegetable peeler. Use shavings in cooking, or sprinkled raw on dishes like pasta, risotto, polenta and omelettes.

From top to bottom, left to right: shiitake; pied bleu; chanterelle, wood ears; pied de mouton

Wild Mushrooms

Cep: *Porcini* "little pig" in Italian, this variety has a chubby shape and bulbous cap.
Chanterelle: Golden-hued and concave, tasting of apricots.
Morel: A slim conical cap and honeycomb exterior, with a sweet intensity to rival truffles.
Pied de mouton (or hedgehog): Cream-coloured and fleshy with tiny white spines under the gills.

Safety First

If you pick wild mushrooms yourself, do not eat anything you cannot positively identify as being edible. Eat wild mushrooms as soon as possible as they quickly deteriorate.

Pods

This classification divides into two types: those that are eaten young and still in the pod, such as mangetouts, runner beans, French beans and okra; and those where the seeds are left to mature and are served shelled, such as garden peas and broad beans.

TRICK OF THE TRADE

Testing for Freshness

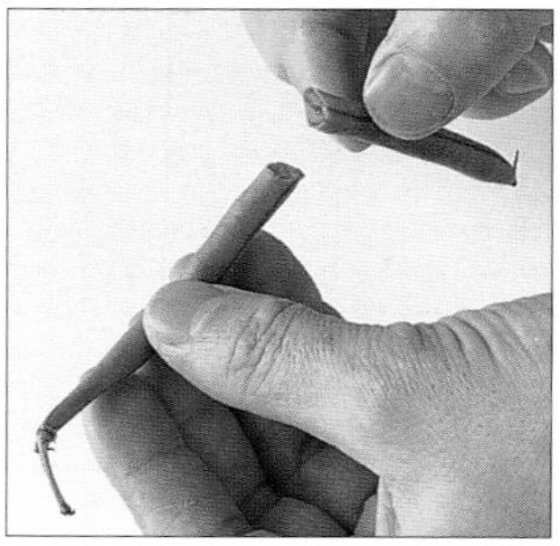

Most fresh green beans, with the exception of broad beans and very young French beans, should snap easily when bent in half. If they do not snap, they have been picked when too old or stored for too long.

Peas

Some pea varieties, such as mangetouts and sugar snap, are cultivated to be harvested young and eaten in the pod. They need only to be stringed before being used raw in salads, or cooked. Other peas are picked later, when the pods are full. They are shelled and the pods discarded. Both types are best cooked briefly, either steamed, boiled or stir-fried.

Stringing
For mangetouts and sugar snaps, break off the stalk and pull off the string.

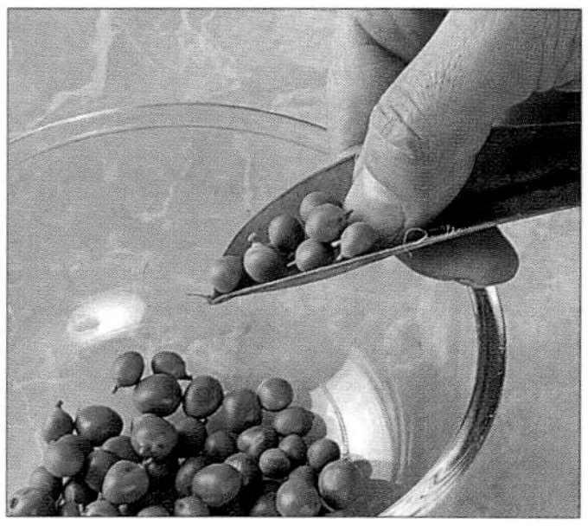

Shelling
Press the base of pea pods to open, then push your thumb up the pod, removing peas.

Green Beans

Runner beans and French beans are eaten whole, including the pod. Runner beans are wide and flat, each containing several mottled purple seeds. They should be trimmed, stringed and sliced before cooking. French beans are long and cylindrical and simply need topping and tailing. They can be left whole, cut into short lengths or sliced on the diagonal.

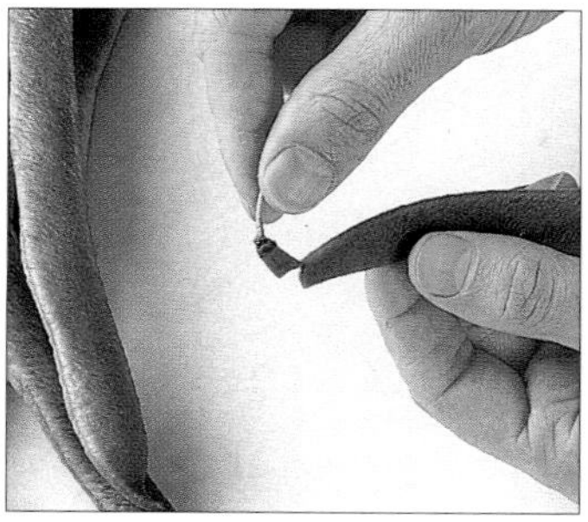

1 Snap the stalk off runner bean and pull the string down the pod. Repeat from the other end.

2 Slice beans diagonally with a chef's knife. Cut thinner slices for quick cooking, such as stir-frying.

Broad Beans

Young broad beans are soft and tender, and can be eaten whole. Always boil or steam them first, as certain beans contain toxins which are only neutralized in cooking. Mature pods are tough, and the beans need to be shelled and skinned following the method here.

Shell mature beans as for peas (see above) and discard the pods. To remove the skins, first blanch beans, then slit the skin around one end using a small knife. Press the other end between your fingers and squeeze the bean out.

OKRA

Also known as "ladies' fingers" and bhindi, *okra are served cooked, usually whole in stir-fries, sliced in curries and stews. They are popular in Caribbean cooking for their natural thickening properties (see box, right).*

To cook whole okra, cut off the end of the stalk. Trim around the stalk to make a cone shape. This prevents the pod being pierced and releasing its sticky juices (see box, right).

SWEETCORN

Every part of sweetcorn may be used. Traditionally, the husked corn is boiled and served "on the cob" with butter, or the kernels are scraped off and cooked. In Mexican cooking, the husks are used to make *tamales*.

COBS AND KERNELS

Sweetcorn can be boiled or barbecued "on the cob", in which case only the husks and silks are removed, or the kernels can be stripped off and cooked separately.

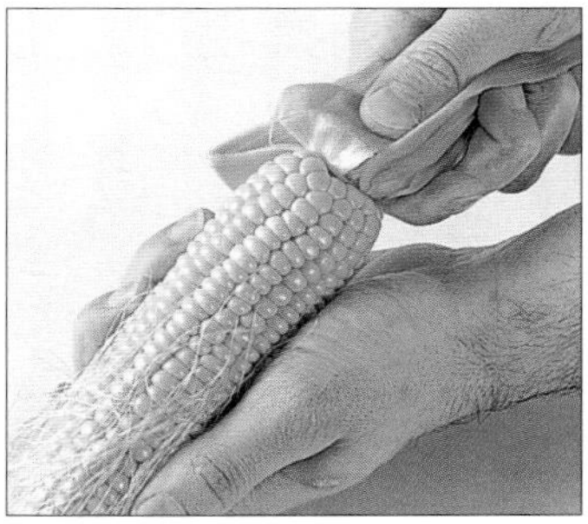

1 To husk the corn, grasp the leaves and pull them firmly back and off the cob.

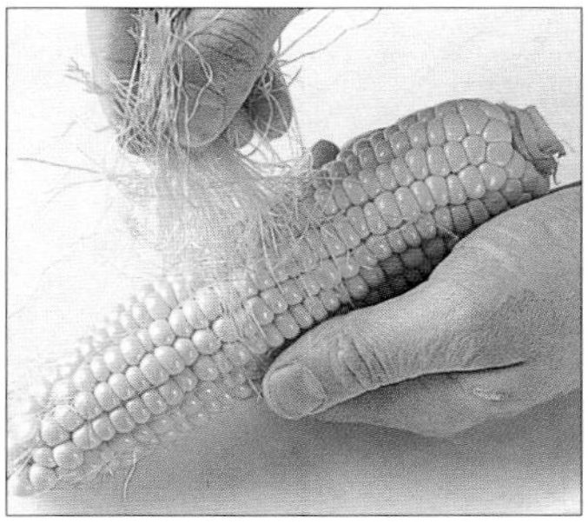

2 Pull off the silk. The corn is now ready for cooking whole "on the cob".

3 To strip the kernels, hold the cob stalk-end down. Cut down in smooth strokes.

USING CORN HUSKS

In Mexico, dried corn husks are used to make tamales *(see recipe box, right). Dried corn husks are not available here, so fresh corn husks are used instead. After removing them from the cobs (see step 1, above), dry them out in the oven at 150°C for about 30 minutes.*

1 Press a piece of cornmeal dough into the widest end of each corn husk with your fingers. Spoon a little of the spicy filling on top of it.

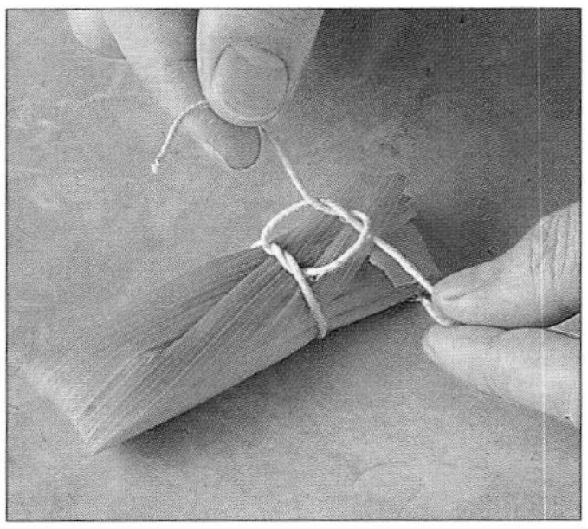

2 Wrap the long sides of the corn husk over the filling. Fold over the short ends and then tie the package neatly with kitchen string.

NATURAL THICKENER

Okra contain a sticky juice that is released when the pod is cut. This gelatinous substance acts as a natural thickener in spicy curries and soups, the most famous of which is the Louisiana gumbo (see page 28). To release the viscous liquid, slice the pod of the okra during preparation. Bear in mind, however, that the juice will become slimy if it is simmered too long. To prevent this, cook okra only until it is just tender, and avoid old and tough pods that tend to be mushy.

TAMALES

40 dried or fresh corn husks
175 g lard
450 g ground cornmeal
3 garlic cloves, chopped
1 onion, chopped
¼ tsp ground cloves
¼ tsp ground cinnamon
2 tbsp butter
450 g minced pork
1 red chilli, deseeded and finely chopped
Salt and freshly ground pepper

If using dried corn husks, soak them in cold water for 1 hour. Lay the husks flat to dry before filling. Mix the lard and cornmeal to form a dough. Press a small piece of dough into the widest end of each husk to make a rectangle.

For the filling, sweat the garlic, onion and spices in the butter. Add the pork and chilli. Cook until the pork browns, 5 minutes. Season well. Spoon the filling along the centre of the dough.

Wrap the husks around the filling and tie with string. Steam for 1 hour. Remove the string before serving. Peel open the husks – the filling is eaten with the fingers.

The Onion Family

Members of the onion family are essential to so many dishes, either as a subtle flavouring or as the star ingredient. When they are prepared correctly, following the methods shown here, they will release their flavour more readily and be more easily digested.

Onions without tears

Once they are cut, the smell of onions can become quite overpowering, and volatile oils released can sting the eyes and make them water. A few time-honoured remedies may help to alleviate the problem.

One method is to peel onions while they are submerged in a bowl of water and then to keep the tap running while chopping.

Another technique is to leave the root end intact during chopping (see below). Chewing a piece of bread while slicing or dicing may also help.

Peeling and Slicing Onions

All onions must be peeled before use to remove the papery skin. Here the technique of slicing a whole onion into rings is shown. For smaller, half-moon slices, cut the onion in half lengthwise, place cut-side down and cut into vertical slices.

1 Trim away the root end without cutting right through. Peel off the skin with a small knife.

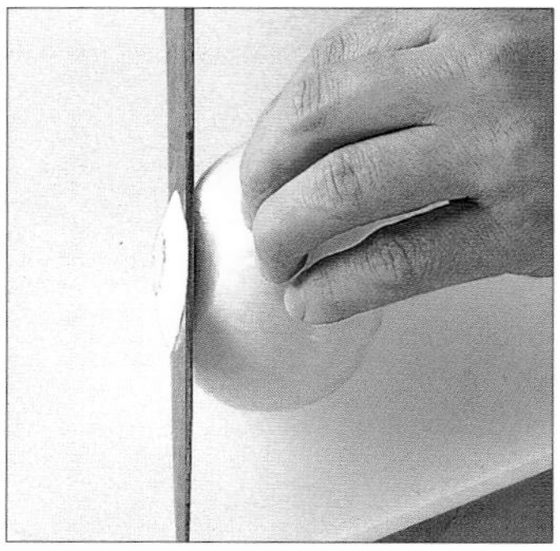

2 Cut off the tough root end with a chef's knife. Reserve for using in stocks.

3 Hold the onion on its side and slice downwards to form rings. Separate into individual rings, if you like.

Dicing Onions

Many recipes call for onions to be diced or chopped. The size of the dice depends on the thickness of the first cuts. Keep the root end intact to prevent the onion from falling apart during chopping; it may also prevent tears (see box, above).

1 Cut peeled onion lengthwise in half. Place cut-side down and make a series of horizontal cuts without cutting the root.

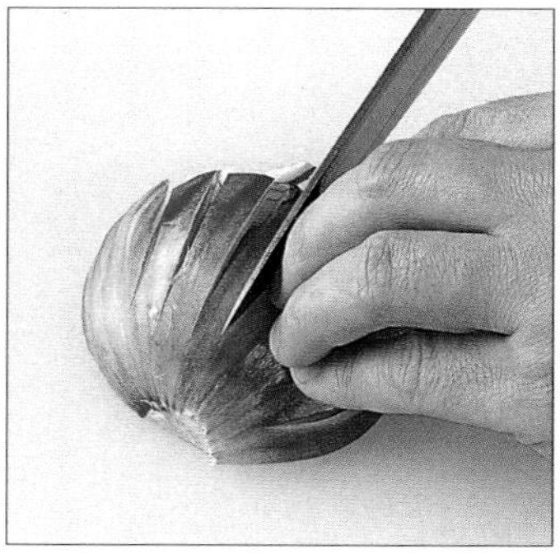

2 Make a series of vertical cuts down through the onion, again making sure the root is not cut.

3 Hold the onion firmly on the cutting board and cut it crosswise into dice. For fine dice, continue to chop until the dice are the desired size. The tough root end that remains can be reserved for use in stocks.

PREPARING PEARL ONIONS

These small onions, also known as baby or button onions, are ideal for braising whole or pickling. The skins are thin and papery and can be difficult to remove. Steeping them in hot water first helps to loosen the skins before peeling.

1 Place the onions in a bowl and cover with hot water. Let steep for a few minutes until the skins begin to soften.

2 Drain the onions, rinse under cold running water, then peel away the skins with a small knife. Keep as much length to the stem ends as possible to prevent the centres from popping out. Discard skins.

CUTTING LEEKS

Trimmed leeks are often cooked whole or gently braised in stock or baked au gratin. *Sliced leeks are baked in quiches or added to soups and stews. Diced leeks are used as a flavouring in classic French cooking (see* mirepoix, *page 166). If you are cooking leeks whole, they must be washed thoroughly to dislodge any earth that may be trapped between the tightly furled leaves.*

1 Slit the green tops. Rinse under cold running water to remove any trace of dirt.

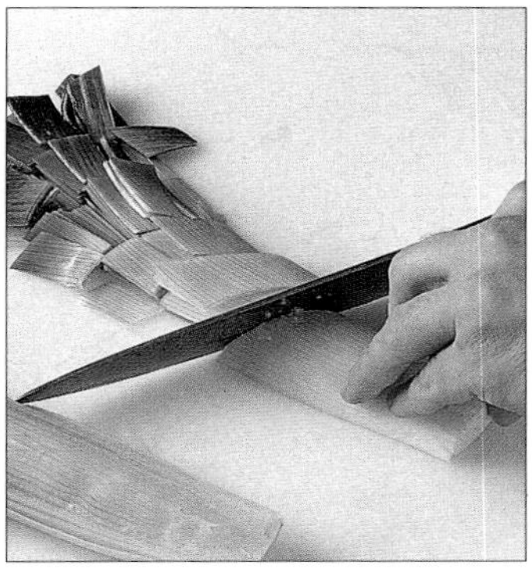

2 Cut leek lengthwise in half. Lay leek flat and slice, thickly or thinly, across.

CRUSHING GARLIC

Choose firm, plump garlic heads and separate them into cloves before peeling.

1 Lay the flat side of a chef's knife over a garlic clove and strike it with your fist.

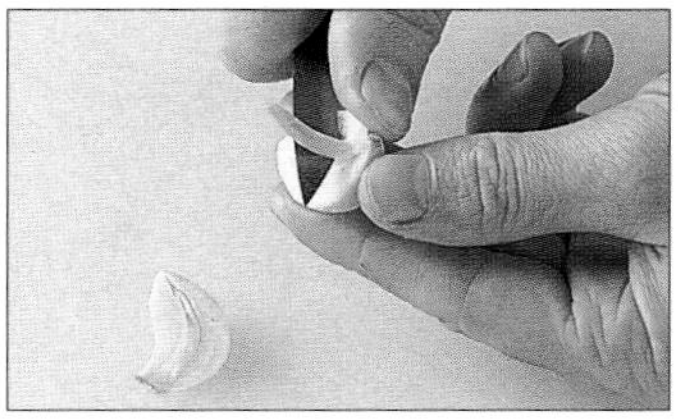

2 Peel the clove and cut it lengthwise in half. Remove the green shoot from centre.

3 Finely chop the clove by moving the knife back and forth in a rocking motion.

CUTTING SPRING ONIONS ASIAN-STYLE

Spring onions are frequently used in Asian cooking, especially in quick stir-fries and soups. Sliced or shredded spring onions, using both the white and green parts, are also used as a flavouring ingredient and a garnish on hot dishes of rice or noodles, or sprinkled over steamed or braised fish and meat dishes.

SHREDDING
Cut off the dark green top. Cut the light part lengthwise in half, then into strips.

ANGLE-SLICING
Start at the dark green top and slice at an angle, using the line of your knuckles as a guide. Slice right down to the root end; discard the root.

UNUSUAL VEGETABLES

Vegetables from Africa, Asia, South America and the Middle East are becoming more widely available. Sometimes these are exotic varieties of more familiar types like aubergines and radishes, but there are also completely new species which require different methods of preparation and cooking. Sea vegetables, in their dried form, are shown opposite.

1 AUBERGINES There are many varieties of aubergine apart from the familiar Mediterranean one. They are all prepared in the same way (see page 178).

2 WHITE & YELLOW AUBERGINES It would seems most likely that the alternative name for aubergine, eggplant, derives from this white variety from Africa, so named for its colouring and shape.

3 LOTUS ROOT Used in Chinese cooking, this vegetable cuts into attractive lacy slices. The skin must be peeled before cooking, then the flesh can be sliced and either steamed or stir-fried.

4 PEA AUBERGINES These are one of the more unusual types of aubergine from Thailand. Add whole to curries or purée for use in spicy dipping sauces.

5 DASHEEN The coarse skin of this tropical root must be peeled off before cooking. The flesh can then be cut into chunks and either baked or boiled.

6 CASSAVA This is a starchy potato-like root vegetable from Africa and South America. Peel and cook as for potatoes.

7 THAI AUBERGINE This green aubergine is prepared like white or purple aubergine (see above). The flesh should be sliced and then fried or roasted. It is also often used for pickling.

8 SALSIFY Also known as oyster plant because of its supposed similarity in taste to the seafood, the skin must be scraped off before the flesh is cooked. To cook, cut into short lengths and boil.

DRIED SEAWEEDS

1 WAKAME Mild in flavour. Good in salads, soups and stir-fries. Can also be toasted and crumbled, over rice dishes.

2 ARAME Delicately flavoured. Used in Japanese *miso* soup.

3 KOMBU A dried form of kelp used in the making of Japanese *dashi* (see page 18).

4 DULSE Salty and spicy tasting, this is particularly good in stir-fries and in salads.

9 MOOLI This vegetable, also called white radish and daikon, is much used in Asian cooking. It can be either shredded and eaten raw or thinly sliced and stir-fried or steamed.

10 LOOFAH An edible gourd generally used in Asian cooking, this vegetable must be peeled before cooking and can then be steamed or stir-fried.

11 CHINESE BITTER MELON A Far Eastern edible gourd, the flesh must be salted (dégorgéd) in order to draw out the bitter juices. The flesh is then best either sautéd or stir-fried.

12 EAST INDIAN ARROWROOT A hard root with tough skin, this is used in South-east Asian stir-fried dishes. Once peeled the flesh can be shredded or diced.

13 EDDO This is a tuber from West Africa and the Caribbean, which can be prepared and cooked like potatoes.

14 ICICLE RADISH Also called green radish, this rather bitter Asian vegetable is used for pickling and preserving but can also be thinly sliced for stir-frying.

15 YARD-LONG BEANS These are an Asian vegetable which can be cooked whole or sliced on the diagonal like runner beans.

16 TARO A hard mealy root vegetable from South-east Asia and India. Peel before cooking and cut into chunks or slices and boil.

17 KOHLRABI This is a slightly unusual European vegetable that should be prepared and cooked like turnip(see page 166).

VEGETABLE FRUITS

Considered fruits by botanists because they contain their own seeds, this colourful group is treated like vegetables in the kitchen. For peppers and chillies, which also contain their own seeds, see pages 180–181.

PEELING, DESEEDING AND CHOPPING TOMATOES

Although often eaten raw or baked in their skins, recipes for sauces, soups and stews often call for tomatoes to be peeled, deseeded and chopped – as in the French concassée *of tomatoes. Core and score a cross in the bottoms before blanching. The bitter seeds are best removed.*

1 Score cored tomatoes and blanch in boiling water for 10 seconds. Drain, then immerse in iced water.

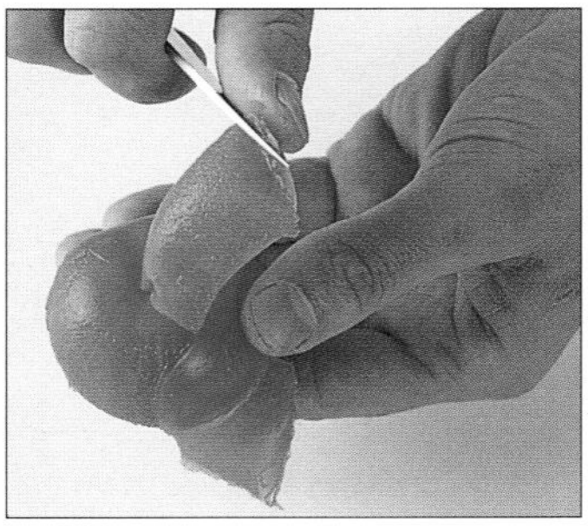

2 Remove tomatoes from the water and peel off the loosened skins, using the tip of a small knife.

3 Cut tomato in half. Taking each half in turn, squeeze out the seeds over a bowl. Remove any core.

4 Put each tomato half cut-side down and cut into strips, then cut across the strips to dice the flesh.

LOVE APPLES

Tomatoes arrived in Europe from the New World in the 1500s following Cortes' conquest of Mexico. One of their early names was "love apples", *pommes d'amour* in French. This may have derived from their reputation as an aphrodisiac. It is possible that early varieties were orange-yellow in colour, hence the corruption of the Italian *pomodoro* – "golden apple" or that the name *pomi di Mori* – "Moorish apples", reflected their route into Europe via Spain.

Cortes (1485-1547)

SALTING AUBERGINES

For most dishes, aubergines do not need peeling. However, they can contain bitter juices which are best extracted before cooking. This technique is called salting or dégorgéing, and is advisable if aubergines are to be fried in oil – it firms the flesh so that less oil is absorbed during cooking.

Slice the aubergine. Spread the slices in a single layer in a colander. Sprinkle salt evenly over the cut surfaces. Leave for about 30 minutes. Rinse under cold running water, then pat dry before cooking.

PREPARING AUBERGINES FOR BAKING

To ensure the flesh of of halved aubergines cooks evenly, the cut surfaces are deeply scored. You can perfume the flesh by inserting razor-thin slices of garlic into the incisions before baking.

Remove the stalk and calyx (the cup around the base of the stalk) and cut the aubergine in half lengthwise using a chef's knife. Cross-hatch the flesh deeply using a sharp pointed knife, then sprinkle with salt (see above).

Preparing Squash

Soft-skinned summer squash that can be eaten raw like courgettes, and marrows, are often left unpeeled. Winter squash, such as pumpkin and butternut, have hard, thick skins which must be peeled, and a firm flesh that must be cooked. Small varieties can be halved before cooking; large squash are often cubed.

Acorn squash
Cut squash in half lengthwise through the stalk. Scoop out seeds and fibrous pulp with a spoon, then peel off skin.

Butternut squash
Cut squash in half. Peel or carve off the skin from each half, then cut the flesh into chunks.

Spaghetti squash
Cut squash in half lengthwise and scoop out the seeds. Brush the cut surfaces with olive oil and season well. Bake at 180°C for 30 minutes. Rake out the flesh using a fork. It will form spaghetti-like strands.

Preparing Cucumber

Mostly eaten raw, cucumbers can also be puréed in soups, stuffed and baked, or stir-fried. In classic French cooking the skin is always removed, and the flesh salted (dégorged).

For a decorative effect, pare evenly spaced narrow strips of skin lengthwise with a canelle knife. Slice cucumber crosswise, dégorge and drain before serving.

Stoning an Avocado

For avocados to be served as halves, with a dressing or filling in the central cavity, the skin is left intact. A chef's technique is shown here; a teaspoon can also be used.

Cut avocado lengthwise in half all around the stone. Twist halves in opposite directions until separated. Carefully strike stone with a chef's knife. Twist to dislodge.

Peeling and Slicing an Avocado

Avocados are usually served raw, but can also be lightly cooked. For purées and dips, the flesh is extracted from a halved and stoned pear (see left) and mashed. For salads, the flesh is peeled and sliced or diced. Using a stainless steel knife or spoon when cutting the flesh and brushing the cut surface with lemon juice helps prevent discoloration.

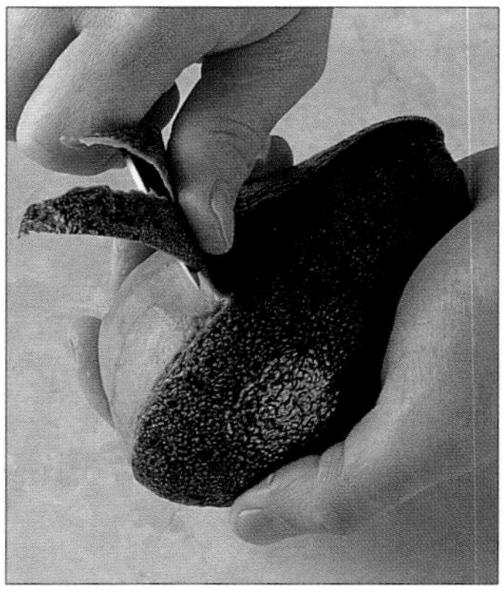

1 Score the skin of a whole avocado lengthwise into quarters, then lift the skin at one end and pull it back in strips, leaving behind as much flesh as possible.

2 Thinly slice the avocado down to and around the stone, lengthwise or crosswise, to remove the flesh. Brush the slices with lemon juice immediately.

PEPPERS

Sweet peppers or capsicums are related to chillies, but they have a mild, not hot, flavour that sweetens as they ripen. They are eaten raw and cooked, and are especially delicious when roasted (see page 189).

SLICING AND DICING PEPPERS

Peppers are kept whole only for stuffing and baking (see below), otherwise they are normally sliced into rings or cut into strips or dice for eating raw or cooked. They need to be cored, halved and deseeded before slicing and dicing.

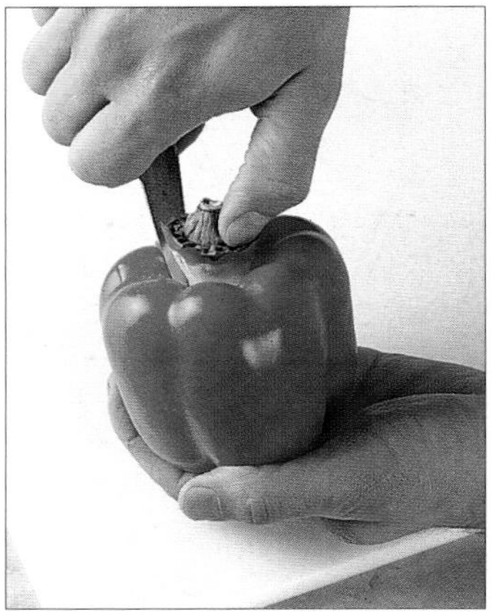

1 Cut around the core with a small knife, pull out and discard. Cut the pepper lengthwise in half. Scrape out the seeds and ribs and discard.

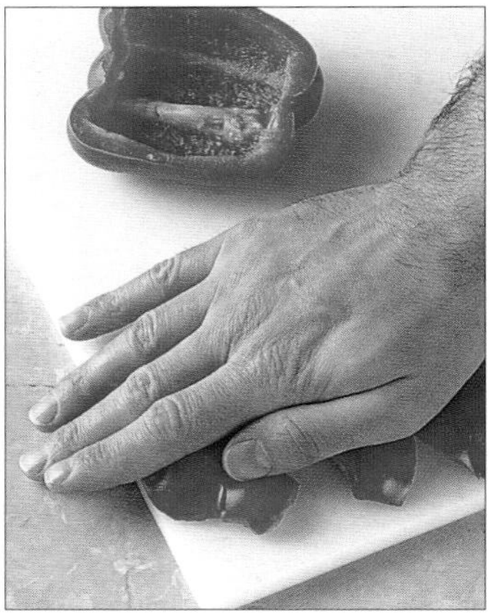

2 Place the pepper flesh-side down on a cutting board and press down firmly to flatten (this will make the pepper easy to slice).

3 Cut each pepper half lengthwise with a chef's knife into thin, even-sized slices or strips.

4 For diced pepper, hold the strips firmly together and slice crosswise to make equal-sized cubes. For larger dice, cut wider strips.

DIFFERENT COLOURS

Peppers come in a dizzying array of colours. Red and green are the most common, but yellow, orange, purple and even white are also available. Often varying hues simply denote peppers at different stages of ripeness. The familiar squat box-shaped pepper, for example, is least ripe when it is green. At this stage it has a fresh grassy flavour. As it matures its colour may change to either red, yellow, orange or purple, and its flavour become sweeter. In general, small green peppers are less sweet and juicy than large ones of other colours.

PREPARING WHOLE PEPPERS FOR BAKING

Sweet peppers make perfect containers for stuffing and baking. They are naturally hollow once the core and seeds have been removed, the sliced-off top makes a convenient lid, and the unskinned flesh will hold firm around the filling during baking. The technique shown here is also used for peppers that are to be sliced into rings.

1 Cut off the top quarter of the pepper that holds the stalk. Do not discard it but reserve it to use as a lid for the stuffed pepper during baking.

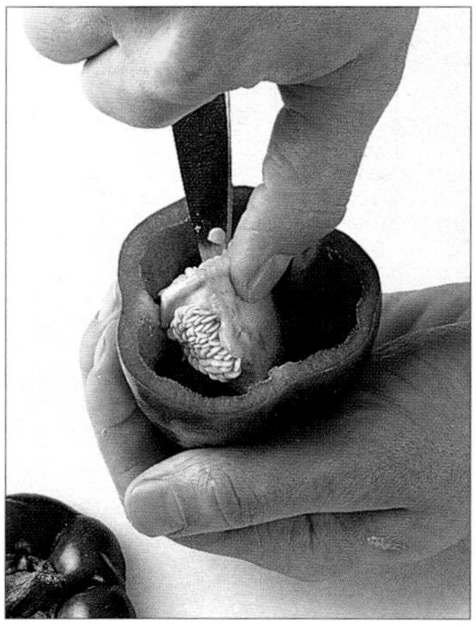

2 Scrape out the seeds with the tip of a small knife blade or a spoon. The pepper can now be filled and the lid replaced ready for baking.

Chillies

The often searingly hot properties of chillies call for careful handling. No matter what the variety, size or colour of the chilli, the preparation techniques are essentially the same.

Preparing Fresh Chillies

Once cut open, chillies sting the skin (see box, right), so prepare them with care. Wash hands, knife and cutting board thoroughly afterwards, and take particular care not to touch your eyes. Some cooks wear rubber gloves for extra protection.

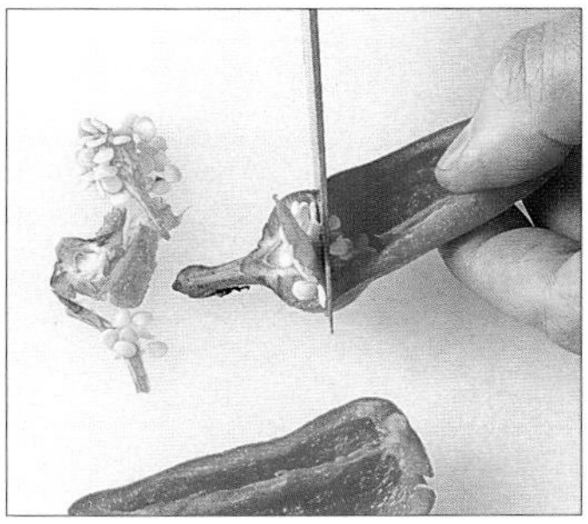

1 Cut chilli lengthwise in half. Scrape out the seeds with a small knife, removing the membrane with them.

2 Flatten the chilli with the palm of your hand and slice lengthwise into strips with a chef's knife.

3 For dice, hold the strips firmly together and slice into equal-sized cubes.

Where is the sting?

The intense fiery heat of chillies comes from the compound capsaicin. This oily substance is present to varying degrees in all parts of the chilli, but is strongest in the membrane and seeds inside the pod. For this reason, these parts are generally removed before cooking.

In some varieties of chilli, capsaicin neutralizes as the fruit ripens, making the heat less intense. As a general guide, green chillies are hotter than red and small chillies are hotter than large ones, but not always. Among the hottest are habañero and the tiny bird's-eye chillies. The mildest include sweet banana and the tapering green Anaheim chillies. Experiment with different kinds until you find those that best suit your needs – new varieties are constantly being introduced.

Rehydrating Dried Chillies

Use dried chillies as a substitute for fresh chillies in cooking. They can be crushed or simply crumbled (with or without the seeds), or soaked and ground into a paste as here.

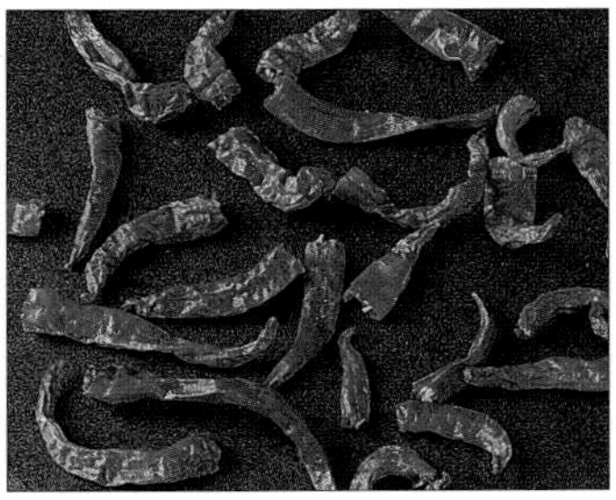

1 Spread dried chillies out on a baking sheet and toast them under a hot grill for 3–5 minutes, turning them frequently.

2 Transfer chillies to a bowl and cover with warm water. Let stand for 1 hour.

3 Drain the chillies and grind them to a paste in a pestle and mortar, then rub the paste through a sieve to remove the skins.

From left to right, top: Scotch bonnet; Jalapeño; Serrano. **Bottom:** Habañero; Bird's-eye chilli; Caribe chilli

Chiles Rellenos

A popular classic from Mexico, chiles rellenos is literally translated as "stuffed peppers". Traditionally for festive occasions, the chillies are dipped in batter and deep-fried, and served as finger food at casual buffets. Here a lighter grilled version, without batter, is also given, so you can mix and match according to personal preference.

SERVES 6–8

26 assorted chillies (jalapeños, poblanos, red and yellow Anaheims, Scotch bonnets)

Vegetable oil, for frying

225 g Monterey Jack or Cheddar cheese, grated

225 g white crabmeat (fresh, defrosted or canned)

2 tbsp chopped fresh coriander

Juice of ½ lime

Prepare the chillies (see box, below). Heat 3 tbsp oil in a frying pan and fry the chillies for 3–5 minutes, turning them so they cook evenly on all sides. Work in batches to prevent the chillies from overcrowding the pan. Let drain on paper towels.

For cheese-stuffed chillies, press grated cheese into jalapeños and poblanos with your fingers, allowing about 1 tbsp cheese for jalapeños and 3 tbsp for poblanos.

For crab-stuffed chillies, pick over the crabmeat to remove any bits of shell or cartilage (if using frozen or canned crabmeat, drain it thoroughly first). Flake the crabmeat with a fork and mix in the chopped coriander and lime juice. Spoon the mixture into yellow Anaheim and Scotch bonnet chillies.

To grill (for all chillies): place chillies on a baking sheet and put under a hot grill for about 2 minutes, just until the cheese is melted.

To deep-fry (for stuffed jalapeños and poblanos and whole red Anaheims): make batter (see box, right). Heat about 8 mm oil in a large frying pan until it is very hot. Holding chillies by their stalks, dip them into the batter to coat, then deep-fry in batches in the hot oil until golden, 2–3 minutes for each batch. Drain on paper towels before serving.

BATTER FOR DEEP-FRIED CHILLIES

100 g plain flour
Pinch of salt
1 egg
100 ml milk

Sift the flour and salt into a bowl and make a well in the centre. Lightly beat the egg and pour into the well. Gradually begin to draw the flour from the sides into the egg, beating with a wooden spoon. When almost all incorporated, beat in the milk to make a smooth batter. If necessary, sieve the batter to remove any lumps (see page 39).

Preparing Chillies

The technique shown here is suitable for jalapeños and poblanos, and red Anaheims if you like. It retains the shape of the chillies so they can be stuffed whole. For round-topped chillies such as yellow Anaheims and Scotch bonnets, cut off the tops and scoop out the cores and seeds. Keep the tops for presentation.

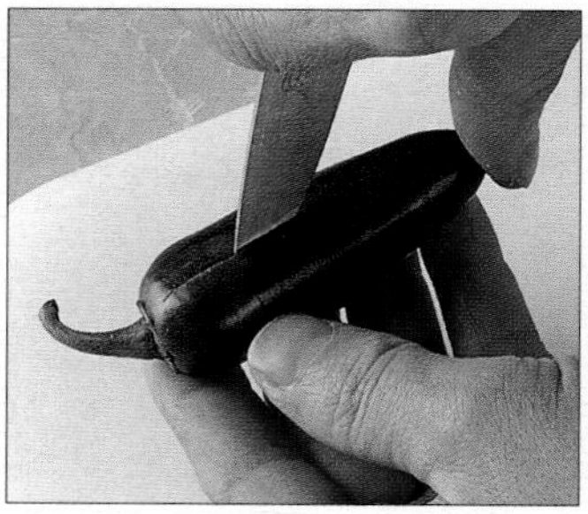

Make a lengthwise slit in the side of each chilli, from the shoulder down, using a small paring knife. With your fingers, carefully open out the slit to expose the seeds in the centre of the chilli.

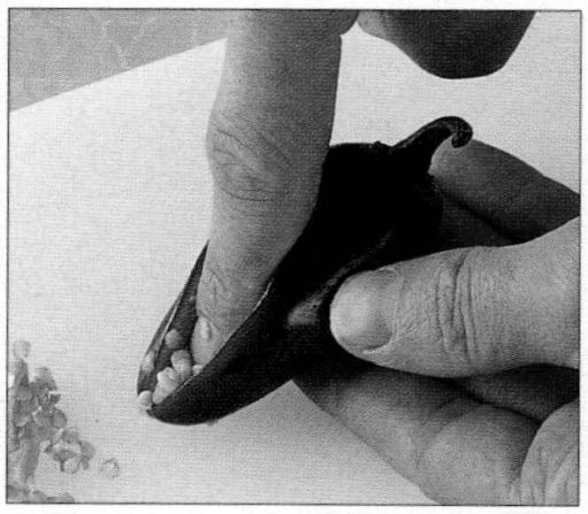

Run your finger down the inside of the chilli to remove the seeds, starting from the shoulder. take care to wash your hands thoroughly afterwards or the juice from the chillies may sting.

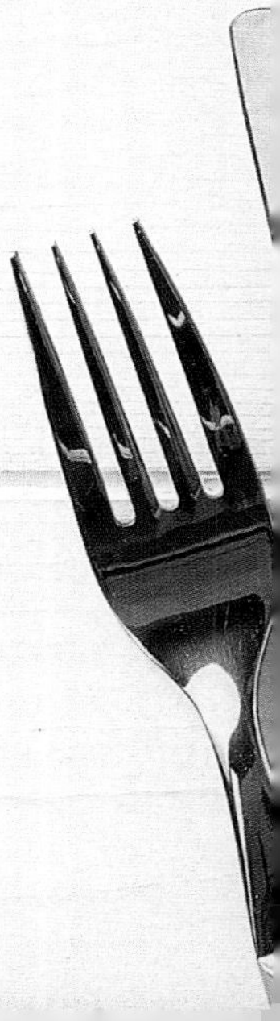

SALAD LEAVES

A beautiful salad depends on more than just the mix of greens. The leaves must be fresh and crisp, and perfectly clean and dry. The techniques for achieving this are shown here. For salad dressings, see page 230.

TRICK OF THE TRADE

DRYING IN A SALAD SPINNER

This dries salad leaves without bruising them. Put the leaves in the basket, close the lid and turn the handle to spin the basket. The water will drain into the drum.

PREPARING LETTUCE

Lettuces have a hard, bitter core which is best removed. The leaves should also be washed to remove dirt and then thoroughly dried. Water left on the leaves will cause them to wilt and dilute any dressing.

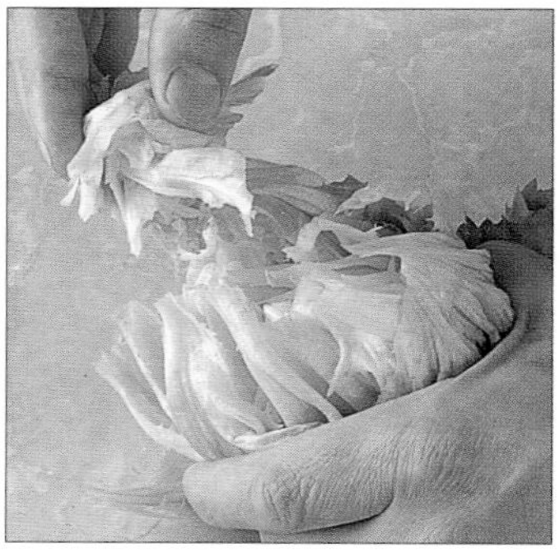

1 Discard any damaged outer leaves. Hold the head of the lettuce in one hand. Grasp the hard core in the other and twist it off.

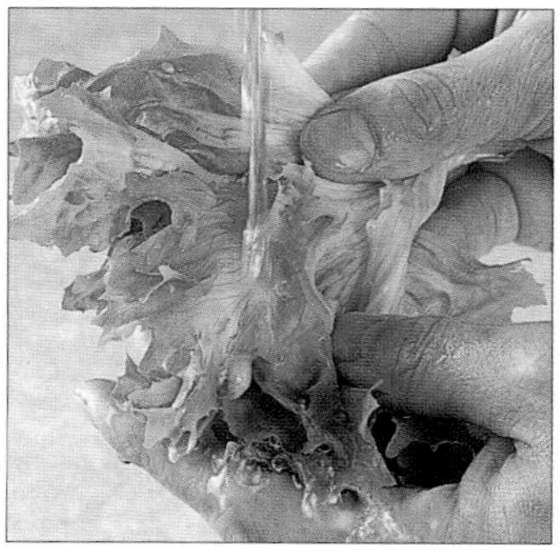

2 Rinse the leaves well under cold running water, then submerge them briefly in a bowl of cold water.

3 Place leaves in a folded tea towel and pat dry (or use a salad spinner, see box left). To crisp, refrigerate for at least 30 minutes.

Outer circle, clockwise from bottom left: red oak leaf; Iceberg; Cos lettuce; lollo rosso; curly leaf; radicchio; frisée; Little Gem lettuce. **Inner circle, clockwise from left:** lamb's lettuce; watercress; green lollo biondo. **Centre:** cress

MAKING A TOSSED SALAD

Choose leaves with flavours, colours and textures that are complementary. Whisk dressing in the salad bowl.

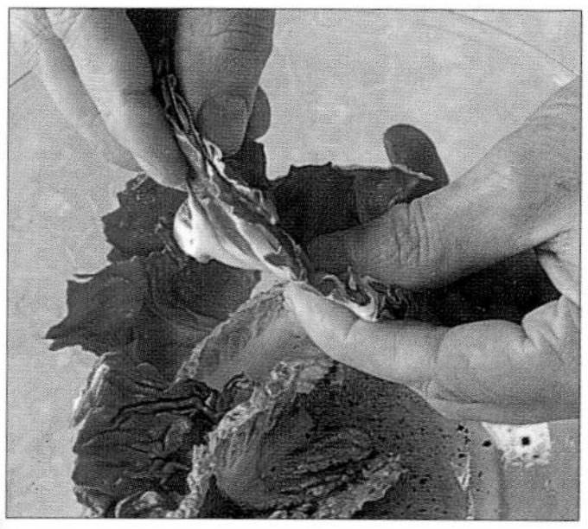

Tear leaves over the bowl; do not cut them or they will bruise. Toss leaves in dressing until lightly and evenly coated.

Fresh Herbs

Fresh herbs are aromatic plants that flavour and garnish both raw and cooked dishes. Here the techniques of chopping, shredding and snipping are shown. For other techniques using herbs, see pages 328–330.

Preparing Fresh Herbs

For maximum flavour, use fresh herbs immediately after picking. Usually only the leaves are used, although stalks are also sometimes included. The aromas come from the essential oils, which are released by cutting.

Chopping
Strip the leaves from the stalks and chop coarsely, bunching the leaves up against a chef's knife.

Shredding
Suitable for soft leaves such as basil. Stack the leaves and roll them tightly. Slice crosswise into shreds.

Snipping chives
Hold a bunch of chives over a bowl or board and finely snip them into small pieces with kitchen scissors.

Cooking with Fresh Herbs

Not all herbs behave in the same way in cooking. Use the points below to make the most of each.

- The flavour of fragile herbs, such as basil, dill and mint, diminishes when heated, so add them at the end of cooking. By contrast, hearty herbs such as thyme and rosemary benefit from long cooking because their perfumes are allowed to slowly permeate the dish.
- The method in which a herb is cut also affects its intensity. Grinding herbs in a pestle and mortar or food processor heightens their flavour. Shredding herbs lends a less pungent taste and is best for soft-leaved herbs like basil.
- Delicate herbs may turn black if chopped too long in advance; this is especially true of mint. To retain colour, cut herbs just before use.

Fines Herbes

This classic mixture of four herbs consists of equal quantities of chives, chervil, parsley and tarragon. The chives should be snipped and the other herbs finely chopped. Fine herbes *should always be added at the end of cooking.*

Snip chives (see above, right). Put chervil, parsley and tarragon leaves on a cutting board and chop them finely together. Combine with the chives before using.

Making a Bouquet Garni

The classic mix for this flavour enhancer is thyme, bay, parsley and celery wrapped in the dark green part of a leek and tied tightly with string. Used in slow-cooked dishes, it gradually releases its flavours.

For the bouquet garni shown here, the green part of the leek is loosely wrapped around a bay leaf, a sprig each of rosemary and thyme and a few stalks of parsley, then tied with string. For easy removal of a bouquet garni at the end of cooking, leave a long end on the string and tie it to the handle of the pan, or enclose the bouquet in a muslin bag.

BOILING

Boiling brings out the natural flavour of vegetables. Root vegetables should be added to cold water and slowly brought to the boil. By contrast, green vegetables should be plunged into rapidly boiling water.

MICROWAVE TIMES

The microwave cooks vegetables quickly with a minimum of water, so they retain nutrients, texture and colour. These cooking times for 225 g quantities are for 600–700 watt ovens set to 100% power. Allow 5 minutes standing time.

- BROCCOLI/CAULIFLOWER (FLORETS) 3½–4 mins
- BRUSSELS SPROUTS 5 mins
- CARROTS (SLICES) 5–6½ mins
- FRENCH BEANS 6–7 mins
- PEAS (SHELLED)/ MANGETOUTS 4–5 mins

ROOT VEGETABLES

It is important to cook root vegetables evenly through to the centre. Undercooked, they will be hard, overcooked they may lose texture and flavour, and even become mushy. For best results, cut them into equal-sized pieces and simmer slowly.

1 Place vegetables in pan. Cover with cold water and add salt to taste. Bring slowly to the boil, then cover.

2 Simmer until tender, 12–20 minutes, depending on type. To test for doneness, pierce the centre of the root with the tip of a knife; it should meet no resistance.

GREEN VEGETABLES

When boiled until just tender, green vegetables have a crisp bite, vibrant colour, optimum nutrients and the freshest flavour. If overcooked, they will turn drab and flabby.

1 Bring a large pan of water to the boil. Add salt to taste, then the vegetables. Simmer uncovered until just tender, 1–4 minutes.

2 Drain the vegetables and immerse in a bowl of iced water to refresh them. Drain and serve cold, or gently reheat with oil or butter.

ASPARAGUS

Asparagus is boiled upright so the thick ends of the stalks cook in simmering water while the tender tips gently steam above. The steamer here is designed specifically for the job, but you can cook asparagus flat, in a deep sauté pan.

Stand asparagus bundles (see page 163) upright in steamer basket. Pour water 10 cm deep into the steamer, bring to the boil and add salt to taste. Place basket in steamer, cover and simmer until stalks are tender, 5–7 minutes. Lift the basket out of the steamer, drain the asparagus and serve with melted butter or hollandaise sauce (see page 226).

STEAMING

Steaming vegetables in the vapour produced by simmering water cooks them gently to crisp-tender perfection while retaining nutrients. You can use a sieve set over a pan, or one of the special steamers shown here.

CONVENTIONAL METHOD

A stainless steel pan with an inset basket for easy lifting makes light work of steaming a variety of vegetables together (carrots, pattypan squash and green beans are shown here). The water should simmer at a quivering, not rolling, boil. Do not sprinkle salt over the vegetables – it draws out moisture and may discolour them.

1 Bring 2.5 cm water to the boil in the bottom pan. Insert the basket containing the vegetables.

2 When the steam rises, cover the pan and cook the vegetables until tender (see chart, right).

3 Remove the basket and refresh the vegetables under cold running water. Reheat and season.

STEAMING TIMES

- BROCCOLI/CAULIFLOWER/ GREEN BEANS 8 mins
- BRUSSELS SPROUTS/ CABBAGE/CARROTS/FENNEL 10 mins
- PEAS 2–3 mins
- POTATOES (NEW) 12 mins
- SPINACH 1–2 mins
- SQUASH/PATTYPAN 5 mins

BAMBOO STEAMER METHOD

Asian-style bamboo steamers fit neatly over woks or other pans and can be stacked in tiers to steam different items separately. For delicately scented and flavoured vegetables, add seasonings such as a bouquet garni, mixed peppercorns, star anise, lemon grass and coriander to the water before steaming.

1 Place firm vegetables in bottom basket, tender ones in the top. Pour water into a wok to just cover the bottom; bring to the boil.

2 Place the stack of baskets on a trivet in the wok. Cover and steam until vegetables are tender (see box, above right).

Roasting & Baking

Many vegetables, particularly fibrous roots and tubers and vegetable fruits, are suited to roasting on their own or baking with an accompanying sauce. The long cooking time renders them tender and intensifies their flavour.

Roasting Potatoes

For a crisp and crunchy outside and soft creamy centre, the trick is to parboil the potatoes first, let them cool, and then roast them. Very hot oil and a very hot oven are essential. For an alternative, Continental, method of roasting potatoes, see opposite page.

1 Peel the potatoes. Leave small ones whole; cut large potatoes into chunks. Parboil in salted water for 10 minutes, then drain and let cool.

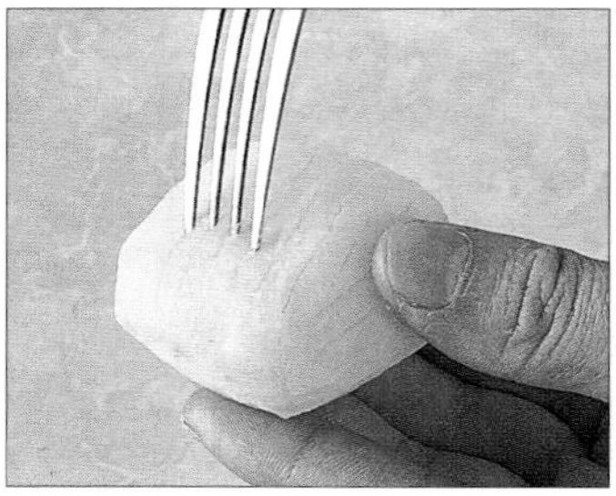

2 Scratch the potatoes with a fork (this helps make them crisp). Pour 1 cm oil into a roasting tin and heat at 200°C until very hot.

3 Add the potatoes and turn them to coat in the oil. Return the tin to the oven and roast the potatoes for 1–1¼ hours, turning them twice. Drain on paper towels.

Roasting Times

The times given below are for roasting vegetables in olive oil at 200°C (see opposite page). All times are approximate.

- AUBERGINES 30 mins
- CARROTS 45 mins
- PARSNIPS 30–45 mins
- SWEET POTATOES 45 mins
- TURNIPS 30–45 mins
- WINTER SQUASH 30–45 mins

Roast Garlic Flowers

Roasting mellows and sweetens the flavour of garlic so that it can be used as a delicious accompaniment as well as a flavouring. Roast whole heads of garlic in their skins at the same time as a joint of meat. If they are trimmed decoratively to form a flower, they also make very attractive garnishes.

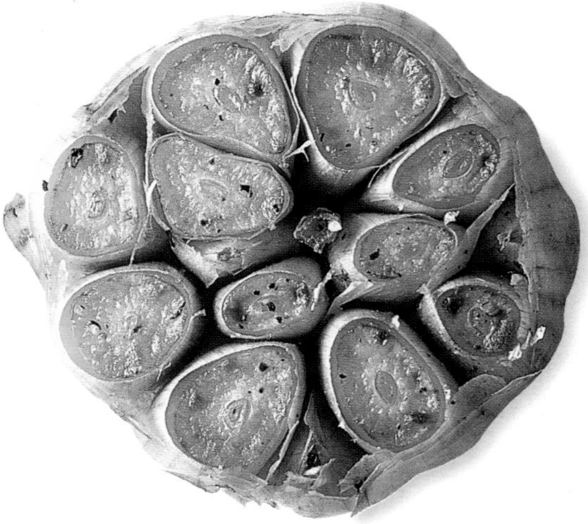

Slice off the top of each head of garlic, cutting through the cloves. Place them cut-side up in a baking dish. Brush with olive oil and roast at 180°C for about 50 minutes.

Roasting Beetroot

Raw beetroot is left unpeeled for roasting so that the colour does not bleed. Cut off the tops, leaving the stalks intact.

Wrap beetroot in foil and roast at 150°C for 1–1½ hours. Let cool slightly and peel. Dot with butter and season with black pepper and coarsely ground sea salt before serving.

ROASTING PEPPERS

When peppers are roasted they acquire an intensely sweet, smoky flavour. The skin is always removed. The flesh, which becomes quite soft, is usually sliced or diced for eating as it is, or for use in composite dishes.

1 Put pepper in a roasting tin. Roast at 200°C, turning once, until skin is charred, 10–12 minutes.

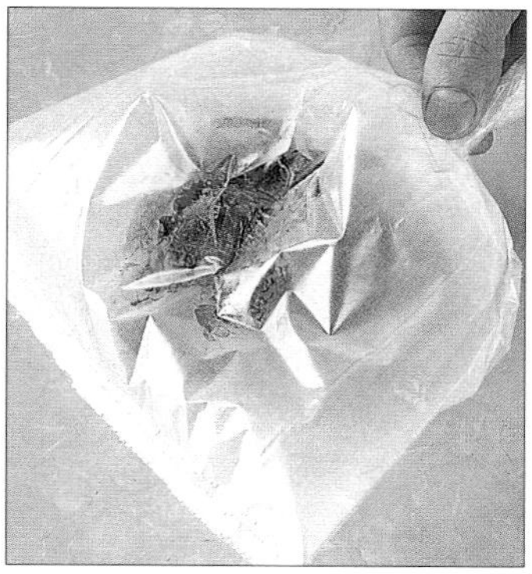

2 Enclose the pepper in a plastic bag. Knot or seal the bag and leave until the pepper is cold.

3 Remove the pepper and core it. Lift the charred skin with a pointed knife, and peel it off.

TRICK OF THE TRADE

QUICK ROASTING

This time-saving method is ideal if you only need to roast one or two peppers.

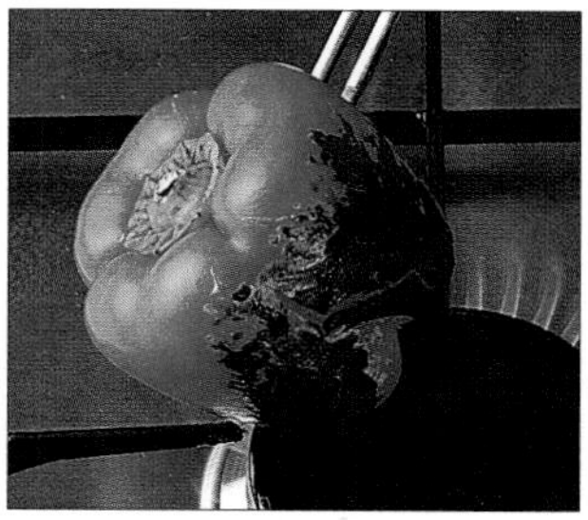

Spear the pepper with a long-handled fork. Hold it over a gas flame and turn it slowly, until the skin is blackened.

ROASTING IN OLIVE OIL

This quick-and-easy technique of roasting vegetables is most often used in Italy and France. For the best flavour, use a good-quality extra virgin olive oil, coarse sea salt, freshly ground black pepper and herbs such as rosemary or thyme.

POTATOES
Put potato chunks (*pommes châteaux* are shown here, see page 168) in a roasting tin. Sprinkle with 2–4 tbsp olive oil, chopped fresh herbs and season with salt and pepper to taste mix well. Roast at 200°C turning once or twice, until well browned, about 45 minutes.

RATATOUILLE
Put sliced courgettes, peppers, aubergines and onions in a roasting tin and add a bouquet garni (see page 185). Sprinkle with 3–4 tbsp olive oil, crushed garlic and salt and pepper to taste; mix well. Roast at 180°C for about 1 hour, turning once or twice.

MAKING A POTATO GRATIN

The term au gratin *refers to any dish topped with cheese and baked in a shallow dish until brown and crispy. The potatoes in the classic* gratin dauphinois *(see box, right), are parboiled in milk before baking. This lends a rich taste and ensures the potatoes cook in the required time.*

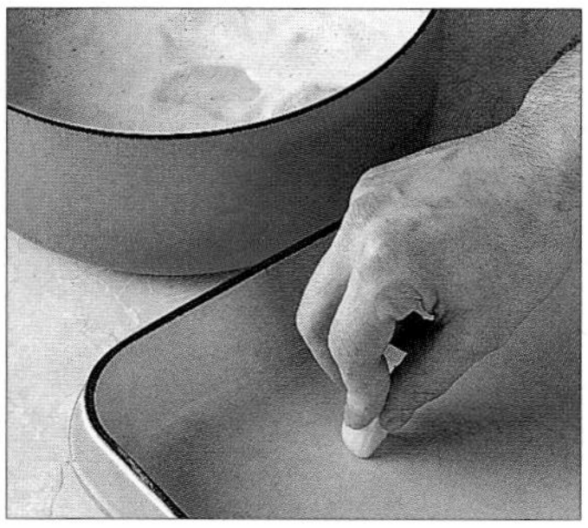

A HINT OF GARLIC
For a subtle garlic flavour, cut a garlic clove in half and rub the cut surfaces over the inside of baking dish. Garlic juices will not be as strong as the actual flesh.

GRATIN DAUPHINOIS

- *1 kg potatoes*
- *1 bouquet garni*
- *Freshly grated nutmeg*
- *Salt and white pepper*
- *500 ml milk*
- *1 garlic clove, halved*
- *25 g butter, softened*
- *150 ml double cream*
- *100 g Gruyère cheese, grated*

Peel the potatoes and thinly slice them. Bring the milk to the boil in a pan. Add the bouquet garni, and nutmeg and salt and pepper to taste. Add the potatoes and return to the boil. Lower the heat and simmer for 10–15 minutes. Drain the potatoes and reserve the milk. Rub the garlic over the inside of a 22- x 33-cm baking dish. Butter the dish and layer the potatoes in it, seasoning each layer. Add the cream to the milk and to the boil and pour over the potatoes. Top with the grated Gruyère cheese and bake at 200°C for about 40 minutes. Serves 4.

FRYING

Vegetables can be shallow-fried, deep-fried or stir-fried; they are also fried as part of other cooking processes – in casserole making for example. All vegetables for frying must be cut into small pieces so they will not burn on the outside before the inside is cooked.

TRICK OF THE TRADE

GREASEPROOF PAPER CARTOUCHE

Fold a square of paper in half, then in half again, then into a triangle. Hold one narrow point in centre of pan; cut level with edge.

SWEATING AND GLAZING

These two techniques are often used in French cooking. Diced flavouring vegetables (see mirepoix, *page 166) are sweated gently at the start of a soup or stew so they cook in their own juices and retain flavour without browning. Greaseproof paper is used as a covering to prevent evaporation – for a snug fit, it can be cut into a cartouche (see box, left). Glazing is the classic technique for finishing off turned vegetables (see page 167). It gives them an attractive glossy presentation.*

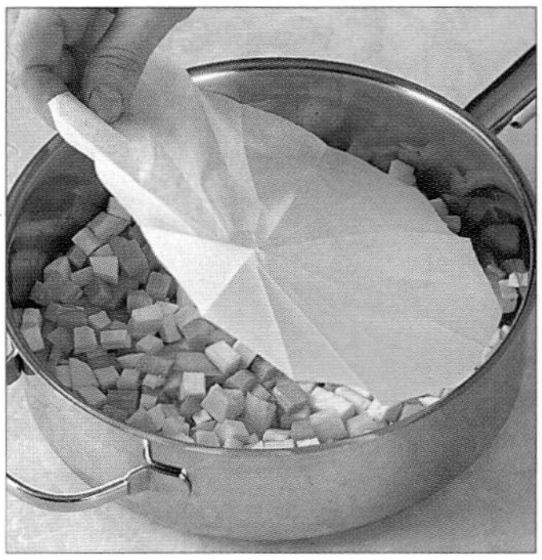

SWEATING
Melt 1-2 tbsp butter in a pan. Add vegetables, sprinkle with water and seasonings. Cover with greasepoof paper. Cook over a low heat, 3-5 minutes.

GLAZING
Melt 2 tbsp butter with 1 tbsp water and 1 tsp sugar. Add blanched vegetables and cook over a high heat, rolling them until glazed, 2-3 minutes.

MAKING VEGETABLE FRITTERS

Vegetables cut into julienne and held together with batter can be shallow-fried to make crisp fritters or rösti. *Here, a mixture of potatoes, carrots and courgettes are shown.*

1 Make a batter of 50 g plain flour, 1 egg and seasonings to taste. Mix in 250 g vegetable julienne. Add spoonfuls to hot, shallow oil in a non-stick pan.

2 Fry the fritters over a moderate heat turning once with a spatula until they are crisp and golden on both sides, 3–4 minutes. Drain thoroughly before serving.

STIR-FRYING

This Asian technique is excellent for vegetables, leaving them crisp, full of nutrients and bright in colour. For best results, cut vegetables into julienne or ribbons (see pages 166-167).

Put prepared firm vegetables (here carrots and mangetouts) in a little hot oil in wok. Toss over a high heat for 2 minutes, then add soft vegetables such as bean sprouts and toss for 1 minute. Add seasonings and serve immediately.

Deep-frying Potatoes

The French way of deep-frying potatoes is to "twice-fry" them, which gives an ultra-crisp result. First they are cooked until tender, then they are left to cool, and then they are fried again at a higher temperature. For different shapes, see page 169. Potato baskets are used in classic French cuisine as containers for diced and tiny vegetables; the bird's nest mould for making them is available at specialist kitchenware shops.

1 Heat the oil to 160°C. Immerse potatoes in the oil for 5–6 minutes. Remove and cool, then increase the oil temperature to 180°C and deep-fry the potatoes again until crisp, 1–2 minutes.

2 Lift the basket out of the oil and let as much oil as possible drain away. Empty the fries out of the basket on to paper towels to absorb any residual oil. Sprinkle with salt before serving.

POTATO BASKET

Press *pommes pailles* (see page 169) into bird's nest mould. Deep-fry in 180°C oil for about 3 minutes until crisp and golden. Drain and unmould.

Making Crispy Seaweed

Although served as seaweed, this Chinese restaurant speciality is in fact a dish of finely shredded spring greens deep-fried until crisp. Remove the tough stalks and wash and dry the leaves before shredding. The drier the cabbage, the easier it is to achieve crispy "seaweed" without it losing its bright green colour.

1 Pour enough oil into a wok to come one-third of the way up the side and heat to 180°C. Reduce the heat slightly, then add shredded greens in batches. Stir constantly with chopsticks to keep the shreds separate.

2 Just at the point the shreds begin to make a tinkling sound, remove with a slotted spoon and drain thoroughly. Serve hot, sprinkled with salt and sugar to taste. If you like, you can also sprinkle the seaweed with the special Chinese seasoning, ground fried fish, as illustrated here.

Safety first

- Use a deep-fat fryer or deep, heavy pan.
- Fill deep-fat fryers no more than half full with oil, and woks no more than one-third full. Use a two-handled wok for optimum stability.
- Dry food well before frying to avoid sputtering.
- Keep pan handles pushed back.
- Clean up spills immediately and ensure that no fat is present on the outside of the pan.
- Never leave the pan unattended.
- Keep a fire blanket close to the stove.

Chargrilling

This technique makes use of a stovetop grill (see page 141) to fry vegetables so that they have an attractive striped "chargrilled" effect.

Cut vegetables (here fennel, courgette, aubergine and red pepper) into chunks and toss them in olive oil, lemon juice, chopped fresh herbs and seasonings. Heat pan until hot but not smoking. Place vegetables on the pan and cook for 5 minutes on each side or until tender.

VEGETABLE MASH AND MOULDS

Softened, cooked vegetables are popular accompaniments to meat, poultry and fish, offering contrast in colour and texture. They can be pressed into a smooth or coarse purée or taken one stage further by being shaped in timbale moulds and baked.

MASH

For the best mashed potatoes you need to select the right type of floury potato (see page 169). Once mash is made, choose from the following – all variations on a similar theme – to create a smooth, creamy mash. Season to taste with salt and freshly ground pepper before serving.

- Hot milk and a generous amount of unsalted butter; cream can also be added.
- Crème fraîche and olive oil.
- Olive oil and crushed garlic.
- Hot creamy milk or cream and roasted garlic flesh (see page 188).
- Cream or creamy milk, unsalted butter and grated Gruyère cheese.

COOKING SPINACH

Clean spinach thoroughly and tear leaves. Although spinach can be cooked in lots of boiling water, it is far better to steam or sauté it to retain its vitamins, minerals and colour. When steaming, only use the water that clings to the leaves after the spinach has been washed; it will cook in minutes. When sautéing, cook the spinach quickly, stirring constantly, in a little olive oil.

MAKING PUREES AND MASH

A food processor or blender can be used for puréeing leafy vegetables (see below). For cooked root vegetables such as carrots, you can use a machine, but sieving after mashing gives a finer texture; use a drum sieve with a very fine mesh. Never put potatoes in a machine – it makes them gluey – use a potato masher or ricer. For the smoothest, fluffiest mashed potatoes, use a drum sieve or a mouli.

DRUM SIEVE
Hold sieve secure over a bowl and firmly press cooked vegetables through the mesh with a plastic scraper.

MOULI
Place cooked potatoes in Mouli set over a bowl; turn handle to force potatoes through into bowl.

MAKING TIMBALES

Puréed vegetables, such as the spinach shown here, make attractive single servings when cooked in small moulds and turned out upside-down. Other suitable vegetables include carrots, broccoli and peas. If you like, you can line the mould with blanched spinach leaves (see page 77); this looks especially effective when the purée inside is a contrasting colour.

1 Purée 300 g cooked spinach in a blender with 3 eggs, 250 ml double cream, nutmeg and seasonings to taste. Spoon into buttered 150 ml timbale moulds.

2 Put the moulds in a bain marie and bake at 190°C for 10 minutes or until firm and a skewer inserted in the centre comes out clean.

3 Remove the moulds from the bain marie and run a knife around the insides to loosen the timbale. Invert on to serving plate. Gently lift off mould.

Pulses, Grains & Nuts

Pulses

Cooking Rice

Cooking Other Grains

Nuts

Coconut

PULSES

Dried beans, peas and lentils, the edible seeds of pod-bearing plants, are known as pulses. Rich in minerals, vitamins and fibre, yet low in fat, they are invaluable in the kitchen. Here's how to prepare and cook them.

COOKING TIMES

All times are approximate and relate to pulses that have been soaked (see right).

- ADUKI BEANS
  30–45 mins
- BLACK BEANS
  1–1½ hrs
- BLACK-EYE BEANS
  1 hr
- BUTTER BEANS
  1 hr
- BROAD BEANS
  1–1½ hrs
- CANNELLINI BEANS
  1¼ hrs
- CHICK PEAS
  1½–2 hrs
- HARICOT BEANS
  1½ hrs
- MUNG BEANS
  45 mins
- PINTO BEANS
  1 hr
- RED KIDNEY BEANS
  1–1½ hrs
- SOY BEANS
  1½–2 hrs

SAFETY FIRST

Many pulses contain harmful toxins, so it is important to boil all beans vigorously for 10 minutes at the beginning of cooking. This destroys toxins and renders the beans harmless.

SOAKING AND COOKING

Dried beans and peas need to be soaked to soften them before cooking; lentils do not. The quick-soak method is an alternative to the one shown here: boil in plenty of water 2 minutes, cover and let soak 2 hours. Always season pulses after cooking or the skins will be tough.

1 Put the beans in a large bowl. Add cold water to cover. Soak for 8–12 hours.

2 Drain the beans into a colander; rinse thoroughly under cold running water.

3 Boil beans in unsalted water, 10 minutes. Simmer for time in chart (see left).

MAKING REFRIED BEANS

These are fried twice, hence their name. Soften chopped onions in oil, then add cooked pinto beans and a little of the bean cooking liquid and fry together, mashing the beans to a paste with a potato masher. Chill the paste overnight, then fry in oil again until crispy.

FIRST FRYING
Add cooked beans to onion and oil and mash to a paste.

SECOND FRYING
Stir bean paste over a high heat just until crisp.

Outer circle from bottom left: soy beans; black-eye beans; black beans; butter beans; red kidney beans; yellow split peas; mung beans. **Inner circle, from bottom left:** aduki beans; chick peas; cannellini beans; haricot beans

Making Patties

Pulses make perfect patties – they purée easily, marry well with flavourings such as garlic, onion, herbs and spices, and hold their shape. Falafel (see box, right) from Israel are the traditional ones, but you can make them with other pulses. Here chick peas and dried broad beans are used together.

1 Soak and boil pulses of your choice, then drain and reserve the cooking liquid. Work to a purée in a food processor, with a little of the reserved liquid. Turn into a bowl and mix with flavourings until well combined.

2 Shape the mixture into even-sized balls with wet hands (this helps prevent sticking), then flatten them into ovals, each one about 2.5 cm thick.

FALAFEL

200 g chick peas, soaked, cooked and puréed
5 garlic cloves, finely chopped
1 onion, finely chopped
4 tbsp chopped fresh coriander
1 tbsp plain flour
1 tsp ground cumin
1 tsp ground allspice
Salt, pepper and cayenne
Vegetable oil, for frying

Mix ingredients; shape into balls. Shallow-fry in hot oil until golden on each side, 3-4 minutes. Drain on paper towels. Serves 4.

Making Pulse Purees

Puréed with olive oil and garlic, cooked pulses make aromatic dips, spreads and creamy side dishes. Here chick peas are used to make the Middle Eastern hummus; other good choices are cannellini beans, black or red kidney beans, or lentils. For a pungent flavour, add a few crushed dried chillies.

1 Purée cooked chick peas in a food processor with a little cooking liquid, and salt and crushed garlic to taste.

2 With machine running, add olive oil through tube. Add lemon juice to taste, and 1-2 tbsp hot water.

Making Dhal

Confusingly, dhal is the name for both this spicy Indian lentil dish and the pulse, of which there are hundreds of different varieties. Here yellow lentils (channa dhal) *are used, but any other type can be substituted. For a special touch, top with the traditional* tadka: *sliced garlic and cayenne fried in ghee.*

1 Fry onions and garlic in ghee with garam masala and chilli powder. Add lentils and stir-fry for 1–2 minutes.

2 Cover with stock or water and simmer until lentils are tender. Stir often and add more liquid, as necessary.

Top row, from left to right: Puy lentils; green lentils; brown lentils **Bottom row:** red lentils; yellow lentils

COOKING TIMES

All timings are approximate. There is no need to soak lentils before cooking.

- BROWN/YELLOW/GREEN (PUY) LENTILS 30–45 mins
- RED LENTILS 20 mins

COOKING RICE

From fragrant pilafs to creamy risottos, rice is foundation of countless dishes. Because not all grains cook the same, it is essential to select the right rice – and cooking technique – for the dish you are making.

TYPES OF RICE

AMERICAN LONG-GRAIN: All-purpose rice; cook by hot water method. White rice takes 15 minutes; brown, 30–35 minutes.
ARBORIO: Italian short-grain; has creamy texture and nutty bite. Cook by risotto method (see page 198), 15–20 minutes.
BASMATI: Aromatic, for use in pilafs and Indian dishes; soak (see step 1, opposite page) before cooking by absorption method, 15 minutes.
EASY-COOK: Processed so the grains stay separate; follow packet instructions, 10–12 minutes.
JAPANESE: Short-grain white rice that is plump, glossy and sticky; see opposite page for cooking.
PUDDING: Short-grain that is very soft when cooked; white rice takes 15-20 minutes., brown, 30-40 minutes. Can also be oven-baked, 1-1½ hours. See page 278 for methods.
THAI: Jasmine fragranced; cook by absorption method, 15 minutes.
WILD: Not a true rice, but an aquatic grass with a nutty flavour; cook by hot water method, 35–40 minutes.

HOT WATER METHOD

White or brown American long-grain rice can be cooked in a large, unmeasured amount of boiling water. After cooking, drain the water off and rinse the rice. Rinsing removes excess starch, leaving the grains separate and dry, and the rice can be left to cool and be reheated without sticking.

1 Bring a pan of water to the boil. Add salt, then the rice. Simmer, uncovered, until tender (see box, left).

2 Turn the rice into a colander or sieve; rinse with boiling water. Toss in butter or oil to reheat.

ABSORPTION METHOD

This method, best for basmati and Thai rice, cooks rice in a measured amount of water that becomes completely absorbed when the rice is cooked. Use $2\frac{1}{2}$ parts water to 1 part rice and cook over a low heat, keeping the pan tightly covered so the rice cooks in its own steam.

1 Put water, rice and salt in a pan; bring to the boil. Stir, lower the heat and cover.

2 Simmer for 15 minutes, then let stand 15 minutes. Fluff up grains with a fork.

Top row, from left to right: wild rice; brown basmati rice; white basmati rice; Thai (jasmine) rice. **Bottom row, from left to right:** American long-grain and easy-cook rice; arborio (or risotto) rice; Japanese rice; pudding rice

MAKING A PILAF

Pilafs are popular in the Middle East and India, and cooks in both areas make them in much the same way – usually by the absorption method. For a main dish, fold in chopped cooked meat, poultry, or seafood and vegetables at the end. Seasonings can be as varied as you like.

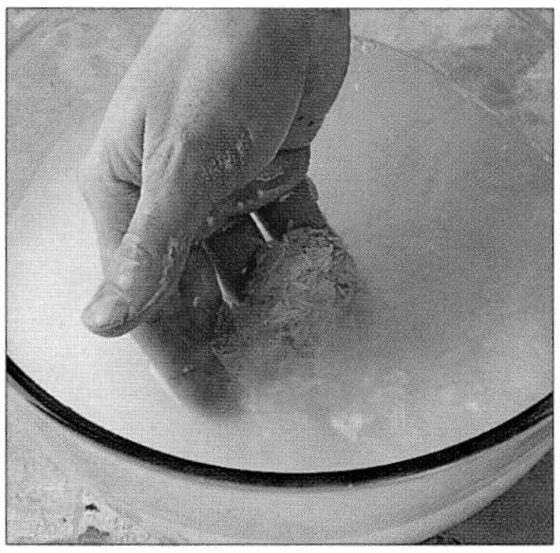

1 Cover rice with cold water and let stand for 1 hour, changing the water several times until clear. Rinse well.

2 Soften chopped onion in oil in a frying pan. Add rice; stir over a moderate heat until grains start to burst.

3 Stir in hot stock (twice the volume of the rice). Add salt, lower the heat and cover. Simmer for 15 minutes.

JAPANESE VINEGARED RICE

The Japanese have a special kind of sticky, short-grain white rice. It is served at the end of every meal, and is also used to make vinegared rice for sushi. To cook Japanese sticky rice, rinse it until the water is clear, then soak it in a pan of water 30 minutes, allowing 600 ml water for 400 g rice. Bring to the boil, cover and simmer over a very low heat 15 minutes, then let stand 15 minutes. For the vinegared rice shown here, let cool to room temperature.

1 Boil 4 tbsp each rice vinegar and sugar with a pinch of salt, stirring until the sugar has melted. Remove from the heat and let cool.

2 Put the cooled, cooked Japanese rice (see left) in a wooden bowl and drizzle the sweetened vinegar syrup evenly over it.

3 Mix the rice and vinegar syrup together with a rice paddle (see box, right) or a wooden spoon. Cool the rice slightly by fanning it with cardboard while fluffing it up with the rice paddle. Use the vinegared rice immediately, or cover with a damp tea towel to retain moisture and use within a few hours.

A special recipe for sushi, using this quantity of vinegared rice, is given on page 64.

RICE ON THE MENU

A staple food in many countries, rice has long been revered for its nutritional qualities – the Chinese word for cooked rice is fan, meaning meal. Vegetarians the world over know that rice, eaten together with pulses, forms a complete protein, equivalent to that in meat.

BIRYANI: Indian favourite pairs fragrant basmati rice with aromatic spices, herbs and meat or vegetables.
DIRTY RICE: Robust Cajun pilaf combines rice with lightly sautéed chicken livers, onions, garlic and green pepper.
KEDGEREE: British classic with curried long-grain rice, smoked haddock and hard-boiled eggs.
PAELLA: Colourful Spanish mix of saffron-stained rice, chicken, seafood, ham, chorizo sausage and tomatoes.
RISI BISI: Rustic Italian dish featuring arborio rice, ham, peas and Parmesan cheese.
STIR-FRIED RICE: A Chinese rice dish flavoured with pork, seafood, vegetables and egg.

RICE PADDLE

In Japan, this small, flat utensil, made out of wood or bamboo, is used to turn cooked sticky rice, a technique that fluffs it up and enhances its appearance.

The paddle is also used to serve rice to guests. It is the custom for each person to get two paddlefuls from a wooden tub, regardless of the quantity of rice that has been cooked.

When fluffing up rice, use a sideways cutting motion.

Seafood Risotto

Here the popular Italian rice dish, risotto, is given an elegant finish with langoustines, scallops, squid and prawns in a creamy sauce. For the creamiest consistency, be sure to use a short-grain risotto rice such as arborio *or* carnaroli.

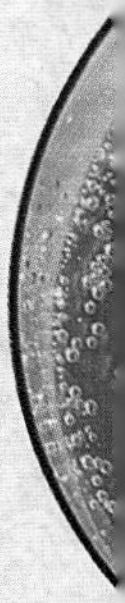

SERVES 4

12 raw langoustines, in their shells

Court bouillon (see page 66)

200 g prepared squid (see page 86), pouch cut into rings

8 shelled scallops

250 ml whipping cream

125 g peeled cooked prawns

Parmesan curls (see page 236), to garnish

FOR THE SEAFOOD STOCK

1 tbsp olive oil

20 g butter

30 g mirepoix *(see page 166) of onion, carrot and celery*

50 ml cognac

1 tbsp tomato purée

1 ripe tomato, chopped

1 garlic clove, crushed

1.5 litres fish stock

1 bouquet garni

Salt and freshly ground pepper

FOR THE RISOTTO

2 tbsp olive oil

½ onion, finely chopped

200 g risotto rice

50 ml dry white wine

50 ml crème fraîche

2 tbsp freshly grated Parmesan cheese

Poach the langoustines in court bouillon, 7–8 minutes; let cool in the liquid, then remove them and pull off the heads and shells. Coarsely crush the heads and shells.

Make the seafood stock: heat the oil and butter in a saucepan over a high heat and sauté the crushed heads and shells with the *mirepoix*. Deglaze the pan with some of the langoustine stock and the cognac. Add the tomato purée, stir for 1–2 minutes, then add the chopped tomato and crushed garlic and cook for a few minutes more. Add the fish stock and bouquet garni and bring to the boil. Lower the heat and simmer until the liquid has reduced to about 1.25 litres. Strain the stock and season lightly.

Pour 900 ml of the stock back into the saucepan and keep it at a low simmer. Pour the remaining stock into another pan and set aside.

Make the risotto: heat the oil in a wide heavy pan and sweat the onion until soft. Add the rice and stir for 1–2 minutes to coat the grains with oil, then start adding the simmering stock, about 150 ml at a time (see box, below). When all the stock has been added, add the wine. The total cooking time will be 20–25 minutes.

While the risotto is cooking, bring the second pan of stock to the boil, then lower the heat. Add the squid and scallops and gently poach them for 3–5 minutes; remove with a slotted spoon.

Reduce the stock by about half, then stir in the whipping cream. Add the langoustines, squid, scallops and prawns and heat through gently. Check the seasoning.

Stir the crème fraîche and grated Parmesan into the risotto, then check the seasoning. Mound the risotto in the centre of warmed serving bowls, doming it neatly, or press it into oiled timbale moulds and turn it out. Surround with the seafood and sauce, garnish with Parmesan curls and serve immediately.

Making Risotto

For a successful risotto, the stock must be added gradually so that the rice, although always kept moist, is not drowned in liquid. Italian cooks literally stand over the pot all the time a risotto is cooking, stirring constantly at first, and then, as the rice cooks, stirring less frequently. This stirring technique ensures a creamy texture and a perfectly cooked risotto.

Add the first 150 ml of stock, regulating the heat so the risotto is bubbling gently. Wait until the stock is almost all absorbed before adding the next 150 ml.

When ready, the rice grains should be separate and firm but tender (*al dente*, like pasta). The starch released from the rice will give the risotto a creamy consistency.

COOKING OTHER GRAINS

Seeds of the grass family, grains are available in a variety of forms, and offer endless preparation possibilities. Choosing the right cooking technique is vital because different cooking processes affect both taste and texture.

POPULAR POLENTA

This sunshine-yellow grain, now seen in fashionable restaurants everywhere, has long been part of the staple diet in northern Italy, where it is usually served to accompany stews and saucy meat dishes, especially game.

Traditional Italian cooks use a special heavy-based copper pan, called a *paiolo*, for cooking polenta. This pan has very tall sides that help contain the spitting and spluttering that characterize polenta cooking. The heavy bottom of the *paiolo* also helps to spread the heat evenly around the pan, and so prevent the polenta catching and burning on the bottom.

POLENTA

Also called cornmeal, it can be served moist, enriched with butter and grated Parmesan cheese as a side dish, or in firm, crisp-crusted pieces that have been pan-fried or chargrilled. These are usually topped with chargrilled vegetables or a fresh tomato sauce.

1 Bring 1.8 litres salted water to the boil. Reduce heat to very low and simmer. Slowly add 300 g polenta, stirring constantly.

2 Cook, stirring, until it pulls away from the pan, 20 minutes. You can now serve the polenta, with butter and Parmesan stirred in.

3 For fried or chargrilled polenta, omit butter and Parmesan and spread polenta 2 cm thick on a work surface. Leave until cold.

4 Trim the rough edges to form a rectangle. Cut lengthwise down the centre of the rectangle, then cut into wedges, as shown here, using a chef's knife.

5 Separate the wedges. Brush the tops with olive oil. Pan-fry or chargrill, turning halfway through and brushing with more oil, until golden brown, about 6 minutes.

COUSCOUS

Most couscous is pre-cooked, and only needs moistening and steaming according to packet instructions. The method shown here gives a richer result. Serve it as a side dish, mixed with finely chopped nuts, dried fruits or fresh herbs.

1 Put 250 g couscous in a lightly buttered pan. Add 500 ml hot water; stir with a fork until well blended.

2 Cook couscous over a medium-high heat for 5–10 minutes. Lower the heat and stir in 50 g butter.

3 Stir with a fork to fluff up and separate the grains, and coat them with the melted butter.

BULGAR

Also known as bulghur wheat, pourgouri and burghul, these are grains of wheat that are boiled until cracked, then dried. The grain is simplicity itself to prepare, but care must be taken to squeeze out as much water as possible after soaking. Bulgar is most often used in Middle Eastern pilafs, and in tabbouleh *and* kibbeh, *all of which will taste insipid if the grain is watery.*

1 Place the bulgar in a bowl. Add enough cold water to completely cover. Let stand for 15 minutes.

2 Tip bulgar into a fine sieve set over a bowl. Squeeze handfuls to remove excess water and place in a bowl.

POPPING CORN

There is nothing quite like the taste of freshly popped corn, tossed in salt, as here, or in sugar or spice, or left just as it is. Only pop a very small quantity at a time – just enough to cover the bottom of the pan to one kernel deep. As it pops, the corn swells up to make a larger amount than you imagine. First measure the volume of the corn, then use oil equal to half that measure.

1 Heat oil in a large pan over a moderate heat until very hot, but not smoking. Add the corn and cover with a tight-fitting lid.

2 Shake the pan over the heat just until the popping stops. Remove from the heat and pour popped corn into a bowl. Sprinkle with salt.

COUSCOUSIERE

In North Africa, the couscous grain gives its name to a spicy dish of meat and vegetables cooked in a special bulbous pot. Called a *couscousière*, this pot comes in two parts. The stew cooks in the bottom part of the pot, while the grain steams in a perforated pot on top, gaining flavour from the heady aromas of the stew beneath. The stew and grain are then served together.

DIFFERENT GRAINS AND THEIR USES

BARLEY: A nutty grain that is most commonly used as a thickener in soups and stews.
BUCKWHEAT (GROATS/KASHA): This fruit used as a grain is most popular in Eastern and Central European cooking. Use as part of a stuffing, as a hot breakfast cereal or a side dish; buckwheat flour is used to make blinis and Breton crêpes.
HOMINY: Served as grits in the American South, hominy is made from yellow or white corn bathed in a lye solution. It must be soaked overnight in water before cooking.
MILLET: Favoured for its crunchy texture and nutty flavour, millet flakes and grains are used in stews, stuffings and curries.
OATS: Rolled and flaked oats are used as the basis for both muesli and porridge.
QUINOA: This has a grassy flavour. Use in soups, salads and breads, and as a substitute for rice.
RYE: Available as grains, flakes and flour, rye is used to make breads and whisky.
WHEAT BERRY: This is the unprocessed kernel of wheat. Use in pilafs instead of rice, and in breads and stuffings.

NUTS

Seeds or fruits with an edible kernel enclosed in a hard shell, nuts add a crunchy texture, flavour and rich colour to a wide range of sweet and savoury dishes. The techniques for shelling, skinning and preparing a selection of nuts are described on these pages.

SHELLING PISTACHIOS

Buy pistachios with partially open shells. If closed, the nut is underripe and the shell will be very difficult to remove.

Prise the shell open with your fingernails to reveal the green-skinned nut. Once the hinge of the shell snaps, the nut will pop out. The pistachios are now ready for blanching and skinning (see right).

Top row, from left to right: peanuts; pistachio nuts; walnuts; pine nuts (*pignoli*).
Bottom row: hazelnuts; pecan; almonds; brazil nuts

BLANCHING AND SKINNING

Almond and pistachio skin is bitter, and will spoil the delicate flavour of the nuts if it is left on. Here almonds are blanched to ease skinning; the technique is the same for shelled pistachios (see left). The nut skins are easiest to remove when still warm after blanching, so do not leave them too long after draining.

1 Cover nuts with boiling water. Let stand, 10–15 minutes. Drain; let cool.

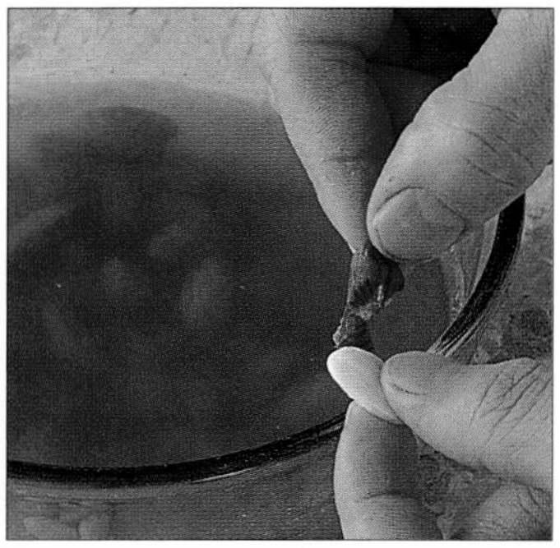

2 Pinch the softened skin between your thumb and index finger and slip it off.

TOASTING AND SKINNING

Hazelnuts and Brazil nuts are best toasted rather than blanched before skinning. Here, hazelnuts are toasted in the oven, but if you like you can toast them by dry-frying them on top of the stove. Put them in a non-stick, heavy frying pan and stir over a low heat until lightly toasted on all sides, 2–4 minutes.

1 Spread the nuts evenly on a baking sheet and toast at 175°C for 10 minutes, shaking the sheet occasionally.

2 Wrap the toasted nuts in a tea towel to steam for a few minutes, then rub to remove the skins.

Shredding and Chopping Nuts

Although most nuts can be bought ready chopped, flaked and shredded, you may not always find what you need. Nuts that are cut just before use will taste fresher and be more moist.

Shredding
Place nut, flat-side down, on a cutting board and cut lengthwise into shreds.

Flaking
Place nut, thin-side down, on a cutting board. Steady one side; cut into long, thin flakes.

Chopping
Put shredded nuts on a board. Steady knife and work blade backwards and forwards.

Peeling Chestnuts

These sweet, starchy nuts have a hard, brittle shell and papery skin, both of which should be removed whether the chestnuts are to be used raw or cooked. Allow plenty of time because the skins tend to stick to the nuts and are difficult to remove. There are three different techniques.

Cutting
Hold nut between your fingers and cut away shell and skin with a sharp knife.

Toasting
Pierce shell with the point of a knife. Grill until the shells split. Cool, then peel.

Blanching
Put nuts in water and bring to the boil. Drain and skin while hot.

Making a Nut Butter

Chilled nut butters make tasty toppings for hot food, and are quick and easy to make in the food processor. Almond butter is good with fish, hazelnut or pistachio with poultry and meat. If sugar and spice are added, nut butters taste good on hot barbecued fruits.

Grind toasted nuts in a food processor fitted with the metal blade. Add twice as much butter as nuts and blend together using the pulse button. Turn out the nut butter and shape into a log on baking parchment, then wrap and refrigerate. Slice as required.

Other Ways with Nuts

Chopping in a food processor: Nuts are best chopped by hand because you can control how fine they are, but for speed you can chop them in a food processsor fitted with the metal blade. Do not overwork them or they release their oil and turn to a paste.
Grinding: For some recipes, such as almond paste, fine-textured ground nuts are required. You can use a food processor for this, or work them in a coffee mill or nut grinder.
Toasting: Spread nuts in grill pan (without rack) and toast 15 cm away from the heat source, shaking the pan frequently, 3-5 minutes. Nuts can also be toasted in the oven at 180°C, 7-10 minutes.

Storing Nuts

Although a good source of fibre, nuts are high in fat, which makes them go rancid very quickly when they are exposed to heat, light and moisture. Store nuts, especially shelled nuts which deteriorate more quickly, in a cool, dark and dry place. Shelled nuts can be kept in the refrigerator for up to six months or the freezer for up to a year.

COCONUT

Exotic in appearance and tropical in taste, coconuts are a staple ingredient in Asian, Caribbean and Latin American kitchens. They have three layers – a hard hairy husk, creamy white meat beneath, and thin milky liquid in the centre. Select coconuts that are heavy for their size and sound full of liquid.

USING COCONUT AND COCONUT MILK

- Use the juice from the middle of the coconut as a drink or a light stock.
- Serve chunks of coconut flesh with fresh fruits in a warm chocolate fondue.
- Top curries, cakes and desserts with toasted coconut shreds.
- Use coconut milk to enrich Thai and Indian curries.
- When making crème anglaise for homemade ice cream (see page 286), use coconut milk instead of cow's milk.
- Use coconut milk to flavour cream sauce (see page 268) and rice (see page 130).

OTHER TYPES OF COCONUT MILK

- Desiccated coconut can be used instead of freshly grated, following the same technique.
- Blocks of creamed coconut work equally well. Chop with a chef's knife, then dissolve in boiling water. This type does not need straining before use.
- Coconut milk powder is very convenient to use. Either mix it to a paste with boiling water, or sprinkle the powder directly into sauces and curries.
- Canned coconut milk has a thick layer of "cream" on the top that can be scooped off and used separately.

PREPARING A WHOLE COCONUT

Before dealing with the flesh of a coconut, you need to crack open the hard shell with a hammer. The technique shown here is much the easiest way. After removing the thin brown skin that surrounds the flesh, shred or grate the flesh according to individual recipes.

1 Pierce a metal skewer through the indentations or "eyes" in the stalk end of the husk. Drain off the juice through the holes.

2 Crack the coconut by tapping it with a hammer all around its girth. Keep turning it around until it splits in half.

3 Prise the flesh out of the shell by working a small knife between them. Pare away the dark outer skin with a vegetable peeler.

MAKING COCONUT MILK

The juice in the centre of a coconut is not the coconut "milk" used in cooking. This is made by steeping the flesh in water, then squeezing it to extract coconut-flavoured "milk". You can steep and squeeze it more than once if you like, each time getting a thinner milk.

1 Rub the coconut flesh against the coarsest grid of a box grater, or grate it in a food processor fitted with the metal blade.

2 Put the grated coconut flesh in a bowl and pour over boiling water to cover. Stir well to mix, then leave to soak for 30 minutes until the water is absorbed.

3 Turn into a muslin-lined sieve set over a bowl and let the "milk" drain through. Draw up the muslin and squeeze hard to extract as much milk as possible.

Pasta

Homemade Pasta
•
Rolling & Cutting
•
Making Fresh Stuffed Pasta
•
Making Gnocchi
•
Cooking Pasta
•
Asian Pasta
•
Spring Rolls

HOMEMADE PASTA

Although there are hundreds of types of commercially made pasta, it is still a uniquely satisfying experience to make your own. Here the techniques are shown for making pasta dough by hand and machine, together with flavouring ideas. To roll and cut the dough, see pages 208-209.

BY HAND

Making pasta by hand is a simple technique that requires only a little time and yet produces quite excellent results. The technique of gentle kneading and the warmth from your hands both help to create a very elastic dough that can be stretched and shaped with ease. Here 450 g egg pasta – pasta all'uovo *– is made, enough for 6–8 for a first course, 4 for a main course.*

1 Sift 300 g strong plain white flour on to a work surface. Make a large well in the centre with your hand. Add 3 lightly beaten eggs, 1 tsp salt and 1 tbsp olive oil to the well.

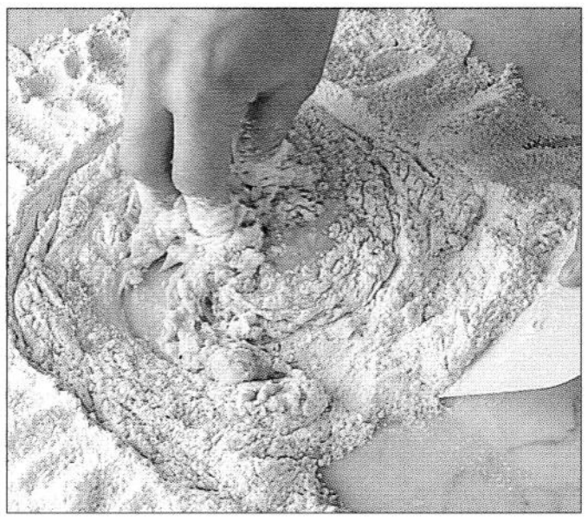

2 Mix the ingredients in the well with your fingertips. Incorporate the flour by pulling it into the centre.

3 Continue incorporating the flour, drawing it in from the sides of the well and using a pastry scraper to mix the dough.

4 Work the ingredients until the egg is absorbed by the flour. The dough should be moist; if sticky, sprinkle over a little more flour.

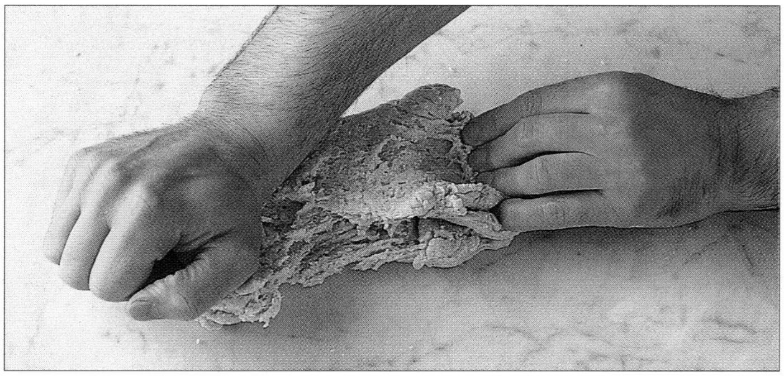

5 Begin kneading the dough by holding one end and pushing the other away from you with the heel of your hand. Continue kneading until smooth and elastic, 10–15 minutes.

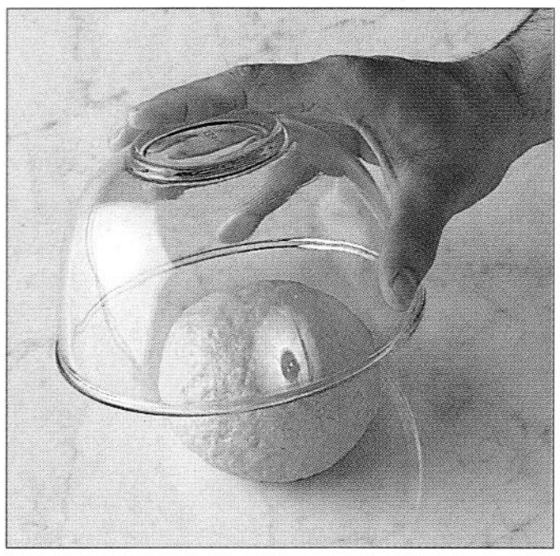

6 Let the dough rest, covered, for up to 1 hour before rolling and cutting.

WHO WAS FIRST?

It is quite widely believed that the 13th-century traveller Marco Polo discovered pasta in China, and brought it back to Italy. What excited his interest was that the Chinese were eating something like macaroni from his homeland.

Pasta was certainly common in Italy by the time the Roman Apicius wrote his famous book *The Art of Cooking* in the first century AD, but it appears that noodles were being eaten in China much earlier than that.

Marco Polo (1254–1324)

FLOUR FOR MAKING PASTA

The very best flour to use is durum wheat or semolina flour, but this is not always easy to obtain and it is also very hard to work with. The next best choice is strong plain flour, either white or wholemeal, the same kind that is used in bread making. Ordinary plain flour can be substituted, but it is best not to use it unless you are using a pasta machine for rolling – it makes a tough dough that is extremely difficult to roll out thinly by hand.

BY MACHINE

If you have a food processor, you can use it, fitted with the metal blade, to make pasta dough. This will save time and effort at the mixing stage, but it is still very important to knead the dough by hand after mixing. Overloading the machine will prevent it from mixing evenly – use a maximum of 450 g flour for any one batch.

1 Put 300 g sifted strong plain white flour and 1 tbsp salt into the food processor bowl. Add 1 tbsp olive oil and 1 egg. Work until the egg is incorporated.

2 With the motor running, add two more eggs, one at a time through the funnel, and work until a dough begins to form.

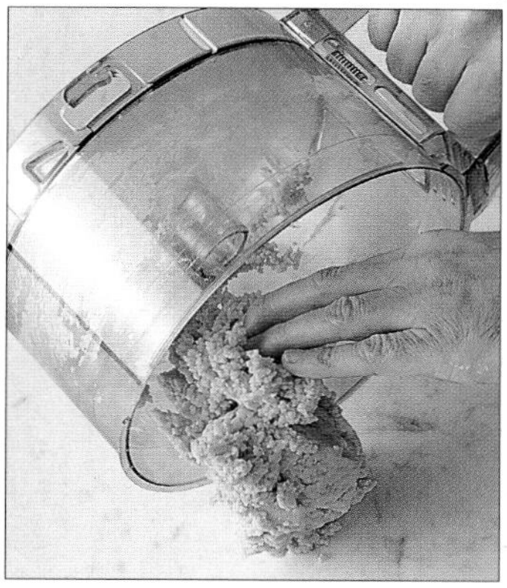

3 Turn the dough out, then knead the dough until it is smooth and elastic (see step 5, opposite page). Cover and let rest for up to 1 hour before rolling and cutting.

ADDING FLAVOURS

To give interest to homemade pasta, you can add different flavourings. Whatever your choice, the only rule is that the flavouring should always be evenly incorporated.

Dry ingredients, such as crushed peppercorns or dried herbs, should be mixed with the sifted flour, while wet ingredients or those that contain more moisture, such as chopped spinach, fresh herbs and squid ink, should be added with the last egg.

BY HAND

SPINACH
Add 2 tbsp finely chopped, well-drained cooked spinach to the wet ingredients in the well and mix thoroughly.

BY MACHINE

TOMATO
Add 1 tbsp sun-dried tomato purée to the dry ingredients at the same time as the oil and the first of the eggs.

SAFFRON STRANDS

FRESH HERBS

CRUSHED PEPPER

TIPS FOR MAKING PASTA

- Depending on the type of flour used you may have to add a little extra oil to bring the dough together.
- Check the flour wall is intact or the eggs will leak out.
- Instead of olive oil you can flavour the pasta with walnut or hazelnut oil.
- When adding wet flavourings, such as chopped spinach, use extra flour if necessary to absorb the extra moisture.
- Flour your hands and the work surface from time to time when kneading the dough to prevent it sticking.
- Don't skimp on the kneading time if you do not have a pasta machine for rolling the dough. The more you knead the more elastic the dough will be, and therefore the easier it will be to roll.
- Once the dough is kneaded, it should have an elastic consistency. Press your finger into the dough: if it is still sticky, add a little more flour.

WHAT'S IN A NAME?

PAGLIA E FIENO: "Straw and hay" – spinach and egg.
PASTA ALL'UOVO: The most popular pasta in northern Italy, made with eggs.
PASTA NERA: Black pasta that gets its colour, and a unique flavour, from squid ink..
PASTA ROSSA: Usually a tomato pasta with an orange tint. Can also be made with a deeper red colour using beetroot.
PASTA VERDE: A green pasta made with spinach, but can also include Swiss chard or basil.
TRICOLORE: "Three colours" – spinach, tomato and egg.

ROLLING & CUTTING

Pasta can be rolled into sheets by hand or, more quickly and thinly, with a pasta machine. After a brief drying time the pasta sheet can then be cut, by hand or using the attachments on the pasta machine, into a wide variety of shapes and sizes, depending on your chosen recipe.

ROLLING PASTA BY HAND

Hand-rolled pasta is thicker than pasta rolled by machine. You will need a spacious work surface: each ball of pasta dough will roll out into a very large sheet. To make handling easier, cut the dough in half, then roll out each half separately, keeping an even thickness.

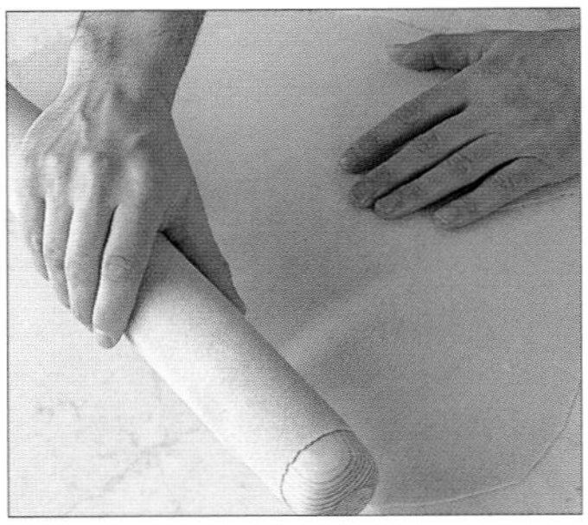

1 Cut rested dough (see pages 206 and 207) in half. Keep one half covered and flatten the other into a round. Roll the dough into a thin round sheet.

2 Bring the edge of the sheet furthest from you up over the pin and use it to help stretch the sheet, as shown. Turn the sheet 45° and repeat seven times.

3 When paper thin, hang the sheet of dough over a suspended floured broom handle. Repeat with the remaining piece of dough. Let dry, about 15 minutes.

ROLLING PASTA BY MACHINE

A pasta machine rolls sheets of pasta until smooth and elastic, and of uniform thickness. Turn the handle and feed the pasta dough through different roller-width settings by progressing one notch at a time. Before and between rollings, flour the pasta sheets and the machine rollers.

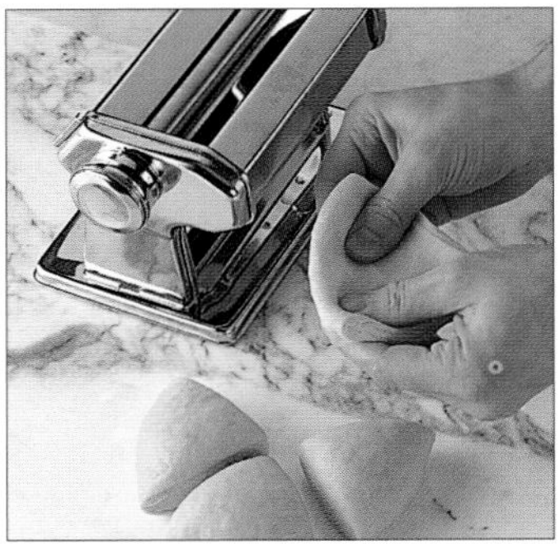

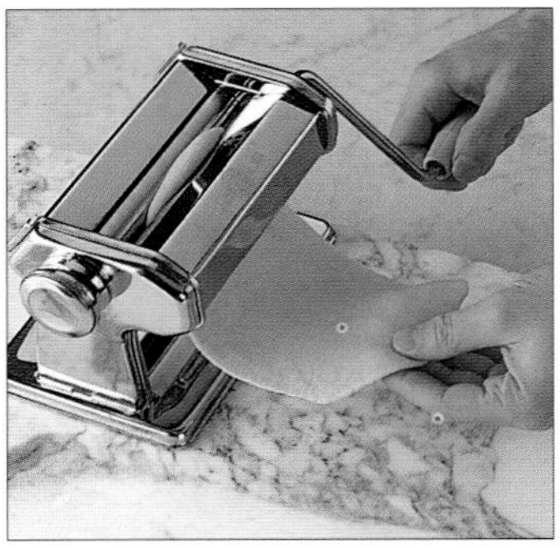

1 Cut rested dough (see pages 206 and 207) into four pieces. Flatten the pieces with your hands to form rectangles, roughly the same width as the machine.

2 Feed one piece of dough through the pasta machine, with the rollers set at their widest setting. Repeat with the remaining pieces.

3 Fold each piece of dough into thirds and roll again. Repeat three or four times without folding, reducing the notch width each time. Let dry as in step 3 above.

TRICK OF THE TRADE

SILHOUETTE PASTA

Place herb leaves such as parsley between two thin layers of pasta. Roll the dough to seal the layers, then cut into squares or rounds around the herbs. Cook in boiling salted water, 2 minutes.

PASTA MACHINE

If you make fresh pasta often, a hand-operated stainless steel pasta machine is a worthwhile investment. You can use it to roll out the pasta into sheets suitable for cutting into rectangles or squares for lasagne and cannelloni, or squares or rounds for ravioli or tortellini. It can also be used to cut the sheets into ribbons and noodles of varying widths. The machine has a set of three rollers with different settings that determine the thickness of the sheet of pasta. A clamp ensures the machine attaches to the work surface, making it very secure.

CUTTING PASTA BY HAND

Handmade pasta must be cut by hand. After drying the rolled out pasta for about 15 minutes, the pasta sheets should feel leathery but supple enough to cut without sticking together. If the pasta is too dry it will be brittle and difficult to cut. Before you start cutting, you can cut the sheets into more manageable-sized pieces, if you like. Use a chef's knife to do this, and try to avoid dragging the dough as you cut it.

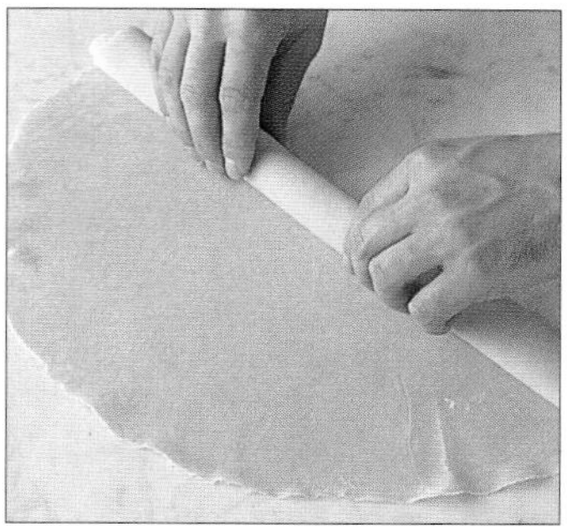

1 Take one sheet of the dried pasta dough and roll it into a loose but even cylinder. Transfer the cylinder to a board.

2 Cut the cylinder crosswise on the diagonal into strips about 10 mm wide. Unroll the strips and dry as in step 3 below, or as bundles (see tagliatelle, right).

CUTTING PASTA BY MACHINE

The great advantage of the pasta machine is that it cuts flat noodles (tagliatelle) cleanly, evenly and quickly. By adjusting the roller settings, the noodles can be cut to varying widths. Keep the dough and rollers lightly floured to prevent sticking.

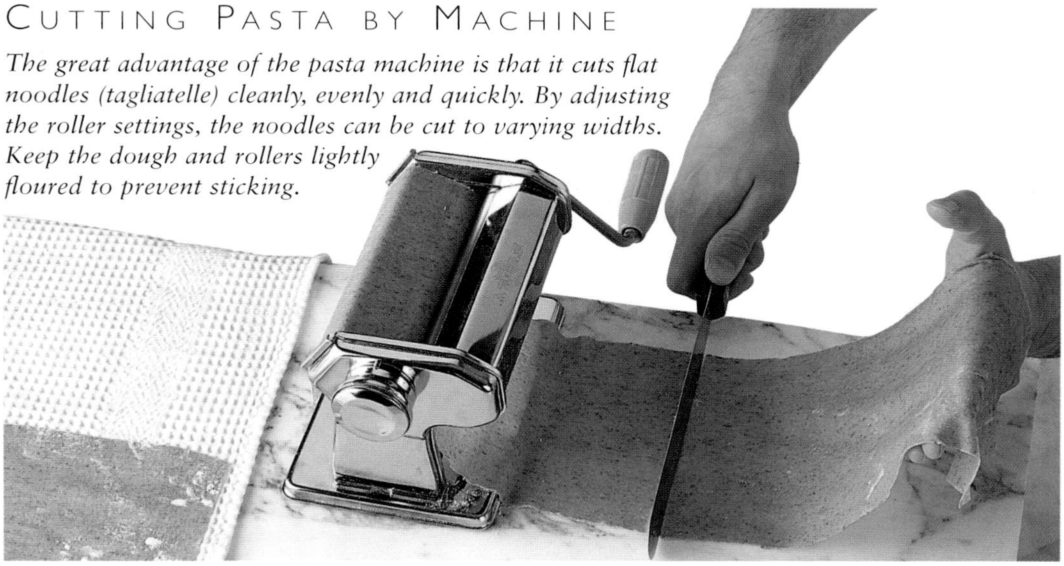

1 Cut the pasta sheet into 30-cm lengths as it passes through the rollers on the thinnest setting. Place the sheets on a floured tea towel until all the dough has been rolled.

2 Feed each length of dough through the machine set on the desired cut.

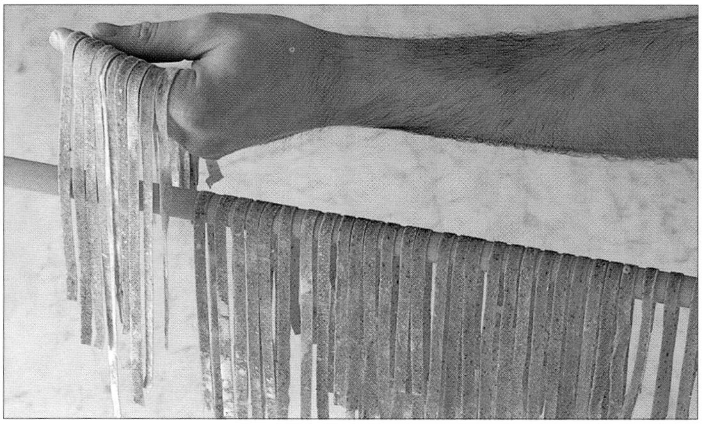

3 Hang the cut pasta over a floured suspended broom handle or over the back of a chair, or lay them flat on floured tea towels. Let dry 1–2 hours.

DRYING PASTA

Fresh egg pasta must be dried thoroughly before storing. Dust it with a little flour and place it in an airtight container in the refrigerator for two days.

TAGLIATELLE
Take a few strands and curl them loosely around your hand to make bundles. Place side by side on a floured dish. Let dry 1–2 hours.

LASAGNE
Put lasagne rectangles or squares side by side on a floured tea towel. Cover with another floured tea towel. Let dry 1–2 hours.

MAKING FRESH STUFFED PASTA

The dough used in stuffed pasta should not be too dry – it must be moist enough to shape easily and seal well. Shapes vary from squares to half moons. Stuffings vary too, but many contain cheese, with egg to bind. Stuffed pasta is usually cooked in water or broth, or baked with a sauce.

RAVIOLI-MAKING EQUIPMENT

Most specialist cookware shops sell equipment specifically designed for making uniformly shaped ravioli. Make sure pasta is not too dry and to prevent it sticking, flour the tools before use.

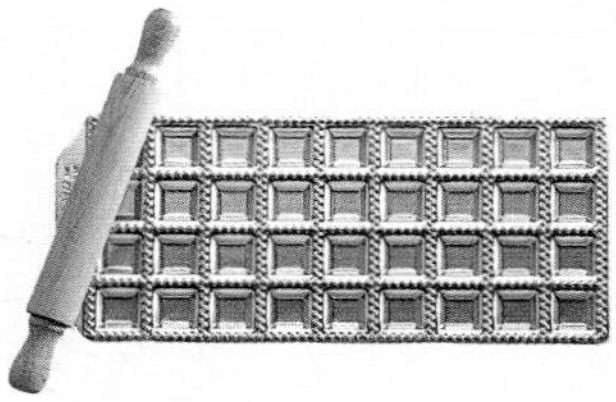

Ravioli moulds come in a variety of sizes and are good for making even-sized ravioli. The metal tray has a series of small indentations with ridged edges – often 40 to a tray. The moulds are usually sold together with a small wooden rolling pin, which is used to flatten the dough on the mould and to seal the ravioli. Use this mould once the dough is cut to size (see step 1, right).

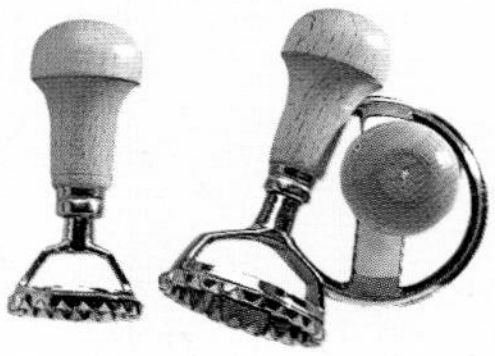

Ravioli cutters have wooden handles with metal cutters attached. They are available in various sizes and cut only one ravioli at a time (see page 216).

MAKING RAVIOLI

Stuffed pillows of pasta can be made by sandwiching the filling between two sheets of pasta (see recipe, page 216) or by folding one large sheet in half, as shown here. Alternatively a special pre-formed mould can be used (see box, left). Cover any pasta that is not being used with a damp tea towel, to keep it moist. Do not overfill. The technique shown here uses rolled-out handmade dough (see rolling pasta by hand, page 208).

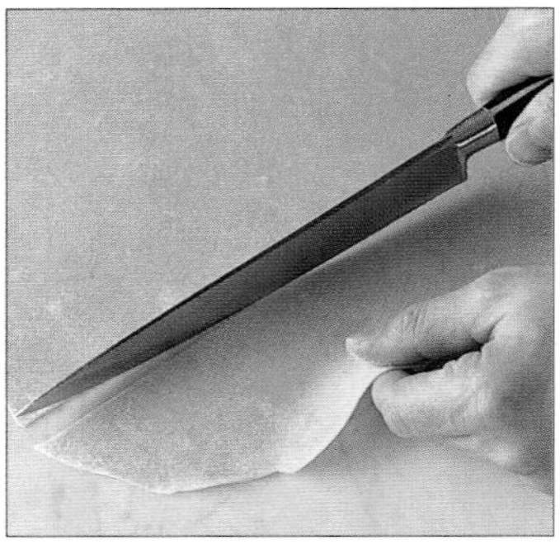

1 Trim one pasta sheet to a 25- x 50-cm rectangle, using a chef's knife. Use the trimmings to make tagliatelle (see page 209).

2 Put 16 rounded teaspoons of filling (see box, opposite page) over half the sheet, making sure that they are evenly spaced.

3 Brush a border around each mound with a little water. This will help the pasta stick together.

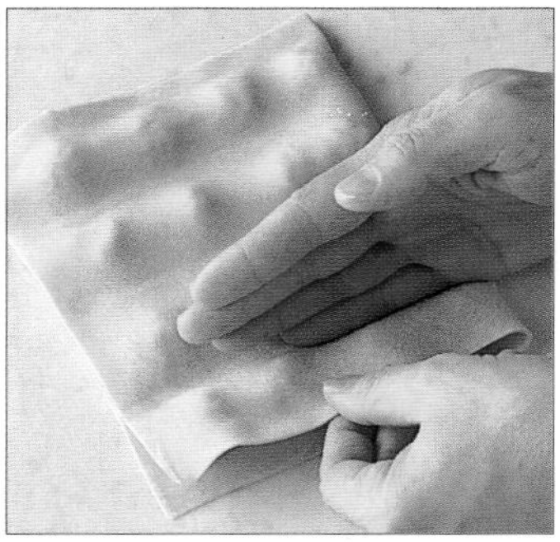

4 Fold over the plain half of the pasta sheet to cover the filling, making sure the edges meet. Press between the mounds of filling using the side of your hand to seal the two layers of pasta and exclude any air.

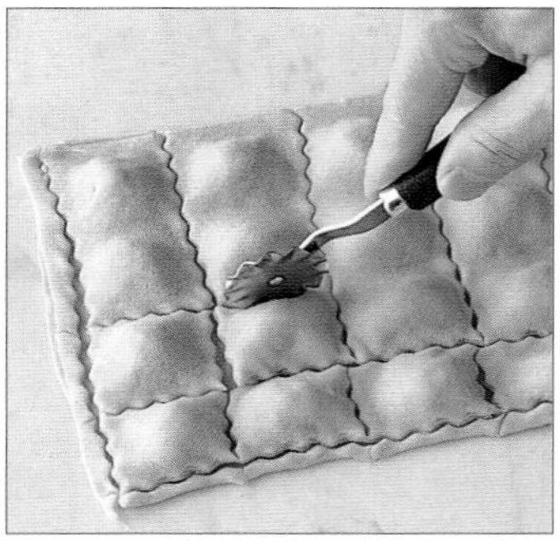

5 Dust a fluted metal pastry wheel lightly with flour. Cut around the edges of the pasta to neaten them and make them square, then cut around the mounds of filling to make the ravioli shapes.

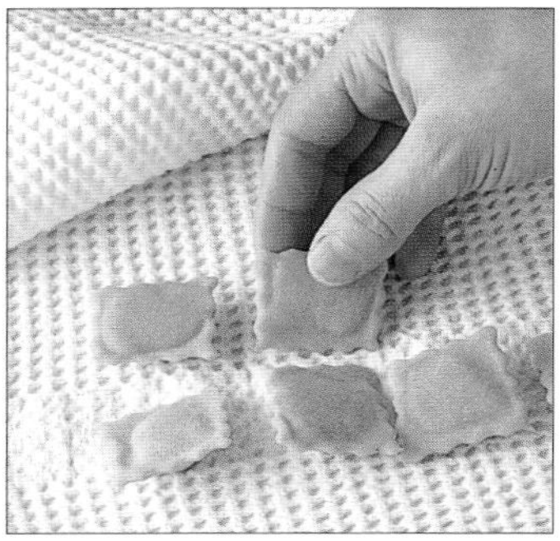

6 Place the ravioli between two floured tea towels. Leave them to dry about 1 hour, turning them halfway through. Meanwhile make another batch of ravioli with the second sheet of pasta and more filling.

Making Tortellini

A speciality of Bologna, tortellini are supposedly modelled on Venus's navel. Shaping them takes some time and practice, but they can be made a day ahead and stored in the refrigerator.

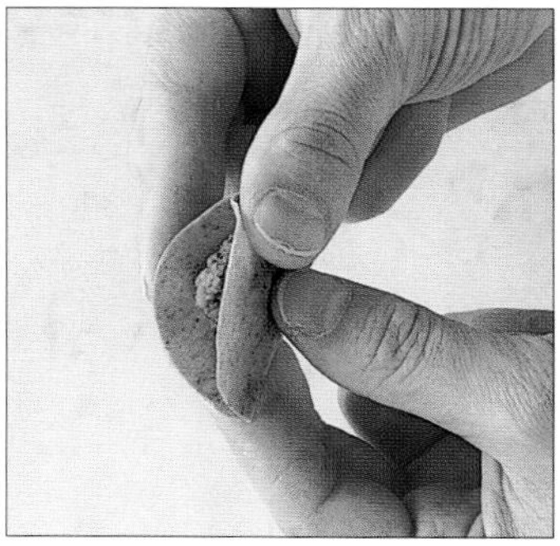

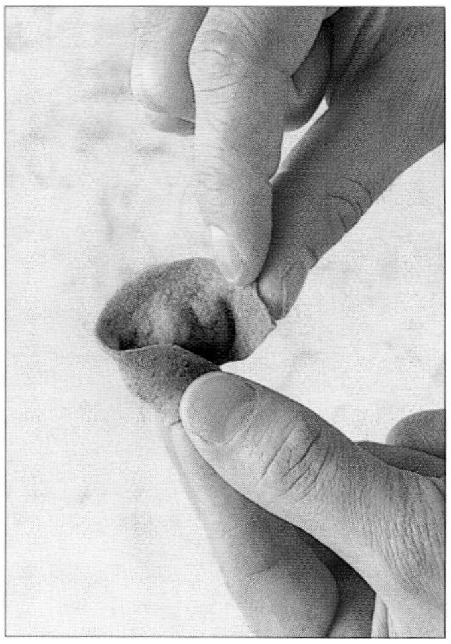

1 Make and roll out pasta dough (see pages 206-208). Cut out rounds from the pasta sheets with a floured 7.5-cm plain ravioli cutter or pastry cutter. Keep rounds covered to prevent them drying out. Put a small spoonful of filling (see box, right) in the centre of each.

2 Using a small brush, dampen the edges of the rounds with a little water. Then pick up each round in your hands and fold it in half, carefully pressing the edges of the dough together to form a sealed crescent around the filling.

3 Wrap the crescent around one index finger, turning the sealed edge upwards at the same time. Pinch the pointed ends firmly together. As you make each one, put the tortellini between two floured tea towels while you make the others. Let them dry for about 1 hour.

Chicken and Sage Filling

125 g skinless boneless chicken breast
1 small onion
2 garlic cloves
Leaves of 1 flat-leaf parsley sprig and 1 sage sprig
Salt and freshly ground pepper
1 egg, lightly beaten

Cut the chicken into pieces. Peel the onion and garlic; cut the onion into quarters. Place in a food processor fitted with the metal blade. Process until roughly chopped, then add the remaining ingredients and process again until finely chopped. Transfer to a bowl, cover and refrigerate until required. Makes about 150 g filling, sufficient for 32 ravioli or tortellini or 4 cannelloni.

Making Cannelloni

Ready-made cannelloni tubes are available but this recipe follows the Neopolitan tradition in which sheets of pasta are boiled, then rolled around a filling.

1 Make and roll out pasta dough (see pages 206-209), then cut the pasta sheets into 10- x 7.5-cm rectangles. Bring a large pan of water to the boil and half fill a large bowl with cold water. Add 1 tbsp oil and 1 tsp salt to the boiling water, then add a few pieces of the pasta. Cook, just until wilted, about 1 minute.

2 Remove the pasta very carefully with a fish slice and immerse immediately in the bowl of cold water. When cool enough to handle, remove the pasta from the cold water and place in a single layer on a tea towel to drain. Repeat with the remaining pieces of pasta.

3 Using a piping bag and a large plain tube, add a line of filling (see box, above) down one long side of each rectangle. Alternatively, use carefully placed spoonfuls. Roll the pasta around the filling, keeping the cylinder as even as possible. Put the cylinders seam-side down in a well-buttered baking dish and coat with the sauce of your choice. Fresh tomato sauce (see page 331) is a classic with cannelloni, so too is béchamel sauce (see page 222). Sprinkle with grated Parmesan cheese and bake at 200°C for 20–30 minutes.

Making Gnocchi

Italian for "little dumplings", these can be made with a variety of ingredients. The two most common are "alla Romana" made with semolina, and the plumper version using potato. Both are a challenge – they must be light in texture but firm enough to shape and not break up when cooked.

Semolina Gnocchi

The semolina is added in a constant stream, stirring all the time, to incorporate air and prevent lumps forming. Infuse the milk first, if you like. Bring it to the boil with seasonings such as onion, cloves and bay leaves, cover and let stand 1 hour. Strain the milk before using.

1 Bring 1 litre milk to the boil in a large pan. Lower the heat and pour in 175 g semolina in a steady stream, stirring constantly with a wooden spoon to prevent lumps forming.

2 Bring the semolina mixture to the boil and cook, stirring constantly, until thick and smooth, about 5 minutes.

3 Whisk together 3 egg yolks. Remove the pan from the heat and beat the eggs, a little at a time, into the semolina mixture until evenly incorporated.

4 Spread the mixture in a lightly oiled shallow dish. Rub the surface with a knob of butter, to prevent a crust forming. Let cool, preferably overnight.

5 Lightly oil a plain pastry cutter and cut the mixture into rounds or use a chef's knife to create shapes of your choice (see left). Arrange the gnocchi shapes, overlapping them slightly, in an oiled baking dish, brush with melted butter and sprinkle with freshly grated Parmesan cheese. Bake at 230°C for 15–20 minutes until golden brown. Serve hot.

Rombi

Stelle

Fiori

Triangoli

POTATO GNOCCHI

It is not easy to make potato gnocchi – Italians say that you need to "feel" the right consistency of the dough rather than measure out the exact quantities of ingredients. The type of potato is very important: floury varieties like King Edward need the addition of flour and egg to moisten them; waxy types, like the Desirée shown here, only require flour. Keep the amount of flour to a minimum, just enough to hold the potato together – too much will make the gnocchi heavy. Cook the potatoes in their skins to reduce the amount of moisture they absorb.

1 Cook 650 g potatoes, in their skins, in boiling salted water for 20 minutes or until tender. Drain, leave until cool enough to handle but still warm, then peel off their skins.

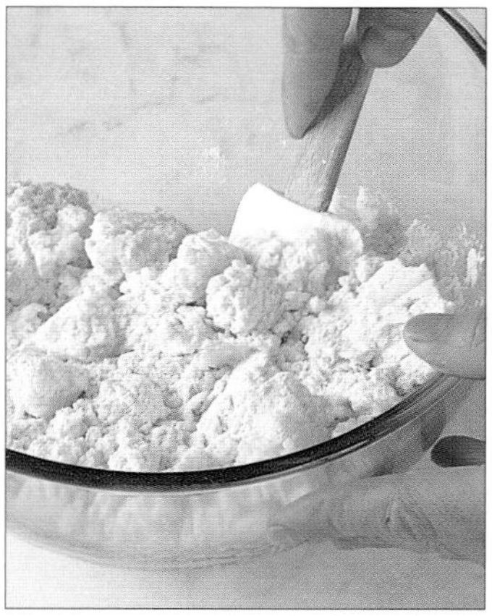

2 Mash the potatoes in a large bowl, then add 175 g plain flour and salt and freshly ground pepper to taste. Mix with a spatula, combining the ingredients evenly to make a dough.

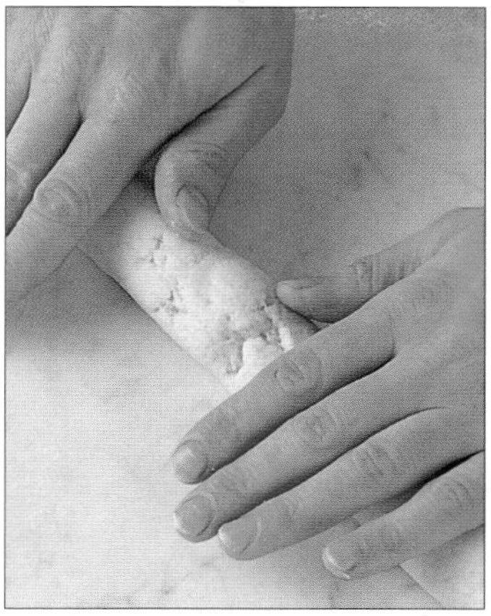

3 Turn the dough on to the work surface and knead with your hands until smooth. Cut the dough in half. Roll each piece into a long sausage shape, about 2 cm in diameter.

4 Cut the lengths of dough crosswise into small pieces. Shape the pieces into ovals by rolling them between your fingers. If the dough feels moist and sticky, lightly flour your fingers, but take care not to use too much flour or the gnocchi will become heavy. Mark the shapes with a fork (see box, right), if you like.

5 Working in batches, drop the gnocchi into a pan of boiling unsalted water and cook them until they rise to the surface, 1–3 minutes. Cook for a further 20 seconds, then remove with a slotted spoon. Serve hot, with melted butter and Parmesan.

WHAT'S IN A NAME?

Gnocchi differ in fillings and names depending on the region they come from.

- *Canederli*, from Trentino, are large gnocchi, each containing a prune.
- *Gnocchi di riso*, a speciality of Reggio Emilia, are made from cooked rice mixed with eggs and breadcrumbs.
- *Gnocchi di zucca*, from Lombardy, are made with cooked pumpkin.
- *Gnocchi verdi* from Emilia-Romagna are made with spinach, ricotta, Parmesan and eggs added to potato.

TRICK OF THE TRADE

MARKING WITH A FORK

The technique of making ridges in gnocchi is not just decorative: it helps compress the gnocchi so that they keep their shape, and the grooves help hold the sauce when the gnocchi are served.

Take a piece of gnocchi and press one side of it against the tines of a large fork, rolling it off the fork on to a board. Repeat with the remaining pieces.

Cooking Pasta

It is important to know how to cook pasta properly: undercooked pasta is chewy and tastes raw; overcooked pasta has a mushy texture. For perfect results, test frequently towards the end of the cooking time.

PASTA EQUIPMENT

A pasta cooker is a worthwhile investment for cooking large quantities, especially as it can be used for other cooking purposes too, such as jam-making and preserving. Made of stainless steel, it consists of a perforated pan which fits inside a solid pan. When the pasta has finished cooking, the inner perforated pan containing the pasta can be lifted out, allowing the water to drain into the outer pan. The pasta can then be transferred safely and easily to a serving dish.

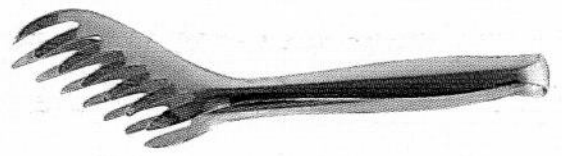

A simple way to lift long strands of spaghetti or tagliatelle out of the cooking water is to use metal tongs. These grasp the pasta without cutting it and are ideal for lifting out one or two strands when testing for doneness.

Cooking Short Pasta

Use a large pan so the pasta shapes can move freely in the boiling water. As an approximate guide, allow 5 litres water and 1 tbsp salt for 450 g pasta. Adding a little oil to the water helps prevent the shapes sticking together during cooking.

1 Bring a large pan of water to the boil. Add salt and 1 tbsp olive oil.

2 Add the pasta all at once, bring the water back to the boil, then start timing (see opposite page).

3 Cook, uncovered, at a rolling boil until the pasta is *al dente* (see box, opposite page), stirring occasionally.

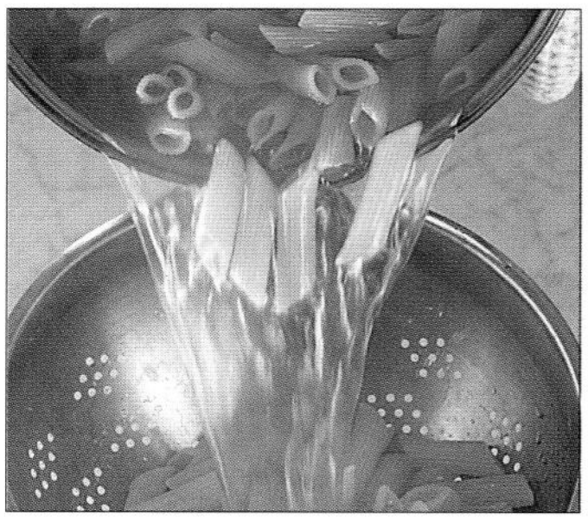

4 Drain the pasta thoroughly in a colander, shaking it vigorously to release all the water. Return it to the pan and reheat with a knob of butter or 1–2 tbsp olive oil. Or turn it into a warmed serving bowl and toss with a sauce.

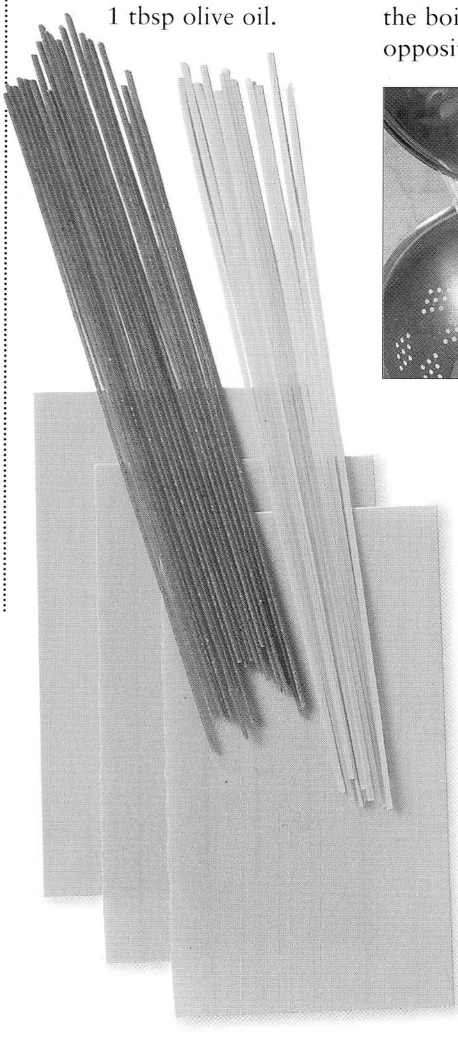

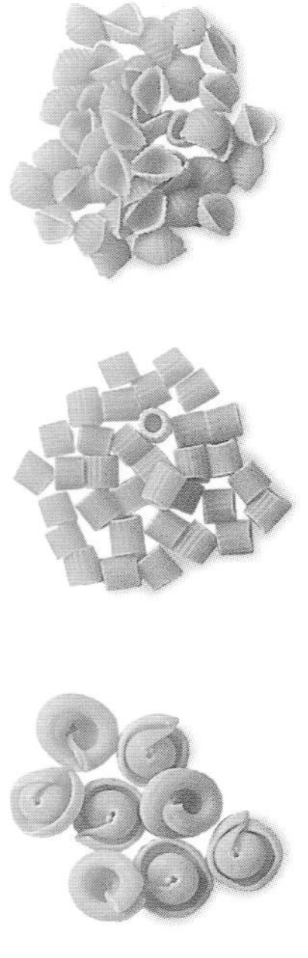

Left from top to bottom: wholewheat spaghetti; plain spaghetti; lasagne sheets. **Middle from top to bottom:** conchiglie; ditalini; orecchiette. **Right from top to bottom:** wholewheat penne; rigatoni; cannelloni

Cooking Long Pasta

The technique for long dried pasta, such as spaghetti, linguine and tagliatelle (unless it has been curled into nests before drying) is to gently ease it into the water. As the pasta becomes submerged in the boiling water it softens and bends so that it can be coiled round in the pan without being broken. The special Italian pasta pot (see box, opposite page) is ideal for cooking long pasta. Calculate the cooking time from the moment the water returns to the boil after all the pasta is submerged.

1 Bring a large pan of water to the boil. Add salt and oil as for short pasta (see opposite page), then take a handful of pasta and dip one end in the water. As the pasta softens, coil until submerged. Cook until *al dente* (see right).

2 Drain the pasta thoroughly. Rinse out the pan then return to the heat and add a knob of butter or 1–2 tbsp olive oil. Return the cooked pasta to the pan and toss over a high heat until the pasta is glistening.

COOKING TIMES

Calculate cooking times of all pasta types from the moment the water returns to the boil after the pasta has been added and always test before draining (see box below). If the pasta is to be cooked further (baked in lasagne, for example), reduce the boiling time slightly.

- FRESH PASTA
  1-3 mins
- FRESH STUFFED PASTA
  3-7 mins
- DRIED PASTA NOODLES
  8-15 mins
- DRIED PASTA SHAPES
  10-12 mins

Cooking Asian Noodles

Most Chinese and Japanese pasta needs to be cooked before it is stir-fried. Exceptions are cellophane and rice noodles, which only require soaking (see page 218). Cook noodles in boiling salted water until just tender, then drain and rinse under cold water to prevent them cooking any further. Drain the noodles again, making sure all the excess water is removed. They are now ready for stir-frying with flavourings of your choice.

Heat a wok until hot but not smoking. Add 1–2 tbsp vegetable oil and heat until hot. Add the noodles and flavourings and stir-fry over a high heat for 2–3 minutes, tossing noodles until they are glistening with oil and warmed through.

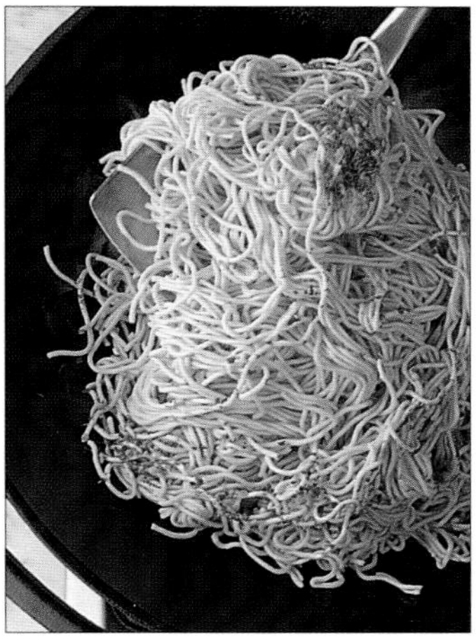

TESTING PASTA FOR DONENESS

Whether it is boiled or baked, pasta should be cooked until it is what Italians call al dente, *which means "firm to bite". If it is overcooked, it will be mushy.*

Just before the end of the recommended cooking time, lift a piece of pasta out of the water with tongs and test it by biting into it. When it is perfectly cooked, the pasta should feel tender, without any hint of rawness, but there should be just a touch of resistance to the bite. If the pasta is done, take it off the heat and drain immediately. If not, continue testing every 30–60 seconds until it is.

Clockwise, from bottom left: fusilli; conchiglie; farfalle; garlic and herb tagliatelle; tortellini; ravioli filled with spinach and ricotta; spinach and herb tagliatelle

Ravioles d'escargots au beurre d'herbes

Tender and tasty snails are often stuffed back in their shells with a herb and garlic butter, then baked or grilled. Here, instead, they are stuffed into pasta pillows with a flavouring of pastis and served with a warm buttery herb and shallot sauce.

SERVES 4 AS A FIRST COURSE

FOR THE PASTA DOUGH

400 g strong plain white flour
1 tsp salt
4 eggs
1 tbsp olive oil

FOR THE FILLING

4 tbsp olive oil
40 g shallots, finely chopped
50 ml pastis, such as Pernod or Ricard
12 canned snails, well drained

FOR THE HERB BUTTER SAUCE

80 g shallots, finely chopped
200 ml dry white wine
2 tbsp white wine vinegar
400 g butter, cut into small pieces
1 bunch of fresh basil, shredded
1 bunch of fresh chervil, shredded
2 tbsp chopped fresh parsley
Salt and freshly ground pepper

TO GARNISH

Carrot and courgette julienne (see page 166), blanched

Make the pasta dough: put the flour and salt in a food processor. Break the eggs into a bowl and whisk them lightly with the olive oil. With the machine running, gradually add the eggs and oil to the flour through the feed tube until a slightly wet, crumb-like dough forms. Turn out the dough and knead and stretch it with the palm of your hand (see step 5, page 206) until it is smooth and elastic. Leave the dough to rest at room temperature, covered with an upturned bowl, for about 1 hour.

Make the filling: heat the oil in a small pan and sweat the shallots. Add the pastis, stir well and bring to the boil. Remove from the heat, add the snails and let cool.

Cut the pasta dough into two equal pieces. Using a pasta machine if available, roll out each piece as thinly as possible to a rectangle measuring 15 x 50 cm.

Put one sheet on a work surface, and cut it in half. Evenly space six spoonfuls of the snail mixture on one half of the dough, allowing one snail per spoonful. Brush the dough around the mounds very lightly with water just to moisten. Lay the second half of the dough on top. Press firmly, then cut out fluted rounds (see box, below). Repeat with the remaining dough and snails. Cover the ravioli and set aside.

Bring a large pan of water to the boil. Meanwhile, make the sauce by combining the shallots, wine and vinegar in a pan and reducing until almost all the liquid has evaporated. Whisk in the butter, a few pieces at a time, to form an emulsified sauce. Add the herbs and season with salt and pepper. Keep the sauce warm.

Add 1 tbsp salt and a splash of olive oil to the boiling water, then add the ravioli. Cook for 3–4 minutes or until *al dente*. Remove with a slotted spoon and drain in a colander.

Arrange three ravioli in each of four warmed bowls and spoon over the herb butter sauce. Garnish with carrot and courgette julienne and serve immediately.

Cutting Ravioli

A ravioli cutter or stamp (see page 210) is the traditional tool for cutting out these stuffed pasta shapes, but you can also use a fluted or plain biscuit cutter.

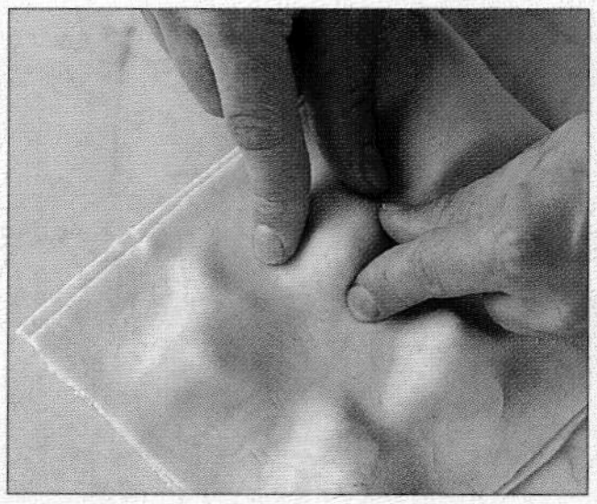

With your fingers, press down firmly around each mound of filling to eliminate any air pockets in the pasta.

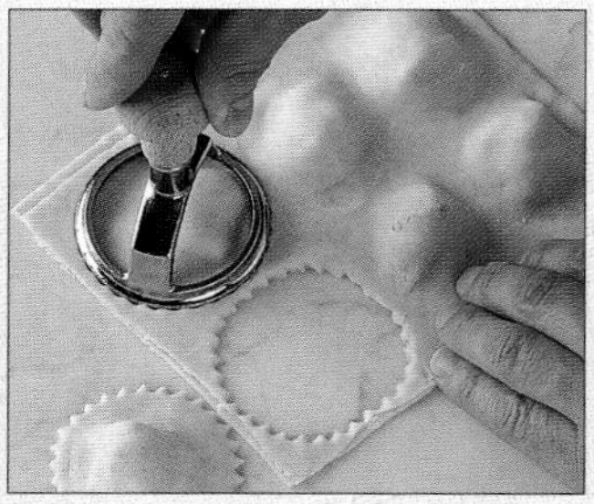

Stamp out the ravioli shapes with the cutter, taking care to keep the mound of filling in the centre.

Asian Pasta

Noodles made from a flour and water paste are common to many cuisines around the world. Asian countries, it is now realized, have an ancient tradition of pasta making even older than that of the Italians. Flours vary in the making of Asian pasta, as do shape and size, but the techniques of making and using Asian pasta differ very little from European methods.

Asian Noodles

Made from a variety of flours, these come in a myriad of shapes, colours and sizes.

Cellophane noodles: Made from ground mung bean flour, these are translucent, very fine shreds. Available dried, they only need soaking before eating. They can also be deep-fried dry.

Egg noodles: Looking like compressed bundles of tagliatelle, these are made from wheat flour and egg. Available fresh and dried, in different thicknesses, they can be boiled, boiled and stir-fried, or added to soups.

Rice noodles: Made from rice flour, these are cut in thick or thin strands. Available dried, they only need soaking before eating, but can also be deep-fried dry.

Rice sticks: Made from rice flour, these are cut like fettuccine. Available fresh and dried, they only need soaking before eating, usually in soups and salads.

Soba noodles: Cut like linguine, these Japanese noodles are made from buckwheat flour. Available fresh and dried, they are mainly used in soups.

Spring roll wrappers: Squares of paper-thin dough made from wheat flour and water. They tear easily, so should be handled with care. Available fresh and frozen.

Wonton wrappers: Sold in 7.5-cm squares, these are made from wheat flour and egg. Available fresh and frozen.

Soaking Dried Noodles

Delicate varieties of Asian noodles, such as the white rice noodles shown here and the translucent cellophane noodles, only require softening in hot water if they are used in stir-fries and salads. They do not need to be cooked further.

Put the noodles in a large bowl and cover them with hot water. Let the noodles soak just until tender and pliable, 5–10 minutes (thinner noodles will require less soaking time than thicker varieties). Drain the noodles thoroughly in a colander and use as required.

Making Purses

Fresh wonton wrappers (see box, left) can enclose savoury fillings to make the Chinese snacks known as dim sum. Use the same filling as in the Chinese dumplings on the opposite page.

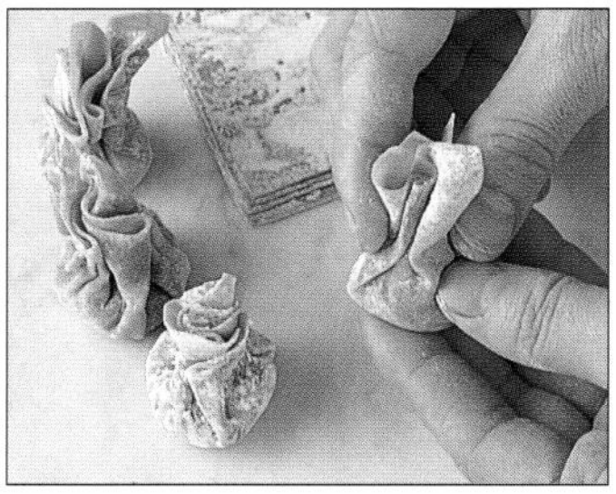

1 Put 1 tbsp filling in the centre of each wonton wrapper. Lightly brush the edges of the wrapper with water. Bring the wrapper up around the filling and pinch and twist to make a purse.

2 Put a few dark leaves of Chinese cabbage in a bamboo steamer, then put the steamer in a wok filled with 1 litre water; bring to the boil. Place the purses well apart on the leaves, cover and steam until tender, about 15 minutes.

Making Chinese Dumplings

Little Chinese dumplings, also known as pot stickers, are fried on one side, then steamed until tender. The techniques shown here, using the recipe in the box, right, are based on a dough that is very easy to handle. Serve the dumplings hot, fried-side up, with soy sauce and hot chilli oil for dipping. Don't be tempted to cut them in half. Eat them whole, to keep in all the juices.

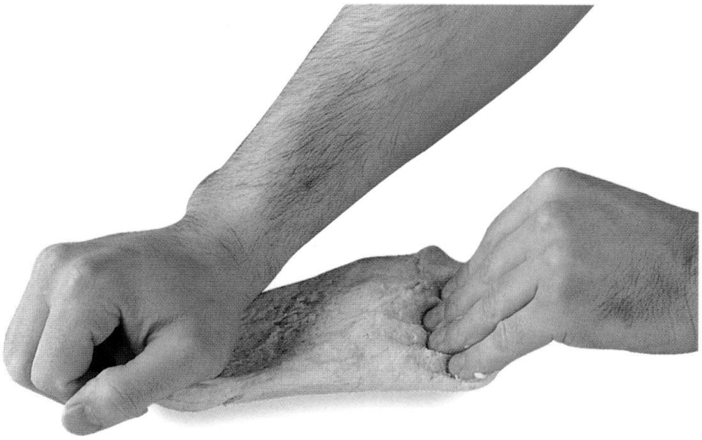

1 Turn the dough on to a lightly floured surface. Begin kneading the dough by holding one end and pushing the other away from you with the heel of your hand. Continue kneading by peeling the dough from the work surface, turning it, and pushing it away from you as before. Stop kneading only when the dough feels smooth and elastic, after about 5 minutes. Let the dough rest, in a bowl covered with a damp cloth, for about 20 minutes.

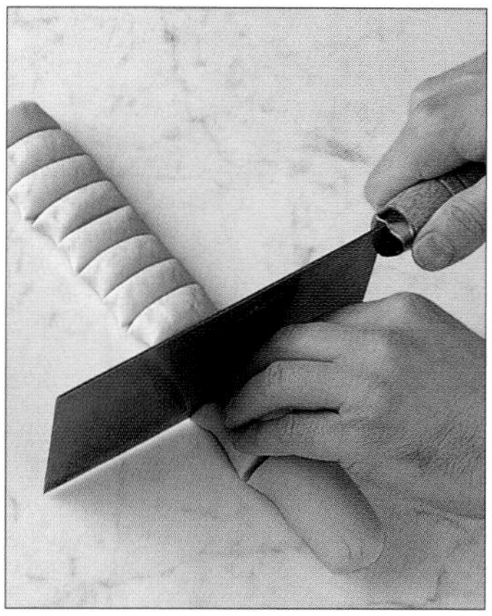

2 Roll the dough into a cylinder, about 2.5 cm in diameter. Cut into even-sized pieces with a cleaver or chef's knife. Form each piece into a ball with your hands, then roll each ball into a 10-cm round with a rolling pin.

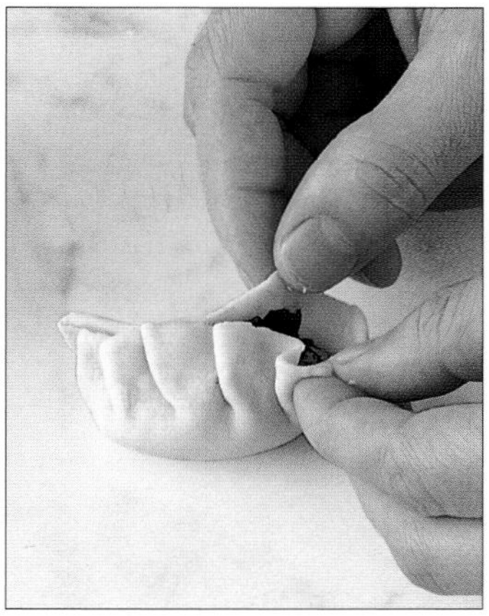

3 Place about 1 tbsp of the prawn and vegetable filling in the centre of each round. Lightly brush the edge of each round with water. Make 4 or 5 pleats on one side of each round, then bring the two sides up and over the filling and press them together to seal in the filling. Heat a wok until hot. Add 1 tbsp vegetable oil and heat until the oil is hot but not smoking.

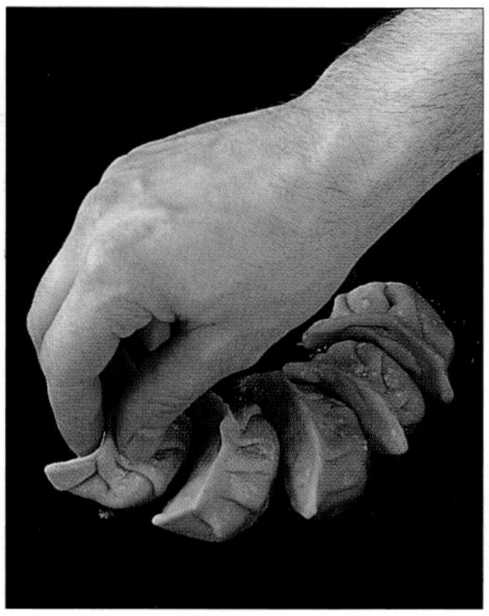

4 Carefully place the dumplings, flat-side down, in the hot oil. Fry over a moderate heat until they are golden brown on the underside, about 2 minutes. Lower the heat, pour about 125 ml cold water into the centre of the wok, and cover tightly with the lid. Let the dumplings steam for about 10 minutes until they feel tender when pierced. Add more water if necessary.

Chinese Dumplings

350 g plain flour
3 spring onions, finely chopped
1.5-cm piece of fresh root ginger, peeled and finely chopped
450 g raw prawns, peeled and finely chopped
2 tsp cornflour
4 tsp soy sauce
4 tsp rice wine or dry sherry
1 tbsp vegetable oil, for frying

Slowly mix 150 ml boiling water into the flour to make a moist, not sticky, dough, adding more flour if necessary. Cover and let rest, 1 hour. Knead, cover and let rest, 20 minutes. Combine the remaining ingredients to make the filling. Roll the dough into 16 rounds, then shape into dumplings around the filling. Fry in the oil in a wok, pour in 125 ml cold water, cover and steam for 10 minutes. Makes 16.

TRICK OF THE TRADE

Using a Dumpling Press

Small plastic dumpling presses are available in most cookware shops. Once the dough and filling are made, shaping the dumplings is simple.

Open the press and lightly brush the fluted rim with vegetable oil. Make the dough and roll into 10-cm rounds (see above).

Place one dumpling round on the press. Spoon 1 tbsp filling on to the centre of the round, then brush the edge of the dough lightly with water.

Close the press, squeezing the handles firmly to seal the dough around the filling. Open the press and remove the dumpling.

Continue with more dough and filling, brushing the rim of the press with more oil as necessary. Fry and steam the dumplings in a wok, as in step 4, left.

Spring Rolls

Fried to a golden-crisp and packed with a tasty mixture of aromatic ingredients, spring rolls are the quintessential Asian treat. The paper-thin wrappers are available in Asian supermarkets in fresh and frozen varieties. Unused wrappers should be quickly resealed and frozen for future use.

SPRING ROLLS

1 red chilli, deseeded
2 small carrots
1 red pepper, cored and deseeded
1 bunch of spring onions
Vegetable oil, for frying
175 g tofu (bean curd)
3 tbsp chopped fresh coriander
A few drops each soy sauce and Chinese rice wine
8 spring roll wrappers

Finely chop the chilli; julienne the carrots, red pepper and spring onions. Heat 1 tbsp oil in a wok, add the vegetables and stir-fry for 1–2 minutes. Transfer to a bowl and cool. Cut the tofu into 2-cm pieces and add to the bowl with the coriander, soy sauce and rice wine; toss well. Enclose the filling in the wrappers, then deep-fry in batches in 180°C oil until golden, about 4 minutes. Makes 8.

Making Spring Rolls

Spring roll wrappers are very fragile and need to be handled with care. Keep them covered with a damp cloth while working with them to prevent them drying out.

1 Put a wrapper on the work surface, arranging it like a diamond with one of the points facing you. Place a little filling across the centre.

2 Fold the point facing you over the filling towards the centre, then fold in the left point followed by the right. Press gently.

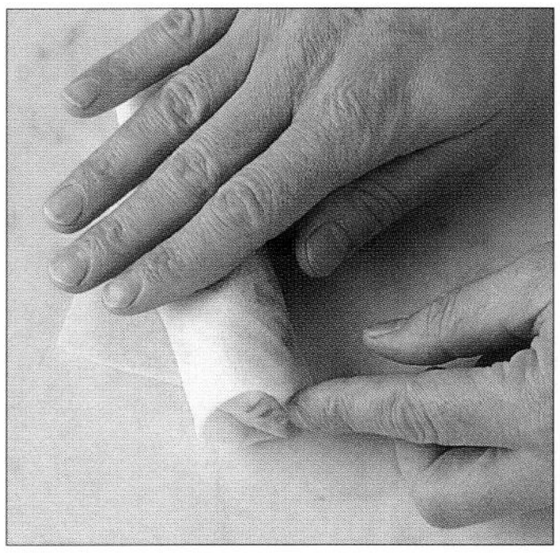

3 Roll the parcel away from you to completely enclose the filling. Seal the edges with a little egg white. Let stand, pointed-end down.

Mini Spring Rolls

These are made by cutting spring roll wrappers into four small squares. You can use the same filling as in the spring rolls above, or one of the suggestions from the box, left.

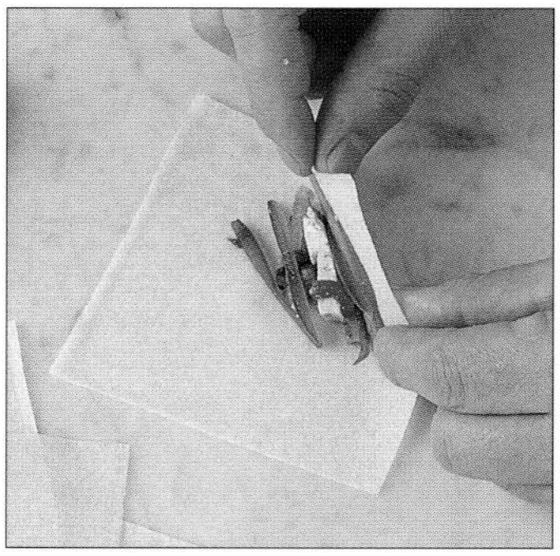

1 Roll the wrappers as in step 1 above, making sure that the filling ingredients are shredded very finely and only a small quantity is used so they do not burst.

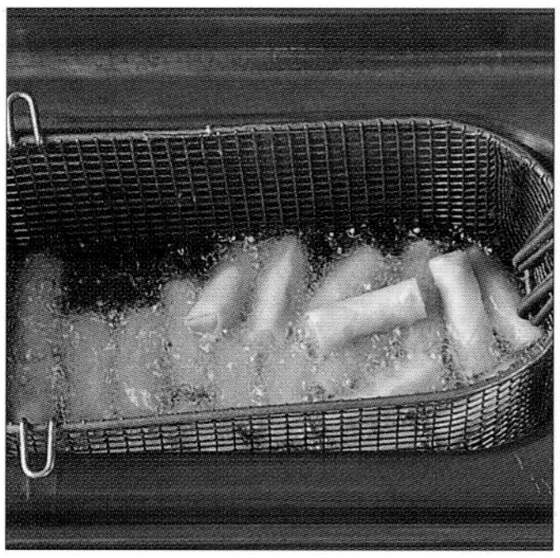

2 Place a batch of spring rolls in a fryer basket and lower gently into 180°C oil. Deep-fry until crisp and golden, 2–3 minutes.

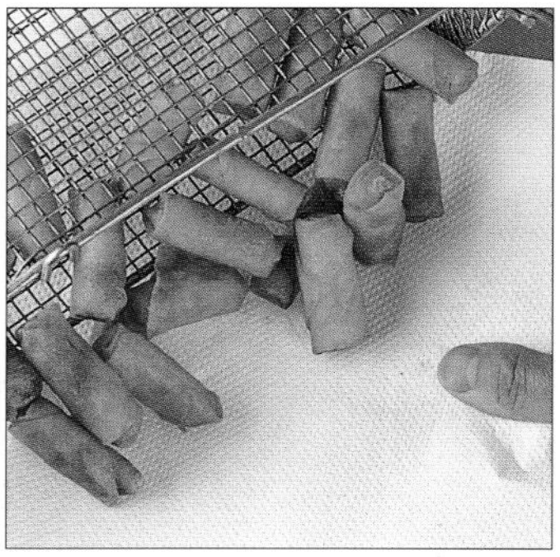

3 Lift the basket out of the fryer and shake to remove excess oil. Tip the spring rolls on to paper towels. Let drain thoroughly before serving.

OTHER FILLINGS FOR SPRING ROLLS

- Flaked white crabmeat, grated lemon zest and juice, soy sauce, crushed garlic, shredded spring onions and fresh ginger.
- Minced pork, chopped fresh coriander, bean sprouts, shredded green pepper, rice wine and sesame oil.
- Chopped prawns, shredded mangetouts, grated fresh ginger, crushed garlic and soy sauce.

Sauces & Dressings

White Sauces

Brown Sauces

Butter Sauces

Mayonnaise

Dressings

Roux-based Sauces

Equal amounts of flour and butter or oil are cooked and used to thicken many sauces. The liquid that is added to make the sauce is milk for a white sauce, infused milk for a *béchamel* and stock for a *velouté*. The term *roux* in French means russet brown and refers generally to the mixture's colour.

Making a White Sauce

For a pouring sauce, use 15 g each butter and flour to 300 ml milk, for a coating sauce, 22 g each butter and flour. Cook flour just long enough to burst the starch grains and avoid a raw taste. To prevent lumps and give an even colour, stir roux constantly over the entire base of pan.

1 Add flour to melted butter. Stir with a wooden spoon over a low heat to create a white roux, 1–2 minutes.

2 Remove pan from heat. Gradually add hot milk, beating constantly to blend it with the roux.

3 Bring to the boil, stirring constantly. Lower the heat and simmer until the sauce reaches the desired thickness.

Infusing Milk

A classic béchamel sauce is simply a white sauce made with milk that has been infused with flavourings. To be absolutely correct, the flavourings should be onion, cloves, bay leaves, freshly grated nutmeg and salt and pepper. There are, however, many variations on the basic sauce.

1 Heat milk and flavourings, stirring occasionally. Remove from the heat. Cover with a plate and let stand for 10 minutes.

2 Strain the infused milk through a sieve. Discard the flavourings. Add hot infused milk to roux, as in step 2, above.

Trick of the Trade

Preventing a Skin Forming
Cover sauce with cling film or buttered greaseproof paper, or do the following.

Rub the surface of warm sauce with a knob of butter to form a coating. Stir in before reheating.

Types of Roux

Roux are cooked for different periods of time depending on the colour required.

White roux: Used to make white and béchamel sauces, this is cooked for 1–2 minutes – long enough for the floury taste to disappear but not take on colour.
Blond roux: This forms the basis of a *velouté* sauce, to which a white stock, such as chicken, veal or fish (see pages 16–17) is added. Cooked for 2–3 minutes, it is a light golden colour.
Brown *(brun)* roux: With its full, rich flavour, this is the base for the classic Freanch *sauce espagnole*. The roux is cooked over a low heat until it is brown in colour, about 5 minutes. The roux used in gumbo (see page 28), a New Orleans speciality, is cooked for at least 15 minutes until nut-brown.

What's in a Name?

Béchamel sauce owes its name to Louis de Béchameil, major domo to Louis XIV. It is unlikely that the aristocrat created the recipe himself, more likely it was devised by one of the king's cooks, then dedicated to Béchameil.

The original sauce paired vast quantities of cream with a thick velouté; today's version is prepared by adding milk to roux.

Making a Veloute Sauce

One of the basic white sauces, a velouté sauce is also the basis for numerous others. After cooking a blond roux and adding a well-flavoured stock, the sauce is skimmed to produce the desired velvety consistency. Use 50 g each butter and flour to 1 litre stock.

1 Add flour to melted butter. Stir with a wooden spoon over a low heat to create a blond roux, 2–3 minutes.

2 Remove from the heat and let cool. Stirring constantly, gradually add hot chicken, veal or fish stock.

3 Bring to the boil, stirring constantly, then lower the heat and simmer, skimming frequently, 10–15 minutes.

Flavouring a Veloute Sauce

There are many classic French recipes based on velouté (see box, right). Some are very complicated and best left to the professional chef. The sauces shown here are simplified versions that can be made quickly and easily at home.

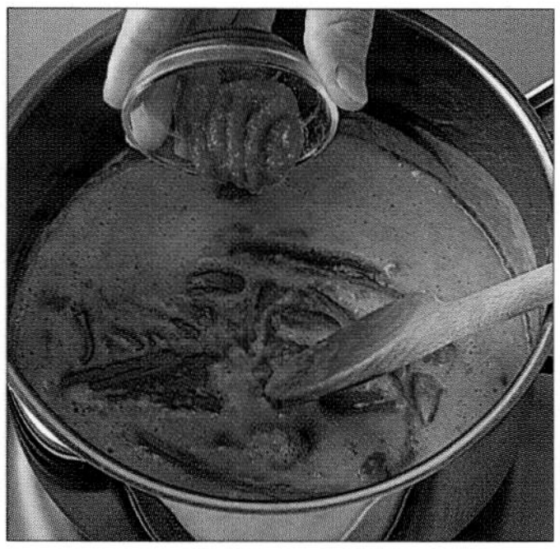

Tomato blush
Cook 2–3 tbsp tomato purée with the roux; add finely chopped tomatoes at the end.

Mock meuniere
Add 3 tbsp lemon juice and 2 tbsp chopped fresh parsley to the sauce before serving.

Sunny citrus
Add 200 ml freshly squeezed orange juice after the stock has been added to the roux.

Tomato

Lemon and parsley

Orange

Trick of the Trade

Correcting a Lumpy Sauce

A sauce that has not been stirred sufficiently may develop lumps.

Pour sauce into a bowl. Whisk with a balloon whisk until smooth. Return to pan; reheat.

Strain sauce through a fine conical sieve held over a bowl. Return to pan; reheat.

What's in a Name?

In classic French cuisine there are many sauces with unusual names; velouté sauces are no exception.

Sauce allemande: Made with veal stock and enriched with egg yolks.
Sauce aurore: Fish velouté, tinted pink with tomato purée.
Sauce cardinale: Made red with lobster coral, enriched with cream and spiced with cayenne.
Sauce poulette: Sauce Allemande with mushroom stock, lemon juice and chopped parsley.
Sauce nantua: Made with crayfish, cream and brandy.

BROWN SAUCES

Generally served with roast meat or game, the basis of any brown sauce is a good homemade brown beef or veal stock; for a rich colour and flavour, this is absolutely essential. A variety of flavouring ingredients, such as finely chopped vegetables, Worcestershire sauce, wine, mustard and tomato purée, can enhance the basic recipe.

THICKENING AGENTS

Use one of the following to thicken a basic brown sauce instead of arrowroot:

- Cornflour.
- Egg yolk and cream liaison.
- Finely chopped foie gras.
- Kneaded butter (see page 128).
- Potato starch.

WHAT'S IN A NAME?

ESPAGNOLE: This classic sauce has its roots in 18th-century French kitchens. It is a complex sauce that traditionally contained Bayonne ham and partridge, and often took several days to complete, although today, a rich meat stock serves to give espagnole its fine rich flavour. Careful skimming or straining is needed to produce its characteristic glossy finish.

DEMI-GLACE: There are different opinions as to what this is made of, how concentrated it should be, or if it is a sauce or a base for other sauces. Some professional chefs use brown meat stock with Madeira, others use white meat stock and wine. The result is a very rich brown sauce that is based on an Espagnole sauce, but is thick enough to coat the back of a spoon. To intensify the flavour of a demi-glace, a little meat glaze is often added.

MAKING A BASIC BROWN SAUCE

As few stocks have sufficient body, it is usually necessary to reduce them until concentrated, rich and dark. Then, instead of a roux, thicken with arrowroot as shown here, or another thickening agent (see box, left). Whatever your choice, it must be whisked in gradually to prevent lumps forming. The quantities given here will make about 750 ml brown sauce.

1 Boil 1 litre brown beef or veal stock (see page 16) for 15–20 minutes until it is reduced and its flavour has become concentrated.

2 Slake $2\frac{1}{2}$ tbsp arrowroot to a paste with 120 ml cold water. Pour into boiling stock, whisking constantly with a balloon whisk.

3 Boil the sauce until thickened, then remove the pan from the heat and skim the sauce with a slotted spoon to remove impurities.

FLAVOURING A BROWN SAUCE

Once the sauce has thickened and been skimmed (see step 3, above), you can add liquid flavourings, such as the Madeira shown here, or wine or Worcestershire sauce. Solid additions such as chopped onions, herbs or bone marrow, can also be included. To prepare marrow before adding it to the sauce, poach a marrow bone in water for 2 minutes, then drain. When cooked in the sauce, the marrow will melt.

USING LIQUIDS
Add about 75 ml liquid flavouring to 750 ml sauce. Stir well to combine, and simmer for 2 minutes.

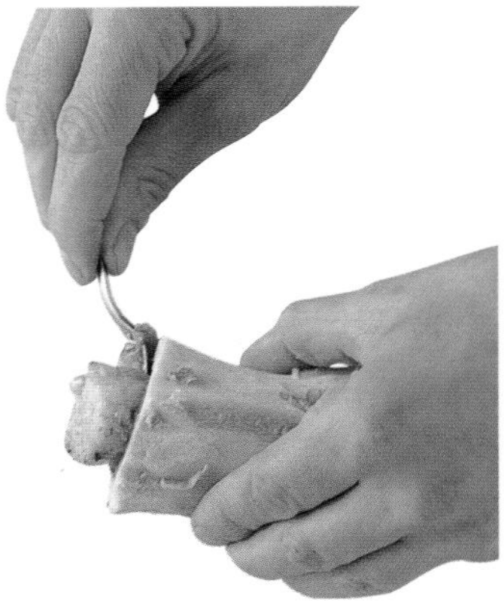

USING POACHED MARROW
Scoop out the marrow from the poached bone with a spoon. Add to the sauce and simmer, stirring, 5 minutes.

Making an Espagnole Sauce

The Carême classic involves many laborious procedures. This extremely simple contemporary version uses just three ingredients – a basic brown sauce, mushrooms and tomato purée. Skimming the sauce helps make it glossy.

1 Heat 750 ml brown sauce (see opposite page) over a moderate heat until simmering and add 150 g finely chopped mushrooms. Stir until well combined.

2 Add 1 tbsp tomato purée and stir until evenly blended into the sauce, then continue simmering over a low heat.

3 Simmer for a total of 15 minutes, skimming often. Strain before using.

What's in a Name?

Espagnole sauce is the base for these sauces, used frequently in classic French cuisine.

Sauce bretonne: Onion, butter, dry white wine, tomato sauce or tomato purée, garlic, parsley.
Sauce charcutiere: Dry white wine, shallots, gherkins, Dijon mustard.
Sauce chasseur: Shallots, butter, mushrooms, dry white wine, tomato sauce, parsley.
Sauce diable: Dry white wine, white wine vinegar, shallots, tomato purée, cayenne.
Sauce perigueux: Truffle juice, diced truffles, Madeira, butter.
Sauce poivrade: Onion, carrot and celery *mirepoix*, dry white wine, vinegar crushed peppercorns, butter.
Sauce robert: Onion, butter, dry white wine, white wine vinegar, Dijon mustard.

Trick of the Trade

Keeping a Brown Sauce Hot

If not serving a brown sauce immediately, this is the best way to prevent a skin forming on top.

Half fill a roasting tin with boiling water. Place the pan of sauce in the roasting tin and stir occasionally to keep it smooth.

Making Chaudfroid

This classic French technique takes its name from the fact that cold food is coated in a cooled cooked sauce, which is then chilled and served cold. Use a béchamel sauce (see page 222) for eggs and fish, or a reduced brown meat stock (see page 16) and liquid aspic (see page 19) for duck, game and red meats. Once set, the chaudfroid can be decorated (see page 105).

Adding aspic
Simmer 500 ml reduced stock, then whisk in 250 ml seasoned liquid aspic until well blended. Leave until cool, but not set.

Coating
Ladle chaudfroid over duck breast slices on a rack set over a dish. Chill until set, then repeat 3-4 times.

Butter Sauces

Light, butter-based sauces, such as hollandaise and béarnaise, rely on an emulsion of egg yolk and butter. The exception to these is white butter sauce, which uses cream. Serve these sauces freshly made, while still warm.

What's in a name?

Hollandaise, famed for serving with fresh asparagus and topping eggs Benedict, a New York breakfast speciality, hails not from Holland but rather from France, where it is sometimes known as *sauce Isigny*, after the home town of France's finest butter.

The origins of béarnaise are somewhat clouded. A reference was made by Collinet in the 1830s to the sauce served at the Pavillon Henri IV, a restaurant in Saint-Germain-en-Laye, near Béarn, the birthplace of Henri IV. However, a similar recipe appears in *La Cuisine des Villes et des Campagnes*, published in 1818.

Additions to Hollandaise

By adding different flavouring ingredients to a basic hollandaise sauce, you can create many other classic sauces.

- Fold in 4 tbsp crème fraîche or lightly whipped double cream to make *sauce mousseline*.
- Stir in 1 tbsp Dijon mustard to make *sauce moutarde*.
- Add the blanched julienned zest of $\frac{1}{2}$ dessert or blood orange and a little of the juice to make *sauce maltaise*.
- Instead of clarified butter, use unsalted butter melted until it is nut-brown in colour; this will make *sauce noisette*.

Making Hollandaise

The technique shown here is very simple. The trick lies in the first step – whisking the egg yolks to the ribbon stage with water. After this, it is really easy to whisk in the clarified butter to make a thick emulsion. A double boiler is not necessary, but a heavy-based saucepan is essential.

By Hand

1 Whisk 3 egg yolks and 3 tbsp hot water to the ribbon stage over a very low heat, about 3 minutes.

2 Add 175 g lukewarm clarified unsalted butter a little at a time, whisking vigorously after each addition.

3 Gradually whisk in the strained juice of $\frac{1}{2}$ lemon. Add salt and white pepper to taste. Makes about 250 ml.

By Machine

Put egg yolks and water in warmed, dry bowl of a food processor fitted with the metal blade. Turn on the machine; add lukewarm clarified butter in a thin stream. Finally, add lemon juice and seasonings.

Trick of the Trade

Fixing Hollandaise and Bearnaise

These butter sauces separate or curdle if the pan is too hot, the butter is added too quickly, or the finished sauce left to stand too long. Here are two remedies.

With the pan off the heat, add an ice cube; whisk quickly, drawing in the sauce as it melts.

Whisk 1 egg yolk and 1 tbsp hot water in a bowl over a *bain marie*; slowly whisk in curdled hollandaise.

Making Bearnaise

The flavour of hollandaise is mild and delicate; its sister sauce, béarnaise, is strong and pungent, yet they both share the same velvety texture. The pungency of béarnaise comes from the reduction of strong-flavoured ingredients – black peppercorns, shallot, tarragon and red wine vinegar, plus a final seasoning of cayenne pepper.

1 Boil the peppercorns, shallot, tarragon and wine vinegar until reduced.

2 Whisk the egg yolks and reduction over a very low heat to the ribbon stage.

3 Add the clarified butter a little at a time, whisking vigorously after each addition.

Bearnaise Sauce

4 black peppercorns, crushed
1 large shallot, finely chopped
2 tbsp chopped fresh tarragon
3 tbsp red wine vinegar
3 egg yolks
175 g unsalted butter, clarified
Salt and cayenne pepper

Boil the peppercorns, shallot, tarragon and vinegar in a heavy pan until reduced by one-third. Remove from the heat and add the egg yolks. Return to a very low heat, whisk for 3 minutes, then whisk in the butter a little at a time. Add salt and cayenne to taste. Makes about 250 ml.

Beurre Blanc

Translated from the French as white butter, this rich sauce is made with the same reduction as the béarnaise sauce above, but crème fraîche is added instead of egg yolks to stabilize the sauce, then it is mounted with butter (see box, right). When thick and creamy, taste and add seasonings. Beurre blanc should always be prepared just before serving.

1 Boil the ingredients as in step 1 above, then add 175 ml crème fraîche and reduce by about one-third.

2 Remove from the heat and whisk in 85 g chilled unsalted butter, a piece at a time. Makes about 250 ml.

Mounting a Sauce with Butter

This professional technique is used to give sauces a glossy, smooth sheen and a fresh, buttery flavour.

To "mount" a sauce, use cubes of chilled unsalted butter and add them off the heat – the warm sauce is enough to melt the butter. Beat each cube into the sauce until it is emulsified before adding the next.

Clarifying Butter

Also known as drawn butter, and ghee in Indian cooking, clarified butter is unsalted butter with its milk solids removed. The result is very pure, with many special uses (see box, right).

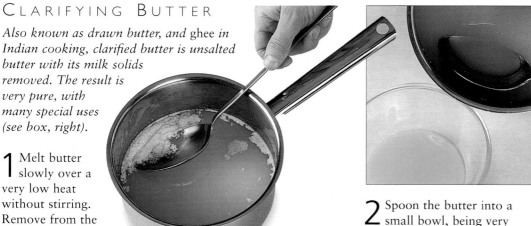

1 Melt butter slowly over a very low heat without stirring. Remove from the heat and skim the foam off the surface.

2 Spoon the butter into a small bowl, being very careful to leave the milky sediment behind in the pan.

Clarified Butter

Because the milk solids have been removed from clarified butter, not only does it keep longer without becoming rancid, it also has a high smoke point and can be heated to higher temperatures than ordinary butter without risk of burning. It is therefore ideal for sautéing and frying. In sauce-making, it is indispensible for giving a high gloss and fine flavour.

Making Mayonnaise

Soft and creamy mayonnaise – a simple emulsion of egg yolks, vinegar, seasonings, and oil – can be made equally successfully by hand or machine, whichever you prefer. Once you have mastered the technique, you will have the confidence to make it again and again. The secrets are to have all ingredients and equipment at room temperature, and not to rush.

MAYONNAISE

1 large egg yolk
1 tbsp Dijon mustard
Salt and freshly ground pepper
150 ml each olive and vegetable oil
About 2 tsp wine vinegar

Bring ingredients to room temperature. Whisk the egg yolk, mustard and seasonings in a bowl. Add the oil drop by drop at first, then in a thin, steady stream, whisking continuously until thickened and emulsified. Whisk in wine vinegar to taste. Store, covered, in the refrigerator for 3–4 days. Makes about 375 ml.

By Hand

Mixing by hand allows you to "feel" the mayonnaise as the oil is added and it begins to thicken. Pour in the oil very slowly, drop by drop at the beginning, until it begins to emulsify, then add the rest in a thin, steady stream. If added too quickly the mayonnaise will separate. Mustard and vinegar help stabilize and emulsify the mayonnaise.

1 Stand a deep bowl on a tea towel to make it stable. Whisk the egg yolk mixture until evenly combined.

2 Whisk in the olive oil a drop at a time until the mixture thickens. Add the remaining oil in a thin stream.

3 Add the vinegar a little at a time, whisking well after each addition to ensure it is completely mixed and emulsified. Check seasoning.

By Machine

Mayonnaise can be made very quickly and easily in a food processor. Although there is less risk of curdling and separating when making by machine – the speed helps to emulsify the egg and oil – a whole egg is used rather than just egg yolks, because the white is needed as a stabilizer. The combination of egg white and speed will give a fresher and lighter mayonnaise than that made by hand.

1 Put 1 tbsp Dijon mustard and 1 whole egg in the machine; work until blended.

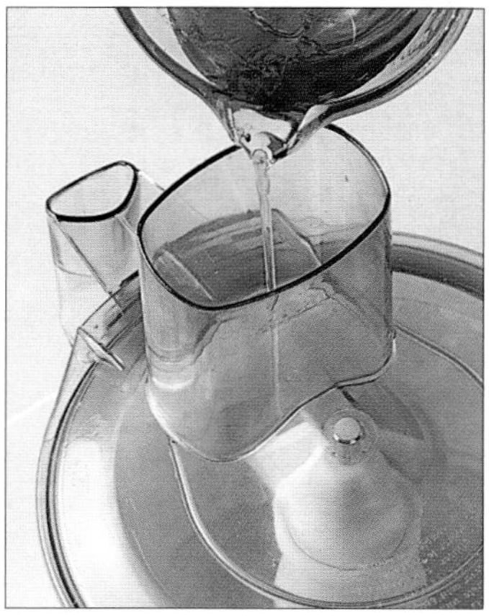

2 While machine is running, add 250 ml olive oil in a thin steady stream.

3 When the mixture begins to thicken, add 2 tsp vinegar and salt and pepper to taste. Work until blended.

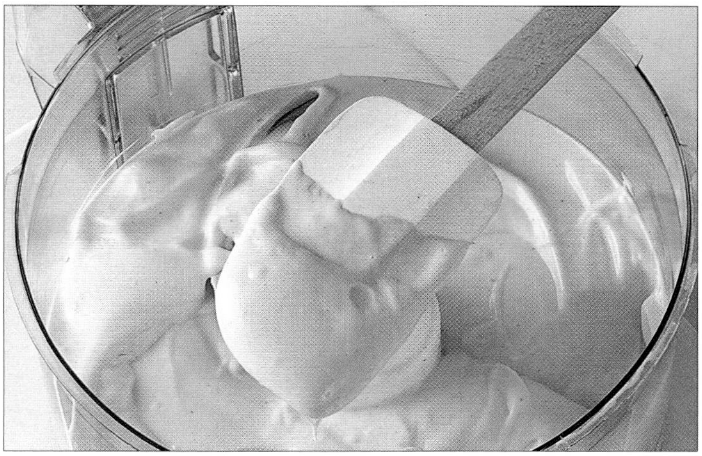

4 With the machine running, add 250 ml vegetable oil, increasing the flow once the mayonnaise becomes pale. Check seasoning. Makes about 650 ml.

Aioli

Chantilly

Andalouse

Herb

Flavoured Mayonnaise

Aioli: Substitute 4 crushed garlic cloves for the mustard and add ½ tsp coarse salt. Serve with cold fish and egg dishes or crudités.
Andalouse: Add 2 crushed garlic cloves and 2 tbsp finely diced red and green pepper. Serve with chargrilled fish or as a topping for burgers.
Chantilly: Fold in 4 tbsp stiffly whipped cream. Serve with cold vegetables or poached fish.
Herb mayonnaise: Stir in finely chopped fresh parsley, tarragon or chervil. Serve with barbecued poultry and meat.

TRICK OF THE TRADE

Fixing Mayonnaise

If the ingredients and equipment are too cold, or if the oil is added too quickly, the mayonnaise may separate and have a curdled appearance. Don't throw it away – it can be rescued by using one of the methods given here.

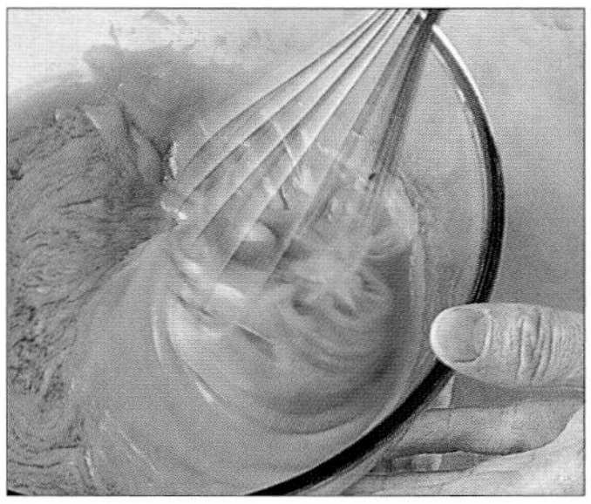

By hand
Mix 1 tbsp cold water or wine vinegar with a little of the mayonnaise, gradually combining more mayonnaise as you go.

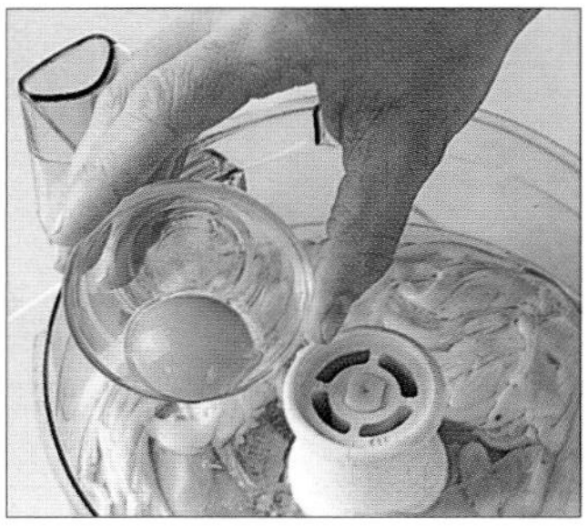

By machine
Add one egg yolk to the curdled mixture, then work the machine with the pulse button until the mayonnaise re-emulsifies.

DRESSINGS

A vital flavour enhancer for salads and many other dishes, dressings invariably contain oil, so be sure to use only the very best quality. Vinaigrette dressings are typically tossed with leafy green and mixed salads (pasta, pulses and seafood for instance); cooked dressings lend a rich taste and a velvety coating to vegetables as well as fish, poultry and meat.

TRICK OF THE TRADE

MATCHING OILS AND VINEGARS

Paired oils and vinegars should complement each other. The rich texture of extra-virgin olive oil, for example, is well-balanced by tart balsamic vinegar. Nut oils are good with fruit vinegars, such as raspberry, while chilli or herb oils benefit from the sharp bite of wine vinegar.

MAKING A VINAIGRETTE

This classic dressing traditionally uses three parts oil to one part vinegar. For different flavours, see box, left. It is important to have all the ingredients at room temperature to ensure they blend evenly. Whisk the vinaigrette as shown, or place in a screw-top jar and shake to blend. See page 184 for making a tossed salad.

1 Put 2 tbsp vinegar in a bowl with 2 tsp Dijon mustard, salt and freshly ground pepper. Whisk to combine and thicken.

2 Slowly add 6 tbsp oil, whisking constantly until the dressing is smooth, thickened and well blended. Check seasoning.

MAKING A COOKED DRESSING

Popular in America – where it was originally made by the Shakers and used for coleslaws and other raw vegetable salads – this simple creamy dressing combines a mixture of egg yolks and sour cream and uses flour to thicken. Although heat is essential to the sauce, to prevent curdling the heat must be very gentle, so the dressing must be cooked over a bain marie.

1 In a heatproof bowl, whisk together 2 egg yolks, 125 ml cider vinegar, 125 ml water and 30 g melted butter. Whisk until well blended, then whisk in 2 tbsp sour cream until smooth.

2 Set the bowl over a pan of simmering water. Add 1 tbsp dry mustard, 1 tbsp plain flour, 70 g caster sugar and ½ tsp salt. Whisk until the dressing is smooth, thickened and well blended.

Bread & Yeast Cookery

Making Bread
•
Italian Breads
•
Flat Breads
•
Enriched Breads
•
Quick Breads
•
Bread Preparations

MAKING BREAD

Making a loaf of leavened bread is one of the most rewarding tasks in the kitchen. Follow the techniques shown here, using the basic white loaf recipe (see box, opposite page), for perfect results every time.

DIFFERENT FLOURS

The flavour and texture of bread can be changed by using flour milled from different cereals and grains. Strong wheat flours, such as white and wholemeal, are used in most breads because of their high gluten content, which produces light loaves with a soft crumb. Denser-textured loaves are made by combining wheat flours with lower gluten flours. You can experiment by replacing some of the strong flour in your basic recipe with one of the following.

BARLEY FLOUR: Adds a creamy grey colour and "earthy" taste.
BRAN WHEAT: Rice and oat brans add a nutty flavour. To boost flavour, toast before use.
BUCKWHEAT FLOUR: Adds a dense texture and stong flavour.
BULGAR WHEAT: Often used in multi-grain loaves for its granular texture. Use in small amounts.
CORNMEAL: Gives a slightly grainy texture and yellow hue, but very little extra flavour.
OATS: Finely ground oats, oat flakes (rolled oats), and oat flour can be used. Adds a slightly grainy texture and oaty flavour.
RYE FLOUR: Must be combined with wheat flour because it contains no gluten. It is often mixed with wholemeal flour.
SOY FLOUR: This fine-textured flour contains no gluten, but it is used in bread doughs for extra flavour and nutrients.
SPELT FLOUR: High in gluten, spelt can be used on its own. It has a slightly sweet flavour and a golden-brown colour.

PREPARING YEAST

Fresh and dried yeast can be used interchangeably in recipes. As a guide, 15 g fresh yeast is equivalent to 1 tbsp dried yeast granules. Both will rise up to a maximum temperature of 30°C – any hotter and the yeast will be killed. Easy-blend yeast is treated differently.

FRESH
Mash in a bowl with a little of the measured warm water from the recipe. Cover and leave until bubbles appear on the surface.

DRIED
Sprinkle granules over a little of the measured warm water from the recipe and stir in ½ tsp sugar. Cover and leave until frothy.

EASY-BLEND
Add straight to the dry ingredients and stir to mix. Add the warm liquid and mix. Read packet; some brands need only one rising.

MAKING DOUGH BY HAND

All flours have different absorption rates, so you may have to add a little less or more liquid than specified in the recipe.

1 Sift flour and salt on to a work surface. Make a well in the centre. Add prepared yeast and remaining water; draw in flour to form dough.

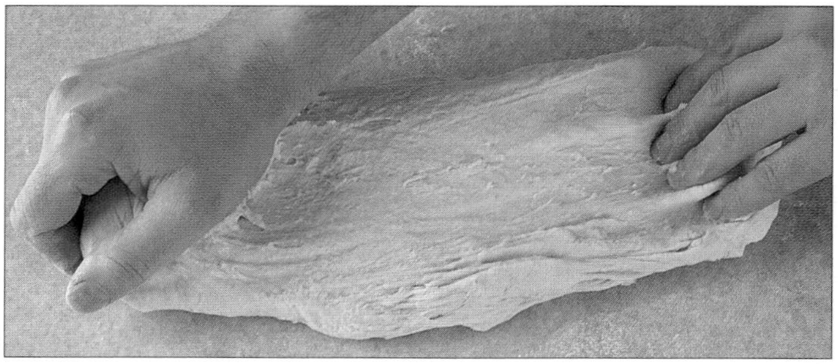

2 Put dough on a floured surface and push it away with one hand, stretching it back with the other.

3 Fold the dough back on itself and give it a quarter turn. Repeat kneading for 10 minutes until the dough is smooth and elastic. Shape it into a smooth ball.

Making Dough by Machine

Using a machine to mix and knead dough makes light work of making bread and saves time, especially when mixing dough for several loaves. A heavy-duty tabletop mixer fitted with a dough hook is ideal.

1 Sift flour and salt. Put three-quarters of the flour in the mixer bowl. Fit the beater and switch on the machine. Add prepared yeast and remaining warm water.

2 Turn off the machine and replace the beater with the dough hook. Add the remaining flour a little at a time, working the machine until a dough forms.

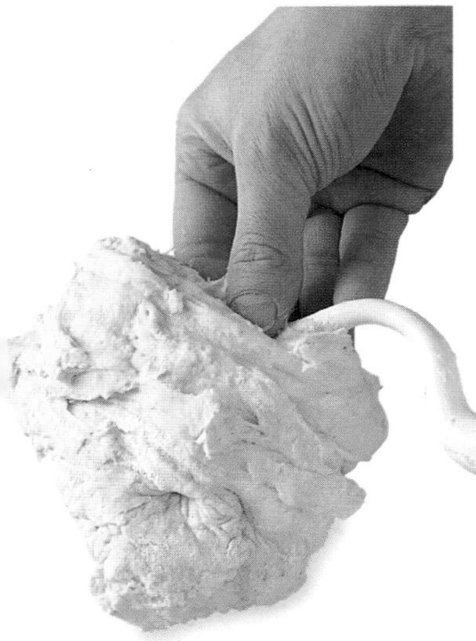

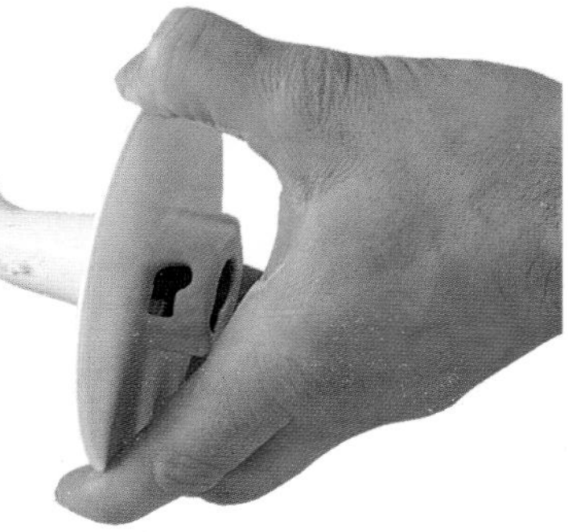

3 Continue until the dough comes away from the side of the bowl and forms a ball around the hook. Remove the hook and dough from mixer. Ease the dough off the hook, leaving it as clean as possible, and knead on a floured surface, 2–3 minutes. Shape into a smooth ball.

Basic White Loaf

15 g fresh yeast, crumbled, or
1 tbsp dried yeast
450 ml warm water
750 g strong plain white flour
2 tsp salt

Prepare the yeast and make and knead the dough by hand or machine. Put the dough in an oiled bowl, cover and let rise in a warm place until doubled in size, 1–2 hours. Punch down the dough and knead lightly, then cover and let rest for 5 minutes. Cut the dough in half. Shape each piece to fit a 900-g loaf tin (see page 234), then cover loosely with oiled cling film, and leave in a warm place for 30–45 minutes until the tins are just full. Glaze and top the loaf, if you like, then bake at 220°C for 20 minutes. Reduce to 180°C and bake for about 15 minutes. Turn out and cool on a rack. Makes two 900 g loaves.

Rising and Punching Down

After kneading, dough needs to be left to rise in a warm, draught-free place until doubled in size. It has risen enough when the impression of a finger pressed into it remains. After rising, the dough is punched down and lightly kneaded again then left to rest for 5 minutes before shaping (see page 234).

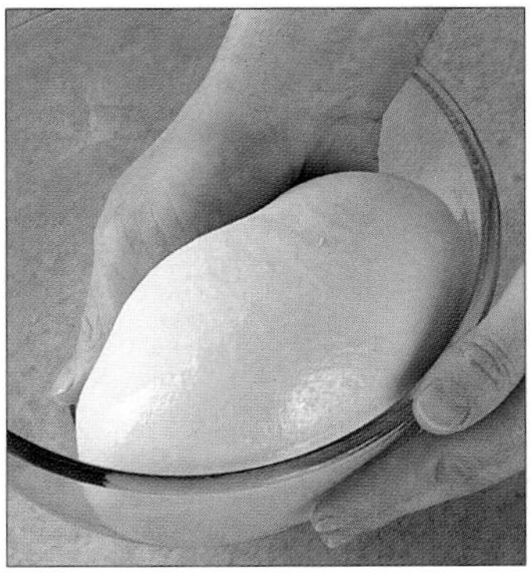

1 To prevent a crust forming, roll the ball of kneaded dough in a lightly oiled bowl. Cover with a damp tea towel to keep dough moist.

2 Let dough stand in a warm place until it expands to double its size, 1–2 hours. If left in a cooler place, it will take longer.

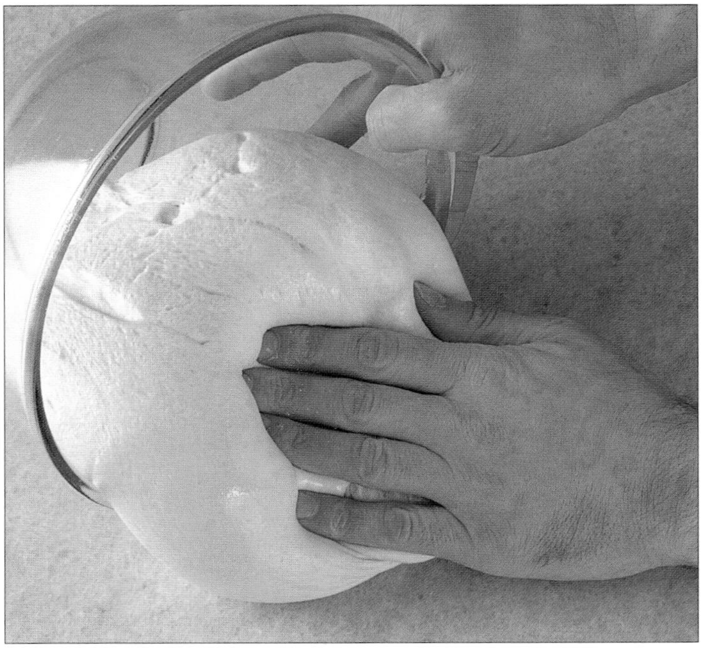

3 Punch the dough with your fist, then turn out on a floured surface. Knead for 2–3 minutes. Punching and kneading distributes the air so the loaf rises evenly and has a soft crumb.

GLAZES

Loaves and rolls can have shiny or matt finishes and thick or thin crusts, depending on the glaze and when it is applied. Do not brush too heavily or the dough will deflate, and do not let the glaze for a loaf baked in a tin seep into the tin, or the loaf will stick and rise unevenly.

- Give bread a golden, shiny finish by brushing it before baking with egg wash (see page 31). Brush again 10 minutes before the end of baking.
- Brush top of bread before baking with milk for a light brown finish and a soft crust.
- Brush baked bread with butter after turning it on to the rack, cover with a tea towel and let cool. This makes a soft crust.
- Brush bread with olive oil before and during baking for a matt finish and soft crust. This is ideal for country-style loaves.

TOPPINGS

Delicate toppings, such as poppy seeds, adhere to dough when lightly pressed. Heavier toppings need a glaze in order to adhere.

- Suitable seeds include fennel, caraway, poppy, sesame and sunflower.
- Sprinkle breads containing oat or barley flour with flakes of the same.
- Chopped pecans, walnuts and hazelnuts make flavourful toppings. Watch carefully or they may burn.
- Finely grate Cheddar or Gruyère cheese over the dough before baking.
- Lightly dust a risen loaf with plain or wholemeal flour for a country-style look.

SHAPING DOUGH

Once the dough has briefly rested it is ready to be shaped for baking. Choose from the traditional loaf shape baked in a tin or freeform shapes placed on floured baking sheets. Dinner rolls are another option (see opposite page).

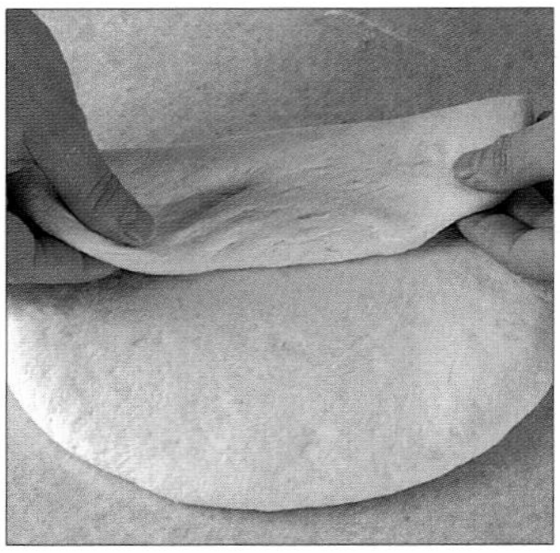

SHAPING FOR A LOAF TIN
Pat dough into an oval. Bring one short side to the centre, then the other. Place join-side down in greased tin.

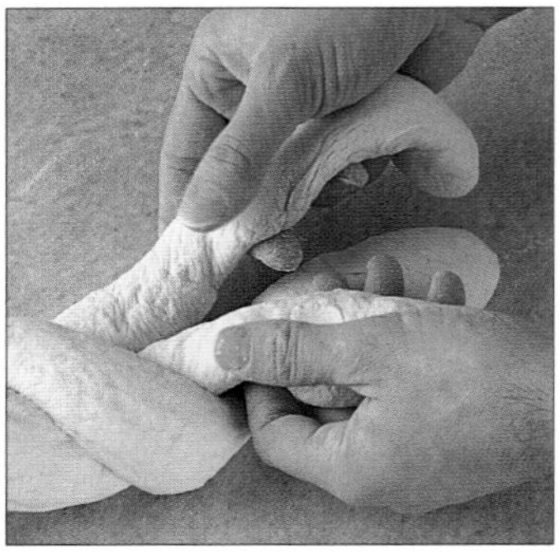

PLAITED LOAF
For an even shape, plait from the centre of the ropes and work towards one end, then the other. Pinch ends to secure.

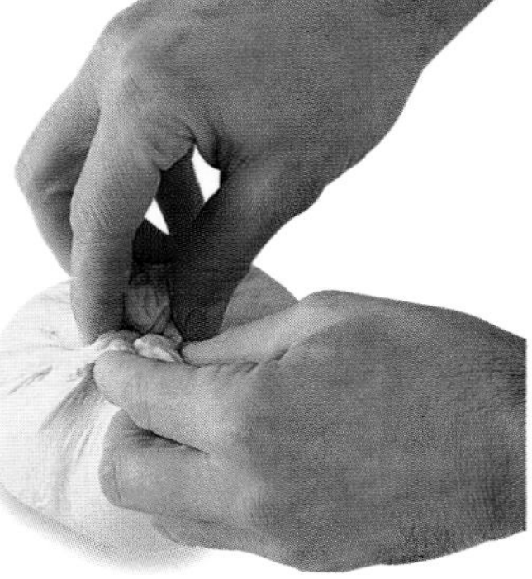

PLAIN ROUND LOAF
Pull the edges of a smooth ball up to meet on top. Pinch the edges to seal and turn the loaf over.

FINISHING LOAVES

Bread can be baked with just a light sprinkling of flour on top, but most breads are finished with a glaze or topping – these can be applied before or after baking (see boxes, left). Another finishing touch is to cut the dough so that it opens out attractively during baking. If several finishes are used, the order to follow is glazing, topping and cutting.

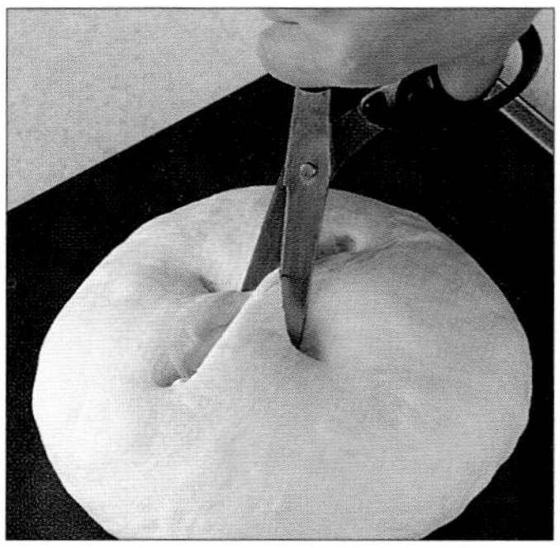

CRISS-CROSS TOP
Cut two snips in the top to form a large X, using kitchen scissors. Each cut should be about 1 cm deep.

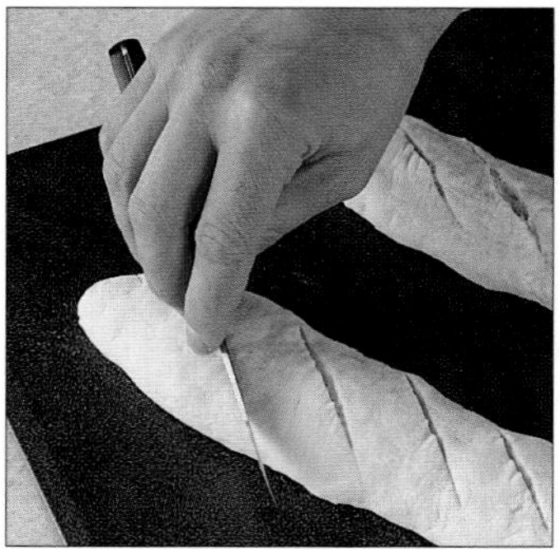

SLASHING
Make slashes 5 mm deep and 4 cm apart, using a small knife. Make smooth strokes to avoid dragging the dough.

GLAZING
Lightly brush the surface with glaze of your choice (see box, above left). Two thin coats are better than one thick one.

TESTING FOR DONENESS

Bread that is not completely baked has an unpleasant, doughy flavour. Exact baking times are difficult, so each loaf should be tested before it is left to cool.

Take the loaf out of its tin, or off the baking sheet, and hold it in a folded tea towel. Tap the bottom with your knuckles. If the loaf is baked through, it will sound hollow. If it sounds dull, return it to the oven for 5 minutes, then test again. At this stage it is not necessary to put loaves back in their tins. Cool the bread on a rack.

Forming Dough into Rolls

It is easy to transform basic bread dough into attractive dinner rolls in a variety of shapes. The rolls can be as simple as balls to more complicated individual plaits. Shape the rolls after the dough has been punched down and rested (see page 233). Use 30–60 g dough for each roll. Place them well apart on lightly floured baking sheets, giving room for them to double in size.

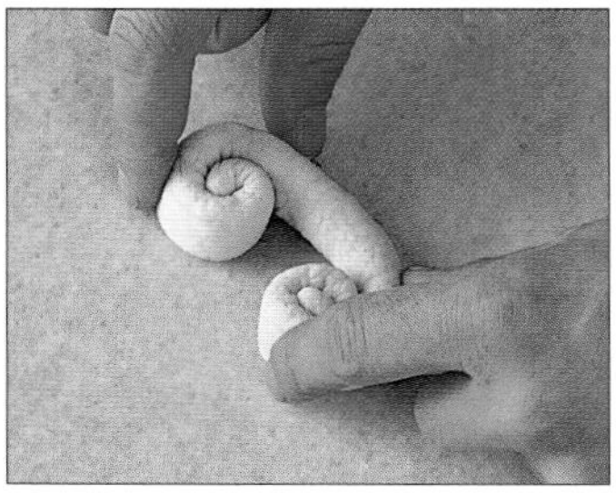

Palmier
Roll a piece of dough into a rope of even width. Coil each end of the rope into the centre to form spirals.

Tourelle
Cut out three rounds of dough, each one smaller than the other. Place the rounds on top of each other.

Snail
Roll a piece of dough into a long rope of even width. Starting at one end, wind the rope into a flat spiral.

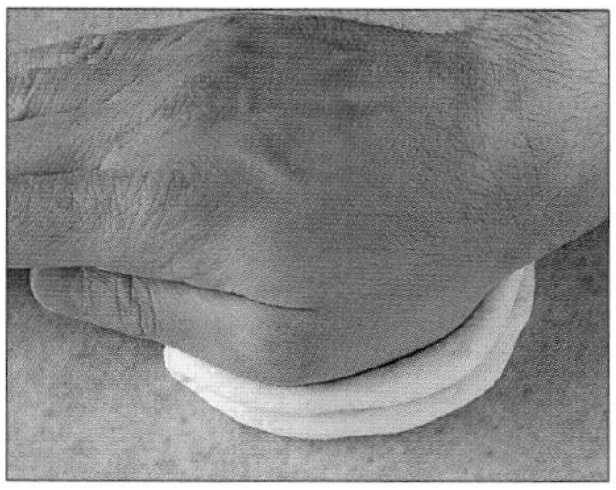

Parker house
Press dough into a 6.25 cm round. Make a crease in the centre with a floured spoon handle, fold over and press firmly to seal.

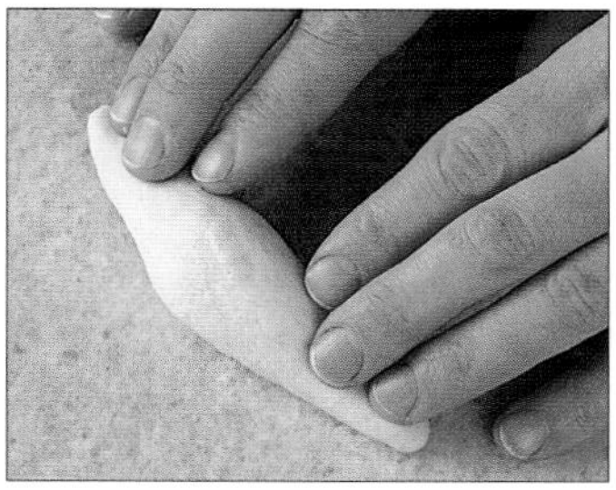

Harvest roll
Form 7-cm lengths of dough into long rolls, each slightly wider in the centre than at the ends. Make three snips along the top.

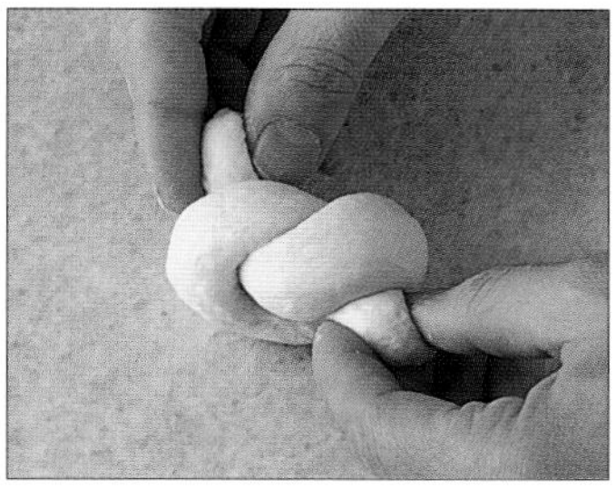

Baker's knot
Roll a piece of dough into a 15-cm long rope. Tie into a knot, pulling each end through the loop.

What's in a name?

Puffy and butter-rich and unusually shaped, Parker House rolls are named after Harvey Parker, the mid-eighteenth century owner of an eponymous hotel in Boston. Legend has it that the hotel's temperamental chef was so irritated with a guest that he lost his concentration and put some unfinished rolls in the oven. These were the result, and they have been an American classic ever since. Recipes for the dough and buttery glaze vary from one cook to another, but the shape is traditional and remains the same.

Trick of the trade

Dividing Dough Equally
Professional bakers weigh each piece of dough to ensure rolls in a batch are the same for even baking.

To divide dough equally without a weighing scale, roll it into a long rope. Cut it in half, then cut each piece in half again. Continue this technique until you have the desired number of pieces.

Bruschetta & Crostini

These Italian toasts make excellent first courses and delicious snacks. Prepare the bruschetta or the slightly thinner crostini following the instructions on page 246, using slices of baguette or halved slices of ciabatta. Each topping below is enough for six. Serve a selection, allowing two or three for each person.

Tiger Prawn and Cherry Tomato

3 red cherry tomatoes, sliced

3 yellow cherry tomatoes, sliced

Olive oil

Salt and freshly ground pepper

6 cooked tiger prawns, peeled and deveined

Fresh coriander leaves, to garnish

Arrange the tomato slices on the bruschetta or crostini, drizzle with a little olive oil and sprinkle with salt and pepper to taste. Top with the prawns and garnish with coriander leaves.

Walnut, Pear and Goat's Cheese

60 g soft goat's cheese

1 small bunch of rocket

1 pear, cored and thinly sliced lengthwise

A little fresh lemon juice

Freshly ground pepper

Walnut halves

Spread a little goat's cheese on each bruschetta or crostini. Cover the cheese with a few rocket leaves and arrange pear slices on top. Sprinkle with lemon juice and pepper and add a walnut half to each.

Parma Ham and Fig

6 slices of Parma ham

2 ripe but firm figs, cut lengthwise into thin wedges

Freshly ground pepper

Fresh chives, to garnish

Place a slice of Parma ham on each bruschetta or crostini, folding the ham slightly. Arrange fig wedges on top and sprinkle with pepper. Garnish with long stems of fresh chive.

Chargrilled Vegetable and Pine Nut

1 red pepper

1 yellow pepper

1 small red onion, quartered

Olive oil

Stoned black olives

30 g pine nuts, toasted

TO GARNISH

Fresh basil leaves

Parmesan curls (see box, left)

Roast the peppers and onion (see page 189). Cut the peppers into thin strips, discarding the cores and seeds. Arrange on the bruschetta or crostini, fanning the onion wedges slightly. Drizzle with a little olive oil. Finish with olives, pine nuts, basil and Parmesan curls.

Making Parmesan Curls

Thin shavings of fresh Parmesan cheese make an attractive and tasty garnish for bruschetta and crostini as well as for salads, pasta dishes and risottos. For best results, use fresh Parmesan at room temperature. The dry, crumbly type of Parmesan will not curl. Pecorino romana can also be used.

Cut a curved triangular shape out of one of the long sides of a piece of Parmesan, using a small sharp knife.

Shave curls out of the indentation with a vegetable peeler. For larger curls, simply increase the size of the triangle.

ITALIAN BREADS

Justly famous the world over for their wonderful flavours and variety, Italian breads are made using the same techniques as basic loaves. Their individuality comes from the addition of traditional Italian ingredients.

BASIC PIZZA

175 g strong plain white flour
1/4 tsp salt
1 tsp easy-blend yeast
150 ml warm water
1 tbsp olive oil

Sift flour and salt into a bowl, stir in the yeast and make a well in the centre. Add warm water and oil and mix to a soft dough. Knead for 5 minutes until smooth and elastic. Cover and let rise, 1–1 1/2 hours. Punch down and knead for 2–3 minutes, then roll into a round on a lightly floured surface. Shape by rotating it between your hands until it is about 25 cm in diameter and 1 cm thick. Place on a lightly floured baking sheet. Cover with a topping of your choice, spread to within 1 cm of the edge. Bake at 220°C until the crust is golden, 15–20 minutes. Serves 4.

MAKING PIZZA

The dough for pizza is much the same as that for white bread, but the addition of olive oil gives the base its thin and crispy crust. Here easy-blend yeast is used for speed, with excellent results, but you can use fresh or dried yeast granules if you like.

1 Add the olive oil to warm water in the well. This will help the oil to blend in more easily and more thoroughly during mixing.

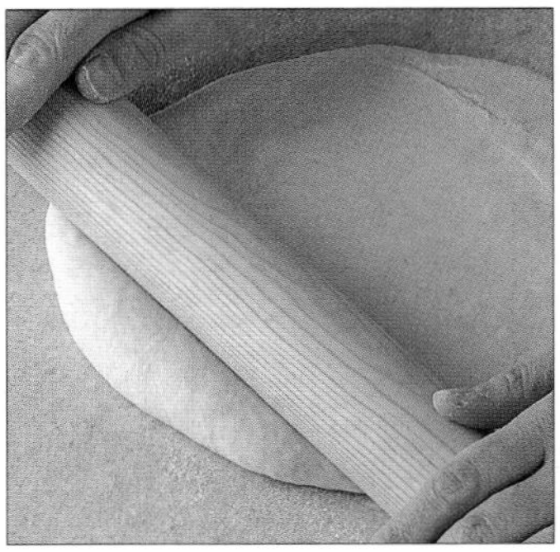

2 For even thickness, work from the centre of the dough to the outside when rolling into a round. Keep turning it as you roll.

3 Slap the dough back and forth with floured hands, rotating it until about 25 cm in diameter and 1 cm thick.

4 Arrange topping ingredients in a regular pattern so that they will cook evenly and look good on the finished pizza.

MAKING CALZONE

Pizza dough can be used for large or small calzone, *a folded pizza enclosing a filling. Cut two slits in the top to let the steam escape during baking.*

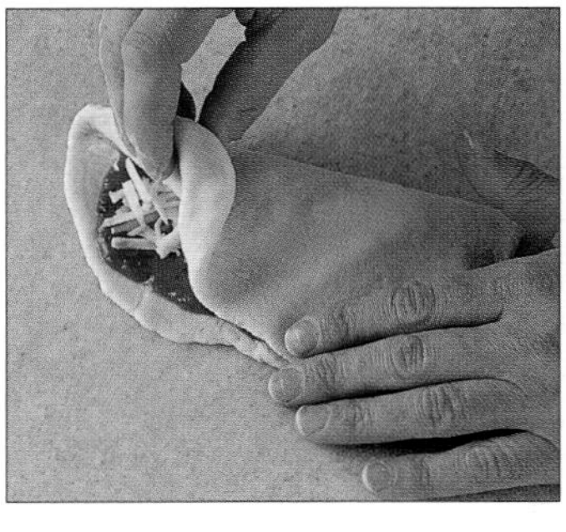

Put filling on half the dough. Moisten edge with water. Fold over plain half to enclose filling. Press edges to seal.

Making Fresh Rosemary Focaccia

Thicker than a pizza, this dimpled bread gets its name from the Latin word focus, *meaning "hearth", because it was originally baked on an open hearth. The dough (see box, right) is made in much the same way as a pizza, but it is enriched with more olive oil. It can be drizzled with another 2 tbsp oil just after baking.*

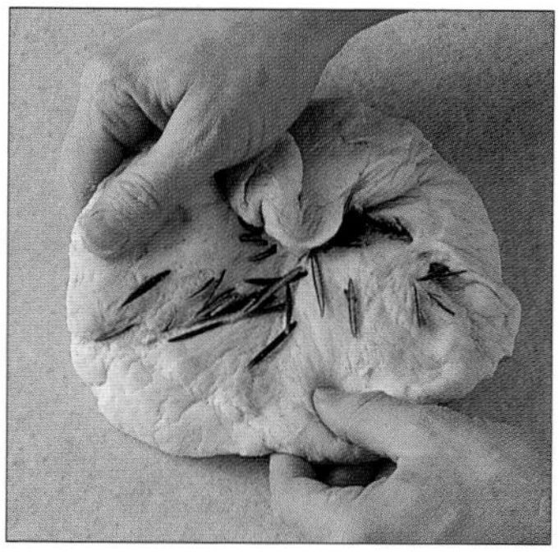

1 Punch down the dough and knead it for 2–3 minutes, working in 3 tbsp fresh rosemary leaves. Let rest for 5 minutes.

2 Pat dough into a floured Swiss roll tin with lightly floured fingers. Cover and let rise until doubled in size, 30–45 minutes.

3 Press your fingers into the dough, then sprinkle the focaccia with coarse sea salt. Bake at 220°C for 30–35 minutes.

FOCACCIA DOUGH

25 g fresh yeast, crumbled, or 1⅔ tbsp dried yeast granules and ½ tsp sugar
300 ml warm water
900 g strong plain white flour
2 tsp salt
4 tbsp olive oil

Prepare the yeast (see page 232). Sift the flour and salt into a bowl and make a well in the centre. Add yeast, remaining water and olive oil. Mix to a dough. Knead the dough on a lightly floured surface for 10 minutes. Shape dough into a ball and roll in an oiled bowl. Cover with a damp tea towel and let rise at 30°C until doubled in size, 1–2 hours.

Making a Flavoured Ring

Italian bakers use focaccia dough (see box, above right) to make many different speciality breads, such as this ring stuffed with fragrant pesto. It can also be filled with any typical Italian ingredient (see box, right), cut into manageable-sized pieces. If you like, you can make your own pesto (see page 330) or use ready-made.

1 Punch down the dough. Knead for 2–3 minutes, then let rest for 5 minutes. Roll the dough into a 40- x 30-cm rectangle and spread the filling evenly over it, leaving a 1-cm border.

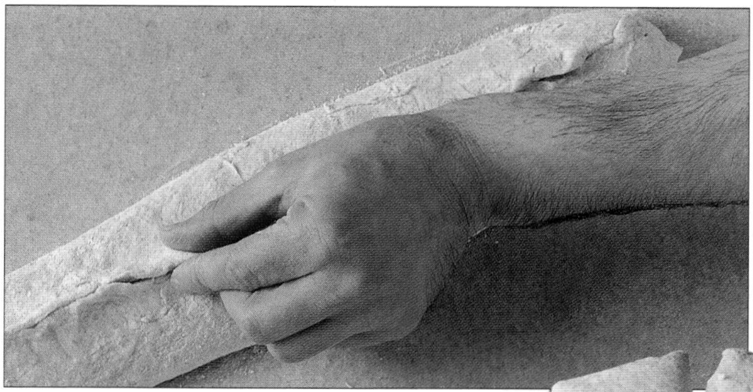

2 Starting from one long side, roll into a cylinder. Pinch the seam to seal, but not the ends. Transfer, seam-side down, to a floured baking sheet, shape into a ring and pinch ends to seal.

3 Slice the ring at 5-cm intervals to within 2 cm of the centre. Gently pull out each slice and twist it over on to one side to show the cut edge. Cover and let rise until doubled in size, 30–45 minutes. Bake at 190°C until golden, 30–40 minutes. Serve warm or cold.

ITALIAN FLAVOURINGS

Any of the flavourings below can be substituted for pesto as a filling for a flavoured bread ring.

- Chopped fresh sage, crushed garlic, coarse sea salt and virgin olive oil.
- Finely chopped black or green olives.
- Roughly chopped spicy salami or Parma ham.
- Chopped sun-dried tomatoes marinated in olive oil, shredded mozzarella and fresh basil.
- Sautéed onions and chopped fresh herbs.

Flat Breads

Made with very little or no yeast, these international breads are known collectively as flat breads because of their appearance. They vary in shapes and flavours and can be made with ordinary plain and wholemeal flour, unlike yeast breads, which need the gluten in strong wheat flour to rise.

Mexican Tortillas

175 g plain flour
½ tsp salt
2½ tbsp vegetable lard or solid shortening, diced
5 tbsp water

Mix flour and salt. Rub in lard. Fork in water to form a dough. Knead until smooth, 3 minutes. Divide into six. Let rest, loosely covered, for 30 minutes. Heat ungreased griddle until a splash of water sizzles on it. Roll out each round. Cook one at a time for 15–30 seconds each side. Serve at once or wrap in foil and keep warm in a low oven. Makes 6.

Making Flour Tortillas

Like most flat breads, Mexican tortillas are easy to make – as long as the lard is properly incorporated into the flour before the water is added. Gradually add the water until a soft dough is formed. You may need to add a little more – or even less – water, depending on the absorption of the flour. The final dough should be pliable and elastic but not sticky.

1 Roll out each tortilla, rotating the dough as you roll it with even pressure, working from the centre outwards. This makes it easier to form an even round.

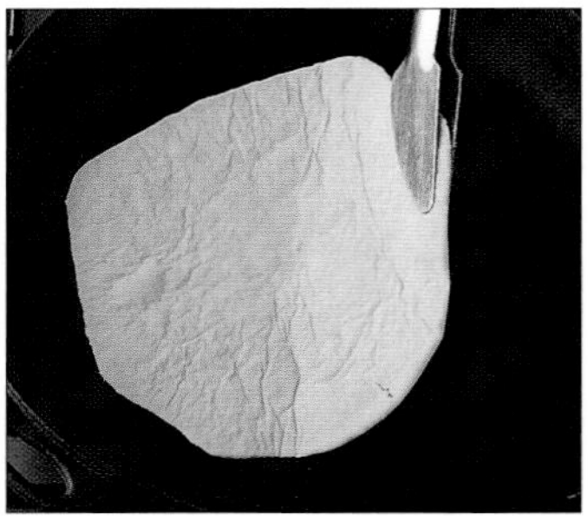

2 Cook the tortilla until the edges begin to curl and brown specks appear on the bottom, 15–30 seconds. Turn over with tongs and cook for a further 15–30 seconds.

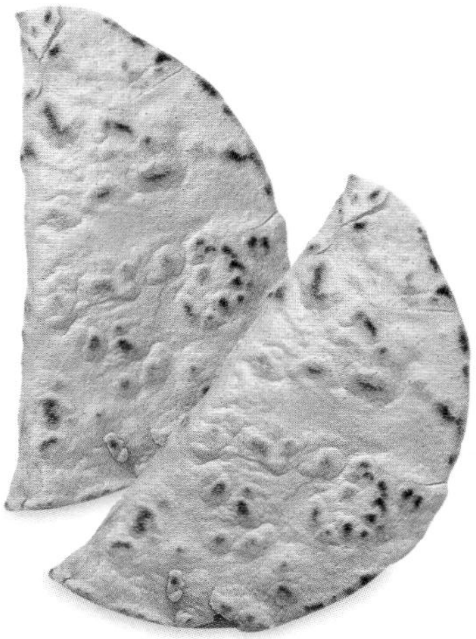

Dough for Chinese Pancakes

175 ml boiling water
250 g plain flour
1 tbsp dark sesame oil

Slowly pour water into a well in the flour; mix and cool. Knead on a floured surface for 5 minutes until smooth. Cover and let rest for 15 minutes. Divide dough into twelve. Roll each piece into a 7.5-cm round and cover with a damp cloth. Take two rounds, brush one side of one with sesame oil and place the other on top. Roll them out to a 12.5-cm pancake and cover again. Repeat with the other ten rounds to produce six pairs.

Making Chinese Pancakes

Paper thin, these are the traditional accompaniment to Oriental roast duck (see page 106). The dough for two pancakes is rolled out and cooked together to keep them moist, then separated while still warm. If the dough is dry, add a little extra boiling water. Do not roll the edges too thin or the pancakes will tear when separated.

1 Place one pair of pancakes in a very hot wok that has been lightly oiled. Cook for 15–30 seconds on both sides, turning with chopsticks.

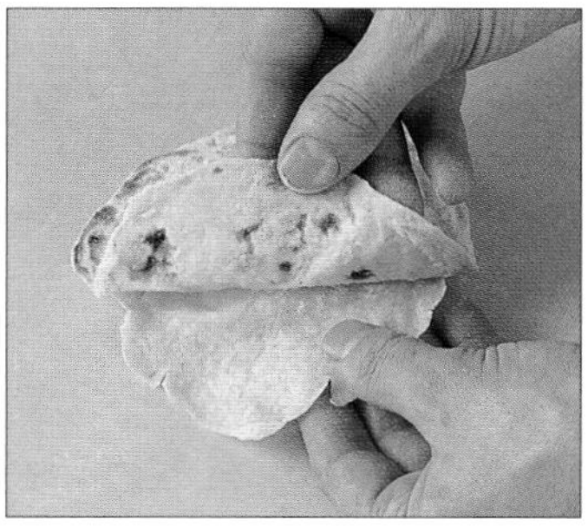

2 When the pancakes are blistered, remove them from the wok. While they are still warm, carefully peel them apart.

MAKING CHAPATIS

These thin Indian breads are dry-fried, then served with melted ghee or clarified butter (see page 227). Use a griddle or heavy frying pan for cooking and heat it until it is very hot to ensure the chapatis puff up and cook quickly.

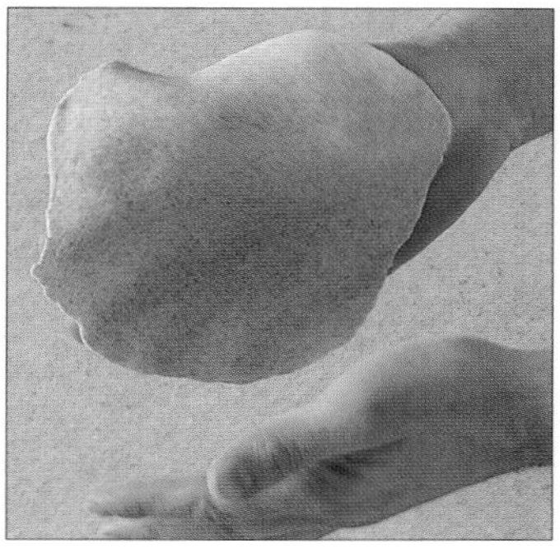

1 Slap the rolled-out dough back and forth between floured hands to stretch it. This will help to keep the dough supple.

2 Heat a griddle until very hot, slap the chapati on to it and cook for 30 seconds until brown specks appear on the bottom. Turn it over.

3 Cook the other side until puffed up and golden, 30–60 seconds, pressing with a fish slice to make sure it cooks evenly.

MAKING POORIS

Although they use the same dough as chapatis, pooris are smaller and more puffy because they are fried in hot oil rather than on a dry griddle. The dough for pooris can be enriched with the addition of 1 tbsp melted ghee or butter, if you like.

Heat 5 cm vegetable oil in a deep frying pan until hot. Add one poori and cook for about 10 seconds until it puffs up. Flip it over and press down with a spoon, then cook for 10 seconds until puffed up and golden. Drain well and serve at once.

DOUGH FOR INDIAN FLAT BREADS

225 g ata flour or wholemeal flour
About 150 ml lukewarm water

Put the flour in a bowl and make a well in the centre. Gradually add water to make a soft dough, if necessary adding extra water a tablespoon at a time towards the end. Turn the dough out on to a lightly floured surface and knead for about 8 minutes until smooth and elastic. Place the dough in a greased bowl and cover with a damp tea towel. Leave to rest for 30 minutes.

For chapatis and parathas, divide the dough into six equal pieces and shape each into a small ball. Roll balls on a lightly floured surface, then stretch them by slapping the dough back and forth between your hands to make 18-cm rounds. Keep covered with a damp cloth.

For pooris, divide the dough into eight equal pieces and roll each on a lightly floured surface into a 12.5-cm round. Keep covered with a cloth.

MAKING PARATHAS

These are the thickest and richest of the Indian flat breads. The same dough (see box, above right) is used as for chapatis and pooris, but melted ghee is spread over it before cooking.

1 Thinly spread about $1\frac{1}{2}$ tsp melted ghee or clarified butter over each round of dough.

2 Fold in the sides to make a square. Sprinkle with flour and roll out on a floured surface to an 18-cm square.

3 Slap the paratha on to a heated griddle. Brush with melted ghee or clarified butter and cook until brown patches appear. Turn over, brush again and cook until golden brown and puffed up into flaky layers. Eat hot, torn into pieces

ENRICHED BREADS

Butter and eggs are worked into the batters of these breads, resulting in more of a cake-like texture, a softer crust, and more flavour than in a basic bread made with only flour, yeast and water. The doughs for kugelhopf and brioche are very soft and require a special kneading technique. Egg-rich bagels on page 244 are dense, with a firm and shiny crust.

KUGELHOPF

250 ml milk
150 g unsalted butter, diced
1 tbsp sugar
20 g fresh yeast, crumbled
450 g strong plain white flour
1 tsp salt
3 eggs, beaten
About 7 walnut halves

Bring the milk just to the boil. Spoon 4 tbsp of the milk into a bowl and let cool slightly. Add the butter and sugar to the remaining milk in the pan and stir to melt. Prepare the yeast with the warm milk (see page 232). Sift the flour and salt into a large bowl and make a well in the centre. Add the yeast, eggs and cooled sweetened milk and mix to a dough. Beat the dough with your hand until elastic. Cover and let rise until doubled in size, 1-1½ hours.

Brush a 1-litre kugelhopf mould with melted butter, then chill in the freezer for about 10 minutes until the butter is firm. Brush with more melted butter to ensure an even coating and arrange the walnuts in the mould.

Punch down the dough, then put it into the mould. Cover and let rise for 30-40 minutes until just above the top of the mould. Bake at 190°C for 40–50 minutes until puffed, very brown and starting to come away from the side of the mould. Let cool in the tin for 5 minutes, then invert on to a rack. Serves 16.

MAKING KUGELHOPF

A speciality throughout Germany, Austria and the Alsace region of France, this cake-like bread is baked in a decorative mould of the same name. The essential techniques for making it are shown here, following the recipe given in the box, left.

1 Draw the flour gradually into the liquid ingredients in the well in the centre of bowl, working with your hands to make a very soft and sticky dough.

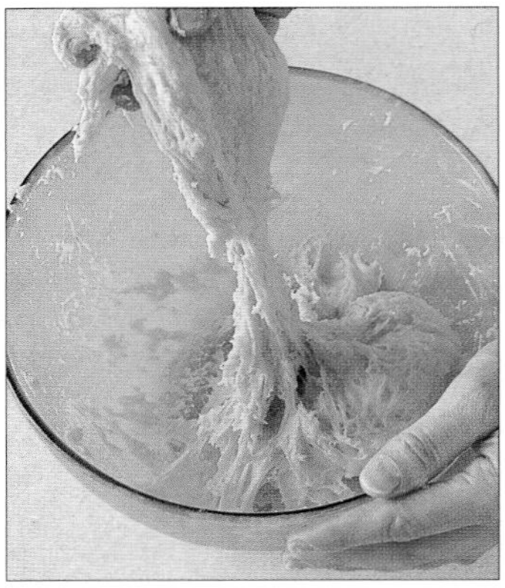

2 Beat the dough with one hand by lifting it and slapping it back into the bowl. Beat in this way for 5–7 minutes until the dough becomes elastic.

3 After the dough has risen, slap it down with your hand for 15–20 seconds – this will knock out all the air before the dough is put into the mould.

4 Arrange walnut halves, rounded-side down, in the depressions in the buttered mould. When the bread is turned out, the nuts will be the right way up.

5 Drop the dough into the mould, taking care not to dislodge the walnuts. Use a pastry scraper to push the dough into all the creases so the mould is evenly filled.

6 Let the kugelhopf cool in the tin for about 5 minutes before unmoulding. This will ensure that the nuts adhere to the bread rather than sticking to the tin.

MAKING BRIOCHE

One of the best loved – and richest – French breads, brioche is made with lavish amounts of butter and eggs. The result is a soft, fine-textured loaf with a distinctive buttery flavour. A special scalloped mould gives brioche its characteristic shape. Because the additional fat creates a very soft dough, brioche requires less liquid than non-enriched breads.

1 Slowly pour the egg and yeast mixture into the well in the centre of the flour, then gradually draw in the flour with your fingers.

2 Lift the dough and throw it down on a lightly floured surface. Repeat this technique until it will form a smooth ball, 8–10 minutes.

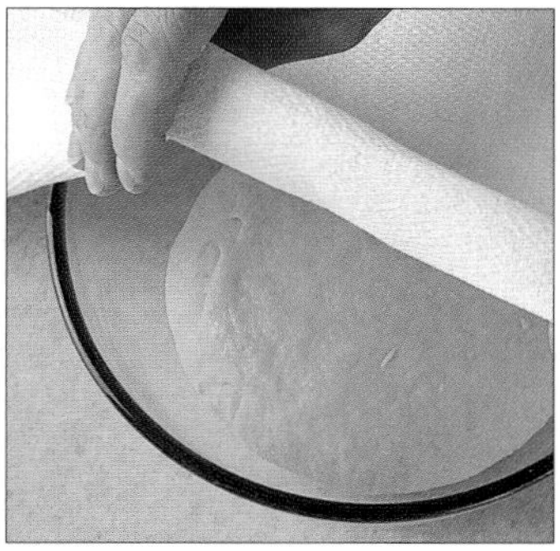

3 Turn the dough in oiled bowl until it is evenly coated. Keep the bowl covered with a damp tea towel while the dough rises.

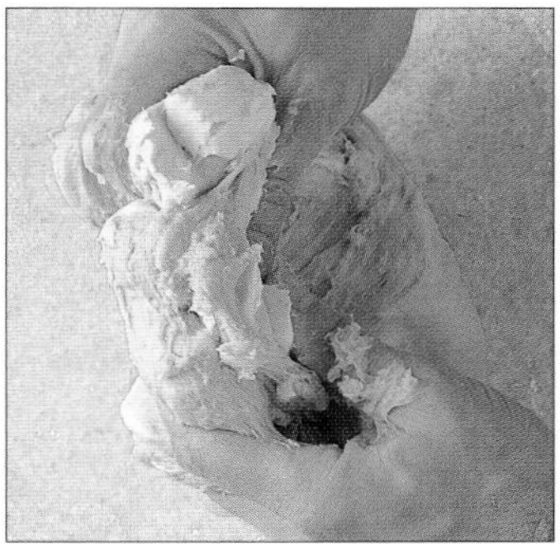

4 Place softened butter on top of punched-down dough. Pinch and squeeze the two of them together until evenly combined.

5 Push a floured forefinger almost all the way through the dough to the bottom of the mould. Rotate the finger to enlarge the hole.

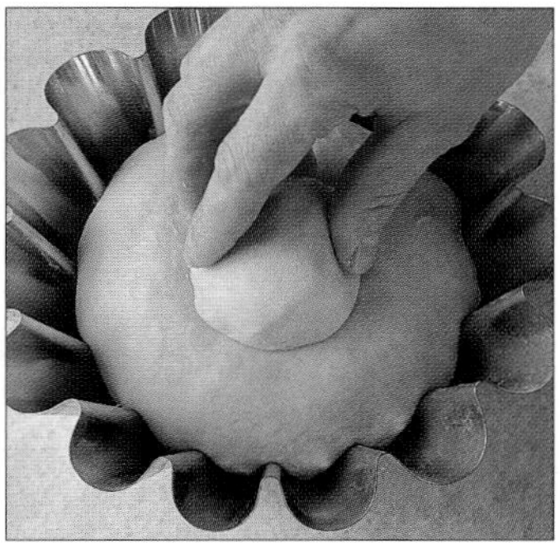

6 Push the teardrop shape, pointed-end down, into the hole with lightly floured fingers. Press down to seal. This will form the characteristic top-knot.

BRIOCHE A TETE

15 g fresh yeast, crumbled
2 tbsp warm milk
375 g stong plain white flour
2 tbsp sugar
1 1/2 tsp salt
6 eggs
175 g unsalted butter, softened

Prepare yeast with milk (see page 323). Sift dry ingredients on to work surface and make a well. Lightly beat 5 eggs, mix with the yeast and pour into the well. Draw in the flour to make a soft, sticky dough, then lift and throw it until it will form a smooth ball. Place in an oiled bowl and turn to coat. Cover and let rise until doubled in size, 1–1 1/2 hours.

Turn out the dough, punch down, cover and let rest for 5 minutes, then add the butter and knead for 3–5 minutes until smooth. Cover and let rest for 5 minutes. Liberally brush two 17.5-cm brioche moulds with melted butter.

Divide the dough in half and pinch one-quarter off each piece. Shape the small pieces into teardrops and the large ones into balls. Place the balls, seam-side down, in the moulds, make holes in the centres and insert the teardrops.

Cover and let rise until the moulds are almost full, about 45 minutes. Glaze with the remaining egg, then bake at 200°C, 25–30 minutes. Turn out and cool on a rack. Makes 2 large brioches.

BAGEL DOUGH

250 ml mixture of water and milk (in equal quantities)
15 g fresh yeast, crumbled
450 g strong plain white flour
2 tsp salt
1 tsp sugar
30 g butter, melted
1 egg, separated

Warm 4 tbsp of the milk mixture and use to prepare the yeast (see page 232). Mix the dry ingredients in a bowl and make a well in the centre. Add the yeast, the remaining liquid and the melted butter. Add the lightly beaten egg white and mix to a soft dough. Knead for 10 minutes until smooth and elastic.

Place the dough in a greased bowl and turn to coat the dough. Cover and let rise until doubled in size, about 1 hour.

Punch down the dough and divide it into 20 equal pieces on a lightly floured surface.

MAKING BAGELS

The dense, chewy texture of traditional Jewish bagels is developed by the unique technique of boiling or simmering the shaped dough before glazing and baking. The moisture prevents the crust from becoming too crisp in the oven.

1 Roll each piece of dough into a 15-cm rope on a lightly floured surface. Brush the ends of each rope with water and push together to make ring shapes, pressing gently to seal. Cover the rings with a damp tea towel and leave to rise for about 10 minutes.

2 Bring a large pan of water to the boil. Reduce the heat. Add the bagels in batches and poach them for about 15 seconds until they are puffed up.

3 Remove bagels with a slotted spoon, shaking it to remove excess moisture, then transfer bagels to a greased baking sheet. Glaze with egg yolk. Bake at 220°C for 25–30 minutes.

QUICK BREADS

Unlike recipes using yeast, quick breads do not require kneading and rising because they are leavened with baking powder or bicarbonate of soda. Quick breads are densely textured so are often enriched with vegetables or fruit.

SODA BREAD

500 g wholemeal flour
2 tsp salt
1 tsp bicarbonate of soda
250 ml buttermilk
About 100 ml warm water

Sift dry ingredients into bowl. Add liquids. Mix to a soft dough. Knead until smooth, shape into a 20-cm round. Score and bake at 220°C, 30–40 minutes. Serves 4.

MAKING SODA BREAD

Traditional Irish soda bread is made without solid fat. White flour, which gives a delicate crumb, can be used instead of the wholemeal flour used here. When mixing, add the buttermilk, then just enough water to form a soft but not sticky dough. Mixing should be quick yet gentle, or the loaf will be heavy.

1 Knead the dough on a lightly floured surface until it is smooth. Shape it in your hands to a smooth round.

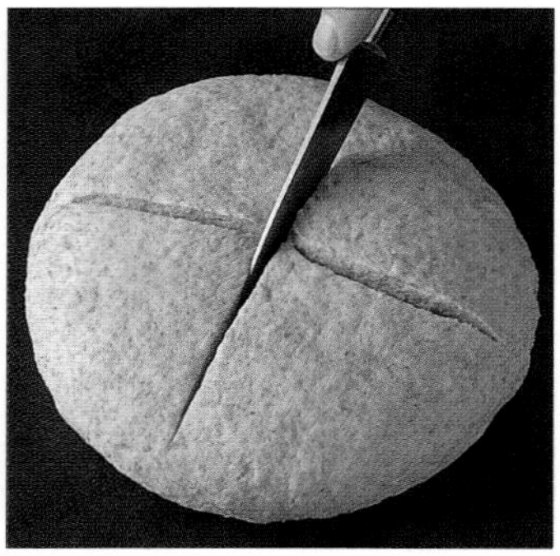

2 Transfer loaf to a baking sheet, then cut a cross in the top, 2 cm deep, with a chef's knife.

MAKING CORNBREAD

Using a method that is typical of the southern United States, this mixture of cornmeal and corn kernels is baked in the oven in a cast-iron frying pan, a method that ensures a crisp, golden crust. Make sure the pan is well greased to prevent the bread sticking. It is best eaten hot.

1 Make a well in the centre of the dry ingredients. Add the corn kernels and stir well to mix. Use a spatula or fork and make sure the corn kernels are evenly distributed.

2 Stir three-quarters of the egg mixture into the dry ingredients until evenly combined. Add the remaining liquid and stir just until the batter is smooth, taking care not to overmix.

3 Brush the top with melted butter before baking to ensure a golden crust and rich flavour. To test for doneness, insert a skewer in the centre of bread – it should come out clean.

MAKING BREAD WITH VEGETABLES

Popular in the United States, these breads have a very moist texture. This recipe uses grated courgettes, but carrots, apples or even puréed pumpkin flesh can be used.

1 Mix together the grated courgettes, eggs, lemon zest and juice and oil, using a spatula. Stir the mixture gently but thoroughly until ingredients are combined.

2 Pour the courgette mixture into the well in the flour mixture and stir gently, gradually drawing in the flour from the sides. Stir gently just until the flour has been incorporated.

3 Spoon the batter into a greased and floured tin, smooth the surface with the back of the spoon, then tap the tin gently on the work surface to remove any air pockets from the batter.

CORNBREAD

175 g plain flour
75 g cornmeal
1 tsp salt
1½ tsp baking powder
100 g fresh or drained corn kernels
250 ml milk
2 eggs, beaten
75 g clear honey
65 g butter, melted

Sift flour, cornmeal, salt and baking powder into a bowl. Fold in corn kernels. Beat together milk, eggs, and honey, and pour three-quarters into dry ingredients. Stir, then mix in remaining liquid. Pour into a greased 20-cm frying pan. Brush with melted butter. Bake at 220°C, 25–30 minutes. Serves 6.

COURGETTE BREAD

375 g courgettes, grated
3 eggs, beaten
Grated zest and juice of 1 lemon
125 ml vegetable oil
375 g plain flour
2 tsp baking powder
1 tsp salt
100 g caster sugar
75 g pine nuts

Combine the courgettes, eggs, lemon zest and juice and oil. Sift flour, baking powder and salt into a bowl. Stir in sugar. Make a well in the centre and add the courgette mixture, then the nuts.

Spoon into a greased and floured 900-g loaf tin and bake at 180°C, 55–60 minutes. Cool on a wire rack. Serves 6–8.

Bread Preparations

Cuisines around the world use different forms of dry bread to add variety to many dishes. Croûtons, for instance, make a crispy garnish, toasted slices become a base for toppings, and crumbs act as a crunchy coating.

Making Breadcrumbs

Breadcrumbs provide a protective coating for fried and baked foods. They also thicken soups and help bind stuffings. For dried crumbs, bake fresh crumbs at 190°C for 3–5 minutes. For fried crumbs to serve with game, fry fresh crumbs in hot oil and butter until golden, 3–5 minutes.

1 To make fresh breadcrumbs, put torn pieces of crustless bread into a food processor and pulse until fine crumbs form.

2 To give the breadcrumbs a fine, even texture and remove any lumps, work them through a fine metal sieve held over a large bowl.

Croutons and Croutes

Croûtons are the small dice of bread that add texture to soups and salads. Croûtes are larger, used to accompany soups, absorb cooking juices from game or meat, or float on top of soups like French onion (see page 20). For the crispest croûtons and croûtes, French chefs use day-old bread. Here croûtons are fried and croûtes toasted.

Frying
Heat 1 cm olive oil with a knob of butter until foaming. Add bread cubes and toss over a high heat until crisp, about 2 minutes. Drain.

Toasting
Toast medium-thick slices of baguette under a hot grill until golden brown, about 2 minutes. Turn over and toast on the other side.

Melba Toast

These thin slices of curled toast triangles are the traditional English accompaniment for rich, smooth pâtés and savoury mousses, as well as creamy soups and salads. The technique works best if you use day-old thinly sliced white bread, lightly toasted on both sides.

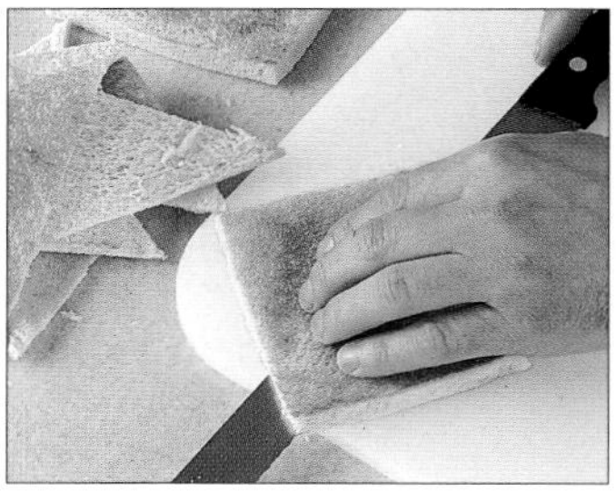

1 Slice horizontally through toast with a serrated knife. Place, untoasted-side up, on a baking sheet.

2 Bake at 190°C until toast is golden and the ends have curled up, 5–10 minutes. Cool on a wire rack.

Bruschetta and Crostini

Italians serve these bread slices with a variety of different toppings (see page 236). The terms are often confused, but crostini are thin, crisp and elegant, and bruschetta are thicker and more rustic. You can use any type of bread – baguette are good for crostini, ciabatta *and* pugliese *for bruschetta.*

Garlic bruschetta
Cut 2-cm thick slices of bread. Rub both sides with the cut side of a peeled and halved garlic clove, then toast.

Olive oil crostini
Toast 5-mm thick slices of bread. While still warm, brush one side of each slice with virgin olive oil.

FRUITS

HARD FRUITS

PINEAPPLE

STONE FRUITS

CITRUS FRUITS

BERRIES

EXOTIC FRUITS

POACHING & PRESERVING

GRILLING & FRYING

BAKING

Choosing Fruit

Where possible choose fruit from a loose display, this will allow you to check the produce and, in the case of some fruits like grapes and cherries, to sample them first. There should be no bruising or mould and avoid any fruit that looks damp and smells musty. Ripe fruit spoils quickly so handle it as little as possible and only buy what you can use within a few days.

Apples should be sweet smelling with firm flesh and smooth shiny skin

Melon smooth skin free of blemishes and bruising, it should feel heavy for its size

Lemons should have smooth glossy skins, even in colour, and feel heavy for their size

Melons

Gallias, honeydews, cantaloupes, charentais, and watermelons are best bought in season to ensure their freshness. Select those that feel heavy, give slightly when gently pressed at the ends and smell aromatic and fragrant

Hard Fruits

Apples and pears should have smooth shiny skins, be free of blemishes and have a good depth of colour, although the evenness of the colour will depend on the variety. The flesh should be firm with no sign of bruising. When buying pears choose those that are underripe, then wrap loosely in a paper bag and allow to ripen at room temperature.

STONE FRUITS

Check the flesh of peaches, nectarines, plums, cherries and apricots is firm but not hard. When fully ripe, the flesh will give slightly to gentle pressure. Select plump well-rounded fruit with an obvious seam, that feel heavy. The velvety skin should not be bruised or cut.

BLUEBERRIES should be plump with a blue/grey "bloom"; check they are firm not soft

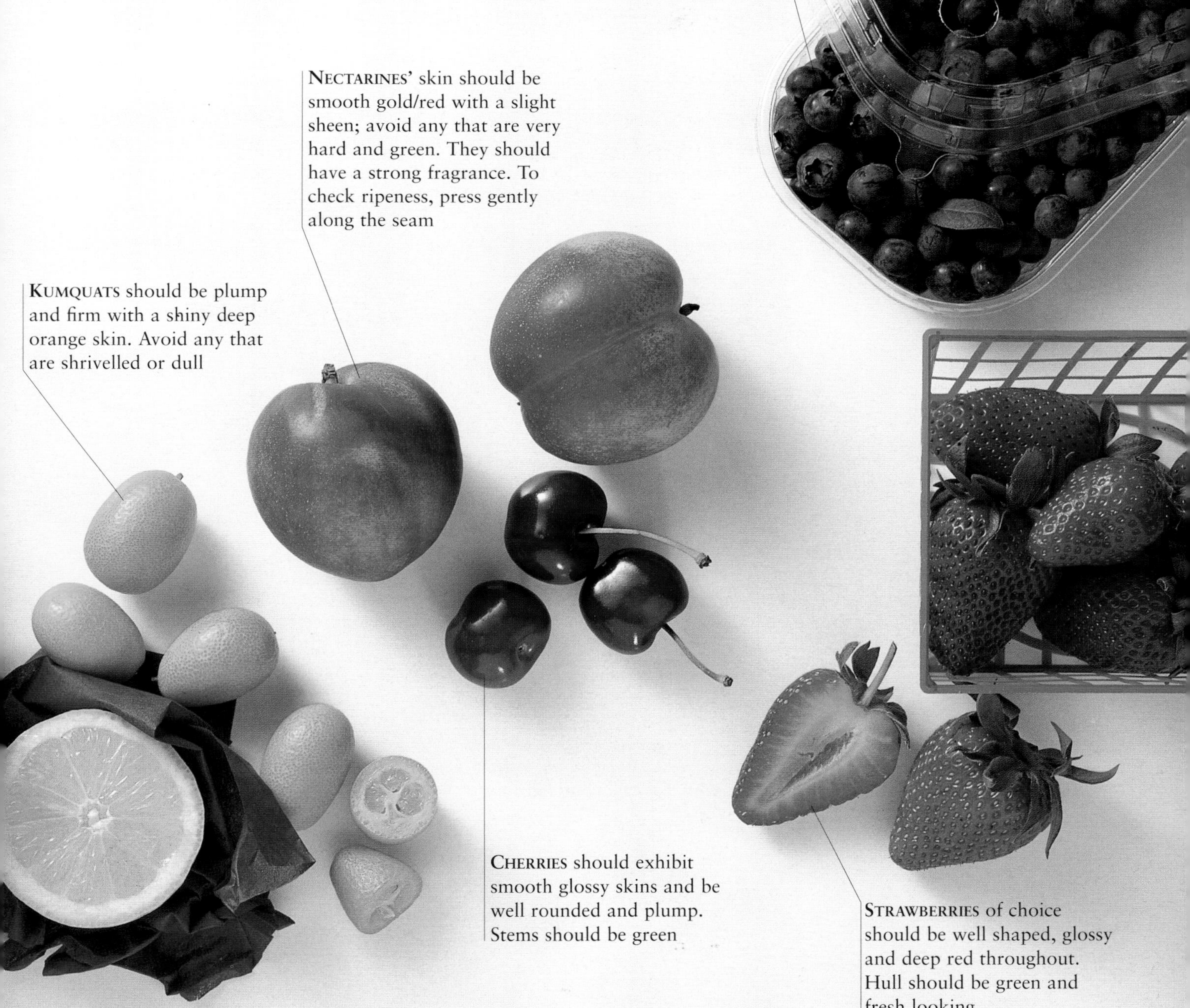

NECTARINES' skin should be smooth gold/red with a slight sheen; avoid any that are very hard and green. They should have a strong fragrance. To check ripeness, press gently along the seam

KUMQUATS should be plump and firm with a shiny deep orange skin. Avoid any that are shrivelled or dull

CHERRIES should exhibit smooth glossy skins and be well rounded and plump. Stems should be green

STRAWBERRIES of choice should be well shaped, glossy and deep red throughout. Hull should be green and fresh looking

CITRUS FRUITS

Choose plump citrus fruits – lemons, limes, oranges, kumquats, grapefruit, satsumas and clementines – and make sure they feel firm and juicy. The skin should have an even colour and look glossy, almost moist. The fruit should be free of blemishes and not shrivelled, and the skin should be unbroken. In general, the smoother the skin, the thinner it will be.

BERRIES

Choose bright coloured black-, blue-, straw-, rasp-, and logan berries that are plump and fragrant. Check for soft or mouldy berries before buying and ensure the punnet is clean and not stained or wet, an indication that the fruit may be damaged underneath. Handle the fruit as little as possible; only wash them if absolutely necessary as this speeds mould.

HARD FRUITS

There are few fruits more versatile than apples and pears. They are both excellent for eating raw, and combine well with cheeses, especially Cheddar with apples and Gorgonzola with pears. They make homely pies or elegant desserts, and can also be cooked with meat, poultry and game.

CHOOSING APPLES

Choose apples that are firm and unblemished, with a sweet smell and taut, unbroken skin. Apples are hard even when ripe.

BRAMLEY'S SEEDLING: Used only for cooking. Good for pies, sauces and purées.
COX'S ORANGE PIPPIN: A dessert apple with a spicy smell. Also good for baking.
DISCOVERY: A crisp dessert apple with a sweet flavour.
GOLDEN DELICIOUS: All-purpose apple. The yellow-skinned types are best for eating raw.
GRANNY SMITH'S: A good eating apple. Also ideal for baking and stewing.

CHOOSING PEARS

Buy pears unripe and ripen them at room temperature – once ripe they should be eaten immediately.

COMICE: Large round sweet pear that turns yellow as it ripens. Best for eating raw.
CONFERENCE: Long, curved fruit with a good sweet flavour when ripe. Good for poaching.
PACKHAM'S: Pale green sweet pear which yellows with ripening. Eat raw.
RED BARTLETT: Rosy-coloured pear with sweet flesh. Eat raw.
WILLIAMS: Yellow-speckled pear. Eat raw or cooked.

PEELING

Peel fruit with a peeler or small knife just before using to prevent discoloration. How to peel can vary – peel around the fruit in a spiral as shown here, or remove a little skin at the top and bottom and peel the remainder vertically.

PLAIN
Core the apple, then peel off the skin, circling round the apple from top to bottom.

DECORATIVE
Use a canelle knife to pare away a single fine strip of skin, spiralling carefully down from the stalk to the bottom.

CORING

A fruit corer is most effective for coring apples and pears whole, but a vegetable peeler will do the job almost as well. A melon baller is the best tool to use for coring halved fruits. Core fruit, unpeeled or peeled, depending on future use.

CORER
Push corer into stalk of apple and through to the bottom. Twist to loosen the core, then pull it out in the corer.

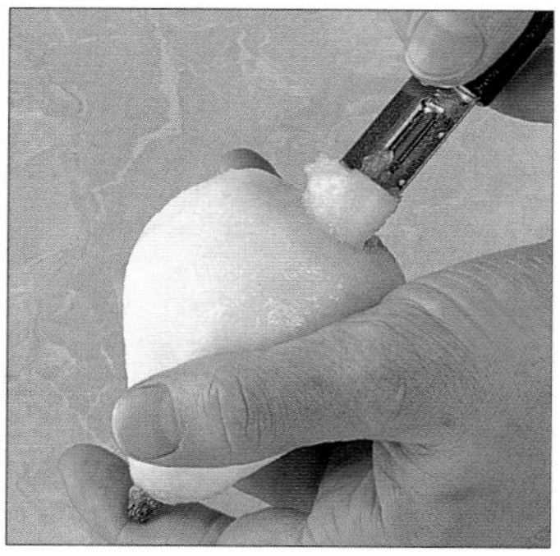

VEGETABLE PEELER
Insert point of peeler into the bottom of pear and twist it so that it cuts around the core. Gently pull out the core.

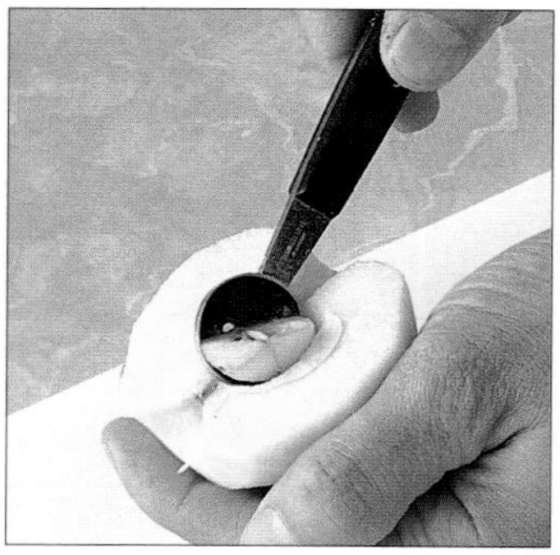

MELON BALLER
Hold halved fruit firmly in one hand and scoop out core and seeds by twisting the melon baller around.

Slicing Apples and Pears

Hard fruits can be sliced as you like, but for classic presentations in tarts and pastries or for poaching, special slicing techniques need to be learnt. Here three of the most commonly used shapes are shown, together with a clever method of chopping that ensures neatly diced fruit with a minimum of waste.

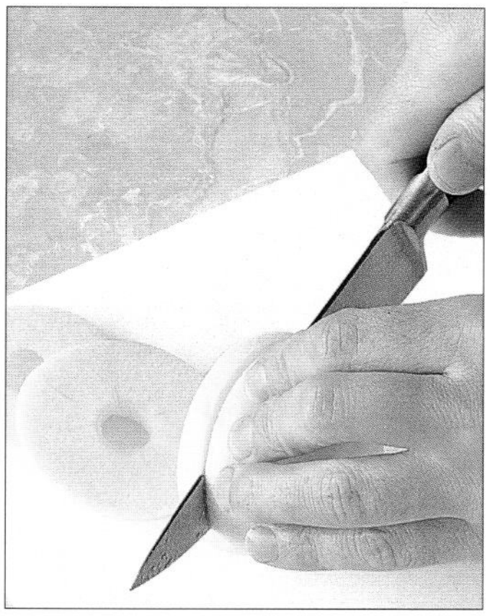

Apple rings
Core and peel an apple, keeping it whole. Hold the apple on its side and slice downwards.

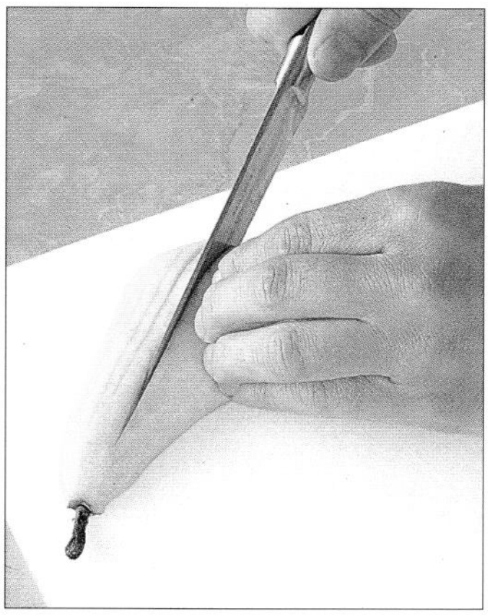

Pear fans
Peel, halve and core pear, leaving stalk intact. Put cut-side down and slice from stalk to bottom. Press with your hand to fan out slices.

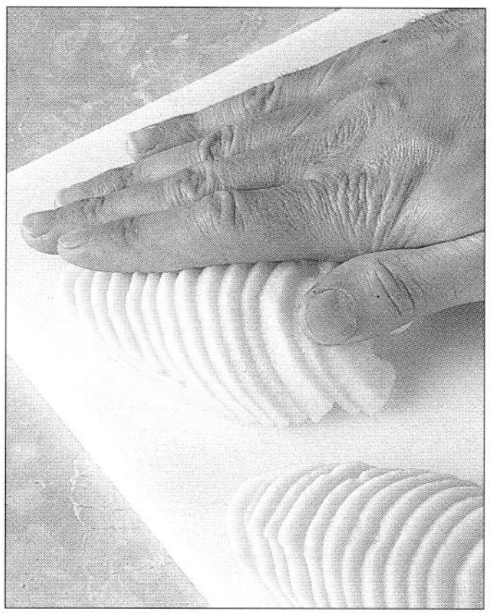

Apple crescents
Core and peel an apple, keeping it whole. Cut in half lengthwise. Put each half cut-side down and cut crosswise into half moons.

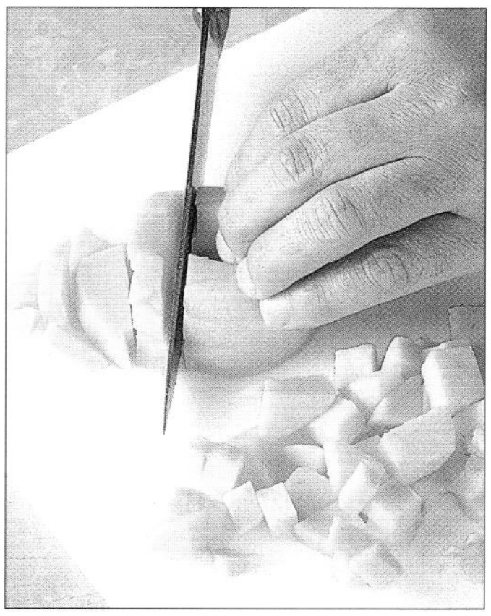

Chopping
Make thick apple rings (see left) and stack them. Slice downwards, holding the stack together, then cut across these slices to make dice.

TRICK OF THE TRADE

Preventing Discoloration

The flesh of apples and pear quickly discolours when exposed to air, so as soon as they are peeled or cut, treat them with an acidic liquid to counteract this. Here the juice of citrus fruit is brushed on the fruit, but you can rub the exposed flesh with the cut surface of a halved citrus fruit if you prefer. Use apples and pears immediately after preparation and, if possible, use stainless steel tools.

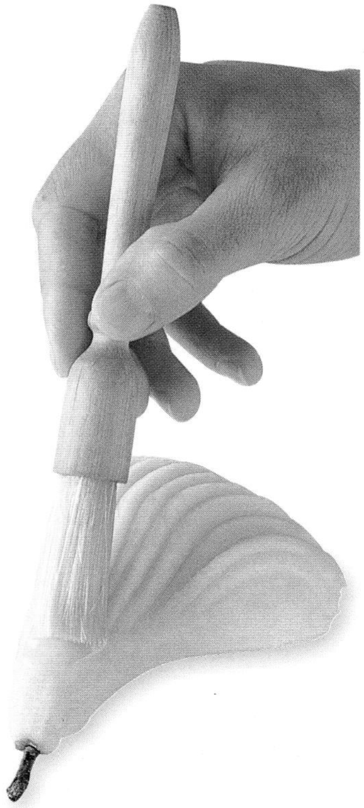

Squeeze the juice of a lemon, lime or orange into a bowl. Dip a pastry brush in the juice, then paint the juice all over the flesh as soon as it is exposed, working it into the crevices.

Rhubarb

Rhubarb bought early in the season is very tender and requires little preparation, but main-crop rhubarb is dark in colour with a more fibrous flesh that needs peeling. If the leaves are still attached, they must be cut off and discarded because they are poisonous. Rhubarb is never eaten raw because it is so tough and tart. It is always cooked with plenty of sugar, or combined with other fruits.

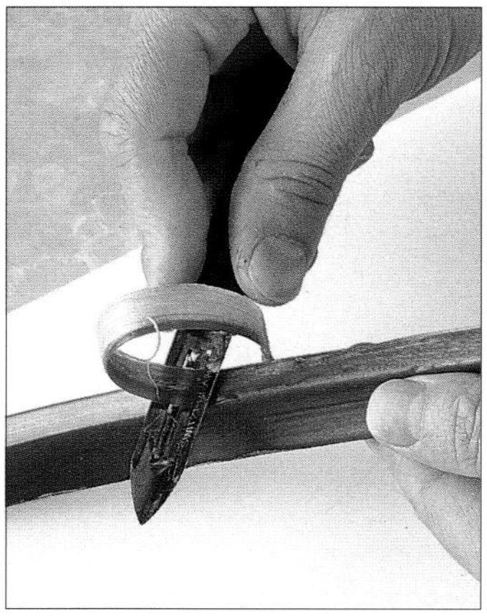

1 Cut off the leaves and discard, then pare away the skin of the rhubarb in long strips using a vegetable peeler. Trim the base of each stalk.

2 Slice the rhubarb crosswise on the diagonal into neat chunks using a chef's knife. The rhubarb is now ready for cooking.

Pineapple

This handsome fruit can be prepared in many ways: the whole fruit can be hollowed to make a shell, or the flesh removed, cored and cut into wedges, rings or chunks. It can be served as it is, or cooked – as a dessert or fragrant accompaniment to meat, especially pork and duck.

Baby Pineapples

Miniature pineapples make attractive containers for individual servings of fruit salad and ice cream, as shown below.

To serve whole baby pineapples topped with their plumes, simply follow steps 1–4, right. Fill with diced pineapple flesh mixed with summer berries and slices of apple and orange. The fruit can be macerated in kirsch or white rum and sugar syrup.

To serve baby pineapple halves, cut the fruit lengthwise in half, scoop out the woody central core and top with a scoop of ice cream. Serve at once.

Making a Shell Container

The shell of a pineapple makes an impressive natural serving bowl that can be filled with diced pineapple flesh mixed with other fruits or ice cream. Removing the flesh in one piece following the technique shown here also allows you to cut perfect rings. To remove cores from slices, see opposite page.

1 Lay the pineapple flat on a cutting board. Slice off the plume with a chef's knife and reserve it for serving.

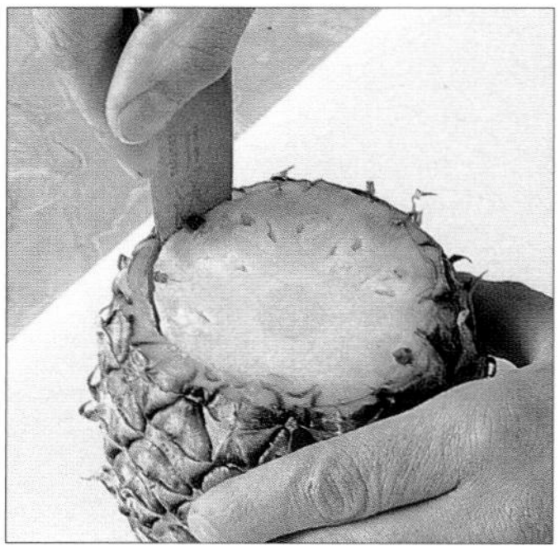

2 Cut down between the skin and flesh, releasing the flesh all round while leaving a firm wall of skin.

3 Turn pineapple over; cut off the bottom to level it and help release the flesh.

4 Cup the pineapple with one hand. Push a fork firmly into the centre of the flesh and pull it out in one piece. To serve the pineapple flesh back in its shell, slice it crosswise, remove the cores (see opposite page) and dice the flesh.

Removing Pineapple Skin

When neither a serving shell nor perfect rings are required (see opposite page), the quickest way to get at the flesh is to strip the skin off the whole fruit. After slicing and coring the fruit, the flesh can then be cut into chunks or dice.

1 Cut off the plume and the bottom of the pineapple. Stand the fruit upright and slice off the skin from top to bottom using a chef's knife.

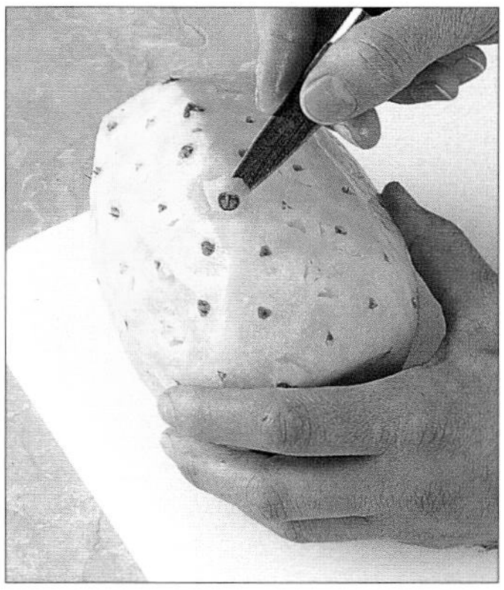

2 Dig out any spikes or eyes left in the flesh with the point of a small knife. Slice the fruit crosswise using a chef's knife.

Coring
Lay each pineapple slice flat and then stamp out the core with a small cutter.

Ring the Changes

Slices or rings of pineapple can be grilled or sautéed with flavourings of your choice.

For a Caribbean flavour, use toasted shredded coconut, rum, fresh orange juice, cinnamon or cloves. For an Asian taste, use star anise or grated lime zest.

Making Wedges

An attractive way to serve a wedge of fresh pineapple is to display the cut fruit in a zigzag pattern, as shown here. Another way, used in classic French cuisine, is to loosen the flesh from the wedge while keeping the core intact – this will help keep it neatly together for serving.

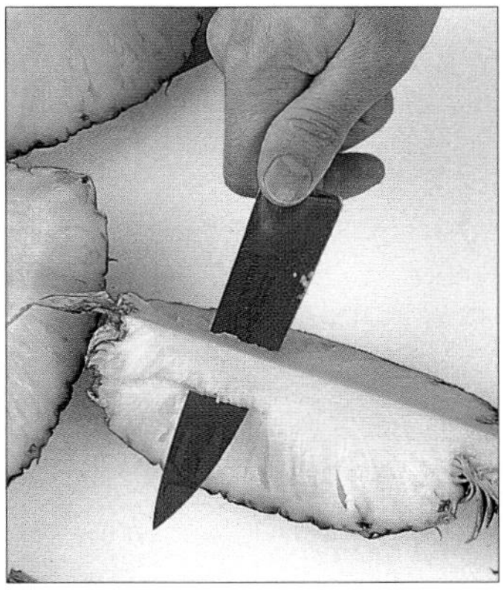

1 Quarter the fruit lengthwise, including the plume. Cut away the core from the centre of each piece.

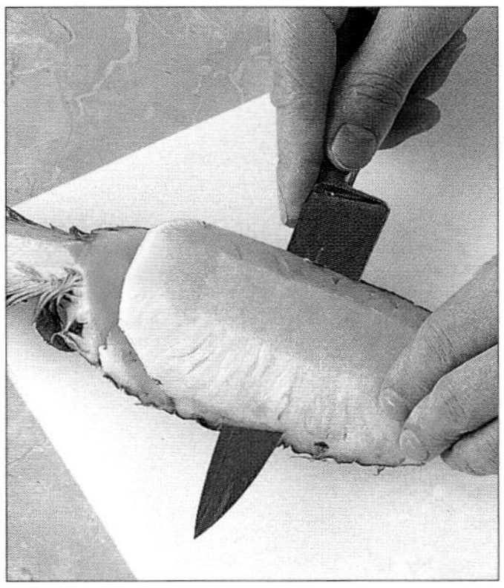

2 Beginning at the plume end of each quarter, cut between the flesh and the skin using a sawing motion.

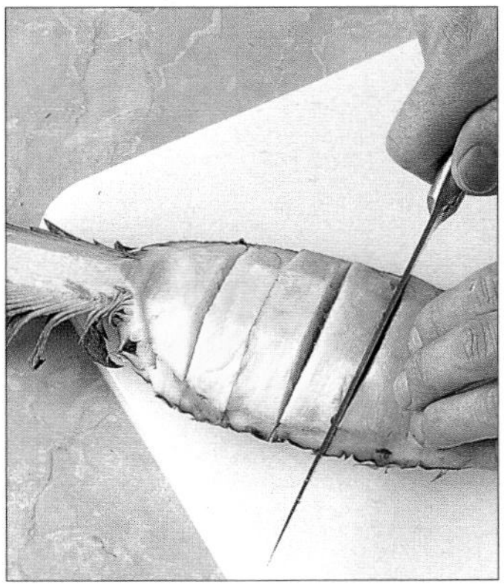

3 Cut the flesh crosswise into even slices. Push the slices out from the shell, changing direction each time.

STONE FRUITS

Many sweet, and a wide range of savoury, dishes owe their distinctive flavour and appearance to luscious, colourful and aromatic stone fruits. Before using them, they need to have their stones removed; this technique is simple but must be done correctly if the fruit is to retain its shape. The thin skin can be left on the fruit or removed before use.

EXTRACTING THE ALMOND FLAVOUR

The small kernel found inside an apricot stone has a distinctive almond flavour. Apricots and almonds make good partners, so add the kernel to apricot jams and jellies, or use to flavour apricot liqueurs.

Place a cutting board on a cloth to steady it. Put the stone on the board and crack it with a small hammer to release the kernel. Blanch the kernel for 1 minute, then refresh in cold water. Pat dry. Cut into slivers or chop finely.

SAFETY FIRST

Do not use the kernels of stone fruits other than apricots. They contain a poisonous acid and should be discarded as soon as they are removed from the fruit.

STONING

When stoning apricots, peaches, plums and nectarines, some of the flesh may cling to the stone, even when the fruits are ripe. The technique shown here helps to combat this problem. If the skin is left on until after stoning this will help you get a good grip on the fruit.

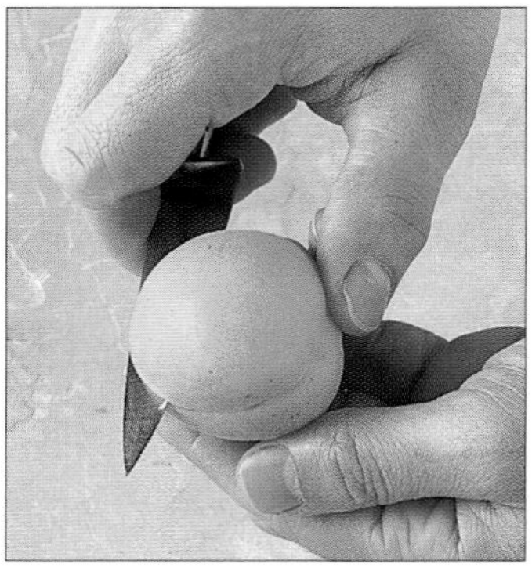

1 Cut around the fruit with a small knife, following the seam and cutting right down to the stone.

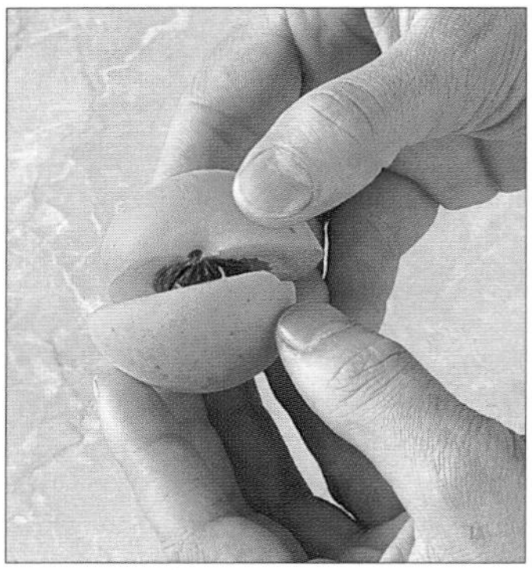

2 Holding the cut fruit, twist each half quite sharply in opposite directions to expose the stone.

3 Prise the stone out of the fruit with the tip of the knife, then lift it out with your fingers.

SKINNING

The skin of stone fruits is notoriously difficult to remove. By far the easiest way is to blanch the fruits first in boiling water, but care must be taken not to cook the fruits, especially if they are really ripe. First score a cross shape in the bottom end of each fruit. Bring a pan of water to the boil and immerse each fruit on a slotted spoon. Count 10 seconds for very ripe fruit, up to 20 seconds for less ripe, just until the skin begins to curl.

1 After immersing the fruit in boiling water, transfer it to a bowl of iced water with a slotted spoon. This stops the heat penetrating the flesh.

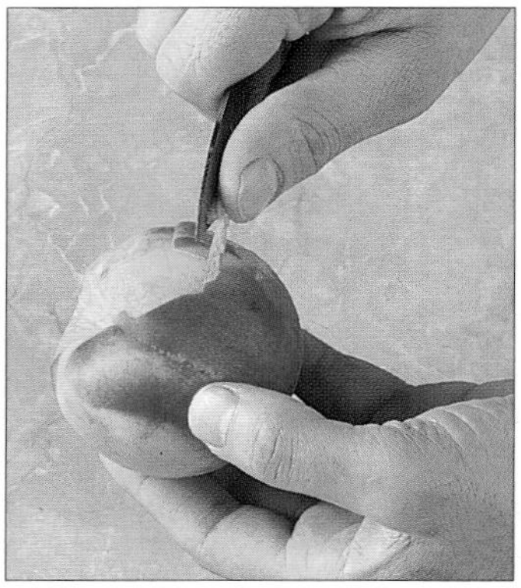

2 Carefully loosen the skin at the stalk end of the fruit with the point of a small knife, then use the knife to help peel the skin away.

Pitting Cherries

A mechanical stoner makes pitting cherries easy. The blunt spike pushes the stone through the flesh, ensuring the fruit retains its shape and precious juices are retained. Alternatively, you can use the point of a vegetable peeler – insert it in the stalk end, rotate it around the stone, then scoop it out.

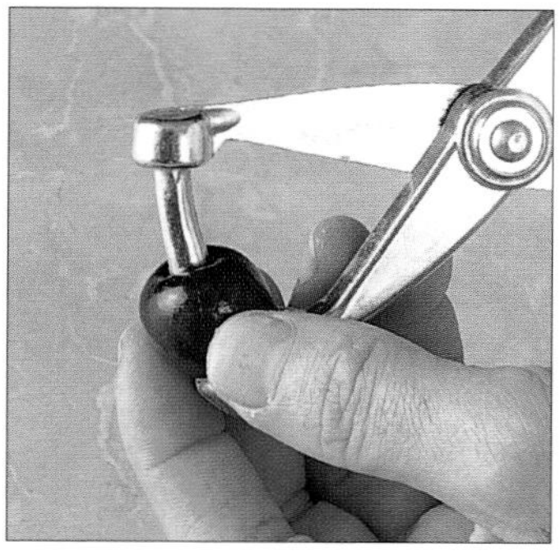

Pull out the stalk and discard. Place the cherry, stalk-end up, in the cupped side of the stoner. Hold the fruit firmly and squeeze both handles of the stoner tightly together until the stone is pushed out.

This pitting technique can also be used for olives – the hole that is left after pitting can be stuffed.

Dicing a Mango

Fibrous mango flesh sticks to the central stone, making it difficult to remove. The technique shown here, commonly known as the hedgehog method, removes most of the flesh by slicing either side of the stone; the sections that remain are then diced separately.

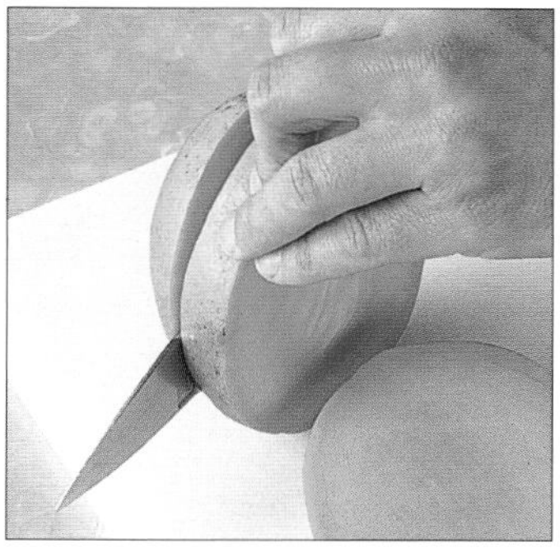

1 Slice the fruit lengthwise on either side of the flat stone, cutting as close to the stone as possible.

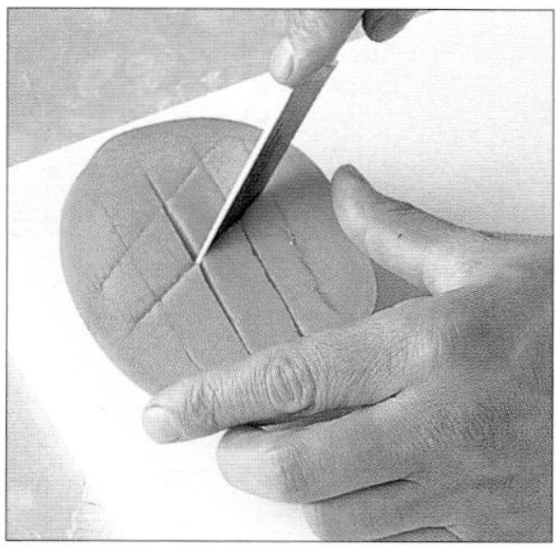

2 Slice the flesh of the two stoneless sections in a lattice pattern, cutting down to the peel but not piercing it.

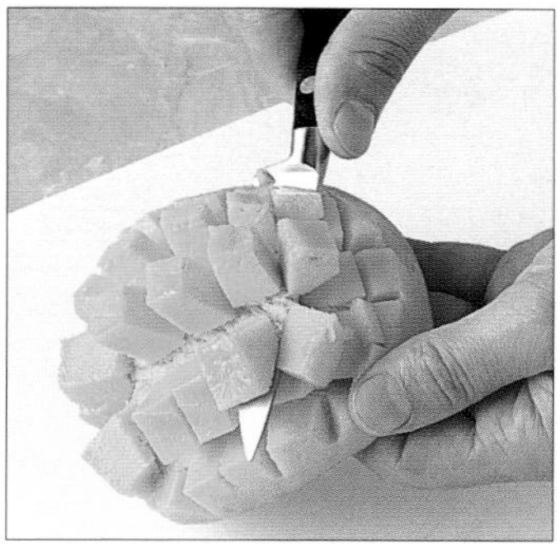

3 Push the peel inside out with your thumbs. Cut away cubes with a small knife. Repeat with the other section.

Slicing a Mango

The easiest way to slice a mango is to peel it first, using a paring knife. This works best with fruit that is only just ripe; if the fruit is over-ripe, it will be slippery and may pulp in your hand, making it difficult to grip. You can simply cut the flesh from the mango and then slice it or cut it into chunks. Alternatively, use the technique shown here for neatly shaped wedges.

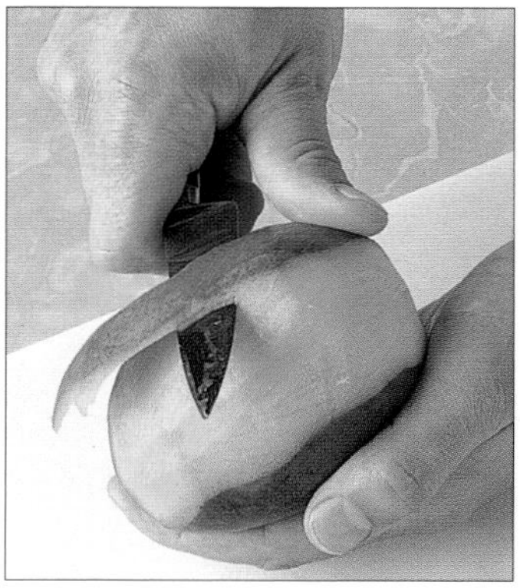

1 Cup mango in your hand and peel skin, lengthwise, as thinly as possible with a paring knife. Work around the fruit, to keep a neat shape.

2 Cut a V-shaped wedge down to the stone. Slice from the V, working around the fruit.

Uses for Mangoes

Eat mango just as it is or add it to sweet or savoury dishes. Its flavour goes particularly well with smoked and salty foods, and it has a cooling effect on spicy ingredients.

- For a refreshing first course, serve sliced mango with smoked meats or fish drizzled with a herb dressing.
- Use puréed ripe mango as a base for mousses, sorbets or ice cream, or mix with some raspberry liqueur and use as a dessert sauce.
- Add to a tropical fruit salad and serve with crème fraîche flavoured with a little coconut.
- Add to a red pepper or chilli sauce to temper the heat.
- For a tangy *salsa*, mix diced mango with diced red onion and avocado and lime juice. Serve with baked fish or *fajitas*.
- Unripe mango is an excellent addition to pickles and chutneys.

CITRUS FRUITS

With their pungent zest, sweet-tasting segments and refreshing tart juices, citrus fruits each have a very distinctive taste. Here's how to use each section correctly to make the most of the fruits.

PEELING AND SLICING

When cutting the peel from citrus fruits, it is important to cut away the bitter white pith with it, leaving the flesh intact. Use a serrated knife if you like, or a chef's knife as shown here, which gives a smoother finish.

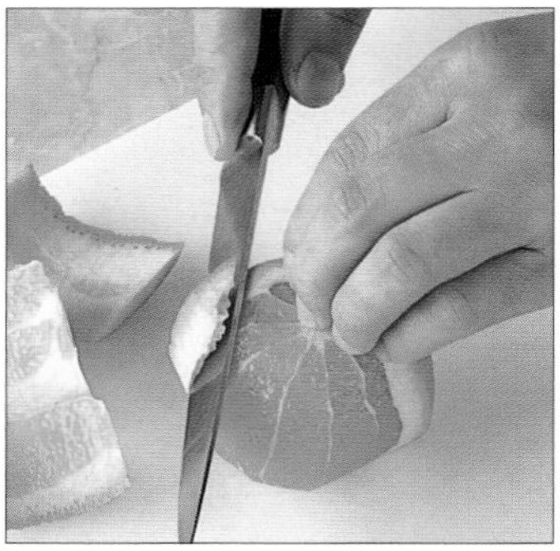

1 Cut a slice of peel from both ends of the fruit to expose the flesh. Stand fruit upright and cut away the peel and white pith, following the curve of the fruit.

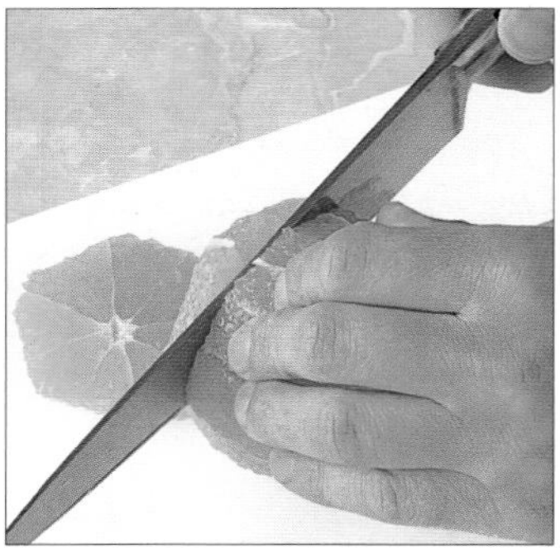

2 Hold the fruit firmly on its side and cut the flesh crosswise into slices about 3 mm thick, using a gentle sawing action with the knife.

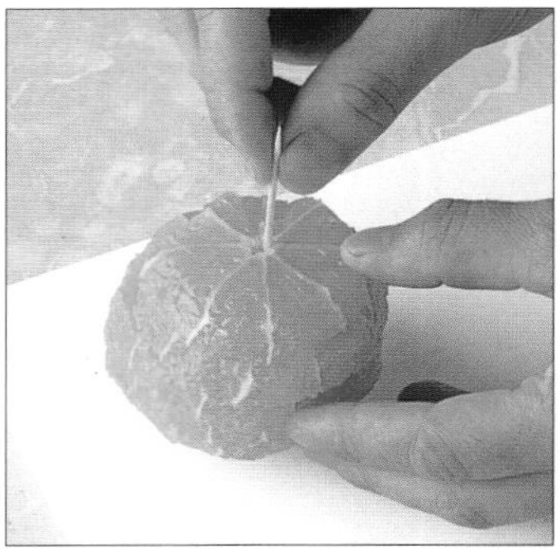

KEEPING SLICES TOGETHER Some dishes, such as oranges in caramel, require the fruit to be reformed for a neat presentation. Stack slices and secure with a cocktail stick.

SEGMENTING

This very simple technique cuts citrus fruits into neat segments so that none of the tough membrane is included. Work over a plate or bowl to collect the juice as it drips from the fruit.

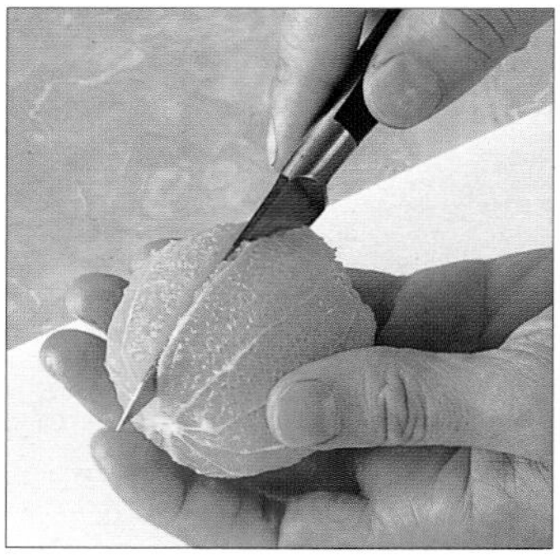

1 Hold the peeled fruit in one hand. Cut down both sides of one white membrane to the core, using a small knife. Try to leave as little flesh as possible attached to the membrane.

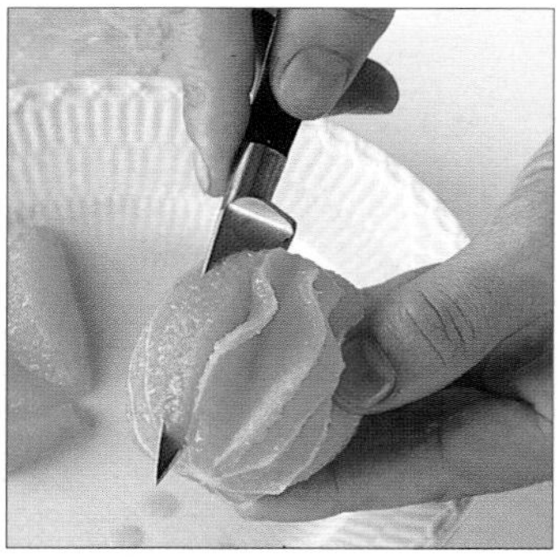

2 Working around the fruit, continue to cut between the membranes and segments, folding the membranes back like the pages of a book as you go to release each segment.

3 Hold the core and membranes over the segments and squeeze tightly in your fist. This will extract as much of the juice from the remaining flesh as possible.

UNUSUAL CITRUS FRUITS

AMALFI LEMON: This southern Italian fruit is much larger than the more common lemon, weighing on average up to 225 g. Available from May until September, it is fully ripened on the tree. Its flesh is juicy and richly flavoured.

BLOOD ORANGE: The distinctive ruby-red flesh and juice are slightly sharper and more strongly flavoured than a standard orange. The sharp refreshing juice can be used to great effect in sorbets and granitas.

CITRON: The thick aromatic peel and pith are the only parts of this fruit that are used – for candied peel and marmalade.

MINEOLA: A hybrid member of the tangerine family, the mineola is the size and colour of an orange but it can be identified by a bulge near the stalk. The skin peels easily and the flesh is sharply flavoured.

ORTANIQUE: A cross between a sweet orange and a tangerine, use just as you would an orange. Ortaniques are delicious whether eaten raw or used in cooked dishes. The thin skin peels easily to reveal sweet juicy flesh.

POMELO: This looks like a large pear-shaped grapefruit with thick skin that is green-yellow in colour; use the sweet-sour flesh as you would grapefruit flesh.

UGLI FRUIT: A hybrid of three other citrus fruits – grapefruit, orange and tangerine – the ugli has an uneven "craggy" skin that fits loosely around its juicy flesh.

Zesting

Citrus zest, the coloured part of the peel not the bitter white pith, is aromatic and full of flavour. It can be taken from the fruit in strips or grated, depending on recipe instructions. For the very fine strips of zest shown here, a tool called a zester is used. Scrub the fruit first, to remove any wax coating.

To cut strips of zest, pull zester towards you applying even pressure.

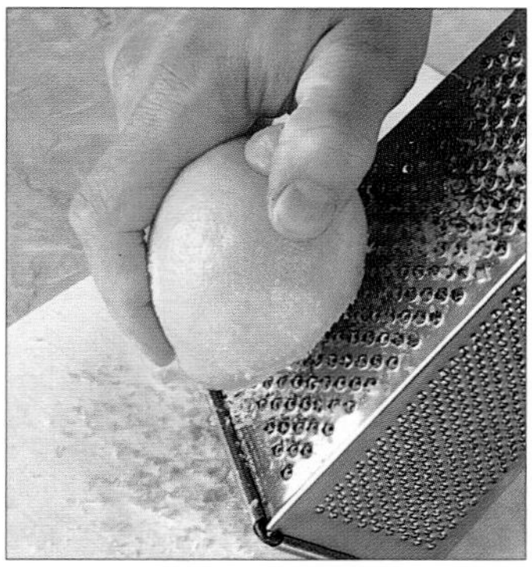

To grate zest, rub fruit over small cutters on grater. Use a brush to remove from grater.

Cutting Julienne

Julienne is a classic French culinary term describing ingredients, such as the lime zest shown here, that have been cut into very thin strips. When using as a decoration, soften the strips first; blanch them in boiling water for 1–2 minutes, drain and refresh in cold water, then pat dry.

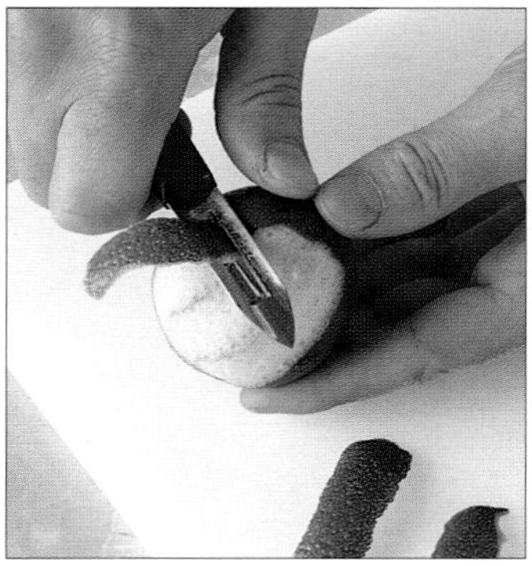

1 Pare zest strips lengthwise from the fruit using a vegetable peeler.

2 Cut strips lengthwise into very fine shreds with a chef's knife.

Extracting Juice

Before juicing, roll the whole fruit on the work surface to soften it – this will yield more juice. The old-fashioned wooden juicer, or reamer, used here, is especially good for extracting juice, and can be used for whole or halved fruits. Strain before use to remove pips and membrane.

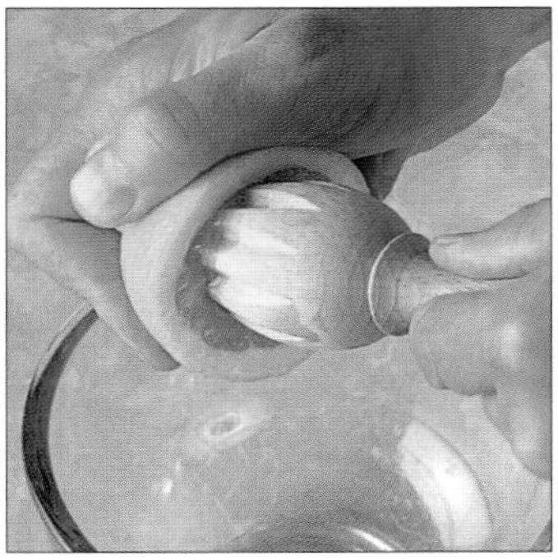

Cut the fruit crosswise in half. Hold one half over a bowl and push the juicer firmly into the flesh. Turn it back and forth in a twisting motion to release the juice. Repeat with other half.

Clockwise from top: lime; lemon; orange; kumquat; satsuma (whole and cut open). **From left to right in foreground:** lemon; ruby grapefruit; kumquat

Berries

A punnet of sweet ripe berries is always a treat, in or out of season. Used in cooking for their beauty and flavour, berries make delicious purées and sauces – and instant desserts with a simple topping of cream.

ALRIGHT FOR SOME

Bursting with vitamin C and iron, potassium for controlling blood pressure, and ellagic acid, a substance thought to fight certain cancers, strawberries are rich in healthy attributes.

Sadly, some people have an intolerance to strawberries, and develop a red skin rash or swollen fingers.

Preparing Strawberries

The hulls of both wild and cultivated strawberries are usually removed, but they can be left intact if the berries are to be used for decoration, or if they are needed to facilitate dipping the fruit in melted chocolate (see page 282).

Removing the hull
Prise out the leafy top (hull) with the tip of a small knife.

Hulls for decoration
Slice the whole fruit in half lengthwise with a chef's knife.

Peeling and Pipping Grapes

When serving grapes in a sauce or as a garnish, both the chewy skin and the pips should be removed. The techniques here are for whole grapes; to remove the pips from grape halves, flick them out with the tip of a small, pointed knife.

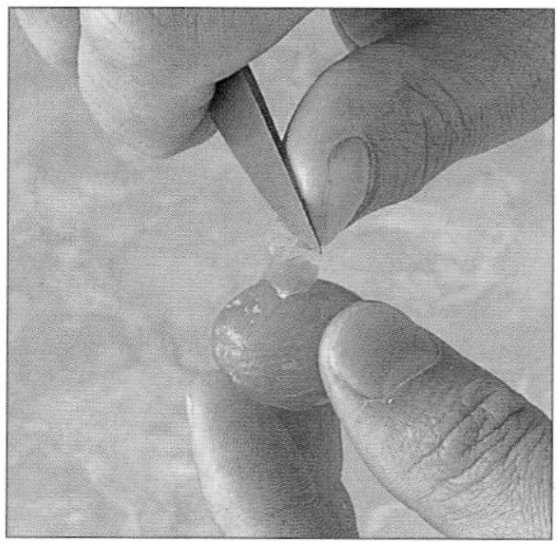

Peeling
Blanch 10 seconds, then strip off skin with a paring knife, starting at stalk end.

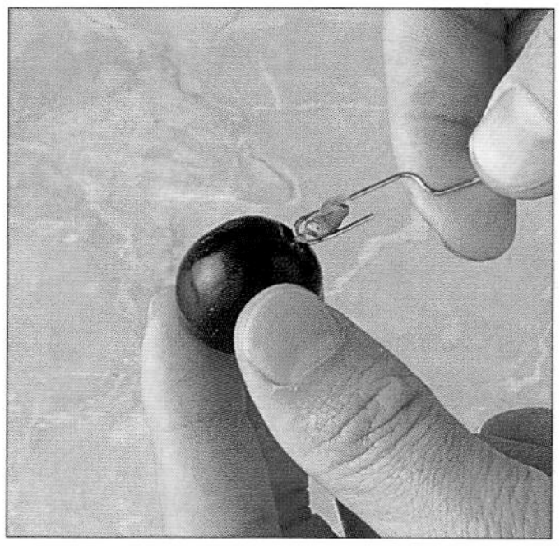

Pipping
Open out a sterilized paper clip and pull out pips with one hooked end.

Top, left to right: strawberries. **Middle:** blackcurrants; raspberries; redcurrants. **Bottom:** loganberries; blackberries

Strigging Currants

Currants need to have their stalks removed before use. The method used here is called strigging – the word strig was the 16th century name for a stalk. The only tool you need for this clever technique is an ordinary kitchen fork.

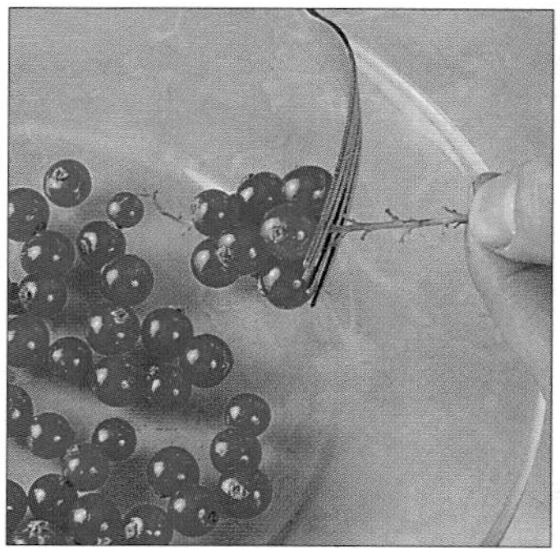

Run the tines of a fork down the stalk – the currants will come away easily.

Making a Berry Puree

Strawberries and raspberries are best puréed raw (firm fruits like currants and cherries need to be cooked); sugar is added after puréeing, depending on the future use of the purée, see box, right. About 250 g fruit will make 250 ml purée.

1 Put hulled and halved strawberries in a blender and purée. There is no need to hull and halve raspberries.

2 Rub purée through a fine sieve set over a bowl to remove seeds. Add icing sugar, if using; stir until dissolved.

Making a Berry Coulis

For an instant coulis, liqueur is added to a sweetened berry purée (left). See box below for presentation ideas.

Add 2 tbsp liqueur to sweetened berry purée – Cointreau with strawberries; kirsch with raspberries.

Uses for Berry Purees

A wide range of desserts can be made with the concentrated flavour of a berry purée.

- Use sweetened purée as a base for cold sweet soufflés, mousses, fools, ice creams, sorbets and granitas.
- Thin unsweetened purée with dry white wine, chill and serve as a refreshing fruit soup topped with a swirl of cream or Greek yogurt.
- Swirl sweetened purée into curd cheese for a fruit-flavoured cheesecake.
- Serve sweetened purée warm over ricotta-filled crêpes.

Pureeing in a Mouli

When berries are worked through a Mouli (food mill) to make a purée, the seeds are left behind in the mill so there is no need to sieve afterwards.

Fit the fine disc into the Mouli and set it over a large bowl. Put berries of your choice (here strigged and cooked redcurrants are used) in the hopper (the top of the Mouli). Hold the handle firmly and turn the crank so that the blade pushes the fruit into the bowl.

TRICK OF THE TRADE

Using Berry Coulis to Good Effect

Professional chefs use coulis for stylish presentations of single servings. Individual slices of desserts, tarts and cakes look especially good this way. Here are two ideas.

Feathers

Ladle a large pool of coulis on to a chilled serving plate. Pipe small dots of cream in two parallel rows on top of the coulis, using a paper piping bag (see box, page 318). Draw the tip of a knife through each of the the cream dots to create a feathered effect.

Yin and yang

Spoon a little coulis on a chilled serving plate. Using the tip of the spoon, pull the coulis out at one point to make a teardrop shape. Repeat with a different-coloured coulis, reversing the shape so the two teardrops come together in the centre.

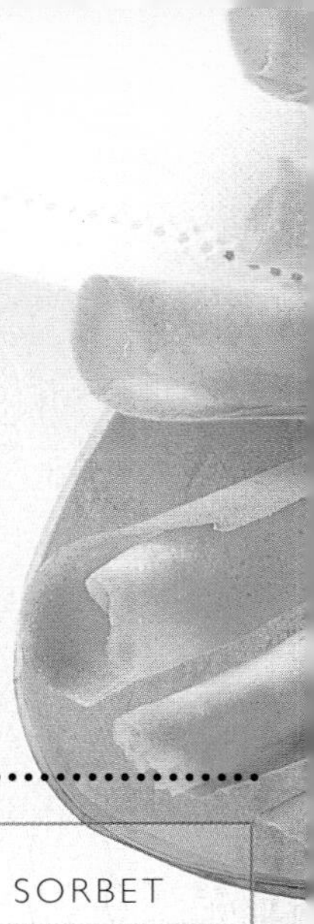

Cantaloupe Surprise

A refreshing salad of melon, mango, pineapple and kiwi in a spiced syrup is served in individual melon cups, topped with melon sorbet. The edges of the melons are attractively vandyked, a quintessentially French technique.

SERVES 4

4 ripe but firm small cantaloupe melons

2 ripe mangos

1 ripe medium pineapple

3 kiwi fruits

150 ml water

150 g caster sugar

Pared zest and juice of 1/2 lemon and 1/2 orange

1 cinnamon stick

1 star anise

1/4 tsp fennel seeds

TO SERVE

Fresh mint leaves

Tuiles and tulipes (see page 326)

Prepare the melons (see box, below) and set the melon balls aside. Chill the melon cups in the refrigerator until ready to serve. Make the melon sorbet (see box, right). Dice the mangos into cubes the same size as the melon balls, using the hedgehog method (see page 255).

Cut the ends off the kiwi fruits, stand the fruits upright and cut just under the skin, following the shape of the fruit. Cut the flesh into cubes.

Remove the flesh from the pineapple (see page 253), then cut it into cubes that are roughly the same size as the mango cubes.

Combine the water, sugar, citrus zest and juice, and spices in a pan and bring to the boil, stirring until the sugar has dissolved. Remove from the heat and add the melon balls and cubes of mango, kiwi and pineapple. Leave to cool, then refrigerate until ready to serve.

Spoon the spiced fruit into the chilled melon cups. Top each cup with a scoop of sorbet, garnish with mint and serve immediately, with tuiles and tulipes handed separately.

MELON SORBET

200 g melon pulp (see box, below)
Juice of 1/2 lemon
30 g caster sugar
2 tbsp water

Purée the melon pulp and lemon juice. Make a sugar syrup (see page 280) with the sugar and water, cool, then mix with the pulp. Freeze in a sorbetière. Or, place in the freezer for 4 hours, whisking as often as possible to break up ice crystals.

CANTALOUPE

Prized for its sweet flavour, the orange-fleshed cantaloupe is easy to recognize from its deeply ridged, craggy skin, which is marked into segments. It must be served ripe, so buy only those fruits which yield to light pressure near the stalk end and which have a fresh melon scent. If cantaloupe melon is not available, use ogen or charentais instead – they are from the same family.

Preparing Melons

Small melons make decorative containers for fruit salads and other desserts, as well as for savoury fruit and poultry or fish combinations. You can cut a slanted vandyked or zigzag edge as shown here, or a straight or scalloped edge.

Mark a slanted zigzag line in the skin of each melon, just above the "equator" line, using the tip of a knife. Cut on the marked lines, inserting the knife through to the centre of the fruit each time.

Gently pull the melons apart. Scoop out the seeds and fibrous flesh using a small spoon; discard. Remove the flesh from the smaller top sections and use to make the melon sorbet (see box, above).

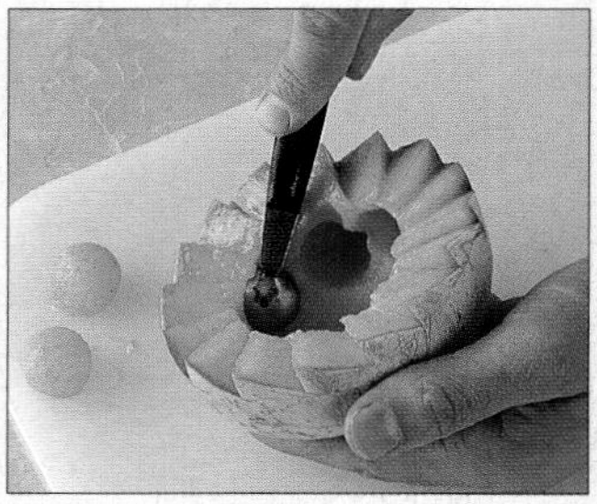

Take out balls of flesh from the bottom sections with a melon baller, pressing it face down into the flesh and rotating it until the flesh is free. Remove the remaining flesh and use for the sorbet.

Exotic Fruits

Many of these fruits originate from the tropical zones of Asia, South America and Africa. Others, such as figs and dates, come from the Mediterranean and have only recently become available as fresh rather than dried fruits. Exotic fruits make intriguing additions to cheese boards and fresh fruit salads, and some make superb ice creams and sorbets.

1 Date Fresh dates can be served whole or stoned (see box, opposite page), or halved, stoned and stuffed with a sweet or savoury filling, or chopped.

2 Kiwi fruit Rich in vitamin C, this is best raw when fully ripe. Cut off the top and scoop out the flesh with a teaspoon (like eating a boiled egg) or peel and slice.

3 Sapodilla This Asian fruit is inedible unless soft and overripe. Peel and eat raw, discarding the seeds in the centre of the fruit.

4 Fig Can be eaten raw, poached or preserved in syrup. Prepared as flowers (see box, opposite page), figs can also be stuffed.

5 Passion fruit Originally from Brazil, this fruit is prized for its fragrant pulp. Slice in half, then scoop out the pulp and edible seeds. Eat as they are or add to fruit salads and sweet sauces.

6 Loquat Also known as Japanese medlar, this sweet, slightly resinous Mediterranean fruit is peeled and eaten raw.

STONING DATES WHOLE

Whole dates look good in fruit salads, but for easy eating it is best to remove the stones first. Hold the date firmly in one hand and pull the stone out by the attached stalk, using the tip of a small knife to help you get a good grip.

MAKING A FIG FLOWER

Trim the stalk end of the fig with a small knife. Cut a deep cross shape in the top of the fig and open it out by pushing the sides slightly with your fingers. Fig flowers can be served plain, or with a filling spooned or piped in the centre.

7 Persimmon The true fruit is best when overripe and jammy in texture. Sharon fruit, a similar variety, can be eaten earlier.

8 Feijoa South American in origin, this fruit is similar to a guava (see below) and can be treated in a similar way.

9 Tamarillo Sour when raw, this fruit is cooked and sweetened or sliced in vegetable salads. Also known as tree tomato.

10 Pepino Sometimes described as a melon, this is related more closely to tomatoes and aubergines. Peel and discard the bitter skin and slice the flesh thinly. Use in fruit salads.

11 Babaco Related to the pawpaw (see below), this has orangey-pink flesh. Eat with a spoon or chop into fruit salads.

12 Curuba From South America, this is a type of passion fruit (see opposite page) and is used in a similar way.

13 Physalis Also called cape gooseberry, this sweet orange berry is encased in an inedible husk of papery leaf-like sepals. Eat raw or cooked, or use as a flower-like decoration.

14 Guava Of South American origin, guavas can be eaten raw or cooked. Good in preserves and ice creams.

15 Pawpaw Green unripe pawpaw (or papaya) is used as a vegetable, often shredded in salads. Orangey-pink ripe pawpaw is eaten raw as a fruit. Peel, halve and remove seeds.

PREPARING A MANGOSTEEN

Use a paring knife to slice the fruit in half, cutting through the thick skin just to the firm flesh. Gently scoop out the white segments of fruit with a small spoon. These segments contain stones which are not edible.

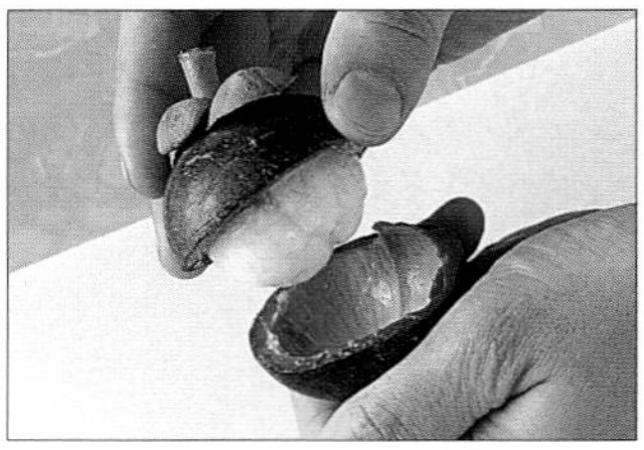

PREPARING A POMEGRANATE

Slice fruit in half. Pressing on the rounded base, invert one half over a sieve set over a bowl. Use fingers to separate the seeds from the pith and membranes. To extract the juice, use the back of a spoon to crush the seeds against the sieve.

1 Mangosteen This hard, round tropical fruit is, surprisingly, not related to the mango. It contains sweet, delicately flavoured succulent white segments that offer a pleasing bite of acidity. They are best eaten raw.

2 Pomegranate Mediterranean in origin, this tough, leathery, shiny red-skinned fruit contains tightly packed seeds surrounded by deep pink, intensely sweet flesh. Use the seeds in fruit salads or press through a sieve and then use the juice to flavour ice creams and mousses. Discard the very bitter skin, pith and membranes.

3 Prickly pear The fruit of a Mediterranean cactus, this can be eaten raw or cooked. It has a yellow or pinkish flesh speckled with crunchy but edible seeds. The fruit has a subtly sweet, mild flavour that benefits from a squeeze of fresh lemon juice. Discard the spiny skin, using gloves to peel it off.

4 Grenadillo This is a type of passion fruit (see page 262). It has a shell-like, hard inedible skin. The flesh can be spooned out and eaten as it is or added to fruit salads, or it can be sieved and used to flavour sorbets and ice creams.

5 Star fruit Of Asian origin, this waxy fruit looks beautiful sliced crosswise in fruit salads or as a decoration. The flavour is refreshing but insipid.

PREPARING A STAR FRUIT

Cut unpeeled fruit crosswise into slices with a small knife. Remove the central seeds. Because the sweetness of the fruit varies (some varieties are quite acidic), taste before adding to salads and adjust dressings accordingly.

PREPARING A LYCHEE

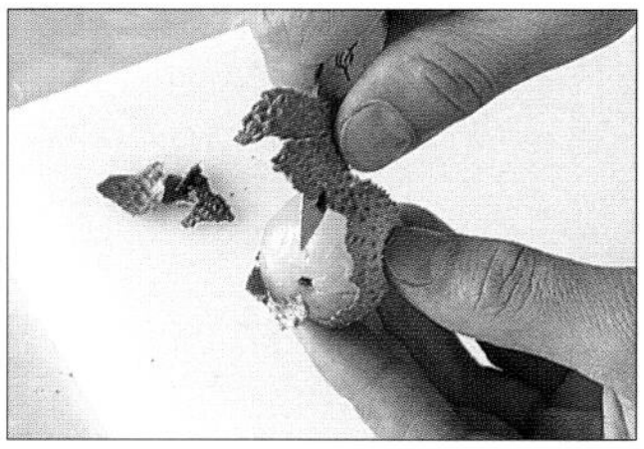

Starting at the stalk end, carefully cut through the rough, brittle skin with a small knife; it will peel off cleanly. The pearly white flesh of the fruit contains a long, brown inedible seed. Ripe fruit has a pink or red blush on its skin.

6 & 7 **Mango** There are thousands of mango varieties – hundreds in Thailand alone. The skin colours vary greatly (here we show a blushing-red variety on the left and an elongated yellow on the right). A ripe mango will have an intense fragrance and should also give slightly when pressed. Unripe mangoes are used as a cooked vegetable in chutneys and curries. Luscious scented ripe mangoes are best eaten raw with a little lime or lemon juice or in fruit salads or *salsas*. They also make delicious sorbets and mousses. See page 255 for two different preparation techniques.

8 **Lychee** The fragrant juicy flesh is encased in a brittle inedible shell which is deep blushing pink when ripe. Eat raw or poached in syrup.

9 **Kiwano** This striking fruit has a spiky inedible orange rind and a green watery interior which is eaten with a spoon.

10 **Rambutan** This Asian fruit looks like a hairy lychee and tastes very similar.

11 **Pitahaya** The fruit of a South American cactus, this can be yellow, ivory or deep pink. Cut in half and spoon out the green or shocking–pink flesh.

12 **Durian** This Indonesian fruit is famed for its unpleasant smell when fully ripe. The flesh is creamy and intensely sweet. It is eaten raw, or used in cakes. Discard the seeds.

Poaching & Preserving

Choose firm fruits for poaching that are not too ripe so they holds their shape. Preserving fruits in alcohol is an ideal way of storing fruits to be eaten later in the year when your favourite fresh fruits are out of season.

Flavours for Poaching Fruits

Serve poached fruits for a simple dessert, or purée and use as the basis of desserts, such as mousses, soufflés and fools. Different flavourings, some subtle, others strong, can be added at the beginning of cooking to infuse the sugar syrup.

- Strips of pared orange, lemon or lime zest.
- Whole spices such as cloves, star anise and cinnamon sticks.
- A split vanilla pod (see page 331).
- Fresh lavender sprigs.
- A slice of fresh root ginger.
- A bruised stalk of lemon grass.

Poaching in Sugar Syrup

Infuse the natural sweetness of fruits with a flavourful poaching liquid. The amount of sugar in the syrup is determined by the fruits to be cooked. A light sugar syrup is suitable for hard and stone fruits, which hold their shape well, while soft berries are best in a heavy syrup, which will help them hold their shape. Sugar syrup quantities are given on page 281. For flavourings, see box, left.

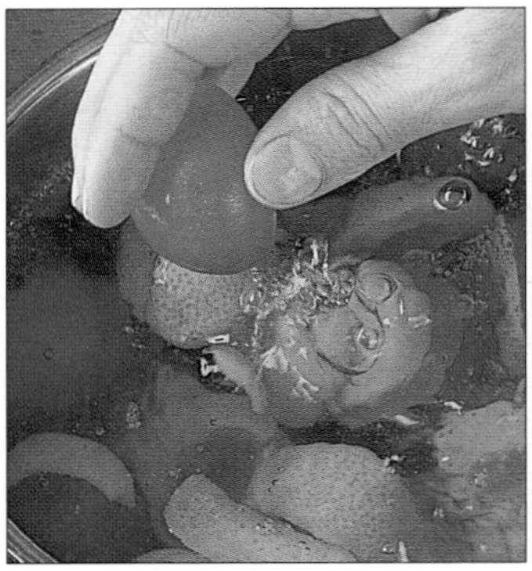

1 Add stoned fruits (here plums are shown) to simmering sugar syrup, making sure the fruits are completely submerged.

2 Poach fruits until tender, 10–15 minutes. Remove with a slotted spoon. Boil the syrup to reduce it, strain and serve poured over the fruits.

Poaching in Wine

Fruits that are poached in wine take on the flavour of the alcohol and, in the case of red wine, the colour. This is the classic French technique for poaching whole pears, as shown here. Before poaching, peel and core pears (see page 250), leaving their stalks intact. This will help to make slicing easy and will give an attractive presentation.

1 Heat wine with flavourings (see box, above left) and sugar until sugar dissolves. Add prepared pears and bring slowly to a simmer. Poach for 15–25 minutes.

2 Remove from the heat, cover and let cool in the liquid. Remove pears with a slotted spoon, reduce liquid and cool. Serve the fruit sliced, on a pool of syrup.

Making a Dried Fruit Compote

A compote is a mixture of fruits poached together to make a delicious blend of colours and flavours. Here, dried fruits are soaked overnight in liquid and flavourings (see box, right). Sugar inhibits the cooking of the fruits, so it is added at the end.

1 Place fruits and soaking liquid in a pan. Add water to just cover fruits. Bring to a gentle simmer, stirring.

2 Poach the fruits gently, just until tender, 15–25 minutes. Remove fruits with a slotted spoon.

3 Sweeten the cooking juices, then reduce by about one-third. Serve fruits with the juices ladled over.

COMPOTE COMBINATIONS

Soaking overnight plumps up dried fruits and allows them to absorb as much flavour as possible. Try the following ideas:

- Make a classic combination of dried apricots, figs, peaches and dates with white wine and honey.
- Mix a tropical blend of dried mango, pineapple and pawpaw, with rum, coconut milk and cinnamon sticks.
- Soak dried apples, pears, apricots and prunes in tea, then cook in orange juice flavoured with cloves.

Preserving and Storing Whole Fruits in Alcohol

Alcohol is used to preserve fruits so they can be kept for an indefinite period of time, although it is advisable to use them within a year in case of fermentation.

Choose fruits that are just ripe and in good condition. For a selection of fruit and alcohol combinations, plus some recommended serving suggestions, see box, right.

Place the prepared fruits in sterilized Kilner jars, and add whole spices, if you like. Pour alcohol into a pan and bring to the boil. Add sugar and stir to dissolve, then remove from the heat and leave to cool. Pour enough of the cooled alcohol into the jars to cover the fruit completely. Seal the jars. Store in a cool dark place for at least 2–3 weeks so that the flavours have time to develop before using.

TRICK OF THE TRADE

Making Rumtopf

A rumtopf *("*rum pot*") is a traditional German method of preserving fruit in alcohol. From summer to autumn, ripened fruits are layered with sugar in stone or glass jars, covered with rum and sealed.*

Sprinkle fruits with sugar and let marinate overnight. Layer fruits (here blueberries and sliced strawberries are shown) in a sterilized Kilner jar, covering each layer with rum. Fill to about 2 cm from the top. Seal and leave to mature for at least 1 month.

FRUITS IN ALCOHOL

Fruits preserved in alcohol make delicious instant desserts all year round. Here are some suggestions for fruit and alcohol partnerships, with ideas for serving them. Citrus fruits need to be peeled first, hard fruits like pears need to be peeled and sometimes poached.

- Cherries with brandy or kirsch. Spoon over vanilla ice cream.
- Grapes with whisky. Fold into whipped cream with crushed meringues.
- Clementines with rum, star anise, cinnamon sticks and cloves. Serve with crème fraîche or warm chocolate sauce.
- Plums with port. Spoon over hazelnut ice cream.
- Mangoes with white rum. Serve with rum and raisin ice cream.
- Pears with vodka. Top with soured cream.
- Summer berries with kirsch. Top with whipped fresh cream.

GRILLING & FRYING

Grilled or chargrilled fruit makes a simple and speedy hot fruit dessert. Fruits can also be deep-fried in batter to make fritters, or sautéed and flambéed. Choose ripe but firm fruits that hold their shape well.

BARBECUING

Cut fruits into slices or wedges, like the pineapple, pawpaw and mango shown here, or cut into chunks and thread on to oiled skewers to make kebabs. Some fruits, such as bananas, can be barbecued whole. Brush the barbecue grid with oil before putting on the fruit. You can also brush the fruit with flavourings such as lemon juice and honey, but use spices sparingly as they can easily scorch.

UNWRAPPED
For a chargrilled effect, cook fruits directly on an oiled grid of the barbecue, turning once, 3–5 minutes.

WRAPPED
For whole fruits to be served *en papillote*, wrap in foil and cook on the barbecue grid for 5–10 minutes.

GRILLING EN SABAYON

Fresh soft fruits, such as the strawberries and blueberries used here, are covered with a sabayon sauce (see page 292) and placed under a hot grill until browned. The sabayon sauce produces a caramelized topping, protecting the sweet juicy fruit below. Choose heatproof bowls that will withstand the intense heat.

1 Arrange prepared fruits decoratively in an even layer in heatproof bowls.

2 Spoon sabayon sauce over fruits – it will melt and spread over the fruits during cooking. Place under a hot grill until lightly browned, 1–2 minutes.

OPPOSITES ATTRACT

A chilled sweet sauce is the perfect accompaniment to a hot fruit dessert. Whipped cream is the traditional choice; here are some alternatives:

- *Crème chantilly* (see page 292) or chilled crème anglaise (see page 276).
- Equal quantities of whipped cream and Greek yogurt or fromage blanc.
- Sugar syrup made with liqueur, sweet wine or citrus juice and flavoured with chopped fresh mint or ground cinnamon.

- Coconut cream sauce (shown above) made following the method for crème anglaise (see page 276) but using coconut milk (see page 204) instead of ordinary milk. Chill the sauce, then top with toasted threads or shavings of coconut just before serving. Serve with tropical fruits.

Coating in a Sugar Glaze

This technique gives fruits a caramelized coating, and is best suited to fruits that are firm enough to hold their shape, such as the orange segments shown here, grapes, cherries, underripe peach or pear slices and wedges or chunks of apple.

Take care when cooking the syrup before the fruits are added. It should be light golden, not brown, or the fruits will taste bitter. Keep the pieces of fruit in a single layer, and do not overcrowd the pan or the fruits will stew and become soggy.

For about 250 g prepared fruits, dissolve 50 g sugar in 100 ml water over a low heat. Add 15 g butter and then heat gently until melted and light golden. Increase the heat and simmer until the syrup bubbles and becomes a glaze, then add fruits. Shake the pan until the fruits are evenly coated with the glaze.

Flambeeing

Flambéed fruits make a spectacular dessert, and have a special intensity of flavour. Grapes or cherries are best suited to this technique, and any high-proof alcohol such as brandy, rum, a fortified wine like Madeira, or a fruit-based liqueur.

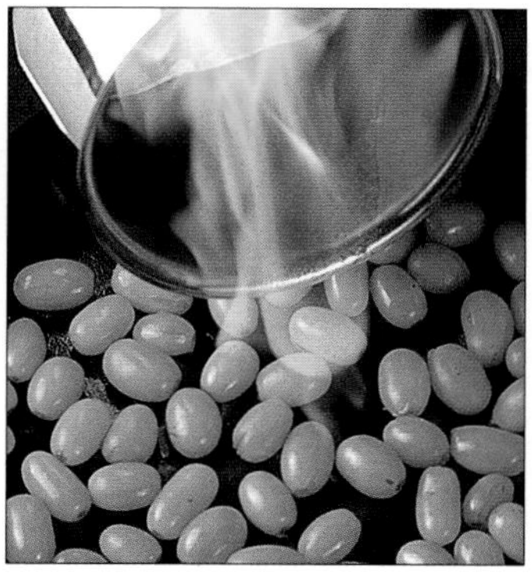

1 Melt butter in a frying pan. Add sugar and prepared fruits; sauté for 1–2 minutes. Warm alcohol in a separate pan and ignite it off the heat, then pour the flaming alcohol over fruits.

2 Baste the fruits constantly with the flaming sauce until the flames have died down, using a long-handled large metal spoon for safety. Serve immediately.

Making Asian Fritters

Fruits deep-fried in Asian-style tempura batter are crisp and light on the outside, sweet and juicy within. The batter is so light that the colour of the fruit shows through. Firm fruits, such as apples and pears, are suitable and tropical fruits like the pineapple, mango, pawpaw and kiwi fruit shown here. Dry the fruit well before coating it or the batter will not adhere.

1 Peel and slice or segment the fruits or cut them into chunks, keeping the shapes as equal in size as possible. Pat the fruits thoroughly dry with paper towels.

2 Prepare tempura batter (see box, right). Dip the fruit pieces in the batter until coated, using a pair of chopsticks or a two-pronged fork. Allow the excess batter to drain back into the bowl. Deep-fry in 190°C oil until the fritters are crisp and golden, 2–3 minutes. Drain before serving.

TEMPURA BATTER

50 g plain flour
50 g cornflour
1½ tsp baking powder
1 egg, beaten
200 ml iced water

Mix the dry ingredients in a bowl. Whisk the egg with the water, then stir into the dry ingredients to form a smooth batter.

BAKING FRUITS

Baking brings out the natural sweetness of fruits and gives them a soft, luscious texture. The fruit requires very little preparation, apart from coring or stoning. Firm, ripe fruits give the best results. Large fruits make perfect containers for sweet stuffings.

BAKING WHOLE APPLES

Cox's Orange Pippin and Granny Smith's are good apple varieties for baking. For filling ideas, see box, right allowing 1–2 tbsp of filling per fruit. After coring the apple, sprinkle the inside with lemon juice to prevent discoloration. Bake in a shallow ovenproof dish to catch the juices.

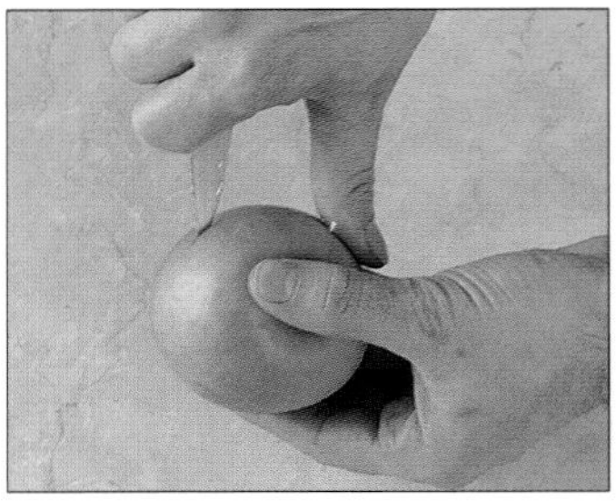

1 Score around the middle of the apple with a small knife to allow the flesh to expand during baking.

2 Place stuffed apples in a baking dish; top with butter and bake at 200°C for 45–50 minutes.

BAKING HALVED FRUIT

This technique works well for stone fruits, such as the peaches shown here. Halve and stone the fruits (see page 254), then sprinkle with lemon juice, to prevent discoloration. Place fruit halves, cut-sides up, in a baking dish in a single layer, taking care not to overcrowd the dish.

1 Spoon the filling of your choice (see box, left) into the cavities in the fruit, mounding it slightly.

2 Bake at 180°C until the flesh of the fruit feels tender when pierced, about 15 minutes.

BAKING EN PAPILLOTE

Baking "en papillote" *helps keep fruit moist by steaming it in its own juices, with sugar and flavourings. A small amount of butter can also be added for richness. Baking parchment or foil can be used; the banana leaf shown here offers an interesting Asian alternative. Bake at 180°C for 15 minutes.*

1 Place fruits in centre of wrapping. Sprinkle with sugar to taste, then sprinkle again with wine or liqueur of your choice.

2 Fold the sides of the wrapping over the filling to form a parcel. Tie with kitchen string to secure.

FILLINGS FOR BAKED FRUITS

Fresh or dried fruits, nuts and spices can be combined to create delicious fillings or toppings for baked fruits. To help the fruits keep their balance in the dish, take a slice off the base to create a flat surface.

- Diced pear, halved raspberries and grated lemon zest.
- Crushed amaretti biscuits, ground almonds and dried cherries.
- Candied fruits and toasted pistachio nuts.
- Chopped walnuts or hazelnuts, brown sugar and honey.
- Snipped dates, dried apricots and cake crumbs soaked in brandy.
- Muesli drizzled with cream.
- Breadcrumbs, raisins and pine nuts moistened with a light sugar syrup and a few drops of orange flower water.

FRUITS FOR BAKING EN PAPILLOTE

- Pineapple, banana and orange.
- Figs and plums, dotted with butter and drizzled with lavender honey.
- Pear, quince and dried cranberries plumped in brandy, sprinkled with cardamom.
- Strawberries, kiwi fruit and peaches.

DESSERTS

MERINGUES
•
COLD MOUSSES, SOUFFLES & JELLIES
•
CUSTARDS & CREAMS
•
HOT PUDDINGS
•
SUGAR
•
CHOCOLATE
•
ICE-CREAM DESSERTS
•
SORBETS & GRANITAS
•
SWEET SAUCES

MERINGUES

A mixture of stiffly beaten egg whites and sugar or a sugar syrup, meringues are the basis of numerous desserts and confections. Although the equipment may vary depending on the type of meringue you are making, the basic techniques and principles are much the same.

TYPES OF MERINGUE

FRENCH: The simplest meringue with a light texture; use for piping and shaping, poaching as in *oeufs à la neige*, or baking as in *vacherin* and nests (see opposite page). Use 115 g sugar to 2 egg whites.
ITALIAN: A firm-textured but velvety meringue, made with a hot sugar syrup that "cooks" the egg whites; use in uncooked desserts, such as cold mousses, soufflés and sorbets. It holds its shape well, so it is also ideal for piping. To make 400 g Italian meringue, make a sugar syrup with 250 g sugar and 60 ml water, boil to the soft-ball stage (118°C) and whisk into 5 stiffly whisked egg whites.
SWISS: Gives a much firmer result than French; use for piping and other decorative effects. Allow 125 g sugar to 2 egg whites.

MAKING MERINGUE

Make sure all utensils are scrupulously clean and free of grease. To ensure maximum volume, allow the egg whites to stand in a covered container at room temperature for one hour before use. There are three ways to make meringue, depending on your recipe and its application.

FRENCH
Whisk egg whites using a balloon whisk until stiff peaks form. Gradually whisk in half the sugar, then fold in the remainder.

ITALIAN
With a tabletop mixer on low speed, whisk hot sugar syrup into whisked egg whites, down the side of the bowl in a steady stream.

SWISS
Whisk egg whites and sugar in a bowl set over a pan of simmering water. Keep turning the bowl to prevent pockets of egg white cooking.

PAVLOVA

3 egg whites
175 g caster sugar
1 tsp raspberry or wine vinegar
1 tsp cornflour

Line a baking sheet with baking parchment. Whisk egg whites until stiff, whisk in half the sugar, then fold in remaining sugar with vinegar and cornflour. Shape into a 20-cm round on paper and bake at 150°C for 1 hour. Let cool in turned-off oven. Serves 6.

MAKING A PAVLOVA

This famous dessert named after the Russian ballerina, Anna Pavlova, celebrated her visit to New Zealand. It is a unique meringue confection that has a squidgy, almost marshmallow texture, created by adding vinegar and cornflour to whisked egg whites and sugar. The relatively short cooking time is another contributing factor, because it ensures that moisture is retained.

SHAPING MERINGUE
Spread into a round with a large metal spoon, making a hollow in centre.

PEELING PARCHMENT
Carefully peel the baking parchment away from bottom of the cooled meringue.

Filling a Piping Bag

Professional chefs fill a piping bag holding it in one hand, as shown here. Another method is to pull the sides of the bag over the rim of a jug to act as a support.

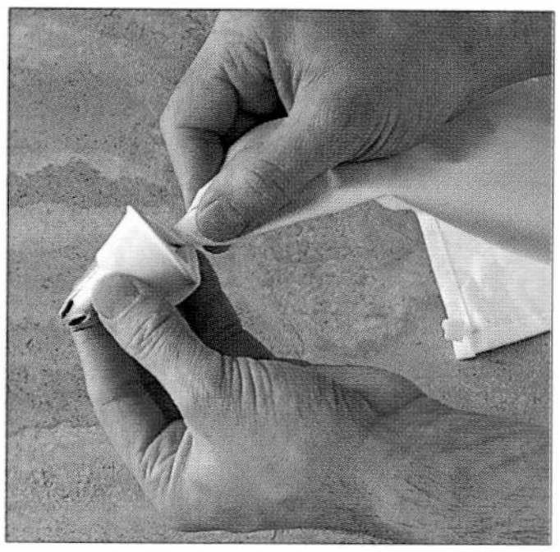

1 Fit the nozzle securely, then twist the bag above the nozzle to prevent leakage.

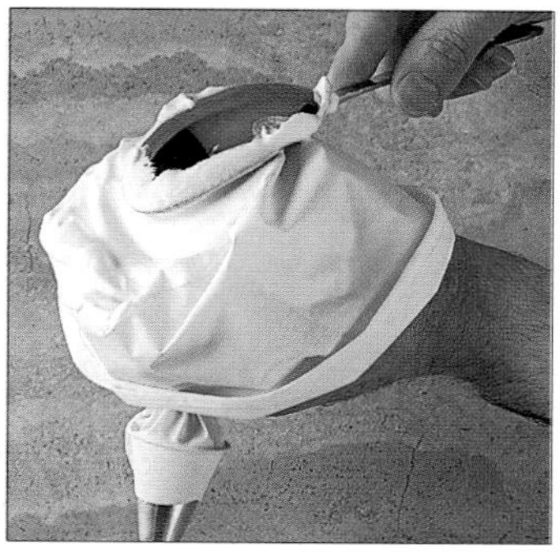

2 Fold the top of the bag over your hand to form a collar; spoon in filling.

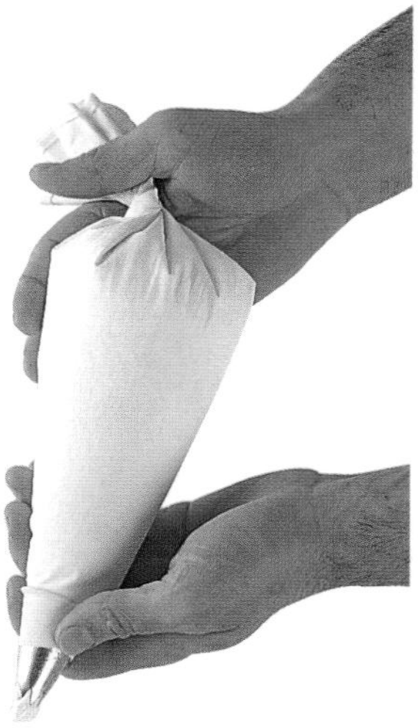

3 Twist the top of the bag, until filling is visible in nozzle, to clear air pockets.

Serving Meringues

Fill or sandwich meringues with flavoured cream or try one of the following ideas:

- Sandwich shells with chocolate ganache (see page 282), sprinkle with chocolate curls (see page 322), then dust with icing sugar and cocoa powder.
- Toss a selection of seasonal fruits in a little Cointreau. Pile high in nests.
- Layer discs with chocolate or fruit mousse to make a gâteau (see page 315).

Making Shapes

The change in consistency of meringue – from soft enough to pipe and shape, to firm enough to stack and hold other ingredients – makes it useful for a wide variety of applications and presentations. A simple French meringue can be used; bake it at 100°C for at least 1 hour. Swiss meringue that has been dried out overnight at 60°C gives a whiter result.

Shells
Pipe small rounds on baking parchment, using a medium or large nozzle.

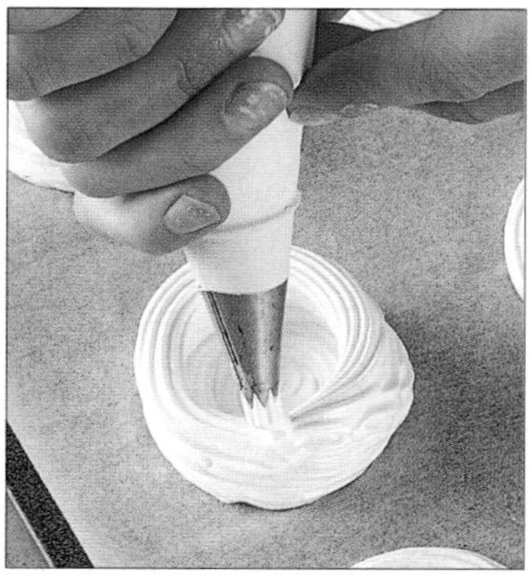

Nests
Mark baking parchment with 5-cm circles. With a star nozzle, pipe the base, working from centre in a spiral. Pipe around edge to create a nest.

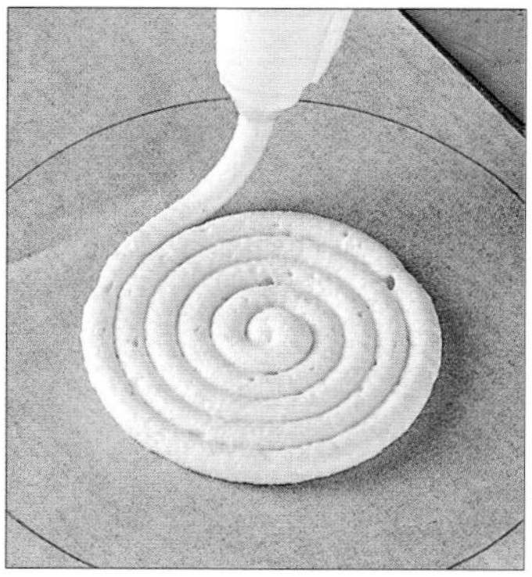

Large disc
On baking parchment, trace a circle the size of the disc you require. Using a small plain nozzle, pipe from the centre of the circle, spiralling outwards.

Cold Mousses, Souffles & Jellies

Light, creamy mousses and sweet soufflés make stunning desserts. Whipped cream, gelatine or Italian meringue, in varying combinations, are required to hold them in shape, but gelatine is vital for a jelly's "wobble".

Dissolving Gelatine

It is necessary to soak both gelatine powder and leaf gelatine before use in order for them to combine evenly with the mixture they are setting. When heating gelatine, never let it boil or the end result will be stringy.

Powder
Sprinkle over 4 tbsp cold liquid. Let stand until spongy, 5 minutes. Place bowl over hot water until liquid is clear.

Leaf
Soften leaves in cold water, 5 minutes. Squeeze out excess water. Transfer leaves to hot liquid to dissolve.

Making a Simple Fruit Mousse

Fruit purées form the base of many mousses. For best flavour, choose strongly flavoured purées such as the apricot shown here; blackcurrants and blackberries are also good. For a lighter mousse, you can fold in 2 stiffly whisked egg whites (see page 31) after the cream.

1 Prepare 15 g gelatine powder in water (see left) and let cool to lukewarm. Stir into 450 ml sweetened fruit purée. Let stand at room temperature until the mixture begins to thicken, 15–30 minutes.

2 Lightly whip 300 ml double cream, then beat 2 tbsp into the fruit mixture to relax it. Fold in the remaining cream using a spatula. Chill for at least 4 hours before serving.

Chocolate Mousse

This quick-and-easy mousse relies on the combination of chocolate, butter and egg whites for setting rather than gelatine. For six servings, melt 450 g unsweetened chocolate with 100 g caster sugar and 2 tbsp butter. Cool, then add 6 egg yolks. Whisk 6 egg whites (see page 31) until they just hold their shape, then fold into the chocolate mixture. Cover and chill for at least 4 hours.

Adding egg yolks
Take care that the melted chocolate mixture is cool before adding the egg yolks. If it is hot, the yolks may cook and curdle.

Folding in egg whites
Beat 2 tbsp of the whisked egg whites into the mixture to relax it slightly, then carefully fold in the remainder until they are evenly incorporated.

Making a Fruit Souffle

This technique combines three ingredients – fruit purée, meringue and cream – and sets them in a dish with a collar to mimic the appearance of a baked soufflé. Here a raspberry soufflé is made with 350 ml purée, 400 g Italian meringue (see page 272) and 400 ml double cream in a 1.5 litre soufflé dish.

1 Put a double collar of baking parchment around dish to extend 3–5 cm above the rim; secure with tape.

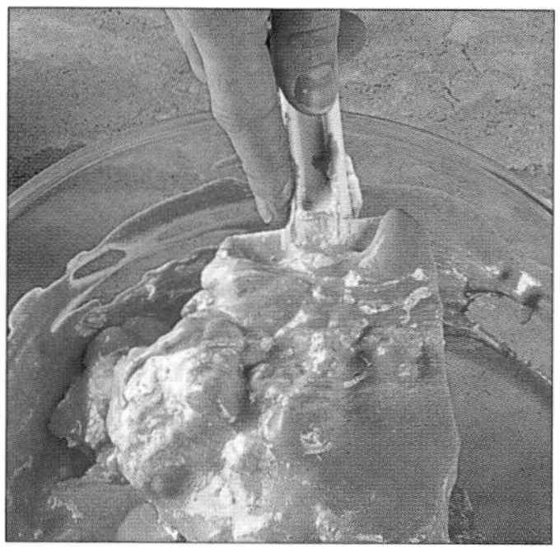

2 Carefully fold Italian meringue into fruit purée with a spatula, then fold in whipped cream.

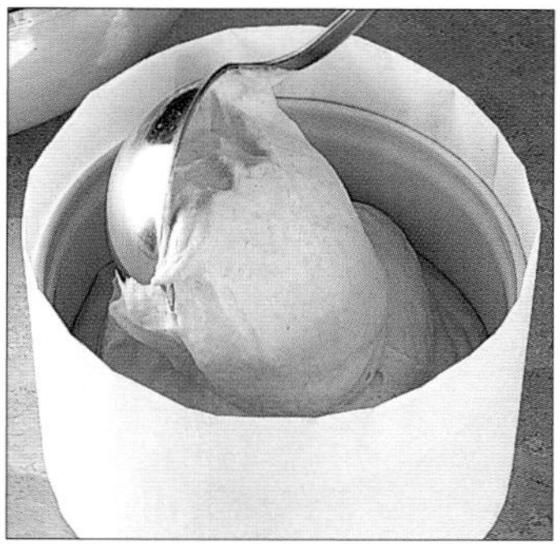

3 Ladle the soufflé mixture into the dish so that it reaches the rim of the collar.

4 Smooth the surface with a palette knife that has been dipped in warm water.

5 Freeze the soufflé for 2 hours until firm. No more than 20 minutes before serving, carefully peel away the paper collar, smooth the edge with a palette knife and decorate.

Making a Fruit Jelly

Fresh fruits suspended in jelly look most appealing, especially if they are layered decoratively with jelly in between. The technique is simple, but time needs to be taken waiting for each layer to set before adding the next. A quick option is to present fruits at random within the jelly – simply fill the mould with fruits and pour in liquid jelly to cover.

1 Prepare 15 g gelatine powder (see opposite page) in water. Add dissolved gelatine to a warm sugar syrup made with 150 g sugar and 150 ml water.

2 Mix 500 ml unsweetened fresh fruit juice with the warm sugar syrup, then stir in 3 tbsp liqueur or spirit of your choice. Let cool.

3 Place 500 g fruits in a single layer in a 1.5-litre mould. Ladle over liquid jelly to cover. Chill 15 minutes or until set; repeat all the way to the top of the mould.

CUSTARDS & CREAMS

The luxurious marriage of milk, sugar and eggs is the foundation for silky sauces, vanilla-scented creams and thick, smooth custards. The following methods make use of similar ingredients, but techniques, cooking times and added enrichments create different tastes and textures.

WHAT'S IN A NAME?

CREME ANGLAISE: This is a rich custard sauce traditionally flavoured with vanilla, although nowadays other flavourings, such as grated citrus zest, chocolate and liqueurs, are often added.
CREME MOUSSELINE: This is a crème pâtissière enriched with butter, used as a filling for sponge cakes and as a base for desserts. It is firmer than crème pâtissière, which is why it is used as a filling for the tiers of choux puffs in croquembouche (see page 300).
CREME PATISSIERE: A term used to describe a custard thickened with both plain flour and cornflour. It can be used as a base for soufflés, and as a filling for cakes, tarts and pastries – especially éclairs.

CREME ANGLAISE

Cooking an egg custard on the stove top requires close attention. So the eggs do not curdle, make sure the milk does not boil while the custard is cooking. Keep the heat gentle and stir constantly around the sides and bottom of the pan to prevent the possibility of scorching.

1 Infuse 500 ml milk with ½ vanilla pod (see page 331). Whisk 5 egg yolks in a bowl with 65 g caster sugar. Remove vanilla pod from the milk and bring the milk to the boil. Whisk milk into eggs, then pour into a clean pan.

2 Heat the custard gently, stirring constantly with a wooden spoon, until it thickens. Test consistency by running your finger through the custard along the back of spoon. It should leave a clear line. Makes about 625 ml.

CREME PATISSIERE

If not using immediately, rub butter over the surface to prevent a skin forming.

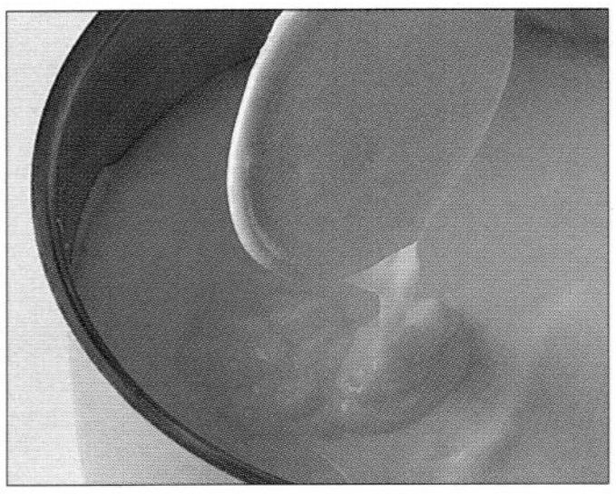

Whisk 6 egg yolks in a bowl with 100 g caster sugar, then whisk in 40 g each plain flour and cornflour. Bring 600 ml milk to the boil and stir into egg mixture. Pour into a pan and bring back to the boil, stirring until large bubbles break on surface. Lower the heat and cook until very thick.

TRICK OF THE TRADE

IF A CUSTARD CURDLES
If the heat is too high when cooking a custard on top of the stove, it will separate and look curdled. To rescue it, remove the pan from the heat and beat with the spoon until blended. Another solution is to strain the custard through a fine sieve into a blender and work it until smooth. Reheat gently.

BAKING CUSTARDS

English custards are baked in a large dish and served hot. Blend 3 egg yolks with 50 g sugar and 25 g each cornflour and plain flour. Add 500 ml milk and cook gently, stirring, until thickened, then pour into dish. In France, custards are baked in pretty little pots and served cold. The custard is the same as the English one, but made with 300 ml double cream and 200 ml milk, plus 2 egg yolks.

TRADITIONAL ENGLISH
Grate nutmeg over top of custard in baking dish and bake in a warm *bain marie* at 170°C for 20-25 minutes. Serve the custard hot.

FRENCH PETITS POTS
Bake individual pots of enriched custard in a cold *bain marie* at 170 °C for 15-20 minutes. Cool, then chill before serving.

Making a Bavarois

This classic French moulded dessert, also called a Bavarian cream, takes crème anglaise *(see opposite page), sets it with gelatine and folds in whipped cream to lighten. The result is a velvety smooth texture that is firm enough to turn out and hold its shape when served.*

1 Prepare 15 g gelatine powder (see page 274) in water, then mix with 3 tbsp Cointreau and stir into 625 ml warm crème anglaise.

2 Transfer custard to a bowl, cover and let cool. When just on the point of setting, fold in 225 ml double cream, lightly whipped.

3 Rinse a 1.5-litre charlotte mould with cold water, then ladle in the bavarois. Chill for 4 hours or until set. Turn out to serve.

Brulee Topping

Rich creams are often topped with a crisp caramel, brûlée *in French. It is cracked open with a spoon at the table.*

Sprinkle 1½ tbsp granulated sugar over each ramekin. Put under a hot grill, as close to heat as possible, 2–3 minutes. Let cool; serve within 2 hours.

Making Creme Caramel

The secret of making these French custards beautifully creamy and smooth is to bake them very gently in a bain marie. *Keep an eye on the water – it should not be allowed to bubble or the custards will turn out dimpled. Follow the techniques here, based on the recipe, right.*

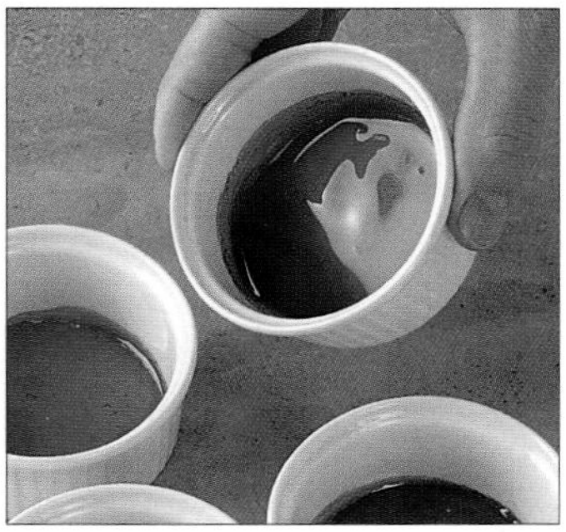

1 Carefully pour hot caramel into ramekins. Working quickly, tip each one so the caramel coats the bottom and sides of the dish.

2 Pour strained custard into prepared ramekins until it comes just below the rims. Place in a roasting tin and pour in hot water to come halfway up sides of ramekins.

3 Run the blade of a small palette knife around the edge of each custard. Hold a dessert plate on top of each ramekin and invert. Lift off the ramekin, letting the caramel sauce form a pool around the custard.

CREME CARAMEL

100 g granulated sugar
60 ml water
2 eggs
4 egg yolks
115 g caster sugar
A few drops of vanilla essence
500 ml milk

Make the caramel (see page 281), using the granulated sugar and water. Use immediately to coat the inside of four 125 ml ramekins. Put the whole eggs, egg yolks, sugar and vanilla in a bowl and stir gently to mix. Heat the milk until hand hot and pour it on to the egg mixture, stirring.

Strain the custard into a jug, then divide equally between the ramekins. Bake, uncovered, in a hot *bain marie* at 170°C for 40–50 minutes until set. Let cool, then chill overnight. Makes 4.

Hot Puddings

These comforting, time-honoured favourites like creamy rice puddings, sensuous sweet soufflés and moulded fruit charlottes are easy to master and so utterly satisfying to prepare.

Making a Stovetop Rice Pudding

Gentle simmering is required for the grains to absorb the milk gradually and acquire a creamy texture. A heavy pan is also essential for the rice to cook evenly, and to prevent scorching. Bring 550 ml milk to the boil, add 115 g pudding rice, 60 g caster sugar and ½ vanilla pod. Simmer gently until thick and creamy, 30 minutes.

Stir often during cooking to distribute the rice in the milk. This will help the rice to cook evenly and prevent it sticking to the bottom of the pan.

Making a Baked Rice Pudding

This English favourite has a thin golden crust. Put 50 g pudding rice in a buttered baking dish with 60 g caster sugar, 1 tsp grated lemon zest, a pinch of salt and 600 ml warm milk. Sprinkle with nutmeg and dot with butter. Bake, uncovered, at 150°C for 1–1½ hours, stirring only once, after the first 30 minutes.

For a rich flavour and crisp skin, dot rice pudding with knobs of butter before baking. Grated nutmeg also adds colour and flavour..

Baked Vanilla Souffles

125 g butter
60 g plain flour
500 ml milk
½ tsp vanilla essence
125 g caster sugar
8 eggs, separated

Make a white sauce using the butter, flour and milk (see page 222). Stir in the vanilla essence and 2 tbsp of the sugar.Remove from the heat and let cool slightly, then beat in the egg yolks. Whisk the egg whites to a soft peak, then gradually whisk in the remaining sugar to form a soft meringue. Gently fold the meringue into the white sauce with a large metal spoon. Spoon the mixture into six prepared 125 ml ramekins and bake at 190°C for 15-20 minutes. Serve immediately, lightly dusted with icing sugar. Makes 6.

Making a Hot Sweet Souffle

The foundation of a baked soufflé is a simple white sauce, and sugar and vanilla are the classic flavourings. The pastry chef's secret is to bake individual soufflés rather than one large one – it is easier to see when they are done, and they are less likely to collapse. Here are two other professional techniques.

Triple coating
To ensure soufflés rise evenly, brush inside ramekins with softened butter, working brush from bottom upwards. Chill until set, then repeat. Half fill ramekin with caster sugar and rotate so the sugar coats the inside, allowing excess sugar to fall into the next ramekin to be coated.

Cleaning rims
For straight-sided soufflés, run thumb around inside of rim.

Making a Hot Charlotte

Like the chilled dessert of the same name (see box, right), this type of charlotte – the pairing of a buttery bread "crust" with a sweet and juicy fruit filling – is traditionally moulded in a bucket-shaped tin of the same name. Stale bread works best because it holds its shape better against the moist fruit.

1 Halve 4-5 slices of bread diagonally, then cut each triangle with a plain biscuit cutter as shown, so they fit in bottom of tin.

2 Halve remaining bread slices as shown. Dip all bread slices in melted butter and overlap them in tin.

3 Put the filling in the centre, packing it down with the back of the ladle, then cover with the remaining bread slices dipped in butter. This will prevent the filling from spilling out when unmoulding.

Steaming a Pudding

Old-fashioned puddings were wrapped in pudding cloths for steaming, but nowadays foil is used. Careful handling is required because the bowl and foil become extremely hot during the long steaming time. The technique shown here reduces the risk of scalding.

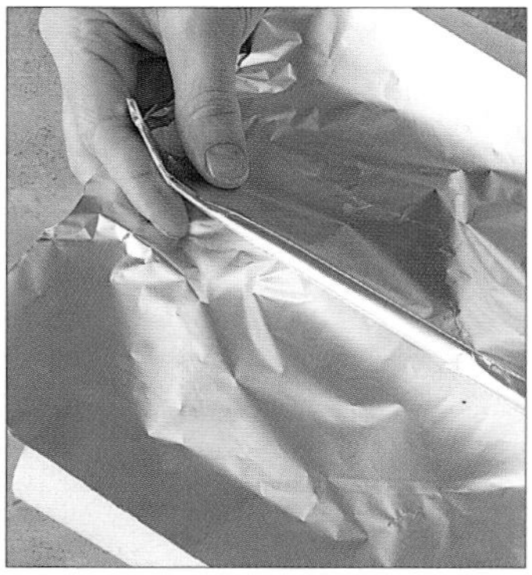

1 Pleat together a piece each of baking parchment and foil large enough to fit comfortably over bowl.

2 Put parchment and foil over bowl and tie string under the lip and over the top of the bowl to make a handle.

3 Use the string handle to lift the pudding in and out of the pan. A trivet in the pan distributes heat evenly.

WHAT'S IN A NAME?

Charlotte is the name of two different desserts: one is hot (as shown here) and the other, a charlotte russe, is cold. The hot pudding was created by a chef during the reign of England's most famous mad king, George III. It was named in honour of Charlotte his wife and queen. The cold version, charlotte russe, was the inspiration of Carême, a famous French pastry chef to the Russian Tzar Alexander in the 19th century. It is an elaborate uncooked dessert made of a rich cream poured into a mould lined with sponge fingers.

Queen Charlotte (d. 1818)

APPLE CHARLOTTE

500 g each cooking apples and Granny Smith's, roughly chopped
100 g unsalted butter
250 g sugar
50 g walnut pieces
10–12 large slices of white bread
Apricot glaze (see page 319)

Sweat the apples and 25 g butter over a low heat for 15 minutes until softened. Stir in the sugar, walnuts and cook until the apples begin to break up. Melt the remaining butter. Remove crusts from bread and cut bread to fit inside a 1.5-litre charlotte tin. Dip bread into butter and use to line tin. Fill with compote; cover with remaining bread. Cover with foil and bake at 190°C for 1 hour or until firm. Turn out on to a serving plate and brush with warm glaze. Serve hot. Serves 6.

Sugar

When it comes to cooking, sugar does more than sweeten. Heated with water it creates syrups that are indispensible in many desserts. Caramelized, it takes on an amber hue, and is used for praline and nougatine.

Sugar Thermometer

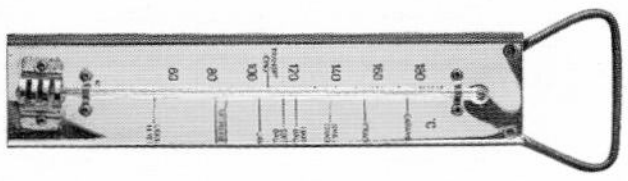

This is invaluable for determining the exact temperature of boiled sugar syrups, and the setting points of jams, jellies and sweets. Take care that the tip of the thermometer touches only the liquid – not the pan.

Making Sugar Syrups

The two essential techniques for a clear, non-grainy sugar syrup are to make sure the sugar has completely dissolved before raising the heat and boiling the liquid, and never to stir the syrup once it is boiling. For different weights of sugar syrups and their uses, see box, opposite page.

1 Put sugar and cold water in a heavy pan; stir over a low heat until sugar dissolves.

2 For a simple syrup, boil for 1 minute. For other boiled syrups, see below.

Boiled Sugar Syrups

If a syrup is left on the heat, water will evaporate and the temperature will rise, creating increasingly thick syrups. During boiling, brush sides of pan with water to prevent crystals forming (see step 2, above). If you have no thermometer, use your fingers: dip them in iced water, then in the syrup, then in iced water. To stop cooking, see step 2 of Caramel, opposite page.

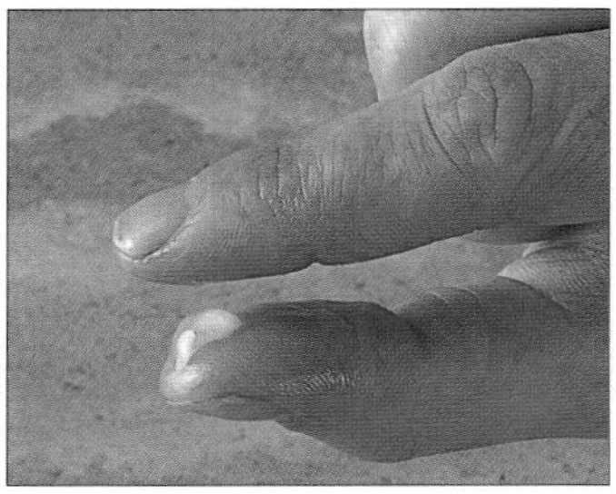

Soft-ball (116–118°C)
The first stage of saturation point; syrup holds its shape but is soft when pressed.

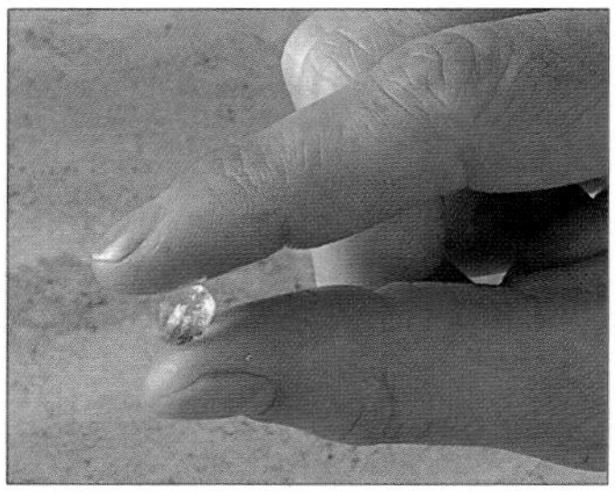

Hard-ball (125°C)
Syrup forms a firm and pliable ball, giving a chewy texture.

Soft-crack (134°C)
Syrup is brittle, but with a soft, pliable texture that will stick to the teeth.

Hard-crack (145°C)
Syrup is very brittle. Beyond this point sugar will quickly caramelize.

From top, left to right; sugar crystals, light muscovado, dark muscovado, demerara sugar. **From bottom, left to right;** icing sugar, sugar cubes, caster sugar, granulated sugar

CARAMEL

Amber-coloured caramel, used as a sauce or a crisp sweet, forms when heavy sugar syrup is heated beyond the hard-crack stage, all the moisture has evaporated, and the syrup takes on a deep brown colour. Light caramel is mild-flavoured; medium caramel is dark golden brown and has a nutty taste. Take care not to cook the caramel beyond 190°C or it will burn. If the caramel sets too quickly, re-warm it briefly.

1 Bring heavy syrup to the boil in a heavy pan. Lower the heat and swirl the pan once or twice so the syrup colours evenly; do not stir.

2 When the caramel is the required colour, plunge base of pan into iced water to stop further cooking; remove pan before caramel sets.

PRALINE

A flavouring for ice creams and other desserts, praline is a mixture of caramel and nuts. Almond praline is traditional, but hazelnuts, or the pecans shown here, are appealing alternatives. Equal amounts of nuts and sugar are usually used, then the praline is cracked into pieces with a rolling pin or ground in a food processor using the pulse button. If the praline is to be rolled out, use fewer nuts.

1 Add whole shelled nuts to boiling golden caramel and heat until they begin to pop and smell toasted.

2 Pour immediately on to a baking sheet lined with baking parchment and spread evenly. Let cool.

SUGAR SYRUPS AND THEIR USES

The temperatures achieved when boiling sugar and water determine its uses – from simple syrups to soft fondants and brittle caramel.

LIGHT SUGAR SYRUP: (250 g sugar to 500 ml water); for fruit salads and poaching fruits.
MEDIUM SYRUP: (250 g sugar to 250 ml water); for candying fruits.
HEAVY SYRUP: (250 g sugar to 225 ml water); for caramel (see left) and ice creams.
SOFT-BALL (116-118°C): For Italian meringue and buttercream icing.
HARD-BALL (125°C): For marzipan, fondant and sweets.
SOFT-CRACK (134°C): For nougat, some caramels and toffee.
HARD-CRACK (145°C): For pulled and spun sugar, rock sugar, straw sugar and glazed fruits.
CARAMEL: In liquid form, for flavouring sauces and using in desserts like crème caramel. Cracked or crushed caramel is used for brittles and toppings.

NOUGATINE

A favourite of pastry chefs, classic nougatine is a mixture of caramel and almonds like praline, but glucose is added so the mixture is malleable, and the nuts are flaked and toasted before mixing with the caramel. Nougatine is mainly used for decorative shaping (see croquembouche, page 300) and to make containers for dessert fillings, but it can be crushed as a topping for ice creams and other desserts. The quantities here make 2 kg.

1 Dissolve 1 kg sugar in 100 ml water, bring to the boil and add 400 g liquid glucose. Cook until a caramel colour. Sprinkle in 500 g toasted flaked almonds; shake pan to coat nuts. Turn on to an oiled surface; let cool slightly. Roll out with a warm, oiled metal rolling pin.

2 When the nougatine is 5 mm thick, cut it into strips with a warm, lightly oiled chef's knife, then cut it into required shapes.

CHOCOLATE

It is important that chocolate is handled correctly because it plays such a major role in dessert making. For best results, always use good-quality chocolate that has a cocoa butter content of at least 32 per cent.

CHOCOLATE

It is easiest to chop and grate chocolate when it is cool and firm. In warm weather, refrigerate it first, and take the extra precaution of holding it in a piece of baking parchment or foil. All utensils should be absolutely dry.

CHOPPING Work blade of chef's knife backwards and forwards over chocolate.

GRATING Hold chocolate firmly; work it down against the coarsest grid.

MELTING

Chocolate is best melted in a bain marie *over a very low heat. If it becomes too hot it will turn grainy and scorch; if splashed with water, it will harden or "seize" and acquire a dull finish.*

Chop chocolate into rough, even-sized pieces. Place the pieces in a dry heatproof bowl and set the bowl over a pan of hot (not simmering) water. When the chocolate starts to melt, stir it with a wooden spoon until smooth.

MAKING GANACHE

This creamy chocolate mixture can be used as an icing and filling for cakes, and can be flavoured with a few drops of liqueur or coffee if you like. For successful results with ganache, use a good-quality chocolate, such as couverture, that contains a high percentage of cocoa butter (see box, left).

1 Chop and melt 300 g chocolate. Heat 150 ml double cream; pour over.

2 Stir the cream and chocolate together using a wooden spoon.

3 When they are evenly combined, beat until smooth and glossy.

TYPES OF CHOCOLATE

Professional pastry chefs use different kinds of chocolate from the home cook. This is because they often need a chocolate that is not only malleable for intricate shaping but also able to hold its shape. The cocoa butter content of chocolate determines its ability to cut and shape, and it also gives the chocolate its flavour.

BAKER'S CHOCOLATE: Also called baker's covering and *pâte à glacer*, this has had all the cocoa butter removed and replaced by hydrogenated vegetable oil, resulting in a chocolate that is very easy to use, with good setting and cutting properties, but a fatty flavour and a matt finish. It is best for making flexible decorations, such as the ribbons on page 284, and can be used without tempering (see opposite page). For stockists, see page 351.
COUVERTURE CHOCOLATE: The pastry chef's favourite for any recipe that calls for chocolate, couverture contains a high percentage of cocoa butter (at least 32%) and so has a high gloss and a fine flavour. It is more difficult to work with than baker's chocolate – it must always be tempered before use – but it looks and tastes much better. If you are unable to get couverture (see stockists, page 351), substitute an unsweetened or semisweet (also called bittersweet and plain) chocolate with the highest cocoa butter content you can find, and temper it before use.

TEMPERING

This technique is for chocolate that has a high cocoa butter content (see box, opposite page). It provides the consistency and sheen required for many decorative items. Melting, cooling and re-warming breaks down the fat to produce glossy, streak-free chocolate that sets very hard.

1 Slowly melt the chocolate in a bowl over a pan of hot (not simmering) water. Stir until smooth, to a temperature of 45°C.

2 Set bowl of chocolate over another bowl filled with ice cubes. Stir until the chocolate cools and the temperature drops to 25°C.

3 Warm the chocolate again over a pan of hot water for 30–60 seconds, until it reaches a working temperature of 32°C.

MAKING CUPS

Pastry chefs dip the outside of dariole moulds covered with cling film in tempered chocolate. Here is an alternative method.

Paint a thin coating of tempered chocolate on the inside of petit four cases. Leave to set, then carefully peel away the paper case.

MAKING SHAPES

When preparing chocolate for cutting, work quickly so the chocolate does not set too soon. Once smoothed and settled to an even layer, you can place a second sheet of baking parchment on top of the chocolate, then invert the paper sheets so the new sheet is on the bottom. This will stop the chocolate curling up as it dries. Peel off the top sheet before cutting. Layer shapes with piped ganache (see opposite page); fill boxes with fresh fruits. For dusting technique, see page 290.

1 Ladle tempered chocolate on to a baking sheet lined with baking parchment.

2 Quickly spread a layer about 2 mm thick, using a paddling motion with a large angled spatula. Cool until cloudy, but not set.

3 Before chocolate sets and becomes brittle, dip a biscuit cutter in hot water, dry, then cut rounds. Use a knife for other shapes. Let shapes set on baking parchment.

Gâteau des Deux Pierre

This spectacular dessert, a truly delicious blend of chocolate and raspberries, is completely encased in rich chocolatey ribbons. Make the separate components one at a time, then assemble the cake at the end.

SERVES 6

FOR THE SPONGE CAKE

85 g plain flour

40 g cocoa powder

4 eggs, separated

125 g caster sugar

FOR THE MOUSSE

50 g caster sugar

75 ml water

4 prepared gelatine leaves (see page 274)

250 g couverture chocolate (see box, page 282), melted

500 ml double cream, lightly whipped

TO FINISH

175 g raspberries

50 ml framboise *(raspberry liqueur)*

Sugar syrup (see page 280), made with 50 g caster sugar and 50 ml water

350 g baker's chocolate (see box, page 282)

Icing sugar

Make the sponge cake: sift the flour and cocoa powder. Whisk the egg whites until soft peaks form. Gradually add the sugar and continue to whisk until smooth. Mix in egg yolks, then gently fold in dry ingredients. Bake in a greased and lined Swiss roll tin at 220°C, 8–10 minutes, then transfer the cake, crust-side up, to a rack and let cool. Place cake crust-side down on a sheet of baking parchment dusted with caster sugar, peel off the lining paper, then cut out 2 discs using a 23-cm metal cake ring as a guide.

Macerate the raspberries in the liqueur.

Make the mousse: put sugar and water in a saucepan and bring to the boil. Remove from the heat and stir in the gelatine, then pour into the chocolate and mix until smooth. Stir one-third of the cream into the chocolate, then fold in the remainder.

Assemble the cake: place a 23-cm metal cake ring on a cake card, then place a sponge disc in the bottom. Spoon the mousse on top, half filling the ring, and smooth the surface. Place a second sponge disc on top of the mousse and press it in. Drain the liqueur from the raspberries and add it to the sugar syrup. Imbibe the sponge with the syrup (see page 315); sprinkle with an even layer of raspberries. Cover with the remaining mousse and smooth the surface. Refrigerate until the mousse has set, about 1 hour. Warm the outside of the metal ring with a blow torch or a hot tea towel. Carefully lift off the ring, then transfer the cake to a serving plate.

Make the ribbons: melt the baker's chocolate and spread over the back of a baking sheet. Leave to cool until almost set, then make ribbons (see box, below). Wrap the ribbons around the cake as each one is made, beginning with the base. Decorate the top of the cake by coiling the ribbons, working inwards from the outer edge. Make a small fan and place it in the centre of the coils. Finish with a dusting of icing sugar.

Making Ribbons

Baker's chocolate, or pâte à glacer, *contains no cocoa butter, and so does not require tempering. Decorations made from baker's chocolate are very flexible and easy to work with. Use a pastry scraper or a clean wallpaper scraper to make the ribbons.*

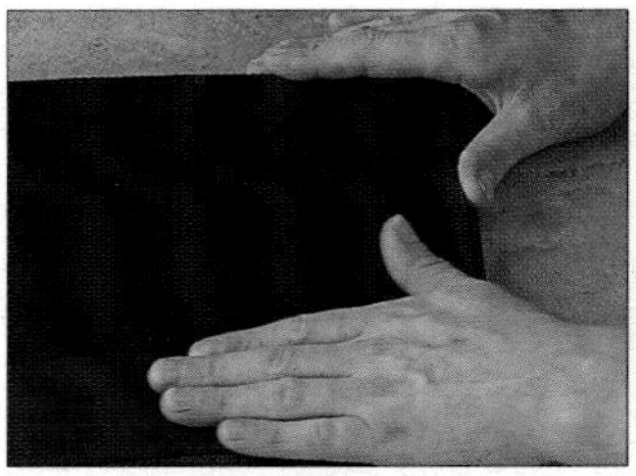

Rub the palm of your hand over the surface of the sheet of chocolate to warm it slightly and make it more malleable.

Working away from yourself, push the scraper shallowly into the sheet of chocolate. Let the end curl over and hold this up gently in your fingers.

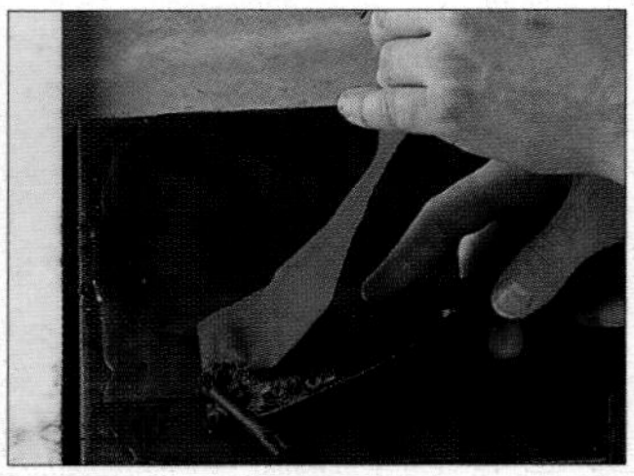

Continue pushing the scraper down the sheet of chocolate to form a long, wide ribbon. Work quickly, and use the ribbon immediately.

ICE-CREAM DESSERTS

Homemade ice cream has a fresh taste unmatched in commercial varieties. Simple to flavour and easy to shape, the techniques shown here create desserts with a professional touch.

ICE CREAM COMES TO AMERICA

Ice cream was introduced to America by Dolley Madison, the wife of James Madison, the fourth US President (1809–1817). The ice cream she was renowned for serving at her grand dinner parties was kept chilled outside in ice houses.

Dolley Madison (1768–1849)

TRICK OF THE TRADE

SHAPING ICE CREAM

Serving ice cream in playful shapes makes a striking presentation, especially when different colours are put together.

Shape ice cream with an ice-cream scoop, then open freeze on a lined baking sheet. To serve, transfer shapes to chilled bowls with a palette knife.

MAKING ICE CREAM

The classic French ice cream is a simple mixture of vanilla custard (crème anglaise) *frozen with whipped cream. An electric ice-cream maker yields the best results, because its constant churning breaks down the ice crystals and produces a creamy texture. Vanilla is the classic flavouring, but 60 g cocoa powder or 200-300 ml fruit purée can be added. Freezing dulls flavours, so additions should be intense – use thick, concentrated fruit purées that won't thin the custard.*

1 Cool 625 ml *crème anglaise* (see page 276) in a bowl set over another bowl filled with ice cubes. Stir frequently during cooling.

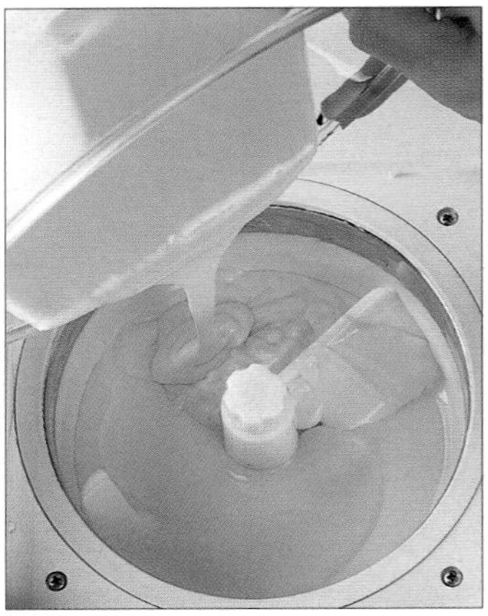

2 Freeze the cooled custard in the ice-cream machine, 30 minutes. Add 250 ml whipping cream and freeze until firm, 20 minutes. Makes 1.5 litres.

COCOA POWDER

FRUIT PUREE

VANILLA

Making Semi-soft Ice cream

By adding liqueur, which slows down the freezing process, to fruit purée, crushed meringue and cream, the Italians make semifreddo, *a "half-frozen" ice cream with a semi-soft texture.*

1 Purée 225 g berries in a blender. Sieve to remove seeds if you like. Blend in 3 tbsp liqueur.

2 Pour the purée into a bowl. Whip 300 ml double cream with 50 g icing sugar, and fold into the purée with 115 g crushed meringue.

3 Freeze the mixture in a 20-cm springform tin lined with baking parchment for at least 6 hours. Turn out, remove paper and slice.

Making Parfaits

A modern interpretation of the classic bombe, these stunning desserts take their name from the French word for perfect. To unmould parfaits, wrap a hot towel around the rings, then remove. Here parfaits are shown with professional-style decorations (see pages 290-291 and page 323).

1 Boil a sugar syrup made with 100 g sugar and 2 tbsp water to the soft-ball stage (see page 280). Whisk into 1 whole egg and 5 egg yolks until thick and cold.

2 Lightly whip 500 ml double cream, then whisk gently into the egg mixture. Tape baking parchment collars around eight 8-cm metal rings.

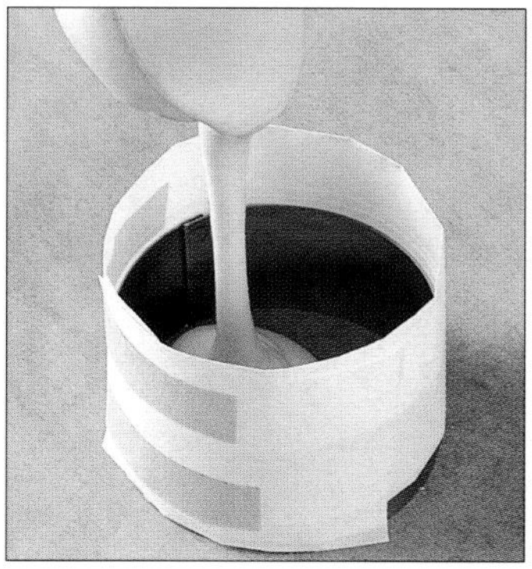

3 Set the metal rings on a baking sheet lined with baking parchment, then ladle in the parfait and tap gently to remove air pockets.

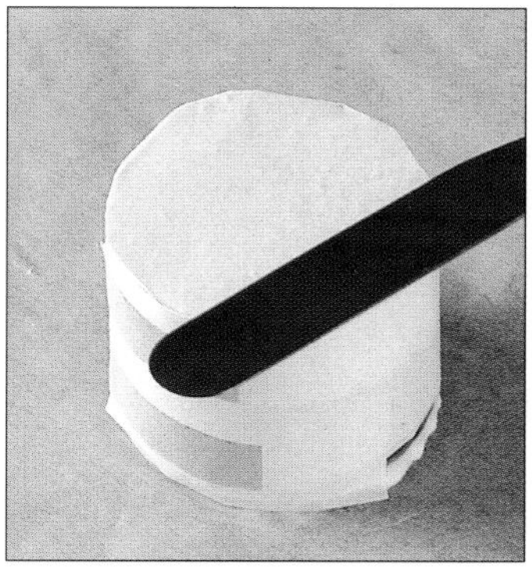

4 Level surface with a warm palette knife. Freeze until firm, at least 6 hours.

Sorbets & Granitas

Icy textures, dazzling colours and clean, lively flavours make sorbets and granitas a refreshing finale to any meal. Techniques for making simple sorbets and granitas are given here, plus clever ways to present them.

Blueberry Sorbet

175 g caster sugar
165 ml water
500 ml sieved blueberry purée
Pinch of black pepper
50 g egg white

Make a sugar syrup (see page 280) with 150 g of the sugar and 150 ml of the water. Remove from the heat and stir in the blueberry purée and pepper. Let cool, then chill in the refrigerator, 2 hours. Put the mixture in a sorbetière and work until partially frozen, 40 minutes. Meanwhile, make an Italian meringue (see page 272) with the egg white and a hot sugar syrup made from the remaining sugar and water. Add to the sorbet and continue working the machine until sorbet is completely frozen, 45 minutes. Makes about 1 litre.

Making a Sorbet By Machine

Using an electric sorbetière speeds up the freezing process and so helps produce an ice that is both fine-textured and smooth, but the real secret of making an ultra-smooth sorbet lies in the addition of Italian meringue.

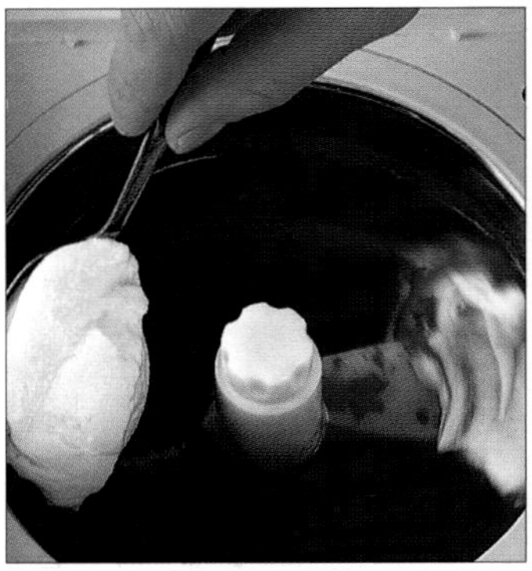

As freezing begins
Add Italian meringue when sorbet is partially frozen, then continue freezing.

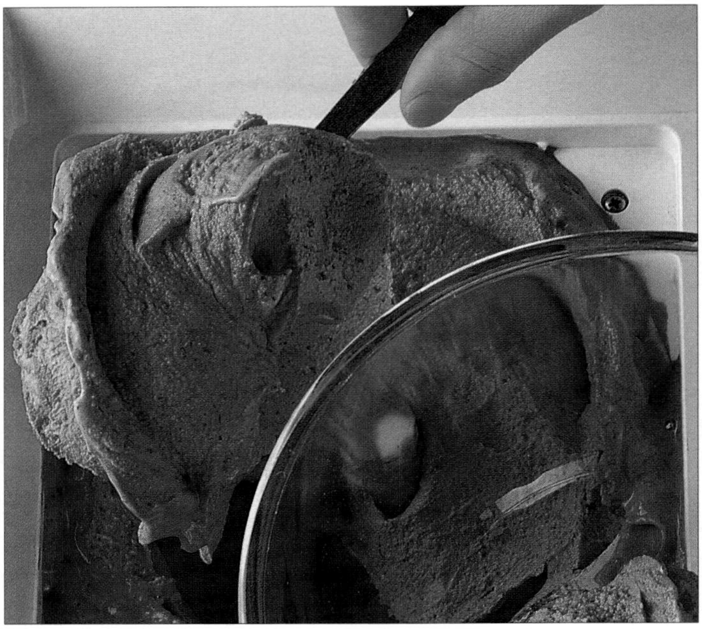

At the end
After 1½ hours in sorbetière, check consistency of sorbet. It should be firm and smooth, with no ice crystals. Decant into a bowl and serve, or store in a rigid container in the freezer.

Flavourings for Sorbets

Choose from the following strongly flavoured ingredients that will stand up well to freezing.

- Fresh blackberry, blackcurrant, raspberry or strawberry purée.
- Poached fresh peach or apricot purée.
- Freshly squeezed orange, lemon or lime juice, or a mixture of these.
- Melon pulp (watermelon, gallia, charentais and ogen are especially good).

Making a Sorbet By Hand

A sorbet is ideally made in a sorbetière, but quite good results can be obtained without a machine if you are prepared to spend some time whisking the mixture during freezing. This is the only way to break down ice crystals and produce a fairly smooth result – the more you whisk the smoother the sorbet will be. Generally speaking, you will get a better result by hand with a fruit purée than with a fruit juice. This is because the high water content of fruit juice produces more ice crystals than a purée.

1 Mix together sugar syrup and fruit purée of your choice and freeze until semi-frozen, about 2 hours.

2 Whisk semi-frozen sorbet with a balloon whisk. Return to freezer. Whisk regularly until frozen, 2 hours.

Making Frozen Fruit Cups

Called fruits givrés *or frosted fruits, these are made by hollowing out fruits and filling them with a sorbet of the same flavour. Lemon is shown here, but lime or orange can also be used. Use the flesh to make the sorbet for the filling – each fruit will take up to 3–4 tbsp sorbet. If not serving the cups the same day, pack them in freezer bags once they have hardened.*

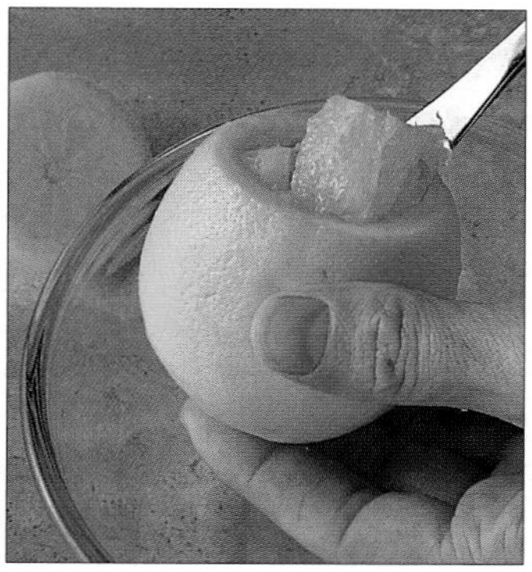

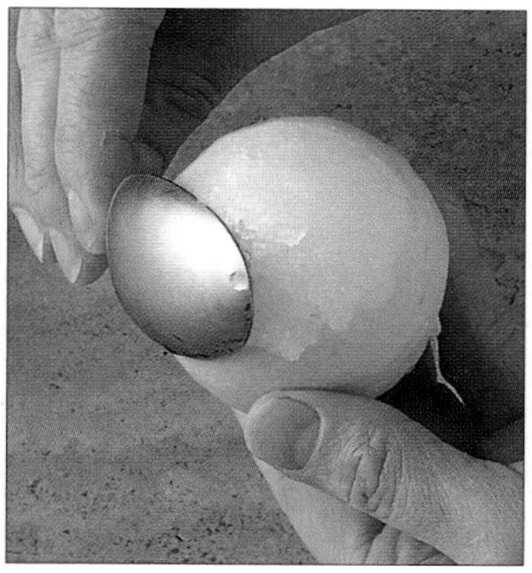

1 Cut off the top of each fruit and a thin slice off the bottom so it will sit level. Remove the flesh. Put the fruit shells in the freezer.

2 Spoon sorbet into centre of each fruit, mounding it 2–4 cm above the rim. Replace tops and place in the freezer until serving time.

Piping Sorbet

Slightly softened sorbet is easy to pipe. For a dramatic effect, use long-stemmed glasses that have been frozen or well chilled. Top with decorations, such as the candied zest used here, to echo the flavour of the sorbet.

Fit a piping bag with a star nozzle, fill with sorbet and pipe into glasses. Place in the freezer until serving time.

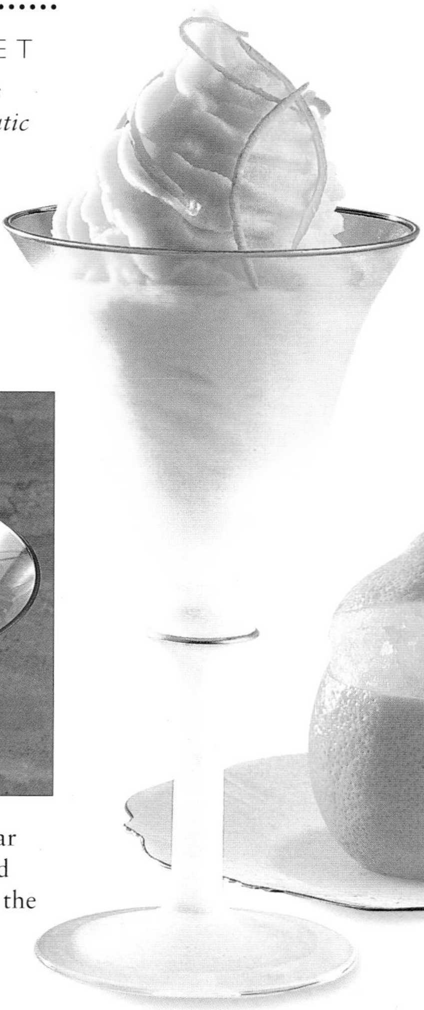

Granita

Granita's signature is its crystalline texture – the name comes from the Italian for granite. Here coffee granita is made, following the recipe in the box, right.

Adding sugar syrup
For sparkling ice crystals, strain the sugar syrup into the cooled coffee mixture, then stir the two together until evenly combined.

Forking through
Break up the ice crystals with a fork several times during freezing so the granita acquires its characteristic slushy texture. To serve, remove the granita from the bowl by scraping it with a spoon.

COFFEE GRANITA

200 g caster sugar
450 ml cold water
50 g instant espresso coffee powder
450 ml boiling water

Make a sugar syrup (see page 280) with the sugar and cold water; let cool. Dissolve coffee powder in boiling water; let cool. Strain cold syrup into coffee and stir to mix thoroughly. Freeze for at least 4 hours until firm, breaking the mixture up with a fork as often as possible during this time. Serves 6–8.

WHAT'S IN A NAME?

Sorbet: A sorbet is a soft-textured water ice made of a sugar syrup combined with a flavouring such as fruit juice or fruit purée, then mixed with Italian meringue or whisked egg whites. Sometimes alcohol is added for extra flavour. Sorbets are most commonly eaten as desserts, but they are also sometimes served as a "refresher" between courses to cleanse the palate.

Sherbet: This is the Western version of *sharbat*, an iced drink that originated in Persia. It is made by pouring fruit syrup over crushed iced, then adding fizzy water. Modern sherbets are often light fruit ices, made with milk, which gives them a creamy texture but without the richness of ice cream.

Spoom: Here, meringue is incorporated into a frozen wine- or champagne-based sherbet to make a spoom – the result is very frothy and sweet. Spooms take longer to freeze than sherbets, because of their alcohol content. An old-fashioned variation is called a shrub.

Finishing Touches

Great garnishes make simple desserts spectacular. The following are best made in advance so they will have time to set or dry. Imaginative chocolate shapes give cakes a professional touch. Drizzled caramel nests and crisp biscuits dress up parfaits, while tuile baskets can cradle ice cream or fruit. Use candied citrus zest to balance rich flavours.

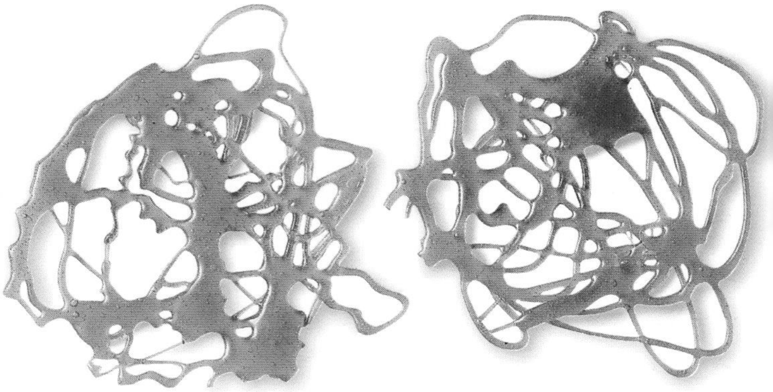

Chocolate rose leaves

Wipe leaves with a damp tea towel; pat dry. Melt 300 g chocolate of your choice. Hold the leaf by the stem and brush a generous coating of chocolate on one side of the leaf – the underside gives best results. Refrigerate until firm, then gently peel the leaf away from the chocolate.

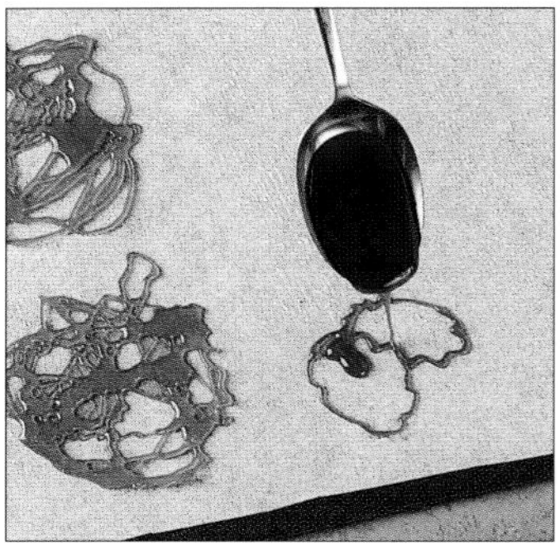

Drizzled caramel shapes

Make a heavy sugar syrup, then cook to a caramel (see page 281). Line a baking sheet with oiled baking parchment. Take a spoonful of caramel and drizzle it on to the parchment, letting it fall from the tip of the spoon. Let the shapes cool, then lift them off the paper.

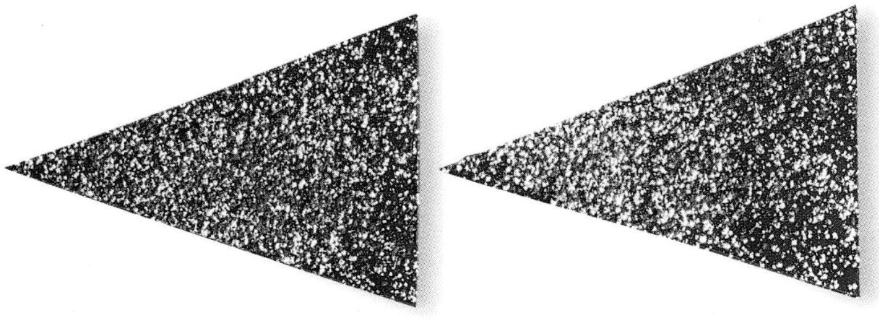

Double-dusted chocolate

Make chocolate shapes (see page 283). Put a little icing sugar in a sieve and gently tap it over the shapes. Put a little cocoa powder in another sieve and dust on top of the icing sugar. You can vary the effect by using cocoa powder first, or by dusting cocoa powder on white chocolate.

Chocolate curls

Hold a block of room-temperature white or dark chocolate firmly and run a vegetable peeler along one edge to make curls. For best results, use chocolate with a low cocoa butter content or baker's chocolate (see box, page 282), both of which are less likely to crack.

Tuile baskets

1 Make a stencil paste (see page 326). Line a baking sheet with baking parchment. Spread 1 tbsp paste in a sunburst shape.

2 Bake, four at a time, at 180°C until edges are golden, 5–8 minutes. Transfer to a bowl. Weight down with a biscuit cutter. Makes 16.

Chocolate cigarettes

1 Spread 300 g tempered couverture chocolate over the back of a baking sheet. Once set, rub the chocolate's surface to warm it slightly.

2 Hold the baking sheet steady and slide a pastry scraper under the chocolate to form cigarette shapes. Makes about 30.

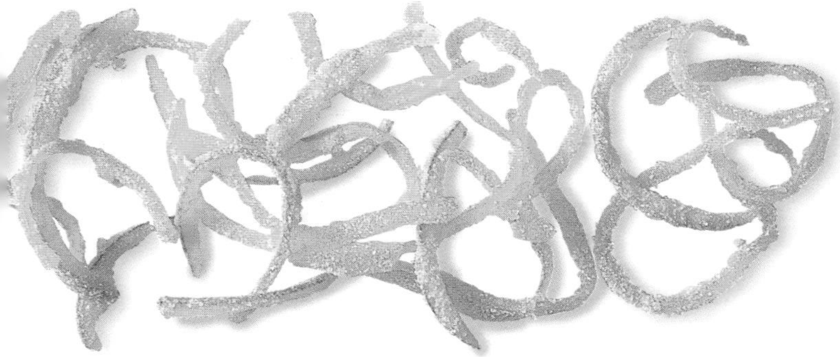

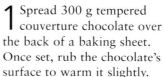

Candied lime zest

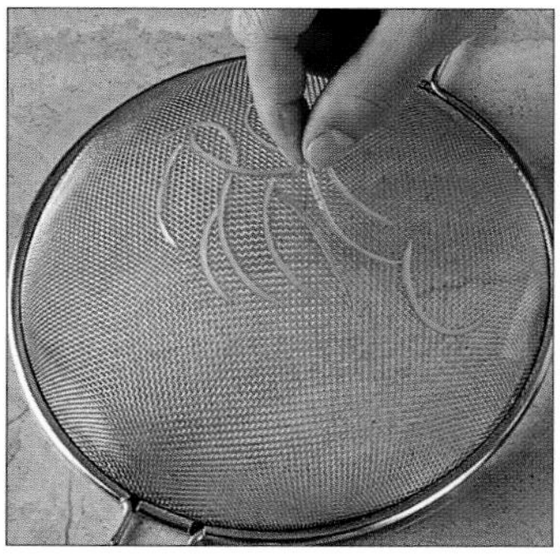

1 Cook blanched zest strips in a light sugar syrup (see page 281), 10 minutes. Add 100 g sugar and simmer for 20 minutes. Drain and let set.

2 Once set, roll the zest in caster sugar and place on a sheet of baking parchment to harden.

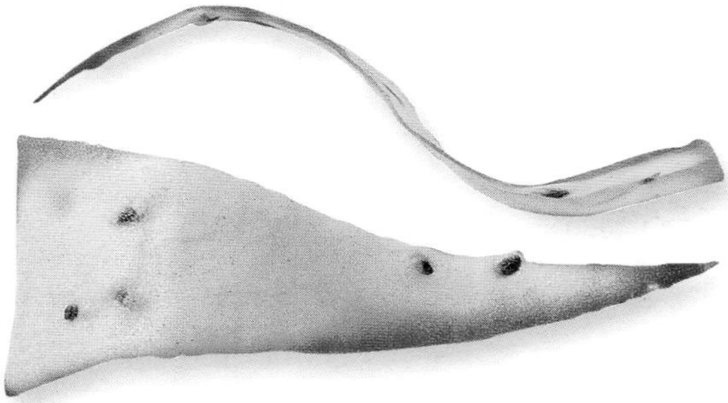

Passion fruit penants

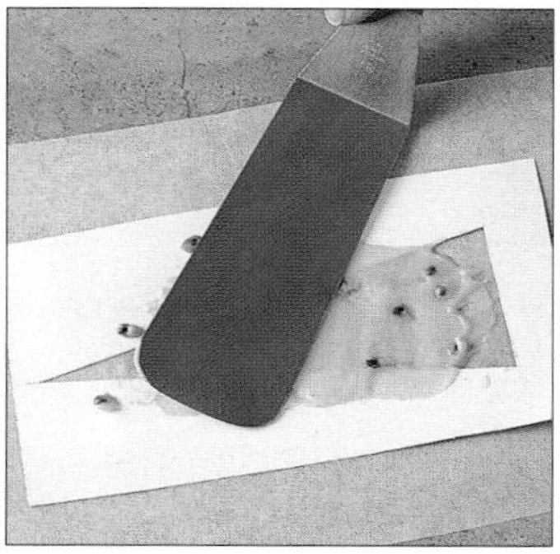

1 Add 60 g passion fruit seeds to stencil paste (see page 326). Spread over stencil on baking parchment. Remove stencil; repeat.

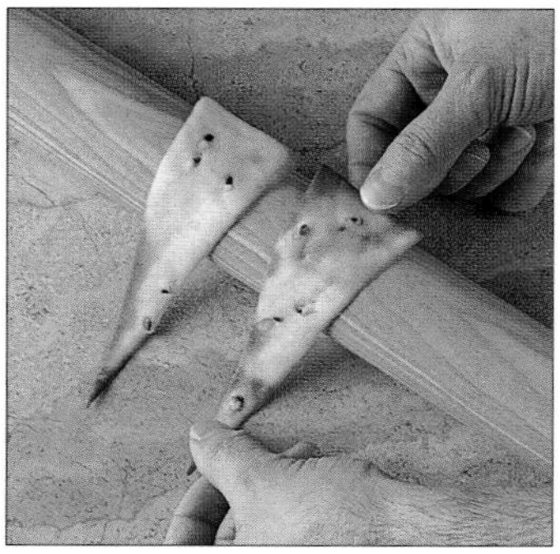

2 Bake, six at a time, at 180°C until edges are golden, 5–8 minutes. Transfer shapes to an oiled rolling pin. Leave to set. Makes 12.

Sweet Sauces

Sweet sauces give desserts a decadent dimension. The technique for silky sabayon, used in classic French desserts and as a sauce, is an absolute must to learn, while the three sauces below provide a year long repertoire – from butterscotch on ice cream to brandy butter with Christmas pudding.

USES FOR SABAYON

Light and delicate, yet full of body, sabayon can be used as a base for parfaits, mousses and buttercream icing, but it is more often used as a sauce.

- Pour over fresh soft fruits, especially berries, and grill until caramelized (see page 268).
- Serve as an accompaniment to warm fruit compotes and poached fruits.
- Serve with warm fruit tarts and pastries.
- Spoon around individual steamed puddings to make a pool of sauce.

Making a Sabayon Sauce

This classic French sauce is a version of the Italian zabaglione. *It is not difficult to make, but care must be taken not to overheat the mixture or it may separate. It is usually served warm, but if you prefer it cold, remove it from the heat and whisk it constantly until it is cold.*

1 Whisk 6 egg yolks and 90 g caster sugar in a heatproof bowl until foamy and pale. Set bowl over a pan of simmering water.

2 Whisk constantly, adding 150 ml white dessert wine or fruit juice a little at a time, until the mixture begins to thicken.

3 Continue whisking until the mixture is thick enough to leave a ribbon trail. Finally, add 1 tbsp Madeira or sherry.

Making Sweet Sauces

These few basic sweet sauces yield surprisingly diverse and sumptuous textures. Brandy butter is melted over hot desserts, butterscotch sauce acts a tawny drizzle, and ethereal crème Chantilly is firm enough to pipe.

Brandy Butter; Butterscotch Sauce; Crème Chantilly

Brandy butter
Cream 175 g softened unsalted butter with a little icing sugar until light and soft. Add 4 tbsp brandy; beat until smooth. Chill.

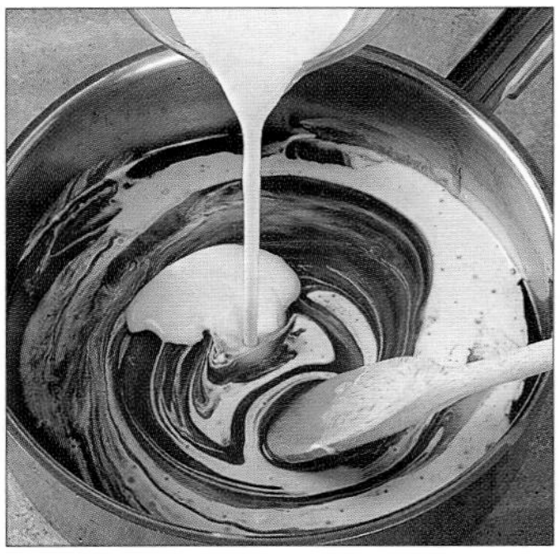

Butterscotch sauce
Stir 85 g butter, 175 g brown sugar and 2 tbsp golden syrup over a low heat until melted. Add 85 ml double cream and bring just to the boil.

Creme chantilly
Whip 250 ml double cream until thickened. Add 2 tbsp caster sugar and a few drops of vanilla essence and whip until stiff peaks form.

PASTRY

SHORTCRUST
•
CHOUX
•
USING FILO & STRUDEL
•
PUFF
•
SHAPING PUFF PASTRY

SHORTCRUST

A rich, flaky dough, shortcrust pastry is the simplest, most versatile pastry. Called *pâte brisée* in French, it is used for flans, tarts and quiches, and for single and double crust pies. It is also ideal for tartlet shells, and for decorative finishes. If sugar is added, it is called *pâte sucrée.*

PATE BRISEE AND PATE SUCREE

200 g plain flour, sifted
1 tsp salt
100 g unsalted butter, diced
1 egg
About 2 tsp water

Mix flour and salt. Rub in butter. Add egg and enough water to make a dough. Wrap and chill, 30 minutes. Makes 400 g.

For *pâte sucrée*, add 1 tbsp caster sugar with the salt.

TRICK OF THE TRADE

USING A PASTRY BLENDER

English shortcrust pastry is slightly different from French *pâte brisée*. Traditionally it is made with equal quantities of butter and lard to double the amount of flour. A special tool, called a pastry blender, with sharp steel wires attached to a handle, is good for cutting in the fat and aerating it at the same time.

MAKING PATE BRISEE

Pâte brisée *for savoury dishes, and* pâte sucrée *for desserts, use identical techniques. For best results, keep utensils and ingredients cool and handle the dough as little as possible. Once worked into a ball, refrigerate dough for 30 minutes to allow it to relax – this helps prevent shrinkage during baking.*

1 Sift flour through a fine sieve into a large bowl. This will aerate the dough and help make the finished pastry crisp and light. Stir in salt.

2 Rub the butter in with your fingers until the mixture is even in colour and resembles fine breadcrumbs.

3 Shake the bowl to ensure all the butter has been incorporated, then make a well in the centre.

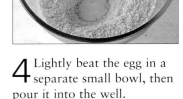

4 Lightly beat the egg in a separate small bowl, then pour it into the well.

5 Work the mixture with a pastry scraper, adding water as necessary, about 1 tsp at a time, until the dough begins to hold together.

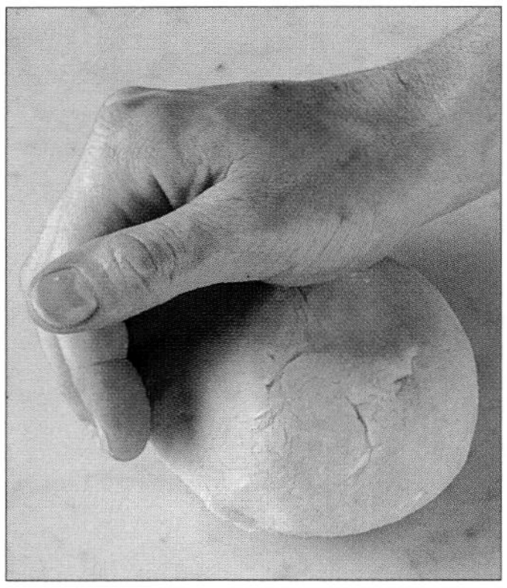

6 Bring the dough together with your hand, then put it on the work surface and shape into a rough ball. Do not overwork the dough or the pastry will be tough.

Lining a Flan Tin

To prevent baked pastry shrinking, take care not to stretch the dough when rolling it out and fitting it into the tin, and chill the shell for at least 30 minutes.

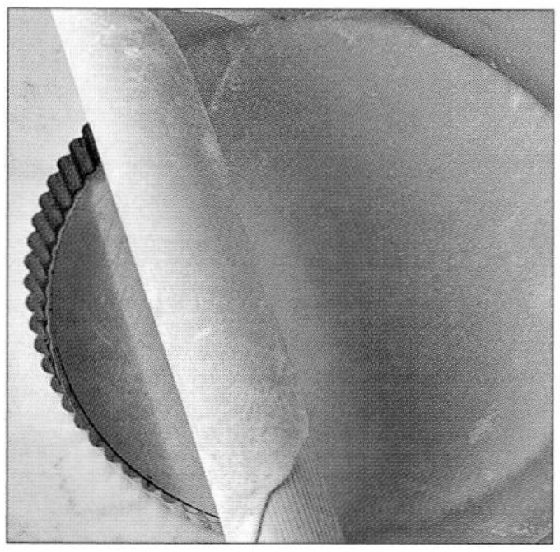

1 Roll dough to a round 5 cm larger than tin and wrap around rolling pin. Unroll loosely over tin.

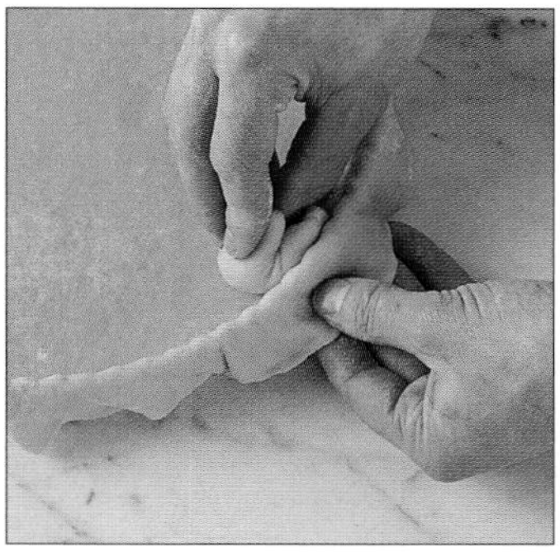

2 Use a small ball of excess dough to press the dough over the bottom and into the seam of the tin.

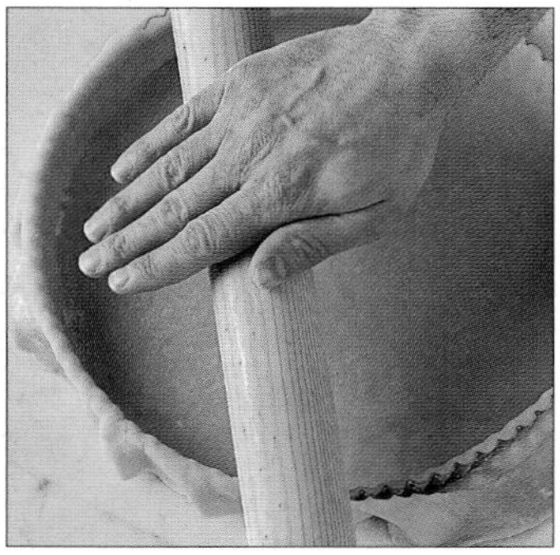

3 Roll the rolling pin over the top of the tin, pressing down firmly with your hand to cut off excess dough.

Baking Blind

Pastry shells for flans, quiches, tarts and tartlets need to be fully baked if the filling does not need to be cooked, or partially baked if the cooking time for the filling is short. The technique of baking an empty shell is called "baking blind".

1 Prick bottom of shell to allow trapped air to escape during baking. Line with parchment, fill with baking beans and bake at 180°C, 10–15 minutes.

2 When pastry is set and rim is golden, remove paper and beans and bake for a further 5 minutes or until lightly browned. Let cool on a wire rack.

BAKING BEANS

When pastry is baked blind – without a filling – it must be held in place by weights to prevent it rising and bubbling up. Place a piece of baking parchment over the bottom, slightly larger than the tin. Fill with an even layer of baking beans – these can be the commercially made china or metal variety, or dried beans or rice, all of which can be re-used.

Making Tartlets

When baking small pastry shells blind, it is easier to weight them down with another mould placed on top of the pastry than to fill individual moulds with paper and baking beans.

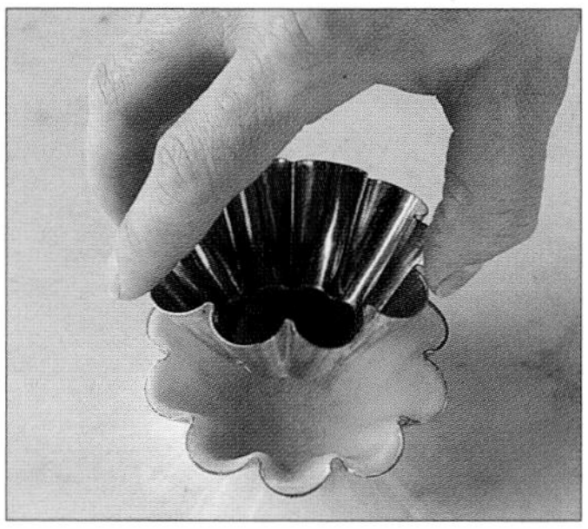

1 Line a tartlet mould with dough; trim. Place another mould inside; press gently to secure. Bake at 180°C, 10 minutes. Remove top mould and bake a further 5 minutes until lightly browned.

2 Unmould and let cool on a wire rack. Fill with crème pâtissière (see page 276), top with fresh fruits and brush with fruit glaze (see page 319).

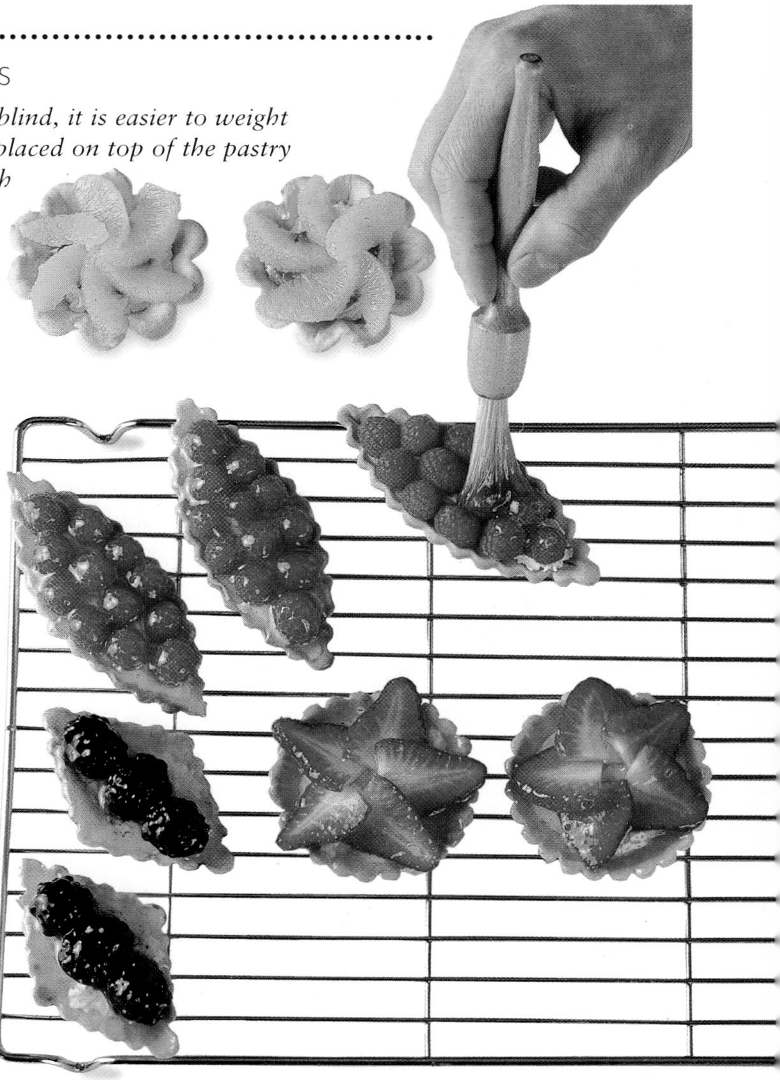

PIE FUNNELS

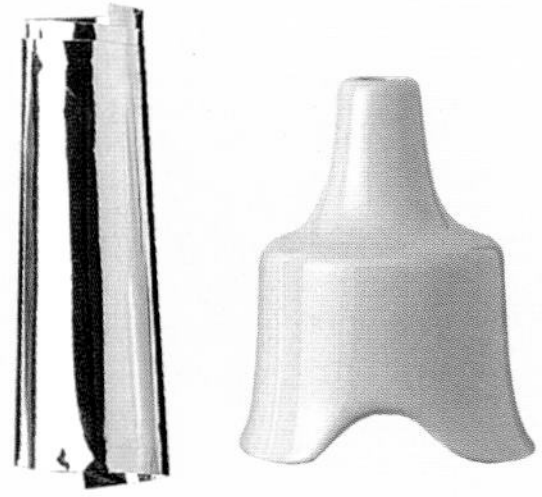

Funnels help support pastry and allow steam to escape. Use a decorative ceramic type, often made in the shape of a bird, or a homemade foil one.

Making a Single Crust Pie

Deep-dish sweet and savoury pies are generally covered with a single, top crust of shortcrust pastry. To ensure the pastry remains secure and does not fall into the filling during cooking, a double collar of dough is made around the edge. For added stability, a pie funnel (see box, left), is set in the centre of the filling to act as a support for the pastry.

1 Roll out dough 2.5–5 cm larger than the dish. Place dish upside-down in the centre. Cut around edge of dish. Cut out a 2-cm collar from the excess dough.

2 Spoon cold filling around funnel. Moisten rim of dish with a pastry brush dipped in water and press on the collar of dough. Brush the collar with water.

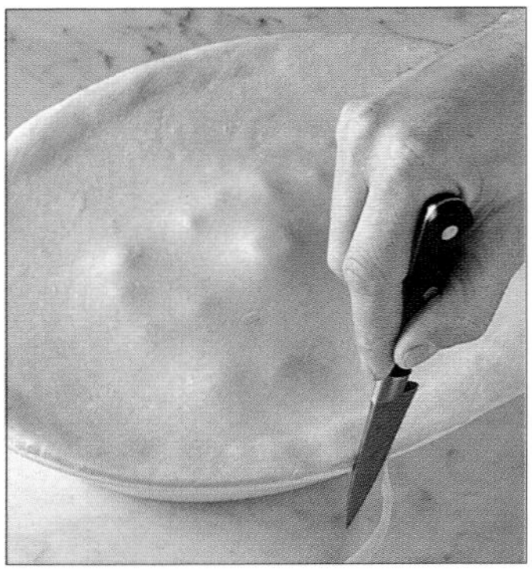

3 Wrap lid over rolling pin and carefully unroll over top of dish. Press on to collar. Trim excess dough by running a knife blade around the edge of the dish.

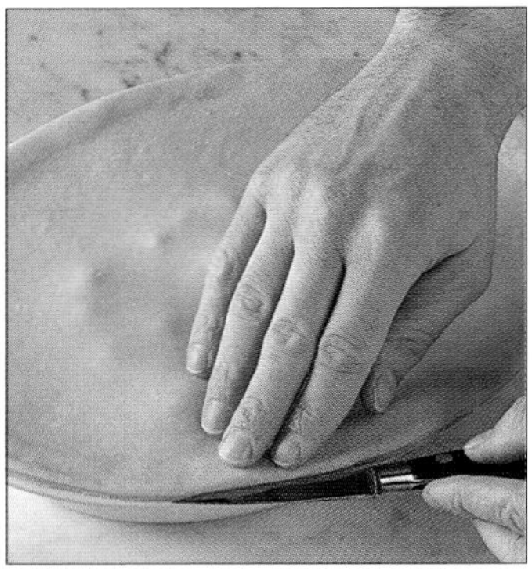

4 "Knock-up" by lightly pressing the rim with your fingers and tapping the back of the knife blade around the edges of the dough to create ridges.

5 Press thumb on rim; draw back a floured knife 1 cm towards centre. Repeat around pie. Cut a hole over funnel, brush lid with egg wash (see page 31).

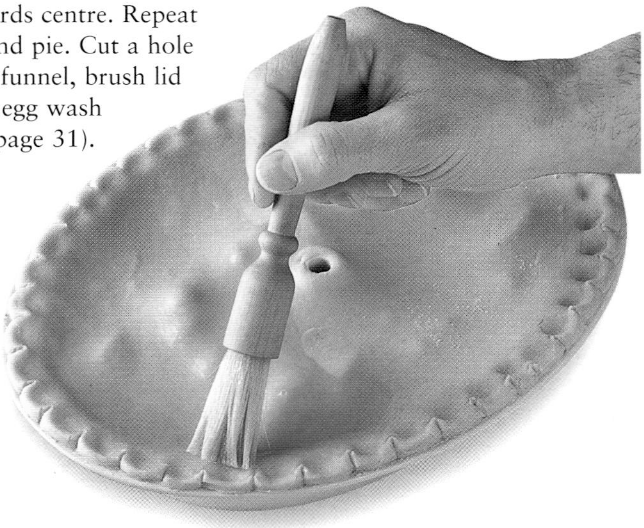

Making a Double Crust Pie

Pies made in shallow dishes or pie plates are often baked with a double crust of pastry – one underneath the filling and another on top. To prevent the bottom layer becoming soggy, brush it with a little lightly whisked egg white before filling, and use a fruit that is firm and not over juicy, such as the rhubarb shown here.

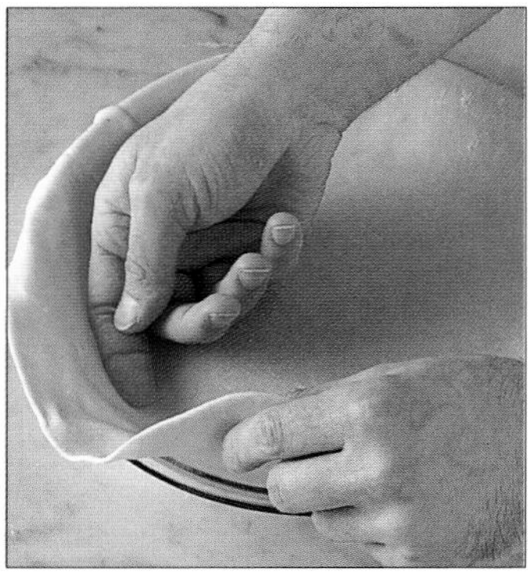

1 Roll out just over half the dough and lay it in the dish. Using the back of your finger, press the dough into the dish; be careful not to stretch it. Trim excess.

2 Spoon in cold filling. Roll out remaining dough slightly larger than dish and wrap around rolling pin. Moisten rim, then unroll dough over filling. Trim and knock-up edges, make steam vents in lid, then glaze (see step 5, above).

DECORATIVE EDGES

Tarts and pies of all types benefit from a prettily shaped edging, or a pastry decoration made from trimmings or an additional sheet of dough. These can be added to the outer edge of the pie or applied as a top crust. Flour your fingers to make the dough easy to handle, and apply an egg wash glaze (see page 31) before baking.

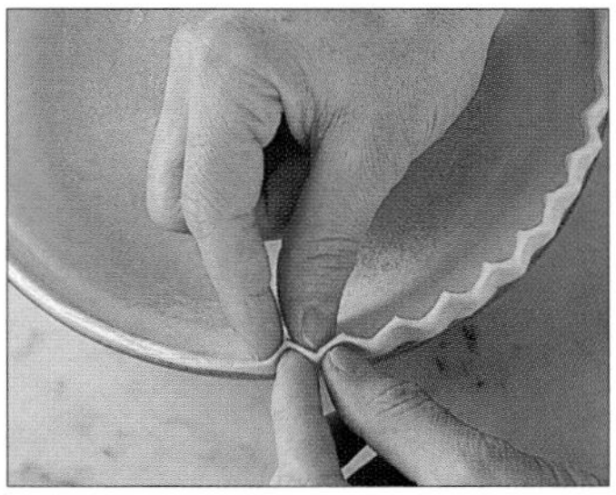

FLUTES
Place one forefinger and thumb inside edge of dough. Pinch between them; sharpen the shape by pinching with your other forefinger and thumb.

LEAVES
Cut out leaves from trimmings. Make veins by lightly scoring the dough with the tip of a knife. Moisten rim and press on leaves, overlapping them slightly.

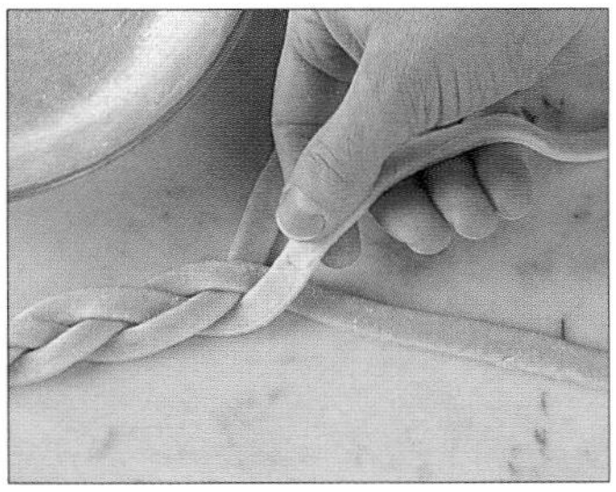

PLAIT
Cut three 1-cm wide strips of dough, about 5 cm longer than the circumference of the dish. Place strips side by side and plait. Brush rim of dough with water and place plait around rim; press lightly to secure and join ends.

LATTICE
Cut 1.5-cm wide strips. Lay across tart, 2 cm apart. Fold back alternate strips until 2 cm from rim and lay a new strip horizontally across the others. Reverse the folded and unfolded strips. Repeat at 2 cm intervals.

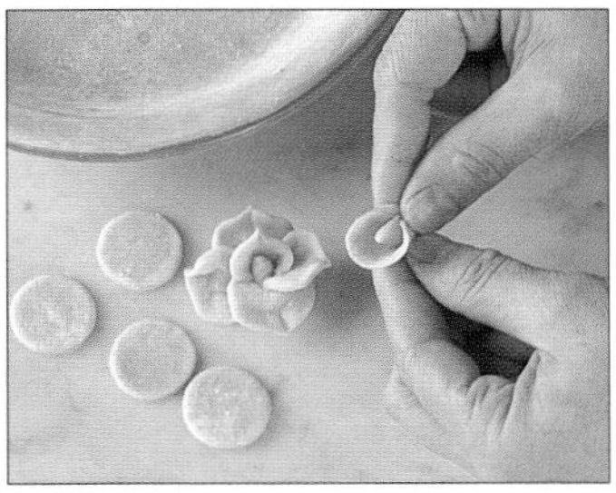

ROSE
Make a 2-cm cone of dough. Cut out five 3-cm rounds for petals. Press your thumb on part of each petal to make it flat. Wrap flat edge around cone; pinch to secure. Repeat, working around cone and overlapping petals slightly.

TARTE TATIN

This classic French dessert is cooked under a pastry lid, then served upside-down.

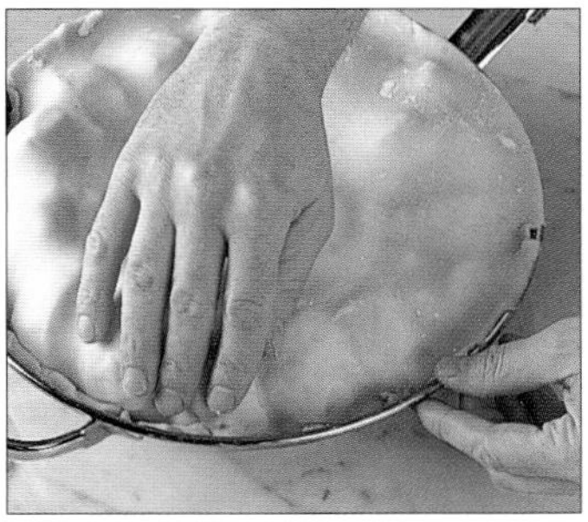

1 Roll out shortcrust dough to a round slightly larger than pan. Place over fruit and trim off excess. Tuck in edges. Bake at 230°C, 20 minutes.

2 Let rest 10 minutes, then place serving plate on top of pan and invert. Carefully remove pan.

Choux

Creating the crisp,·airy shells for buns and eclairs, dazzling desserts like croquembouche (see page 300) and many savoury hors d'oeuvre, *pâte à choux*, a dough that is cooked twice, is unlike any other pastry.

Choux Paste

The essential technique is to cook the paste until it begins to puff up, then add the eggs very slowly off the heat, beating to incorporate as much air as possible. The paste should be just warm enough to cook the eggs slightly but not so hot that it sets the mixture. This quantity of choux paste will make 40 buns (see below) or 30 eclairs (see opposite page).

1 Bring 100 g unsalted butter and 250 ml water just to the boil; remove the pan from the heat.

2 Add 150 g plain flour sifted with 1 tsp each salt and sugar and beat.

3 When dough is smooth, return to heat until it is dry, forms a ball and pulls away from the side of the pan.

4 Slowly add four beaten eggs, off the heat so they do not cook, beating well after each addition.

5 Continue beating until paste is thick and shiny. It should drop off spoon when shaken.

Choux Buns

These small balls of choux paste are piped, baked, then cooled and either cut in half and sandwiched together again with a filling, or pierced in the bottom and piped with a filling (see box, opposite page). Before baking, lightly butter baking sheets and chill in the refrigerator – so the mixture will not slip when piped. Bake at 200°C, until golden, about 20 minutes.

1 Pipe mounds on buttered baking sheet with 1-cm plain nozzle; space well apart.

2 Lightly brush tops with a small amount of egg wash (see page 31).

3 Slightly flatten balls with a fork dipped in egg wash to form rounded top.

ECLAIRS

Choux paste is piped into 8-cm lengths for eclairs. Use a 1-cm plain nozzle and space them apart on chilled, lightly buttered baking sheets. Bake at 200°C for 20–25 minutes until golden brown, then cool on a rack. Here eclairs are pierced and piped with crème pâtissière (see page 276) flavoured with melted couverture chocolate. For other fillings, see box, right.

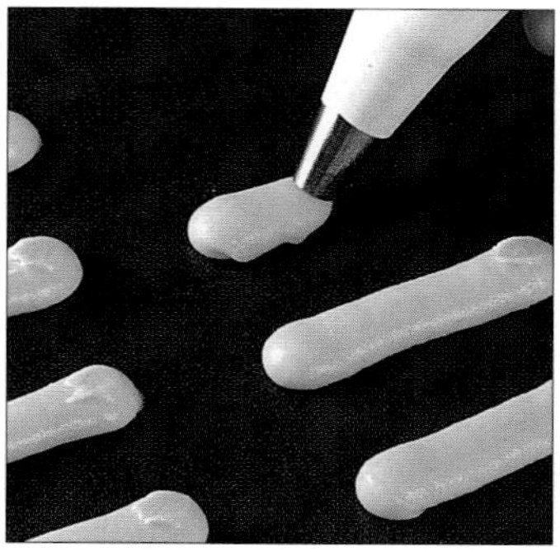

1 Pipe choux directly on to baking sheet, applying even pressure to keep shapes as uniform as possible.

2 Brush the choux fingers with egg wash (see page 31) and score with a fork dipped in egg wash.

3 Let eclairs cool on rack. When ready to fill, pierce eclairs at each end with tip of small knife or piping nozzle.

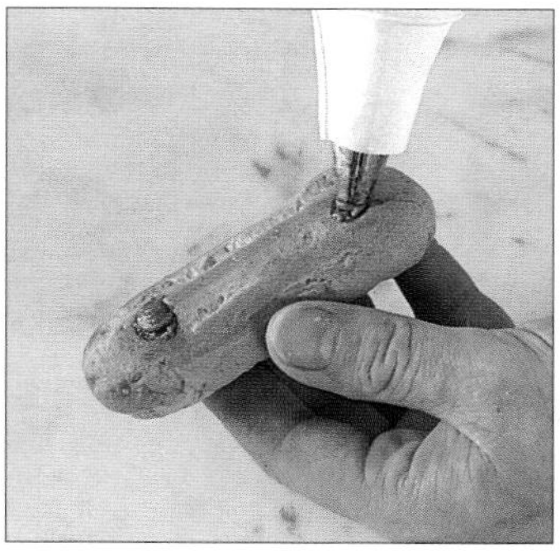

4 Pipe filling into one of the holes with a 5-mm nozzle. Stop piping when filling starts to come out of the other hole.

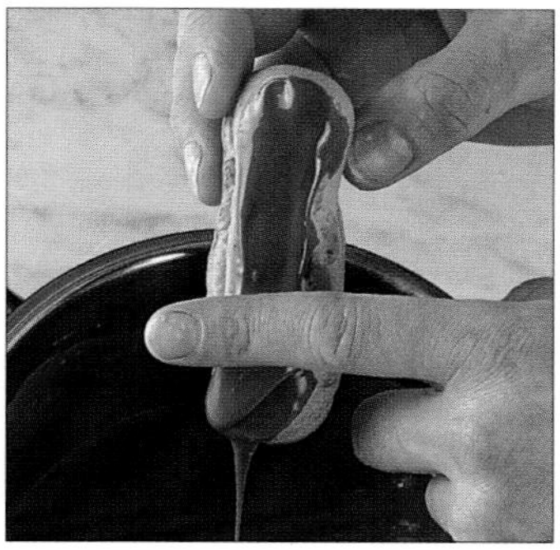

5 Dip into softened fondant icing (see page 338) or tempered couverture (see page 283); remove excess.

SERVING CHOUX BUNS

- Sandwich split choux buns with piped crème Chantilly and sliced fresh fruits. Dust tops with icing sugar.
- Present choux buns with a caramel topping. Place almond slivers on a buttered baking sheet. Make caramel (see page 281). Dip the top of each choux bun in the caramel, then place caramel-side down on top of an almond. Leave to set.
- Make chocolate profiteroles by filling choux buns with ice ceam or crème Chantilly, then drizzling over hot chocolate sauce or melted couverture.
- Fill choux buns with piped crème mousseline and use to make croquembouche (see page 300).
- Pipe patterns on top of fondant and tempered chocolate icing. Use melted chocolate or glacé icing and pipe from a paper piping bag.

TRICK OF THE TRADE

DEEP-FRYING CHOUX

Examples of deep-fried doughs include Mexican churros, *New Orleans* beignets, *and Italian* cenci. *When cooked in the same way, choux paste gives similar results. Serve dusted with icing sugar or caster sugar and cinnamon.*

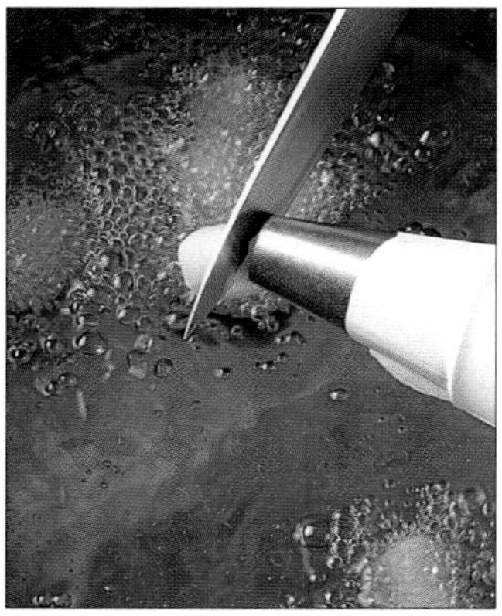

Heat 7.5 cm oil to 190°C. Fill a piping bag fitted with a plain 1.5-cm nozzle with choux paste. Hold the bag over the hot oil and squeeze it to extrude a piece of dough about 3 cm long. Cut off the dough close to the nozzle, using a chef's knife, so the dough falls directly into the oil. Deep-fry for 3–5 minutes until puffed and golden. Remove with a slotted spoon and drain on paper towels. Serve warm.

Croquembouche

Traditionally prepared for weddings in France, this spectacular confection consists of tiers of choux buns filled with an enriched crème pâtissière and embellished with caramel. Croquembouche is straightforward to make; each element is prepared individually before the final assembly.

SERVES 20

2 kg nougatine (see page 281)

Nibbed sugar, to decorate

FOR THE ROYAL ICING

250 g icing sugar

1 egg white

1 tbsp lemon juice

FOR THE CHOUX BUNS

500 ml water

200 g unsalted butter

10 g salt

15 g caster sugar

300 g plain flour

8–9 eggs

FOR THE EGG WASH

1 egg

1 egg yolk

Pinch of salt

FOR THE CREME MOUSSELINE

12 egg yolks

300 g caster sugar

100 g plain flour

100 g cornflour

1.5 litres milk infused with 1 vanilla pod (see page 331)

200 g unsalted butter, softened

90 ml liqueur of your choice

FOR THE CARAMEL

1 kg caster sugar

200 ml water

300 g glucose

Make the nougatine and roll it out thinly (see step 1, page 281). Using a 30-cm cake card as a guide, cut out a large disc of nougatine – this will be the base of the croquembouche; set the disc aside on the card. Using a 10-cm metal cutter, cut out 2 discs of nougatine and 3 quarter moons for the top.

Make royal icing (see page 318) using the ingredients listed left; pipe around the edge of the large disc (see box, below), and around the edges of the 2 small discs.

Make 100 choux buns (see page 298), using the ingredients listed left and brushing with egg wash before baking. Let cool.

Make the *crème mousseline* as for *crème pâtissière* (see page 276), whisking in the butter and liqueur a little at a time at the end; let cool. Using a small plain nozzle, pipe the crème through the hole in each choux bun.

For the caramel, dissolve the sugar in the water and bring to the boil. Skim off any scum, then stir in the glucose. Lower the heat and cook, swirling the pan occasionally, until turned to a blond caramel. Plunge base of pan into iced water to cool slightly, then dip tops of buns in the caramel and place them caramel-side down on a tray to set. Dip a few of the buns into nibbed sugar.

Cover a large cone-shaped mould with foil and oil it well. Wrap a roll of foil around the base to support the bottom tier of buns.

Arrange buns for the bottom tier: dip the sides of the buns in caramel and stick them to each other not the foil. Add the next tier of buns (see box, below). Continue building tiers; place the buns with nibbed sugar at random. Leave to harden.

Unmould croquembouche (see box, below); set it on the nougatine base and decorate the top, sticking the shapes on with caramel.

Assembling the Croquembouche

The key to success is to take your time and work with care. The assembled croquembouche should be kept in a cool place for no longer than 4–6 hours until serving time. It should not be stored in the refrigerator because the caramel will become sticky.

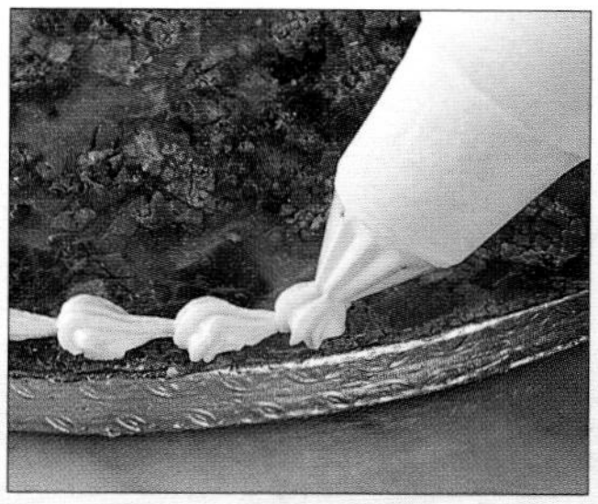

Using a small star nozzle, pipe a border of royal icing shells around the edge of the large nougatine base.

Arrange tiers of choux buns around the cone, sticking them side by side and to the previous tier, not to the foil.

Gently lift the croquembouche off the mould, then carefully remove the roll of foil followed by the foil lining.

Using Filo & Strudel

Both these doughs bake into irresistible paper-thin layers. Creating them demands speed and practice – which is why filo is normally bought ready-made. The following methods offer ways to make the most of purchased filo, plus step-by-step instructions for homemade strudel.

Layering Filo

In the Middle East, filo pastry is often baked in layers with a tasty filling in between. The technique is easy, as long as you keep the filo covered with a damp cloth because it dries out very quickly. Here a baklava is made with 450 g filo, 100 g melted butter and a filling of chopped nuts, sugar and cinnamon. Bake at 170°C, 1¼ hours. Coat with a honey syrup while warm.

1 Layer half the filo sheets in buttered dish, brushing melted butter over each layer. Add filling; continue layering.

2 For a rich, gooey result, make sure top layer of filo is thoroughly drenched in melted butter before baking.

3 Before baking, score top layers in a diamond pattern with a sharp knife to make filo easy to serve.

Shaping Filo

Paper-thin filo is perfect for wrapping around fillings, sweet or savoury. As with layering (see above), keep filo covered with a damp cloth to prevent it drying out. Brush with melted butter after shaping and bake at 180°C, about 30 minutes.

Cigar
Brush an 8-cm wide strip of filo with melted butter. Put 1 tsp filling in centre of one end. Fold over edges of the strip lengthwise to neaten. Roll up into a cigar.

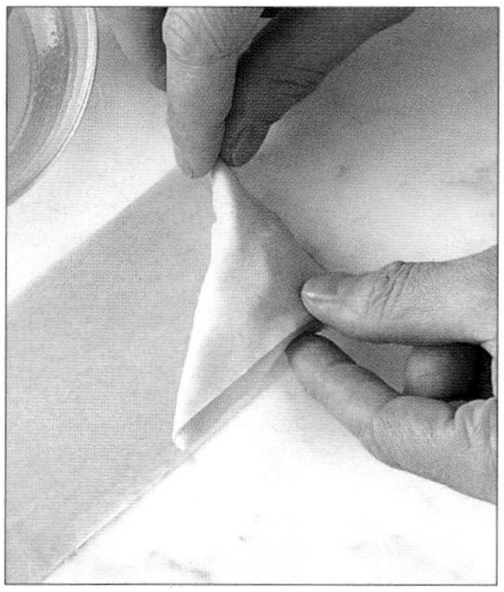

Triangle
Brush an 8-cm wide strip of filo with melted butter. Put 1 tsp filling in one corner of one end. Bring other corner diagonally over filling to make a triangle. Repeat folding to other end of strip.

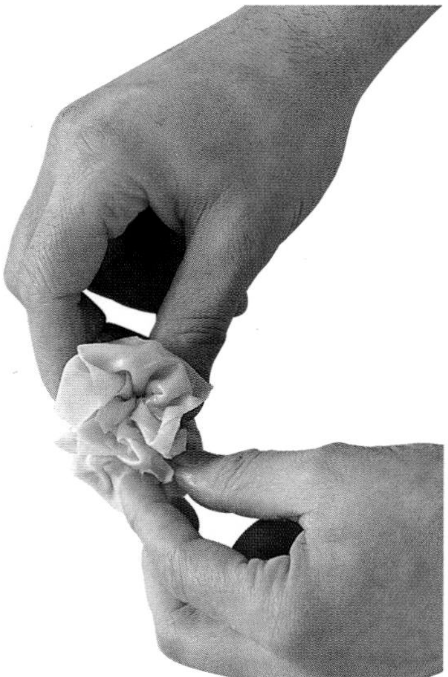

Purse
Brush an 8-cm square of filo with melted butter. Put 1 tsp filling in centre and gather up the corners over the filling. Twist the pastry gently just above the filling to seal without splitting the pastry.

Making Strudel

Kneading the dough thoroughly develops the gluten; letting it rest sufficiently makes it easier to stretch out. Work quickly when stretching the dough, because it dries out quickly. A simple recipe for apple strudel is given in the box, below right, using these techniques.

1 Add liquids to well in flour and quickly work into a soft ball of dough.

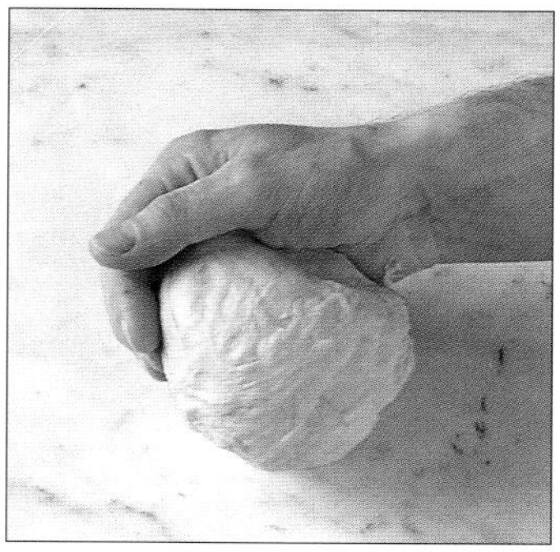

2 Knead dough on floured surface: pick it up and throw it down until smooth.

3 After the dough has rested, start rolling it out on a floured surface.

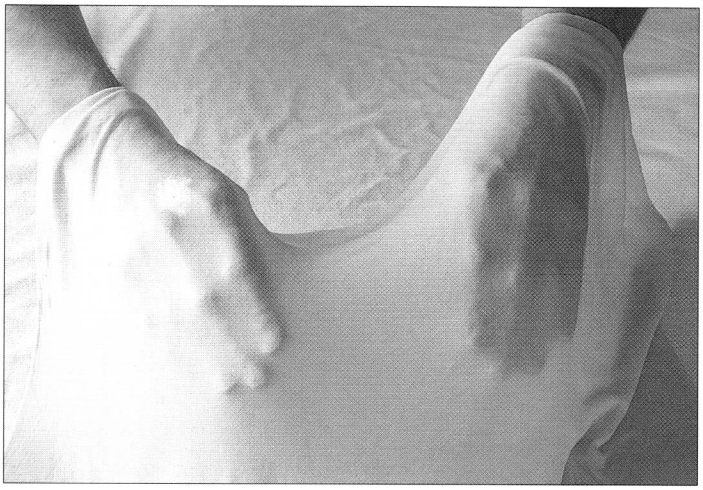

4 Working over a floured sheet, begin stretching the dough. Use the floured backs of your hands and work from the centre outwards until dough is a very thin rectangle and you can see your hands through it.

5 Sprinkle the filling over dough. Starting at one long end and using the sheet to help, roll up the dough.

6 Carefully lift the rolled strudel and place seam-side down on a buttered baking sheet. Shape into a horseshoe by curving round the ends of the roll. Brush with melted butter before baking. Serve strudel warm or cold, dusted with icing sugar and cut crosswise into thick slices. Chilled crème Chantilly (see page 292) makes a good accompaniment.

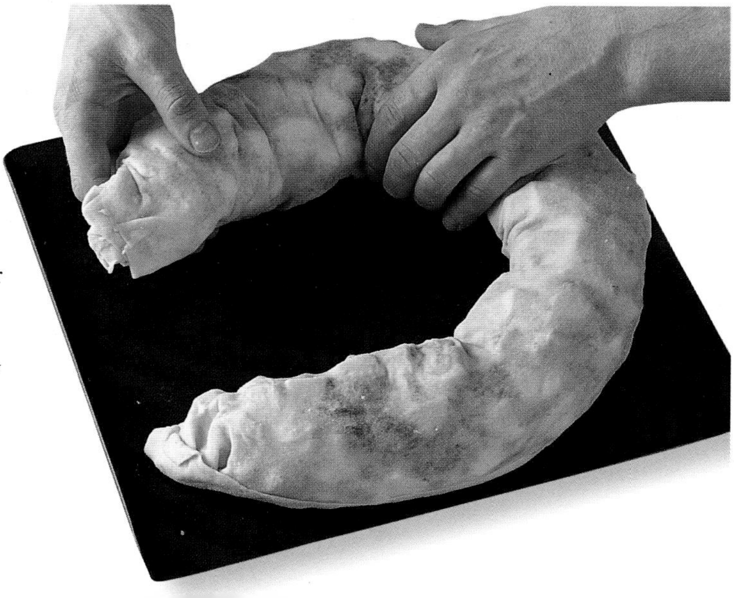

TRICK OF THE TRADE

Letting Dough Rest

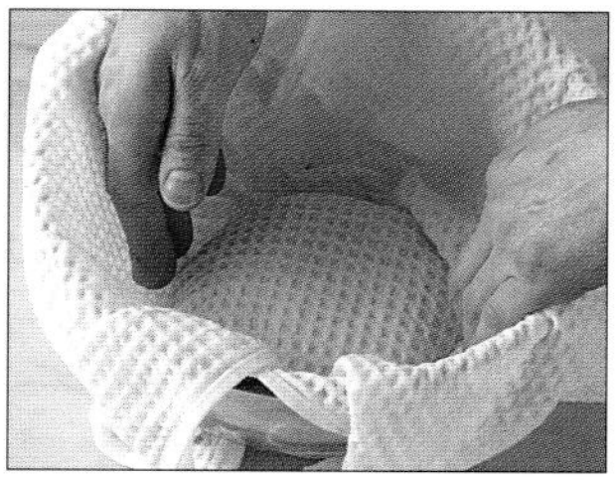

When resting dough after kneading, put it in a bowl and tuck a damp tea towel around it.

APPLE STRUDEL

300 g strong plain white flour
1 tsp salt
40 ml vegetable oil
200 ml warm water
500 g cooking apples, peeled, cored and chopped
About 150 g butter, melted
150 g demerara sugar
100 g raisins
100 g walnuts, toasted and chopped
1 tsp ground cinnamon
50 g cake crumbs or fresh breadcrumbs

Sift flour and salt; add oil and water; work into ball. Knead for 5–7 minutes until smooth. Cover; let rest for up to 2 hours. Sweat apples in half the butter. Add remaining ingredients for the filling and let cool.

Roll out dough with a rolling pin, cover with a damp tea towel and let rest 15 minutes. Transfer to sheet-covered work table and stretch into a large rectangle; brush with butter. Spread filling to within 3 cm of edges. Roll up and transfer to baking sheet. Brush with butter. Bake at 190°C for 30–40 minutes. Serves 8–10.

PUFF

There are three major stages in preparing the light, flaky and buttery pastry used for sweet and savoury tarts, bouchées and feuilletés. These are creating the *détrempe* or foundation, adding the butter, and then rolling, folding and turning the dough. For best results, keep the dough chilled.

PUFF PASTRY

500 g strong plain white flour
250 ml cold water
75 g melted unsalted butter
2 tsp salt
300 g unsalted butter

Make a dough with the flour, water, melted butter and salt. Soften the 300 g butter slightly and shape into a 2-cm thick square. Flatten dough on a lightly floured chilled surface, add the butter and enclose it in the dough. Roll, fold and turn the dough six times, chilling it in the refrigerator for 30 minutes after every second turn.
Makes 1.25 kg.

MAKING THE DETREMPE

The first stage of making the dough (détrempe *in French) is working together the flour, salt, water and melted butter to the point where it forms a ball. It is then wrapped and chilled.*

1 Sift flour on to chilled work surface and make a well in centre. Add water, melted butter and salt. Mix together with fingertips.

2 Using a pastry scraper, work flour-and-butter mixture until loose crumbs form. Add more water if dough becomes dry.

3 Shape dough into a ball. Cut an "X" on top to prevent shrinkage. Wrap dough in floured parchment; chill 30 minutes.

ADDING THE BUTTER

Before incorporating the butter into the dough, flatten it to a 2-cm thick square under a sheet of baking parchment or cling film, using a rolling pin.

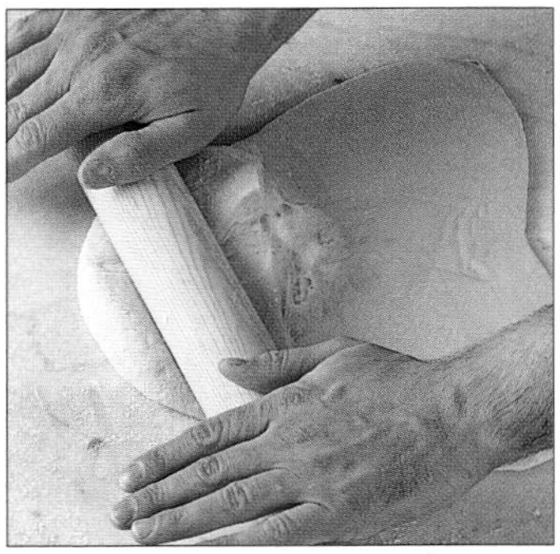

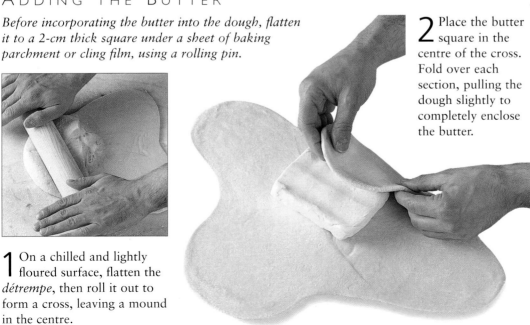

1 On a chilled and lightly floured surface, flatten the *détrempe*, then roll it out to form a cross, leaving a mound in the centre.

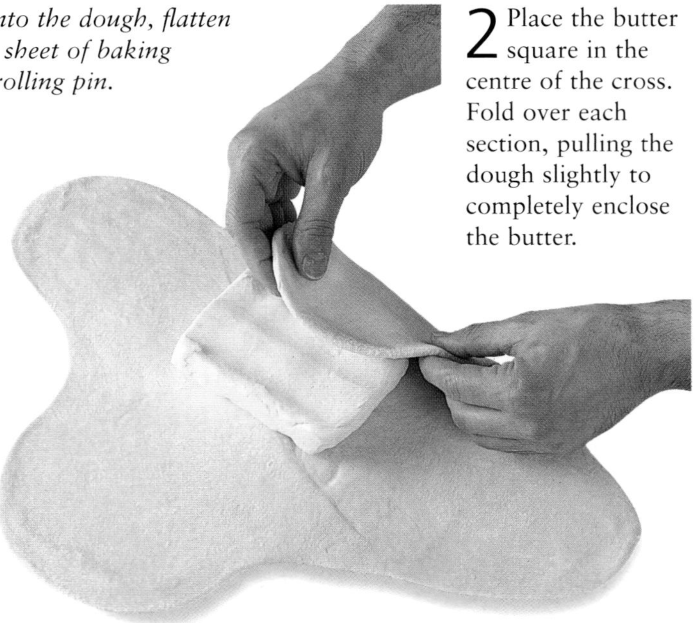

2 Place the butter square in the centre of the cross. Fold over each section, pulling the dough slightly to completely enclose the butter.

3 Lightly flour the work surface and roll over the top of the dough to seal the edges, then roll the dough into a rectangle.

Rolling and Folding the Dough

In this stage, the dough is rolled out, then folded like a letter. It is important to keep the edges even and straight. Roll dough away from you with firm, even strokes.

1 Roll the dough into a 20- x 45-cm rectangle. Fold the bottom-third up towards the middle.

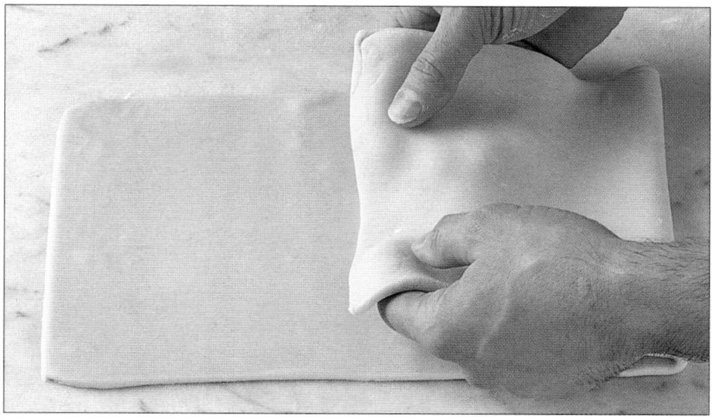

2 Bring the top-third of the dough over the folded thirds, and brush off any excess flour.

3 The dough should be square, have three layers and the edges should align. It now needs turning.

Quick Tips for Puff Pastry

For best results, always work with puff pastry in a cool room and on a marble surface.

- Whenever possible, make puff pastry the day before it is to be used. This additional resting time makes the final dough easier to shape for baking.
- Perfect dough depends on the right proportion of ingredients. Some pastry chefs weigh the *détrempe* after mixing, then incorporate exactly half its weight in butter.
- Once the butter is wrapped in the *détrempe* package, chill it for an additional 30 minutes to bring them to the same temperature (this ensures a more even mixing).
- To ensure even rising, thorough chilling is essential after each second turn and the pastry should be scored before baking – this encourages the layers to rise evenly.
- As a further safeguard, chill the pastry one final time for 30 minutes after it has been cut into desired shape.
- Use an oven thermometer to ensure the pastry is baked at the proper temperature. If the oven is too cool, the butter in the dough will melt and the pastry will not rise properly.

Turning the Dough

Puff pastry dough needs to be rolled, folded and turned a total of six times if it is to puff up and separate into layers. Mark the dough every "second" turn before chilling.

1 Give the square a quarter turn so that the exposed edge is on your right, as if the dough were a book. Gently press the edges to seal.

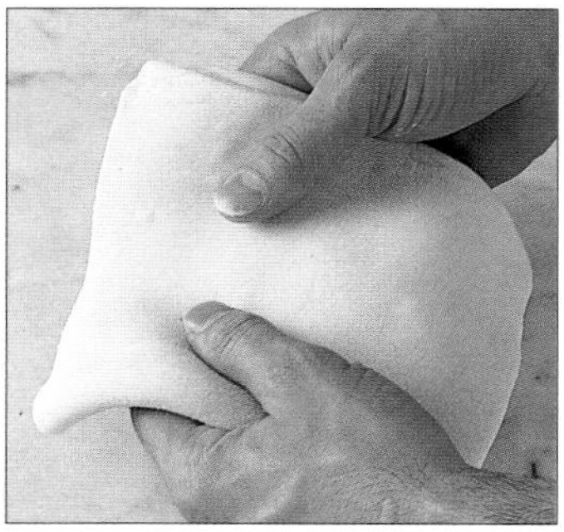

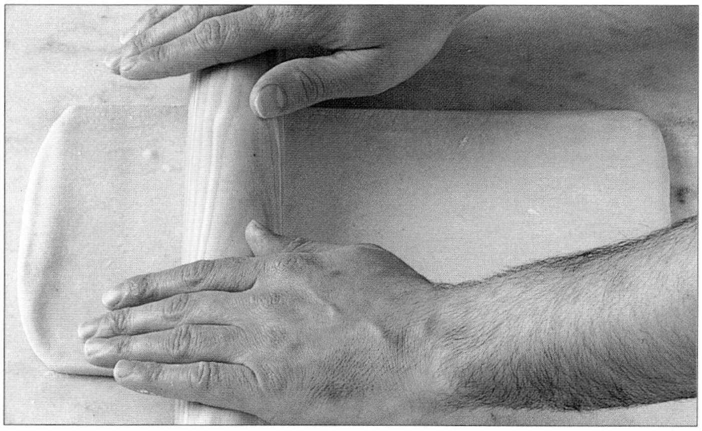

2 Roll out the dough into a 20- x 45-cm rectangle. Fold it again into thirds; seal edges. Chill for 30 minutes. Repeat rolling, folding and turning twice more.

Marking the dough
Use your fingers to record how many turns you make.

Shaping Puff Pastry

In classic French cuisine, puff pastry (see pages 304–305) is cut into shapes such as rectangles, rounds and diamonds and decoratively scored to make elegant crusts and airy, golden containers for sweet and savoury fillings.

Making Bouchees

These little cases are so-called because of their size – bouchée *means mouthful. Bake on dampened baking sheets at 220°C, 20–25 minutes. To ensure straight rising, put a metal cutter at all four corners of the sheet and place another sheet on top. As bouchées rise, the top sheet prevents them toppling over.*

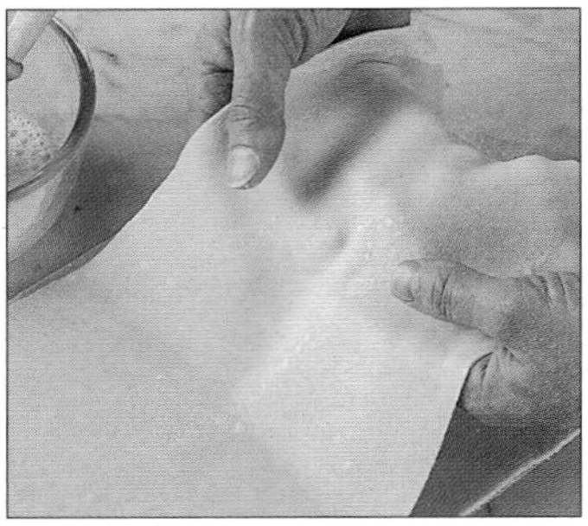

1 Roll out two 3-mm thick sheets of dough. Lay one on top of the other; brush with egg wash (see page 31).

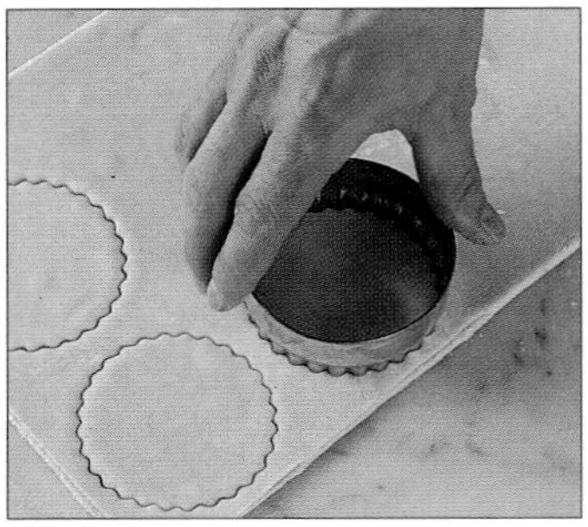

2 Chill or freeze pastry, then cut through both layers of dough with a 7.5-cm fluted pastry cutter.

3 Cut out the centres in the top layer of dough with an oiled 3.5-cm plain cutter.

Making a Tranche

Named after the French for slice, this decorative puff pastry case is used in classic French cuisine as a container for crème pâtissière and glazed fresh fruits, although other fillings can be used. Brush with egg wash (see page 31) and place on a dampened baking sheet before baking at 220°C for 8–12 minutes, then at 190°C for 12–15 minutes. Cool on a rack before filling.

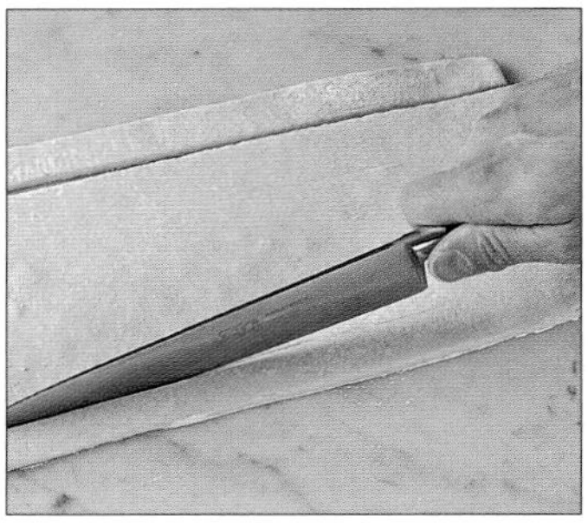

1 Cut a 3-mm thick 14- x 30-cm rectangle.Trim edges neatly. Cut two 1-cm strips from the long edges.

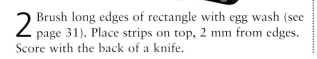

2 Brush long edges of rectangle with egg wash (see page 31). Place strips on top, 2 mm from edges. Score with the back of a knife.

Making Feuilletes

These diamond-shaped pastries make stunning containers for creamy fillings and fresh fruits. Bake on dampened baking sheets at 220°C for 8–12 minutes, then at 190°C for 12–15 minutes. Cool on a rack before filling.

1 Roll out dough 3 mm thick. Cut into 13-cm squares. Fold each square in half diagonally to form a triangle.

2 Starting 1 cm in at the folded side, cut a 1-cm wide border along the open sides. Leave 1 cm uncut at end so strips remain attached.

3 Unfold the triangle and brush the edges of the inner square with egg wash (see page 31). Lift border strips and slip one strip under the other. Pull across the base to the opposite corners, then attach the points of the strips to the corners of the base with egg wash.

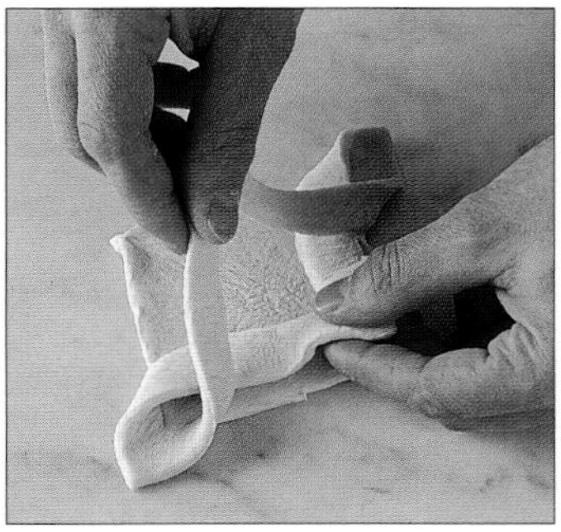

Cakes & Biscuits

Cake Making
•
Basic Cakes
•
Whisked Cakes
•
Special Cakes
•
Cheesecakes
•
Cake Icing
•
Petits Fours
•
Biscuits

Cake Making

A perfectly baked cake requires more than just a good recipe and skilled mixing. It is vital to use the correct tins and to prepare them correctly. It is also essential to know how to tell just when a cake is fully baked.

Best Ingredients for Cakes

Eggs: Use fresh, medium-sized eggs. Take them from the refrigerator at least one hour before using – eggs at room temperature will incorporate more air and give a lighter result than eggs taken straight from the refrigerator.

Fat: Use unsalted butter, unless otherwise stated in recipe. For creamed cakes made by the all-in-one method (see page 310), use soft-tub margarine.

Flour: Most recipes specify plain flour plus an added raising agent such as baking powder or bicarbonate of soda. Self-raising flour includes its own raising agent and should only be used in recipes specifically calling for it.

Sugar: For most recipes, use fine sugars such as caster or soft brown, both of which cream easily. Granulated sugar is not generally used, except for cakes made by the rubbing-in method.

Greasing and Flouring a Cake Tin

For simple creamed cakes, such as Victoria sandwich, tea breads and fruit loaves, greasing and flouring is sufficient to prevent the batter sticking to the tin during baking and for the cake to turn out easily. Use melted unsalted butter, unless your recipe states otherwise.

1 Brush an even, thin layer of melted butter over the bottom, into the corners and up the sides of the cake tin.

2 Sprinkle with plain flour and rotate to coat evenly. Turn tin upside-down and tap centre to remove excess.

Lining a Tin

Some cakes, especially whisked sponges that have a tendency to stick, benefit from having a paper lining between them and the tin. For cakes such as sachertorte (see page 318), where a clean edge is important for perfect presentation, lining is vital. Non-stick baking parchment gives best results. Use the same technique for round, square and Swiss roll tins.

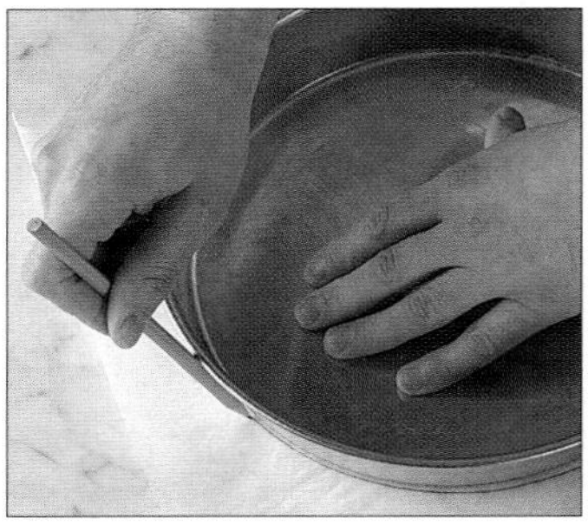

1 Stand tin on a sheet of baking parchment; draw around base with a pencil. Cut just inside the pencil line.

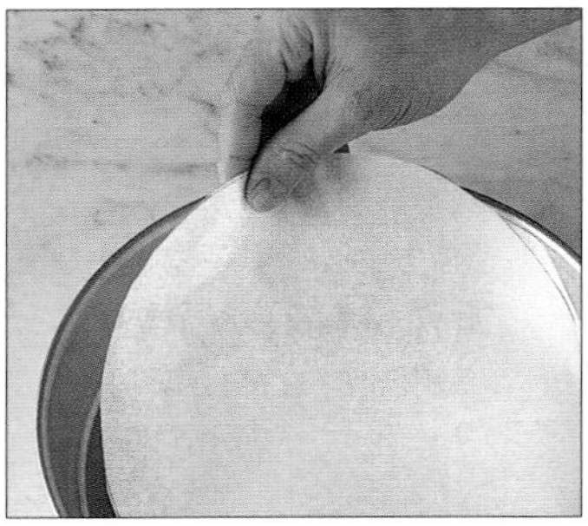

2 Grease the inside of the tin (see step 1, above), then place the baking parchment in the bottom.

Double Lining a Deep Tin

Some rich fruit cakes have very long baking times, so to protect them from the oven's heat use a double lining. This will prevent the fruit burning and the crust overcooking. Once double lined, place a base liner (see above) into the tin. For extra protection, tie a folded newspaper around the outside of the tin.

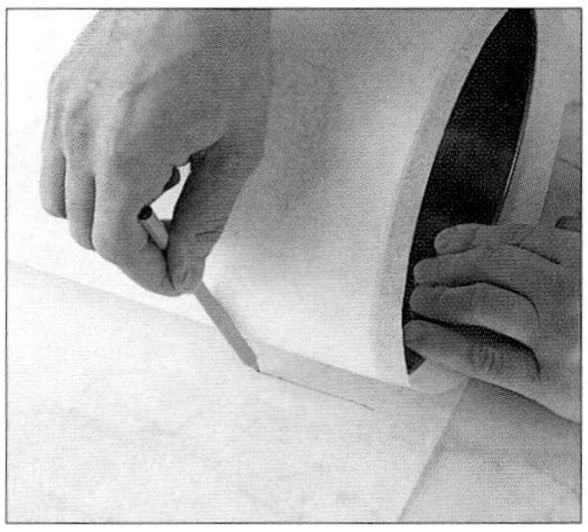

1 Fold baking parchment sheet lengthwise in half. Wrap around tin. Mark 2 cm longer than circumference.

2 Snip 2-cm diagonal cuts along the folded edge, 3 cm apart. Secure inside tin, cut-edge down to line base.

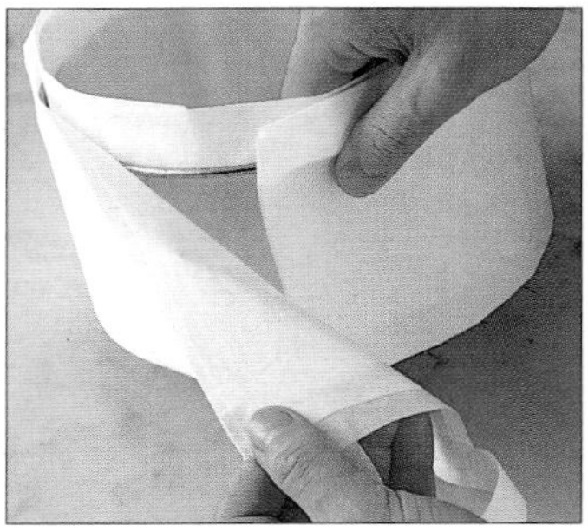

3 Fold another baking parchment sheet in half, lengthwise. Wrap around tin and secure with tape.

LINING A LOAF TIN

Use the method shown here for lining a deep or shallow rectangular loaf tin. The cut corners of the lining paper will overlap in the tin, so use greaseproof paper, which is thinner then baking parchment, to reduce the bulk. Cut the paper to twice the size of the tin and centre the tin on the paper with the long sides of the tin parallel to the long sides of the paper.

1 Place tin in centre of the greaseproof paper. Make a diagonal cut from each corner to the corners of the tin.

2 Place the greaseproof paper inside tin and overlap the corners. Press into the corners and sides of tin.

TESTING FOR DONENESS

The cake should be golden and risen and shrinking slightly from the sides of the tin. There are two further tests, depending on the cake you are baking.

SPONGE CAKE
Lightly press the centre of the cake with your fingertips: it should spring back.

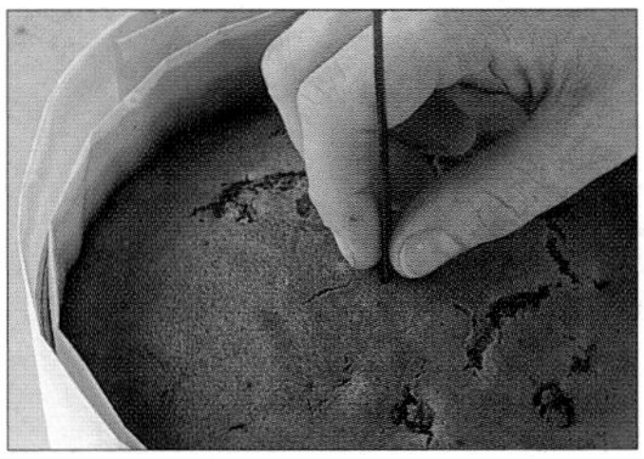

FRUIT CAKE
Insert a metal skewer in the centre of the cake: it should come out clean.

ADDING BATTER BEFORE BAKING

Soft light batters, such as creamed mixtures and whisked sponges, should be poured or spooned into tins, filling them half to two-thirds full. Heavy or dense batters, such as those for rich fruit cakes, need to be spooned in, filling the tin three-quarters full. Once the batter is in the tin, gently smooth the surface level to encourage even rising.

FRUIT CAKE BATTER
To prevent peaking and cracking, make a dip in centre with back of metal spoon.

SPONGE CAKE BATTER
Swirl with back of metal spoon. Mixture will find its own level during baking

TURNING OUT AND COOLING

After baking, let cakes stand in their tins for a while before turning out – sponge cakes need about 5 minutes standing, fruit cakes 30 minutes. Cooling on a wire rack ensures the bottom of the cake dries out and does not steam in its own heat.

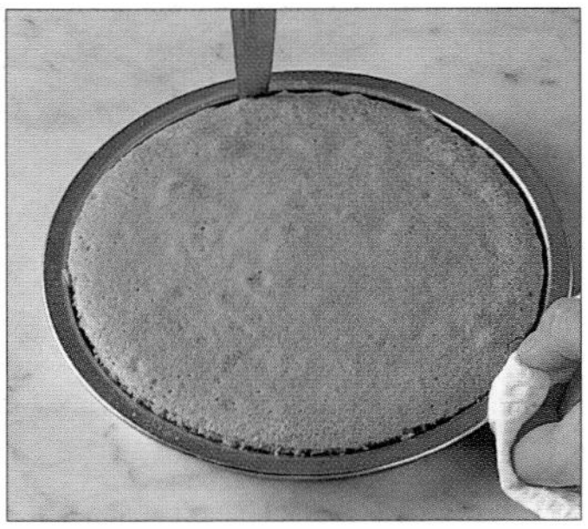

1 Run a knife between the cake and the tin. Use one even movement. Short strokes could damage the cake crust.

2 Place wire rack on top of cake. Hold with tea towel and invert the rack and tin so cake falls out on to rack.

3 Carefully peel off lining paper. Turn cake over and let cool on rack.

Basic Cakes

The texture of a cake relies on both the ratio of its ingredients (varying amounts of fat, sugar, flour and eggs) and the method in which they are mixed. The techniques shown here produce three cakes of different densities and richness, all of which are easy to make.

Victoria Sandwich

225 g self-raising flour
Pinch of salt
225 g butter, softened
225 g caster sugar
4 eggs
4 tbsp strawberry jam

Grease and flour two 20-cm round cake tins (see page 308). Sift the flour and salt together. Put the butter and sugar in a large bowl and cream together. In another bowl, lightly beat the eggs, then add them gradually to the creamed mixture. Gently fold in the flour. Spoon mixture into the prepared tins and bake at 190°C for 25 minutes. Turn out and let cool on a rack, then sandwich the cakes together with jam and dust cake top with caster sugar. Serves 6–8.

Flavourings for Victoria Sandwich

Any of these can be added to the batter. For dry ingredients, replace a little of the flour; in the case of liquids, add them drop by drop.

- Grated citrus zest.
- Cocoa powder.
- Instant coffee granules dissolved in a little water.
- Vanilla or almond essence.
- Orange-flower water.
- Liqueurs, such as Cointreau.

The Creaming Method

The aim of using this technique is to incorporate as much air as possible. When mixing by hand, this is achieved by creaming the butter and sugar until almost white in colour, beating in the eggs slowly, then folding in the flour gently. For the all-in-one method shown in the tabletop mixer below, soft-tub margarine is needed to lighten the batter, plus baking powder to lift it.

By Hand

1 Beat the butter and sugar together using a wooden spoon until the mixture is very light and fluffy.

2 Add eggs a little at a time, beating well after each addition. If mixture starts to curdle, add 1–2 tbsp flour.

3 Fold in the flour with a large metal spoon. Use a figure-of-eight movement to avoid knocking out air.

By Machine

1 Put ingredients in a table-top mixer, using soft-tub margarine instead of butter. Add 1½ tsp baking powder.

2 Beat together on medium speed until the batter is creamy, smooth and well blended, 2–3 minutes.

Trick of the Trade

Making a Lighter Batter

Fold 1–2 tbsp warm water into the batter immediately before spooning it into the cake tin.

The Rubbing-in Method

The essential technique here is to rub the fat into the flour until evenly distributed – stop rubbing when the mixture resembles fine breadcrumbs.

1 Rub the butter into the flour between your fingers and thumbs. Lift your hands up out of the bowl as you rub. This will incorporate air into the mixture.

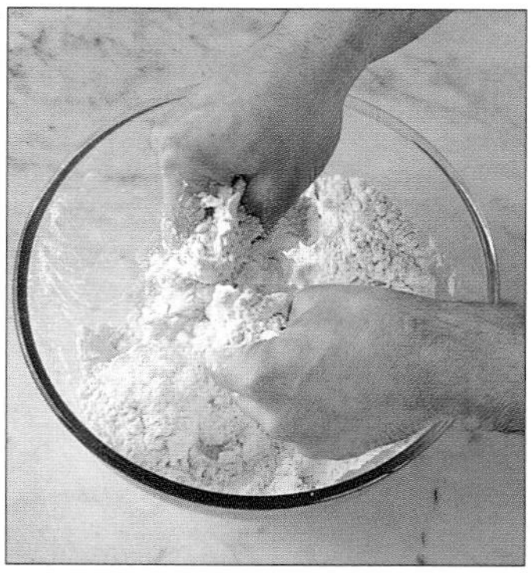

2 Add the sugar and mixed dried fruits and stir until all of the ingredients are evenly mixed.

3 After adding the egg and milk, incorporate the flour from the sides gradually and mix together well.

Trick of the Trade

Preventing Fruits Sinking

Dried fruits are heavy and tend to sink to the bottom of cake batters; this simple but clever technique helps combat the problem.

Toss the fruits in a little of the measured flour before starting to make the batter. The flour creates a dry coating around the fruits which helps to suspend them within the cake mixture and prevent them absorbing too much of the liquid.

Mixed Fruit Cake

450 g plain flour
1 tsp ground mixed spice
1 tsp ground ginger
1 tsp bicarbonate of soda
225 g mixed dried fruits
175 g butter, softened
225 g brown sugar
1 egg, beaten
About 300 ml milk

Grease and line a deep 23-cm round cake tin (see page 308). Sift the flour, ground spices and bicarbonate of soda into a bowl. Remove 2 tbsp and mix this with the fruits (see box, left).

Rub the butter into the flour to resemble fine breadcrumbs. Stir in the sugar and dried fruits.

Make a well in the centre, add the egg and milk and mix to a soft dropping consistency, adding a little more milk if necessary. Spoon into the prepared tin and level the surface. Bake at 170°C for about 1 hour 40 minutes. Turn the cake out and let cool on a rack. Serves 10–12.

The Melting Method

This is one of the simplest of cake-making techniques, relying on a melted mixture of butter, sugar and treacle for moistness and bicarbonate of soda for lightness. Measure the treacle accurately – too much will result in a heavy cake. The bicarbonate of soda will begin to work as soon as the ingredients are mixed, so work quickly.

1 Stir butter, sugar and treacle over a low heat with a wooden spoon until just melted. Let cool slightly.

2 Pour slightly cooled melted mixture into egg and milk, mix well, then start to stir in flour from sides.

3 Beat with a wooden spoon until the mixture is smooth, with a dropping consistency.

Gingerbread

250 g each butter, dark brown sugar and black treacle
375 g plain flour
1 tbsp ground ginger
1 tsp each ground mixed spice and nutmeg
2 tsp bicarbonate of soda
1 egg, beaten
300 ml milk

Grease and line a 23-cm square cake tin (see page 308). Melt butter, sugar and treacle. Cool slightly. Sift dry ingredients into a bowl, add egg, milk and melted mixture and beat well. Pour into prepared tin. Bake at 170°C for about 1½ hours. Turn out and let cool on a rack. Serves 10–12.

WHISKED CAKES

A whisked sponge boasts the lightest texture of all cakes. Its volume relies on the amount of air incorporated when eggs are whisked with sugar over a gentle heat. Butter can be included for richness.

BASIC WHISKED SPONGE CAKE

4 eggs
120 g caster sugar
120 g plain flour, sifted with a pinch of salt

Grease, flour and line a 20-cm round cake tin (see page 308). Whisk the eggs and sugar in a heatproof bowl over a pan of hot water until the mixture is thick. Remove the bowl from the pan of hot water and continue whisking off the heat until the mixture is cool. Sift and fold in the flour. Pour into the prepared tin and bake at 170°C for about 25 minutes. Turn out, remove paper and let cool on a wire rack. Serves 6–8.

SERVING A WHISKED SPONGE

A plain whisked sponge can be simply layered with whipped cream and jam and sprinkled with caster or icing sugar, or it can be elaborately decorated. Try one of the following ideas.

- Fill with raspberry mousse and whole raspberries (as shown in the Swiss roll, opposite page).
- Imbibe with sugar syrup and liqueur, then layer and coat with whipped cream and fruit purée (see page 315).
- Fill and decorate with crème Chantilly and fresh fruits (see page 321).

MAKING A WHISKED SPONGE

Pastry chefs use a very large balloon whisk to incorporate as much air as possible, but you can use a hand-held electric whisk if you prefer. To speed up the thickening process, the bowl is set over hot water – take care not to let it touch the water or the mixture will start to cook.

1 Put the eggs and sugar in large heatproof bowl and whisk vigorously for a few seconds to break up the eggs and start mixing them with the sugar.

2 Put the bowl over a pan of hot water and whisk until the mixture is thick enough to leave a figure-of-eight ribbon trail on the surface when the whisk is lifted.

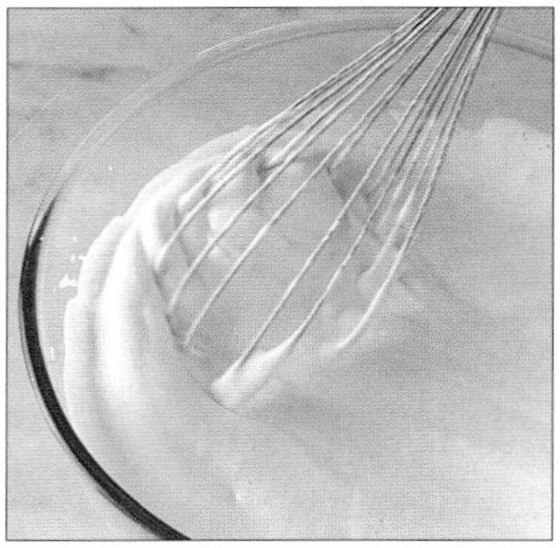

3 Remove the bowl from the heat and continue whisking until the mixture has cooled and is very thick, 3–5 minutes.

4 Fold in flour in batches with a rubber spatula. Cut cleanly through, to avoid knocking out the air.

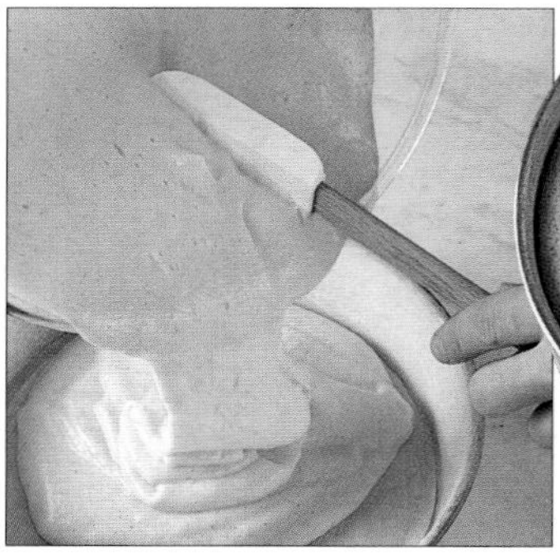

5 Pour finished batter slowly into the prepared tin, gently guiding it in with the spatula.

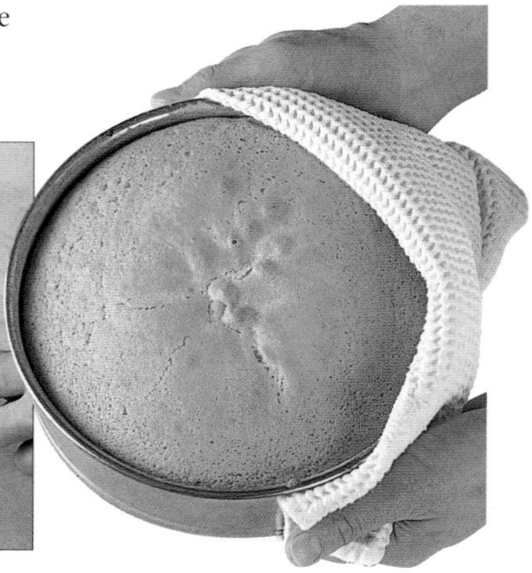

6 When fully cooked, the sponge will be golden, well risen and firm but springy to the touch.

ENRICHING A WHISKED SPONGE

Add melted butter to the basic whisked sponge mixture to enrich the batter and make it more moist. Take care that the butter is thoroughly cooled after melting and add it to the whisked mixture slowly, after the flour has been folded in. Bake the cake as soon as possible after mixing or batter may deflate.

1 Melt 20 g unsalted butter and let cool. Pour slowly over the surface of the whisked mixture.

2 Gently fold in the butter, cutting through the mixture with a spatula so as not to knock air out of it, until evenly incorporated.

WHAT'S IN A NAME?

A whisked sponge is often called a Genoese sponge cake or *génoise* in French. Considered one of the great French classics in cake making, it actually originated in Genoa, northern Italy, hence its name. Recipes vary – some are fatless, while others enriched with melted butter. For layered cakes, the fatless sponge is lighter – butter gives a denser texture.

MAKING A SWISS ROLL

The sponge for a Swiss roll is baked in a shallow rectangular tin, then turned out, cooled and rolled around a filling. Follow the whisked sponge technique on the opposite page, using 4 eggs, 125 g sugar and 75 g plain flour. Bake in a 22- x 33-cm Swiss roll tin at 190-200°C, 4–5 minutes. For fillings, see box, opposite page.

1 Lift sponge out of tin on lining paper and place on wire rack. Let cool.

2 Place crust-side down on parchment dusted with sugar. Peel off lining paper.

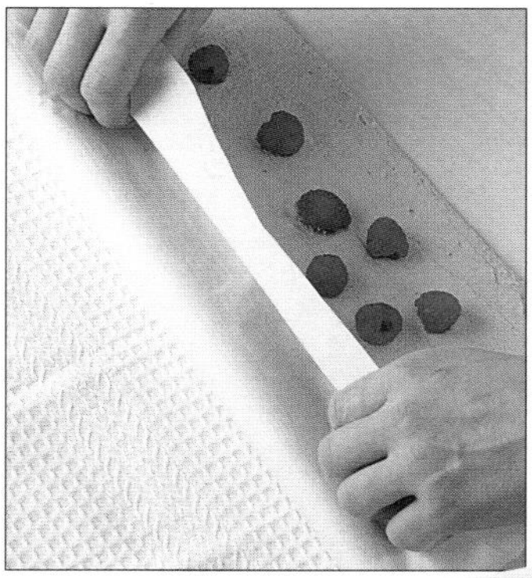

3 Transfer sponge, still on the baking parchment, to a tea towel. Spread over your chosen filling. Fold over 2 cm of sponge along one long edge, using the parchment to guide you. This will make rolling easier.

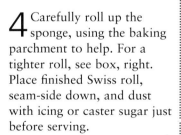

4 Carefully roll up the sponge, using the baking parchment to help. For a tighter roll, see box, right. Place finished Swiss roll, seam-side down, and dust with icing or caster sugar just before serving.

TRICK OF THE TRADE

Use this chef's technique to tighten a Swiss roll for a neat presentation.

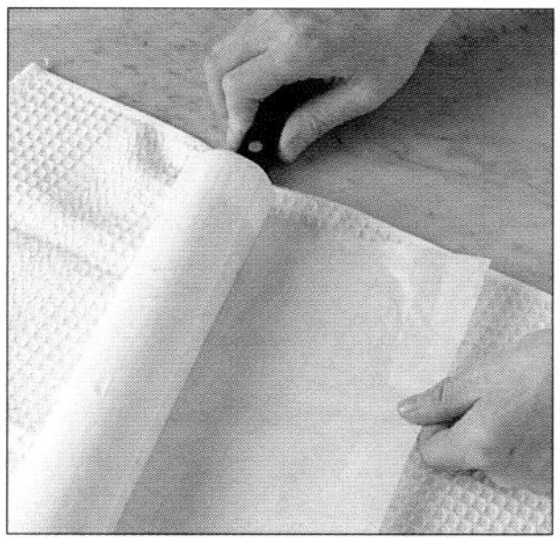

Push a palette knife under the sponge in the parchment. Pull the parchment away from the knife.

SPECIAL CAKES

These cakes rely on special techniques involving the ingredients used, and the way the cakes are made and assembled. Added interest and flavour are achieved pastry-chef style by imbibing layers and stacking them.

ANGEL FOOD CAKE

12 egg whites (about 350 ml)
1½ tsp cream of tartar
280 g caster sugar
85 g plain flour, sifted
25 g cornflour, sifted
1 tsp vanilla essence

Whisk the egg whites until foaming, then add the cream of tartar and continue whisking until stiff. Add the sugar, 1 tbsp at a time, whisking after each addition to form a stiff meringue. Fold in the flour, cornflour and vanilla. Pour into an ungreased angel cake or tube tin and bake at 175°C for 40–45 minutes. Invert tin and leave cake to cool in the tin. Serves 10–12.

MAKING AN ANGEL FOOD CAKE

This famous American cake is unusual in that it is made with just egg whites, no yolks, which is why it is so light and airy. Cream of tartar is whisked with the whites to stiffen them and give the meringue body, and the cake is cooled upside down in the tin to prevent shrinkage and preserve the shape.

1 Fold flour, cornflour and vanilla into meringue with a spatula until just blended. Do not overmix or air will be knocked out.

2 Pour batter into an ungreased and unfloured angel cake tin. Level the surface with the spatula and bake immediately.

3 After baking, invert cake in tin on to its feet. If tin has no feet, invert tin on to a funnel or bottle neck. Cool completely, then unmould.

CHOCOLATE TORTE

225 g unsalted butter, softened
150 g soft brown sugar
4 eggs, separated
200 g chilled unsweetened chocolate, grated
200 g ground hazelnuts
25 g ground almonds
50 g caster sugar

Grease and line a 23-cm round cake tin (see page 308). Cream butter and sugar, then beat in egg yolks. Add grated chocolate and ground nuts and beat well to mix. Whisk egg whites in a separate bowl until stiff, then whisk in sugar. Fold into chocolate mixture. Pour into tin and bake at 150°C, 50 minutes. Serves 10–12.

MAKING A CHOCOLATE TORTE

Austrian-style tortes have no flour, hence their rich, dense textures. In such flourless cakes, nuts replace the flour, ground very fine so they release some of their oil and give the cake a close crumb. Good-quality chocolate with a high cocoa butter content is absolutely essential.

1 Beat grated chocolate and ground nuts into creamed ingredients until they are evenly mixed.

2 Fold the meringue very carefully into the nut mixture, in 3–4 batches, using a spatula.

3 Press centre of baked cake with your finger: it should feel slightly soft. During cooling, texture will firm up.

Cutting and Imbibing

For a layered cake to have a neat finish, the layers must be cut accurately. The technique used here ensures even layers that line up perfectly when the cake is reassembled (see right). Imbibing the layers with sugar syrup and liqueur is the professional way to give moistness and flavour.

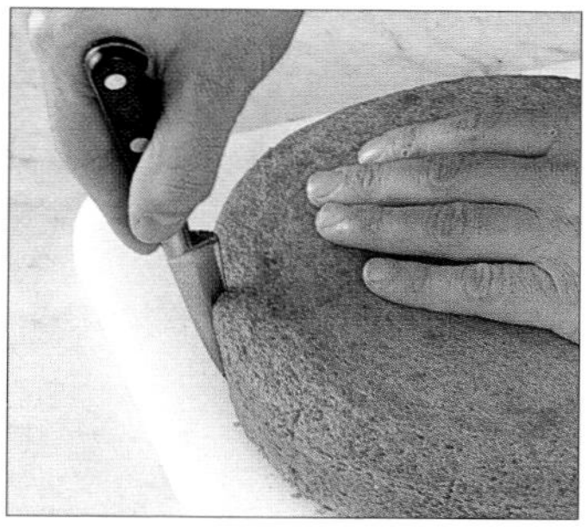

1 Make a notch down the side of the cake with the blade of a small knife.

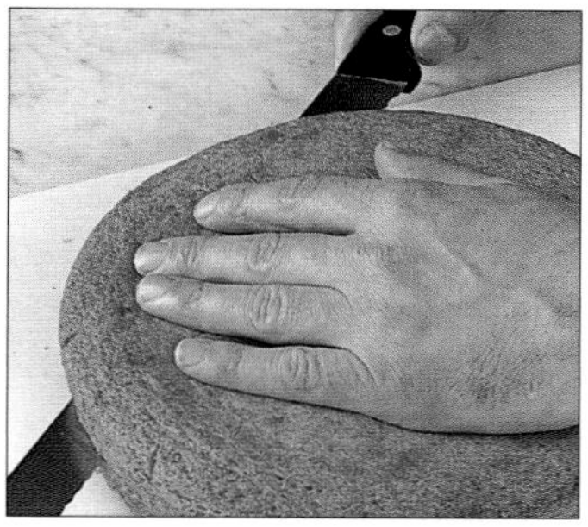

2 Cut cake into two or three layers, using a serrated knife and a sawing action.

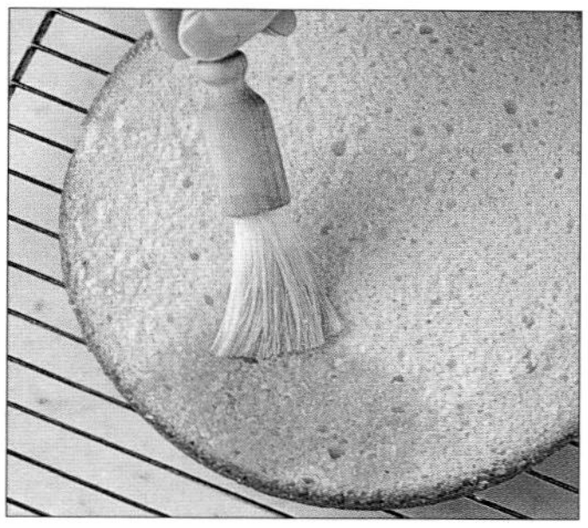

3 Brush cut surfaces with a light sugar syrup (see page 281) and 2–3 tbsp liqueur.

Filling and Layering

After cutting and imbibing (see left), cake layers can be reassembled with the filling of your choice. Whipped cream and raspberry purée are shown here; for other filling ideas, see box, page 312. Save the base of the cake for the last, top layer because it has the flattest surface.

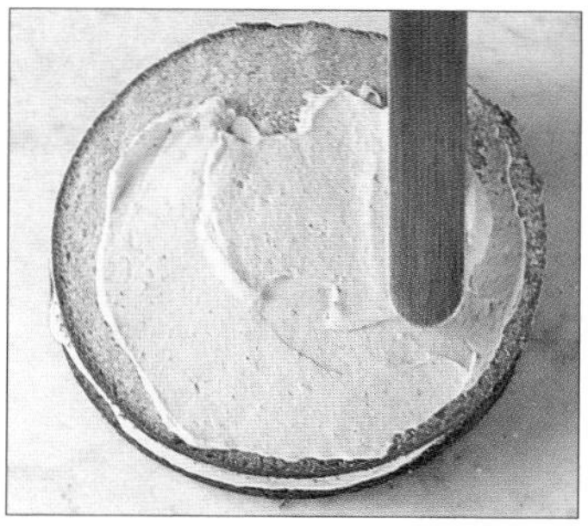

1 Spread filling over one cake layer. Top with next layer, lining up notches, and repeat.

2 Top with the last cake layer, cut-side down, again matching up notches.

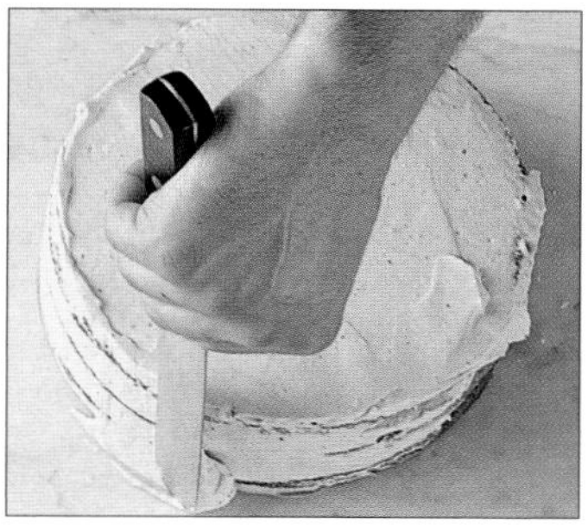

3 Spread the top and sides of the cake with filling, using a warm palette knife.

Making a Meringue Cake

Pastry chefs use this professional layering technique to create cakes with a very precise finish. Here meringue discs (see page 273) are layered with the chocolate mousse from the Gâteau des Deux Pierre (see page 284), but you can use the same technique for the layers of sponge cake and cream filling shown above. For the technique of making the chocolate cigarettes for the decoration, see page 323.

1 Place a meringue disc on a cake card in a metal ring. Add a layer of mousse to cover it. Cover with another disc and continue the layers, finishing with mousse. Chill in the refrigerator until set.

2 Wrap a warm cloth around the metal ring for 1–2 minutes, then carefully lift the ring off the cake.

Cheesecakes

Baked or unbaked, with biscuit crumb or pastry crust, ever-popular cheesecakes are very easy to make. The cake itself can be light and fluffy, or sumptuous and rich, depending on the method and type of cheese used.

RASPBERRY CHEESECAKE

250 g digestive biscuits, crushed
60 g butter, melted
15 g gelatine powder
4 tbsp water
125 ml double cream
500 ml unsweetened berry purée
125 g caster sugar
250 g curd cheese

Base-line a 25-cm springform tin with biscuits and butter and chill. Prepare gelatine (see page 274) in the water. Whip cream. Mix remaining ingredients, stir in dissolved gelatine, then fold in cream. Pour into tin. Chill at least 4 hours; unmould. Serves 6–8.

Making a Crumb Base

Biscuit crumb bases, held together by melted butter, are usually chilled in the refrigerator until set and used for refrigerator cheesecakes as here, but they can also be used for baked cheescakes (see opposite page). If you like you can crush the biscuits in a food processor.

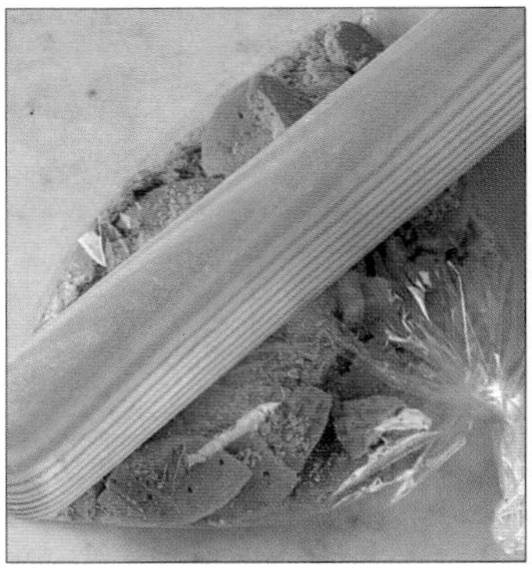

1 Break the biscuits into pieces. Place them in a heavy-duty plastic bag and crush them by tapping and rolling with a rolling pin.

2 Transfer the crushed biscuits to a large bowl, pour in the melted butter and stir with a metal spoon until they are evenly mixed.

3 Press the biscuit crust into the bottom of the tin with the back of the metal spoon, smoothing and flattening it so the layer is even.

Making a Chilled Cheesecake

Fruit purée, curd cheese and whipped cream are set with gelatine to make a mousse-like texture that is firm enough to slice. This type of cheesecake, also called a refrigerator cheesecake, is lighter than the baked variety. A simple recipe using this technique is given above.

Adding gelatine
Stir cooled, dissolved gelatine into berry purée and cheese mixture until evenly mixed, using a spatula.

Releasing clip
Slowly release the spring on the side of the tin; this will loosen the edge and free the cheesecake.

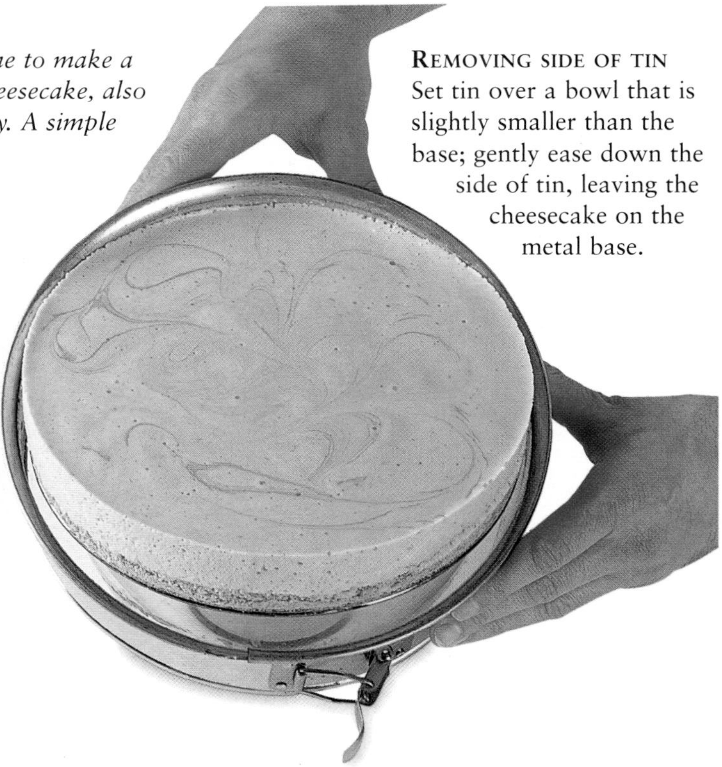

Removing side of tin
Set tin over a bowl that is slightly smaller than the base; gently ease down the side of tin, leaving the cheesecake on the metal base.

Making a Baked Cheesecake

This type of cheesecake is traditionally baked in a pastry case. Here a crisp, sweet Austrian-style pastry that has been enriched with cream cheese is used, but you can use a plain pâte brisée or sweet pâte sucrée if you prefer. Pastry cases should always be baked blind first, to prevent the filling making them soggy.

1 Make the filling: beat the cream cheese, cottage cheese and sugar with a wooden spoon until well blended, then add the remaining filling ingredients and stir together until the flour and the cornflour are evenly incorporated.

2 Line bottom of tin with a circle of pastry, then line side with a deep strip. Make sure all edges are sealed, to prevent the filling leaking out during baking.

3 After removing foil and baking beans, ladle the cheese filling into the partially baked crust. It should come almost to the top of the pastry case.

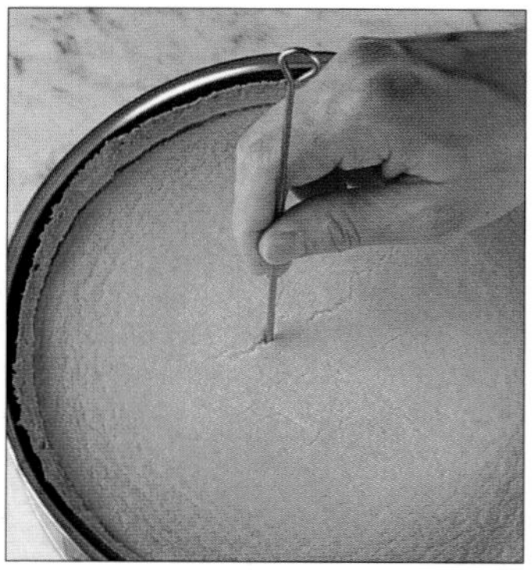

4 When the cheesecake is cooked, the pastry case will have shrunk away from the side of the tin and a fine skewer inserted into the centre will come out clean.

5 To decorate, place a paper doily on top of cake. Put icing sugar in a small fine sieve and shake gently over top of cheesecake. Carefully remove the doily. Alternatively, cover top of cheesecake with glazed berries or chocolate curls (see page 290).

Austrian Cheesecake

375 g cream cheese
350 g cottage cheese
175 g caster sugar
4 eggs, lightly beaten
125 ml sour cream
215 g plain flour
1 tbsp cornflour
2–3 tbsp water

Make the filling: beat 250 g cream cheese with the cottage cheese and 100 g sugar. Stir in the eggs, sour cream, 2 tbsp of the flour and the cornflour.

Make the pastry: rub the remaining cream cheese into the remaining flour. Stir in the remaining sugar and enough water to bind the dough. Chill for 30 minutes. Roll out and line the base and sides of a 25-cm springform tin. Bake blind at 180°C for 10–15 minutes. Pour in filling and bake for 45–50 minutes until set. Cool in the tin, then unmould. Serves 12.

Cake Icing

Even the plainest of cakes can be transformed into a real treat with the addition of icing – either simply swirled or skilfully piped. Glacé, royal, chocolate and buttercream are the easy-to-master basics, while the art of whipped crème Chantilly is one of the pastry chef's best-kept secrets.

Making a Paper Piping Bag

Use baking parchment. The tip of the bag can be cut to vary its size.

Cut a 25-cm square of paper in half diagonally. Bring one point of triangle to centre to form cone.

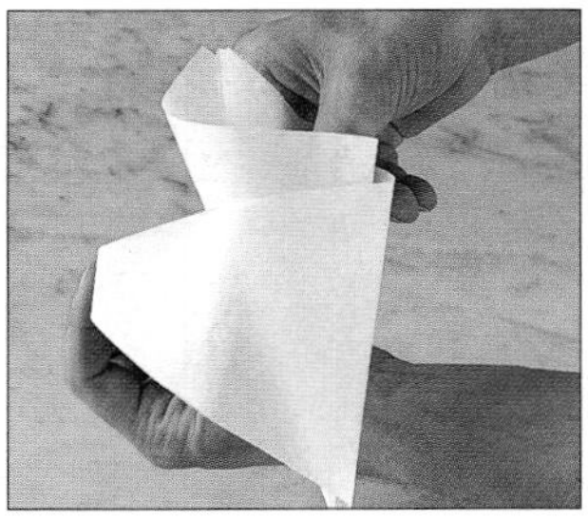

Wrap the remaining point of the triangle around to meet the other two points.

Pull all 3 points tightly together to create a sharp tip and fold flap inside; crease to hold the shape.

Making Glace Icing

This simple icing is traditionally made with icing sugar and warm water, but many pastry chefs like to cut its sweetness by using fruit juice or a liqueur instead. To coat the top and sides of a 20-cm cake, use 175 g icing sugar and 1–2 tbsp liquid. Use the icing immediately after making.

1 Sift icing sugar into a bowl. Work hard lumps through with a metal spoon.

2 Add a little warm water or flavouring of your choice and whisk vigorously.

3 Continue whisking until smooth, adding more liquid as necessary.

Making Royal Icing

To delay setting and make icing easy to work with, the trick of the trade is to add glycerine. For the top and sides of a 24-cm cake, use 500 g icing sugar, 2 egg whites, 2 tbsp lemon juice and 2 tsp glycerine. Cover icing with cling film, let stand overnight and stir before using.

1 Put sifted icing sugar in a bowl and make a well in the centre. Add lightly beaten egg whites and lemon juice.

2 Whisk until stiff and glossy, about 10 minutes, then whisk in glycerine.

MAKING CHOCOLATE ICING

A glossy professional-looking icing, as on the sachertorte below, is easy to make following the technique here. Good-quality unsweetened chocolate is essential – here couverture buttons (pistoles) are used for ease of melting. Glaze the cake (see box, below) before making the icing.

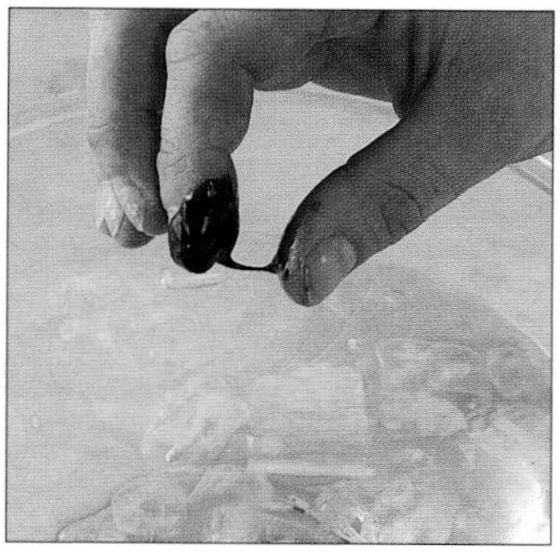

1 Add chocolate to sugar syrup, then whisk over a moderate heat until well combined and smooth.

2 To test for the thread stage, dip fingers in iced water, then into chocolate. Pull apart to see thread.

3 Stand pan on tea towel and tap lightly to knock out any air bubbles. Use immediately (see below).

CHOCOLATE ICING

150 g caster sugar
150 ml water
300 g chocolate pistoles

Make a sugar syrup (see page 280) with the sugar and water. Add the chocolate pieces and whisk until combined. Cook over a low heat for 3–5 minutes until just before the soft-ball stage, when the "thread" stage is reached (110°C). Remove pan from heat and tap on the work surface to eliminate air bubbles. Use immediately. Makes enough icing to coat a 25-cm cake.

TRICK OF THE TRADE

MAKING A GLAZE
Jam glazes are used to coat cakes before icing to give a smooth finish and add moisture; they are also used over fruits in tarts and tartlets to keep them fresh and give sparkle.

Melt 100 g jam (use apricot for chocolate cakes; red fruit jam for fruits). Work warm jam through a sieve to remove lumps of fruit. Return to pan, add 50 ml water and bring to the boil, stirring. To glaze cake, place on a rack and brush warm glaze all over.

COATING WITH CHOCOLATE ICING

For a flawless finish, work quickly, and with a steady hand. Before the cake is iced, place it on a wire rack over baking parchment to catch the drips and prevent the icing from pooling around the bottom of the cake. After it has set, the icing will be glossy and smooth.

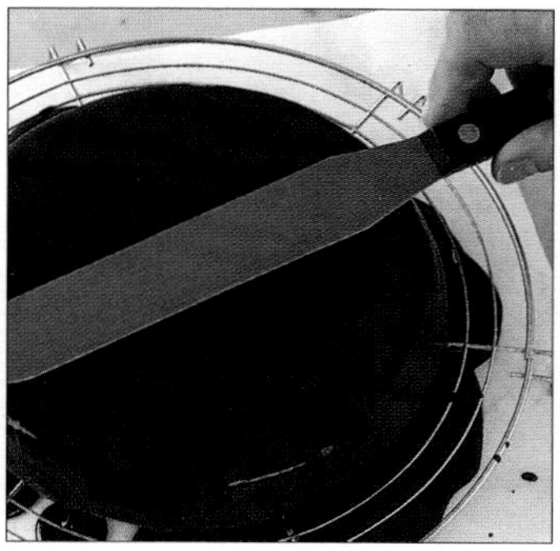

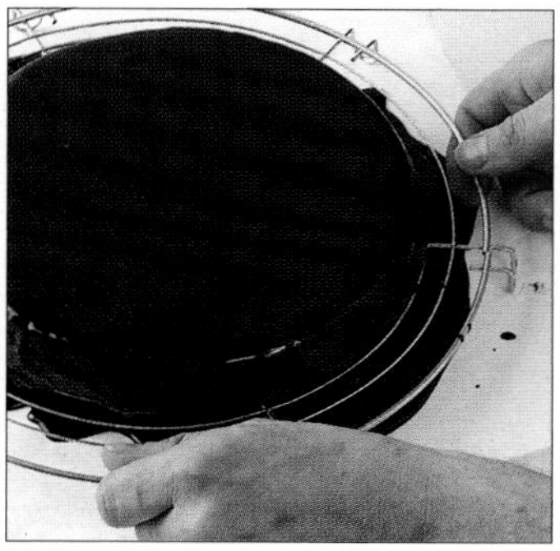

1 Ladle warm chocolate icing (see above) over the centre of cake coated with apricot-jam glaze (see left).

2 Quickly smooth icing across top of cake with a warm palette knife. Allow excess to run down sides.

3 Tap rack on work surface so icing settles. Leave to set, about 5–10 minutes.

FINISHING

Melted chocolate is easy to pipe from a paper piping bag and it looks very effective. A classic example of this is shown on the Austrian sachertorte, *simply but elegantly decorated with its name.*

Fill a paper piping bag (see opposite page) with melted chocolate. Fold over the top to seal, then trim the tip. Squeeze the chocolate out of the bag as you write the name.

BUTTERCREAM ICING

160 g caster sugar
85 ml water
2 egg yolks
1 egg
250 g unsalted butter, softened

Make a sugar syrup with the sugar and water and heat to the soft-ball stage (see page 280). Lightly beat the egg yolks and egg in a tabletop mixer fitted with the whisk attachment. With the motor running, pour a thin, steady stream of sugar syrup down the side of the bowl. Whisk until the mixture is mousse-like, pale in colour and cool. Cut butter into chunks and gradually add to the bowl. Increase to full speed and whisk for 3–4 minutes until butter is incorporated. When pale and fluffy, add flavouring if you like. Makes enough icing to coat a 24-cm cake.

MAKING BUTTERCREAM ICING

This ultrasmooth rich frosting is made by whisking butter into a sabayon *of eggs and sugar syrup. The sabayon should be at cool room temperature before adding the butter – too hot and the butter will melt, too cold and it will set. Buttercream can be used as a cake filling or coating, plain or flavoured with vanilla or coffee essence, or with a liqueur or praline paste.*

1 Boil the sugar syrup to the soft-ball stage (see page 280). To test without a thermometer, dip your fingers in iced water, then quickly into the syrup – the syrup that sticks to your fingers should hold its shape but feel soft when pressed.

2 Whisking on medium speed, pour the hot sugar syrup in a thin steady stream down the side of the mixer bowl into the egg yolks and egg. Continue whisking on medium speed to make a sabayon (see page 292) that is pale, thick and cool.

3 With the machine whisking on full speed, add chunks of softened butter to the mixture, making sure that each piece is completely blended in before adding the next. When the butter is incorporated, whisk in the flavouring of your choice.

4 Lift whisk out of bowl and scrape off buttercream. Refrigerate for 5–10 minutes to firm up the butter in the mixture. The buttercream is now ready to use.

MAKING BUTTERCREAM

This simple frosting is most often used for children's birthday cakes and novelty cakes. Made as a simple alternative to the professional buttercream above, it is particularly favoured because it requires no special skill or equipment.

Cream 125 g unsalted butter with a wooden spoon until soft. Gradually beat in 250 g sifted icing sugar until the mixture is smooth and pale, then add a few drops of flavouring or colouring if you like. Continue beating until the mixture is very pale and fluffy, adding a little warm water if the icing is too stiff.

ICING WITH CREAM

One of the quickest, easiest and most effective ways to fill and ice a cake is with whipped cream. Pastry chefs frequently use crème Chantilly (see page 292) – its vanilla flavour goes well with plain sponge cake and fresh fruits to make a truly fabulous dessert. Here a whisked sponge cake (see page 312) is used, cut into three layers and imbibed with sugar syrup and kirsch. For a 25-cm cake, you will need about 500 ml cream and 200 g fruit.

1 Cut and imbibe the cake (see page 315); place on a cake card. Spread the layers with crème Chantilly and top with thinly sliced fresh fruits, arranging them in even layers.

2 Smooth any excess filling around the sides of the cake with a palette knife, then spread an even layer of crème Chantilly over the top of the cake, making the surface as smooth as possible.

3 Using a "paddling" motion with the tip of the palette knife, spread more cream on the sides, rotating the cake with the help of a turntable if available.

4 Use a flat scraper to smooth off the sides. Keep it at a 45° angle as you rotate the cake. Repeat with a toothed scraper to make a decorative ridged edge.

5 Transfer cake to a smaller card. Place the cake on an icing turntable over a sheet of paper; gently press chopped toasted nuts around the base.

6 Score the top of the cake into twelve equal sections with the tip of a sharp knife, then pipe a rosette of cream on each section using a large star nozzle.

7 Decorate the top of the cake as shown, with strawberry halves dipped in red jam glaze (see box, page 319) and nuts. Alternatively, experiment with fruits, nuts, and flavourings of your choice.

TRICK OF THE TRADE

SOFTENING JAM

Pastry chefs use this technique to prevent jam from tearing cakes when it is spread over layers.

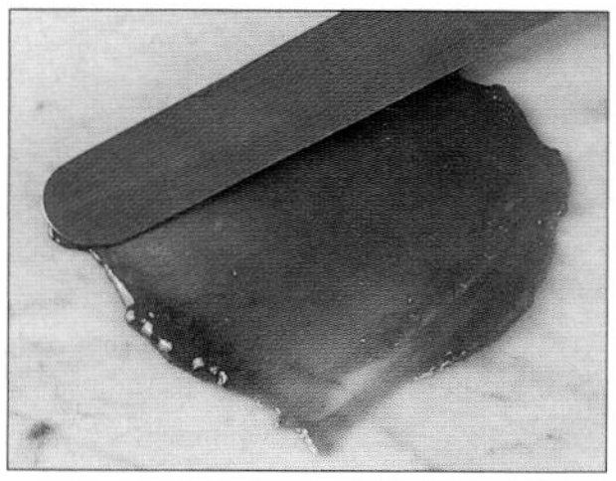

Put seedless or sieved jam on the work surface or a clean, smooth board and work it back and forth with a palette knife until it has a very soft, spreading consistency. This technique is especially useful for whisked sponge cakes made without fat, because they have a delicate crumb. The thin layer of cake in a Swiss roll (see page 313) is particularly delicate and may break up if spread with unsoftened jam.

Petits Fours

Dainty, demure and splendidly frivolous, these playful bites are the debutantes of desserts. Petit fours – a range of delicate and exquisite cakes, biscuits, fruits and chocolate – demand close attention to detail; even the simplified versions. Bake with care; they scorch easily.

LACE TUILES

70 ml orange juice
Grated zest of 1 orange
50 ml Grand Marnier
250 g caster sugar
100 g unsalted butter, melted
200 g nibbed almonds
125 g plain flour

Mix all the ingredients in a bowl. Butter a baking sheet and place small spoonfuls of mixture on to the sheet, five at a time. Flatten each one with a fork and bake at 180°C, 5 minutes. Remove the tuiles and place on oiled rolling pins to set shapes as you make the next five. Makes 25.

FINANCIERS

30 g raisins
3 tbsp rum
60 g unsalted butter, melted
60 g egg whites
60 g caster sugar
30 g plain flour
30 g ground almonds

Butter six small oval tartlet moulds and chill. Soak the raisins in rum for at least 15 minutes. Mix all the ingredients together until smooth. Add raisins. Divide one-quarter of the mixture between the moulds and bake at 200°C, 10 minutes. Remove from oven and repeat three times with the remaining mixture. Imbibe with remaining rum. Makes 24.

LACE TUILES
Tuile is the French word for roof tile and these delicious delicacies are so-called because of their shape.

OPERETTAS
Make a Swiss roll sponge (see page 313) and cut cake into three. Spread one piece with ganache (see page 282). Cover with another piece and imbibe with a coffee-flavoured sugar syrup. Spread sponge with buttercream icing (see page 320) and top with the remaining sponge. Coat with chocolate fondant (see page 337) and let set. Cut into squares and top each one with gold leaf. Makes 21.

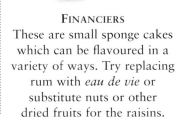

FINANCIERS
These are small sponge cakes which can be flavoured in a variety of ways. Try replacing rum with *eau de vie* or substitute nuts or other dried fruits for the raisins.

CARAMEL-COATED PHYSALIS
Gently peel back the leaves of physalis (see page 263) and twist at the base. Make a light caramel syrup (see page 281). Dip each berry into the caramel, leaving the leaves uncoated, and allow any excess to drip off. Place upright on greased baking parchment and allow to set.

Ice-cream balls

Use a melon baller to shape ice cream into small balls. Working quickly to keep ice cream solid, place balls on baking parchment and insert a cocktail stick in each one. Freeze balls for 10 minutes. Dip ice-cream balls into cooled melted chocolate until balls are evenly coated, then place at an angle on baking parchment and leave to set.

Citron tartlets

Make half the pâte sucrée (see page 294). Line 6 tiny tartlet moulds with pastry and bake at 180°C, about 7–10 minutes. Unmould and repeat five times. Make half the crème patissière (see page 277) and add the juice of 2 lemons. Pour custard into each tart and sprinkle with icing sugar. Caramelize tops with a blow torch. Makes 30.

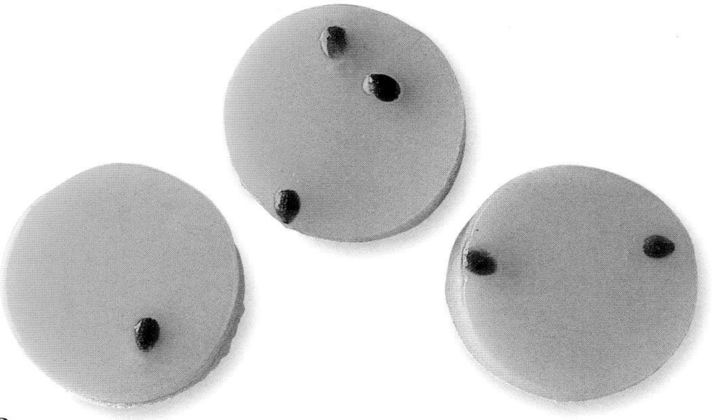

Passion fruit miroirs

1 Make a fruit mousse (see page 275) with passion fruit and set in a tin. Coat with a fruit jelly (see page 275). Chill until set.

2 Cut out miroirs using 4-cm metal cutters. Place miroirs on baking parchment and chill in the refrigerator until serving time.

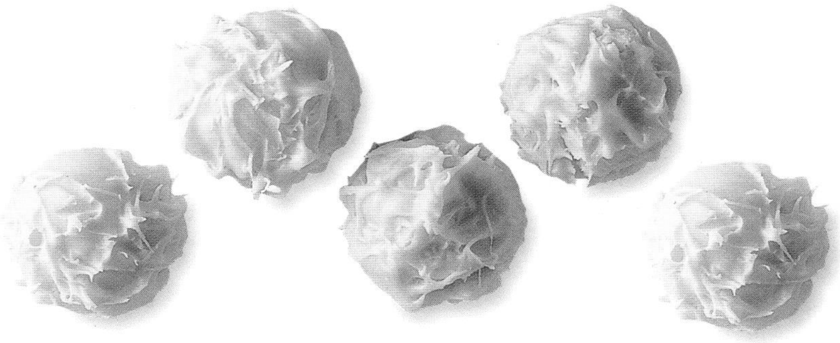

Almond truffles

1 Shape almond paste into small balls with a melon baller and dip into ganache (see page 282) made with white chocolate until coated.

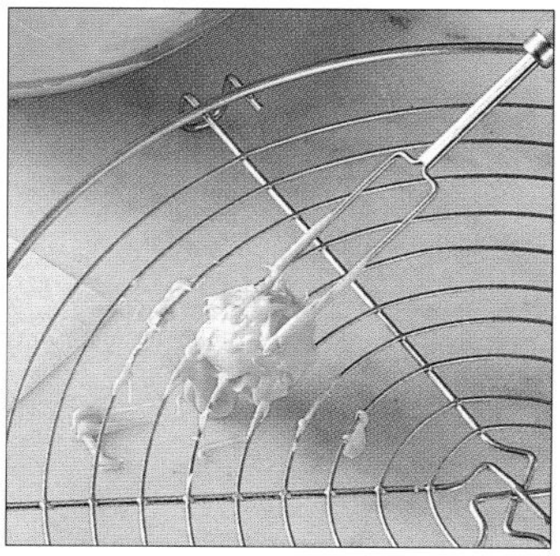

2 Roll each truffle over a wire cooling rack to create a spiked effect. Leave truffles on rack to set, then place in petit-four cases.

BISCUITS

From simple rolled, sliced and piped biscuits based on similar doughs, to buttery shortbread, crisp brandy snaps and classic French sponge fingers and *tuiles*, biscuits appear in a seemingly endless array of shapes, textures and flavours. The following techniques reveal some of the best.

BASIC DOUGHS

ROLLED BISCUITS: Soften 125 g unsalted butter and cream with 150 g caster sugar. When smooth, beat in 2 egg yolks and 225 g plain flour. Add 50 g raisins, currants or sultanas. Shape biscuits; bake at 180°C, 15 minutes. Makes 12–15.

DROPPED BISCUITS: Melt 125 g unsalted butter. Add 150 g caster sugar. When cool, mix in 2 egg whites, then 100 g plain flour and 125 g ground almonds. Shape biscuits, then bake at 180°C, 15 minutes. Makes 12–15.

SHORTBREAD

115 g butter, softened
55 g caster sugar
115 g plain flour

Cream the butter and sugar until light and fluffy. Stir in the flour. Spoon the mixture into a buttered 31- x 21-cm tin and press down with your fingertips to compress and level the dough.

Mark the dough into bars of equal size, without cutting through to the base of the tin. Bake at 170°C for 35 minutes or until shortbread is pale golden brown. Cool in the tin for about 5 minutes, then sprinkle with sugar and cut into bars. Let cool in the tin for about 1 hour, then lift out and cool completely on a wire rack. Makes 18 bars.

ROLLED BISCUITS

For these biscuits, the dough (see box, left) is firm enough to roll and cut out, or roll and slice. It spreads very little on the baking sheet during cooking, so there is no need to space the shapes very far apart. Lightly knead the dough until it just comes together, then chill. Re-roll trimmings only once – any more than this and the biscuits will be tough.

ROLLING AND CUTTING
Chill dough, then roll out. Cut out shapes using a floured biscuit cutter.

ROLLING AND SLICING
Roll dough into a log, then wrap and chill in the refrigerator until firm. Cut the dough log crosswise into even slices with a knife.

MAKING SHORTBREAD

This shortbread is made with ground rice, which gives it a crisp texture, but you can use semolina instead. If you like, shape the mixture in a round on a baking sheet, either freeform or, more precisely, inside a metal ring. Round shortbreads traditionally have crimped edges.

1 Press dough firmly into buttered tin with your fingertips, making sure that it is even in thickness.

2 While still warm, sprinkle shortbread with caster sugar, then cut into bars with a large chef's knife.

3 After cooling shortbread in tin for 5 minutes, transfer bars to a rack and let cool completely.

Dropped Biscuits

These biscuits are made with a slacker dough than the rolled biscuits (see box, opposite page), soft enough to be dropped from a spoon or piped on to a baking sheet, without needing to be rolled out first. Make sure the shapes are the same size to ensure even baking, and space them well apart as the dough tends to spread.

Free-form
Place mounds or drop teaspoonfuls of the dough on to the baking sheet.

Piped
Fill a piping bag fitted with a star nozzle with dough. Pipe rosettes on to baking sheet.

Brandy Snaps

These light, lacy-textured biscuits are shaped after baking, while they are still warm and malleable. If you work quickly they should not harden, but if they do, pop them back in the oven to soften for about 30 seconds.

1 Space teaspoonfuls of batter well apart on baking sheet; press each one with your fingertips to spread it out to a 3-cm round.

2 Let the biscuits rest for one minute after baking, then lift off the baking sheet with a palette knife.

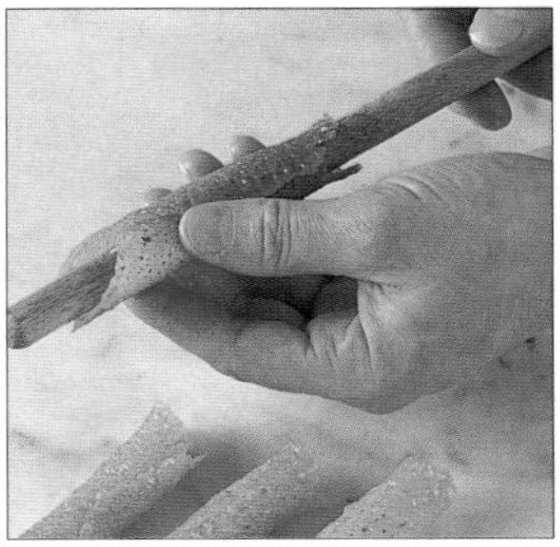

3 Curl each brandy snap, lacy-side out around the greased spoon, overlapping the edges slightly. Slip off and cool on a wire rack.

Finishing

To enhance the appearance, flavour and texture of biscuits, try the following.

Sprinkling sugar
For a crunchy texture, sprinkle demerara sugar on to shapes before baking. For extra crunch, add more sugar after baking, if you like.

Chocolate covering
Spread melted chocolate over one side of biscuits after baking, then mark with a fork if you like. Let set, chocolate-side up, on a rack.

BRANDY SNAPS

115 g butter
115 g demerara sugar
2 tbsp golden syrup
115 g plain flour
1 tsp ground ginger
1 tsp brandy

Melt butter, sugar and syrup. Stir in flour, ginger and brandy. Put four well-spaced teaspoonfuls of mixture on a greased baking sheet. Bake at 180°C for 7–10 minutes. Shape one at a time around a greased wooden spoon handle while still warm. Repeat five times. Makes 20.

SPONGE FINGERS

3 eggs, separated
100 g caster sugar
75 g plain flour, sifted
Icing sugar, for dusting

Grease a baking sheet and line with baking parchment. Whisk egg whites until soft peaks form, then gradually whisk in half the caster sugar until stiff and glossy. In a separate bowl, lightly beat egg yolks with the remaining caster sugar, then fold into the meringue followed by the flour. Pipe on to prepared baking sheet and dust with icing sugar in two batches. Bake at 180°C until golden brown, 10 minutes. Let cool on a wire rack. Makes 10–12.

STENCIL PASTE

3 egg whites
100 g icing sugar
100 g plain flour
60 g unsalted butter, melted
Vanilla essence (optional)

Whisk the egg whites and icing sugar together until smooth. Stir in the flour and whisk lightly until just combined. Pour in melted butter, and a few drops of vanilla essence if using, and stir gently until smooth. Cover and let rest in the refrigerator, 30 minutes. For *tuiles*, grease a baking sheet and a rolling pin. Place six teaspoonfuls of batter on baking sheet; spread into 5-cm circles with a wet fork. Bake at 200°C for 5–8 minutes until golden at the edges. Shape while warm on greased rolling pin; repeat with remaining mixture. Makes 18. For *tulipes*, bake as for *tuiles*, using tablespoonfuls of batter and spreading each one into a 10-cm circle. While warm, shape in two moulds. Makes 8–10.

MAKING SPONGE FINGERS

These light, airy sponge fingers are made by enriching a meringue mixture with egg yolks. Gently fold the ingredients together to prevent knocking out the air. The double dusting technique creates the characteristic "pearls" of sugar on top of the fingers.

1 Pipe batter fingers with a 2-cm plain nozzle on baking parchment. Make them 10 cm long and 5 cm apart.

2 Before baking, dust fingers with half the icing sugar. Let stand until sugar has dissolved, then dust again.

3 Holding the parchment in place, lift one side of the baking sheet and tip off the excess sugar.

MAKING TUILES

Pastry chefs use a classic French stencil paste (see box, left) to make these delicate, curved biscuits, named after the French word for roof tiles. Shape the mixture straight from the oven, while still soft.

SHAPING BATTER
Use the back of a fork dipped in cold water to prevent the batter sticking.

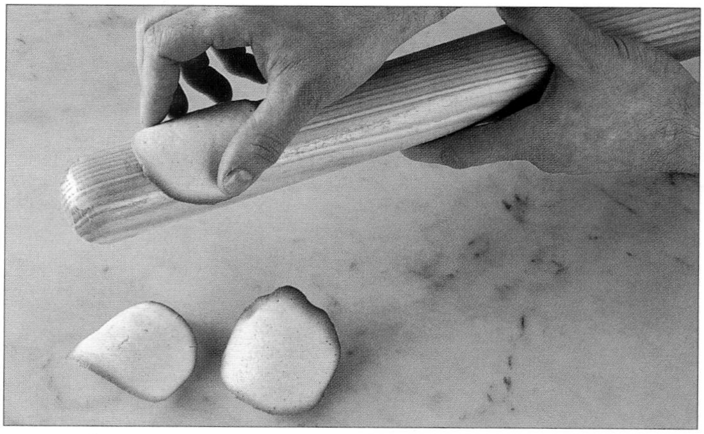

SHAPING BISCUITS
Immediately after baking, shape the biscuits around a greased rolling pin to form curved *tuiles*. Let cool on a wire rack.

MAKING TULIPES

These ruffled biscuits are made from the same stencil paste as tuiles *(see left), but they are shaped to make containers – for filling with fruits and ice creams.*

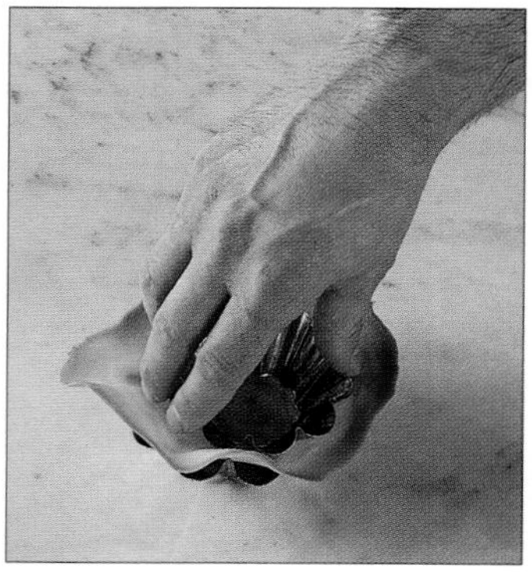

Immediately after baking, press each shape into a small fluted mould then, while the shape is still warm, gently press a smaller mould inside the first to form a tulip-shaped container. Carefully remove the moulds and place the *tulipe* on a wire rack until cold and firm.

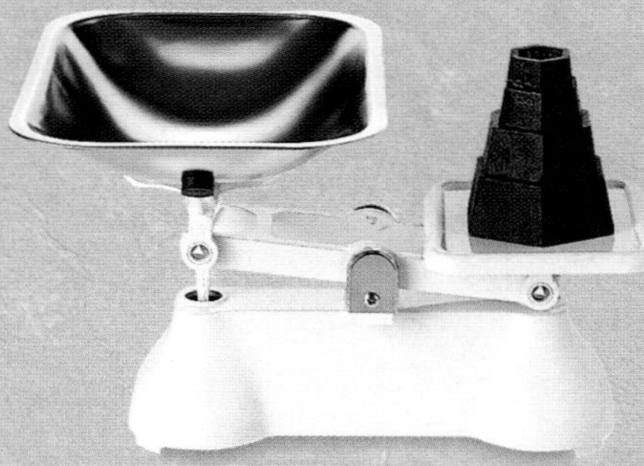

General Information

East–West Flavours
•
Herbs & Spices
•
Measurement Charts
•
Glossary

East-West Flavours

Certain herbs, spices and condiments characterize particular cuisines. For example, pesto is pure Italian, ginger suggests the Orient, and mint is popular in the Middle East. Contemporary chefs recognize few boundaries these days, and fuse ingredients from both East and West.

Curry Mixtures

Although the term curry is often applied to a single spice, it actually refers to a mixture of seasonings. Curry is most famous for its role in Indian cooking, but different powders and pastes are used in many other Asian cuisines.

Indian curry powders, called masalas, are sultry mixtures of native spices. They typically include pepper, cardamom, cinnamon, cumin and coriander (see opposite page).

Thai dishes are characterized by fiery curry blends. Pastes of garlic, lemon grass, chillies, galangal, shrimp paste, fish sauce, coriander and lime zest are common. The green curry paste shown below uses fresh green chillies, while the red uses fiery hot dried red bird's eye chillies.

Chinese curry powder is a mild mix, relying on cinnamon, fennel and coriander seeds, star anise, Sichuan pepper, turmeric and ginger. A small quantity of chilli powder can be included.

Preparing Ginger

Fresh root ginger is used in many Asian dishes to impart a spicy, mildly hot flavour. Choose plump pieces with smooth, firm skin. The pale yellow flesh is slightly fibrous. To preserve freshness, only peel off the skin covering the flesh to be immediately used. Peeled ginger can be sliced, chopped, grated or crushed.

Removing the skin
Use the sharp, heavy blade of a cleaver to scrape away the tough outer skin.

Grating the flesh
A wooden Japanese grater or *oroshigane* is authentic, but a metal box grater will do.

Preparing Thai Flavourings

These ingredients offer the intense aromatic flavours that characterize Thai cuisine. Lemon grass, coriander and galingal can be found fresh in most supermarkets. Tamarind can be bought as pods, blocks or concentrate. The latter is most convenient. If bought as pods, the flesh is removed and soaked, to make sour tamarind water.

Lemon grass
Bruise stalks to release flavour and use in curries, or chop finely for stir-fries.

Coriander stems
Trim stems and roots; chop finely. Use in curries for pungent flavour.

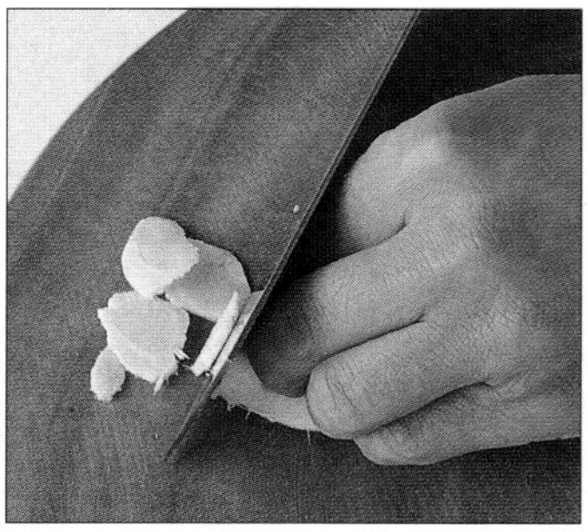

Galingal
Like ginger but hotter and more peppery, galingal is first peeled then sliced.

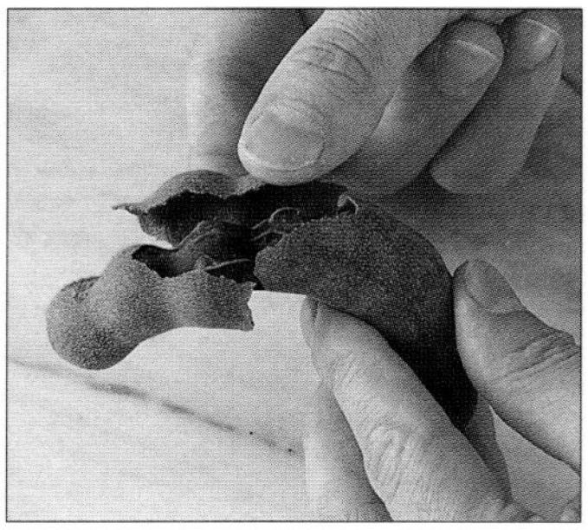

Tamarind
Remove pulp from pods; soak pulp in hot water 30 minutes, then strain. Use liquid.

Green curry paste

Red curry paste

MAKING GARAM MASALA

Meaning "a warm blend of spices", this spice mixture is traditionally used in north Indian dishes; it has many variations. Dry-roasting before crushing intensifies the flavour.

1 Combine mace, cinnamon, bay leaf, cardamom, cumin, peppercorns and coriander; stir over a low heat until spices darken.

2 When cool, place toasted spices in a mortar and grind with a pestle until powdery. Store in an airtight container.

PREPARING DRIED SEAWEED

Highly nutritious, dried seaweed is widely used in Japanese cuisine. Toasted dried nori can be crumbled over dishes or used as a wrap; wakame is used in soups, salads and stir-fries.

NORI
Toast sheets over a flame or in the oven for a sweet, delicate flavour.

WAKAME
Soak shreds in warm water to reconstitute; drain thoroughly before use.

SOAKING SAFFRON

This golden-hued, expensive spice is sold in thin, wiry threads that require soaking before use if they are to impart colour and flavour.

Place a pinch of threads in a bowl and pour over hot water. Let soak 10 minutes, then strain; use liquid in sauces and curries.

TOASTING SESAME SEEDS

A popular garnish for Chinese dishes, sesame seeds become rich and nutty when dry-fried. An authentic wok and chopsticks are used here, but a frying pan and wooden spoon can be used instead.

Heat a wok until hot but not smoking, add a handful of sesame seeds and dry-fry over a low heat until golden brown, stirring constantly with chopsticks.

A SELECTION OF ASIAN SPICES AND SEEDS

ASIAN CONDIMENTS

These highly flavoured ingredients are as essential as curry paste in Asian cuisine.

CHINESE FIVE-SPICE POWDER: A fragrant, finely ground blend of star anise, fennel seeds, fagara, cassia and cloves. Used throughout China and Vietnam, usually on roast meat and poultry and in marinades.

JAPANESE SEVEN-SPICE POWDER: A mix of sansho (Japanese pepper), seaweed, chilli, orange zest, poppy seeds and white and black sesame seeds. This mixture is most commonly sprinkled over noodles and soups.

WASABI: A hot flavouring generally served with sushi or sashimi or combined with mayonnaise-based dressings and sauces. Can be grated fresh from horseradish root or prepared from a powder mixed with water.

HERB BUNDLES

The most well-known herb mixture is the bouquet garni (see page 185). This classic combination of thyme, bay, parsley and celery is encompassed in a leek leaf and used to flavour a wide variety of dishes. Here are some suggestions for bouquets garnis to use with specific foods.

BEEF: Pared orange zest, rosemary, thyme and parsley.
FISH AND SHELLFISH: Tarragon, dill and pared lemon zest.
LAMB: Sprigs of rosemary, thyme, savory, mint and parsley.
PORK: Sprigs of fresh sage, thyme and marjoram.
POULTRY: Celery stick with a sprig each of parsley, thyme, marjoram, tarragon and a bay leaf. With game birds, add 6 juniper berries and secure in a muslin bag.
VEGETABLE DISHES AND PULSES: Bay leaf, savory, sage, marjoram, oregano and parsley.

HERB MIXTURES

Western chefs traditionally use specific herb combinations to flavour certain dishes. French dishes are often perfumed with herbes de Provence *and* persillade, *while Italian specialities such as* osso buco *are served with pungent* gremolada.

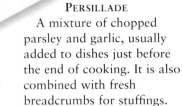

CHOPPING LEMON ZEST FOR GREMOLADA
Rock the curved blade of a *mezzaluna* over pared strips of lemon zest.

HERBES DE PROVENCE
A mixture of fresh or dried aromatic herbs consisting of thyme, rosemary, bay, basil, savory and even lavender. Delicious as a seasoning for roast lamb and pork.

GREMOLADA
A flavouring from Milan, usually made with finely chopped lemon zest, garlic and parsley. Add at the end of cooking to *osso buco* and other Italian stews.

PERSILLADE
A mixture of chopped parsley and garlic, usually added to dishes just before the end of cooking. It is also combined with fresh breadcrumbs for stuffings.

MAKING PESTO

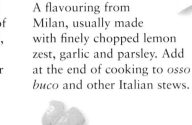

For enough pesto to serve with 250 g pasta, use 60 g fresh basil, 4 tbsp each extra-virgin olive oil and freshly grated Parmesan cheese, 2–4 garlic cloves, and 30 g pine nuts. Make small quantities by hand, large quantities by machine.

BY HAND

Grind the basil, cheese, garlic and pine nuts in a pestle and mortar. Add the oil gradually to form a granular paste.

BY MACHINE

Work basil, nuts, cheese and garlic with half the oil in a food processor; slowly add remaining oil.

Making a Tomato Sauce

A quick-cooking tomato sauce is indespensable – not only can it can be used on pizza and pasta, vegetables and meat, but it also forms the base of many classic European dishes. Here fresh plum tomatoes are used; in winter, use canned Italian plum tomatoes.

1 Sweat finely chopped garlic, onion and carrot in olive oil over a moderate heat, 5–7 minutes.

2 Add chopped ripe tomatoes, a little sugar and salt and pepper. Cook until soft, 10–15 minutes.

3 Check seasoning. Use sauce as it is – or, to remove skins and seeds, work through a sieve to a *coulis* consistency.

Spice Mixtures

These traditional aromatic blends are greatly favoured by European cooks, who use them to flavour meat and poultry dishes, as well as cakes, biscuits and puddings. The old-fashioned English pickling spice mixture is used in vinegars and a variety of condiments.

Grinding spices
Electric spice or coffee grinders quickly work whole spices to a fine powder.

Mixed spice
Also known as pudding spice. Finely grind 1 tbsp coriander seeds, 1 tsp each allspice berries and cloves, and 1 cinnamon stick; mix with 1 tbsp grated nutmeg and 2 tsp ground ginger.

Pickling spice
Combine 2 tbsp ground ginger with 1 tbsp each black peppercorns, white mustard seeds, dried red chillies, allspice berries, dill seed and crushed mace. Add 1 cinnamon stick, crushed, 2 bay leaves, crushed, and 1 tsp whole cloves.

Quatre-epices
A mix of four spices. Combine 1 tbsp black peppercorns, 2 tsp each whole cloves and grated nutmeg and 1 tsp ground ginger. Variations may use allspice and cinnamon.

Mixed spice **Pickling spice** **Quatre-epices**

Vanilla

Both the pod and seeds of the vanilla bean can be used as flavourings; the seeds impart a stronger flavour than the pod.

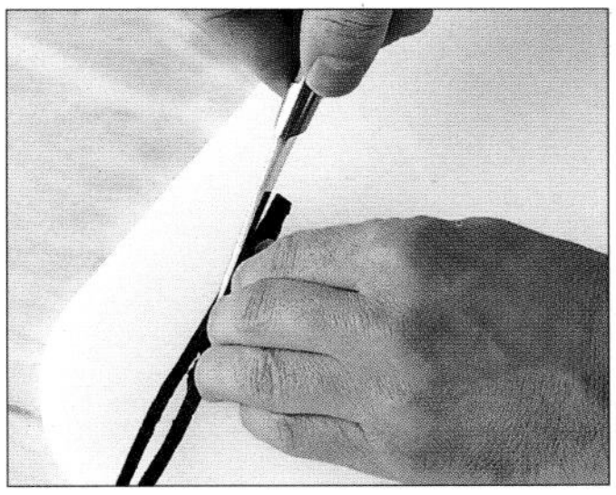

Splitting the pod
Halve pod lengthwise; infuse in warm milk, 30 minutes, or bury in jar of caster sugar.

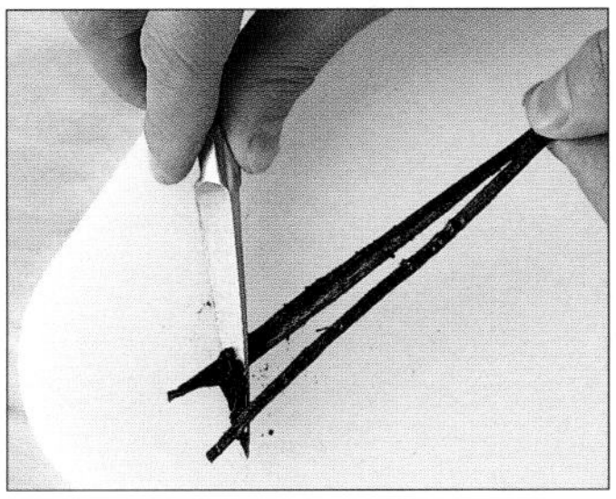

Removing the seeds
Scrape out seeds from halved bean with tip of knife; use as for pod above.

USING HERBS & SPICES

An invaluable addition to the kitchen, fresh herbs and aromatic spices give dishes distinctive taste and ethnic personality. These charts help pair flavourings with the foods they best enhance.

STORING HERBS

Because they do not keep well, fresh herbs are best used straight after picking. The following methods of storage will help keep them fresh and prolong their life, essential techniques in the summer months if you have a herb garden.

- For short storage of 1-2 days, pack freshly picked herbs in plastic bags in the refrigerator. Delicate varieties, such as basil, benefit from being wrapped in slightly damp paper towels before they are placed in bags.
- To dry herbs, hang them up by their stalks in a dry, well-ventilated room. This position concentrates the flavour in the leaves. Once dried, store herbs in airtight containers.
- Fresh herbs can be frozen with excellent results. For best flavour, use young herbs picked before the flowering stage. Gather them in the early morning when the dew has dried and the leaves are at their most aromatic. Strip off the leaves and chop them finely (bay, rosemary, sage and thyme should not be chopped, but snipped into small sprigs). Place chopped herbs in ice-cube trays, cover with iced water and freeze. When solid, pack herb ice cubes in freezer bags, ready to drop into liquids straight from the freezer. Sprigs of herbs should be frozen as they are, in airtight containers.

HERBS AND THEIR USES

	FLAVOUR	USE WITH
BASIL	*Sweet, warm, softly spicy, aromatic*	White fish, veal, chicken, seafood, salad greens, eggs, tomatoes, pesto and other pasta sauces
BAY	*Aromatic, pungent*	Soups, stocks, stews, casseroles, sauces (especially béchamel)
CHERVIL	*Delicate, slightly anise-like*	Fish, chicken, omelettes, sauces
CHIVES	*Mild, oniony*	Fish, eggs, cheese, salads, creamy soups, potatoes
CORIANDER	*Intensely aromatic, spicy*	Asian, Middle Eastern and Mexican dishes, carrots, salads, yogurt
CURRY LEAVES	*Spicy "curry" flavour*	Indian curries, casseroles, soups, seafood, stuffings
DILL	*Delicate, anise-like*	Salmon, soused herring, veal, carrots, cucumbers, potatoes, mayonnaise, soured cream, soft fresh cheeses
FENNEL	*Anise-like*	Fish soups, pork, seafood, eggs
MARJORAM/ OREGANO	*Sweet, aromatic, pungent*	Grilled meats, chicken, tomato sauces, eggs. cheese, flavoured oils and marinades
MINT	*Strong, sweet, clean*	Cucumber, potatoes, peas, cheese, melon, chilled soups, lamb, yogurt
PARSLEY	*Fresh, slightly spicy*	Eggs, fish, soups, poultry, meat
ROSEMARY	*Pungent, oily, aromatic*	Lamb, chicken, pork, bread, potatoes
SAGE	*Aromatic, slightly bitter*	Pork, veal, duck, goose, turkey, pulses, eggs, ricotta, Parmesan cheese, risotto, pasta
SUMMER SAVORY	*Pungent, lemony*	Pulses, broad and French beans, eggs, cheese, grilled meats, tomato sauce
TARRAGON	*Aromatic, anise-like, cooling*	Chicken, eggs, tomatoes, béarnaise
THYME	*Intensely aromatic*	Poultry and meat roasts and casseroles, roast potatoes

Spices and Their Uses

	Flavour	Form	Use With
Allspice	*Hints of clove and cinnamon*	Whole berries or ground	Caribbean meat stews, game, lamb, onions, cabbage, spiced vinegar, poached fruits, cakes, breads, and pies
Caraway	*Aromatic, strong hints of fennel*	Whole seeds or ground	Meat stews, sausages, cabbage, pork, sauerkraut, breads, cheese, rich fruit cakes
Cardamom	*Pungent, lemony*	Pods, loose seeds or ground	Indian and Middle Eastern curries, stews, pickling brines, pastries, cakes, fruit dishes, quick breads
Cayenne/ Chilli powder	*Spicy, very hot*	Ground	Indian, Mexican, Cajun, Caribbean and Creole dishes, seafood, béarnaise sauce
Cinnamon	*Sweet, warm aromatic*	Sticks or ground	Middle-Eastern dishes, curries, fruit desserts, cakes and breads, milk and rice puddings, chocolate desserts
Cloves	*Sweet, strong*	Whole buds or ground	Ham and pork, sweet potatoes, pumpkin, spiced cakes, apples and other fruits, stocks
Coriander	*Fragrant, lemony*	Whole berries or ground	Indian and Oriental dishes, meat, chicken, pickled fish, mushrooms, breads, cakes, pastries and custards
Cumin	*Pungent, warm, earthy*	Whole seeds or ground	Indian and Mexican dishes, pork, chicken, lamb, cheese, bean soups, rice pilafs
Fennel seed		Sweet, licquorice-flavoured	Mediterranean fish soups and stews, grilled fish
Ginger	*Pungent, spicy*	Fresh root or ground	Oriental and Indian dishes, chicken, vegetables, particularly pumpkin and carrots, fruits such as melon and rhubarb, cakes and biscuits
Juniper	*Pungent, clean, pine-scented*	Berries	Sausage, pork and game dishes, pâtés and terrines, particularly venison, cabbage, stuffings
Mace	*Sweet, fragrant*	Whole blades or ground	As for nutmeg
Mustard	*Pungent, hot*	Whole seeds or ground	Beef and pork, chicken, rabbit, vegetables, pickles and relishes, sauces and dressings
Nutmeg	*Sweet, fragrant*	Whole or ground	Stuffed pastas, meat and béchamel sauces, spinach and potato gratins, cakes and biscuits, milk puddings and custards, mulled wine
Paprika	*Pungent, sweet or hot*	Ground	Meat and poultry, especially Eastern European dishes, eggs, vegetables, cream cheese
Pepper	*Pungent, mild or hot*	Berries (peppercorns) or ground	Almost every savoury dish and a few sweet ones, such as strawberries and sorbets
Poppy seeds	*Nutty, sweet*	Whole and ground	Breads, cakes, pastries, salads, coleslaws, egg noodles, sauces for meat and fish
Star anise	*Warm, aromatic, spicy-sweet*	Whole, broken, seeds and ground	Oriental-style dishes, especially Chinese, pork, duck and chicken, fish and shellfish dishes, marinades
Turmeric	*Warm, mild aroma*	Whole and ground	Adds subtle flavouring and a distinctive yellow colour, used in curry powders, rice, pulse dishes and chutneys

Measurement Charts

Accurate measurements are crucial to the success of any dish. The following charts give quick and easy reference for gauging oven temperatures and converting metric and imperial units for ingredients and equipment.

Oven Temperatures

Celsius	Fahrenheit	Gas	Description
110°C	225°F	¼	Cool
120°C	250°F	½	Cool
140°C	275°F	1	Very low
150°C	300°F	2	Very low
160°C	325°F	3	Low
170°C	325°F	3	Moderate
180°C	350°F	4	Moderate
190°C	375°F	5	Moderately hot
200°C	400°F	6	Hot
220°C	425°F	7	Hot
230°C	450°F	8	Very hot

US Cups

Cups	Metric
¼ cup	60 ml
⅓ cup	70 ml
½ cup	125 ml
⅔ cup	150 ml
¾ cup	175 ml
1 cup	250 ml
1½ cups	375 ml
2 cups	500 ml
3 cups	750 ml
4 cups	1 litre
6 cups	1.5 litres

Spoons

Metric	Imperial
1.25 ml	¼ tsp
2.5 ml	½ tsp
5 ml	1 tsp
10 ml	2 tsp
15 ml	3 tsp/1 tbsp
30 ml	2 tbsp
45 ml	3 tbsp
60 ml	4 tbsp
75 ml	5 tbsp
90 ml	6 tbsp

Volume

Metric	Imperial	Metric	Imperial	Metric	Imperial
25 ml	1 fl oz	300 ml	10 fl oz/½ pint	1 litre	1¾ pints
50 ml	2 fl oz	350 ml	12 fl oz	1.2 litres	2 pints
75 ml	2½ fl oz	400 ml	14 fl oz	1.3 litres	2¼ pints
100 ml	3½ fl oz	425 ml	15 fl oz/¾ pint	1.4 litres	2½ pints
125 ml	4 fl oz	450 ml	16 fl oz	1.5 litres	2¾ pints
150 ml	5 fl oz/¼ pint	500 ml	18 fl oz	1.7 litres	3 pints
175 ml	6 fl oz	568 ml	20 fl oz/1 pint	2 litres	3½ pints
200 ml	7 fl oz/⅓ pint	600 ml	1 pint milk	2.5 litres	4½ pints
225 ml	8 fl oz	700 ml	1¼ pints	2.8 litres	5 pints
250 ml	9 fl oz	850 ml	1½ pints	3 litres	5¼ pints

Weight

Metric	Imperial	Metric	Imperial
5 g	⅛ oz	325 g	11½ oz
10 g	¼ oz	350 g	12 oz
15 g	½ oz	375 g	13 oz
20 g	¾ oz	400 g	14 oz
25 g	1 oz	425 g	15 oz
35 g	1¼ oz	450 g	1 lb
40 g	1½ oz	500 g	1 lb 2 oz
50 g	1¾ oz	550 g	1 lb 4 oz
55 g	2 oz	600 g	1 lb 5 oz
60 g	2¼ oz	650 g	1 lb 7 oz
70 g	2½ oz	700 g	1 lb 9 oz
75 g	2¾ oz	750 g	1 lb 10 oz
85 g	3 oz	800 g	1 lb 12 oz
90 g	3¼ oz	850 g	1 lb 14 oz
100 g	3½ oz	900 g	2 lb
115 g	4 oz	950 g	2 lb 2 oz
125 g	4½ oz	1 kg	2 lb 4 oz
140 g	5 oz	1.25 kg	2 lb 12 oz
150 g	5½ oz	1.3 kg	3 lb
175 g	6 oz	1.5 kg	3 lb 5 oz
200 g	7 oz	1.6 kg	3 lb 8 oz
225 g	8 oz	1.8 kg	4 lb
250 g	9 oz	2 kg	4 lb 8 oz
275 g	9¾ oz	2.25 kg	5 lb
280 g	10 oz	2.5 kg	5 lb 8 oz
300 g	10½ oz	2.7 kg	6 lb
315 g	11 oz	3 kg	6 lb 8 oz

Linear Measurements

Metric	Imperial	Metric	Imperial
2 mm	1/16 in	17 cm	6½ in
3 mm	⅛ in	18 cm	7 in
5 mm	¼ in	19 cm	7½ in
8 mm	⅜ in	20 cm	8 in
10 mm/1 cm	½ in	22 cm	8½ in
1.5 cm	⅝ in	23 cm	9 in
2 cm	¾ in	24 cm	9½ in
2.5 cm	1 in	25 cm	10 in
3 cm	1¼ in	26 cm	10½ in
4 cm	1½ in	27 cm	10¾ in
4.5 cm	1¾ in	28 cm	11 in
5 cm	2 in	29 cm	11½ in
5.5 cm	2¼ in	30 cm	12 in
6 cm	2½ in	31 cm	12½ in
7 cm	2¾ in	33 cm	13 in
7.5 cm	3 in	34 cm	13½ in
8 cm	3¼ in	35 cm	14 in
9 cm	3½ in	37 cm	14½ in
9.5 cm	3¾ in	38 cm	15 in
10 cm	4 in	39 cm	15½ in
11 cm	4¼ in	40 cm	16 in
12 cm	4½ in	42 cm	16½ in
12.5 cm	4¾ in	43 cm	17 in
13 cm	5 in	44 cm	17½ in
14 cm	5½ in	46 cm	18 in
15 cm	6 in	48 cm	19 in
16 cm	6¼ in	50 cm	20 in

Glossary of Terms

Al dente: Italian for "to the tooth"; describes just-cooked vegetables or pasta that offer slight resistance when bitten.

Albumen: The protein-rich white of an egg; contains the chalazae, the stringy cord which anchors the yolk to the shell.

Aromat: Any spice or herb (basil, cumin, rosemary) which gives flavour and fragrance to food.

Aspic: A clear fish, poultry or meat jelly made of clarified stock or consommé and gelatine; used as a base for moulded dishes or as a glaze for cold food.

Ata/atta flour: An extremely fine wholemeal flour used in making flat breads; found in Asian shops.

Bain marie: A "water bath" made by placing a pan or bowl of food in or above a larger pan of boiling water. Used in the oven or on top of the stove.

Bake: To cook food in an oven. For best results, use an oven thermometer – most ovens heat to temperatures other than their gauges read.

Bake blind: To bake a pastry crust before it is filled. To keep its shape, the shell is often pricked and lined with parchment or foil and baking beans.

Ballotine: Meat, poultry or fish that has been boned, stuffed, rolled and tied in a bundle; usually poached or braised.

Bard: To wrap pieces of fat (typically back fat or bacon) around lean cuts of meat to keep them moist.

Baste: To spoon or brush a liquid stock (pan juices or fat) over foods during cooking; adds flavour and moisture.

Batter: The uncooked mixture of crêpes, pancakes and cakes. Can be thick or thin. Also used to describe a coating for foods to be fried, such as fish.

Beurre manie: French for "kneaded butter". A paste made from equal parts flour and butter, used as a thickener for sauces, soups and stews.

Blanc: A stock containing water, flour and lemon juice that is used to cook and preserve the colour of vegetables; most often used for globe artichokes.

Blanch: To plunge vegetables or fruits into boiling – then iced – water to stop them cooking, loosen skins, set colour and remove bitterness. Also reduces salt content in bacon or other cured meats.

Blend: To use a spoon, beater or electric blender to evenly combine two or more ingredients.

Boil: "Bring to the boil" refers to heating a liquid until bubbles break the surface (100°C). The term also means to cook food in a boiling liquid.

Braise: To brown foods in fat, then cook them, tightly covered, in a small amount of flavourful liquid, at low heat, for a lengthy period of time.

Brochette: French for "skewer"; food threaded or moulded on to a metal or wooden skewer and grilled or barbecued.

Brunoise: Finely diced carrot, celery, leek or courgette, used singly or together as the classic garnish for consommé.

Butterfly: To split a food (leg of lamb, chicken breast, prawns) down the centre, cutting almost – but not completely – through. The two halves are then opened out to resemble a butterfly.

Canelle (Caneller): A decorative effect for the skins of fruits or vegetables made with a canelle knife. When sliced, these have grooved borders.

Caramelize: The process of heating sugar until it liquefies and becomes a syrup, ranging in colour from golden to dark brown. Sugar can also be caramelized by being sprinkled on food and grilled until it melts (as for crème brûlée). This term also often applies to onions and leeks that are sautéed in fat.

Caul: A thin membrane taken from an animal's stomach, normally a pig. Used to encase and moisten lean meats and minced meat mixtures during cooking.

Chargrill: To prepare foods on a metal grid that is set over hot coals, or by using a stovetop grill pan.

Chiffonade: Leafy vegetables or herbs that have been rolled together and then sliced crosswise into thin strips.

Chinois: A fine-meshed conical sieve that requires the food to be pushed through with a ladle or spoon. Most often used to strain sauces.

Chop: To cut food, more coarsely than mincing, using a knife. The knife tip is held stationary with one hand, while the other moves the handle up and down.

Clarify: To rid a liquid of impurities. The process usually involves simmering egg whites (and shells) with stock; the whites attract foreign particles. Also applies to the process of slowly heating butter and removing the milk solids.

Coat: To cover food with an outer coating, such as flour, beaten eggs, breadcrumbs, mayonnaise or icing.

COMPOTE: A mixture of fruits that is slowly cooked, often in a sugar syrup infused with spices or liqueur.

CONCASSEE: A coarsely chopped mixture, usually tomatoes that have been peeled, seeded and chopped.

CONFIT: A method of cooking meat (usually duck, goose or pork) very slowly in its own fat, then storing it in the fat. Vegetables, such as baby onions, can also be cooked in the fat.

COULIS: A sieved purée or sauce, often made with tomatoes, or fruits combined with a sweetener and a small amount of lemon juice.

CREAM: To beat ingredients together until light, fluffy and smooth. Typically involves creaming a fat, such as butter, with sugar.

CROSS-HATCH: To score criss-crossing diagonal lines on the surface of food to create a diamond pattern. This allows food to absorb marinades, drain excess fat, or be more easily removed from their skins (as with mangoes).

CURE: To preserve a food by treating it with salt, smoke, acid-based brines or bacteria.

CUTLET: A cut of meat, such as lamb, pork or veal, that is taken from the leg or rib sections.

DARNE: A thick cross-section slice of a large round fish, such as salmon or tuna.

DEGLAZE: After sautéing, food and excess fat are removed from the pan and a small amount of liquid stirred into the pan juices to dilute them and form a sauce.

DEGORGE: To soak meats, poultry and fish in cold water with salt or vinegar to expel impurities and blood. Also the process of sprinkling some vegetables (especially aubergines) with salt to draw out the juices.

DEMI-GLACE: A thick, intensely flavoured sauce, or base for a sauce, made from concentrated stock, wine and sometimes meat glaze.

DETREMPE: A French term for the initial paste made from flour, salt, melted butter and water in the first stage of making puff pastry.

DICE: To cut food into small, equal-sized cubes.

DOUGH: A flour and water mixture, often with other ingredients, worked until it is firm enough to hold its shape but malleable enough to mould by hand.

DRESS: To pluck, clean and truss poultry or game for cooking. The term also applies to adding a dressing such as vinaigrette to a salad, reparing a whole crab or lobster, or putting food on a plate and decorating it before serving.

DROPPING CONSISTENCY: This term describes a mixture, usually a cake batter, that is soft enough to be dropped by spoonfuls, yet firm enough to hold its shape.

DRY-FRY: Frying without the use of fats or oils. This method is often used for Indian spices and flat breads, and for Mexican tortillas.

DUXELLES: Clasically, a mixture of finely chopped mushrooms and shallots or onions cooked in butter until quite dry.

EMULSION: To combine liquids by the dispersion of one in another. In cookery, to emulsify is to add one liquid to another in a slow, steady stream while stirring vigorously.

ENRICH: Adding cream or egg yolks to a sauce or soup, or butter to a dough to create a rich texture or flavour. Also used to describe flour that has had nutrients returned to it after being lost in the milling process.

ENTRECOTE: French for "between the ribs", this tender cut of beef is usually grilled or sautéed.

ESCALOPE: Thin slice of meat, such as veal or chicken, or fish.

FEUILLETE: A puff pastry case that is cut into the shape of a diamond, triangle, square or round.

FLAKE: Using a fork to separate food into small pieces; also used to test fish for doneness.

FLAMBE: French for "flamed". Liqueur is set alight, usually for a spectacular table presentation. Also used to burn off the alcohol content of a dish.

FOLD: To mix together a light, airy mixture with a heavier one. The lighter is placed on the heavier, then a large metal spoon or a rubber spatula is used in a gentle figure-of-eight motion, which combines the mixtures without losing air.

FONDANT ICING: A soft-textured mixture of water, sugar and glucose, cooked to the soft ball stage then worked until flexible and smooth and used to decorate eclairs. Not to be confused with the decorative icing commonly used for novelty cakes, which is made from sugar, water and cream of tartar.

FONDUE: French for "melt", this term refers to food cooked in a single vessel (a fondue pot) at the table. Traditionally, it involves dipping cubes of bread into melted cheese; variations include dipping meat in hot oil (fondue bourguignonne) and cubes of cake into melted chocolate.

FORCEMEAT: Old-fashioned term for stuffing, from the French word "farce", meaning stuff; a mixture of finely minced meat mixed with breadcrumbs.

FRITTER: A small piece of fruit or meat that is coated in batter and deep-fried. A fritter can also refer to a julienne of vegetables that is fried.

FRY: Cooking food in hot fat. Deep-fried foods are submerged in fat. Sautéed or pan-fried foods are cooked in just enough fat to coat the bottom of the pan and prevent food from sticking. Stir-frying describes small pieces of food that are tossed over a very high heat, traditionally in a wok.

FUMET: A well-flavoured stock, that is usually made from fish bones, usually white, or occasionally game, that is used for flavouring mild-tasting liquids. Used frequently in classic French cuisine

GLAZE: To coat food with a thin liquid (either sweet or savoury) that will be smooth and shiny after setting. Coatings include reduced meat stock (aspic), melted jam, egg wash or chocolate. Also refers to well-reduced meat or fish stocks.

GLUTEN: A protein found in flour that provides elasticity. High-gluten flour is best suited for the kneading process required in bread making. Low gluten flour, such as cake flour, has a softer and less elastic quality.

GLYCERINE: A syrup form of alcohol added to food to maintain moisture. It is often added to royal icing to prevent crystallization.

GOLD/SILVER LEAF (ALSO CALLED VARAK): Ultra-thin, edible sheets of gold or silver used as a decoration for desserts. Sold in speciality baking shops and Indian stores, gold or silver leaf comes in fragile sheets.

GRATIN: A dish topped with grated cheese and dotted with butter, and sometimes breadcrumbs, grilled or baked in a shallow dish until crisp.

GREASE: Coating a tin with fat (usually butter or oil in the case of cake tins) to prevent sticking.

GRIND: To reduce food to powder or to tiny pieces, using a pestle or mortar or a food processor. Special grinders can be used for spices or coffee beans.

ICE-BATH: A bowl containing ice cubes and water; used to cool mixtures and stop the cooking process.

IMBIBE: To soak a cake with a flavoured sugar syrup or liqueur; usually applied with a pastry brush.

INFUSE: To flavour a liquid by steeping it with aromatic ingredients, such as spices, citrus zest or vanilla.

JULIENNE: To cut food into fine strips, most commonly used with vegetables to ensure quick, even cooking and provide an attractive presentation.

KNEAD: A pressing and folding technique used to make dough firm and smooth. Kneading stretches the gluten in flour, providing elasticity.

KNOCK-UP: To create ridges around the edge of pies by pressing with your fingers and tapping with the back of a knife blade.

KNOCK BACK: To push back yeast doughs after they have risen.

LARD: Inserting strips of fat (usually pork) into lean cuts of meat, creating a more succulent, flavourful dish.

LARDON: Pork fat or bacon cut into small cubes and used to flavour soups, stews or salads.

LEAVENER: A substance used to raise doughs and increase the volume of baked goods. For bread, the most common leavener is yeast. For cakes, baking powder and bicarbonate of soda are used.

LIAISON: A mixture of egg yolk and cream used to thicken sauces, soups and stews. Always added off the heat just before serving to prevent curdling.

LINE: To coat a tin with butter or oil and/or flour or baking parchment to prevent sticking. Foods, such as bacon rashers, spinach leaves and sponge fingers, can also be used as linings.

MACERATE: To soak foods in a liquid, usually a spirit or liqueur, to soften the texture and infuse them with flavour.

MARBLING: Used to describe the mixing of two different batters in a cake, usually of different colours. Also the flecks or lines of fat found in meat.

MARINATE: To steep foods in a highly-flavoured liquid. Marinades add flavour and moisture and often tenderize.

MEDALLION: A small, round nugget of meat. Typically tender and lean, it calls for a short cooking time.

MELANGE: French for a mixture, this term usually refers to a combination of two or more fruits or vegetables that are prepared together.

MEUNIERE: The French term to describe a dish cooked in butter, seasoned with salt, pepper and lemon juice, and then garnished with parsley.

MINCE: To reduce pieces of food, usually meat, into small pieces. Knives and mincing machines can be used.

MIREPOIX: Rough dice of mixed vegetables (traditionally carrot, onion, celery and leek) that is used to flavour sauces, soups and stews.

MOUSSE: A light, airy dish of whisked sweet or savoury ingredients, folded together until evenly blended. Often set in a decorative mould and usually served turned out, either hot or cold.

MOUSSELINE: A term used to describe a very rich mousse-like mixture, usually with whipped cream added to it. Crème mousseline is crème pâtissière enriched with butter.

NOISETTE: A small tender slice of lamb taken from the "eye" of the rack, encased in a thin strip of fat and often tied with string. The name comes from the French for "hazelnut", and is also used to describe nut-brown butter – as in beurre noisette.

OPEN FREEZE: To freeze foods, such as peas or beans, uncovered in a single layer. When frozen solid, the items can be packed together and will remain free flowing. This term can also refer to liquids frozen in ice-cube trays.

PASTE: Food that is ground to an extremely fine texture. Commonly used for almonds, as in almond paste.

PATE (pâte): Used to describe a pastry mixture, for instance pâte brisée (shortcrust pastry); pâte sucrée is the sweetened version.

PATE (pâté): A smooth or coarse textured mixture, traditionally made of meat and/or liver, but can be vegetable or fish, seasoned or spiced and set in a mould.

PAYSANNE: A mixture of vegetables (usually potatoes, carrots, turnips, and cabbage) cut into small squares, triangle, diamonds or rounds. Traditionally used to garnish soups, meat, fish or omelettes.

Poach: To cook food by submerging it in liquid (water, sugar syrup, alcohol) that is just below boiling point.

Pot roast: To cook meat slowly in a covered container in the oven with little or no liquid.

Prick: To pierce foods (fruit and vegetable skins) to allow them to release air or moisture during baking. Duck skin is pricked before cooking to release fat.

Prove: To create a non-stick surface on a pan. To prove, heat pan then rub with salt. Wipe clean and repeat with oil. Also, to prove whether yeast is alive by allowing it to grow, usually in a dough

Puree: Food that is blended or sieved to form a smooth pulp. An electric blender is normally used, but a Mouli or sieve achieves the same results.

Quenelles: Ovals of a soft mixture such as fish mousse or ice cream shaped using two spoons. The term also refers to dumplings of the same shape.

Reduce: To rapidly boil down liquids in an uncovered pan. This evaporates the liquid and concentrates the flavour.

Refresh: To plunge an item (typically green vegetables) into iced water after blanching to prevent further cooking and retain a vibrant colour.

Render: To refine the fat in meat by cooking it over a low heat until it runs free from the connective tissue. The rendered fat can be used for frying.

Ribbon: A term used to describe the consistency of an egg-sugar mixture, beaten until extremely thick. When the whisk is lifted the batter runs down in smooth, thick ribbons. Also the term for the shavings of vegetables, such as carrots and courgettes, made with a vegetable peeler.

Roast: To cook food in an oven in either in its own juices or with added fat. It is usually uncovered so it browns.

Roux: A flour and fat mixture cooked slowly and stirred constantly over a low heat. Used as a base for, and a thickening agent in, many sauces and soups. There are three classic roux: white, blond and brown; colour and flavour are determined by cooking time.

Rubs: A name for finely ground or minced mixtures of flavourful ingredients that are "rubbed" into the surface of foods before cooking.

Saddle: A tender cut (usually of lamb, mutton or veal), of unseparated loin (from rib to leg). The cut is expensive, and prized for its appearance.

Score: To make incisions in the skin, flesh or fat of foods, such as meat, fish or vegetables, before cooking.

Sear: To brown meat, poultry or fish quickly over a high heat while keeping the centre of the cut slightly rare.

Shred: To separate food by cutting or pulling into thin lengths using a chef's knife or cleaver, or a grater. You can also use a food processor fitted with the shredding disc. Poached chicken and Oriental roast duck are shredded with two forks.

Shuck: An American term used to describe the removal of oysters and clams from their shells; also used for removing the husk from corn, and peas and beans from their shells.

Sift: To work dry ingredients through a sieve so that larger pieces are retained in the sieve and separated from the fine powder. Used frequently in baking to aerate ingredients.

Simmer: To cook food in a liquid that is kept just below boiling point – where the surface of the liquid quivers rather than bubbles.

Snip: This term refers to cutting herbs (most typically chives) or leafy greens into small-sized pieces.

Skim: To use a spoon or ladle to remove scum, fat or other impurities from the top of simmering liquids.

Sour: To add an acidic liquid, usually lemon juice or tamarind water, to make the flavour tart.

Steep: To soak dried ingredients in hot liquid to rehydrate the food and/or infuse the liquid with its flavour.

Stock: The aromatic liquid created when foods are simmered in water.

Sweat: To gently cook vegetables in fat or water until soft but not brown.

Tenderize: To break down the tough fibres of meat by either pounding it with a mallet or using acid-based marinades.

Tepid: Used to describe the temperature of a liquid when it is luke warm or blood heat (37°C).

Terrine: A mould or the food contained within it. Often a pâté-like mixture of blended ingredients.

Tian: A French word describing a shallow earthenware dish, as well as the food that is cooked in one.

Timbale: A small mould commonly used to shape custards and rice mixtures.

Tranche: French for slice, this term usually refers to a slim, rectangular-shaped piece of puff pastry.

Troncon: French term used to describe a steak cut from a large flat fish.

Turn: A classic French technique for cutting vegetables, such as carrots or turnips, into neat barrel shapes.

Whisk: To incorporate air into ingredients, such as cream or eggs, as a result of beating them with a wire whisk.

Zest: The outermost, coloured skin of citrus fruits (the bitter white portion of the peel is called pith).

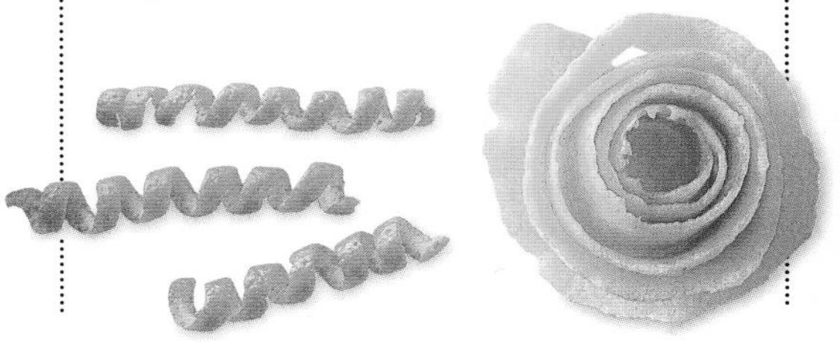

INDEX

A

Accompaniments
for burgers 152
for game birds 103
for meat 138
Acorn squash 179
Aduki beans
cooking times 194
Al dente 215
Alcohol
preserving fruits in 267
Almonds
extracting the flavour from apricot stone, 254
truffles 323
American long-grain rice 196
Anchovies, desalting 62
Andouille 151
Andouillette 151
Apple(s)
baking whole 270
choosing 248, 250
chopping 251
crescents 251
preventing discoloration 251
rings 251
slicing 251
varieties 250
Apricot(s)
extracting almond flavour 254
stoning 254
Arame 177
Arborio rice 196, 198
Artichoke(s)
baby 165
cooking 164
fillings for 164
globe 164
hearts, preparing 165
Jerusalem 167
preparing 164
stalks 164
Asian
condiments 329
equipment 12
noodles
cooking 215
soaking 218
varieties 218
Asparagus
boiling 186
choosing 159
preparing 163
white 163
Aspic 19
Aubergines 176
pea 176
preparing 178
roasting times 188
salting 178
Thai 176
white and yellow 176
Avocado
peeling 179
slicing 179
stoning 179

B

Babaco 263
Baby
artichokes 165
pineapples 252
Bacalao/bacalhau 62
Bacon *(see also Pork; Ham)*
green 151
types of 151
unsmoked 151
using in cooking 151
Bacteria, salmonella 31
Bagels 244
Bain marie 32, 36, 76
Baker's
chocolate 282
knot 235
Bakeware 13
Baking
beans 295
eggs 32
fish 72
en papillote 73
in a salt crust 73
in leaves 73
fruits 270
vegetables 188
Baklava 302
Bamboo steamer 70, 187
Barbecuing
beef and veal 127
butterflied leg of lamb 141
crosshatch steaks 127
fruit 268
lamb
cutlets 140
kebabs 140
tips 113
whole bird 113
whole fish 71
Barding 120
Barley 201
flour 232
Basmati rice 196
Batterie de cuisine 10
Batters 38
deep-frying fish in 75
griddle pancakes 39
making a smooth batter 39
tempura batter 269
Yorkshire puddings 39
Bavarois 277
Beans *(see also Dried beans)*
broad 172
French 172
freshness 172
green 172
microwave times 186
steaming times 187
refried 194
runner 172
yard-long 177
Bearding mussels 51, 82
Béarnaise sauce 226, 227
Béchamel sauce 222
Beef & Veal 118–131
à point 127
barbecuing 127
barding 120
Beef Wellington 125
bien cuit 127
bleu 127
boning breast of veal 121
braising 129
buying 118
calf's liver 154
carving
rib of beef 124
rolled joint 124
chargrilling fillet steak 127
châteaubriand 122
choosing 118
coating steaks 126
cooking
in clay pot 129
methods 119
salt beef 129
crosshatch steaks 127
cuts 119
cutting meat for stewing 122
fajitas 126
flavoured butters for 127
freezing 118
grilling 127
times for steaks 127
handling 118
joints, preparing 120
kneaded butter for 128
larding 120
meat thermometer 124
mincing 123
pan-frying 126
pot roasting 128
preparing 120
quick cooking 124
roasting
beef en croûte 125
rib of beef 124
times 124
whole fillet of beef 125
rolling, stuffing and tying 121
rolling veal escalopes 123
saignant 127
slicing wafer thin 122
slow cooking 128
steak(s)
au poivre 126
preparing 120
tartare 123, 153
stewing 128
stuffing
fillet 125
veal escalopes 123
tender steaks 122
tournedos 122
trimming and slicing 122
Beetroot, roasting 188
Berries 258 *(see also Fruits)*
making a coulis 259
making a purée 259
uses for purées 259
Beurre
blanc 227
manié 128
noisette 74
Bhindi 173
Bird's-eye chilli 181
Biryani 197
Biscuits
dropped 325
finishing 325
rolled 324
shortbread 324
sponge fingers
tuiles 326
tulipes 326
Bisque 25
Black-eye beans
cooking times 194
Blanching
bones of chicken 16
nuts 202
Blini pans 38

Blood orange 256
Blue cheese 41
Bockwurst 151
Boiling
crab 80
eggs 32
vegetables 186
whelks 85
Bombe 287
Boning
breast of veal 121
large bird 96
loin of pork 146
quail 98
round fish 54
shoulder of lamb 134
Bonito 18
Bouchées 306
Boudin
blanc 151
noir 151
Bouquet garni 185, 330
Braising
beef and veal 129
fish 58
pork in milk 149
shoulder of lamb 137
Bramley's seedling 250
Bran wheat 232
Brandy
butter 292
snaps 325
Brassicas 160
Bread & Yeast Cookery 231–246
Bread(s) *(see also Rolls)*
dough
making by hand 232
making by machine 232
punching down 233
rising 233
shaping 234
enriched 242
finishing loaves 234
flat 240
glazes 234
Indian flat 241
Italian 238
Italian flavourings for 239
making 232
preparations 246
quick 244
soda 244
testing for doneness 234
toppings 234
with vegetables 245
Breadcrumbs 246
Brill
baking en papillote 73
filleting 57
Brioche 243
Broad beans 172
cooking times (dried) 194
Broccoli
choosing 159
microwave times 186
nutrients in 161
preparing 161
steaming times 187
Brochettes 153
Brown
sauce 224
stock 16
Brunoise 166
Bruschetta 236, 246
Brussels sprouts
microwave times 186
preparing 161
steaming times 187
Buckwheat 201
flour 232
Bulgar 201
wheat 232
Burgers
accompaniments for 152
making 152
Butter beans
cooking times 194
Butter, clarifying 227
Buttercream 320
icing 320
Butterflied leg of lamb
barbecuing 141
grilling times 140
Butterflying a leg of lamb 134
Buttermilk 46
Butternut squash 179
Butterscotch sauce 292
Buying
beef and veal 118
fish 48
lamb 132
pork 144
poultry 88
shellfish 49

C

Cabbage
coring 160
red, setting the colour of 160
shredding 160
steaming times 187
Cajun cooking 80
Cajun-style fried fish 74
Cakes and Biscuits 307–326
Cake(s)
angel food 314
cooling 309
cheesecake
baked 317
chilled 316
chocolate torte 314
creaming method 310
cutting and imbibing 315
filling and layering 315
fillings for 312
flavourings for 310
glazing 319
icing 318
melting method 311
meringue cake 315
preparing the tin 308
rubbing-in method 311
Swiss roll 313
testing for doneness 309
turning out 309
whisked sponge 312
enriching 313
serving 312
Calzone 238
Camembert 40, 45
Cannellini beans
cooking times 194
Cannelloni 211
Cantaloupe 260
Cape gooseberry 263
Caper flowers 68
Capon, roasting times 100
Capsaicin 181
Caramel 281
shapes, drizzled 290
Carciofi alla giudea 165
Cardoon 163
Caribe chilli 181
Carnaroli rice 198
Carré d'agneau 135
Carrot(s)
choosing 158
flowers 139
-flower soup 21
microwave times 186
roasting times 188
steaming times 187
Cartouche 190
Carving
duck 102
Chinese method 107
leg of lamb on the bone 137
rack of lamb 137
rib of beef 124
roasted bird 101
rolled joint 124
Cassava 176
Casseroling
beef and veal 128
chicken in wine 114
Caul 153
making crépinettes 153
pan-frying in 153
Cauliflower
microwave times 186
preparing 161
preventing discoloration 161
steaming times 187
Caviar eggs 32
Celeriac, preparing 167
Celery, preparing 163
Cellophane noodles 218
Ceps 171
Cervelat 151
Ceviche 51
Chanterelles 171
Chapatis 241
Chargrilling *(see also Grilling)*
fillet steak 127
lamb 141
pork chops 150
poultry escalopes 109
vegetables 191
Charlotte
making a hot 279
russe 279
Châteaubriand 122
Chaudfroid 225
de canard 105
Cheese
blue 41
choosing 40
coatings for fresh 42
deep-frying 45
feta 43
flavourings for fresh 43
fondue 45
goat and sheep 41
goat's 43, 45
grater, rotary 44
grating 44
grilling 45
halloumi 45
hard 40
making fresh 42
melting 44
Parmesan curls 236
piping fresh cheese 43
soft 40
soft, testing for ripeness 41
Cheesecake(s)
baked 317
chilled 316
crumb base 316
Cherries
choosing 249
pitting 255
Chervil 332
Chestnuts, peeling 203
Chick peas
cooking times 194
Chicken *(see also Poultry)*
cooking methods 89
dishes 89
liver pâté 116
roasting times 100
stock 16
Chiffonade 162
Chilli(es) 181
bean sauce 58
flowers 139
preparing 181
preparing for stuffing 182
rehydrating dried 181

Chinese
  bitter melon 177
  dish "red, green and yellow" 33
  dumplings 219
  five-spice powder 329
  flavourings 21
  mustard greens 162
  pancakes 240
  seasoning mix 106
  -style fish 58
  -style soup 21
Chipolatas 151
Chive(s) 332
  coated cheese 42
  snipping 185
Chocolate 282
  baker's 282, 284
  cigarettes 291
  couverture 282
  curls 290
  ganache 282
  icing
    coating with 319
    making 319
  leaves 290
  making shapes 283
  melting 282
  mousse 274
  ribbons 284
  shapes
    double-dusted 290
  tempering 283
Choosing
  beef and veal 118
  cheese 40
  fruit 248
  lamb 132
  pork 144
  poultry 88
  vegetables 158
Chopping
  apples 251
  herbs 185
  mushrooms 170
  pears 251
Choux
  buns 298
    fillings and icings for 299
  pastry 298
Chowder 28
Citron 256
  tartlets 323
Citrus fruits 256
  (see also Fruits)
Clams
  buying 49, 51
  chowder 28, 51
  cooking 51
  opening 84
Clarifying butter 227
Clay pot, cooking beef in a 129
Cleaning
  mussels 51, 82
  truffles 171
Clotted cream 46
Coating(s)
  fish with a herb crust 74
  for fried fish 74
  fruit in sugar glaze 269
  steaks 126
Cobs, sweetcorn 173
Cockles
  buying 49, 51
  cooking 51
Coconut
  milk 204
  preparing 204
  using and storing 204
Cod, salt 62
Coleslaw 160
Comice 250
Compote
  dried fruit 267
Concassée of tomatoes 178
Conchiglie 215
Conference 250
Consommé 19
Conversion charts 334
Cooking
  artichokes 164
  Asian noodles 215
  dried beans and peas 194
  lamb 133
  live lobster 78
  pasta 214
  pork 145
  poultry and game 89
  sausages 151
  times
    dried beans and peas 194
    lentils 195
    pasta 215
  with fresh herbs 185
Cookware
  bakeware 13
  ovenware 13
  stovetop 12
Coquilles Saint-Jacques 85
Coral (scallops) 85
Corer 250
Coriander root 328
Coring
  cabbage 160
  fruit 250
  pineapple 253
Corn, popping 201
Corn, see Sweetcorn
Cornbread 245
Cornichons 153
Cornmeal 200, 232
Cos lettuce 184
Côte d'agneau 135
Cottage cheese 41, 42
Coulis
  decorative effects with 259
  making a berry 259
Courgette
  boats 139
  fireworks 139
  scales 69
Couronne 135
Court bouillon 66
Couscous 201
Couscousière 201
Couverture chocolate 282
Cox's orange pippin 250
Crab
  boiling 80
  buying 49, 51
  cooking 51
  dressing 80
  removing meat from shell 80
Crackling, pork 148
Crayfish 81
Cream
  cheese 41
  clotted 46
  decorating soups with 27
  enriching soups 25
  sour 46
  types of 46
Crème
  anglaise 268, 276
  brûlée 277
  caramel 277
  Chantilly 268, 292
  fraîche 46
    enriching soups with 25
  mousseline 276
  pâtissière 276
Creole cooking 80
Crêpe(s)
  cigarettes 38
  fans 38
  making 38
  pannequets 38
  pans 38
Crépine 153
Crépinettes 153
Cress 184
Croquembouche 298, 300
Crostini 236, 246
Crottins de Chavignol 43
Croûtons and croûtes 246
Crown roast of lamb 135
Crushing garlic 175
Cucumber
  crowns 139
  preparing 179
  twirls 69
Cuillère parisienne 168
Cumberland sausages 151
Curly leaf lettuce 184
Currants, strigging 258
Curry
  leaves 332
  mixtures 328
Curuba 263
Custards
  and creams 276
  baking 276
Cutting
  bird into eight pieces 93
  duck into four pieces 92
  fish
    escalopes 60
    steaks 60
  leeks 175
  pasta 209
  poultry for stir-frying 95
  roll method 166
  spring onions
    Asian-style 175
  up a rabbit 93
  up a roasted bird 101

D

Dariole mould 76
Darnes 60
Dasheen 176
Dashi 18
Dates 262
  stoning 263
Dead man's fingers 81
Deep-fat thermometer 75
Deep-frying
  cheese 45
  eggs 33
  fish 58
    in batter 75
  potatoes 191
  safety 191
Dégorgéing 17, 179
Demi-glace 224
Desalting anchovies 62
Desserts 271–292
Desserts, garnishes for 290
Détrempe 304
Dhal 195
Dicing
  mango 255
  onions 174
  peppers 180
  vegetables 166
Discoloration
  fruit, preventing 251
  vegetables,
    preventing 161, 179
Doneness, testing for
  beef and veal 124
  roast poultry 101
Dough
  filo and strudel 302
  forming into rolls 235
  making by hand 232

making by machine 233
rising and punching
down 233
shaping 234
Dover sole
fish plaits 61
skinning 56
Dressing a crab 80
Dressings
cooked 230
vinaigrette 230
Dried
beans and peas
cooking times 194
soaking and cooking 194
chillies 181
cheese coated with 42
fish, bonito 18
fruit compote 267
yeast 232
Drumsticks
grilling chicken 112
Dry-frying breast of duck 108
Drying pasta 209
Duck *(see also Poultry)*
breast
pan-frying 108
preparing whole 95
carving, Chinese method 107
chaudfroid de canard 105
cutting into four pieces 92
Oriental roast 106
Peking 106
preparing
for roasting 102
whole breast of 95
roasting
and carving 102
times 102
Dulse 177
Dumplings, Chinese 219
Durian 265
Durum wheat flour 206
Duxelles 170

E

East Indian arrowroot 177
Easy-blend yeast 232
Easy-cook rice 196
Eclairs
fillings and icings for 299
making 299
Eddo 177
Eggah 35
Eggs, Cheese & Creams 29–46
Egg(s)
baking 32
batters 38
Benedict 226
blending albumen strands 31
boiling 32
crêpes 38
deep-frying 33
egg wash 31
eggah 35
flavourings for omelettes 34
folded omelette 34
free-range 30
freshness, testing for 30
frittata 35
griddle pancakes 39
hard-boiled 32
Japanese omelette 34
noodles 218
nutritional value of 31
omelette shreds 35
omelettes 34
pasta 206
poaching 32
safety 31
scrambling 33
separating yolk and white 30
shallow-frying 33
shell colours 30
soufflé omelette 35
Spanish tortillas 35
storing 31
testing for freshness 30
whisking egg whites 31
yolk liaison
enriching soups with 25
Yorkshire puddings 39
Emmenthal 40
Emperor fish 49
En bellevue 78
En crapaudine 92
En papillote 73
barbecued fruit 268
Enriched breads 242
Enriching soups 25
Equipment *(see also Cookware)*
Asian 12
general 10
measuring 10
pasta 214
ravioli making 210
mixing, rolling and
decorating 14
sieves, strainers and sifters 14
Escalopes, poultry 94
Espagnole sauce 225
Exotic fruits 262

F

Fajitas 119
making 126
Falafel 195
Farfalle 215
Feijoa 263
Fennel
preparing 163
steaming times 187
Feta 41
cheese 43
Feuilletés 306
Figs 262
making a fig flower 263
Filet de boeuf en croûte 125
Fillet of beef, see Beef and veal
Filleting
flat fish 57
round fish 55
Fillings
for cakes 312
for choux buns
and eclairs 299
for stuffed fish 61
Filo pastry 302
Financiers 322
Fines herbes 185
Finishing loaves 234
Fish & Shellfish 47–86
Fish
baking 72
en papillote 73
in a salt crust 73
in foil 72
in leaves 73
barbecuing 71
batters for 75
braising 58
buying 48
cakes 77
coating(s)
with a herb crust 74
for fried 74
cutting
escalopes 60
steaks 60
deep-frying 58
in batter 75
en papillote 73
escalopes 60
fillets 60
flat
cooking methods 50
filleting 57
scaling 56
skinning 56
flavouring(s)
steamed 70
for open baking 72
frying 74
Cajun-style 74
with nut-brown butter 74
garnishes 68
goujons 75
gravadlax 63
grilling 71
handling 48
kettle 66
microwave cooking times 66
mixtures 76
mousse 76
open baking 72
packages 60
paupiettes 61
pillows 61
plaited monkfish 73
plaits 61
poached 66
preparing for serving 67
presenting a whole fish 68
quenelles 76
racks 71
roe 62
preparing smoked 62
round
boning 54
cooking methods 50
filleting 55
gutting 53
scaling 52
scoring 53
slipperiness 52
trimming 52
vandyking 52
salsa 71
salt cod, preparing 62
salted 62
shallow pan-frying 74
shallow poaching 66
smoked 62
poaching 67
salmon, slicing 63
steaks, cutting 60
steaming 70
stock 17
stuffing 72
terrine, making a layered 77
timbales 76
unusual 49
Flambéing fruits 268
Flat breads 240
Indian 241
Flavourings
Chinese 21
for baking fish 72
for fresh cheese 43
for Italian breads 239
for omelettes 34
for poaching fruits 266
for sponge cakes 310
fresh cheeses 43
lamb joints 136
steamed fish 70
Fleurons, pastry 68
Flour for pasta 206
Focaccia
making 239
ring 239
Foil, baking fish in 72
Fondue 36
Swiss cheese 45
Fontina 44
Frankfurter 151
Freezing stock 17

French
beans 172
dandelion 162
meringues 272
Fresh cheese 41
flavourings for 43
making 42
marinades for 43
piping 43
Fresh
herbs, preparing 185
yeast 232
Frisée 184
Frittata 35
Fritters
Asian-style fruit 268
vegetable 190
Fromage frais 41
enriching soups 25
Frozen fruit cups 289
Fruits 247–270
Fruit(s)
baking en papillote 270
baking halved 270
barbecuing 268
choosing 248
citrus 256
extracting juice 257
julienne 257
peeling 256
segmenting 256
slicing 256
unusual 256
zesting 257
coating in sugar glaze 269
coring 250
cups, frozen 289
dried fruit compote 267
exotic 262
flambéing 268
fritters, Asian-style 269
frosted 289
frying 268
grilling en sabayon 268
jelly 275
kebabs 268
mousse 274
peeling 250
poaching 266
preserving 266
in alcohol 267
skinning 254
soufflé 275
soups 24
star fruit 264, 265
stoning 254
Frying *(see also Deep-frying; Pan-frying; Shallow-frying; Stir-frying)*
chicken breast 108
fish 74
Cajun-style 74
coating with a herb crust 74
with nut-brown butter 74
fruit 268
poultry 108
Frying vegetables 190
Fusilli 215

G

Galingal 328
Game
cooking methods 89
cutting up a rabbit 93
garnishes for 104
rabbit terrine 116
stock 18
Game birds
accompaniments for 103
pot-roasting 115
preparing 103
roasting 103
Game birds see also Poultry
Ganache 282
Garam masala 329
Garde d'honneur 135
Garlic
bruschetta 246
crushing 175
flavouring roast vegetables 189
flowers, roasting 188
inserting in lamb joints 136
Garnishes 26
for desserts 290
for fish 68
for game 104
for meat 138
for soups 26, 68
Oriental 69, 139
Gelatine 19
dissolving 274
General Information 327–339
Genoese sponge 313
Ghee 227
Giblets 90
Gigot d'agneau 133
Ginger root
deep-fried 69
preparing fresh 328
Ginger rose, pickled 69
Glaze(s)
coating fruit in a sugar 269
for loaves and rolls 234
for spareribs 149
making 319
Glazing vegetables 190
Globe artichokes 164
Gnocchi
making 212
potato 213
semolina 212
Goat's cheese 41, 43, 44
Golden Delicious 250
Goose *(see also Poultry)*
preparing for roasting 102
roasting times 102
Goujons 75
Goulash 119
Grains 200
Granita 289
Granny Smith's 250
Grape(s)
leaves 162
peeling 258
pipping 258
Gratin
dauphinois 189
topping 44
Grating cheese 44
Gravy, making poultry 101
Green bacon 151
Green beans 172
microwave times 186
steaming times 187
Green lollo biondo 184
Green vegetables, boiling 186
Greens see Leafy green vegetables; individual names
Gremolada 330
Grenadillo 264
Grey mullet 58
Griddle pancakes 39
Grilling *(see also Chargrilling)*
beef and veal 127
cheese 45
chicken drumsticks 112
fish 71
fruits en sabayon 268
lamb
cutlets 140
times for 140
pork chops 150
sausages 151
small birds 113
steaks, times for 127
stovetop 141, 150
Grinding nuts 203
Groats 201
Grouse 90 *(see also Game birds; Poultry, small birds)*
pot roasting 115
roasting times 102
Gruyère 44
Guard of honour 135
Guava 263
Guinea fowl *(see also Game birds; Poultry, small birds)*
roasting times 100
Gumbo 28
Gurnard 49
Gutting round fish 53

H

Habañero chilli 181
Halloumi 45
Ham 151 *(see also Bacon; Pork)*
preparing and presenting 152
Handling
beef and veal 118
lamb 132
pork 144
poultry 88
Hangtown fry 33
Hard cheese 40
Hard-boiled eggs 32
Haricot beans
cooking times 194
Harvest roll 235
Hasselback potatoes 168
Heart
preparing for pan-frying 155
stuffing 155
Herb(s)
bouquet 69
bundles 330
chopping 185
cooking with fresh 185
deep-fried 69
mixtures 330
preparing fresh 185
shredding 185
storing 332
using 332
Herbes de Provence 330
Hollandaise sauce 226
Homemade pasta 206
Hominy 201
Huevos rancheros 32
Hummus 195

I

Ice cream
balls 323
making 286
semi-soft 287
shaping 286
Iceberg lettuce 184
Icicle radish 177
Icing(s)
buttercream 320
chocolate 319
crème Chantilly 321
for choux buns and eclairs 299
glacé 318
piping bag 318
royal 318
with cream 321
Indian flat breads 241
Ink, squid 86

Italian
breads 238
focaccia 239
flavourings for bread 239
meringues 272

J

Jalapeño chilli 181
Japanese
horseradish 64
ingredients
bonito 18
dashi 18
kombu 18
nori 64, 329
wakame 177, 329
wasabi 64, 329
medlar 262
omelette 34
rice 196
seven-spice powder 329
soups 21
sushi 64, 86
vinegared rice 197
Jelly, fruit 275
Jerusalem artichokes 167
Jointing and cutting up poultry 92
Julienne 166
citrus fruits 257
truffle 19

K

Kalamari 51
Kasha 201
Kebabs
fruit 268
lamb 140
preparing thigh meat for 95
Kedgeree 67, 197
Kernels, sweetcorn 173
Kettle, barbecue 113
Kibbeh 201
Kidneys
and suet 155
preparing 155
Kilner jar 43, 267
Kiwano 265
Kiwi fruit 262
Knackwurst 145, 151
Knife (knives) 11
smoked salmon 63
Kohlrabi 167, 177
Kombu 18, 177
Kugelhopf 242
Kumquat 257
cups 68

L

Lace tuiles 322
Ladies' fingers 173
Lamb 132–143
barbecuing cutlets 140
boning a shoulder 134
braising 136
shoulder of lamb 137
butterflying a leg 134
buying 132
carving
leg on the bone 137
rack of lamb 137
chargrilling 141
choosing 132
chops, grilling times 140
cooking
butterflied leg 141
methods 133
crown roast 135
cutlets, grilling times 140
cuts 133
dishes 133
flavouring joints 136
freezing 132
grilling
cutlets 140
times 140
guard of honour 135
handling 132
kebabs 140
grilling times 140
liver 154
marinating 140
noisettes
cutting 142
grilling times 140
pan-frying in caul 141
preparing
for cooking 134
rack 135
quick cooking 140
rack of 135, 137
roasting 136
sautéing 141
stuffing 136
shoulder of lamb 137
tagine 133
tunnel boning a leg 134
wrapping a joint 136
Lamb's lettuce 184
Larding 120
Lardons 151
Lasagne 209
Leafy green vegetables 161
choosing 159
Leaves,
baking fish in 73
salad 184
Leeks
crispy 138
cutting 175
Lemon(s)
choosing 248
garnishes for fish 68
zest, chopping 330
rose 69
Lemon grass 328
Lentils
cooking times 195
dhal 195
Lettuce, preparing 184
Lime
butterflies 68
zest, candied 291
Lincolnshire sausages 151
Little Gem lettuce 184
Livarot 40
Liver(s)
pâté, chicken 116
pig's, soaking 154
poultry 94
preparing 154
types of 154
Loaves, finishing 234
Lobster
buying 49, 51
cooking 51, 78
crackers 79
humane killing 78
parts of 79
removing from half-shell 79
removing tail meat 78
Lollo rosso 184
Long-grain rice 196
Loofah 177
Loquat 262
Lotus root 176
Louisiana crab boil 80
Lychees 265

M

Magret (duck breast) 95
Maltose 107
Mandolin 167, 169
Mangetouts 172
microwave times 186
Mango(es) 265
dicing 255
salsa 255
slicing 255
uses for 255
Mangosteen 264
Manhattan chowder 28
Marinades
for fresh cheeses 43
for poultry 112
for tough birds 115
Marinating
chicken in wine 114
lamb 140
poultry for kebabs 95
Mascarpone 41, 42
Mashed
potatoes 192
vegetables 192
Mayonnaise
flavoured 229
making by hand 228
making by machine 229
Measurement charts 334
Measuring equipment 10
Meat 117–156
Meat *(see also Bacon; Beef and Veal; Burgers; Ham; Lamb; Minced Meat; Offal; Pork; Sausages)*
accompaniments 138
garnishes 138
thermometer 124, 136
Meatballs 153
Medallions of lobster 78
Melba toast 246
Melon(s)
baller 250
cantaloupe 260
Chinese bitter 177
choosing 248
preparing 260
sorbet 260
Melting
cheese 44
chocolate 282
Meringues
making 272
making shapes 273
serving 273
types of 272
Mexican tortillas 240
Microwave times
for fish 66
for vegetables 186
Millet 201
Minced meat
brochettes 153
burgers 152
meatballs 153
meatloaf 153
using 152
Mincing beef and veal 123
Mineola 256
Mirepoix 166
Miroirs, passion fruit 323
Mixed spice 331
Mixing, rolling and decorating tools 14
Monkfish
boning 55
plaited 73
Mooli 177
julienne 69
Morel 171
Mouli 259
grater 44
-légumes 10

Mousse
chocolate 274
fish 76
fruit 274
Mung beans
cooking times 194
Mushrooms 170
choosing 158
chopping 170
dried, reconstituting 171
preparing 170
slicing 170
wild
safety 170
varieties 170
Mussels
buying 49, 51
cleaning 82
cooking 51
removing rubbery ring 83
serving on the half-shell 83
steaming 83

N

Nectarines
choosing 249
stoning 254
New England chowder 28
Noisettes
lamb 135
cutting lamb 142
making pork 147
Nori 64, 329
Nougatine 281
Nut butter 203
Nut-brown butter 74
Nutrients in broccoli 161
Nutritional value of eggs 31
Nuts 202
blanching 202
chopping 203
flaking 203
grinding 203
shredding 203
skinning 202
storing 203
toasting 202, 203

O

Oats 201, 232
Octopus
buying 51
cooking 51
Oeufs en cocotte 32
Offal 154 *(see also Heart; Kidneys; Livers; Oxtail; Pig's Trotters; Sweetbreads; Tongue; Tripe)*
freshness 154
Okra 173
Olive oil crostini 246
Omelette(s) 34
flavourings for 34
folded 34
Japanese 34
shreds, making 35
soufflé 35
Onion(s)
choosing 158
dicing 174
family 174
pearl, preparing 174
peeling 174
slicing 174
spring
cutting Asian-style 175
tassel 69
Opening and preparing
scallops 85
clams 84
Operas 322
Oriental
garnishes 69, 139
greens 160
roast duck 106
Ortanique 256
Osso buco 119, 129
Oven temperatures 334
Ovenware 13
Oxtail
preparing and cooking 156
Oyster mushrooms 171
Oysters
buying 49, 51
cooking 51
shucking 84

P

Packages, fish 60
Packham's 250
Paella 51, 197
Paglia e fieno 207
Paiolo 200
Pak choi 160
Palmier 235
Palourdes 84
Pan-frying
breast of duck 108
fish 74
lamb in caul 141
preparing heart for 155
veal 126
Pancakes *(see also Batters; Crêpes; Griddle pancakes)*
Chinese 240
Pancetta 151
Papaya 263
Parathas 241
Parfaits 287
Parker House 235
Parmesan 40
curls 236
grating 44
Parsnips, roasting times 188
Partridge(s) 90 *(see also Game birds; Poultry, small birds)*
roasting times 102
Passion fruit 262
miroirs 323
penants 291
Pasta 205–220
all'uovo 206, 207
cannelloni 211
cooking 214
times 215
cutting 209
drying 209
egg 206
equipment 214
flour 206
fresh stuffed 210
homemade 206
in brodo 20
machine 208
making by hand 206
making by machine 207
nera 207
ravioli
cutting 216
making 210
rolling 208
rossa 207
silhouette 208
spinach 207
testing for doneness 215
tomato 207
tortellini 211
verde 207
Pastry 293–306
baking blind 295
blender, using 294
choux 298
decorative edges 297
double crust 296
filo 302
fleurons 68
lattice 297
lining with 295
puff 304
shaping 306
shortcrust 294
single crust 296
strudel 303
tartlets 295
wrapping a lamb joint in 136
Pâte
à glacer 282, 284
brisée 294
sucrée 294
Pâtés, poultry and game 116
Paupiettes
fish 61
veal 123
Pavlova 272
Pawpaw 263
Pea aubergines 176
Peaches, stoning 254
Pearl onions, see Onions
Pears
choosing 250
chopping 251
fans 251
slicing 251
varieties 250
Peas 172 *(see also Dried peas)*
choosing 159
mangetouts 172
microwave times 186
shelling 172
steaming times 187
stringing 172
sugar snap 172
Pecorino 40, 41
Peeling
avocado 179
chestnuts 203
citrus fruits 256
fruits 250
grapes 258
onions 174
pineapple 253
Peking duck 106
Pen (of squid) 86
Pepino 263
Peppers 180
colours 180
dicing 180
preparing 180
roasting 189
slicing 180
Périgueux sauce 225
Persillade 330
Persimmon 263
Pesto 330
Petit sale 151
Petits fours 322
Pheasants 90 *(see also Game birds; Poultry, small birds)*
keeping moist 100
preparing and roasting 103
roasting times 102
Physalis 263
caramel-coated 322
Pickling spice 331
Pie funnels 296
Pied bleu 171
Pied de mouton 171
Pig's trotters 156
Pilaf 197
Pilgrim scallops 85
Pineapples 252
baby 252
coring 253

making wedges 253
removing skin 253
shell container, making 252
Pinto beans, cooking times 194
Pinwheels (poultry) 94
Pipérade 33
Piping bag
filling 273
paper 318
Piping fresh cheese 43
Pipping grapes 258
Pistachios, shelling 202
Pitting cherries 255
Pizza 238
Plums, stoning 254
Poached fish, preparing for serving 67
Poaching
ballotine 97
chicken (Asian style) 111
eggs 32
fish 66
fruits 266
pinwheels (poultry) 111
sausages 151
smoked fish 67
whole bird 110
Pod vegetables 172
Polenta 200
Pomegranates 264
Pomelo 256
Pommes
allumettes 169
châteaux 168, 189
frites 169
gaufrettes 169
parisiennes 168
pont neuf 169
soufflés 169
Pont l'Evêque 40
Pooris 241
Popping corn 201
Porcini 171
Pork 144–150
boning a loin 146
braising in milk 149
buying 144
choosing 144
chops
chargrilling 150
grilling 150
stuffing 147
cooking methods 145
crackling 148
cuts 145
dishes 145
fillet, preparing 147
freezing 144
handling 144
joint, roasting 148
noisettes 147
pig's liver 154
preparing 146
pork fillet 147
tenderloin 147
quick cooking 150
roasting
a joint of 148
pork chops 149
spareribs 149
tenderloin 148
times 148
sparerib chops 149
spareribs
glazes for 149
roasting 149
stir-frying 150
stuffing(s)
for boned loin 146
pork chops 147
tenderloins 147
tunnel 146
tenderloin
preparing a 147
roasting 148
stir-frying 150
stuffing 147
tunnel stuffing 146
Port Salut 40
Pot roasting game birds 115
Potato gnocchi 213
Potato(es) 168, see also Pommes
baking 168
basket 191
choosing 158
deep-frying 191
gratin 189
hasselback 168
mashed 192
new, steaming times 187
piped 138
preparing
for deep-frying 169
for roasting 168
pricking for baking 168
roasting 188
in olive oil 189
scrubbing 168
varieties 169
Poule au pot 110
Poulette sauce 223
Poultry & Game 87–116
Poultry
ballotine 96
barbecuing a whole bird 113
boning a large bird 96
breasts 94– 95, 108–112
buying 88
carving
a roasted bird 101
duck (Chinese) 107
duck 102
chargrilling escalopes 109
chicken livers 154
choosing 88
cooking methods 89
cutting
bird into eight pieces 93
against the grain 95
up a roasted bird 101
drumsticks, grilling 112
duck
carving (Chinese style) 107
cutting into four pieces 92
Oriental roast 106
Peking 106
preparing 106
roasting 106
whole breast of 95
escalopes 94
fatty bird
preparing for roasting 102
frozen 88
frying 108
game bird
preparing 103
roasting 103
giblets 90
gravy 101
grilling
drumsticks 112
small bird 113
handling 88
jointing and cutting 92
kebabs, preparing 95
keeping moist 100
large birds
boning 96
carving 101
stuffing and rolling 97
trussing 91
livers 94 ,154
marinades 112
for tough birds 115
marinating 95
casseroling in wine 114
pan-fried liver pâté 116
poaching
and slicing a ballotine 97
pinwheels 111
whole bird 110
pot roasting game birds 115
preparing
fatty bird for roasting 102
pieces 94
thigh meat for kebabs 95
whole birds 90
whole breast of duck 95
removing
tendons 94
wishbone 90
roasting
duck 102
fatty bird 102
game bird 103
testing for doneness 101
times 100, 101
whole bird 100
saté 112
sautéing pieces 109
schnitzels 108
shears 93
shredded, using 110
small birds
cutting up 101
grilling 113
pot-roasting 115
spatchcocking 92
trussing 90
spatchcocking a bird 92
stir-frying strips of 109
stuffing(s) 100
chicken breast 108
and rolling 97
suprêmes 94
tendons, removing the 94
terrines and pâtés 116
thighs 95
trussing
large birds 91
needle 91
quick 91
small birds 90
using shredded 110
whole birds, preparing 90
Pounding steaks 122
Poussin(s) 90, 92, 113 *(see also Poultry, small birds)*
roasting times 100
Praline 281
Prawns
buying 49, 51
cooking 51
preparing 81
soup 21
Presenting
a ham 152
a whole fish 68
Preserving fruits 266
in alcohol 267
Pricking sausage skins 151
Prickly pear 264
Proving a pan 38
Pudding
hot 278
rice 196, 278
steaming a 279
Puff pastry 304
shaping 306
Pulses, Grains & Nuts 193–204
Pulses 194
patties 195
purées of 195
Pumpkin 179
Purée(d)
berry 259
fish mixtures 76
fish soup 25
pulses 195
vegetable soups 24
vegetables 192

Puréeing
  making soup 24
  methods of (for soups) 24

Q

Quahogs 84
Quail(s) 90 *(see also Game birds; Poultry, small birds)*
  boning a 98
  pot roasting 115
  roasting times 102
Quatre-épices 331
Quenelles 76
Quick breads 244
Quinoa 201

R

Rabbit
  cutting up 93
  terrine 116
Rack of lamb 135
  carving 137
Radicchio 184
Radish
  icicle 177
  roses 139
Rambutan 265
Ratatouille 189
Ravioli 215
  cutting 216
  making 210
Reamer 257
Reblochon 40
Reconstituting mushrooms 171
Red Bartlett 250
Red cabbage, see Cabbage
Red kidney beans
  cooking times 194
Red snapper 58
  baking 72
  fish plaits 61
  steaming 70
Refried beans 194
Rehydrating
  dried chillies 181
Removing
  crabmeat from the shell 80
  lobster from the half-shell 79
  tail meat (lobster) 78
  tendons (poultry) 94
  wishbone (poultry) 90
Rhubarb 251
Rib of beef, see Beef & Veal
Ribbons, vegetable 167
Rice *(see also Risotto)*
  arborio 198
  carnaroli 198
  cooking 196
  Japanese vinegared 197
  moulds 138
  noodles 218
  paddle 197
  pilaf 197
  pudding, baked 278
  pudding, stovetop 278
  sticks 218
  types of 196
Ricotta 41, 42
Risi bisi 197
Rising and punching down (bread dough) 233
Risotto 198
Roast pork 145
Roasting
  beetroot 188
  duck 102
    Peking duck 106
  game bird 103
  garlic flowers 188
  joint of pork 148
  leg of lamb 136
  peppers 189
  pork 146
    chops 149
    tenderloin 148
  potatoes 188
  preparing a fatty bird for 102
  rib of beef 124
  spareribs 149
  times
    beef and veal 124
    lamb 136
    pork 148
    poultry 100, 102
    vegetables 188
  vegetables 188
    in olive oil 189
  whole fillet of beef 125
    en croûte 125
Roe, preparing smoked 62
Roll cutting vegetables 166
Rolling
  boneless joints 121
  pasta 208
  veal escalopes 123
Rolls, forming dough into 235
Root vegetables, boiling 186
Roots and tubers 166
Roquefort 41
Rösti 190
Rouille 22
Roux 28
  types of 222
Rumtopf 267
Runner beans 172
Rye 201
  flour 232

S

Sabayon sauce 268
  making 292
Sachertorte 319
Saffron, soaking 329
Salad(s) *(see also Vegetables and Salads)*
  leaves 184
  choosing 159
  making a tossed 184
  spinner 184
Salade tiède 130
Salisfy 176
Salmon
  boning 54
  escalopes 60
  filleting 55
  gravadlax 63
  knife 63
  packages 60
  pillows 61
  slicing smoked 63
Salmonella bacteria 31
Salsa
  for fish 71
  mango 255
Salt
  beef, cooking 129
  cod, preparing 62
  crust, baking fish in 73
Salted fish 62
  gravadlax 63
Saltimbocca 123, 126
Salting aubergines 178
Samphire 84
Sapodilla 262
Sardines
  boning 54
  grilling 71
Sashimi 64
Saté, chicken 112
Satsuma 257
Sauces & Dressings 221–230
Sauce(s) *(see also Sweet Sauces)*
  allemande 223
  aurore 223
  béarnaise 226, 227
  béchamel 222
  beurre blanc 227
  bretonne 225
  brown
    flavouring 224
    making 224
  cardinale 223
  charcutière 225
  chasseur 225
  chilli bean 58
  diable 225
  espagnole 225
  hollandaise 226
  mounting 227
  nantua 223
  périgueux 225
  poivrade 225
  poulette 223
  robert 225
  sabayon 268, 292
  tomato 331
  velouté 223
    flavouring 223
  white 222
Sausages
  bacon and ham 151
  casings and fillings 154
  cooking 151
  grilling 151
  making 154
  poaching 151
  pricking the skins 151
  varieties 151
Sautéing
  poultry pieces 109
  tender cuts of lamb 141
Scaling
  flat fish 56
  round fish 52
Scallops
  buying 49, 51
  cooking 51
  opening and preparing 85
Schnitzels (poultry) 108
Scoring round fish 53
Scotch
  bonnet chilli 181
  pancakes 39
Scrambled eggs 33
  additions to 33
Sea bass 58
  cutting steaks 60
Sea bream 49 *(see also Fish)*
Seafood, choosing fresh 48 *(see also Fish & Shellfish; individual names of fish and shellfish)*
Seaweed
  crispy 191
  kombu 18
  nori 64, 329
  preparing 329
  stock 18
  wakame 329
Segmenting citrus fruits 256
Semifreddo 287
Semolina
  flour 206
  gnocchi 212
Separating
  egg yolk from white 30
Serrano chilli 181
Serving
  mussels on the half shell 83
  whole poached fish 67
Sesame seeds, toasting 329
Shallots
  confit 138
  roast 138

Shallow poaching fish 66
Shallow-frying eggs 33
Shaping bread dough 234
Shark 49
Sheep cheese 41
Shellfish 78–86
  buying 49
  cooking methods 51
  handling 48
  what to look for 51
Shelling
  peas 172
  pistachios 202
Sherbet 289
Shiitake mushrooms 171
Shortcrust pastry 294
Shredding
  cabbage 160
  celeriac 167
  herbs 185
  poached poultry 110
Shucker (shellfish) 84, 85
Shucking oysters 84
Sieves, strainers and sifters 14
Silhouette pasta 208
Silver dollar pancakes 39
Skate wings 74
Skimming stock 17
Skinning
  fish fillet 57
  flat fish 56
  fruits 254
  nuts 202
Slicing
  apples 251
  avocado 179
  ballotine 97
  beef, wafer thin 122
  citrus fruits 256
  kohlrabi 167
  mango 255
  mushrooms 170
  onions 174
  pears 251
  peppers 180
  truffles 171
Smoked
  cod, poaching 67
  fish 62
    roe 62
    using poached 67
  haddock, poaching 67
  salmon, slicing 63
Snail (bread roll) 235
Snails 216
Snipping chives 185
Soaking
  dried beans and peas 194
  liver 154
  mushrooms 170
  wakame 329
Soba noodles 218
Soda bread 244
Soft cheese 40
  testing for ripeness 41
Sole paupiettes 61
Sorbet(s) 289
  flavourings for 288
  making by hand 288
  making by machine 288
  piping 289
Sorbetière 288
Sorrel 162
Soufflé 36
  fruit 275
  hot 278
  omelette 35
Soupe de poissons 25
Soups
  carrot-flower 21
  clear
    Chinese-style 21
    Japanese 21
    variations 20
  consommé 19
  decorating with cream 27
  enriching 25
  French onion soup 20
  fruit 24
  garnishes for 26, 68
  prawn 21
  puréed
    fish 25
    vegetable 24
  simple additions to stock 20
Sour cream 46
Soy
  beans, cooking times 194
  flour 232
Spaghetti alle vongole 51
Spaghetti squash 179
Spanish tortillas 35
Spareribs
  glazes for 149
  roasting 149
Spatchcocking a bird 92
Spelt flour 232
Spices
  grinding 331
  mixtures 331
  using 332
Spinach
  choosing 159
  cooking 192
  pasta 207
  preparing 162
Sponge
  fingers 326
  whisked 312
Spoom 289
Spring onions, see Onions
Spring roll(s)
  fillings 220
  making 220
  mini 220
  wrappers 218
Squash
  acorn 179
  butternut 179
  preparing 179
  spaghetti 179
  steaming times 187
  winter, roasting times 188
Squid
  buying 51
  calamares en su tinta 86
  cooking 51
  ink 86
  kalamari 51
  preparing 86
  stuffing 86
Stalks
  and shoots (vegetables) 163
  artichokes 164
Star fruit 264
  preparing 265
Steak *(see also Beef and Veal)*
  au poivre 126
  barbecueing 127
  cross-hatch 127
  grilling 127
  tartare 123, 153
  tenderizing 122
Steaming
  fish 70
  mussels 83
  pudding 279
  vegetables 187
Stewing
  beef and veal 128
  cutting beef or veal for 122
  cutting poultry for 95
  pork 150
Stir-frying
  strips of poultry 109
  vegetables 190
Stocks & Soups 15–28
Stock(s)
  basic 16
  brown 16
  chicken 16
  cubes 17
  fish 17
  freezing 17
  game 18
  quick skimming 17
  seaweed 18
  simple additions to 20
  special 18
  vegetable 18
Stoning
  avocado 179
  dates 263
  fruits 254
Storing
  eggs 31
  herbs 332
  nuts 203
Stovetop grill 141
Strawberries *(see also Berries)*
  choosing 249
  preparing 258
Strigging currants 258
Stringing peas 172
Strudel 303
Stuffing(s)
  and rolling a bird 97
  boneless joints 121
  chicken breast 108
  fillet of beef 125
  fish 72
  fish through the back 72
  for boned loin of pork 146
  for heart 155
  for pork chops 147
  for poultry 100
  for veal escalopes 123
  heart 155
  leg of lamb 136
  pork chops
  pork tenderloins 147
  shoulder of lamb 137
  squid 86
Suet 155
Sugar snap peas 172
Sugar
  syrups 280, 281
  thermometer 280
Summer savory 332
Suprêmes 94
Sushi 64, 197
Sweating vegetables 190
Sweetbreads 156
Sweetcorn 173
  using corn husks 173
Sweet potatoes
  roasting times 188
Swiss
  chard 162, 163
  cheese fondue 45
  meringues 272
  roll 313
Syrups, sugar 280, 281

T

Tabbouleh 201
Tadka 195
Tagine 129
Tagliatelle 209, 215
Tamales 173
Tamarillo 263
Tamarind 328
Tandoori chicken 89
Taramasalata 62
Taro 177
Tarte Tatin 297
Tartlets 295
Tempering chocolate 283
Tempura batter 269
Tenderizing steaks 122

Terrine(s)
making a layered fish 77
poultry and game 116
Testing
eggs for freshness 30
for doneness
bread 234
cake 309
pasta 215
roast poultry 101
Thai
aubergine 176
flavourings, preparing 328
rice 196
Thermometer
deep-fat 75
meat 124
sugar 280
Tian 142
Tilapia 49
Timbales 76, 192
Toasting nuts 202, 203
Tomalley 79
Tomato(es)
choosing 158
concassée of 178
pasta 207
preparing 178
sauce 331
Tongue
preparing and cooking 156
Toppings for bread 234
Tortellini 215
making 211
Tortilla(s)
flour 240
Spanish 35
Tossed salad 184
Tourelle 235
Tournedos 122
Tranches 306
Tricolore 207
Trimming and slicing
(beef fillet) 122
round fish 52
Tripe 156
Tronçons 60
Trout *(see also Fish)*
barbecuing 71
boning 55
Truffles (fungi) 171
Truffles, almond 323
Trussing
large birds 91
needle 91
poultry, quick 91
small birds 90
Tuile(s) 326
baskets 291
Tulipes 326
Tuna, sushi rolls 64
Tunnel
boning a leg of lamb 134
stuffing pork 146
Turkey *(see also Poultry)*
roasting times 100
Turning vegetables 167
Turnips
roasting times 188
stuffed baby 139
Tying boneless joints
beef and veal 121

U

Ugli fruit 256
Unsmoked bacon 151
Unusual
citrus fruits 256
vegetables 176

V

Vandyking 52
Vanilla 331
Veal, see Beef & Veal
Vegetables & Salads 157–192
Vegetable(s) *(see also individual names)*
baby 138
baking 188
boiling 186
bread with 245
bundles 138
chargrilling 191
choosing 158
dicing 166
fritters 190
fruits 178
frying 190
glazing 190
julienne 166
knobbly, preparing 167
mandolin 167, 169
mashed 192
microwave times 185
peeler 250
potatoes 168
purées 192
ribbons 167
roasting 188
in olive oil 189
flavouring with garlic 189
times 188
roll cutting 166
roots and tubers 166
spirals 139
steaming 187
stir-frying 190
stock 18
sweating 190
timbales 192
turning 167
unusual 176
Velouté sauce 223
Vinaigrette 230
Vongole 84

W

Wakame 177, 329
Wasabi 64, 329
Watercress 184
Wheat berry 201
Whelks 85
buying 51
cooking 51
Whisked sponge 312
Whisking egg whites 31
White
asparagus 163
sauce 222
Wild mushrooms, see Mushrooms
Wild rice 196
Williams 250
Winkles
buying 51
cooking 51
Winter squash, roasting times 188
Wok 58, 70
Wonton wrappers 218
Wood ears 171
Wrapping
chicken in banana leaves 270
fish, en papillote 73
fruit in banana leaves 270
lamb joint in pastry 136

Y

Yard-long beans 177
Yeast
dried 232
easy-blend 232
fresh 232
preparing 232
Yogurt 46
enriching soups 25
Yorkshire puddings 39

Z

Zest
candied 291
chopping 330
Zesting citrus fruits 257

Speciality Suppliers

The Grove Bakery
28-30 Southbourne Grove
Bournemouth BH6 3RA
Phone: 01202 422 653
Speciality: cake decorating Supplies (fondant icing)

Keylink Ltd.
Blackburn Road
Rotherham S61 2DR
South Yorkshire
Phone: 01790 550 206
Speciality: chocolate (ingredients, equipment, moulds)

Pages
121 Shaftesbury Avenue
London WC2H 8AD
Phone: 0171 379 6334
Speciality: equipment

Peter Nisbet
Sheene Road
Bedminster
Bristol BS3 4EG
Phone: 0117 966 9131
Speciality: mail order source, equipment

Divertimenti (mail order) Ltd.
P.O. Box 6611
London SW6 6XU
Phone: 0171 386 9911
Speciality: equipment and ingredients

Recipe Index

Aïoli 229
Almond truffles 323
Angel food cake 314
Apple charlotte 279
Apple strudel 303
Asian fritters 269
Austrian cheesecake 317

Bagels 244
Baked fruits 270
Baked rice pudding 278
Baked vanilla soufflés 278
Baklava 302
Barbecued fruits 268
Bavarois 277
Béarnaise sauce 227
Beef carpaccio 122
Blueberry sorbet 288
Braised lamb with herb stuffing 137
Brandy butter 292
Brandy snaps 325
Brioche à tête 243
Brown sauce 224
Brown stock 16
Bruschetta and crostini 236
Burgers 152
Buttercream 320
Buttercream icing 320
Butterflied leg of lamb 141
Butterscotch sauce 292

Cailles rôties farcies Madame Brassart 98
Cajun fish 74
Cannelloni 211
Cantaloupe surprise 260
Chapatis 241
Chargrilled chicken escalopes 109
Chaudfroid de canard 105
Cheese fondue 45
Cheese soufflés 36
Chicken and sage filling 211
Chicken ballotine 96
Chicken liver pâté 116
Chicken saté 112
Chicken stock 16
Chiles rellenos 182
Chinese dumplings 219
Chinese pancakes 240
Chocolate icing 319
Chocolate mousse 274
Chocolate torte 314
Choux buns 298
Choux pastry 298
Citron tartlets 323
Coconut rice 130
Coffee granita 289
Consommé 19
Cooked dressing 230
Coq au vin 114

Cornbread 245
Courgette bread 245
Court bouillon 66
Couscous 201
Cranberry sauce 148
Crème anglaise 276
Crème caramel 277
Crème Chantilly 292
Crème d'ail 98
Crème pâtissière 276
Creole Bouillabaisse 22
Creole gumbo
Crêpes 38
Crispy seaweed 191
Croquembouche 300

Dashi 18
Deep-fried eggs Escoffier style 33
Deep-fried fish 75
Dhal 195
Dim sum 218
Dropped biscuits 324

Eclairs 299
Eggah 35
English baked custard 276
Espagnole sauce 225

Fajitas 126
Falafel 195
Fillet of beef en croûte 125
Financiers 322
Fish cakes 77
Fish goujone 75
Fish mousse 76
Fish quenelles 76
Fish stock 17
Fish terrine 77
Fish timbales 76
Flambéed fruits 269
Focaccia ring 239
Forcemeat stuffing 96
French onion soup 20
French petits pots 276
Fresh cheese 42
Fresh rosemary focaccia 239
Frittata 35
Frozen fruit cups 289
Fruit jelly 275
Fruit soufflé 275
Fruit tartlets 295
Fruits in alcohol 267

Game stock 18
Ganache 282
Gâteau des deux Pierre 284
Gingerbread 311
Glacé icing 318
Glazed ham 152
Gratin dauphinois 189

Gravadlax 63
Griddle pancakes 39
Grilled chicken drumsticks 112
Grilled fruits en sabayon 268

Herb-crusted fish 74
Hollandaise sauce 226
Hummus 195

Ice cream 286

Japanese vinegared rice 197

Kugelhopf 242

Lace tuiles 322
Lamb kebabs 140

Mayonnaise 228
Melon sorbet 260
Meringue cake 315
Mexican tortillas 240
Mixed fruit cake 311
Moules à la marinière 82
Mussels on the half-shell 83

Noisettes d'agneau au thym, tian provençale 142
Nougatine 281

Operas 322
Oriental roast duck 105
Osso buco 129

Pan-fried breast of duck 108
Pan-fried lamb in caul 141
Parathas 241
Parfaits 287
Passion fruit miroirs 323
Pasta 206
Pâte brisée 294
Pâte sucrée 294
Pavlova 272
Pesto 330
Petits tians 142
Pilaf 197
Pizza 238
Poached chicken pinwheels 111
Polenta 200
Pooris 241
Pork in milk 149
Port sauce 98
Potato gnocchi 213
Pot-roasted game birds 115
Poule au pot 110
Puff pastry 304
Puréed fish soup 25

Rabbit terrine 116
Raspberry cheesecake 316

Ravioles d'escargots 216
Ravioli 210
Refried beans 194
Roast chicken 100
Roast duck 102
Roast fillet of beef 125
Roast leg of lamb 136
Roast pheasant with wine gravy 103
Roast pork 148
Roast pork spareribs 149
Roast pork tenderloin 148
Roast rib of beef 124
Rolled biscuits 324
Rouille 22
Royal icing 318
Rumtopf 267

Sabayon sauce 292
Saltimbocca 126
Sashimi 64
Sautéed lamb 141
Schnitzels 108
Seafood risotto 198
Semifreddo 286
Semolina gnocchi 212
Shortbread 324
Sichuan fish 58
Simple fruit mousse 274
Soda bread 244
Spinach timbales 192
Sponge fingers 326
Spring rolls 220
Steak tartare 153
Stencil paste 326
Stir-fried pork 150
Stovetop rice pudding 278
Strawberry and cream gâteau 321
Stuffed fried chicken breasts 108
Sugar-glazed fruits 269
Sushi rolls 64
Swiss roll 313

Tagine 129
Tamales 173
Taramasalata 62
Tempura batter 269
Thai beef 130
Tomato sauce 331
Tortellini 211

Vegetable stock 18
Velouté sauce 223
Victoria sandwich 310
Vinaigrette 230

Whisked sponge cake 312
White loaf 233
White sauce 222

Yorkshire puddings 39

ACKNOWLEDGEMENTS

Food consultant Christina Harlan
Food preparation Maddalena Bastianelli

IT manager John Clifford

Picture research Sandra Schneider
Index Madeline Weston

Contributing writers Kate Fryer, Arlene Sobel, Norma MacMillan, Beverley Le Blanc

Additional editorial assistance Simon Warmer
Additional design assistance Paul Stradling

Carroll & Brown would also like to thank the chefs of all the Le Cordon Bleu schools without whose knowledge and expertise this book would not have been possible, especially: Chef Michel Cliche, Meilleur Ouvrier de France (Paris), Chef Andrew Males (London), Chef Didier Chantefort (Tokyo), Chef Hervé Boutin, Meilleur Ouvrier de France (Sydney) and Chef Philippe Guiet (Ottawa) and also the major co-ordinators Chef Michel Cliche and Chef Andrew Males. **And for their administrative assistance:** Carole Jory, Kathy Shaw

Picture credits: p52 Sir Anthony van Dyke, Prado, Madrid/Bridgeman; p110 Henry IV, King of France and Navarre, Lauros-Giraudon/Bridgeman; p125 The Duke of Wellington, Wallace Collection, London/Bridgeman; p168 Sir Francis Drake, National Maritime Museum, London/ Bridgeman; p176 Hernando Cortes, Museo de America, Madrid/Bridgeman; p206 Marco Polo, Biblioteca Nazionale, Turin/Bridgeman; p279 Queen Charlotte, Guildhall Art Gallery, Corporation of London/Bridgeman; p286 Dolley Payne Madison, National Portrait Gallery, Smithsonian Institution/ Bridgeman.

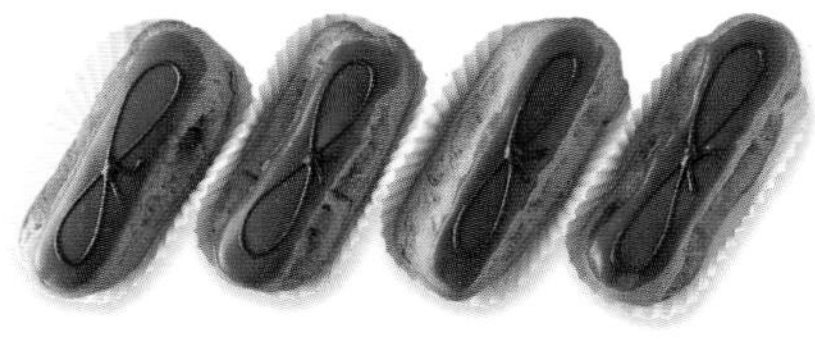

Le Cordon Bleu London, 114 Marylebone Lane, London, W1M 6HH, England. Tel 44/171 935 3503. Fax 44/171 935 7621.

Le Cordon Bleu Paris, 8 Rue Leon Delhomme, 75015 Paris, France. Tel 33/1 53 68 22 50. Fax 33/1 48 56 03 96.

Le Cordon Bleu Tokyo, ROOB-1, 28-13 Sarugaku-cho, Daikanyama, Shibuya-ku, Tokyo 150, Japan. Tel 81/3 5489 01 41. Fax 81/3 5489 01 45.

Le Cordon Bleu (US Headquarters), 404 Airport Executive Park, Nanuet, NY 10954, USA. Tel 1/914 426 7400. Fax 1/914 426 0104 (Toll Free Number USA 1-800-457 CHEF).

Le Cordon Bleu Sydney, Ryde College of TAFE, 250 Blaxland Road, Ryde, Sydney, NSW 2112, Australia. Tel 61/2 808 8307. Fax 61/2 809 3346.